DORSET COUNTY LIBRARY
204935027 W

THE COOK'S BOOK OF EVERYTHING

THE COOK'S BOOK OF EVERYTHING

MURDOCH BOOKS

··CONTENTS··

THE COOK'S BOOK OF...

Everything? Yes, you're right, we can't possibly have included everything. As one of our friends pointed out, there's no information on how to cook with yak milk or carve a model ship from a potato. And, if there was, this book would be so heavy you wouldn't be able to lift it down from the shelf.

But if you're searching for a book, just one book, that holds a huge array of recipes — both modern and traditional, western and Asian, complicated and simple, quick and elaborate — together with a wealth of information, *The Cook's Book of Everything* is written for you. This is where you'll find a recipe for classic kedgeree; instructions, and photographs to go with them, on how to clean and debeard mussels and make sure they're safe to serve to your friends; recipes to make your own curry pastes that will blow the commercial varieties right out of your pantry; and hints and tips to make baking cakes and bread simpler than you ever thought.

You might be an experienced cook who wants a well researched, one-stop point of reference, or a beginner, maybe setting up your first home, or perhaps you want to streamline your cookbooks, or have just one that you can take on weekends away. We've tried to make *The Cook's Book* as user-friendly as possible. You can pick it up and flick through for recipes that fit with what you've got in the fridge, or use the comprehensive index to track down something specific, either a recipe or an ingredient.

Chapters are divided into general categories such as Soup, Vegetables, Poultry, Baking and Desserts and, where appropriate, some chapters start with the Basics: information on different varieties and cuts; how to buy and store; prepare or cut up; cook and keep. Then you'll find the recipes, some with step photography, others with helpful cooking tips. You'll also find footnotes on interesting ingredients and snippets of food history and lore interspersed among the recipes. So, next to the recipe for Thai green chicken curry you'll find a footnote and photograph of galangal, because it's an interesting ingredient in that recipe that you might want to know more about.

But we did have to draw a line somewhere, so if you're looking for a picture of hyssop or a guide to using geranium leaves to line a cake tin, you'll need to seek out a specialist herb manual. But if you want a photograph of garam masala and a recipe for making your own, turn to our Herbs and Spices chapter.

Oh, and for information on milking a yak, there's always the internet.

CHAPTER ONE
SOUP

••STOCK••

Stock is one of the essential building blocks of many savoury dishes, forming the basis of most soups, sauces and casseroles. There are many commercial stocks on the market, but you will find most are over-salted, under-flavoured and packed with preservatives.

HOW TO... MAKE PERFECT STOCK

* Stock can be made from raw or cooked meat and poultry, but fish stock should be made from raw non-oily fish.
* The quality of stock depends on the type of bones that you use — marrow bones, pigs' trotters and chicken wings will produce a jellied stock (when cold) as they contain collagen.
* Vegetables should be aromatics (leek, onion, carrot, celery), as should herbs (bay leaves, thyme and parsley). For clear stock, use whole spices such as black peppercorns rather than ground pepper. Vegetables that give off starch, such as potatoes, will turn your stock cloudy.
* Stock must be simmered for a long time (although not as long for fish) and never boiled — boiled stock becomes cloudy and greasy as the fat is incorporated into the liquid.
* As your stock simmers, skim off any scum that rises to the surface. To bring scum (fat and impurities) to the surface, add a little cold water at regular intervals.

VEGETABLE STOCK

METHOD

1 Put 500 g (1 lb 2 oz) mixed chopped carrots, celery, onions and leeks in a stockpot. Add a bouquet garni and 10 peppercorns.

2 Add 2.5 litres (10 cups) cold water, bring to the boil and then simmer for 1–2 hours. Skim off any scum regularly.

3 Press the solids to extract all the flavour, then strain and cool in the fridge.

FISH STOCK

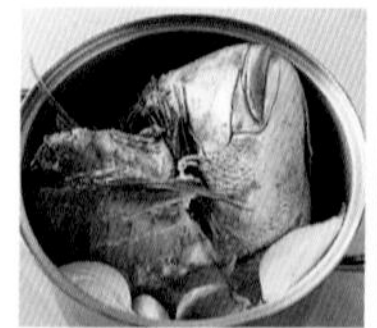

METHOD

1 Put 2 kg (4 lb 8 oz) fish bones and heads in a stockpot with a bouquet garni, 1 chopped onion and 10 peppercorns.

2 Add 2.5 litres (10 cups) cold water, bring to the boil and then simmer for 20–30 minutes. Skim off any scum.

3 Strain the stock, then cool in the fridge. When cool, lift off any congealed fat.

BEEF (BROWN) STOCK

METHOD

1 Roast 1.5 kg (3 lb 5 oz) beef or veal bones in a single layer in a large roasting tin at 220°C (425°F/Gas 7) for 20 minutes. Do not burn the bones or your stock will be bitter.
2 Add 1 quartered onion, 2 chopped carrots, 1 chopped leek and 1 chopped celery stalk and roast for a further 20 minutes.
3 Transfer to a stockpot with 10 peppercorns and a bouquet garni. Cover with 4 litres (16 cups) cold water. Bring to the boil.
4 When the stock boils, turn it down to a simmer and skim off the scum.
5 Skim regularly — adding a little cold water to the pot will help any impurities rise up to the surface so they can be skimmed off.
6 After 6–8 hours, strain the stock and leave it to cool in the fridge. When cool, lift off any congealed fat.

CHICKEN STOCK

METHOD

1 Put 1 kg (2 lb 4 oz) chicken carcasses into a stockpot with a bouquet garni, 1 quartered onion, 1 chopped carrot and 10 peppercorns.
2 Add 4 litres (16 cups) cold water and bring to the boil. When the stock boils, turn it down to a simmer and skim off the scum.
3 Skim regularly — adding a little cold water to the pot will help any impurities rise up to the surface so they can be lifted off.
4 Strain the stock and remove any fat by dragging a sheet of paper towel over the stock surface.
5 If not using immediately, cool in the fridge. When cool, lift off any congealed fat.
6 Once made, a stock can be reduced (by boiling) for freezing. The stock can then be poured into ice cube trays and frozen. Reconstitute with water before use. Store stock in the fridge for up to 3 days, or frozen for up to 6 months.

HOME-MADE VERSUS READY-MADE

The flavour of soup is improved by using home-made stock, plus you know exactly what ingredients have gone into your dish. If possible, make stock a day in advance and store it in the fridge. This will improve the flavour and you'll find the fat solidifies on top and can be easily lifted off with a spoon.

••CLEAR SOUP••

Clear soup, based mainly on a flavoursome broth, can be served as a first course or a light meal. Perfect, clear consommé was once the hallmark of a top chef; today we are not as concerned with the clarity as the flavour and fabulous 'comfort food' value of this soup.

CHICKEN CONSOMME

SERVES 4

INGREDIENTS

STOCK

1 kg (2 lb 4 oz) chicken carcasses, halved
185 g (6½ oz) chicken legs
1 carrot, chopped
1 onion, chopped
1 celery stalk, chopped
2 parsley sprigs
20 black peppercorns
1 bay leaf
1 thyme sprig

CLARIFICATION MIXTURE

2 chicken drumsticks
1 carrot, finely chopped
1 leek, finely chopped
1 celery stalk, finely chopped
10 black peppercorns
1 parsley sprig, chopped
2 tomatoes, chopped
2 egg whites, lightly beaten
sea salt

METHOD

1 To make the stock, remove any skin and fat from the chicken carcasses and legs, and put the carcasses in a large heavy-based saucepan with 3 litres (12 cups) cold water. Bring to the boil and skim any fat that floats to the surface. Add the remaining stock ingredients. Simmer for 1½ hours, skimming occasionally. Strain the stock (you should have about 1.5 litres/6 cups) and pour it back into the clean saucepan.

2 To make the clarification mixture, remove the skin and meat from the chicken drumsticks and discard the skin. Chop the meat finely (you will need about 150 g/5½ oz) and mix with the carrot, leek, celery, peppercorns, parsley, tomato and egg white. Add 200 ml (7 fl oz) of the warm stock to loosen the mixture.

3 Add the clarification mixture to the strained stock and whisk in well. Bring to a gentle simmer. As the mixture simmers the clarification ingredients will bind with any impurities and form a 'raft'. As the raft rises, gently move it with a wooden spoon to one side of the pan away from the main movement of the simmering stock (this will make it easier to ladle out the stock later). Simmer for 1 hour, or until the stock is clear.

4 Ladle out the chicken stock, taking care not to disturb the raft, and strain through a fine sieve lined with damp muslin. Place sheets of paper towel over the top of the consommé and then quickly lift away to remove any remaining fat. Season with coarse sea salt (or other iodine-free salt, as iodine will cloud the soup).

5 Reheat before serving, season and garnish with parsley or cooked julienned carrot and leek.

VEGETABLE SOUP WITH PISTOU

SERVES 4–6

INGREDIENTS

1.75 litres (7 cups) chicken stock (page 11)
1 celery stalk, diced
1 carrot, diced
1 zucchini (courgette), diced
75 g (2½ oz) small green beans, trimmed and chopped
125 g (4½ oz) vermicelli, broken into pieces

PISTOU

6 garlic cloves
80 g (2¾ oz) basil leaves
100 g (3½ oz/1 cup) grated parmesan cheese
200 ml (7 fl oz) olive oil

METHOD

1 To make the pistou, put the garlic, basil and parmesan in a food processor and process until finely chopped. With the motor running, slowly add the olive oil, until you have a thick paste. Alternatively pound the ingredients using a mortar and pestle. Cover with plastic wrap and set aside.
2 Heat the stock in a large saucepan over medium heat, add the celery, carrot and zucchini and cook for 10 minutes.
3 Add the beans and stir in the vermicelli and cook for a further 10 minutes, or until the vermicelli is cooked. Season and stir through a spoonful of pistou, to taste.

NOTE: Store leftover pistou, covered with a layer of oil, in a sealed jar in the fridge.

STRACCIATELLA ALLA ROMANA

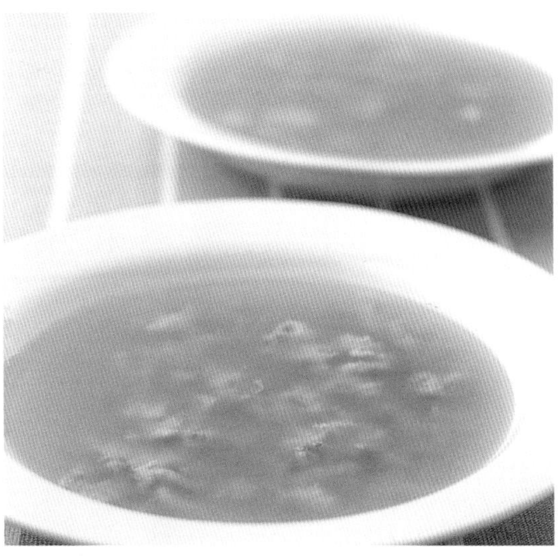

This traditional Roman soup is made from a paste of eggs and cheese dropped into hot chicken or beef broth. In Italian, *stracciatella* means 'little rags', referring to the ribbon-like strands that form as the paste cooks.

SERVES 4

INGREDIENTS

2 litres (8 cups) beef or chicken stock (page 11)
3 eggs
50 g (1¾ oz/½ cup) grated parmesan cheese
1½ tablespoons fresh breadcrumbs
2 tablespoons finely chopped parsley

METHOD

1 Put the stock in a saucepan, bring to the boil and then lower the heat to a simmer.
2 Lightly beat the eggs, then beat in half the parmesan, the breadcrumbs and parsley.
3 Drizzle the egg into the stock. When it's set, stir in the remaining parmesan and serve.

••VEGETABLE SOUP••

Since man first learnt to boil water, we've been throwing a few vegetables into the pot and heating them up to make soup — a dish that really lives up to the phrase 'greater than the sum of its parts'. There are few more simple ways to prepare a meal.

PUMPKIN SOUP

SERVES 4

INGREDIENTS

1 kg (2 lb 4 oz) pumpkin (winter squash)
60 g (2¼ oz) butter
1 onion, chopped
1 litre (35 fl oz/4 cups) chicken stock (page 11)
185 ml (6 fl oz/¾ cup) cream

METHOD

1 Peel the pumpkin and chop into chunks. Heat the butter in a large saucepan, add the onion and cook gently for 15 minutes, or until softened.
2 Add the pumpkin and stock and simmer, covered, for 20 minutes, or until the pumpkin is tender. Allow to cool a little, then process in batches in a food processor or blender until smooth. Return the soup to the pan.
3 Stir in the cream and stir over low heat to heat through. Season to taste. If you like, swirl in a little more cream to serve.

› THAI PUMPKIN AND COCONUT MILK SOUP

SERVES 4

INGREDIENTS

2 tablespoons olive oil
1 onion, finely chopped
1 tablespoon red curry paste
1 tablespoon tomato paste (concentrated purée)
450 g (1 lb) peeled pumpkin (winter squash), cubed
400 ml (14 fl oz) coconut milk
500 ml (17 fl oz/2 cups) vegetable stock (page 10)
coriander (cilantro) leaves, to garnish
sliced red chilli, to garnish

METHOD

1 Heat the oil in a large saucepan and gently fry the onion for 5 minutes, or until softened. Add the curry paste and tomato paste and fry for 30 seconds.
2 Add the pumpkin and fry for 5 minutes, then add the coconut milk and stock. Cover and simmer for 15 minutes, then remove the lid and simmer for a further 5 minutes.
3 Allow to cool a little, then process in batches in a food processor or blender until smooth. Return the soup to the pan and reheat. Garnish with coriander and chilli and serve.

FRENCH ONION SOUP

SERVES 6

INGREDIENTS

- 50 g (1¾ oz) butter
- 750 g (1 lb 10 oz) onions, thinly sliced
- 2 garlic cloves, finely chopped
- 45 g (1½ oz/⅓ cup) plain (all-purpose) flour
- 2 litres (8 cups) beef or chicken stock (page 11)
- 250 ml (9 fl oz/1 cup) white wine
- 1 bay leaf
- 2 thyme sprigs
- 12 slices day-old baguette
- 100 g (3½ oz/¾ cup) finely grated gruyère cheese

METHOD

1. Melt the butter in a heavy-based saucepan and add the onion. Cook over low heat, stirring occasionally, for 25 minutes, or until the onion is deep golden brown and beginning to caramelise.
2. Add the garlic and flour and stir continuously for 2 minutes. Gradually blend in the stock and the wine, stirring all the time, and bring to the boil. Add the bay leaf and thyme and season. Cover the pan and simmer for 25 minutes. Remove the bay leaf and thyme and check the seasoning. Preheat your grill (broiler).
3. Toast the bread, then put two slices in each of six warm soup bowls, and ladle the soup over the top. Sprinkle with the cheese and place under the hot grill until the cheese melts to golden brown. Serve immediately.

CREAM OF TOMATO SOUP

SERVES 4

INGREDIENTS

- 1.25 kg (2 lb 12 oz) ripe tomatoes
- 1 tablespoon olive oil
- 1 onion, chopped
- 375 ml (13 fl oz/1½ cups) chicken stock (page 11)
- 2 tablespoons tomato paste (concentrated purée)
- 1 teaspoon sugar
- 250 ml (9 fl oz/1 cup) cream, plus extra to serve
- chopped parsley, to serve

METHOD

1. To peel the tomatoes, score a cross in the base of each tomato. Put in a heatproof bowl and cover with boiling water. Leave for 30 seconds, then transfer to cold water and peel the skin away from the cross. Cut the tomatoes in half horizontally and scoop out the seeds with a teaspoon. Roughly chop the flesh.
2. Heat the oil in a large saucepan over medium heat, add the onion and cook for 3 minutes, or until soft. Add the tomato and cook, stirring occasionally, for 5 minutes, or until very soft. Stir in the stock, bring to the boil, reduce the heat and simmer for 10 minutes.
3. Cool slightly, then transfer to a food processor or blender. Process in batches until smooth, then return to the pan. Add the tomato paste and sugar and bring to the boil, stirring. Reduce the heat and stir in the cream. Season and serve with a swirl of cream and a little parsley.

GAZPACHO

SERVES 4

INGREDIENTS

- 1 kg (2 lb 4 oz) ripe tomatoes
- 2 slices day-old white Italian bread, crusts removed, broken into pieces
- 1 red capsicum (pepper), seeded and chopped
- 2 garlic cloves, chopped
- 1 small green chilli, chopped (optional)
- 1 teaspoon sugar
- 2 tablespoons red wine vinegar
- 2 tablespoons extra virgin olive oil
- 8 ice cubes

METHOD

1. To peel the tomatoes, score a cross in the base of each tomato. Put in a heatproof bowl and cover with boiling water. Leave for 30 seconds, then transfer to cold water and peel the skin away from the cross. Cut in half and scoop out the seeds. Roughly chop the flesh.
2. Soak the bread in cold water for 5 minutes, then squeeze out the water. Put the bread in a food processor with the tomato, capsicum, garlic, chilli, sugar and vinegar, and process until smooth.
3. With the motor running, add the oil to make a smooth mixture. Season well. Refrigerate for at least 2 hours. Serve in bowls with the ice cubes.

MUSHROOM SOUP

SERVES 2

INGREDIENTS

- 20 g (¾ oz) butter
- ½ onion, finely chopped
- 700 g (1 lb 9 oz) large field mushrooms (about 6)
- 1 garlic clove, crushed
- 1 tablespoon dry sherry
- 500 ml (17 fl oz/2 cups) chicken or vegetable stock (page 10–11)
- 1 tablespoon finely chopped parsley
- 2 tablespoons cream

METHOD

1. Melt the butter in a saucepan, add the onion and fry until it is softened but not browned. Add the mushrooms and garlic and continue frying. The mushrooms will give off some liquid, so keep frying for a further 10 minutes or so, until the liquid is absorbed back into the mixture.
2. Add the sherry to the pan, increase the heat and bring to the boil to burn off the alcohol. Allow to cool slightly, then transfer to a blender. Blend to form a smooth paste, then add the stock and blend until smooth.
3. Add the parsley and cream and blend together. Return to the pan and heat gently. Serve with crusty bread.

VICHYSSOISE

This rich potato and leek soup, thickened with cream and often served chilled, was created in New York in the 1920s by the French chef, Louis Diat. It was named, nostalgically, for his birthplace near Vichy.

SERVES 6

INGREDIENTS

- 50 g (1¾ oz) butter
- 1 onion, finely chopped
- 3 leeks, white part only, sliced
- 1 celery stalk, finely chopped
- 1 garlic clove, finely chopped
- 200 g (7 oz) potatoes, peeled and chopped
- 750 ml (26 fl oz/3 cups) chicken stock (page 11)
- 200 ml (7 fl oz) cream
- 2 tablespoons snipped chives

METHOD

1. Melt the butter in a large saucepan and add the onion, leek, celery and garlic. Cover the pan and cook over low heat, stirring occasionally, for 15 minutes, or until the vegetables are softened but not browned. Add the potato and stock and bring to the boil, then reduce the heat and leave to simmer, covered, for 20 minutes. Cool a little before puréeing in a blender or food processor. Return to the clean saucepan.
2. Bring the soup gently back to the boil and stir in the cream. Season with salt and white pepper and reheat without boiling. Serve hot or well chilled, garnished with chives.

CROUTONS AND CROUTES

Croutons are small cubes of toasted or fried bread, usually served as an accompaniment to soups or as a garnish in salad. Translated from the French, crouton means 'little crust'. Croûtes are larger, used to accompany soups, to absorb cooking juices from meat, or to float on top of soups such as French onion soup.

To make fried croutons, heat 1 cm (½ inch) oil and a knob of butter in a frying pan over high heat. Add the bread cubes (day-old bread is best) and toss for 2 minutes, until crisp and golden. For toasted croûtes, put slices of baguette under a hot grill (broiler) and cook for 2 minutes, until golden brown, then turn over and cook the other side.

THICK VEGETABLE SOUP

SERVES 6

INGREDIENTS

100 g (3½ oz/½ cup) dried red kidney beans or borlotti beans
1 tablespoon olive oil
1 leek, chopped
1 small onion, diced
2 carrots, chopped
2 celery stalks, chopped
1 large zucchini (courgette), chopped
1 tablespoon tomato paste (concentrated purée)
1 litre (35 fl oz/4 cups) vegetable stock (page 10)
400 g (14 oz) pumpkin (winter squash), cubed
2 potatoes, peeled and cubed
3 tablespoons chopped parsley

METHOD

1 Put the beans in a large bowl, cover with cold water and soak overnight. Rinse, then transfer to a saucepan, cover with cold water and cook for 45 minutes, or until just tender. Drain.

2 Meanwhile, heat the oil in a large saucepan. Add the leek and onion and cook over medium heat for 2–3 minutes until softened but not browned. Add the carrot, celery and zucchini and cook for 3–4 minutes. Add the tomato paste and stir for a further 1 minute, then pour in the stock and 1.25 litres (5 cups) water and bring to the boil. Reduce the heat to low and leave to simmer for 20 minutes.

3 Add the pumpkin, potato, parsley and kidney beans and simmer for a further 20 minutes, or until the vegetables are tender and the beans are cooked. Season to taste and serve with crusty bread.

NOTE: To save time, use 420 g (15 oz) tin red kidney beans. Rinse well before use.

CURRIED PARSNIP SOUP

SERVES 4

INGREDIENTS

2 tablespoons olive oil
2 large parsnips (about 550 g/1 lb 4 oz), peeled and chopped
1 onion, chopped
2 teaspoons curry paste, such as Madras
750 ml (26 fl oz/3 cups) vegetable stock (page 10) or water
60 ml (2 fl oz/¼ cup) cream

METHOD

1 Heat the oil in a large saucepan over medium heat. Add the parsnips and onion and cook for 5 minutes. Add the curry paste and cook, stirring, for 1 minute. Pour in 500 ml (17 fl oz/ 2 cups) of the stock.

2 Cover, bring to the boil, then simmer for about 20 minutes, or until the parsnips are tender. Cool slightly, then transfer to a food processor and blend until smooth. Return to the saucepan, stir in the remaining stock and the cream. Season well and serve hot with crusty bread.

‹ WATERCRESS SOUP

SERVES 4

INGREDIENTS

30 g (1 oz) butter
1 onion, finely chopped
250 g (9 oz) potatoes, peeled and diced
625 ml (21 fl oz/2½ cups) chicken stock (page 11)
1 kg (2 lb 4 oz) watercress, trimmed and chopped
125 ml (4 fl oz/½ cup) cream
125 ml (4 fl oz/½ cup) milk
pinch of ground nutmeg
watercress leaves, to garnish

METHOD

1 Melt the butter in a large saucepan and add the onion. Cover the pan and cook over low heat until the onion is softened but not browned. Add the potato and chicken stock and simmer for 12 minutes, or until the potato is tender. Add the watercress and cook for 1 minute.
2 Allow to cool a little before puréeing until smooth in a blender or food processor. Return to the clean saucepan.
3 Bring the soup gently back to the boil and stir in the cream and milk. Season with nutmeg, salt and pepper and reheat without boiling. Serve garnished with a few small watercress leaves.

PANCOTTO

SERVES 4

INGREDIENTS

900 g (2 lb) ripe tomatoes
2 tablespoons olive oil
3 garlic cloves, crushed
1 white onion, finely chopped
200 g (7 oz) day-old ciabatta, torn into pieces
875 ml (30 fl oz/3½ cups) chicken stock (page 11)
20 basil leaves, shredded
parmesan cheese shavings, to garnish

METHOD

1 To peel the tomatoes, score a cross in the base of each tomato. Put in a bowl and cover with boiling water. Leave for 30 seconds, then transfer to cold water and peel the skin away from the cross. Cut in half, remove the seeds and chop.
2 Heat the oil in a large saucepan. Cook the garlic and onion over low heat until softened but not browned. Add the tomatoes and season well. Cover and simmer for 30 minutes. Add the bread and simmer, stirring once or twice, for 5 minutes.
3 Slowly stir in the stock and stir until the bread has broken down. Remove from the heat and add the basil. Cover and leave for 1 hour. Serve at room temperature or warm, with parmesan.

• • MAIN-COURSE SOUP • •

These bowls of hearty, warming soup usually have a carbohydrate ingredient (perhaps pasta, beans or potato), making them substantial enough to eat as a meal in themselves. Most taste better after a day or so, letting you make a panful to last.

PEA AND HAM SOUP

SERVES 4–6

INGREDIENTS

- 440 g (15½ oz/2 cups) green split peas
- 750 g (1 lb 10 oz) ham bones
- 1 celery stalk, including leaves, chopped
- 1 carrot, peeled and chopped
- 1 onion, chopped
- 3 leeks, white part only, sliced
- 1 potato, peeled and chopped

METHOD

1. Put the split peas in a large bowl, cover with water and leave to soak for 4–8 hours. Drain.
2. Put the split peas, ham bones, celery, carrot and onion in a large saucepan with 2.5 litres (10 cups) water. Bring to the boil, then reduce the heat and simmer, covered, for 2 hours, or until the split peas are very soft.
3. Add the leek and potato to the pan and cook for 30 minutes, or until the vegetables are tender and the ham is falling off the bone.
4. Remove the ham bones from the soup. When the bones are cool enough to handle, cut off all the meat and finely chop.
5. Transfer the soup to a bowl to cool, then push it through a large wire sieve. (For a chunkier soup, don't push the mixture through a sieve — mash lightly with a potato masher.) Return the soup to the pan, stir in the chopped ham and reheat the soup to serve.

CAULIFLOWER, BEAN AND PROSCIUTTO SOUP

SERVES 4

INGREDIENTS

- 2 tablespoons olive oil
- 100 g (3½ oz) prosciutto, chopped
- 1 onion, chopped
- 1 garlic clove, crushed
- 800 g (1 lb 12 oz) cauliflower, cut into florets
- 2 x 400 g (14 oz) tins cannellini beans, rinsed
- 125 ml (4 fl oz/½ cup) cream
- snipped chives, to serve

METHOD

1. Heat 1 tablespoon of the oil in a large saucepan over medium–high heat. Add the prosciutto and sauté until crisp. Drain half the prosciutto on paper towel, leaving the rest in the saucepan.
2. Reduce the heat to medium. Add the remaining oil and the onion to the saucepan and fry for 5 minutes, or until softened. Add the garlic and cauliflower and fry for 3 minutes.
3. Add the beans and 1 litre (35 fl oz/4 cups) water and season well with salt and pepper. Bring to the boil, then reduce the heat and simmer, covered, for 15 minutes, until the cauliflower is tender. Set aside to cool for 10 minutes.
4. Purée the soup until smooth. Season with salt and plenty of pepper. Stir in the cream and gently reheat the soup. Serve immediately, with the crisp prosciutto and chives sprinkled on top.

PANCETTA, CABBAGE AND PASTA SOUP

SERVES 6

INGREDIENTS

- 50 g (1¾ oz) butter
- 1 onion, finely chopped
- 1 garlic clove, crushed
- 200 g (7 oz) pancetta, cubed
- 2 celery stalks, sliced
- 2 carrots, peeled and sliced
- 1 teaspoon tomato paste (concentrated purée)
- 400 g (14 oz) tin chopped tomatoes
- 2 tablespoons chopped parsley
- 2 litres (8 cups) chicken stock (page 11)
- 150 g (5½ oz) small soup pasta
- ½ savoy cabbage, shredded
- 200 g (7 oz/1⅓ cups) fresh or frozen peas
- grated parmesan cheese, to serve

METHOD

1. Heat the butter in a frying pan over medium heat, add the onion, garlic and pancetta and fry until soft and golden in colour.
2. Add the celery, carrot, tomato paste, tomatoes and parsley and stir to combine. Add the stock and bring to the boil. Simmer for 1¾ hours, then add the pasta and cook for 5 minutes.
3. Add the cabbage and peas to the pan and cook for a further 2 minutes, or until the pasta is *al dente* and the cabbage and peas are cooked. Taste for seasoning and serve with grated parmesan.

MINESTRONE

Minestrone is Italian for vegetable soup. Each region has its own recipe for minestrone, but most use onions, tomatoes, zucchini, beans and celery. The vegetables are cooked for 2 to 3 hours so their flavours are completely blended. In some recipes, grated parmesan or spoonfuls of pesto are added at the end of cooking. In the south of Italy, the soup is thickened with pasta; in the north, rice is used. Although minestrone can be served as a starter, it is so thick and filling that a bowl usually constitutes a meal in itself.

MINESTRONE ALLA GENOVESE

SERVES 6

INGREDIENTS

- 220 g (7¾ oz) dried borlotti beans
- 50 g (1¾ oz) butter
- 1 large onion, finely chopped
- 1 garlic clove, finely chopped
- 1 large handful parsley, finely chopped
- 2 sage leaves
- 100 g (3½ oz) pancetta, cubed
- 2 celery stalks, sliced
- 2 carrots, peeled and sliced
- 3 potatoes, peeled but left whole
- 1 teaspoon tomato paste (concentrated purée)
- 400 g (14 oz) tin chopped tomatoes
- 8 basil leaves
- 3 litres (12 cups) chicken or vegetable stock (page 10–11)
- 2 zucchini (courgettes), sliced
- 220 g (7¾ oz) fresh or frozen peas
- 120 g (4¼ oz) green beans, cut into 4 cm (1½ inch) lengths
- ¼ cabbage, shredded
- 150 g (5½ oz) small soup pasta
- 1 quantity pesto (page 265)
- grated parmesan cheese, to serve

METHOD

1. Put the borlotti beans in a large bowl, cover with cold water and leave to soak overnight. Drain and rinse under cold water.
2. Melt the butter in a large saucepan and add the onion, garlic, parsley, sage and pancetta to make a 'sofrito'. Cook over low heat, stirring once or twice, for about 10 minutes, or until the onion is soft and golden.
3. Add the celery, carrot and potatoes and cook for 5 minutes. Stir in the tomato paste, tomatoes, basil and borlotti beans. Season with plenty of freshly ground black pepper. Add the stock and bring slowly to the boil. Cover and leave to simmer for 2 hours, stirring once or twice.
4. If the potatoes haven't already broken up, roughly crush them with a fork against the side of the pan. Taste for seasoning and add the zucchini, peas, beans, cabbage and pasta. Simmer until the pasta is *al dente*. Serve with a dollop of pesto and the parmesan.

NOTE: The 'sofrito' forms the base of most Italian stews, soups, risottos and sauces. It may contain any or all of the following: finely chopped pancetta, ham or pork, garlic, onion, carrot, celery, tomatoes or capsicums. These are slowly cooked in oil to release their flavours.

SAUSAGE AND BORLOTTI BEAN SOUP

SERVES 4

INGREDIENTS

2 tablespoons olive oil
3 thin Italian sausages
100 g (3½ oz) thickly sliced pancetta, cut into 5 mm x 2 cm (¼ x ¾ inch) strips
2 onions, chopped
1 leek, white part only, sliced
2 garlic cloves, chopped
2 celery stalks, chopped
2 carrots, chopped
2 large thyme sprigs
1 litre (35 fl oz/4 cups) chicken or vegetable stock (page 10–11)
400 g (14 oz) tin borlotti beans, rinsed
400 g (14 oz) tin chopped tomatoes
2 large handfuls parsley, chopped

METHOD

1 Heat a little of the oil in a large frying pan over medium heat. Fry the sausages for 5–6 minutes, or until browned all over. Add the pancetta halfway through cooking the sausage. Remove from the heat and set aside.
2 Heat the remaining oil in a large heavy-based saucepan and add the onion, leek, garlic, celery and carrot. Stir for 2 minutes to coat the vegetables in the oil. Reduce the heat, cover and simmer, stirring occasionally, for 10 minutes. Do not allow the vegetables to brown.
3 Add the thyme and stock. Slowly bring to the boil, then reduce the heat and simmer, covered, for 20 minutes. Remove the thyme. Stir in the beans, then remove the saucepan from the heat.
4 Roughly purée the soup in a blender and return to the pan. Dice the sausages and add them to the soup along with the pancetta and tomatoes. Gently reheat, stir in the parsley and season with salt and pepper.

› LENTIL AND SPINACH SOUP

SERVES 6

INGREDIENTS

280 g (10 oz/1½ cups) brown lentils, washed
1 litre (35 fl oz/4 cups) chicken stock (page 11)
60 ml (2 fl oz/¼ cup) olive oil
1 large onion, finely chopped
4 garlic cloves, crushed
850 g (1 lb 14 oz) spinach or silverbeet, stems removed, shredded
35 g (1¼ oz) finely chopped coriander (cilantro)
80 ml (2½ fl oz/⅓ cup) lemon juice
lemon wedges, to serve

METHOD

1 Put the lentils in a large saucepan, add the stock and 1 litre (35 fl oz/4 cups) water. Bring to the boil, then reduce the heat and simmer, covered, for 1 hour.
2 Heat the oil in a saucepan over medium heat, add the onion and cook for 3–4 minutes. Add the garlic and cook for 1 minute, then toss in the spinach and heat until wilted. Stir the mixture into the lentils.
3 Add the coriander and lemon juice and season well. Simmer, covered, for 15–20 minutes. Serve with lemon wedges.

MULLIGATAWNY

SERVES 6

INGREDIENTS

30 g (1 oz) butter
375 g (13 oz) boneless, skinless chicken thighs
1 large onion, finely chopped
1 apple, peeled, cored and diced
1 tablespoon Indian curry paste
2 tablespoons plain (all-purpose) flour
750 ml (26 fl oz/3 cups) chicken stock (page 11)
3 tablespoons basmati rice
1 tablespoon mango chutney
1 tablespoon lemon juice
60 ml (2 fl oz/¼ cup) cream
chopped coriander (cilantro), to serve

METHOD

1 Heat the butter in a large heavy-based pan and brown the chicken for 5 minutes, then remove. Add the onion, apple and curry paste to the pan, cook for 5 minutes, until the onion is soft, then stir in the flour. Cook for 2 minutes, stirring, then add half the stock. Stir until it boils and thickens.
2 Return the chicken to the pan with the remaining stock. Stir until boiling, then reduce the heat, cover and simmer for 1 hour.
3 Add the rice for the last 15 minutes. Remove the chicken, dice and return to the soup. Add the chutney, lemon juice and cream and garnish with coriander to serve.

BORSCHT

SERVES 6

INGREDIENTS

1 tablespoon oil
1 small onion, chopped
1.5 kg (3 lb 5 oz) beetroot, peeled and chopped
1.25 litres (5 cups) vegetable stock (page 10)
2 teaspoons caraway seeds
2 tablespoons horseradish cream
250 g (9 oz/1 cup) sour cream

METHOD

1 Heat the oil in a heavy-based saucepan. Add the onion and cook over medium heat for 5 minutes, or until soft.
2 Add the beetroot, stock and caraway seeds and bring to the boil. Simmer, partially covered, for 40 minutes. Cool, then process in batches until smooth. Reheat gently and stir in the horseradish and sour cream to serve.

HARIRA

SERVES 4

INGREDIENTS

- 2 tablespoons olive oil
- 2 small onions, chopped
- 2 large garlic cloves, crushed
- 500 g (1 lb 2 oz) lamb shoulder steaks, trimmed of excess fat and sinew, cut into small chunks
- 1½ teaspoons ground cumin
- 2 teaspoons paprika
- ½ teaspoon ground cloves
- 1 bay leaf
- 2 tablespoons tomato paste (concentrated purée)
- 1 litre (35 fl oz/4 cups) beef stock (page 11)
- 600 g (1 lb 5 oz) tin chickpeas, rinsed
- 2 x 400 g (14 oz) tins chopped tomatoes
- 30 g (1 oz) finely chopped coriander (cilantro), plus extra leaves to garnish

METHOD

1. Heat the oil in a large heavy-based saucepan or stockpot, add the onion and garlic and cook for 5 minutes, or until softened. Add the meat, in batches, and brown over high heat. Return all the meat to the pan.
2. Add the spices and bay leaf and cook until fragrant. Add the tomato paste and cook for 2 minutes, stirring constantly. Pour in the stock, stir well and bring to the boil.
3. Add the chickpeas, tomatoes and chopped coriander to the pan. Stir, bring to the boil, then reduce the heat and simmer for 2 hours, or until the meat is tender, stirring occasionally. Season with salt and freshly ground black pepper. Garnish with coriander and serve with bread.

OXTAIL SOUP

SERVES 4

INGREDIENTS

- 2 oxtails, chopped (ask your butcher to do this)
- 2 tablespoons oil
- 3 onions, chopped
- 4 garlic cloves, chopped
- 1 tablespoon plain (all-purpose) flour
- 1 litre (35 fl oz/4 cups) beef stock (page 11)
- 2 bay leaves, torn in half
- 2 tablespoons tomato paste (concentrated purée)
- 2 teaspoons worcestershire sauce
- 4 potatoes, peeled and chopped
- 2 parsnips, peeled and chopped
- 2 carrots, peeled and chopped
- 3 tomatoes, chopped
- 2 tablespoons chopped parsley

METHOD

1. Cut the excess fat from the oxtail. Heat the oil in a heavy-based saucepan and brown the oxtail in batches. Return all the meat to the pan. Add the onion and garlic and cook until just softened.
2. Add the flour and cook, stirring, for 1 minute. Mix in half the stock and bring to the boil, stirring. Remove from the heat and refrigerate the soup for 2 hours, or until the fat can be spooned from the surface.
3. Add the remaining stock, 1 litre (35 fl oz/4 cups) water, bay leaves, tomato paste, worcestershire sauce and season with salt and pepper. Bring to the boil, then reduce the heat to low and simmer, covered, for 2 hours, stirring occasionally.
4. Add the potato, parsnip and carrot and simmer for 10 minutes, or until tender. Remove the bay leaves before serving. Garnish with the chopped tomato and parsley.

••SEAFOOD SOUP••

Clam chowder, bouillabaisse and crab bisque — these are some of the seafood dishes that are known and loved in their home countries and the world over. Just because you're putting the seafood in a soup doesn't mean you shouldn't buy good-quality produce. And, if you keep the trimmings to make your own stock, you'll lift your soup to a higher level.

BOURRIDE

SERVES 4

INGREDIENTS

GARLIC CROUTONS
½ day-old baguette, sliced
60 ml (2 fl oz/¼ cup) olive oil
1 garlic clove, halved

¼ teaspoon saffron threads
1 litre (35 fl oz/4 cups) dry white wine
1 leek, white part only, chopped
2 carrots, peeled and chopped
2 onions, chopped
2 long pieces orange zest
2 teaspoons fennel seeds
3 thyme sprigs
2.5 kg (5 lb 8 oz) whole firm white fish such as monkfish, sea bass, cod, perch, sole or bream, filleted, skinned and cut into 4 cm (1½ inch) pieces (reserve the trimmings)
1 quantity aïoli (page 422)
3 egg yolks

METHOD

1 Preheat the oven to 160°C (315°F/Gas 2–3). To make the garlic croutons, brush the bread with oil and bake for 10 minutes until crisp. Rub one side of each slice with garlic.
2 To make the stock, combine the saffron and 1 tablespoon of hot water in a bowl. Set aside for 15 minutes. Put the saffron and its soaking water, wine, leek, carrot, onion, orange zest, fennel seeds, thyme and fish trimmings in a large saucepan with 1 litre (35 fl oz/4 cups) water. Cover and bring to the boil, then simmer for 20 minutes, skimming occasionally. Strain into a clean saucepan, pressing the solids with a wooden spoon to extract all the liquid.
3 Bring the stock to a gentle simmer, add half the fish pieces and poach for 5 minutes. Remove with a slotted spoon and keep warm while you cook the rest of the fish. Remove the fish from the pan and return the stock to the boil. Boil for 5 minutes, or until slightly reduced. Remove from the heat.
4 Put half the aïoli and the egg yolks in a bowl and mix until smooth. Whisk in a ladleful of hot stock, then gradually add five ladlefuls, stirring constantly. Pour back into the pan holding the rest of the stock and whisk over low heat for 3–5 minutes, or until the soup is hot and slightly thicker (don't let it boil or it will curdle). Season with salt and pepper.
5 To serve, put two garlic croutons in each bowl, top with a few pieces of fish and ladle over the hot soup. Serve the remaining aïoli separately.

MANHATTAN CLAM CHOWDER

SERVES 4

INGREDIENTS

- 1 kg (2 lb 4 oz) large clams (vongole)
- 1 tablespoon olive oil
- 100 g (3½ oz) bacon, chopped
- 1 onion, chopped
- 2 celery stalks, chopped
- 1 potato, peeled and diced
- 1 leek, white part only, chopped
- 1 bay leaf
- 400 g (14 oz) tin chopped tomatoes
- 750 ml (26 fl oz/3 cups) fish stock (page 10)

METHOD

1. Soak the clams in a bucket of salted cold water for 1–2 hours to rid them of sand, then rinse under running water. Discard any clams that are broken or any that are open and do not close when tapped on the work surface.
2. Put 1 cm (½ inch) water in a large saucepan and bring to the boil. Add the clams, cover and cook for 3 minutes, until they all open — discard any closed ones. Take out the clam meat and strain the liquid into a bowl.
3. Heat the oil in a frying pan over low–medium heat, add the bacon, onion, celery, potato and leek and fry for 10 minutes. Add the bay leaf, the reserved clam liquid, tomatoes and stock. Simmer for 10 minutes, or until the potato is cooked. Season, then stir in the clams. Remove the bay leaf and serve.

CHOWDER AND BISQUE

Originally chowder was a thick soup made from fish or shellfish, but the term is now applied to any rich, chunky soup, with corn chowder being a popular example. Chowder comes from the French word *chaudière*, the cauldron used by fishermen to cook their soup. Clam chowder is popular in North America — the New England version uses a milk or cream base while Manhattan chowder has a tomato and herb base.

Like chowder, bisque is a rich, thick soup, usually made from shellfish and flavoured with white wine or cognac and cream. Typically, bisque is made using crab, lobster or oysters. Today, the term bisque is misused to mean any smooth, creamy soup, including vegetable or chicken.

‹ CRAB BISQUE

SERVES 4

INGREDIENTS

- 1 kg (2 lb 4 oz) live crabs
- 50 g (1¾ oz) butter
- ½ carrot, finely chopped
- ½ onion, finely chopped
- 1 celery stalk, finely chopped
- 1 bay leaf
- 2 thyme sprigs
- 2 tablespoons tomato paste (concentrated purée)
- 2 tablespoons brandy
- 150 ml (5 fl oz) dry white wine
- 1 litre (35 fl oz/4 cups) fish stock (page 10)
- 60 g (2¼ oz/⅓ cup) medium-grain rice
- 60 ml (2 fl oz/¼ cup) cream
- ¼ teaspoon cayenne pepper, or to taste

METHOD

1. Freeze the crabs for 2 hours to immobilise them, then drop them into boiling water and cook just until the shells turn red. Remove with tongs and set aside until cool enough to handle.
2. Following steps 3–5 on page 210, cut the crab and pick out the meat from the body. Reserve four crab claws and pick the meat out of the rest. Reserve the meat and shells separately.
3. Heat the butter in a large saucepan. Add the vegetables, bay leaf and thyme and cook over medium heat for 3 minutes, without allowing the vegetables to colour. Add the reserved crab shells, the tomato paste, brandy and wine and simmer for 2 minutes, or until reduced by half.
4. Add the stock and 500 ml (17 fl oz/2 cups) water and bring to the boil. Reduce the heat and simmer for 5 minutes. Remove the shells and finely crush them with a mortar and pestle (or in a food processor with a little of the stock). Return the crushed shells to the soup with the rice and the reserved crabmeat. Bring to the boil, reduce the heat, cover and simmer for about 20 minutes, or until the rice is soft.
5. Immediately strain the bisque into a clean saucepan through a fine sieve lined with damp muslin, pressing down firmly on the solids to extract all the soup. Add the cream and season with salt and cayenne pepper, then gently reheat. Ladle into warmed soup bowls and garnish with the crab claws.

PRAWN BISQUE

SERVES 4–6

INGREDIENTS

- 60 g (2¼ oz) butter
- 500 g (1 lb 2 oz) raw prawns (shrimp), peeled and deveined (heads and shells reserved)
- 2 tablespoons plain (all-purpose) flour
- 2 litres (8 cups) fish stock (page 10)
- ½ teaspoon paprika
- 250 ml (9 fl oz/1 cup) cream
- 80 ml (2½ fl oz/⅓ cup) dry sherry
- 1–2 tablespoons cream, extra, to serve
- paprika, extra, to garnish

METHOD

1. Heat the butter in a large saucepan, add the prawn heads and shells and cook, stirring, over medium heat for 5 minutes, lightly crushing the heads with a wooden spoon.
2. Add the flour to the pan and stir until combined. Add the stock and paprika and stir over medium heat until the mixture boils. Reduce the heat and simmer, covered, over low heat for 10 minutes.
3. Strain the mixture through a fine sieve set over a bowl, then return the liquid to the pan. Add the prawns and cook over low heat for 2–3 minutes. Cool slightly, then process in batches in a food processor until smooth.
4. Return the mixture to the pan. Add the cream and sherry to the pan and stir to heat through. Season with salt and pepper. Serve topped with a swirl of cream and sprinkled with paprika.

NEW ENGLAND CLAM CHOWDER

SERVES 4

INGREDIENTS

- 1.5 kg (3 lb 5 oz) clams (vongole) or pipis, in their shells
- 2 teaspoons oil
- 3 slices bacon, chopped
- 1 onion, chopped
- 1 garlic clove, crushed
- 750 g (1 lb 10 oz) potatoes, diced
- 310 ml (10¾ fl oz/1¼ cups) fish stock (page 10)
- 500 ml (17 fl oz/2 cups) milk
- 125 ml (4 fl oz/½ cup) cream
- 3 tablespoons finely chopped parsley

METHOD

1. Soak the clams in a bucket or bowl of salted cold water for 1–2 hours to rid them of sand, then rinse under running water. Discard any clams that are broken or any that are open and do not close when tapped on the work surface. Drain the clams and put in a large heavy-based saucepan with 250 ml (9 fl oz/1 cup) water. Cover and simmer over low heat for 5 minutes, or until the clams open. Discard any that do not open. Strain and reserve the liquid. Remove the clam meat from the shells.
2. Heat the oil in a clean saucepan. Add the bacon, onion and garlic and cook, stirring, over medium heat until the onion is soft and the bacon is golden. Add the potato and stir well.
3. Measure the reserved clam liquid and add water to make 310 ml (10¾ fl oz/1¼ cups). Add to the pan along with the stock and milk. Bring to the boil, then reduce the heat, cover and simmer for 20 minutes, or until the potato is tender. Uncover and simmer for 10 minutes, or until slightly thickened. Add the cream, clam meat and parsley and season to taste. Heat through gently before serving, but do not allow to boil or the liquid may curdle.

› CREAMY CLAM SOUP

SERVES 4

INGREDIENTS

- 1.8 kg (4 lb) clams, cleaned (page 202)
- 1 litre (35 fl oz/4 cups) fish stock (page 10)
- 60 g (2¼ oz) butter
- 1 onion, chopped
- 1 celery stalk, chopped
- 1 large carrot, chopped
- 2 large leeks, sliced into rings
- 1 bay leaf
- 85 g (3 oz) long-grain white rice
- 185 ml (6 fl oz/¾ cup) cream

METHOD

1. Put the clams in a large heavy-based saucepan with 250 ml (9 fl oz/1 cup) water. Place over high heat, bring to the boil, then reduce the heat to medium, cover and simmer for 5 minutes, or until the clams open. Discard any that do not open. Strain and reserve the liquid. Add enough fish stock to make 1 litre (35 fl oz/4 cups).
2. Rinse the saucepan, then return to the heat, add the butter and cook the onion, celery, carrot and leek over medium heat, covered, for 10 minutes, stirring occasionally. Add the stock and bay leaf, bring to the boil, then reduce the heat and simmer for 10 minutes. Add the rice, return to the boil, then cover and cook for 15–20 minutes, or until the rice and vegetables are tender.
3. Remove all but eight of the cooked clams from the shells. When ready, remove the soup from the heat and stir in the clam meat. Remove the bay leaf. Cool slightly, then process in batches in a blender until smooth (a food processor can be used but it will not achieve the same smooth consistency). Rinse the saucepan. Pass the soup through a sieve back into the pan. Stir in the cream and season with salt and pepper. Gently reheat and serve, garnishing with the reserved clams.

CIOPPINO

Cioppino is a version of the Ligurian fish stew, *ciuppin*, which originated in the bay area of San Francisco. Like bouillabaisse, cioppino was first made by fishermen from the leftovers when their catch had been sold. It can be made with any variety of fish and seafood, and is then poured over chunks of stale bread to serve.

SERVES 4

INGREDIENTS

- 2 dried Chinese mushrooms
- 1 kg (2 lb 4 oz) firm white fish fillets (hake, cod, snapper, ocean perch)
- 375 g (13 oz) raw large prawns (shrimp)
- 1 raw lobster tail (about 400 g/14 oz)
- 12–15 black mussels
- 60 ml (2 fl oz/¼ cup) olive oil
- 1 large onion, finely chopped
- 1 green capsicum (pepper), finely chopped
- 2–3 garlic cloves, crushed
- 400 g (14 oz) tin chopped tomatoes
- 250 ml (9 fl oz/1 cup) white wine
- 250 ml (9 fl oz/1 cup) tomato juice
- 250 ml (9 fl oz/1 cup) fish stock (page 10)
- 1 bay leaf
- 2 parsley sprigs
- 2 teaspoons chopped basil
- 1 tablespoon chopped parsley

METHOD

1. Place the mushrooms in a small bowl, cover with boiling water and soak for 20 minutes. Cut the fish into bite-sized pieces, removing the bones.
2. Peel the prawns, leaving the tails intact. Gently pull out the dark vein from each prawn back, starting at the head end.
3. Starting at the end where the head was, cut down the sides of the lobster shell on the underside with kitchen scissors. Pull back the flap, remove the meat and cut into small pieces.
4. Scrub the mussels with a stiff brush and pull out the hairy beards. Discard any broken mussels, or open ones that don't close when tapped on the work surface. Rinse well.
5. Drain the mushrooms, squeeze dry and chop finely. Heat the oil in a heavy-based saucepan, add the onion, capsicum and garlic and stir over medium heat for about 5 minutes, or until the onion is soft. Add the mushrooms, tomato, wine, tomato juice, stock, bay leaf, parsley sprigs and basil. Bring to the boil, reduce the heat, then cover and simmer for 30 minutes.
6. Layer the fish and prawns in a large pan. Add the sauce, then cover and leave on low heat for 10 minutes, or until the prawns are pink and the fish is cooked. Add the lobster and mussels and simmer for another 4–5 minutes. Season with salt and pepper. Discard any unopened mussels. Sprinkle with parsley before serving.

TINNED TOMATOES AND TOMATO PASSATA

Tinned peeled tomatoes are available chopped, whole, crushed and pulped. Unless you have ripe flavoursome tomatoes to hand, tinned tomatoes make a perfectly good substitute. You might need to add a pinch of sugar to counteract their acidity.

Tomato passata is a bottled tomato sauce made from fresh, ripe tomatoes that have been peeled, seeded and slowly cooked with fresh basil, onion and garlic. The thickened sauce is then passed through a sieve before it is bottled.

BOUILLABAISSE

Traditionally, bouillabaisse was made by cooking pieces of white fish in a broth of tomatoes, oil, garlic, saffron and herbs, but it is now common to include shellfish as well. Bouillabaisse was once a humble affair, made by French fishermen on their boats as a way to use up fish that weren't suitable for market. The soup and the fish can be served separately, the soup followed by the fish, but it is more usual to see them eaten together.

A good bouillabaisse is said to include at least seven different types of fish, and debate still takes place over which varieties are best to use. The people of Marseilles, the home of the bouillabaisse, consider the strong-tasting racasse to be the quintessential element. You can use any seafood combination to make the soup. Use the shellfish and fish as suggested in the recipe or add shellfish such as crab (pictured) — whatever seafood is freshest and in season.

BOUILLABAISSE

SERVES 4

INGREDIENTS

- 300 g (10½ oz) raw prawns (shrimp)
- 16–18 black mussels
- 200 g (7 oz) scallops
- 1.5 kg (3 lb 5 oz) assorted white fish fillets (such as red rock cod, snapper, mullet, monkfish, john dory, sea bass, bream)
- 5 ripe tomatoes
- 2 tablespoons oil
- 1 fennel bulb, thinly sliced
- 1 onion, chopped
- 1.25 litres (5 cups) fish stock (page 10)
- pinch of saffron threads
- 1 bay leaf
- 1 bouquet garni
- 5 cm (2 inch) strip of orange zest
- 1 tablespoon chopped parsley

ROUILLE

- 1 small red capsicum (pepper)
- 1 red chilli
- 1 slice white bread, crusts removed
- 2 garlic cloves
- 1 egg yolk
- 80 ml (2½ fl oz/⅓ cup) olive oil

METHOD

1. Peel the prawns and gently pull out the dark vein from each prawn back, starting at the head end. Scrub the mussels with a stiff brush and pull out the hairy beards. Discard any broken mussels, or open ones that don't close when tapped on the work surface. Slice or pull off any vein, membrane or hard white muscle from the scallops, leaving any roe attached. Cut the fish into large bite-sized pieces. Refrigerate the seafood, covered.
2. To peel the tomatoes, score a cross in the base of each tomato. Put in a heatproof bowl and cover with boiling water. Leave for 30 seconds, then transfer to cold water and peel the skin away from the cross. Cut the tomatoes in half horizontally and scoop out the seeds with a teaspoon. Roughly chop the flesh.
3. Heat the oil in a large saucepan over medium heat, add the fennel and onion and cook for 5 minutes, or until golden. Add the tomato and cook for 3 minutes. Stir in the stock, saffron, bay leaf, bouquet garni and orange zest. Bring to the boil and boil for 10 minutes. Reduce the heat to simmer and add the scallops, prawns, mussels and fish. Simmer for 4–5 minutes, or until the mussels open. Discard any unopened mussels. Remove the bouquet garni and orange zest.
4. To make the rouille, cut the capsicum and chilli into large flattish pieces. Remove the seeds and membrane and cook, skin side up, under a hot grill (broiler) until the skin blackens and blisters. Place the capsicum and chilli in a plastic bag and leave to cool, then peel.
5. Soak the bread in 60 ml (2 fl oz/¼ cup) water, then squeeze out any excess. Process the capsicum, chilli, bread, garlic and egg yolk in a food processor. With the motor running, add the oil in a thin stream, until the mixture is thick and smooth.
6. Ladle the bouillabaisse into bowls, sprinkle with parsley and serve with the rouille and crusty bread.

••ASIAN SOUP••

Asian soup can be hearty, noodle-filled, meals-in-a-bowl, tangy, clear and palate-cleansing or soothing comfort food, rich with coconut milk. In Asia, soup is enjoyed throughout the day, even for breakfast.

SEAFOOD LAKSA

A spicy noodle soup popular in Malaysia, Singapore and the Philippines, laksa is a blend of Chinese, Indian and Malaysian cuisines. Laksa can be made with ready-made laksa paste, sold in supermarkets. The recipe below gives the method for making the paste yourself.

SERVES 4–6

INGREDIENTS

- 1 kg (2 lb 4 oz) raw prawns (shrimp)
- 80 ml (2½ fl oz/⅓ cup) oil
- 2–6 red chillies, seeded, finely chopped
- 1 onion, roughly chopped
- 3 garlic cloves, halved
- 2 cm (¾ inch) piece ginger or galangal, chopped
- 1 teaspoon ground turmeric
- 1 tablespoon ground coriander
- 3 lemongrass stems, white part only, chopped
- 1–2 teaspoons shrimp paste
- 625 ml (21 fl oz/2½ cups) coconut cream
- 2 teaspoons grated palm sugar (jaggery) or soft brown sugar
- 4 kaffir lime leaves, lightly crushed
- 1–2 tablespoons fish sauce
- 200 g (7 oz) packet fish balls
- 190 g (6¾ oz) packet tofu puffs
- 250 g (9 oz) dried rice vermicelli
- 250 g (9 oz) bean sprouts
- chopped mint, to serve
- coriander (cilantro) leaves, to serve

METHOD

1. Peel the prawns and gently pull out the dark vein from each prawn back, starting at the head end. Keep the shells, heads and tails. Cover the prawn meat and refrigerate.
2. To make the prawn stock, heat 2 tablespoons of the oil in a large, heavy-based saucepan or wok and add the prawn shells, heads and tails. Stir until the heads are bright orange, then add 1 litre (35 fl oz/4 cups) water. Bring to the boil, reduce the heat and simmer for 15 minutes. Strain through a fine sieve, discarding the shells. Clean the pan.
3. Put the chilli, onion, garlic, ginger, ground turmeric and coriander, lemongrass and 60 ml (2 fl oz/¼ cup) of the prawn stock in a food processor and process until finely chopped.
4. Heat the remaining oil in the clean pan and add the chilli mixture and shrimp paste. Stir over low heat for 3 minutes, or until fragrant. Pour in the remaining stock and simmer for 10 minutes. Add the coconut cream, sugar, lime leaves and fish sauce. Simmer for 5 minutes.
5. Add the prawns and simmer for 2 minutes, until just pink. Add the fish balls and tofu puffs and simmer gently until just heated through. Soak the rice vermicelli in a bowl of boiling water for 2 minutes, drain and divide among the serving bowls. Top with bean sprouts and ladle over the soup. Sprinkle with the mint and coriander.

WON TON SOUP

SERVES 6

INGREDIENTS

- 250 g (9 oz) prawns (shrimp)
- 80 g (2¾ oz) tinned water chestnuts, chopped
- 250 g (9 oz) lean minced (ground) pork
- 70 ml (2¼ fl oz) light soy sauce
- 70 ml (2¼ fl oz) Chinese rice wine
- 1½ teaspoons sesame oil
- 1 teaspoon finely chopped ginger
- 1½ tablespoons cornflour (cornstarch), plus extra for dusting
- 30 square or round won ton wrappers
- 1.5 litres (6 cups) chicken stock (page 11)
- 2 spring onions (scallions), finely chopped

METHOD

1 Peel the prawns and gently pull out the dark vein from each prawn back, starting at the head end. Place in a cloth and squeeze out the moisture. Put the prawns in a food processor and process to a coarse paste.

2 Put the prawn meat, water chestnuts, pork, 2 teaspoons of the soy sauce, 2 teaspoons of the rice wine, ½ teaspoon of the sesame oil, the ginger and cornflour in a bowl. Season well and stir vigorously to combine.

3 Put a teaspoon of filling in the centre of a wrapper. Brush the edge with a little water, fold in half and bring the two folded corners together; press firmly. Put on a tray dusted with cornflour.

4 Bring a saucepan of water to the boil. Cook the won tons, covered, for 5–6 minutes, until they rise to the surface. Remove with a slotted spoon and divide among six bowls.

5 Put the stock in a saucepan with the remaining soy sauce, rice wine, sesame oil and 1 teaspoon salt, and bring to the boil. Pour the stock over the won tons and sprinkle with the spring onion.

CHICKEN NOODLE SOUP

SERVES 4–6

INGREDIENTS

- 2.5 litres (10 cups) chicken stock (page 11)
- 1 star anise
- 4 x 5 mm (¼ inch) slices ginger
- 600 g (1 lb 5 oz) boneless, skinless chicken breasts
- 375 g (13 oz) Shanghai noodles
- 200 g (7 oz) asparagus, cut into 3 cm (1¼ inch) pieces
- 1 tablespoon julienned ginger
- 1½ tablespoons light soy sauce
- 1 tablespoon Chinese rice wine
- ½ teaspoon sugar
- 4 spring onions (scallions), thinly sliced
- ¼ teaspoon sesame oil

METHOD

1 Pour the stock into a wok and bring to the boil. Reduce the heat to medium, add the star anise, ginger and chicken and poach the chicken for 15–20 minutes, or until cooked through. Remove the chicken with a slotted spoon and cool. Leave the stock in the wok.

2 Bring 2 litres (8 cups) water to the boil in a large saucepan and cook the noodles for 3 minutes. Drain and refresh under cold water.

3 Cut the chicken across the breast into 5 mm (¼ inch) slices. Return the stock to the boil and add the asparagus, ginger, soy sauce, rice wine, sugar and ½ teaspoon salt. Reduce the heat, add the noodles and simmer for 2 minutes. Add the chicken and heat through for 1 minute.

4 Remove the noodles from the liquid with tongs and divide among serving bowls. Divide the chicken, asparagus and spring onion among the bowls, then ladle the broth on top. Drizzle with sesame oil and serve with soy sauce.

MISO

Miso is a rich, earthy paste made from fermented soya beans. The beans are boiled and then ground into a thick paste, with wheat, barley or rice added to it. The mixture is injected with yeast and left to ferment. There are many different grades and colours of miso, each suited to a particular recipe. Generally the lighter the colour, the sweeter and less salty the taste.

MISO SOUP

SERVES 4

INGREDIENTS

DASHI STOCK

10 cm (4 inch) square piece kombu seaweed

20 g (¾ oz/1 cup) bonito flakes

1½ teaspoons dried wakame pieces

200 g (7 oz) silken firm tofu, cut into 1.5 cm (⅝ inch) cubes

1 spring onion (scallion), thinly sliced on the diagonal

100 g (3½ oz/⅓ cup) aka (red) or shiro (white) miso, or a mixture of both

METHOD

1. To make the dashi stock, wipe the kombu with a damp cloth but do not rub off the white powdery substance that will become obvious as it dries.
2. Cut the kombu into strips. Put the kombu and 1.5 litres (6 cups) cold water into a saucepan and slowly bring to the boil. Quickly add 60 ml (2 fl oz/¼ cup) cold water to stop the boiling process. Add the bonito, return to the boil, then reduce the heat and simmer for 15 minutes.
3. Remove from the heat. Allow the bonito to sink to the bottom of the pan, then strain the liquid through a fine sieve. You will need about 875 ml (30 fl oz/3½ cups) dashi stock for the soup.
4. Soak the wakame in cold water for 5 minutes, or until rehydrated and glossy. Drain well, then divide among four small soup bowls. Divide the tofu and the spring onion among the bowls.
5. Pour the dashi into a saucepan and bring to the boil. Combine the miso with 250 ml (9 fl oz/ 1 cup) of the hot dashi in a bowl and whisk until smooth. Return the miso mixture to the pan and stir until combined — be careful not to boil the broth, as this will diminish the flavour of the miso.
6. Ladle into the bowls until they are two-thirds full and serve immediately. To drink the miso, sip the soup from the bowl — rest the bowl in your left hand and tilt to your lips with your right. Then use chopsticks to eat the solid ingredients.

TYPES OF MISO

HATCHO MISO

This is a very dark, strongly flavoured, salty miso that is most often used in soups. It is made using only soya beans and water.

AKA OR INAKA MISO

Also called red miso, this has barley mould added. It is used in soups and stews and can be either sweet or salty.

SHINSHU MISO

This is one of the most commonly found misos outside Asia. It is smooth, yellow and salty and can be used in most recipes.

SHIRO MISO

Also called white miso, this is actually more yellow than white. Its sweet, mild taste makes it good for dressings and soups.

THOM KHA GAI

This soup is one of the classic dishes of Thailand. It translates literally as 'boiled galangal chicken' — which doesn't really do justice to its absolutely perfect blend of hot, sour, sweet and salty. You can make this with prawns or fish instead of chicken.

SERVES 4

INGREDIENTS

- 750 ml (26 fl oz/3 cups) coconut milk
- 2 lemongrass stems, white part only, bruised
- 5 cm (2 inch) piece galangal, cut into several pieces
- 4 red Asian shallots, crushed with the flat side of a knife
- 400 g (14 oz) boneless, skinless chicken breasts, thinly sliced
- 2 tablespoons fish sauce
- 1 tablespoon grated palm sugar (jaggery)
- 200 g (7 oz) cherry tomatoes, halved
- 150 g (5½ oz) straw mushrooms or button mushrooms
- 60 ml (2 fl oz/¼ cup) lime juice
- 6 kaffir lime leaves, torn in half
- 3–5 bird's eye chillies, stems removed, bruised, or 2 long red chillies, seeded and thinly sliced
- coriander (cilantro) leaves, to garnish

METHOD

1. Put the coconut milk, lemongrass, galangal and shallots in a saucepan or wok over medium heat and bring to the boil.
2. Add the chicken, fish sauce and palm sugar and simmer, stirring constantly for 5 minutes, or until the chicken is cooked through.
3. Add the tomatoes and mushrooms and simmer for 2–3 minutes. Add the lime juice, lime leaves and chillies in the last few seconds, taking care not to let the tomatoes lose their shape. Taste, then adjust the seasoning if necessary. Serve garnished with coriander leaves.

NOTE: Don't worry when the coconut milk splits; it's supposed to.

HOW TO... MAKE COCONUT MILK

The flesh from a young fresh coconut is soft and jelly-like, becoming white and harder as the nut matures. The milk contained within the nut is not the sweet, heavy liquid used in cooking, but a thin, watery milk that makes a refreshing drink. Coconut milk, made from the flesh of the coconut, is sold in tins and cartons, and in solid blocks or as a powder. The milk is often thinner than the cream but this can vary between brands. Light coconut milk has a thinner consistency and is lower in fat.

You can make your own coconut milk at home by soaking grated fresh coconut in hot water or milk. Pour into a sieve lined with muslin, then gather into a ball and squeeze out the remaining coconut milk.

THOM YAM GOONG

SERVES 4

INGREDIENTS

- 350 g (12 oz) raw prawns (shrimp)
- 1 tablespoon oil
- 3 lemongrass stems, white part only, bruised
- 3 thin slices galangal
- 2 litres (8 cups) chicken stock (page 11)
- 5–7 bird's eye chillies, stems removed, bruised
- 5 kaffir lime leaves, torn
- 2 tablespoons fish sauce
- 70 g (2½ oz) straw mushrooms, or quartered button mushrooms
- 2 spring onions (scallions), sliced
- 60 ml (2 fl oz/¼ cup) lime juice
- coriander (cilantro) leaves, to garnish

METHOD

1. Peel the prawns, leaving the tails intact, and gently pull out the dark vein from each prawn back, starting at the head end. Keep the shells, and heads. Heat the oil in a large stockpot or wok and add the prawn heads and shells. Cook for 5 minutes, or until the prawn shells turn bright orange.
2. Add one lemongrass stem to the pot with the galangal and stock or water. Bring to the boil, then reduce the heat and simmer for 20 minutes. Strain the stock and return to the pot. Discard the shells and flavourings.
3. Finely slice the remaining lemongrass and add it to the liquid with the chillies, lime leaves, fish sauce, mushrooms and spring onions. Cook gently for 2 minutes.
4. Add the prawns and cook for 3 minutes, or until the prawns are firm and pink. Take off the heat and add the lime juice. Taste, then adjust the seasoning with extra lime juice or fish sauce if necessary. Garnish with coriander leaves.

PORK NOODLE SOUP

SERVES 4

INGREDIENTS

- 200 g (7 oz) dried egg noodles
- 1.5 litres (6 cups) chicken stock (page 11)
- 8 thin slices ginger
- 4 spring onions (scallions), thinly sliced
- 200 g (7 oz) bok choy (pak choy), chopped
- soy sauce, to serve
- hoisin sauce, to serve
- 150 g (5½ oz) Chinese barbecued pork, thinly sliced
- coriander (cilantro) leaves, to garnish

METHOD

1. Cook the egg noodles in boiling water for 4 minutes, or until tender. Drain well.
2. Put the stock in a saucepan with the ginger and spring onions. Bring to the boil, then add the bok choy and cook for 2 minutes.
3. Divide the noodles among four large bowls, pour in the stock and then top with a drizzle of soy sauce and hoisin and a few slices of pork. Garnish with the coriander.

PHO

Pho is Vietnam's favourite noodle soup. Street vendors selling bowls of freshly prepared soup are a common sight on the country's roadsides. The fresh rice noodles, called *banh pho*, are usually rinsed in boiling water and put in bowls. Boiling broth is poured over them, and then slices of raw beef, herbs such as Vietnamese mint and coriander, and bean sprouts and chilli are added to the bowl by each customer.

❮ BEEF PHO

SERVES 4

INGREDIENTS

1 kg (2 lb 4 oz) beef shin bones
1 star anise
4 cm (1½ inch) piece ginger, sliced
½ onion, studded with 2 cloves
2 lemongrass stems, bruised
2 garlic cloves, crushed
¼ teaspoon ground white pepper
1 tablespoon fish sauce
200 g (7 oz) fresh rice noodles
300 g (10½ oz) beef fillet, partially frozen, thinly sliced
90 g (3¼ oz/1 cup) bean sprouts, tailed
2 spring onions (scallions), thinly sliced

TOPPINGS

coriander (cilantro) leaves
Vietnamese mint leaves
1 red chilli, thinly sliced
2 limes, quartered

METHOD

1 Put the shin bones, star anise, ginger, onion, lemongrass, garlic, white pepper and 2 litres (8 cups) water in a wok and bring to the boil. Reduce the heat to very low and simmer, covered, for 30 minutes. Strain, return to the wok and stir in the fish sauce.
2 Meanwhile, put the noodles in a heatproof bowl, cover with boiling water and gently separate. Drain well, then refresh under cold running water.
3 Divide the noodles among four soup bowls, then top with beef slices, bean sprouts and spring onion. Ladle on the hot broth — the broth will cook the thinly sliced beef.
4 Put the coriander and mint leaves, chilli and lime quarters on a platter. Each diner chooses their own toppings, and can also add sauces such as sweet chilli and hoisin to their soup if desired.

CONGEE

Congee is eaten in China for breakfast or as an all-day snack. Plain congee is served with lots of different condiments to sprinkle over it and often a fried dough stick. Fried dough sticks are available in Chinese shops and are sold as long thin sticks, best eaten fresh on the day they are made, or grilled until crisp again.

SERVES 4

INGREDIENTS

200 g (7 oz) short-grain rice
2.25 litres (9 cups) chicken stock (page 11) or water
light soy sauce, to taste
sesame oil, to taste
white pepper, to taste

TOPPINGS

3 spring onions (scallions), chopped
1 handful coriander (cilantro), chopped
30 g (1 oz) sliced pickled ginger
4 tablespoons finely chopped preserved turnip
4 tablespoons roasted peanuts
2 one-thousand-year-old eggs, cut into slivers
2 tablespoons sesame seeds, toasted
2 fried dough sticks, diagonally sliced

METHOD

1 Put the rice in a bowl and, using your fingers as a rake, rinse under cold running water to remove any dust. Drain the rice in a colander. Place in a clay pot, casserole or saucepan and stir in the stock or water. Bring to the boil, then reduce the heat and simmer very gently, stirring occasionally, for 1¾–2 hours, or until it has a porridge-like texture and the rice is breaking up.
2 Add a sprinkling of soy sauce, sesame oil and white pepper to season the congee. The congee can be served plain, or choose a selection from the toppings listed and serve in bowls alongside the congee for guests to help themselves.

CHAPTER TWO

EGGS AND CHEESE

••EGGS••

Man has been eating eggs for thousands of years, both for their nutritional value and also for the lightening and raising properties they bring to baking. Eggs are a versatile, high-protein food — one large egg provides about 15 per cent of the daily recommended protein intake for an adult, with no carbohydrate and only about 59 calories (247 kilojoules).

TYPES OF EGGS

hen

quail

bantam

duck

ostrich

HEN

Brown and white hen eggs have the same nutritional value and flavour: the shell colour is dependent on the breed of the hen. Brown eggs are usually a bit larger than white eggs, which is what makes them a little more expensive. The size of an egg is influenced by many factors, the major one being the age of the hen — older hens lay bigger eggs. There is a wide variety of eggs available, with many consumers making the choice not to buy those from battery-farmed hens or hens which have been given antibiotics to prevent disease in cramped conditions. Free-range eggs are generally popular, but the term 'free-range' can vary in each country and you need to check the packaging carefully and do your own research. Organic, free-range eggs, we can assume, have been produced by the happiest chickens of all.

QUAIL

Quail eggs are beautiful small speckled eggs, about a third of the size of regular hen eggs. They make perfect canapés and garnishes, or can be added to salads. Quail eggs are usually eaten poached, or soft- or hard-boiled with celery salt.

BANTAM

The Bantam is a smaller breed of hen, which thus lays a smaller egg. Bantam eggs are used in exactly the same way as regular hen eggs, but are particularly good if you want a small portion, perhaps for children.

DUCK

Duck eggs, with their pretty pale blue or chalk-white shells, are larger and have a stronger flavour than hen eggs. Their richness makes them particularly good in custards, pasta dishes and cakes, but the whites will not whisk well, making them unsuitable for meringues or soufflés. Goose eggs are similar to duck eggs but milder.

OSTRICH

An ostrich egg can be used in just the same way as a hen egg — except one ostrich egg is equivalent to about two dozen hen eggs.

HOW TO... TEST FOR FRESHNESS

Egg shells are porous; designed to let in air so that the chick inside can breathe. The small air pocket between the egg membrane and the shell increases in size as the egg ages. This air pocket can provide a useful means of testing for freshness. To test, put the egg in a glass of water: if it lies horizontally on the bottom, it is fresh. If it floats vertically, this shows that the air pocket has grown and the egg may well be stale. When cracked, a fresh egg will have a rounded yolk sitting in a gelatinous white that has a thinner rim of white around its edge. A staler egg will have a flatter yolk and a runny white.

Fresh eggs with good gelatinous whites are best for poaching or frying: cooking methods that depend on the egg holding together well. Eggs that are a couple of days older have slacker membranes and so contain more air — this makes them easier to peel when hard-boiled. They also separate and whisk more easily. Eggs more than a week old should be used in baking rather than as the main feature of a dish.

HOW TO... STORE EGGS

Eggs quickly lose their freshness at room temperature, so keep them in the fridge in their box or in a covered container to prevent them losing moisture and absorbing fridge odours through their porous shells. They will keep for 3 weeks in the fridge. Bring them out 30 minutes before use and let them come to room temperature.

Don't wash an egg unless you are going to use it immediately. Washing removes the egg's protective film and will cause it to deteriorate more rapidly.

EGG SIZES

Eggs are graded into sizes according to the minimum weight of each egg in the carton. These range from the largest, size 1, to the smallest, size 7. Eggs graded as 'small' weigh about 45 g (1½ oz), 'medium' about 55–60 g (2 oz), 'large' 60–65 g (2¼ oz) and 'very large' about 90 g (3¼ oz). The standard egg used in most recipes is size 3, weighing 60 g (2¼ oz). For most dishes this is of little importance, but when you are baking, you should try to use standard-sized eggs.

HOW TO... BOIL AN EGG

The satisfaction gained from producing a perfectly boiled egg is not to be scoffed at. It's not hard either; apart from ignoring the instruction in the name — eggs are simmered not boiled (and keep an eye on the clock).

METHOD

1 To soft-boil an egg, bring a small saucepan of water to the boil. Put the egg onto a spoon and gently lower it into the water. Adjust the heat so that the water is simmering, not boiling and jiggling the egg around in the pan.
2 Cook for 4 minutes and then use a spoon to scoop out the egg. Transfer to an egg cup, slice the top off, and eat. The yolk will be soft and runny, and the white just set.
3 For a medium-boiled egg, follow the above method but cook the egg for 5–6 minutes before lifting it out. The yolk, though still soft, will be almost cooked and the white fully set.
4 For a hard-boiled egg, put the egg in a saucepan and cover with cold water. Bring to the boil, then reduce the heat and simmer for 8 minutes. Lift out the egg, run under cold water to cool and then peel away the shell. The yolk should be fully cooked and only slightly soft in the centre. The white will be fully cooked.

HOW TO... POACH AN EGG

The perfect poached egg is much sought after, and suggestions abound as to how to ensure success. Whichever method you favour, it is essential that only really fresh eggs are used.

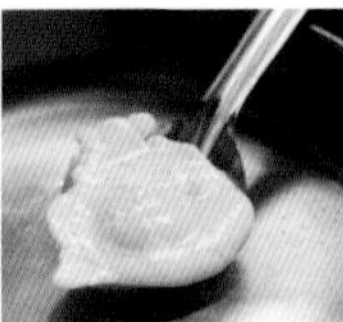
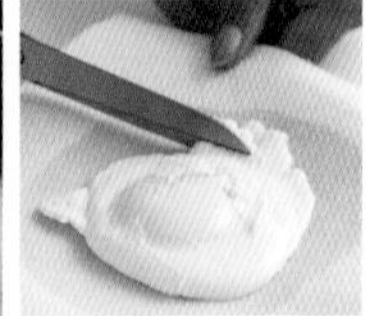

METHOD

1 Bring about 5 cm (2 inches) water to the boil, or pour boiling water from the kettle into the frying pan, then reduce the temperature to the lowest simmering point possible.
2 Break the egg into a small bowl and, once the water is still, gently slide the egg in. The egg can be broken directly into the water, but using a bowl gives greater control. Do not crack the egg until it is needed.
3 Cook the egg for 3–4 minutes, until the white has set and the yolk is just set on the surface but soft inside. Lift out with a slotted spoon and drain on paper towel. Cut away any trailing bits of egg white, if you like.
4 If you're poaching quail eggs, break the egg into a large spoon rather than a bowl. Rest the spoon just under the water for 30–40 seconds, then lift out and the egg should be perfectly poached.

TIPS

* Store your eggs in the fridge but always bring them to room temperature before boiling. The shell of a fridge-cold egg may crack when added to the simmering water.
* Choose a saucepan that is just big enough to hold the eggs in a single layer. If too big, the eggs will move around too much and possibly crack.

TIPS

* Adding a few drops of vinegar to the boiling water will help set the egg white.
* Before adding the egg, some cooks prefer to wait until the bubbles on the pan base have disappeared. Another option is not to wait at all, but remove the pan from the heat once the water boils, add the egg, cover, and leave for 3 minutes to set.

HOW TO... FRY AN EGG

Most people feel confident about frying an egg. However, there is a big difference between a well-fried egg and a rubbery one. Add a little oil to the butter to prevent the butter burning.

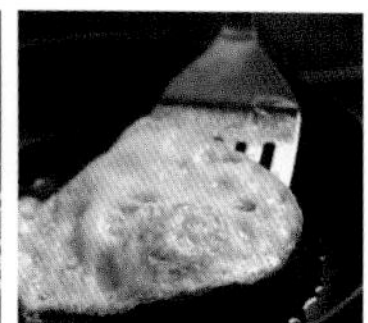

METHOD

1 Heat a heavy-based non-stick frying pan and add some oil and a knob of butter. When the butter is sizzling, carefully break the egg into the pan and gently fry over medium heat, swirling the pan occasionally.
2 For eggs 'sunny side up', cook for 1 minute, until the white is set. As the egg cooks, spoon some hot oil over the yolk so that the surface sets. Turn off the heat and leave to stand for 1 minute.
3 For eggs 'over easy', cook for 1 minute until the white is set, then use a spatula to turn the egg over. Cook for 30 seconds (no more) over low heat. For fully hard yolks, cook for 1 minute.
4 Lift out the egg with a metal spatula, drain on paper towels and season well before serving.

HOW TO... SCRAMBLE EGGS

The wonder of scrambled eggs is that they can keep everyone happy, from purist to hedonist. A gentle hand will achieve best results.

METHOD

1 Break 2 eggs into a clean dry bowl and beat lightly with a fork. Add 2 tablespoons of milk and season with salt and pepper. Mix with a fork, depending on your preference — mix thoroughly for even yellow scrambled eggs, or just stir through for a streaky consistency.
2 Melt a knob of butter in a heavy-based saucepan or frying pan over medium heat. Swirl to coat the pan with the butter, making sure it doesn't burn or turn brown.
3 Add the eggs and cook for 30 seconds. With a flat-ended wooden spoon, slowly but constantly fold the mixture around as it cooks. Cook for about 1 minute, lifting and folding, until the eggs are softly scrambled.
4 Remove the pan from the heat while there is still a little liquid left in the base — the eggs will continue to cook in the heat of the pan. Season and serve immediately.

TIPS

* Use only the very freshest, room-temperature eggs for frying — both white and yolk will hold their shape better when completely fresh.
* The trick to frying eggs is to strike the right balance of heat — high enough that the egg sets before spreading out too much, but low enough that the underside doesn't burn before the yolk is cooked.

TIPS

* The amount of milk or cream added to eggs to make a creamier, softly scrambled dish is important. If too much liquid is added, the proteins in the eggs become fully saturated if overheated and will squeeze the liquid out, forming a mass of solids in a pool of liquid. The recommended amount is 2–4 teaspoons of liquid per egg.

❮ EGGS BENEDICT

SERVES 4

INGREDIENTS

HOLLANDAISE SAUCE
175 g (6 oz) butter
4 egg yolks
1 teaspoon tarragon vinegar

8 very fresh eggs
4 thick slices rye bread or 4 English muffins
8 slices leg ham

METHOD

1 To make the hollandaise sauce, put the butter in a small saucepan and bring to a simmer. Skim off any scum that comes to the surface, then pour the butter into a jug, leaving the whitish sediment behind.
2 Put the yolks, 2 tablespoons water and tarragon vinegar in a small food processor or blender and, with the motor running, gradually pour in the melted butter. Whizz until the sauce is thick, creamy and buttery.
3 Put 5 cm (2 inches) water in a deep saucepan and bring to the boil. Immediately reduce the heat to very low and wait until the water is still and there are only a few tiny bubbles on the base of the pan. Break the eggs, one by one, into a small bowl or saucer and then gently slide them into the water. Cook the eggs for about 3 minutes, or until the white has set. Cook the eggs in batches.
4 Meanwhile, toast the bread or muffins. Arrange on plates and top with the ham. Using a slotted spoon, remove the eggs from the pan and drain on paper towels. Cut away any trailing bits of egg white. Set the poached eggs on the ham, pour over the hollandaise sauce, add plenty of freshly ground black pepper and serve.

NOTE: Instead of ham, use wilted baby spinach, smoked salmon or steamed fresh asparagus.

PIPERADE

SERVES 4

INGREDIENTS

2 tablespoons olive oil
1 large onion, thinly sliced
2 red capsicums (peppers), seeded and cut into batons
2 garlic cloves, crushed
750 g (1 lb 10 oz) tomatoes
pinch of cayenne pepper
8 eggs, lightly beaten
20 g (¾ oz) butter
4 thin slices ham
buttered toast, to serve

METHOD

1 Heat the oil in a large, heavy-based frying pan, then add the onion. Cook for about 3 minutes, or until soft. Add the capsicum and garlic, cover and cook for 8 minutes, stirring frequently to ensure the mixture doesn't brown.
2 To peel the tomatoes, score a cross in the base of each tomato. Put in a heatproof bowl and cover with boiling water. Leave for 30 seconds, then transfer to cold water and peel the skin away from the cross. Chop the flesh and discard the cores. Add the chopped tomato and cayenne to the capsicum mixture, cover the pan and cook for a further 5 minutes.
3 Uncover the pan and increase the heat. Cook for 3 minutes, or until the juices have evaporated, shaking the pan often. Season well with salt and freshly ground black pepper. Add the eggs and scramble into the mixture until just cooked.
4 Heat the butter in a small frying pan and fry the ham. Place the buttered toast on four plates, arrange the piperade on top, lay the cooked ham alongside, and serve.

SCRAMBLED EGGS AND SALMON ON BRIOCHE

SERVES 2

INGREDIENTS

- 4 eggs
- 80 ml (2½ fl oz/⅓ cup) cream
- 40 g (1½ oz) butter
- 125 g (4½ oz) sliced smoked salmon
- 2 teaspoons finely chopped dill
- 2 small brioche or 2 croissants, warmed

METHOD

1. Crack the eggs into a bowl, add the cream and beat together well. Season with salt and pepper.
2. Melt the butter in a non-stick frying pan. When it starts to sizzle, add the eggs and reduce the heat to low. Using a flat-ended wooden spoon, push the mixture around until it starts to set, then fold in the salmon and dill. Continue to cook until the eggs are mostly cooked, and just a little liquid is left in the pan.
3. Cut the tops off the brioche, scoop out some of the filling, then pile the scrambled eggs on top. If using croissants, cut them in half and fill with the egg.

FRENCH TOAST

SERVES 4

INGREDIENTS

- 60 ml (2 fl oz/¼ cup) cream or milk
- 3 eggs
- 3 tablespoons caster (superfine) sugar
- pinch of ground cinnamon
- 8 thick slices bread
- 85 g (3 oz) butter
- 1 tablespoon olive oil
- 12 slices prosciutto
- maple syrup, to serve

METHOD

1. Put the cream, eggs, sugar and cinnamon in a wide, shallow bowl and mix together. Soak the bread in the egg mixture, one slice at a time, shaking off any excess.
2. Melt some of the butter in a frying pan over medium heat. When the butter is sizzling, add the bread to the pan and cook until golden brown on both sides.
3. Transfer the cooked French toast to a warm plate and cover with foil or keep warm in a low oven. Cook the remaining bread in batches, adding more butter as needed.
4. In a separate frying pan, heat the oil. When hot, add the prosciutto and fry until crisp. Remove and drain on paper towels. Place the prosciutto on top of the French toast, drizzle with maple syrup and serve.

OEUFS EN COCOTTE

SERVES 4

INGREDIENTS

20 g (¾ oz) butter, melted
125 ml (4 fl oz/½ cup) cream
4 button mushrooms, finely chopped
40 g (1½ oz) ham, finely chopped
40 g (1½ oz) gruyère cheese, finely chopped
4 eggs
1 tablespoon finely chopped herbs such as chervil, parsley and chives

METHOD

1. Preheat the oven to 200°C (400°F/Gas 6) and put a baking tray on the top shelf.
2. Grease four ramekins with melted butter. Pour half the cream into the ramekins and then put a quarter of the mushrooms, ham and cheese into each. Break an egg into each ramekin. Mix the remaining cream with the herbs and pour over the top.
3. Bake for 15–20 minutes on the hot baking tray, depending on how runny you like your eggs. Remove from the oven while still a little runny as the eggs will continue to cook. Season well and serve immediately with crusty toasted bread.

SCOTCH WOODCOCK

This is a scrambled egg dish served on toast flavoured with anchovies or anchovy paste. The egg is softly scrambled with the addition of cream. Scotch woodcock was a great favourite in Victorian times and was served as a first course.

SERVES 4

INGREDIENTS

4 slices bread
30 g (1 oz) anchovy fillets
30 g (1 oz) butter, softened
4 egg yolks
200 ml (7 fl oz) cream
1 tablespoon finely chopped parsley
pinch of cayenne pepper

METHOD

1. Toast the bread. Meanwhile, mash the anchovies with the butter and spread it onto the toast, then place the toast on four plates.
2. Whisk together the egg yolks, cream, parsley and cayenne pepper. Pour the egg mixture into a buttered frying pan and stir gently over low heat until the mixture is creamy and just set. Spoon over the toast and serve.

SCOTCH EGGS

As its name suggests, these are a Scottish invention, dating from the nineteenth century. To make them, a peeled hard-boiled egg is encased in sausage meat, coated in flour, egg and breadcrumbs, then deep-fried until crisp and golden. To serve, the Scotch egg is cut in half or quarters to display the egg filling. They are served hot or cold as a starter and, uncut, make excellent picnic fare.

QUAILS EGGS EN CROUSTADE

MAKES 12

INGREDIENTS

- sliced white bread
- 45 g (1½ oz) butter, melted
- 12 quail eggs
- ½ quantity hollandaise sauce (page 55)

METHOD

1. Preheat the oven to 170°C (325°F/Gas 3).
2. Cut out 12 circles of bread to fit in a mini tartlet tin. Brush both sides of the bread with the melted butter, then press the rounds into the tin. Bake for 15 minutes.
3. Meanwhile, poach 12 quail eggs. Put 5 cm (2 inches) water in a small, deep frying pan. Bring to the boil, then lower the heat to very low. Crack each quail egg, one at a time, onto a large spoon. Hold the spoon on the surface of the water for 15 seconds until the egg white sets, then gently lower the spoon into the water, immersing the egg. Hold for 20–25 seconds until the yolk is firm but still runny.
4. Put the egg in the croustade and drizzle with the hollandaise sauce. Serve as canapés.

HUEVOS RANCHEROS

SERVES 2

INGREDIENTS

- 1 tablespoon olive oil
- 1 small onion, finely chopped
- ½ green capsicum (pepper), finely chopped
- 1 red chilli, finely chopped
- 1 garlic clove, crushed
- ½ teaspoon dried oregano
- 1 tomato, chopped
- 400 g (14 oz) tin chopped tomatoes
- 4 eggs
- 2 flour tortillas
- 50 g (1¾ oz/⅓ cup) crumbled feta cheese

METHOD

1. Put the olive oil in a frying pan over medium heat. Add the onion and capsicum and fry for 2 minutes, or until soft.
2. Add the chilli and garlic and stir briefly, then add the oregano, fresh and tinned tomatoes, and 90 ml (3 fl oz) water. Bring to the boil, then reduce the heat and simmer for 5 minutes, or until the sauce thickens. Season with salt and black pepper.
3. Smooth the surface of the mixture, then make four hollows with the back of a spoon. Break an egg into each hollow and put the lid on the pan. Cook the eggs for 5 minutes, or until set.
4. While the eggs are cooking, heat the tortillas according to the instructions on the packet and cut each into quarters.
5. Serve the eggs with some feta crumbled over them and the tortillas on the side.

EGG SANDWICHES

EACH RECIPE MAKES 2 SANDWICHES

INGREDIENTS

CURRIED EGG

3 hard-boiled eggs, cooled and peeled
1½ tablespoons mayonnaise
2 teaspoons softened butter
2 teaspoons curry powder
4 slices rye bread, buttered, crusts removed

EGG AND WATERCRESS

3 hard-boiled eggs, cooled and peeled
1½ tablespoons mayonnaise
1 teaspoon softened butter
1 tablespoon finely chopped chives
1 small handful watercress, leaves only
4 slices wholegrain bread, buttered, crusts removed

EGG, OLIVE AND ROCKET

3 hard-boiled eggs, cooled and peeled
1½ tablespoons mayonnaise
1 teaspoon softened butter
2 tablespoons finely shredded basil
1 tablespoon chopped kalamata olives
4 slices white bread, buttered, crusts removed
1 handful baby rocket (arugula), washed and dried

METHOD

1 To make the curried egg sandwiches, put the eggs, mayonnaise, butter and curry powder into a bowl. Mash together with a fork until evenly mixed but still slightly chunky. Season well with salt and freshly ground black pepper. Spread the egg mixture onto two slices of bread, top with the remaining slices of bread, cut into quarters and serve.

2 To make the egg and watercress sandwiches, put the eggs, mayonnaise, butter and chives into a small bowl. Add salt and freshly ground black pepper, then mash together with a fork until evenly and well mixed but still slightly chunky. Wash and dry the picked watercress leaves. Spread the egg mixture onto two slices of bread, top with the watercress and the remaining slices of bread. Cut into quarters and serve.

3 To make the egg, olive and rocket sandwiches, put the eggs, mayonnaise and butter into a small bowl. Mash together with a fork until evenly mixed but still slightly chunky, then add the basil leaves and olives. Stir well, then season to taste. Spread the egg mixture onto two slices of bread, top with the rocket, then the remaining slices of bread. Cut into quarters and serve.

EGGNOG

Based on egg and cream and laced with a spirit such as brandy, bourbon or whisky, eggnog is a traditional Christmas drink. To make eggnog, beat 6 egg yolks with 200 g (7 oz) icing (confectioners') sugar until creamy, then add 250 ml (9 fl oz/1 cup) brandy. Whisk 6 egg whites until soft peaks form and slowly stir in the egg yolk mixture. Sprinkle with ground nutmeg. Serves 6

••OMELETTES••

There are many versions of the omelette, with perhaps the most typical being the savoury French omelette, made from lightly beaten eggs that are cooked in a frying pan until just firm. Some omelettes are folded around fillings such as cheese or ham; others are flavoured with herbs, cooked spinach or bacon mixed into the raw eggs. A tortilla, or Spanish omelette, is a thick omelette of potato, onion and often garlic. A frittata, or Italian omelette, is cooked on both sides, and often eaten as a snack or antipasto.

HOW TO... MAKE THE PERFECT OMELETTE

* An omelette pan is best if you make omelettes often, but if you haven't got one just use a good heavy-based, non-stick frying pan. Don't make it any larger than it needs to be; a pan 15–20 cm (6–8 inches) across is sufficient for a two- or three-egg omelette.
* Add a little oil to the butter in the pan to prevent the butter burning too easily.
* When you add the beaten egg, and as you are cooking it, tilt the pan to distribute the egg evenly. Work quickly — the finished omelette should be golden on the outside but still soft and almost custard-like on the inside. Speed is the key to success here.
* As an alternative to folding the omelette into traditional thirds, when the top is still moist, add the filling to one half, then fold the other half over the top (just as good as thirds, but easier to do). Cook gently for 1–2 minutes, then slide the omelette out of the pan. Omelettes can also be rolled or left flat, cooked on one side or both.
* A soufflé-type omelette involves beating the egg whites separately before folding them into the yolks — this gives a fluffier texture.

BASIC OMELETTE

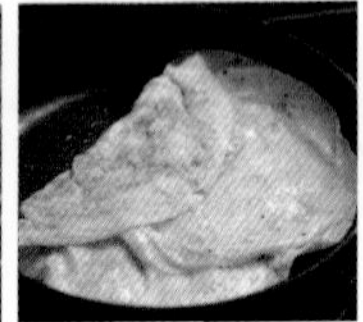
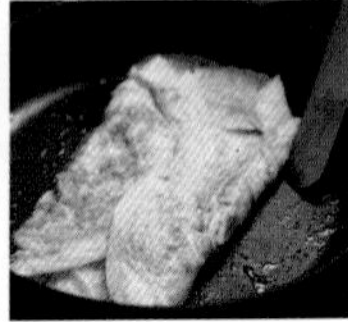

METHOD

1 Break 3 eggs into a bowl and season well with salt and pepper. Put a knob of butter and a little oil in an omelette pan or small frying pan and heat until the butter is foaming. Meanwhile, lightly beat the eggs with a fork to aerate slightly.
2 When the butter is foaming, add the eggs and cook for about 20 seconds, allowing them to set slightly on the base, then stir the egg with a fork. Work quickly, drawing away some of the cooked egg from the bottom, tilting the pan a little as you work so that the uncooked egg runs into the space. If you're making an omelette with a filling, add it now to the middle of the just-set eggs.
3 When most of the egg is set and the underside is golden, slide a small palette knife under the cooked egg to loosen it. Fold one-third of the omelette over the centre, then fold the remaining third over the top. This will encase the filling if you've added one. The omelette should be soft on the inside and golden on the outside. Cook for 1 minute more, if you think it's necessary.
4 Slide the omelette from the pan onto a plate and let it sit for a minute before serving.

ZUCCHINI AND PARMESAN OMELETTE

SERVES 2

INGREDIENTS

10 g (1/4 oz) butter
1 tablespoon olive oil
1 small zucchini (courgette), sliced
1 small leek, white part only, sliced
small pinch of ground nutmeg
1/2 teaspoon finely chopped basil

OMELETTE
20 g (3/4 oz) butter
1 1/2 tablespoons olive oil
6 eggs
20 g (3/4 oz) shaved parmesan cheese

METHOD

1 Heat the butter and oil in a small frying pan over medium heat. Fry the zucchini and leek for 5–6 minutes, until golden. Season, add the nutmeg and basil, then remove from the pan.
2 To make the omelette, heat the butter and oil in a small frying pan. Beat the eggs and season well. Pour the eggs into the pan and cook gently over high heat, pulling the mixture in from the sides until it begins to set in small, fluffy clumps. Reduce the heat and shake the pan from side to side to prevent the omelette sticking.
3 When the omelette is almost set, scatter the parmesan onto one half, spoon the zucchini and leek on top, then fold the omelette over to enclose the filling. Cook for 10–12 seconds, shaking the pan once or twice. Slide onto a warm plate and serve.

SPRING ONION AND DOLCELATTE OMELETTE

Blue cheeses have been treated with spores to develop blue or green veins on the inside, giving the cheese its characteristic strong flavour. These vary from the harder stilton and shropshire blue, through gorgonzola and roquefort, to blue de bresse and the beautifully creamy dolcelatte, used here. Substitute any other soft blue cheese if dolcelatte is unavailable.

SERVES 2

INGREDIENTS

20 g (¾ oz) butter
6 eggs
1 spring onion (scallion), chopped
60 g (2¼ oz) dolcelatte cheese, cubed

METHOD

1 Heat half the butter in a small frying pan over medium heat. Beat the eggs and season well. Pour half the egg into the frying pan and cook gently over high heat, pulling the mixture in from the sides until it begins to set. Reduce the heat and shake the pan from side to side to prevent the omelette sticking.
2 When the omelette is almost set but still soft on the surface, scatter half of the spring onion and half of the cheese into the centre, fold into thirds and cook for a further 10–12 seconds, shaking the pan once or twice.
3 Slide the omelette onto a warm plate and serve at once. Repeat with the remaining egg, spring onion and cheese.

› OMELETTE AUX FINES HERBES

SERVES 4

INGREDIENTS

15 g (½ oz) butter
2 French shallots, finely chopped
1 garlic clove, crushed
2 tablespoons chopped parsley
2 tablespoons chopped basil
2 teaspoons chopped tarragon
2 tablespoons cream
8 eggs, lightly beaten
oil, for frying

METHOD

1 Melt the butter in a frying pan and cook the shallots and garlic over low heat until tender. Stir in the herbs and then tip into a bowl. Mix in the cream and eggs and season well.
2 Heat a little oil in a non-stick frying pan. Pour a quarter of the egg mixture into the pan and cook gently, constantly pulling the set egg around the edge of the pan into the centre, until the omelette is set and browned underneath and the top is just cooked.
3 Fold the omelette into three and slide it out of the pan onto a plate with the seam underneath. Serve hot, for someone else to eat while you cook up the remaining three omelettes.

TORTILLA

This simple 'potato omelette' is a Spanish classic — it's really more about potatoes than eggs, and debate abounds as to whether garlic and onion should be included. Nowadays, recipes might include many other ingredients, such as salmon, chorizo or vegetables and herbs. Try the tortilla hot, cold, or eaten as a sandwich between chunks of bread.

❮ SMOKED SALMON TORTILLA

SERVES 2

INGREDIENTS

- 1 tablespoon olive oil
- 200 g (7 oz) potatoes, peeled and cut into small cubes
- 1 small onion, finely chopped
- 4 eggs
- 2 tablespoons chopped parsley
- 1 tablespoon finely chopped dill
- 1 tablespoon chopped chives
- 4 slices smoked salmon, roughly chopped
- 2 tablespoons mascarpone cheese

METHOD

1. Heat the oil over low heat in a non-stick frying pan with a flameproof handle (a pan about 15–20 cm/6–8 inches in diameter is fine). Add the potato and gently fry for 10 minutes, or until cooked through to the middle and brown on all sides. Cut a cube open to see if it is cooked through completely.
2. When the potato is cooked, add the onion and cook for a few minutes until translucent. Preheat the grill (broiler) to high.
3. Break the eggs into a bowl and whisk them together with the parsley, dill and chives. Season well with salt and pepper.
4. Add the smoked salmon pieces to the frying pan, then the mascarpone in blobs. Using a wooden spatula, make sure the mixture is evenly distributed over the base of the pan and level it off. Pour the eggs over the top. Lightly swirl the blobs of mascarpone with a spoon. Cook for 4 minutes, or until the tortilla is just set.
5. Put the frying pan under the hot grill for 1 minute to lightly brown the top of the tortilla. Gently slide the tortilla out of the frying pan and cut it into quarters. Serve with a salad if desired. If taking on a picnic, leave to cool, then wrap in foil.

POTATO TORTILLA

SERVES 4

INGREDIENTS

- 500 g (1 lb 2 oz) potatoes, peeled and cut into 1 cm (½ inch) slices
- 60 ml (2 fl oz/¼ cup) olive oil
- 1 onion, thinly sliced
- 4 garlic cloves, thinly sliced
- 2 tablespoons finely chopped parsley
- 6 eggs

METHOD

1. Put the potato slices in a large saucepan, cover with cold water and bring to the boil over high heat. Boil for 5 minutes, then drain and set aside.
2. Put the oil in a deep-sided non-stick frying pan over medium heat. Add the onion and garlic and cook for 5 minutes, or until the onion softens.
3. Add the potato and parsley to the pan and stir to combine. Cook over medium heat for 5 minutes, gently pressing on the mixture.
4. Whisk the eggs with 1 teaspoon each of salt and pepper and pour evenly over the potato. Cover and cook over low–medium heat for 20 minutes, or until the eggs are just set. Slide onto a serving plate or serve directly from the pan.

FRITTATA

Just like an omelette, but flashed under the grill to finish off the cooking, the Italian frittata can vary from thin and pancake-like, to thick with a golden crust and creamy centre. Frittatas can be filled with cheese, vegetables, meat or seafood. And, just like tortillas, they can be eaten warm or cold, or in squares as part of an antipasti plate.

ARTICHOKE FRITTATA

SERVES 4

INGREDIENTS

- 175 g (6 oz) broad (fava) beans, fresh or frozen
- 1 onion
- 400 g (14 oz) tin artichoke hearts, drained
- 60 ml (2 fl oz/¼ cup) olive oil
- 6 eggs
- 2 tablespoons chopped parsley
- 45 g (1½ oz/½ cup) grated pecorino cheese
- pinch of ground nutmeg

METHOD

1. Bring a small saucepan of water to the boil and add a large pinch of salt and the broad beans. Boil for 2 minutes, then drain and rinse under cold water. Peel the skins off the beans.
2. Halve the onion and slice thinly. Cut the artichoke hearts from bottom to top into slices about 5 mm (¼ inch) wide. Discard any slices that contain the tough central choke.
3. Heat the oil in a 30 cm (12 inch) frying pan and fry the onion over low heat for 6–8 minutes, without allowing it to brown. Add the artichoke slices and cook for a further 1–2 minutes. Stir in the broad beans.
4. Preheat the grill (broiler). Lightly beat together the eggs, parsley, pecorino and nutmeg and season well with salt and pepper. Pour over the vegetables in the frying pan and cook over low heat until three-quarters set, shaking the pan often to stop the frittata sticking.
5. Finish the top off under the grill and leave to cool before serving in wedges.

MINI SWEET POTATO AND LEEK FRITTATAS

MAKES 12

INGREDIENTS

- 1 kg (2 lb 4 oz) orange sweet potato, cubed
- 1 tablespoon olive oil
- 30 g (1 oz) butter
- 4 leeks, white part only, thinly sliced
- 2 garlic cloves, crushed
- 250 g (9 oz/1⅔ cups) crumbled feta cheese
- 8 eggs
- 125 ml (4 fl oz/½ cup) cream

METHOD

1. Preheat the oven to 180°C (350°F/Gas 4). Grease twelve 125 ml (4 fl oz/½ cup) muffin tin holes. Cut small rounds of baking paper and place in the base of each hole. Boil or steam the sweet potato until tender, then drain well and set aside.
2. Heat the oil and butter in a large frying pan, add the leek and cook for about 10 minutes, stirring occasionally until very soft and lightly golden. Add the garlic and cook for 1 minute more. Cool, then stir in the feta and sweet potato. Divide the mixture evenly among the muffin holes.
3. Whisk the eggs and cream together and season with salt and freshly ground black pepper. Pour the egg mixture into each hole until three-quarters filled, then press the vegetables down gently. Bake for 25–30 minutes, or until golden and set. Leave in the tin for 5 minutes, then ease out of the tin with a knife and cool on a wire rack before serving.

SALMON FRITTATA

SERVES 4–6

INGREDIENTS

2 red onions, cut into 5 mm (¼ inch) slices
2 tablespoons olive oil
150 g (5½ oz) baby English spinach leaves
8 eggs
2 spring onions (scallions), finely chopped
200 g (7 oz) sliced smoked salmon
100 g (3½ oz) ricotta cheese

METHOD

1 Preheat the grill (broiler) to high. Spread the onion on a lightly greased tray, lightly brush the onion with a little oil and cook for 2–3 minutes, until browned. Flip the onion over, brush with a little more oil and grill for 2–3 minutes. Remove from the tray and set aside. Turn the grill down to medium.
2 Blanch the spinach in a pan of boiling water for 30 seconds. Drain, refresh in cold water, then squeeze out any liquid. Chop the leaves.
3 Beat the eggs in a bowl, season, then stir in the spinach and onion. Heat the remaining oil in a 20 cm (8 inch) non-stick frying pan, add the spring onion and sauté over medium heat for 1 minute, until soft. Stir the spring onion through the egg, then pour the mixture into the pan. Arrange the salmon and ricotta over the frittata.
4 Cook the frittata on the stovetop over medium heat for 10 minutes, moving the pan around over the heat. When the frittata is half cooked, put the pan under the grill and cook for a further 5–10 minutes, or until the top is golden brown and the frittata is cooked through. If it starts to brown too quickly, cover it with a piece of foil.
5 Turn out onto a plate and cut into wedges. This is good with sour cream on the side.

··SAVOURY SOUFFLES··

Soufflés have developed a reputation as difficult and unpredictable creations, but they are actually not hard to make. The secret lies in beating the egg whites to the right stiffness, preparing the dish correctly, and serving the soufflé straight from the oven.

HOW TO... PREPARE THE DISH

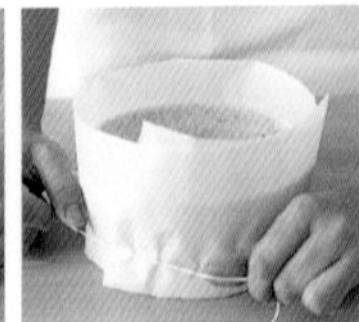

METHOD

1 To prepare your soufflé dish, first melt a little butter and use a pastry brush to brush this lightly over the base and side of the dish. Then tip in a tablespoon or so (depending on the size of the dish) of dried breadcrumbs, turn the dish around so they cling to the butter and coat the base and side. Tip out the excess. This will help the soufflé cling to the side of the dish and rise evenly.

2 You can prepare a paper collar for your dish to help the soufflé rise straight and high. Simply wrap a double layer of baking paper around the outside of the dish and tie with kitchen string.

HOW TO... WHISK EGG WHITES

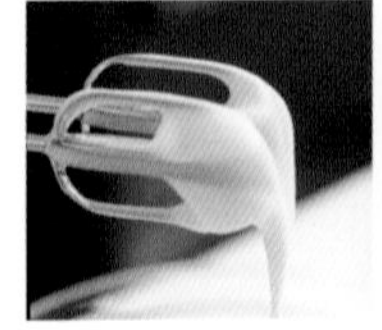
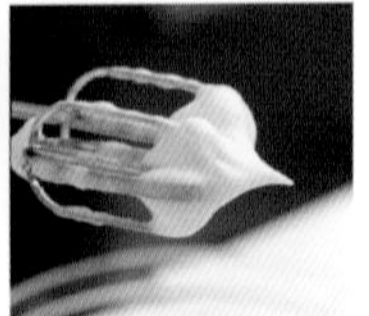

METHOD

1 You need perfectly whisked eggs to make a soufflé. Get them out of the fridge and separate the yolks from the whites (this is easier when they are cold). Let the whites come to room temperature (cold egg white will not whisk well). The slightest trace of fat will prevent the egg whites whisking properly, so use a very clean and dry glass or metal (copper is classic) bowl.

2 Whisk the whites gently at first, then more vigorously until they have tripled in volume. At 'soft peak', the peaks on the egg white will flop; at 'stiff peak', only the very tops will flop.

TIPS

* Use very fresh eggs for soufflés. The older the egg, the weaker the membrane around the yolk, and thus greater the chance of a little yolk getting into the egg white.
* When separating eggs, give each one a firm crack, rather than crushing it. This way, there will be less chance of small bits of shell falling into the bowl. Only whisk egg whites when you are ready to use them.
* While underbeaten egg whites will not hold their shape, overbeaten whites will have the appearance of 'cracking' and be lumpy. If this happens, there is nothing else for it but to start again with a fresh batch of whites.
* If you're using cheese in a soufflé, finely grate it so that it melts quickly without forming bubbles of oil.
* When you tip your soufflé mixture into the dish, run a knife or a finger quickly around the dish between the mixture and the edge of the dish — this will help the soufflé rise.

CHEESE SOUFFLES

SERVES 6

INGREDIENTS

- melted butter, for brushing
- 25 g (1 oz/¼ cup) dried breadcrumbs
- 20 g (¾ oz) butter
- 3 tablespoons plain (all-purpose) flour
- 250 ml (9 fl oz/1 cup) milk
- 25 g (1 oz/¼ cup) grated parmesan cheese
- 90 g (3¼ oz/¾ cup) grated cheddar cheese
- 1 teaspoon dijon mustard
- 3 eggs, separated

METHOD

1 Preheat the oven to 180°C (350°F/Gas 4). Prepare six 125 ml (4 fl oz/½ cup) soufflé dishes with melted butter and breadcrumbs (see opposite).

2 Heat the butter in a small saucepan. Add the flour and stir over low heat for 2 minutes, or until lightly golden. Remove from the heat and add the milk gradually, stirring until smooth. Return to medium heat and stir until the sauce boils and thickens. Boil for 1 minute, then remove from the heat and add the parmesan, cheddar and mustard. Beat in the egg yolks, then transfer the mixture to a large bowl.

3 Place the egg whites in a small, clean dry mixing bowl. Beat until soft peaks form. Using a metal spoon, gradually fold the egg whites gently through the cheese mixture, then pour immediately into the soufflé dishes.

4 Bake for 10–15 minutes, or until the soufflés are puffed and golden. Serve immediately.

NOTE: To make one large soufflé, cook the mixture in a 14 cm (5½ inch) soufflé dish for approximately 45 minutes.

PARMESAN

This hard cow's milk cheese is widely used in Italian cooking, either grated and added to dishes or shaved to use as a garnish. Always buy parmesan in a chunk and grate it as you need it, rather than use ready-grated. Parmigiano Reggiano, from Parma in northern Italy, is widely regarded as the most superior variety. It is produced following strictly governed methods and the use of the name is restricted by law.

‹ ZUCCHINI SOUFFLE

SERVES 4

INGREDIENTS

- melted butter, for brushing
- 1½ tablespoons dried breadcrumbs
- 350 g (12 oz) zucchini (courgettes), chopped
- 125 ml (4 fl oz/½ cup) milk
- 30 g (1 oz) butter
- 2 tablespoons plain (all-purpose) flour
- 75 g (2½ oz) gruyère or parmesan cheese, finely grated
- 3 spring onions (scallions), finely chopped
- 4 eggs, separated

METHOD

1 Prepare a 1.5 litre (6 cup) soufflé dish with melted butter and breadcrumbs (page 68).

2 Cook the zucchini in boiling water for 8 minutes until tender. Drain, then put in a food processor with the milk and mix until smooth. Preheat the oven to 180°C (350°F/Gas 4).

3 Melt the butter in a heavy-based saucepan and stir in the flour. Cook, stirring, for 2 minutes over low heat without browning. Remove from the heat and add the zucchini purée, stirring until smooth. Return to the heat and bring to the boil. Simmer, stirring, for 3 minutes, then remove from the heat. Pour into a bowl, add the cheese and spring onion and season well. Mix until smooth, then beat in the egg yolks until smooth again.

4 Whisk the egg whites in a clean dry bowl until soft peaks form. Spoon a quarter of the egg white onto the soufflé mixture and quickly but lightly fold it in, to loosen the mixture. Lightly fold in the remaining egg white. Pour into the soufflé dish. Bake for 45 minutes, or until the soufflé is well risen and wobbles slightly when tapped. Test with a skewer through a crack in the side of the soufflé — the skewer should come out clean or slightly moist. If it is slightly moist, the soufflé will be cooked in the centre by the time it reaches the table. Serve immediately.

CRAB SOUFFLES

SERVES 6

INGREDIENTS

- melted butter, for brushing
- 1½ tablespoons dried breadcrumbs
- ½ small onion, studded with 4 cloves
- 2 bay leaves
- 10 black peppercorns
- 500 ml (17 fl oz/2 cups) milk
- 30 g (1 oz) butter
- 2 spring onions (scallions), finely chopped
- 2 tablespoons plain (all-purpose) flour
- 6 egg yolks and 5 egg whites
- 250 g (9 oz) cooked crabmeat
- pinch of cayenne pepper
- 3 teaspoons lime juice

METHOD

1 Prepare six 125 ml (4 fl oz/½ cup) soufflé dishes with melted butter and breadcrumbs (page 68). Preheat the oven to 200°C (400°F/Gas 6).

2 Put the clove-studded onion in a small pan with the bay leaves, peppercorns and milk. Bring to the boil, then remove from the heat and leave to infuse for 10 minutes. Strain and set aside.

3 Melt the butter in a heavy-based pan, add the spring onion and cook, stirring, for 3 minutes until softened. Add the flour and cook, stirring, for 3 minutes over low heat. Remove from the heat and gradually stir in the milk. Return to the heat and simmer for 3 minutes, stirring. Beat in the egg yolks, one at a time. Add the crabmeat and stir until the mixture thickens. Pour into a heatproof bowl, then add the cayenne, lime juice and season with salt and pepper.

4 Whisk the egg whites until soft peaks form. Spoon a quarter of the egg white onto the soufflé mixture and fold it in, then fold in the remaining egg white. Divide the mixture between the dishes. Transfer to a baking tray. Bake for 12–15 minutes, or until the soufflés have risen and wobble slightly when tapped. Serve immediately.

••CHEESE••

Cheese is made by coagulating or curdling milk with rennet so that it separates into curds (solids) and whey (liquid). The curds are usually then separated, processed and matured. Different countries categorise their cheeses in different ways: French cheese is categorised according to the method of production, type of rind and producer. Italian cheeses are listed by their milk (cow, sheep, goat) first, then by consistency and method of production. The 'families' listed below contain cheeses that taste similar and can be used interchangeably.

CHEESE CATEGORIES

NATURAL-RIND CHEESES

Rinds vary from a young, wrinkled cream colour to a mature, blueish-grey. These are mostly goat's cheeses such as crottin de chavignol.

WASHED-RIND CHEESES

These are washed with saline or alcohol to remove any grey mould and encourage the growth of an orange sticky bacteria that helps mature the cheese from the outside. These are often smelly and have a strong flavour. They include époisses, livarot, munster, maroilles and limburger and gubeen.

DOUBLE AND TRIPLE CREAM CHEESES

These have been enriched with cream during production. Double cream cheeses have 60 per cent fat content and triple creams have 75 per cent. These include jindi, petit suisse, brillat-savarin, blue castello and bavarian blue.

HARD CHEESES

These have a thick rind, which may be waxed or wrapped in cloth. Textures vary greatly. Cheeses include cheddar, parmesan, grana padano, emmental, cantal, gruyère, cheshire, manchego, leicester and wensleydale.

SEMI-SOFT CHEESES

These have an elastic, rubbery texture and buttery flavour. Some are wax covered. Cheeses include fontina, raclette, edam, jack and taleggio.

SMOKED CHEESES

These are treated with flavouring and may include smoked cheddar and mozzarella, and applewood.

GOAT'S AND EWE'S MILK CHEESES

These are made in a variety of sizes and shapes such as pyramids, cones and cylinders. The goat or sheep flavour can be mild or pronounced depending on how long the cheese has been aged. These can be classed under other categories (feta is a fresh cheese, and many goat's cheeses have natural rinds). Chèvre is the term for fresh goat's cheese.

WHEY CHEESES

These are made from the whey left behind when curds are drained. Ricotta is made by heating whey and adding a coagulant to make a cheese similar to fresh cheeses like cottage cheese.

SOFT-RIND CHEESES (BLOOMY OR FLOWERY RIND)

These have white mould growth, which may be speckled with pink, yellow or grey on their rinds and a creamy smooth pâte that bulges when ripe. Brie, camembert, bonchester, coulommiers and chaource, and some blue cheeses fit into this category.

BLUE CHEESES

These are treated with spores to develop the veins which give the characteristic strong flavour. They vary from the harder stilton and shropshire blue, through gorgonzola and roquefort, to blue de bresse and torta dolcelatte.

HOW TO... SERVE A PERFECT CHEESEBOARD

* Cheese should be cut in such a way that each part, from the rind to the heart, can be enjoyed.
* Always serve cheese at room temperature, so take it out of the fridge at least 4 hours before serving.
* Keep cheeseboards simple and don't clutter them up with too many accompaniments. Choose a crisp pear, some muscatels, or a slice of candied citron, one good bread and two or three varieties of cheese.

HOW TO... STORE CHEESE

Cheese needs to be stored carefully. It needs humidity, yet it must not get wet. Never freeze cheese, or wrap it in plastic. If you buy it packed in plastic wrap, remove it immediately and wrap it in waxed paper, foil or in a cloth cheese bag. If the cheese comes properly wrapped by the cheesemaker, use that wrapping. After that, store it in an unsealed box in the vegetable crisper of your fridge.

Washed-rind cheeses should be wrapped as above and kept in cool, damp humid conditions. Blue cheese can be stored at colder temperatures, preferably wrapped in wax paper, and must not be stored touching other foods. Store cut hard cheeses (such as cheddar) and grain cheeses (such as parmesan) in a cloth cheese bag, or cover the cut surface (never the rind) with waxed paper or foil. Store fresh cheese at cooler temperatures (about 4°C/39°F), but try to eat them fairly quickly.

BUYING RIPE CHEESE

Pre-packed (shrink-wrapped) cheese or cheese packed in containers will have a 'best before' or 'use-by' date (expiry date) or 'sell-by' date (pull date). It is assumed that, in the right conditions, the cheese will continue to mature up until the 'use-by' date and from then on it will start to deteriorate. The 'sell-by' date is rather more arbitrary and may mean that the cheese will keep for a few more days or even weeks — the shop just has to have sold it by that date.

When you're buying packaged cheese, check the date to make sure it will be ready on the day you want to eat it. This means that, if you're buying from the supermarket, you may have to buy your cheese some days in advance and mature it yourself. Specialist cheese shops will look after the maturing process and sell you cheese that will be perfectly mature on the day you want to eat it. As a general rule, add at least one week to a sell-by date. (As a tip, with cheese, you can usually save money and get more mature cheeses by buying special offers when the use-by date has expired.)

unripe

medium

very ripe

CHEESE FONDUE

SERVES 4–6

This classic Swiss dish is made by melting one or more cheeses with dry white wine, and often kirsch, nutmeg or cinnamon. Fondue is served in a special pot over a gas burner with a fork for each person and cubes of bread for dipping. Similarly, raclette is made by melting a chunk of Swiss raclette cheese over heat. This is traditionally served with potatoes, dark bread and pickles.

INGREDIENTS

½ garlic clove
1 bottle dry white wine
500 g (1 lb 2 oz) gruyère cheese, grated
500 g (1 lb 2 oz) emmental cheese, grated
2 tablespoons cornflour (cornstarch)
shot of kirsch
pinch of ground nutmeg
cubes of bread

METHOD

1. Rub the inside of the fondue pot with the garlic. Pour in the wine and bring to the boil on the stovetop. Stir in the cheeses and the cornflour and melt the cheese slowly, stirring constantly.
2. Fire up the fondue burner and carefully transfer the pot onto the fondue burner, then stir in the kirsch and season with the nutmeg.
3. Supply a large bowl of bread cubes and some forks, then dip the bread, one cube at a time, into the cheese fondue.

NOTE: Switzerland's oldest and most famous cheese, emmental, is named after the valley where it was originally made. Emmental is a buttery, nutty cheese, characterised by its marble-sized holes, and is suitable for both cooking and as a table cheese.

FRESH CHEESE DIP

Beat 500 g (1 lb 2 oz) fromage blanc (fromage frais) or curd cheese with a wooden spoon. Add 2 tablespoons olive oil and 1 finely chopped garlic clove and beat into the cheese. Add 2 tablespoons chopped chervil, 4 tablespoons chopped parsley, 2 tablespoons chopped chives, 1 tablespoon chopped tarragon and 4 finely chopped French shallots and mix together well. Season and serve with toast or bread, perhaps after dessert, as you would cheese and biscuits. Serves 8

CROQUE-MONSIEUR

A popular French café snack, croque-monsieur is simply a grilled ham and cheese sandwich. The sandwiches are either lightly fried in butter or cooked in a sandwich iron. If the croque-monsieur is served with a fried egg on top, it becomes a croque-madame.

‹ CROQUE-MONSIEUR

SERVES 2

INGREDIENTS

1 egg
1 tablespoon milk
30 g (1 oz) butter, softened
4 slices white bread
1 teaspoon dijon mustard
4 slices gruyère cheese
2 slices leg ham
2 teaspoons vegetable oil

METHOD

1. Crack the egg into a wide, shallow bowl, add the milk and lightly beat. Season with salt and freshly ground black pepper.
2. Spread one-third of the butter over the bread, then spread two slices with mustard. Place a slice of cheese on top, then the ham and then another slice of cheese. Top with the other slices of bread to make sandwiches.
3. Heat the remaining butter and the oil in a large non-stick frying pan. While the butter is melting, dip one sandwich into the egg and milk mixture, coating the bread on both sides. When the butter is sizzling but not brown, add the sandwich and cook for 1½ minutes on one side, pressing down firmly with a spatula. Turn over and cook the other side.
4. Transfer the sandwich to a plate and keep warm while you cook the other sandwich, adding more butter and oil to the pan if necessary.

WELSH RAREBIT

There are many variations of this dish, and arguments over both its name and exact ingredients are ongoing, but it is essentially a mixture of a cheesy white sauce or cheese, butter, mustard or worcestershire sauce and beer or wine. The mixture can be spread over toast and grilled, or melted and then poured over toast. Welsh rarebit also goes by the name 'Welsh rabbit'. The question 'why a rabbit?' has never been answered satisfactorily (the alternative name, rarebit, was perhaps invented for those confused by the inexplicable rabbit).

SERVES 4

INGREDIENTS

225 g (8 oz) cheddar cheese, grated
30 g (1 oz) butter
60 ml (2 fl oz/¼ cup) beer
1 tablespoon dried mustard
dash of worcestershire sauce
4 thick slices toast

METHOD

1. Melt the cheddar, butter and beer in a small saucepan over low heat. Stir in the mustard and worcestershire sauce, and season with salt and pepper.
2. Preheat the grill (broiler) to high. Spoon the mixture over the buttered toast, place under the grill and cook until bubbling and golden brown.

LABNA

Labna, or labneh, is made by draining yoghurt through muslin to produce a soft, creamy cheese that is rolled into balls, sometimes coated with paprika or herbs and served as part of a meze, preserved in jars of olive oil or mixed with oil and eaten as a spread. In the Middle East, labna is eaten for breakfast with olives and bread.

MAKES 18 BALLS

INGREDIENTS

1.5 kg (3 lb 5 oz) Greek-style yoghurt
1 garlic clove, crushed
two 50 cm (20 inch) square pieces of muslin
2–3 handfuls herbs, such as mint and parsley, finely chopped
2 bay leaves
3 thyme sprigs
2 oregano sprigs
500 ml (17 fl oz/2 cups) olive oil

METHOD

1. Put the yoghurt in a bowl with the garlic and 2 teaspoons salt and mix well. Put the muslin squares one on top of the other and place the yoghurt mixture in the centre. Gather up the corners of the muslin and tie securely with string, then suspend it over a bowl. Refrigerate and leave to drain for 3 days.
2. Once drained, the yoghurt will have become the texture and consistency of ricotta cheese. Remove from the cloth and place in a bowl.
3. Using wet hands, roll tablespoons of the mixture into balls and place on a large tray. You should have 18 balls. Cover and refrigerate for 3 hours, or until firm. Roll the labna in the chopped herbs.
4. Place the labna in a clean dry 1 litre (35 fl oz/4 cup) glass jar with the bay leaves, thyme and oregano. Fill the jar with the olive oil to cover the labna. Seal and refrigerate for up to 1 week. Return to room temperature for serving.

HERB BAKED RICOTTA

SERVES 6–8

INGREDIENTS

1 kg (2 lb 4 oz) wedge fresh full-fat ricotta cheese (see Note)
2 tablespoons thyme
2 tablespoons chopped rosemary
2 tablespoons chopped oregano
1 large handful parsley, chopped
15 g (½ oz/¼ cup) chopped chives
2 garlic cloves, crushed
125 ml (4 fl oz/½ cup) olive oil

METHOD

1. Pat the ricotta dry with paper towels and put in a baking dish.
2. Mix the herbs, garlic, oil and 2 teaspoons of cracked pepper in a bowl. Spoon the herb mixture onto the ricotta, pressing with the back of a spoon. Cover and refrigerate overnight.
3. Preheat the oven to 180°C (350°F/Gas 4). Bake for 30 minutes, or until the ricotta is golden. Serve with crusty bread.

NOTE: It is best to buy fresh ricotta from a delicatessen or speciality cheese shop. If you can't buy ricotta in a wedge, drain the wet ricotta in a colander overnight over a large bowl. Spread half the herb mixture in a 1.25 litre (5 cup) loaf (bar) tin, then spoon the ricotta in and spread with the remaining herbs before baking.

CHEESE FILO TRIANGLES

MAKES 30

INGREDIENTS

250 g (9 oz) feta cheese
180 g (6½ oz) gruyère cheese, grated
2 eggs, lightly beaten
white pepper
15 sheets filo pastry
125 ml (4 fl oz/½ cup) olive oil
125 g (4½ oz) butter, melted

METHOD

1 Preheat the oven to 180°C (350°F/Gas 4). Put the feta in a bowl and mash with a fork. Add the gruyère, egg and pepper and mix.
2 Cut the filo sheets in halves widthways. Keep the unused pastry covered with a damp tea towel to prevent it drying out. Place a half-sheet of filo lengthways on the work surface. Brush with the combined oil and butter, then fold into thirds lengthways to form a long, thin strip. Brush with the oil and butter. Place 1 tablespoon of the cheese mixture on the corner of the strip. Fold this corner over the filling to form a small triangle. Repeat the fold to make another triangle, continuing like this to the end of the strip. Repeat with the remaining pastry and filling.
3 Place the triangles on a lightly greased baking tray and brush them with the oil and butter mixture. Bake for 20 minutes, or until crisp.

MARINATED FETA

SERVES 6

INGREDIENTS

350 g (12 oz) feta cheese
1 tablespoon dried oregano
1 teaspoon coriander seeds
1 tablespoon cracked black pepper
125 g (4½ oz) sun-dried tomatoes in oil
4 small red chillies
3–4 rosemary sprigs
olive oil

METHOD

1 Pat the feta dry with paper towels, and cut into 2 cm (¾ inch) cubes. Place in a bowl and sprinkle with the oregano, coriander seeds and black pepper.
2 Drain the sun-dried tomatoes over a bowl so that you retain all of the oil — you should have about 60 ml (2 fl oz/¼ cup) oil.
3 Arrange the feta, chillies, rosemary and sun-dried tomatoes in a sterilised 750 ml (26 fl oz/3 cup) wide-necked jar with a clip-top lid. Cover with the reserved sun-dried tomato oil and top up with olive oil to cover. Seal and refrigerate for 1 week. Serve at room temperature. Marinated feta will keep in the refrigerator for 1–2 months.

FETA

This fresh, salty, crumbly Greek cheese is made from the milk of goat, sheep or, increasingly nowadays, cow. Its texture can vary from soft to firm, depending on the manufacturer, and it is usually sold in brine. Feta is probably best known for its inclusion in traditional Greek salads. Marinated feta has become popular and is now widely available.

INSALATA CAPRESE

SERVES 4

INGREDIENTS

- 8 ripe roma (plum) tomatoes
- 3–4 mozzarella balls, preferably buffalo mozzarella
- 2 tablespoons extra virgin olive oil
- 1 handful small basil leaves

METHOD

1. Slice the tomatoes, pouring off any excess juice, and cut the mozzarella cheese into slices of a similar thickness.
2. Arrange alternating rows of tomato and mozzarella on a serving plate. Sprinkle with salt and freshly ground black pepper and drizzle the olive oil over the top. Scatter with basil leaves, tearing any large ones, and serve immediately.

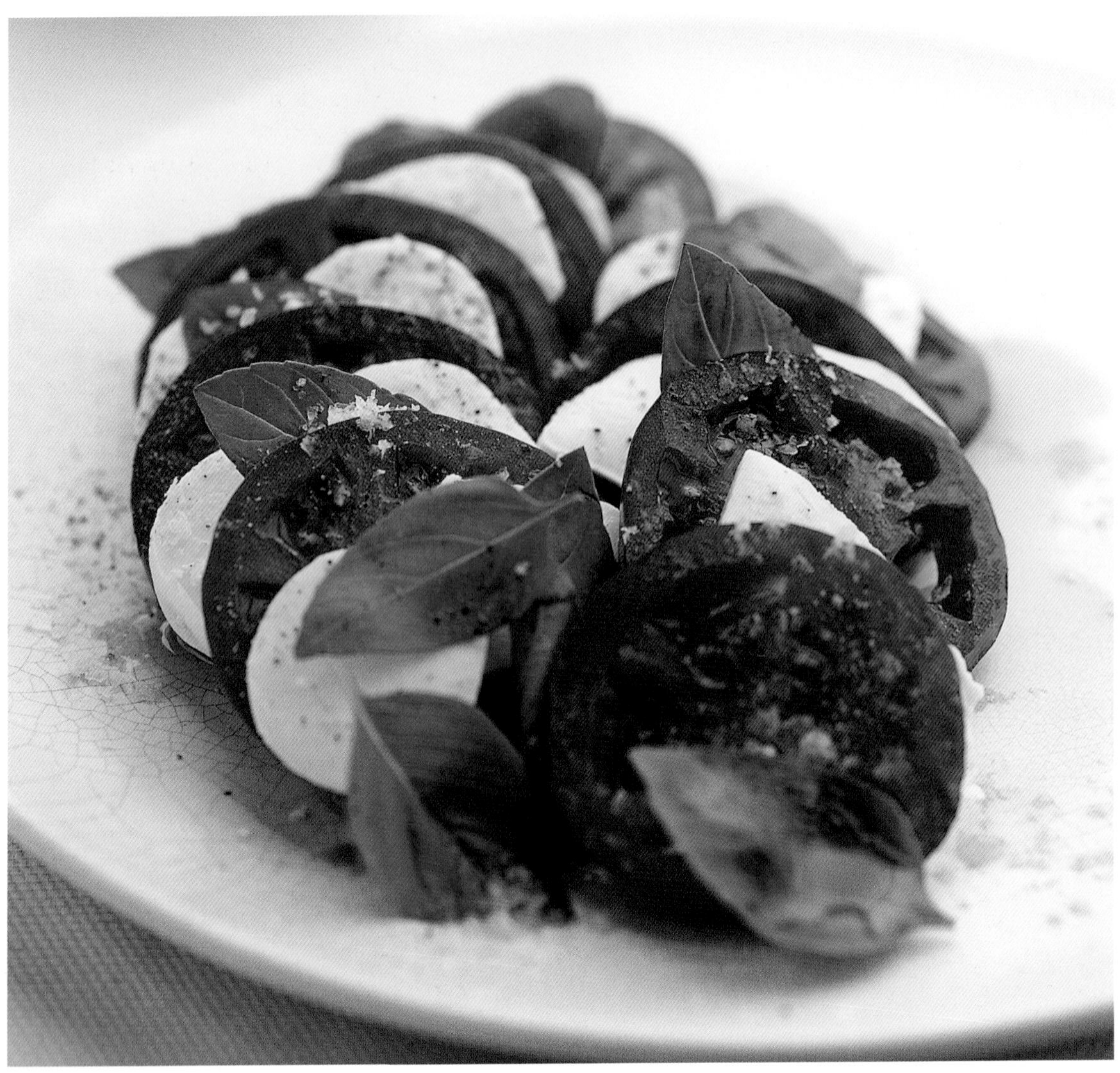

MARINATED BOCCONCINI

SERVES 8

INGREDIENTS

- 400 g (14 oz) bocconcini (fresh baby mozzarella cheese), sliced
- 150 g (5½ oz) jar sun-dried capsicums (peppers) in oil
- 1 handful small basil leaves
- extra virgin olive oil
- 60 ml (2 fl oz/¼ cup) lemon juice

METHOD

1. Dry the bocconcini with paper towels. Drain the capsicums, reserving the oil, and cut the capsicums into strips. Gently crush the basil leaves. Pour the reserved oil and 250 ml (9 fl oz/1 cup) of the olive oil into a saucepan and gently heat for 5 minutes. Stir the lemon juice into the oil.
2. Put a layer of bocconcini slices in a sterilised 750 ml (26 fl oz/3 cup) wide-necked jar with a clip-top lid. Sprinkle with freshly ground black pepper. Put a thin layer of crushed basil leaves on top of the cheese and cover with some of the capsicum. Continue layering, then cover with the warmed oil, topping up with a little more olive oil if necessary.
3. Seal the jar and leave to marinate in the fridge for 3 days. Return to room temperature and drain before serving.

GRILLED HALOUMI SALAD

SERVES 4

INGREDIENTS

- 1 Lebanese (short) cucumber, seeded and diced
- 3 tomatoes, seeded and diced
- 40 g (1½ oz/¼ cup) pitted kalamata olives
- 2 tablespoons capers, rinsed
- 1 small red onion, finely diced
- 1 garlic clove, roughly chopped
- 1 small handful basil
- 1 small handful parsley
- 60 ml (2 fl oz/¼ cup) olive oil
- 2 tablespoons lemon juice
- 300 g (10½ oz) haloumi cheese, cut into 1 cm (½ inch) slices

METHOD

1. Combine the cucumber, tomato, olives, capers and onion in a serving dish.
2. To make the herb dressing, crush the garlic with a pinch of salt using a mortar and pestle. Add the basil and parsley and pound until a paste starts to form. Add a little of the oil and pound for another 10 seconds. Stir in the remaining oil and lemon juice and season with pepper.
3. Heat a barbecue grill and cook the haloumi for 1–2 minutes on each side, until it is starting to soften but not melt. Cut into thick strips and arrange on top of the salad. Spoon over the dressing. Serve while the haloumi is still hot.

HALOUMI

This salty, semi-hard, sheep's milk cheese is popular in countries such as Lebanon, Syria and Cyprus, where much of the supply comes from. It has a distinctive, almost rubbery texture when fresh, and is squeaky when cooked. Haloumi is often thickly sliced and grilled or fried, then served with a squeeze of lemon juice or a sprinkling of mint. Taken with a glass of ouzo, this is a classic Greek meze dish.

CHAPTER THREE

POULTRY

••BASICS••

Which came first: the chicken or the egg? Surprisingly, while we've been eating eggs for thousands of years, it is only relatively recently that chicken became the widely farmed meat it is today. Descended from the aggressive red jungle fowl of Asia, chickens reached Europe in about 500 BC and scavenged quietly on farmyards and small holdings. In the nineteenth century chicken's popularity as a meat suddenly took off in Europe and North America, but it was a special-occasion food, available only to the wealthy (or farmers) until the mass-production and battery-farming of the twentieth century.

THE MODERN CHICKEN

Free-range, organic and corn-fed chickens are now widely available and, as well as the obvious ethical advantages, have a better flavour than intensively farmed birds. Free-range chickens can be identified by a label stating that they've been reared humanely with room to roam. Corn-fed chickens have a yellowy skin and flesh, but are not necessarily free-range. Organic birds are usually free-range and have not been fed the antibiotics given to battery-farmed chickens to prevent disease in their cramped conditions. You will pay more for any of these varieties but this should be compensated for by the quality and taste.

WHITE MEAT OR DARK?

Chicken breasts can be bought on the bone or as 'fillets' (bone removed). Both can have the skin on or removed and both are available as single or double (joined) breasts. In our recipes, when we ask for '1 boneless, skinless chicken breast' we mean a single breast fillet.

White breast meat is very lean and can dry out quickly so it's best for cooking methods that will help retain its moisture, such as poaching, grilling with the skin on, or roasting at high heat. Boneless chicken breast fillets are perfect for quick cooking such as pan-frying or stir-frying. Underneath the fillet is a long thin strip of white meat called the tenderloin, which can be easily detached. In some places you can buy tenderloins by the kilo; perfect for stir-fries and satays. But for casseroles, a whole chicken jointed (cut into pieces that contain bone, see right), or 'darker' more succulent meat such as legs or thighs (or Marylands, which are joined leg and thigh), will cook slowly and retain flavour.

HOW TO... STORE CHICKEN

* Fresh chicken should be taken out of its packaging, covered loosely with plastic wrap and put on a plate to catch any drips. Keep it in the fridge, and not where it can drip onto other food. Cook it within 2 days.
* Frozen chicken must be solid and tightly wrapped when you buy it. Chicken can be frozen for up to 3 months, sealed in a bag with the air squeezed out (write the date on a label).
* Thaw chicken carefully as bacteria, such as salmonella, can be activated if it gets too warm. Thaw in the fridge, not at room temperature. (And not in a bowl of warm water because you forgot to do it earlier!)
* Use thawed chicken within 12 hours and never refreeze. Store cooked chicken in the fridge for up to 3 days.

HOW TO... JOINT A CHICKEN

Cutting a whole chicken into pieces is called 'jointing'. The flavour of a dish will often be better if, rather than buying pieces, you cut up a whole bird. Large birds can be cut into four, six, eight or ten pieces.

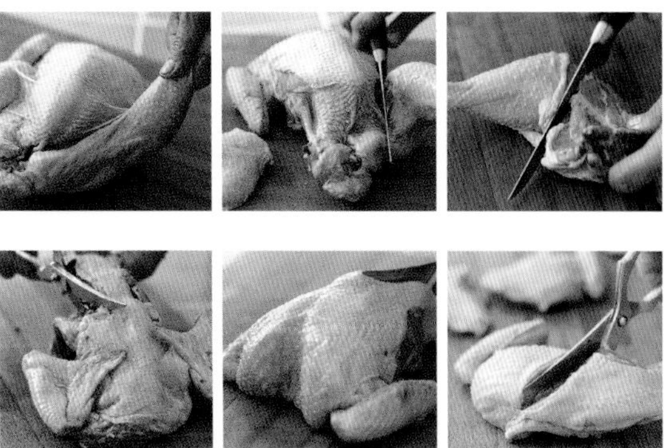

METHOD

1 Lay the bird on a board with the cavity end facing you. Pull both legs away from the carcass and twist the thigh bones out of their body sockets.
2 Cut through the flesh to remove the leg. Keep the small piece of meat, known as the oyster, that is found at the back of the body attached to the leg meat.
3 Cut between the drumstick and the thigh along the natural fat line, which is visible on the underside of the thigh. Your knife should slide easily through the joint.
4 Cut down either side of the backbone and lift it out (easier with a pair of poultry scissors).
5 Turn the bird over, remove the wishbone and cut down the centre of the breastbone.
6 Cut through each piece of breast at an angle so it makes two equal pieces. Leave the wing attached to one piece and trim off the wing tips and any straggly pieces of skin.

HOW TO... BONE A CHICKEN

Some special-occasion recipes call for a chicken to be boned and then stuffed and rolled for spectacular presentation. These dishes are usually served cold.

METHOD

1 Pull the flap of skin from the neck down around the shoulder to expose the wishbone and joint where the wing bone joins the shoulder. Carefully cut around the wishbone and snap it out.
2 Turn the bird over. Cut through the joints between the wings and backbone but leave the wing bones in.
3 Remove the shoulder bones by scraping away any flesh and cutting though the cartilage that joins them to the breastbone. Pull on the shoulder bones: they are attached together but both ends should now be loose.
4 Once the shoulder bones are out, use your knife to scrape down the bones of the carcass, making sure the flesh comes away in one piece. Angle the blade of the knife towards the bones so it doesn't slip and cut through the flesh.
5 When you reach the legs, pull the thigh bones out of their sockets. Leave the bones in the legs to give them more definition when cooked.
6 Carry on scraping down the carcass until you reach the bottom. Sever the cartilage at the bottom of the breastbone on one side and cut through the bottom vertebra on the other. You should now be able to lift out the carcass.

••ROASTS••

Although chicken was once a dish available only to the wealthy, food has long been a route to people's hearts. In his coronation speech of 1594, France's Henry IV courted favour by promising every peasant of the land 'a chicken in his pot every Sunday'. Since then, the Sunday roast chicken has become probably the most popular family meal of them all.

ROAST CHICKEN WITH ROSEMARY

SERVES 4

INGREDIENTS

- 2 rosemary sprigs
- 3 garlic cloves
- 1 teaspoon balsamic vinegar
- 1.5 kg (3 lb 5 oz) chicken
- 80 ml (2½ fl oz/⅓ cup) olive oil
- 125 ml (4 fl oz/½ cup) chicken stock (page 11)

METHOD

1 Preheat the oven to 200°C (400°F/Gas 6). Put one rosemary sprig, the garlic and balsamic vinegar inside the cavity of the chicken. Season with salt and pepper. Truss the legs together.

2 Rub half of the olive oil over the chicken skin. Pour the remaining oil into a roasting tin and put the chicken in the tin, breast side up. Put the second sprig of rosemary on top. Transfer to the oven and roast for 1 hour, turning the chicken and basting with the pan juices every 15 minutes.

3 Put the chicken on a warm serving plate and discard the rosemary sprig. Spoon off the fat from the roasting tin and place the tin over high heat on the stovetop. Add the stock and deglaze the pan. Boil until reduced and thickened. Check the seasoning, adding salt and pepper if needed, then pour into a gravy boat. Carve the chicken and serve with the gravy.

ROAST CHICKEN PIECES WITH HERBED CHEESE

SERVES 4

INGREDIENTS

- 150 g (5½ oz) herbed cream cheese
- 1 teaspoon finely grated lemon zest
- 4 chicken leg quarters or breasts, skin on
- 2 leeks, cut into chunks
- 2 parsnips, cut into chunks
- 2 teaspoons olive oil

METHOD

1 Preheat the oven to 200°C (400°F/Gas 6). Mix the cream cheese with the lemon zest. Loosen the skin from the leg quarters or breasts and use your fingers to spread the cream cheese between the skin and flesh. Press the skin back down and season it.

2 Bring a saucepan of water to the boil and cook the leek and parsnip for 4 minutes. Drain, then put in a single layer in a roasting tin. Drizzle with the oil and season well. Put the chicken on top.

3 Transfer to the oven and roast for 40 minutes, until the skin is browned and the cream cheese has mostly melted out to form a sauce over the vegetables. Check that the vegetables are cooked and tender. (If they need a little longer, remove the chicken, cover the tin with foil and cook for another 5 minutes. Keep the chicken warm under foil in the meantime.) Serve with roast potatoes and a green salad.

ROAST LEMON GARLIC CHICKEN

SERVES 4

INGREDIENTS

- 1.5 kg (3 lb 5 oz) chicken
- 80 ml (2½ fl oz/⅓ cup) lemon juice
- ½ lemon
- 9 garlic cloves, whole and unpeeled
- 80 ml (2½ fl oz/⅓ cup) olive oil
- 1 kg (2 lb 4 oz) roasting potatoes, cut into 5 cm (2 inch) pieces
- 4 red onions, cut into quarters
- 8 small zucchini (courgettes), trimmed and cut in half lengthways
- 250 ml (9 fl oz/1 cup) chicken stock (page 11)

METHOD

1. Preheat the oven to 220°C (425°F/Gas 7). Wash the chicken and pat dry inside and out with paper towels, then place in a large roasting tin. Pour 1 tablespoon of the lemon juice over the chicken, then place the lemon half and 1 garlic clove inside the chicken cavity. Brush the outside with 1 tablespoon of the oil. Season.
2. Arrange the potato and remaining garlic cloves around the chicken. Brush the potatoes with 2 tablespoons of the oil and roast for 20 minutes. Reduce the heat to 190°C (375°F/Gas 5). Put the onion around the chicken, turning the potatoes at the same time. Return to the oven for a further 30 minutes.
3. Put the zucchini, cut side down, on a baking tray and brush with the remaining oil, then place in the oven. Baste the chicken with the pan juices and pour the remaining lemon juice over the top. Turn the onion and potatoes and roast for 20 minutes, or until the chicken is golden and the juices run clear when pierced between the breast and thigh.
4. Transfer the chicken, potatoes, garlic and onion to a serving plate, cover with foil and keep warm for 10 minutes. Check the zucchini are tender — they may need to stay in the oven.
5. To make the gravy, put the roasting tin over high heat and add the stock. Stir to scrape up any sediment and boil until it reduces and thickens.
6. To serve, remove the lemon and garlic from the cavity and discard. Serve the chicken with the onion, garlic, zucchini, potatoes and gravy.

HOW TO... ROAST A PERFECT CHICKEN

* First make sure that there is nothing inside the cavity (the giblets are sometimes stored in there in a plastic bag, which could lead to disaster). Rinse inside and out and dry with paper towels.
* You can truss the chicken to help it keep its shape and cook evenly — tie its legs together with kitchen string and tuck its wings back under the body.
* For even roasting, turn the bird over halfway through cooking time. Baste as often as you can.
* When the chicken is cooked the juices from the cavity and from a skewer pushed into the thigh will run clear.
* Leave the chicken to 'rest' loosely covered with foil for 10 minutes before carving to let the juices settle. Some people leave the chicken upside down for the juices to run into the breast.

ROAST TURKEY WITH PISTACHIO STUFFING

SERVES 6–8

INGREDIENTS

PISTACHIO STUFFING

45 g (1½ oz/⅓ cup) shelled pistachio nuts
100 g (3½ oz) prosciutto, finely chopped
200 g (7 oz) minced (ground) pork
200 g (7 oz) minced (ground) chicken
1 egg
80 ml (2½ fl oz/⅓ cup) thick (double) cream
150 g (5½ oz) chestnut purée
½ teaspoon finely chopped sage or ¼ teaspoon dried sage
pinch of cayenne pepper

3 kg (6 lb 12 oz) turkey
300 g (10½ oz) butter, softened
1 onion, roughly chopped
4 sage leaves
1 rosemary sprig
½ celery stalk, cut into 2–3 pieces
1 carrot, cut into 3–4 pieces
250 ml (9 fl oz/1 cup) dry white wine
125 ml (4 fl oz/½ cup) dry Marsala
250 ml (9 fl oz/1 cup) chicken stock (page 11)

METHOD

1 To make the pistachio stuffing, preheat the oven to 170°C (325°F/Gas 3). Spread the nuts on a baking tray and toast for 6–8 minutes. Place in a bowl with the other stuffing ingredients, season well and mix together thoroughly.
2 Fill the turkey cavity with the stuffing and join the cavity with a skewer. Cross the legs and tie them together, then tuck the wings under the body.
3 Rub the skin with 100 g (3½ oz) of the butter. Put the onion in the centre of a roasting tin and place the turkey on top, breast side up. Add another 100 g (3½ oz) of butter to the tin along with the sage, rosemary, celery and carrot. Pour the wine and Marsala over the top. Roast for 2½–3 hours, basting several times. Once the turkey skin becomes golden brown, cover with buttered foil.
4 When cooked, transfer the turkey to a carving plate, cover with foil and leave to rest.
5 Put the vegetables from the tin into a food processor and blend, or push them through a sieve. Add the pan juices and scrapings from the bottom of the tin and blend until smooth. Transfer the mixture to a saucepan, add the remaining butter and the stock and bring to the boil. Season and cook until thickened to a gravy consistency. Transfer to a gravy boat. Carve the turkey and serve with stuffing and gravy.

PISTACHIO NUTS

These yellow–green nuts are enclosed inside a soft fruit of a native Asian tree. The fruit grow in clusters, encasing a beige, brittle shell, which hold the nuts. As the nuts mature, the shells open slightly, revealing the nuts inside. Pistachios can be eaten from the shell, added to sweet and savoury dishes, or used in salads and stuffings and to flavour ice cream and cassata.

ROAST TURKEY WITH RICE AND CHESTNUT STUFFING

SERVES 6–8

INGREDIENTS

CHESTNUT STUFFING

12 prunes, pitted
180 g (6½ oz) whole fresh chestnuts
40 g (1½ oz) butter
1 red onion, finely chopped
2 garlic cloves, crushed
60 g (2¼ oz) pancetta (including any fat), finely chopped
100 g (3½ oz) wild rice blend
60 ml (2 fl oz/¼ cup) chicken stock (page 11)
3 dried juniper berries, lightly crushed
2 teaspoons finely chopped rosemary
3 teaspoons finely chopped thyme

3 kg (6 lb 12 oz) turkey
1 large red onion, cut into 4–5 slices
30 g (1 oz) butter, softened
375 ml (13 fl oz/1½ cups) dry white wine
1 carrot, quartered
1 celery stalk, quartered
1 large rosemary sprig
2 teaspoons finely chopped thyme
250 ml (9 fl oz/1 cup) chicken stock
2 tablespoons plain (all-purpose) flour

METHOD

1 Preheat the oven to 170°C (325°F/Gas 3). To make the stuffing, soak the prunes in hot water for 20 minutes. Meanwhile, to prepare the chestnuts, make a small cut in the skin on the flat side, then brown on all sides under a hot grill (broiler). Transfer to a bowl lined with a damp tea towel and cover with the towel. Peel when cool enough to handle. (Don't let the chestnuts cool completely or they will become harder to peel.) Roughly chop the prunes and chestnuts.

2 Melt the butter in a large saucepan and add the onion, garlic and pancetta. Cook over low heat for 5–6 minutes, or until the onion is softened, then add the wild rice, stock, juniper berries, prunes and chestnuts. Stir well, then pour in 375 ml (13 fl oz/1½ cups) water. Bring to the boil and cook, covered, stirring once or twice, for 20–25 minutes, or until the rice is tender and the liquid has absorbed. Remove from the heat, stir in the rosemary and thyme, and season.

3 Fill the turkey cavity with the stuffing and join the cavity with a skewer. Cross the legs and tie them together, then tuck the wings under the body. Arrange the onion in the centre of a large roasting tin, then sit the turkey on top, breast side up. Season and dot with butter. Pour 250 ml (9 fl oz/1 cup) of the wine into the tin and scatter the carrot, celery, rosemary and half the thyme around the turkey.

4 Roast for 2–2½ hours, until cooked through and the juices run clear, basting every 30 minutes. After 1 hour, pour half the stock into the tin. Once the skin becomes golden brown, cover with buttered foil.

5 When cooked, transfer the turkey to a carving plate, cover with foil and leave to rest.

6 Pour the juices into a small saucepan and reduce for 8–10 minutes. Stir in the flour, then add a little of the remaining stock, stirring to form a paste. Slowly add the rest of the stock and wine, stirring constantly. Stir in the remaining thyme. Bring to the boil and simmer for 8 minutes, or until reduced by a third. Season to taste. Transfer to a gravy boat. Carve the turkey and serve with the stuffing and gravy.

NOTE: Do not stuff the turkey until you are ready to cook it. The stuffing can be made ahead of time and frozen if necessary. If you are using warm stuffing, cook the bird immediately.

CHICKEN WITH FORTY CLOVES OF GARLIC

SERVES 4

INGREDIENTS

- 2 celery stalks, including leaves
- 2 rosemary sprigs
- 4 thyme sprigs
- 4 parsley sprigs
- 1.6 kg (3 lb 8 oz) chicken
- 40 garlic cloves, unpeeled (see Note)
- 2 tablespoons olive oil
- 1 carrot, roughly chopped
- 1 small onion, cut into 4 wedges
- 250 ml (9 fl oz/1 cup) white wine
- 1 baguette, cut into slices

METHOD

1. Preheat the oven to 200°C (400°F/Gas 6). Put a chopped celery stalk and 2 sprigs each of the rosemary, thyme and parsley into the chicken cavity. Add 6 garlic cloves. Tie the legs together and tuck the wing tips under.
2. Brush the chicken liberally with some of the oil and season well. Scatter about 10 more garlic cloves over the base of a large casserole dish. Put the remaining herb sprigs, chopped celery, carrot and onion in the dish.
3. Put the chicken in the dish. Scatter the remaining garlic cloves around the chicken and add the remaining oil and the wine. Cover and bake for 1 hour 20 minutes, or until the chicken is tender and the juices run clear when the thigh is pierced with a skewer.
4. To serve, carefully lift the chicken out of the casserole dish. Strain off the juices into a small saucepan. Use tongs to pick out the garlic cloves from the strained mixture. Spoon off the fat from the juices and boil for 2–3 minutes to reduce and thicken a little.
5. Cut the chicken into serving portions, pour over a little of the juices and scatter with the garlic. Toast the baguette slices and serve, with the bread to be spread with the soft flesh squeezed from the garlic cloves.

NOTE: This sounds frighteningly overpowering but roasting causes the garlic cloves to mellow and sweeten.

COOKING WITH GARLIC

* Raw garlic is more potent than cooked garlic. When garlic is cooked, some of the starch converts to sugar, making it less pungent.
* Be careful not to overbrown or burn garlic or it will become very bitter.
* Crush a whole garlic clove by putting it under the flat blade of a knife then banging the knife with your fist.
* Flavour oil with garlic by frying slices in the oil, then straining the oil.

ROAST DUCKLING

SERVES 2

INGREDIENTS

- 1.8 kg (4 lb) duckling
- 1 bouquet garni
- 30 g (1 oz) clarified butter (page 120)
- 1 carrot, chopped
- 1 celery stalk, chopped
- ½ large onion, chopped
- 2 teaspoons sugar
- 8 French shallots
- 8 baby turnips
- 80 ml (2½ fl oz/⅓ cup) white wine
- 500 ml (17 fl oz/2 cups) chicken stock (page 11)
- 2 teaspoons softened butter
- 2 teaspoons plain (all-purpose) flour

METHOD

1. Preheat the oven to 200°C (400°F/Gas 6) and put a roasting tin in the oven to heat up. Truss the duckling, prick all over, put the bouquet garni in the cavity and season with salt and pepper.
2. Heat the butter in a large frying pan and brown the duckling. Lift out of the pan and pour all but a tablespoon of the fat into a jug. Add the carrot, celery and onion to the pan and soften over low heat, then brown. Remove the vegetables.
3. Add another 2 tablespoons of duck fat to the pan. Add the sugar and let it dissolve over low heat. Turn up the heat and add the shallots and turnips. Caramelise over high heat, then remove from the pan. Pour in the wine and boil, stirring, for 30 seconds to deglaze the pan.
4. Put the carrot, celery and onion in the middle of the hot roasting tin, put the duckling on top and pour in the wine and the stock. Add the turnips, then roast for 45 minutes. Baste well, add the shallots and roast for 20 minutes. Baste again and roast for a further 25 minutes.
5. Lift out the duck, turnips and shallots and keep warm. Pour the sauce into a sieve, pressing the chopped vegetables in the sieve to extract all the juices, then throw away the chopped vegetables. Pour the strained sauce into a saucepan and boil rapidly to reduce by half. Mix together the butter and flour and whisk it into the sauce and boil, stirring, for 2 minutes until thickened. Put the duckling, turnips and shallots on a serving plate and serve with the sauce.

ROAST GOOSE

SERVES 6

INGREDIENTS

- 3 kg (6 lb 12 oz) goose
- 1 tablespoon plain (all-purpose) flour
- 2 tablespoons brandy
- 375 ml (13 fl oz/1½ cups) chicken stock (page 11)
- bread sauce (page 428), to serve

METHOD

1. Preheat the oven to 180°C (350°F/Gas 4). Remove any excess fat from the cavity of the goose. Place in a large pan, cover with boiling water, then drain. Dry with paper towels.
2. Place the goose, breast side down, on a rack in a large roasting tin. (If the goose sits directly in the tin it will be very greasy.) Prick the skin all over, being careful to pierce only the skin, not the flesh. Roast for 1 hour, then remove from the oven and drain off any excess fat. Turn the goose over and bake for another 30 minutes, or until the outside is golden and crisp. Remove from the roasting tin, cover loosely with foil and leave for 5–10 minutes.
3. To make the gravy, drain all but 2 tablespoons of fat from the tin. Place the tin on the stovetop. Add the flour, stirring constantly over medium heat until browned. Remove from the heat and gradually stir in the brandy and stock. Return to the heat and stir until the gravy boils and thickens. Season with salt and pepper. Serve the goose with the gravy and bread sauce.

DUCK A L'ORANGE

SERVES 4

INGREDIENTS

- 5 oranges
- 2 kg (4 lb 8 oz) duck
- 2 cinnamon sticks
- 15 g (½ oz) mint leaves
- 95 g (3¼ oz/½ cup) light brown sugar
- 125 ml (4 fl oz/½ cup) cider vinegar
- 80 ml (2½ fl oz/⅓ cup) Grand Marnier
- 30 g (1 oz) butter

METHOD

1. Preheat the oven to 150°C (300°F/Gas 2). Halve two of the oranges and rub them all over the duck. Place the halved oranges inside the duck cavity along with the cinnamon sticks and mint. Tie the legs together and tie the wings together. Prick all over with a fork so that the fat can drain out as the duck cooks.
2. Put the duck on a rack, breast side down, and put the rack in a shallow roasting tin. Roast for 45 minutes, turning the duck halfway through.
3. Meanwhile, zest and juice the remaining oranges (if you don't have a zester, cut the orange peel into thin strips with a sharp knife). Heat the sugar in a saucepan over low heat until it melts and then caramelises: swirl the pan gently to make sure it caramelises evenly. When the sugar is a rich brown, add the vinegar (be careful as it will splutter) and boil for 3 minutes. Add the orange juice and liqueur and simmer for 2 minutes.
4. Blanch the orange zest in boiling water for 1 minute, three times, changing the water each time. Refresh under cold water, then drain.
5. Remove the excess fat from the roasting tin. Increase the oven to 180°C (350°F/Gas 4). Spoon some of the orange sauce over the duck and roast for a further 45 minutes, spooning the remaining sauce over the duck every 10 minutes or so, and turning the duck to baste all sides.
6. Remove the duck from the oven, cover with foil and strain the juices from the roasting tin into a saucepan. Skim off any excess fat and add the blanched orange zest and butter to the saucepan. Stir to melt the butter. Reheat the sauce and serve over the duck.

GOOSE

This domesticated wild bird is traditionally eaten at Christmas in Northern Europe. The goose is a useful bird — the liver becomes foie gras, preserved goose is a necessary addition to cassoulet, and goose fat is highly prized in France especially. Geese are best roasted. Remove visible fat and prick the skin to allow the fat to run off during cooking. Like all water birds, geese appear large, but yield little meat. A 6 kg (13 lb) bird should feed 8 people.

VINE LEAVES

These large green leaves of the grape vine are used in Middle Eastern and Greek cookery as food wrappers, mainly in dolmades, where they wrap a meat or rice mixture before the whole parcel is steamed over stock. They are also used to wrap small game birds or fish before braising or baking. Vine leaves are sold fresh, or tinned in brine. Fresh leaves need blanching in hot water until soft enough to be pliable. Tinned vine leaves should be rinsed in cold water before use to remove the salty brine.

QUAIL WRAPPED IN VINE LEAVES

Quail have delicate flesh that can dry out in the oven. Here they are wrapped in vine leaves before roasting, to give flavour as well as keep the meat moist.

SERVES 4

INGREDIENTS

- 4 rosemary sprigs
- 4 quail
- 2 tablespoons olive oil
- 1 tablespoon balsamic vinegar
- 2 teaspoons soft brown sugar
- 4 large vine leaves

METHOD

1. Preheat the oven to 180°C (350°F/Gas 4). Stuff a sprig of rosemary into each quail and then tie its legs together. Tuck the wings behind the back.
2. Heat the olive oil in a large frying pan and add the quail. Brown them all over and then add the vinegar and sugar. Cook, allowing the sauce to bubble, for a few minutes. Remove the quail.
3. Blanch the vine leaves in a bowl of boiling water for 15 seconds and then wrap one leaf around each quail. Put the wrapped quail in a roasting tin, seam side down, and bake for 15 minutes, or until cooked through.

QUAIL STUFFED WITH WILD RICE

SERVES 4

INGREDIENTS

- 50 g (1¾ oz/¼ cup) wild rice
- 250 ml (9 fl oz/1 cup) chicken stock (page 11)
- 1 onion, finely chopped
- 20 g (¾ oz) butter
- 1 tablespoon finely chopped dried apricots
- 1 tablespoon finely chopped prunes
- 1 tablespoon chopped mixed parsley and chervil
- 4 quail
- 80 ml (2½ fl oz/⅓ cup) olive oil

METHOD

1. Preheat the oven to 200°C (400°F/Gas 6). Put the rice and stock in a pan and bring to the boil. Simmer for 30 minutes, until tender, then drain.
2. Sauté the onion in the butter for 5 minutes, or until softened but not browned. Then add the apricots, prunes, parsley and chervil. Add the wild rice and season well.
3. Loosely fill the quail with the rice stuffing and fasten them closed with toothpicks.
4. Heat the oil in a frying pan and brown the quail all over — you may need to do this in batches. Transfer the quails to a roasting tin and roast for 15–20 minutes, or until a skewer inserted into the cavity comes out very hot.

••STARTERS AND SALADS••

Chicken is the ideal ingredient if you're making a starter for a special dinner: the leanness of the meat means it doesn't tend to fill anyone up too much before the main course, it is seen as a healthy low-fat choice, fits into just about any style of cuisine and tends to be universally enjoyed.

CHICKEN LIVER PATE

SERVES 6

INGREDIENTS

- 500 g (1 lb 2 oz) chicken livers
- 80 ml (2½ fl oz/⅓ cup) brandy
- 90 g (3¼ oz) unsalted butter
- 1 onion, finely chopped
- 1 garlic clove, crushed
- 1 teaspoon chopped thyme
- 60 ml (2 fl oz/¼ cup) thick (double) cream
- 4 slices white bread

METHOD

1. Trim the chicken livers, cutting away any discoloured bits and veins. Rinse them, pat dry and cut in half. Place in a small bowl with the brandy, cover and leave for a couple of hours. Drain the livers, reserving the brandy.
2. Melt half of the butter in a frying pan, add the onion and garlic and cook over low heat until the onion is soft and transparent. Add the livers and thyme and stir over medium heat until the livers change colour. Add the reserved brandy and simmer for 2 minutes. Cool for 5 minutes.
3. Place the livers and liquid in a food processor and process until smooth. Add the remaining butter, chopped, and process again until smooth. (Alternatively, roughly mash the livers with a fork, then push them through a sieve and mix with the melted butter.) Pour in the cream and process until just incorporated.
4. Season the pâté and spoon into an earthenware dish or terrine, or small individual ramekins, and smooth the surface. Cover and refrigerate until firm. If the pâté is to be kept for more than a day, chill it and then pour clarified butter (page 120) over the surface to seal. Garnish with a bay leaf, if desired. Serve with bread or melba toast.

FOIE GRAS

Although now made in several countries, foie gras ('fat liver') is traditionally a French product. To make it, geese and ducks are force-fed grain, which encourages their livers to grow abnormally large. Once removed, the liver is cleaned, seasoned, spiced and cooked. It is sold fresh, preserved, semi-cooked and pasteurised in tins, or preserved (in its own fat) in jars. Pâté de foie gras is puréed liver (minimum 75 per cent foie gras). Fresh foie gras will keep for a week in the fridge. Jars of preserved foie gras can keep for years in a cold, dark, dry place.

MELBA TOAST

These very thin, dry triangles of toast are used as an accompaniment for soups, pâtés and salads. The bread for melba toast can be cooked either in the oven or under a grill but the colour should be as even as possible. Because the edges of the toast curl slightly, melba toast also makes a good base for hors d'oeuvres.

To make melba toasts, remove the crusts from fresh white bread. Roll out thinly with a rolling pin and slice in half horizontally, then cut into triangles. Space on a baking tray and bake at 200°C (400°F/Gas 6) for 15 minutes, or until golden. Alternatively, preheat the grill (broiler) and cut the crusts off the bread. Toast the bread on both sides, slice horizontally with a sharp serrated knife, then cut into triangles to give eight pieces.

DEEP-FRIED QUAIL WITH SPICY SALT AND PEPPER

SERVES 4

INGREDIENTS

4 quail
1 tablespoon salt
2 teaspoons ground sichuan peppercorns
1 teaspoon Chinese five-spice
1 teaspoon sugar
1 tablespoon light soy sauce
1 tablespoon Chinese rice wine
2–3 tablespoons plain (all-purpose) flour
oil, for deep-frying
1 spring onion (scallion), finely chopped
1 red chilli, finely chopped

METHOD

1. Split each quail in half down the middle and clean. Combine the salt, pepper, five-spice, sugar, soy sauce and rice wine. Add the quail and marinate for 2–3 hours in the fridge.
2. Coat each quail piece in the flour. Fill a wok one-quarter full of oil and heat to 190°C (375°F), or until a cube of bread fries golden brown in 10 seconds. Reduce the heat and fry the quail for 3 minutes on each side. Drain on paper towel.
3. Soak the spring onion and chilli in the hot oil (with the heat turned off) for 2 minutes. Remove, drain and then sprinkle over the quail pieces.

SWEET CHILLI CHICKEN WINGS

SERVES 10

INGREDIENTS

2 kg (4 lb 8 oz) chicken wings
2 garlic cloves, crushed
1 tablespoon oil
60 ml (2 fl oz/¼ cup) sweet chilli sauce
2 tablespoons honey
1 tablespoon white vinegar
60 ml (2 fl oz/¼ cup) soy sauce
2 teaspoons grated ginger
1 tablespoon soft brown sugar

METHOD

1. Trim the chicken of excess fat and sinew. Cut each wing into three sections, discarding the tips (you can freeze them and use for making stock).
2. Mix together the remaining ingredients in a large bowl. Season with salt and pepper, then add the chicken wings and stir until coated. Cover and refrigerate overnight (or for several hours).
3. Preheat the oven to 180°C (350°F/Gas 4). Drain the chicken wings and reserve the marinade. Put the chicken on a roasting rack over a baking tray or in a deep baking tin. Bake for 1 hour, or until the chicken is crisp and cooked through. Brush the pieces with the reserved marinade several times during cooking. Serve hot.

CHICKEN WITH LEMON MAYONNAISE

Fry 2 chicken breasts for 3–4 minutes on each side, or until cooked through. When cold, shred the chicken into long strips. Combine 100 g (3½ oz) whole-egg mayonnaise, 1 teaspoon finely grated lemon zest and 1 tablespoon lemon juice in a bowl. Cut 8 slices from a sourdough loaf and spread 4 slices with the lemon mayonnaise. Top with some watercress, thinly sliced cucumber and chicken. Season with salt and freshly ground black pepper and top with the remaining slices of bread. Serves 4

BUFFALO WINGS

SERVES 4

INGREDIENTS

8 large chicken wings
2 teaspoons garlic salt
2 teaspoons onion powder
2 teaspoons black pepper
oil, for deep frying
125 ml (4 fl oz/½ cup) tomato sauce (ketchup)
2 tablespoons worcestershire sauce
1 tablespoon melted butter
2 teaspoons sugar
Tabasco sauce, to taste

RANCH DRESSING

125 g (4½ oz/½ cup) mayonnaise
125 g (4½ oz/½ cup) sour cream
2 tablespoons lemon juice
2 tablespoons chopped chives

METHOD

1 Wash the chicken wings and pat dry with paper towels. Cut the tip off each wing and discard. Bend each wing back to snap the joint and cut through to create two pieces. Combine the garlic salt, onion powder and pepper and rub into the wings.
2 Fill a deep heavy-based saucepan one-third full of oil and heat to 180°C (350°F), or until a cube of bread dropped into the oil turns golden brown in 15 seconds. Deep-fry the chicken in batches for 2 minutes. Drain on paper towels.
3 Transfer the chicken to a shallow non-metallic dish. Combine the sauces, butter, sugar and Tabasco and pour over the chicken, stirring to coat. Cover and refrigerate for at least 3 hours.
4 Heat a lightly oiled barbecue grill or hotplate and cook the chicken for 5 minutes, turning and brushing with the marinade.
5 To make the ranch dressing, combine the mayonnaise, sour cream, lemon juice and chives. Season and serve with the chicken wings.

THAI CHICKEN CAKES

MAKES 15

INGREDIENTS

DIPPING SAUCE

115 g (4 oz/½ cup) caster (superfine) sugar
2 teaspoons rice wine vinegar
1 tablespoon sweet chilli sauce
½ small Lebanese (short) cucumber, seeded and diced

500 g (1 lb 2 oz) minced (ground) chicken
4 spring onions (scallions), chopped
2 garlic cloves, chopped
2 teaspoons green curry paste
4 kaffir lime leaves, shredded
1 large handful coriander (cilantro)
1 tablespoon fish sauce
60 ml (2 fl oz/¼ cup) coconut cream
50 g (1¾ oz) snake (yard-long) beans, cut into 5 mm (¼ inch) slices
oil, for deep-frying

METHOD

1 To make the dipping sauce, put the sugar and 125 ml (4 fl oz/½ cup) water in a small saucepan. Stir over low heat until the sugar has dissolved. Bring to the boil and cook for 5 minutes, or until thick and syrupy. Cool, then stir in the vinegar, sweet chilli sauce and cucumber.
2 Put the chicken, spring onion, garlic, curry paste, lime leaves, coriander, fish sauce and coconut cream in a food processor and process until well combined. Fold in the sliced beans. Using 2 tablespoons of mixture at a time, form into small cakes.
3 Fill a wok one-third full of oil and heat to 180°C (350°F), or until a cube of bread dropped into the oil turns golden brown in 15 seconds. Deep-fry the chicken cakes in batches for 2–3 minutes, or until lightly golden and cooked through. Remove with a slotted spoon and drain on paper towels. Serve with the dipping sauce.

YAKITORI

Japanese in origin, yakitori (meaning 'grilled chicken') is made with pieces of chicken, sometimes interspersed with leek or spring onion, threaded onto skewers. These are basted in a marinade and traditionally grilled over charcoals.

MAKES 8 SKEWERS

INGREDIENTS

- 100 ml (3½ fl oz) Japanese soy sauce
- 2 tablespoons mirin
- 2 tablespoons vegetable oil
- 2 tablespoons sake or rice wine
- 2 tablespoons sugar
- 6 boneless, skinless chicken thighs, trimmed and cut into 4 cm (1½ inch) pieces
- 6 spring onions (scallions), cut into 3 cm (1¼ inch) pieces

METHOD

1. Soak eight wooden skewers in water for 30 minutes to prevent them burning.
2. Put the soy sauce, mirin, oil, sake and sugar in a saucepan and bring to the boil, stirring. Turn off the heat and allow the marinade to cool. Transfer half the marinade to a bowl, large enough to fit the chicken skewers.
3. Thread the chicken onto the skewers alternating with the spring onion, and place the skewers in the marinade. Turn to coat completely, then lift out and drain, reserving the marinade.
4. Preheat and lightly oil a barbecue grill or chargrill pan and cook the chicken skewers for 8–10 minutes, turning and brushing with the marinade. Put the remaining marinade in a saucepan and bring to the boil. Simmer for 3–4 minutes, or until reduced a little. Serve as a dipping sauce.

CHICKEN SATAYS

MAKES 8

INGREDIENTS

- 1 tablespoon honey
- 60 ml (2 fl oz/¼ cup) soy sauce
- 2 teaspoons sesame oil
- 1 teaspoon ground coriander
- 1 teaspoon ground turmeric
- ½ teaspoon chilli powder
- 500 g (1 lb 2 oz) chicken tenderloins, halved lengthways

SATAY SAUCE

- 1 tablespoon oil
- 1 small onion, finely chopped
- 125 g (4½ oz/½ cup) crunchy peanut butter
- 2 tablespoons soy sauce
- 125 ml (4 fl oz/½ cup) coconut cream
- 2 tablespoons sweet chilli sauce

METHOD

1. Soak eight wooden skewers in water for 30 minutes to prevent them burning.
2. In a shallow non-metallic dish, combine the honey, soy sauce, sesame oil, coriander, turmeric and chilli powder.
3. Thread the chicken lengthways onto the skewers and place the skewers in the marinade. Cover and refrigerate for at least 2 hours.
4. Meanwhile, make the satay sauce. Heat the oil in a saucepan, add the onion and cook for 5 minutes, or until softened. Stir in the peanut butter, soy sauce, coconut cream and sweet chilli sauce. Cook gently until smooth and heated through.
5. Preheat a barbecue grill or chargrill pan and cook the chicken satays for 5–7 minutes, turning and basting with the marinade frequently. Serve warm with the satay sauce.

PAPRIKA GARLIC CHICKEN

SERVES 6

INGREDIENTS

- 1 kg (2 lb 4 oz) boneless, skinless chicken thighs
- 1 tablespoon paprika
- 2 tablespoons olive oil
- 8 garlic cloves, unpeeled
- 60 ml (2 fl oz/¼ cup) brandy
- 125 ml (4 fl oz/½ cup) chicken stock (page 11)
- 1 bay leaf
- 2 tablespoons chopped parsley

METHOD

1. Trim any excess fat from the chicken and cut the thighs into thirds. Combine the paprika with some salt and pepper in a bowl, add the chicken and toss to coat.
2. Heat half the olive oil in a large frying pan over medium heat. Add the garlic and cook for 1–2 minutes, until brown. Remove from the pan. Increase the heat to high and cook the chicken in batches for 5 minutes each batch, or until brown. Return all the chicken to the pan, add the brandy and boil for 30 seconds, then add the stock and bay leaf. Reduce the heat, cover and simmer over low heat for 10 minutes.
3. Meanwhile, peel the garlic and put it in a mortar or small bowl. Add the parsley and pound with the pestle or crush with a fork to form a paste. Stir into the chicken, then cover and cook for 10 minutes, or until tender. Serve hot.

PEKING DUCK

SERVES 6

INGREDIENTS

- 2.5 kg (5 lb 8 oz) duck
- 2 tablespoons maltose or honey, dissolved in 2 tablespoons water
- 24 Mandarin pancakes (see Note)
- 125 ml (4 fl oz/½ cup) hoisin sauce or plum sauce
- 6–8 spring onions (scallions), trimmed and thinly sliced lengthways
- ½ cucumber, thinly sliced lengthways

METHOD

1. Cut the wing tips off the duck. Rinse the duck, drain, and then remove any fat from the cavity opening and around the neck. Cut off and discard the parson's nose. Plunge the duck into a pot of boiling water for 2–3 minutes to tighten the skin. Remove and drain, then dry thoroughly.
2. While the skin is still warm, brush the duck all over with the maltose mixture, then hang it up to dry in a cool and airy place for at least 6 hours, or overnight, or leave it uncovered in the fridge.
3. Preheat the oven to 200°C (400°F/Gas 6). Put the duck, breast side up, on a rack in a roasting tin, and cook without basting or turning for 1½ hours. Check to make sure the duck is not getting too dark — if it is, cover loosely with foil.
4. To serve, remove the crispy duck skin in small slices using a carving knife, then carve the meat, or carve both together. Arrange on a plate.
5. To assemble the pancakes, spread 1 teaspoon of the hoisin sauce or plum sauce in the centre of a pancake, add a few lengths of spring onion and cucumber, some duck skin and meat, then roll up the pancake and turn up the bottom edge to prevent the contents from falling out.

NOTE: Mandarin pancakes are available in Asian food stores, fresh or frozen, or from restaurants that sell takeaway barbecued ducks and meats.

CHICKEN AND PAPAYA SALAD

SERVES 4

INGREDIENTS

- 2 poached or barbecued chicken breasts, shredded
- 1 large papaya, peeled, seeded and chopped or sliced
- 1 Lebanese (short) cucumber, diced
- 2 spring onions (scallions), shredded
- 1 large handful mint
- 1 large handful coriander (cilantro)
- 80 g (2¾ oz/½ cup) peanuts, chopped

DRESSING

- 25 g (1 oz) tamarind pulp
- 1 teaspoon soy sauce
- 2 teaspoons finely grated ginger
- 1 tablespoon grated palm sugar (jaggery) or soft brown sugar
- 1 large red chilli, seeded and thinly sliced

METHOD

1. To make the dressing, put the tamarind pulp in a bowl and cover with 125 ml (4 fl oz/½ cup) boiling water. Leave to steep for 30 minutes, stirring occasionally, then strain, reserving the tamarind water.
2. Put the tamarind water in a large bowl with the soy sauce, ginger, sugar and chilli, stirring until the sugar has dissolved. Add the chicken and toss to coat in the dressing.
3. Combine the papaya, cucumber, spring onion and herbs in a bowl. Transfer to a serving platter and top with the chicken. Pour over any remaining dressing. Scatter with the peanuts.

VIETNAMESE CHICKEN SALAD

SERVES 2

INGREDIENTS

- 1 boneless, skinless chicken breast or 2 thighs
- 1 tablespoon lime juice
- 1 tablespoon fish sauce
- pinch of sugar
- 1 red bird's eye chilli, finely chopped
- 1 garlic clove, crushed
- 1 French shallot, thinly sliced
- 1 handful bean sprouts, blanched
- 1 large handful shredded Chinese cabbage
- 2 tablespoons chopped Vietnamese mint

METHOD

1. Bring a saucepan of salted water to the boil. Add the chicken, return to the boil, then cover and remove from the heat. Leave the chicken in the water to poach for 1 hour. Drain the chicken well and when cool enough to handle, shred the meat into long pieces.
2. To make the dressing, combine the lime juice, fish sauce, sugar, chilli, garlic and shallot.
3. Mix the bean sprouts with the cabbage, mint and chicken. Pour the dressing over the salad, toss together and serve.

CHICKEN AND GRAPEFRUIT SALAD

SERVES 4

INGREDIENTS

4 x 200 g (7 oz) boneless, skinless chicken breasts
80 ml (2½ fl oz/⅓ cup) virgin olive oil
2 teaspoons balsamic vinegar
2 pink grapefruit
½ teaspoon dijon mustard
1½ tablespoons pickled pink peppercorns, drained and rinsed
1 tablespoon snipped chives
rocket (arugula) leaves, to serve

METHOD

1 Put the chicken between two sheets of plastic wrap and pound each with a mallet or rolling pin until 1.5 cm (⅝ inch) thick. Put 2 tablespoons of the oil in a shallow dish with the vinegar, and season with salt and pepper. Toss in the chicken, then cover and marinate in the refrigerator for 15 minutes, turning once.
2 Preheat a barbecue grill and brush with oil. Drain the chicken and cook for 7–8 minutes, or until cooked through, turning once. Remove from the heat, cool to room temperature, then slice.
3 Peel the grapefruit, removing all the bitter white pith. Working over a bowl to catch the juices, cut the grapefruit into segments between the membrane, removing any seeds. Reserve a tablespoon of the juice and whisk in the mustard and remaining oil to make a dressing. Add the peppercorns and chives and season with salt and pepper to taste.
4 Arrange the rocket on four plates and top with the chicken and grapefruit. Drizzle with the dressing and serve.

CHICKEN SALAD WITH ROCKET

SERVES 4

INGREDIENTS

80 ml (2½ fl oz/⅓ cup) lemon juice
3 garlic cloves, crushed
1 handful basil, finely chopped
1 teaspoon soft brown sugar
125 ml (4 fl oz/½ cup) olive oil
4 boneless, skinless chicken breasts
400 g (14 oz) tin cannellini beans, rinsed
100 g (3½ oz) small rocket (arugula) leaves

METHOD

1 To make the dressing, whisk together the lemon juice, garlic, basil, sugar and olive oil. Season with salt and pepper.
2 Pour a third of the dressing over the chicken breasts to coat. Preheat a barbecue grill or chargrill pan and cook the chicken, in batches, over medium heat for 10 minutes, or until cooked through, turning once.
3 Meanwhile, combine the beans and rocket with the remaining dressing, toss well and season. Slice the chicken across the grain into 1.5 cm (⅝ inch) pieces. Arrange the chicken pieces over the rocket and beans and serve.

COLD CHICKEN AND MANGO SALAD

SERVES 4

INGREDIENTS

HONEY DRESSING

60 ml (2 fl oz/¼ cup) rice vinegar
2 tablespoons honey
3 cm (1¼ inch) piece ginger, chopped
60 ml (2 fl oz/¼ cup) grapeseed oil
1 teaspoon sesame oil

125 g (4½ oz) mixed Asian salad leaves
1 large mango, thinly sliced
125 g (4½ oz/¾ cup) yellow or red cherry tomatoes, halved
½ small red onion, sliced into thin wedges
1 cold barbecued chicken, fat and skin removed, meat shredded
1 handful snow pea (mangetout) sprouts
2 teaspoons sesame seeds, toasted

METHOD

1. To make the honey dressing, put the vinegar, honey and ginger in a mini processor and process in short bursts for 20 seconds, or until finely chopped. With the motor running, slowly pour in the oils and whizz for 20 seconds, or until the dressing is thick and creamy.
2. Arrange the salad leaves on individual plates and top with the mango, tomatoes, onion, chicken and snow pea sprouts. Drizzle with the dressing and sprinkle with the sesame seeds. Serve immediately.

ROAST DUCK SALAD WITH CHILLI DRESSING

SERVES 4

INGREDIENTS

CHILLI DRESSING

½ teaspoon chilli flakes
2½ tablespoons fish sauce
1 tablespoon lime juice
2 teaspoons grated palm sugar (jaggery) or soft brown sugar

1 Chinese roasted duck
1 small red onion, thinly sliced
1 tablespoon julienned ginger
4 tablespoons chopped coriander (cilantro)
4 tablespoons chopped mint
80 g (2¾ oz/½ cup) roasted unsalted cashew nuts
8 butter lettuce leaves

METHOD

1. To make the chilli dressing, put the chilli flakes in a frying pan and dry-fry over medium heat for 30 seconds, then grind to a powder using a mortar and pestle or spice grinder. Put the powder in a small bowl with the fish sauce, lime juice and sugar. Mix well to dissolve the sugar and set aside.
2. Remove the flesh from the duck, cut it into bite-sized pieces and put it in a bowl. Add the onion, ginger, coriander, mint and cashews. Pour in the dressing and toss together gently.
3. Arrange the lettuce on a serving platter, or use the leaves to line individual serving bowls. Top with the duck salad and serve.

••FRIES AND GRILLS••

For quick cooking such as pan-frying, deep-frying and stir-frying, breast meat is generally the most suitable. Grilling or barbecuing can make chicken skin crisp and give it a wonderful flavour. Grilling is also ideal for small birds such as quail or poussins because they cook quickly and the flesh remains tender and moist. Whether you're using a frying pan or a barbecue, make sure the oil or the hotplate or grill is very hot, to give the poultry a crisp coating without drying out the meat.

CAJUN CHICKEN WITH SALSA

SERVES 4

INGREDIENTS

- 2 sweet corn cobs
- 2 tomatoes, diced
- 1 Lebanese (short) cucumber, diced
- 2 tablespoons chopped coriander (cilantro)
- 4 boneless, skinless chicken breasts
- 35 g (1¼ oz) Cajun seasoning
- 2 tablespoons lime juice
- lime wedges, to serve

METHOD

1. Cook the corn in a saucepan of boiling water for 5 minutes, or until tender. Remove the kernels using a knife and place in a bowl with the tomato, cucumber and coriander. Season and mix well.
2. Preheat a barbecue grill and brush with oil. Pound each chicken breast between two sheets of plastic wrap until 2 cm (¾ inch) thick. Lightly coat the chicken with the Cajun seasoning and shake off any excess. Cook the chicken for 5 minutes on each side, until just cooked through.
3. Just before serving, stir the lime juice into the salsa. Place a chicken breast on each plate and spoon the salsa on the side. Serve with the lime wedges, a green salad and crusty bread.

CHICKEN CORDON BLEU

SERVES 4

INGREDIENTS

- 4 boneless, skinless chicken breasts
- 4 thick slices Swiss cheese
- 4 slices double-smoked ham
- seasoned flour, for dusting
- 1 egg, lightly beaten
- 50 g (1¾ oz/½ cup) dry breadcrumbs
- 125 ml (4 fl oz/½ cup) oil

METHOD

1. Slice through the middle of each chicken breast without cutting right through. Open it out flat and season well.
2. Place a slice of cheese and ham on one half of each fillet and fold the other half over.
3. Coat the chicken in the seasoned flour, shaking off the excess. Dip into the egg, then coat with the breadcrumbs. Place on a foil-lined tray. Cover and refrigerate for 30 minutes.
4. Heat the oil in a large frying pan over medium heat. Working in batches, add the chicken and cook for 5 minutes on each side, or until golden and cooked through. Serve immediately.

CHICKEN KIEV

SERVES 6

INGREDIENTS

- 125 g (4½ oz) butter, softened
- 1 garlic clove, crushed
- 2 tablespoons chopped parsley
- 2 teaspoons lemon juice
- 2 teaspoons finely grated lemon zest
- 6 small boneless, skinless chicken breasts
- 60 g (2¼ oz/½ cup) plain (all-purpose) flour
- 400 g (14 oz/4 cups) dry breadcrumbs
- 2 eggs, beaten
- 60 ml (2 fl oz/¼ cup) milk
- oil, for frying
- lemon wedges, to serve

METHOD

1. Mix together the butter, garlic, parsley, lemon juice and zest. Spoon onto a sheet of foil and shape into a rectangle 5 x 8 cm (2 x 3 inches). Roll up the foil and chill until firm.
2. Place each piece of chicken between two sheets of plastic wrap and use a meat mallet or rolling pin to gently flatten to 5 mm (¼ inch) thick.
3. Cut the chilled butter into six pieces. Place a piece in the centre of each chicken slice, fold in the edges and roll up to completely enclose. Fasten with toothpicks and chill until firm.
4. Place the flour and breadcrumbs on separate plates or pieces of baking paper. Toss the chicken in the flour, dip in the combined egg and milk, then coat with the breadcrumbs. Chill on a paper-lined tray in the fridge for 1 hour, then toss in the egg and breadcrumbs again.
5. Half-fill a heavy-based frying pan with oil and cook the chicken in batches for 5 minutes on each side, or until golden and cooked through. Drain on paper towels, remove the toothpicks and serve with the lemon wedges.

SOUTHERN FRIED CHICKEN

SERVES 4

INGREDIENTS

- 1 kg (2 lb 4 oz) chicken pieces
- 500 ml (17 fl oz/2 cups) buttermilk
- oil, for deep-frying
- 185 g (6½ oz/1½ cups) plain (all-purpose) flour, seasoned

METHOD

1. Put the chicken in a bowl and pour in the buttermilk. Mix well. Cover and refrigerate for 2 hours, turning occasionally.
2. Half-fill a deep heavy-based saucepan with oil and heat to 180°C (350°F), or until a cube of bread dropped into the oil turns golden brown in 15 seconds. Place the flour in a shallow dish. Remove the chicken from the buttermilk, shake off any excess, dip the pieces into the flour and coat well.
3. Lower the chicken into the oil, in small batches, and deep-fry for 12 minutes on each side, making sure that the oil is not too hot or the chicken will brown on the outside before it is cooked through. Drain well on paper towels before serving.

GRILLED SPATCHCOCK

SERVES 4

To 'spatchcock' describes the method of preparing a chicken or other bird by either cutting it in half along each side of the backbone, or splitting it along the breastbone. The chicken can then be opened out and flattened, seasoned and grilled. The word is thought to have come from an old English innkeeping term, 'to dispatch cock', meaning that the chicken was killed, then split so it could be cooked quickly for a traveller. The spatchcock can be skewered to keep it flat, then brushed with oil and grilled (broiled) or barbecued. It can be marinated or have a paste of softened butter and herbs pushed under the skin. In some countries, such as Australia, the term spatchcock has come to mean a small or young chicken (poussin).

INGREDIENTS

- 4 x 450 g (1 lb) baby chickens (poussin)
- 120 g (4¼ oz) butter
- 4 tablespoons finely chopped parsley
- 2 garlic cloves, crushed
- 2 tablespoons lemon juice
- pinch of cayenne pepper

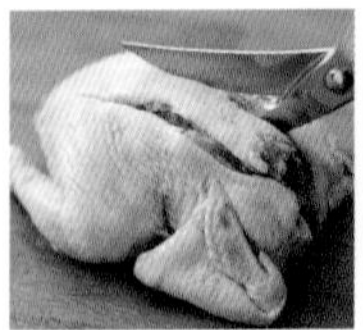
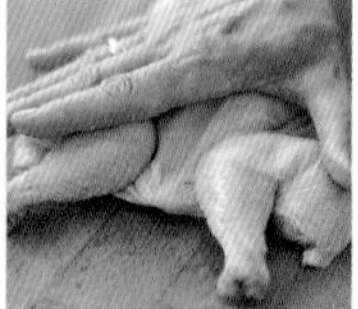

METHOD

1. To spatchcock the birds, split them by cutting down each side of the backbone with poultry shears or a pair of poultry scissors.
2. Put the bird, cut side down, on your chopping board and press firmly down on the ribcage, squashing it out flat.
3. Trim off the wing tips and any excess fat or skin and set aside.
4. In a bowl, mash together the butter, parsley and garlic. Season with salt and pepper. Push two fingers under the skin of the spatchcock breasts to loosen the skin, then push the mixture under the skin of each breast.
5. Combine the lemon juice, cayenne pepper and some salt and pepper and brush over the spatchcocks, then set aside for 1 hour.
6. Brush the spatchcocks with olive oil and then cook, breast side up, under a hot grill (broiler) or on a barbecue grill until golden brown. Turn over and cook for a further 7 minutes, or until the juices run clear.

TANDOORI CHICKEN

SERVES 4

INGREDIENTS

1.5 kg (3 lb 5 oz) whole chicken or skinless chicken thighs and drumsticks
cucumber raita, to serve (page 159)

MARINADE

2 teaspoons coriander seeds
1 teaspoon cumin seeds
1 onion, roughly chopped
3 garlic cloves, roughly chopped
5 cm (2 inch) piece ginger, roughly chopped
250 g (9 oz/1 cup) Greek-style yoghurt
finely grated zest of 1 lemon
60 ml (2 fl oz/¼ cup) lemon juice
2 tablespoons white vinegar
1 teaspoon paprika
2 teaspoons garam masala
½ teaspoon tandoori food colouring (optional)

METHOD

1 Remove the skin from the whole chicken and cut the chicken in half. Using a sharp knife, make 2.5 cm (1 inch) long diagonal incisions on each limb and breast, taking care not to cut through to the bone. Thread two metal skewers through each chicken half to keep the pieces flat. If using thighs and drumsticks, trim away any excess fat and make an incision in each piece.
2 To make the marinade, place a frying pan over low heat and dry-roast the coriander seeds until aromatic. Remove and dry-roast the cumin seeds. Grind the seeds to a fine powder using a spice grinder or mortar and pestle. In a food processor, blend all the marinade ingredients to form a smooth paste. Season with salt.
3 Marinate the chicken in the yoghurt marinade for 8 hours, or overnight, turning the chicken occasionally in the marinade to coat all sides.
4 Preheat a barbecue grill and brush lightly with oil. If using the skewered chicken halves, cook for 40–45 minutes, turning every 10 minutes and basting with the marinade, until cooked through. If using chicken thighs and drumsticks, cook them for 20–25 minutes, turning frequently. Serve the chicken with cucumber raita.

CHICKEN TIKKA

SERVES 4

INGREDIENTS

450 g (1 lb) boneless, skinless chicken breasts, cubed
lemon wedges, to serve

MARINADE

2 teaspoons paprika
1 teaspoon chilli powder
2 tablespoons garam masala
¼ teaspoon tandoori food colouring
juice of 1 lemon
4 garlic cloves, crushed
1 tablespoon grated ginger
1 small handful coriander (cilantro), chopped
125 g (4½ oz/½ cup) Greek-style yoghurt

METHOD

1 To make the marinade, blend all the ingredients in a food processor until smooth, or chop the garlic, ginger and coriander more finely and mix with the rest of the marinade. Season with salt.
2 Put the chicken in a bowl with the marinade and mix thoroughly. Marinate overnight in the fridge.
3 Thread the chicken pieces onto four metal skewers and grill, barbecue or bake in a 200°C (400°F/Gas 6) oven for 15–20 minutes, or until the chicken is cooked through and browned. Serve with lemon wedges.

❮ DUCK WITH WILD RICE

SERVES 4

INGREDIENTS

DRESSING

80 ml (2½ fl oz/⅓ cup) olive oil
2 tablespoons orange juice
2 teaspoons walnut oil
1 teaspoon finely grated orange zest

95 g (3¼ oz/½ cup) wild rice
2 teaspoons oil
50 g (1¾ oz) pecans, roughly chopped
½ teaspoon ground cinnamon
65 g (2¼ oz/⅓ cup) long-grain white rice
2 tablespoons finely chopped parsley
4 spring onions (scallions), thinly sliced
2 duck breasts
finely grated zest of 1 orange

METHOD

1 To make the dressing, combine the ingredients. Season with salt and pepper. Set aside.
2 Put the wild rice in a pan with 300 ml (10½ fl oz) water. Bring to the boil, then cook, covered, for 30 minutes, until tender. Drain off any water.
3 Heat the oil in a large frying pan. Cook the pecans, stirring, until golden. Add the cinnamon and a pinch of salt, and cook for 1 minute.
4 Bring a large saucepan of water to the boil. Add the white rice and cook, stirring occasionally, for 12 minutes, or until tender. Drain and mix with the wild rice and pecans in a large, shallow bowl. Add the parsley and spring onion. Add half the dressing and toss well.
5 Put the duck, skin side down, in a cold frying pan, then heat the pan over high heat. Cook for 5 minutes, or until crisp, then turn over and cook for another 5 minutes. Tip out any excess fat and add the remaining dressing and the orange zest, and cook until bubbling. Transfer the duck to a serving dish and slice on the diagonal. Serve with the rice, drizzled with any juices.

CHICKEN WITH OLIVES AND PRESERVED LEMON

SERVES 4

INGREDIENTS

60 ml (2 fl oz/¼ cup) olive oil
1.6 kg (3 lb 8 oz) chicken
1 onion, chopped
2 garlic cloves, chopped
625 ml (21 fl oz/2½ cups) chicken stock (page 11)
½ teaspoon ground ginger
1½ teaspoons ground cinnamon
pinch of saffron threads
100 g (3½ oz) green olives
¼ preserved lemon (page 668), rinsed, pith and flesh removed, zest thinly sliced
2 bay leaves
2 chicken livers
3 tablespoons chopped coriander (cilantro)

METHOD

1 Preheat the oven to 180°C (350°F/Gas 4). Heat 2 tablespoons of the oil in a large frying pan, add the whole chicken and brown on all sides. Place the chicken in a deep baking dish.
2 Heat the remaining oil, add the onion and garlic to the pan and cook over medium heat for 3–4 minutes, or until softened. Add the stock, ginger, cinnamon, saffron, olives, lemon zest and bay leaves and pour around the chicken. Transfer to the oven and bake for 45 minutes, adding a little more water or stock if the sauce gets too dry. Remove the chicken from the dish, cover with foil and leave to rest.
3 Pour the contents of the baking dish into a frying pan, add the chicken livers and mash into the sauce as they cook. Cook for 5–6 minutes, or until the sauce has reduced and thickened. Add the coriander. Cut the chicken into four pieces and serve with the sauce.

(pictured page 82)

CHINESE LEMON CHICKEN

SERVES 6

INGREDIENTS

500 g (1 lb 2 oz) boneless, skinless chicken breasts
1 tablespoon light soy sauce
1 tablespoon Chinese rice wine
1 spring onion (scallion), finely chopped
1 tablespoon finely chopped ginger
1 garlic clove, finely chopped
1 egg, lightly beaten
100 g (3½ oz) cornflour (cornstarch)
oil, for deep-frying

LEMON SAUCE

2 tablespoons lemon juice
2 teaspoons sugar
½ teaspoon sesame oil
60 ml (2 fl oz/¼ cup) chicken stock (page 11)
½ teaspoon cornflour (cornstarch)

METHOD

1 Cut the chicken into slices. Place in a bowl, add the soy sauce, rice wine, spring onion, ginger and garlic, and toss lightly. Marinate in the fridge for at least 1 hour, or overnight.
2 Add the egg to the chicken mixture and toss lightly to coat. Drain off the excess and coat the chicken pieces with the cornflour. The easiest way to do this is to put the chicken and cornflour in a plastic bag and shake it.
3 Fill a wok one-quarter full of oil and heat to 190°C (375°F), or until a cube of bread dropped into the oil turns golden brown in 10 seconds. Add half the chicken, a piece at a time, and fry, stirring constantly, for 3–4 minutes, or until golden brown. Remove with a wire sieve or slotted spoon and drain. Repeat with the remaining chicken. Reheat the oil and return all the chicken to the wok. Cook until crisp and golden brown. Drain the chicken. Pour off the oil and wipe out the wok.
4 To make the lemon sauce, combine the lemon juice, sugar, ½ teaspoon salt, sesame oil, stock and cornflour.
5 Reheat the wok over medium heat until hot, add the lemon sauce and stir constantly until thickened. Add the chicken and toss lightly in the sauce.

CHICKEN WITH CHILLI JAM

SERVES 4

INGREDIENTS

2 teaspoons fish sauce
2 tablespoons oyster sauce
60 ml (2 fl oz/¼ cup) coconut milk
½ teaspoon sugar
2½ tablespoons vegetable oil
6 garlic cloves, finely chopped
1–1½ tablespoons chilli jam (page 430), to taste
500 g (1 lb 2 oz) boneless, skinless chicken breasts, thinly sliced
1 handful Thai basil leaves
1 long red or green chilli, seeded and thinly sliced, to garnish

METHOD

1 Mix the fish sauce, oyster sauce, coconut milk and sugar in a small bowl.
2 Heat the oil in a wok or frying pan and stir-fry half the garlic over medium heat until light brown. Add half the chilli jam and stir-fry for 2 minutes, or until fragrant. Add half of the chicken and stir-fry over high heat for 2–3 minutes. Remove from the wok. Repeat with the remaining garlic, chilli jam and chicken. Return all the chicken to the wok.
3 Add the fish sauce mixture to the wok and stir-fry for a few more seconds or until the chicken is cooked. Taste, then adjust the seasoning if necessary. Stir in the basil leaves and garnish with chilli slices.

CHICKEN WITH CASHEW NUTS

This popular dish is typically Chinese but appears on many Thai restaurant menus (the cashews are actually a Thai addition). Frying the cashew nuts separately brings out their flavour and adds a more 'nutty' taste to the dish.

SERVES 4

INGREDIENTS

- 1–2 dried long red chillies
- 1 tablespoon fish sauce
- 2 tablespoons oyster sauce
- 60 ml (2 fl oz/¼ cup) chicken or vegetable stock (page 10–11), or water
- ½–1 teaspoon sugar
- 80 ml (2½ fl oz/⅓ cup) vegetable oil
- 85 g (3 oz/½ cup) cashew nuts
- 4–5 garlic cloves, finely chopped
- 500 g (1 lb 2 oz) boneless, skinless chicken breasts, thinly sliced
- ½ red capsicum (pepper), cut into thin strips
- ½ carrot, sliced diagonally
- 1 small onion, cut into 6 wedges
- 2 spring onions (scallions), chopped
- ground white pepper, to sprinkle

METHOD

1. Take the stems off the dried chillies, cut each chilli into 1 cm (½ inch) pieces with scissors or a sharp knife and discard the seeds.
2. Mix the fish sauce, oyster sauce, stock and sugar in a small bowl.
3. Heat the oil in a wok over medium heat and stir-fry the cashews for 2–3 minutes, or until light brown. Remove with a slotted spoon and drain on paper towels.
4. Stir-fry the chillies in the same oil over medium heat for 1 minute. They should darken but not blacken and burn. Remove from the wok with a slotted spoon.
5. Heat the same oil again and stir-fry half the garlic over medium heat until light brown. Add half the chicken and stir-fry over high heat for 4–5 minutes, or until the chicken is cooked. Remove from the wok and repeat with the remaining garlic and chicken. Return all the chicken to the wok.
6. Add the capsicum, carrot, onion and the sauce mixture to the wok and stir-fry for 1–2 minutes. Taste, then adjust the seasoning if necessary. Add the cashews, chilli and spring onion and toss well. Sprinkle with white pepper.

CASHEW NUTS

Native to Brazil, cashew nuts are encased in kidney-shaped hard shells and develop inside fruit called cashew apples. Each apple only produces one nut and, when the nut is ripe, the nut and shell protrude below the fruit. Removing the cashew nut from the shell is a slow and laborious task as the shells contain a caustic oil known as 'cashew balm', which is highly toxic and can irritate the skin and eyes. The whole nuts are removed from the apples and heated before the nut can be safely extracted.

Cashew nuts, sold shelled, have a rich, buttery flavour. They can be eaten roasted and salted, or added raw to curries or stir-fries. They are high in fat and should be stored in the fridge to prevent them turning rancid. The tart cashew apple can be eaten raw, and is used to make jams, wine and liqueurs.

••STEWS, CASSEROLES AND CURRIES••

Chicken pieces on the bone (either bought that way, or by jointing a whole bird) are perfect for long, slow cooking. As with most other long-cooked dishes, these stews and casseroles benefit from being made a day in advance and left in the fridge overnight for the flavours to develop. Just reheat gently without boiling. (And if you do make your stews in advance you'll find you can lift off the layer of fat that solidifies on top of the dish when it's cooled.)

COQ AU VIN

SERVES 8

INGREDIENTS

- 2 x 1.6 kg (3 lb 8 oz) chickens, each jointed into 8 pieces (page 85)
- 1 bottle red wine
- 2 bay leaves
- 2 thyme sprigs
- 250 g (9 oz) bacon, diced
- 60 g (2¼ oz) butter
- 20 baby onions
- 250 g (9 oz) button mushrooms
- 1 teaspoon oil
- 30 g (1 oz/¼ cup) plain (all-purpose) flour
- 1 litre (35 fl oz/4 cups) chicken stock (page 11)
- 125 ml (4 fl oz/½ cup) brandy
- 2 teaspoons tomato paste (concentrated purée)
- 30 g (1 oz) butter, softened
- 1 tablespoon plain (all-purpose) flour
- 2 tablespoons chopped parsley

METHOD

1. Put the chicken, wine, bay leaves, thyme and some salt and pepper in a bowl. Cover and leave to marinate overnight.
2. Blanch the bacon in boiling water, then drain, pat dry and sauté in a large frying pan until golden. Lift out onto a plate. Melt a quarter of the butter in the pan, add the onions and sauté until browned. Lift out and set aside.
3. Melt another quarter of the butter, add the mushrooms, season with salt and pepper and sauté for 5 minutes. Remove and set aside.
4. Drain the chicken, reserving the marinade, and pat the chicken dry. Season. Add the remaining butter and the oil to the frying pan, add the chicken and sauté until golden. Stir in the flour.
5. Transfer the chicken to a large saucepan and add the stock. Pour the brandy into the frying pan and boil, stirring, for 30 seconds to deglaze the pan. Pour the brandy over the chicken, then add the marinade, bacon, onions, mushrooms and tomato paste. Cook over medium heat for 45 minutes, or until cooked through.
6. If the sauce needs thickening, lift out the chicken and vegetables and bring the sauce to the boil. Mix together the butter and flour and whisk into the sauce. Boil, stirring, for 2 minutes until thickened. Return the chicken and vegetables to the sauce. Sprinkle with the parsley and serve.

CHICKEN CHASSEUR

SERVES 4

INGREDIENTS

1.6 kg (3 lb 8 oz) chicken
1 tablespoon oil
60 g (2¼ oz) butter
2 French shallots, finely chopped
125 g (4½ oz) button mushrooms, sliced
1 tablespoon plain (all-purpose) flour
125 ml (4 fl oz/½ cup) white wine
2 tablespoons brandy
2 teaspoons tomato paste (concentrated purée)
250 ml (9 fl oz/1 cup) chicken stock (page 11)
2 teaspoons chopped tarragon
1 teaspoon chopped parsley

CROUTONS
2 slices bread
olive oil

METHOD

1 Joint the chicken into eight pieces by removing both legs and cutting between the joint of the drumstick and the thigh. Cut down either side of the backbone and lift it out. Turn the chicken over and cut through the cartilage down the centre of the breastbone. Cut each breast in half, leaving the wing attached to the top half.
2 Heat the oil in a frying pan or saucepan and add half the butter. When the foaming subsides, add the chicken and sauté in batches on both sides until browned. Lift out onto a plate and keep warm. Pour the excess fat out of the pan.
3 Melt the remaining butter in the pan, add the shallots and cook gently until softened but not browned. Add the mushrooms and cook, covered, over medium heat for 3 minutes.
4 Add the flour and cook, stirring constantly, for 1 minute. Stir in the wine, brandy, tomato paste and stock. Bring to the boil, stirring constantly, then reduce the heat and add the tarragon. Season with salt and pepper.
5 Return the chicken to the pan, cover and simmer for 30 minutes, or until the chicken is tender and cooked through. Sprinkle with parsley to serve.
6 To make the croutons, trim the crusts from the bread and cut the bread into moon shapes with a biscuit cutter. Heat the oil in a frying pan and fry the bread until golden. Drain the croutons on paper towels and serve hot with the chicken.

SPICY APRICOT CHICKEN

SERVES 4

INGREDIENTS

750 g (1 lb 10 oz) boneless, skinless chicken thighs, cut into 5 cm (2 inch) pieces
flour, for coating
2 tablespoons oil
2 teaspoons red curry paste
2 spring onions (scallions), sliced
415 g (15 oz) tin apricot halves in light syrup
125 ml (4 fl oz/½ cup) chicken stock (page 11)
200 g (7 oz) plain yoghurt
2 tablespoons chopped coriander (cilantro)

METHOD

1 Lightly coat the chicken in the flour. Heat the oil in a saucepan, add the curry paste and stir over low heat for 1 minute. Add the spring onion and chicken and cook, stirring, over medium heat for 2–3 minutes, or until the chicken is golden.
2 Drain the apricots and reserve 125 ml (4 fl oz/½ cup) of the juice. Add the reserved juice, apricots and chicken stock to the pan. Bring to the boil, then reduce the heat and simmer for 10 minutes, or until the chicken is tender.
3 Mix together the yoghurt and coriander and place a spoonful of the mixture over each serving of chicken. Serve with couscous or rice.

CHICKEN CACCIATORE

SERVES 4

INGREDIENTS

- 60 ml (2 fl oz/¼ cup) olive oil
- 1 large onion, finely chopped
- 3 garlic cloves, crushed
- 1 celery stalk, finely chopped
- 150 g (5½ oz) pancetta, finely chopped
- 125 g (4½ oz) button mushrooms, thickly sliced
- 4 chicken drumsticks
- 4 chicken thighs
- 80 ml (2½ fl oz/⅓ cup) dry vermouth or white wine
- 2 x 400 g (14 oz) tins chopped tomatoes
- ¼ teaspoon soft brown sugar
- 1 oregano sprig, plus 4–5 sprigs to garnish
- 1 rosemary sprig
- 1 bay leaf

METHOD

1. Heat half the oil in a large flameproof casserole dish. Add the onion, garlic and celery and cook, stirring from time to time, over low heat for 6–8 minutes, or until the onion is golden.
2. Add the pancetta and mushrooms, increase the heat and cook, stirring occasionally, for 4–5 minutes. Spoon onto a plate and set aside.
3. Add the remaining oil to the dish and lightly brown the chicken pieces, a few at a time. Season them as they brown. Spoon off any excess fat and return all the pieces to the casserole. Add the vermouth, increase the heat and cook until the liquid has almost evaporated.
4. Add the tomatoes, sugar, oregano, rosemary, bay leaf and 70 ml (2¼ fl oz) cold water. Bring to the boil, then stir in the reserved pancetta mixture. Cover and simmer for 20 minutes, or until the chicken is tender but not falling off the bone.
5. If the liquid is too thin, remove the chicken from the casserole, increase the heat and boil until thickened. Discard the sprigs of herbs and season with salt and pepper. Toss in the extra oregano sprigs and serve.

CHICKEN STEW WITH APPLE POTATO MASH

SERVES 4

INGREDIENTS

- 1 kg (2 lb 4 oz) boneless, skinless chicken thighs, cut into 2 cm (¾ inch) cubes
- 1½ tablespoons finely chopped thyme
- 1 tablespoon oil
- 90 g (3¼ oz) butter
- 3 French shallots, thinly sliced
- 375 ml (13 fl oz/1½ cups) apple cider
- 1 kg (2 lb 4 oz) all-purpose potatoes, cubed
- 2 large green apples, peeled, cored and sliced into eighths
- 170 ml (5½ fl oz/⅔ cup) cream

METHOD

1. Season the chicken with 2 teaspoons of the thyme and salt and black pepper. Heat the oil and 20 g (¾ oz) of the butter in a large saucepan over medium–high heat. Cook the chicken in two batches for 2–3 minutes, or until evenly browned. Remove from the pan.
2. Add the shallots and the remaining thyme to the pan and sauté for 2 minutes. Pour in the cider, then bring to the boil, stirring well. Return the chicken to the pan and cover. Reduce the heat to medium–low and cook for 35–40 minutes, or until the chicken is tender and the sauce has reduced (check occasionally to see if any water needs to be added).
3. Cook the potato and apple in a saucepan of boiling water for 15–20 minutes, or until tender. Drain and return to the pan over low heat for 1 minute to evaporate any water. Remove from the heat and mash. Stir in 2 tablespoons of the cream and the remaining butter with a wooden spoon, then season with salt and pepper.
4. Gently stir the remaining cream into the chicken stew and cook for 2–4 minutes, or until the sauce has thickened. Serve with the potato and apple mash.

CREAMY CHICKEN WITH TARRAGON AND MUSTARD

SERVES 4

INGREDIENTS

1.5 kg (3 lb 5 oz) chicken, jointed into 8 pieces (page 85)
2 tablespoons wholegrain mustard
1 teaspoon chopped tarragon, plus extra to garnish
45 g (1½ oz) butter
2 teaspoons olive oil
85 g (3 oz) bacon slices or mild pancetta, chopped
3 French shallots, finely chopped
2 garlic cloves, finely chopped
1 tablespoon plain (all-purpose) flour
185 ml (6 fl oz/¾ cup) dry white wine
300 ml (10½ fl oz) chicken stock (page 11)
125 ml (4 fl oz/½ cup) cream

METHOD

1 Put the chicken pieces in a bowl. Mix half the mustard with the tarragon and rub over the chicken. Cover and refrigerate overnight.

2 Preheat the oven to 180°C (350°F/Gas 4). Melt the butter and oil in a frying pan over medium–high heat and brown the chicken in batches until the skin is golden. Transfer to a flameproof casserole dish.

3 Add the bacon, shallots and garlic to the pan and cook until the bacon starts to brown. Stir in the flour and cook for 1 minute. Add the wine, stock and remaining mustard and cook for 5 minutes, until the sauce is smooth. Pour over the chicken, then cover, transfer to the oven and bake for 1 hour. Remove the chicken from the dish. Put the dish on the stovetop and stir the cream into the sauce, and reduce over high heat until thickened.

4 Return the chicken to the sauce and stir to coat. Serve on a platter with the sauce poured over the chicken. Garnish with extra tarragon. Serve with mashed potato and green vegetables.

BRAISED CHICKEN WITH WINE AND LEEKS

SERVES 4

INGREDIENTS

1.2 kg (2 lb 10 oz) chicken pieces
2 tablespoons oil
1 leek, white part only, thinly sliced
5 spring onions (scallions), thinly sliced
1 tablespoon marjoram
125 ml (4 fl oz/½ cup) white wine
400 ml (14 fl oz) chicken stock (page 11)
100 ml (3½ fl oz) cream

METHOD

1 Score the chicken drumsticks (if using). Heat 1 tablespoon of the oil in a frying pan and cook the chicken in batches for 3–4 minutes, or until browned.

2 Heat the remaining oil in a large flameproof casserole dish and cook the leek, spring onion and marjoram for 4 minutes, or until soft. Add the chicken and wine, and cook for 2 minutes. Add the stock, cover and bring to the boil. Reduce the heat and simmer for 30 minutes. Stir in the cream and simmer, uncovered, for 15 minutes, or until the chicken is tender. Season with salt and pepper. Serve with rice.

CHICKEN GUMBO

This cross between a soup and a stew is a speciality of Cajun cuisine. Traditionally, gumbo is served in deep bowls, each containing a few tablespoons of cooked rice in the bottom.

SERVES 4–6

INGREDIENTS

- 80 ml (2½ fl oz/⅓ cup) vegetable oil
- 30 g (1 oz/¼ cup) plain (all-purpose) flour
- 600 g (1 lb 5 oz) boneless, skinless chicken thighs
- 60 g (2¼ oz) unsalted butter
- 100 g (3½ oz) smoked ham, diced
- 150 g (5½ oz) chorizo sausage, thinly sliced
- 2 onions, chopped
- 2 garlic cloves, finely chopped
- 2 celery stalks, thinly sliced
- 1 red capsicum (pepper), finely chopped
- 400 g (14 oz) tin chopped tomatoes
- 500 ml (17 fl oz/2 cups) chicken stock (page 11)
- 1 bay leaf
- 2 teaspoons thyme
- Tabasco sauce, to taste
- 350 g (12 oz) okra, cut into 1 cm (½ inch) slices

METHOD

1. Heat 3 tablespoons of the oil in a small, heavy-based saucepan, add the flour and stir to make a smooth paste. Stir over low heat for 1 hour, or until the roux turns very dark brown, but is not burnt. This requires a great deal of patience and stirring but provides the gumbo with its dark look and rich flavour — when it is done, the roux should be the colour of dark chocolate. Remove from the heat.
2. Pat dry the chicken with paper towels, cut into quarters and lightly season with salt and pepper. Heat the remaining oil and half the butter in a heavy-based frying pan over medium heat. Cook the chicken for about 5 minutes, or until golden brown. Remove the chicken with a slotted spoon. Add the ham and chorizo and cook for another 4–5 minutes, or until lightly golden. Remove, leaving as much rendered fat in the pan as possible.
3. Add the remaining butter to the same pan and cook the onion, garlic, celery and capsicum over medium heat for 5–6 minutes, or until the vegetables have softened but not browned.
4. Transfer the vegetables to a heavy-based, flameproof casserole dish and place on the stovetop over medium heat. Add the tomato and the roux to the vegetables and stir well. Gradually stir the stock into the dish. Add the herbs and season with the Tabasco. Bring to the boil, stirring constantly.
5. Reduce the heat, add the chicken, ham and chorizo to the casserole dish and simmer, uncovered, for 1 hour. Add the okra and cook for another hour. Skim the surface as the gumbo cooks because a lot of oil will come out of the chorizo. The gumbo should thicken considerably in the last 20 minutes as the okra softens. Remove the bay leaf and serve with rice.

RED CURRY DUCK WITH LYCHEES

SERVES 4

INGREDIENTS

- 60 ml (2 fl oz/¼ cup) coconut cream
- 2 tablespoons red curry paste (page 438)
- ½ roasted duck, boned and chopped
- 400 ml (14 fl oz) tin coconut milk
- 2 tablespoons fish sauce
- 1 tablespoon grated palm sugar (jaggery) or soft brown sugar
- 225 g (8 oz) tin lychees, drained
- 115 g (4 oz) cherry tomatoes
- 7 kaffir lime leaves, torn in half
- 1 handful Thai sweet basil leaves
- 1 long red chilli, seeded and thinly sliced

METHOD

1 Put the coconut cream in a wok or saucepan and simmer over medium heat for 5 minutes, or until the cream separates and a layer of oil forms on the surface. Add the curry paste, stir well to combine and cook until fragrant.

2 Add the duck and stir for 5 minutes. Add the coconut milk, fish sauce and sugar and simmer over medium heat for another 5 minutes.

3 Add the lychees and tomatoes and cook for 1–2 minutes. Add the lime leaves. Taste, then adjust the seasoning if necessary. Spoon into a serving bowl and sprinkle with the basil leaves and sliced chilli. Serve with rice.

THAI GREEN CHICKEN CURRY

SERVES 4

INGREDIENTS

- 60 ml (2 fl oz/¼ cup) coconut cream
- 2 tablespoons green curry paste (page 438)
- 350 g (12 oz) boneless, skinless chicken thighs, sliced
- 400 ml (14 fl oz) tin coconut milk
- 2½ tablespoons fish sauce
- 1 tablespoon grated palm sugar (jaggery)
- 350 g (12 oz) mixed Thai eggplants (aubergines), quartered, and pea eggplants
- 50 g (1¾ oz) galangal, julienned
- 7 kaffir lime leaves, torn in half
- 1 handful Thai sweet basil leaves
- 1 long red chilli, seeded and thinly sliced

METHOD

1 Put the coconut cream in a wok or saucepan and simmer over medium heat for 5 minutes, or until a layer of oil forms on the surface. Add the curry paste, stir to combine and cook until fragrant.

2 Add the chicken and stir for a few minutes. Add nearly all of the coconut milk, the fish sauce and sugar and simmer for 5 minutes.

3 Add the eggplants and cook, stirring, for about 5 minutes, or until cooked. Add the galangal and lime leaves. Taste, then adjust the seasoning if necessary. Spoon into a serving bowl and sprinkle with the last bit of coconut milk, as well as the basil and chilli. Serve with rice.

GALANGAL

This spicy root, similar to ginger in appearance and preparation, is used in Southeast Asian cooking, particularly in Thailand, Indonesia and Malaysia. Galangal has a tougher, woodier texture than ginger and needs to be chopped or sliced very thinly before use. Use in soups, curry pastes or in recipes that call for ginger. Buy galangal with pinker stems as these are fresher than the browner ones.

THAI RED CHICKEN CURRY

SERVES 4

INGREDIENTS

60 ml (2 fl oz/¼ cup) coconut cream
2 tablespoons red curry paste (page 438)
5 cm (2 inch) piece ginger, julienned
400 ml (14 fl oz) tin coconut milk
125 ml (4 fl oz/½ cup) chicken stock (page 11)
4 kaffir lime leaves
600 g (1 lb 5 oz) boneless, skinless chicken breasts, cut into thin strips
125 g (4½ oz) green beans, halved
2 tablespoons fish sauce
1 tablespoon grated palm sugar (jaggery)
1 tablespoon lime juice
sliced chilli and coriander (cilantro), to garnish

METHOD

1 Put the coconut cream in a wok or saucepan and simmer over medium heat for 5 minutes, or until a layer of oil forms on the surface. Add the curry paste and ginger, stir to combine and cook for 2 minutes, or until fragrant.
2 Add the coconut milk, stock and lime leaves. Bring to the boil, then reduce the heat and simmer for 10 minutes, or until reduced and thickened a little.
3 Add the chicken and green beans. Simmer for 5 minutes, or until the chicken is cooked and the beans are just tender. Stir in the fish sauce, palm sugar and lime juice and garnish with the chilli and coriander. Serve with rice.

BUTTER CHICKEN

SERVES 6

INGREDIENTS

- 2 cm (¾ inch) piece ginger, roughly chopped
- 3 garlic cloves, roughly chopped
- 75 g (2½ oz) blanched almonds
- 170 g (6 oz/⅔ cup) Greek-style yoghurt
- ½ teaspoon chilli powder
- ¼ teaspoon ground cloves
- ¼ teaspoon ground cinnamon
- 1 teaspoon garam masala
- 4 cardamom pods, lightly crushed
- 400 g (14 oz) tin chopped tomatoes
- 1 kg (2 lb 4 oz) boneless, skinless chicken thighs, cut into fairly large pieces
- 60 g (2¼ oz) butter or ghee
- 1 large onion, thinly sliced
- 1 handful coriander (cilantro), finely chopped
- 80 ml (2½ fl oz/⅓ cup) cream

METHOD

1 Put the ginger and garlic in a food processor and blend to form a paste, or finely grate the ginger and crush the garlic and mix together. Grind the almonds in a food processor or finely chop with a knife.

2 Put the paste and almonds in a bowl with the yoghurt, chilli powder, cloves, cinnamon, garam masala, cardamom pods, tomato and 1 teaspoon salt, and blend together with a fork. Add the chicken pieces and stir to coat thoroughly. Cover and marinate for 2 hours, or overnight, in the fridge.

3 Preheat the oven to 180°C (350°F/Gas 4). Heat the butter in a deep, heavy-based frying pan, add the onion and fry until softened and brown. Add the chicken mixture and fry for 2 minutes, then stir in the coriander.

4 Put the mixture into a shallow baking dish, pour in the cream and stir with a fork. Transfer to the oven and cook for 1 hour. If the top is browning too quickly during cooking, cover with a piece of foil. Leave to rest for 10 minutes before serving. The oil will rise to the surface.

5 Just before serving, place the dish under a hot grill (broiler) for about 2 minutes to brown the top. Before serving, tip the dish a little and spoon off any excess oil. Serve with rice and roti or naan bread.

GHEE AND CLARIFIED BUTTER

Butter chicken, or *murgh makhni*, is a Moghul dish. The butter in the name refers to ghee, a richly aromatic clarified butter that has a high burning point and is common in Indian cooking. It can be bought in tins or tubs at large supermarkets or from specialist shops. To make clarified butter, melt unsalted butter in a pan, bring it to a simmer and cook for 30 minutes to evaporate off any water. Skim any scum from the surface, then drain off the clarified butter (leaving the white sediment behind) and leave to cool.

BALTI CHICKEN

SERVES 6

INGREDIENTS

- 80 ml (2½ fl oz/⅓ cup) oil
- 1 large red onion, finely chopped
- 4–5 garlic cloves, finely chopped
- 1 tablespoon grated ginger
- 2 teaspoons ground cumin
- 2 teaspoons ground coriander
- 1 teaspoon ground turmeric
- ½ teaspoon chilli powder
- 400 g (14 oz) tin chopped tomatoes
- 1 kg (2 lb 4 oz) boneless, skinless chicken thighs, trimmed, each thigh cut into 4 or 5 pieces
- 1 green capsicum (pepper), chopped
- 1–2 small green chillies, seeded and finely chopped
- 1 handful coriander (cilantro), chopped
- 2 spring onions (scallions), chopped

METHOD

1. Heat a large wok over high heat, add the oil and swirl to coat the side. Add the onion and stir-fry over medium heat for 5 minutes, or until softened but not browned. Add the garlic and ginger and stir-fry for 3 minutes.
2. Add the spices to the wok, with 1 teaspoon salt and 60 ml (2 fl oz/¼ cup) water. Increase the heat to high and stir-fry for 2 minutes, or until the mixture has thickened. Take care not to burn it.
3. Add the tomatoes and 250 ml (9 fl oz/1 cup) water and cook, stirring often, for a further 10 minutes, or until the mixture is thick and pulpy and the oil comes to the surface.
4. Add the chicken to the wok, reduce the heat and simmer, stirring often, for 15 minutes. Add the capsicum and chilli and simmer for 25 minutes, or until the chicken is tender. Add a little water if the mixture is too thick. Stir in the coriander and garnish with the spring onion. Serve with rice.

CHICKEN TIKKA MASALA

SERVES 6

INGREDIENTS

- 1 tablespoon oil
- 1 onion, finely chopped
- 2 cardamom pods
- 2 garlic cloves, crushed
- 400 g (14 oz) tin diced tomatoes
- ¼ teaspoon ground cinnamon
- 1 tablespoon garam masala
- ½ teaspoon chilli powder
- 1 teaspoon grated palm sugar (jaggery) or soft brown sugar
- 310 ml (10 fl oz/1¼ cups) cream
- 1 tablespoon ground almonds
- 1 quantity chicken tikka (page 107)
- 1 tablespoon chopped coriander (cilantro)

METHOD

1. Heat the oil in a heavy-based saucepan over low heat. Add the onion and cardamom pods and fry until the onion is soft and starting to brown.
2. Add the garlic to the saucepan, cook for 1 minute then add the tomatoes and cook until the paste is thick.
3. Add the cinnamon, garam masala, chilli powder and sugar to the pan and cook for 1 minute. Stir in the cream and almonds, then add the cooked chicken tikka and gently simmer for 5 minutes to heat through. Sprinkle with the coriander and serve with steamed rice.

CHAPTER FOUR

MEAT

••BEEF••

Meat usually takes the starring role in the meal, so we should take great care in the choosing and buying of it. Most chefs will say that the most important aspect of preparing a meal is choosing the best ingredients, so a good butcher is a vital component of any cook's tools. The quality of beef varies according to breed, diet and farming technique. Specialist beef, such as organic or grass-fed beef, produces higher quality meat than mass-produced beef reared on grain. Often beef is hung for 2–3 weeks to allow its flavour to mature and let the meat become more tender. Prime cuts are more expensive and have been aged to improve both flavour and texture, while cuts for stewing are sold younger.

CUTS OF BEEF

The best beef should be dark-red moist meat with creamy white fat (bright red meat usually indicates that it has not been aged sufficiently). A beef carcass is divided into sections from which numerous cuts are made (the names of these cuts vary from country to country). If you are buying beef for a stew, casserole or curry you don't need to buy the most expensive cuts.

FRONT CUTS

Cuts from the front of the animal contain the muscles that do the most work and are therefore the toughest. These are the cuts that need the longest cooking time and slowest methods (pot-roasting, braising or stewing). Front cuts include: neck, chuck, blade and shin.

CENTRE CUTS

Cuts from the top and centre of the animal are the tenderest because they are the least muscled. These can be cooked quickly (roasting, grilling or frying). Cuts include: fore rib, wing rib, sirloin, fillet and rump.

BACK CUTS

The back and underside of the animal fall in between in tenderness and need a reasonably long cooking time, making them also good for stewing, braising or pot-roasting. Cuts include: top rump, topside, silverside, brisket, skirt and shin.

HOW TO... TRIM A FILLET OF BEEF

METHOD

1. Try to buy a piece of beef fillet that is of even thickness along its length so it cooks evenly. Using a small sharp knife, trim off any fat.
2. Trim off any membrane by sliding the blade of your knife underneath while pulling the membrane taut. Neaten any straggly pieces.
3. If your fillet is uneven along its length, fold the thinner end back under the thicker part to make it an even thickness. If you are roasting your beef, tie it all the way along with kitchen string.

HOW TO... COAT MEAT WITH FLOUR

When you're cooking stews and casseroles the recipe will often call for the meat to be coated with seasoned flour before browning, then adding the liquid. The flour will then work as a thickener for the stew. An easy and clean way to do this is to put the seasoned flour in a small plastic bag, add the meat and shake. Then pull out the meat, shaking off the excess flour.

HOW TO... CHOOSE BEEF FOR ROASTING

Choose joints from the back, ribs, fillet or sirloin for roasting. Meat should be well marbled with fat and slightly larger than you need, as it will shrink slightly when cooked. A covering of fat will baste the meat well as it roasts. Beef cooked on the bone cooks faster than a rolled joint and the bones also add extra flavour and can then be used for stock (page 11). If you ask your butcher to chine (loosen the backbone from the ribs) your joint, it will be easier to carve it when cooked. Season and sear the joint before cooking.

HOW TO... STORE BEEF

Wipe any blood off the beef, put it on a plate, cover with plastic wrap and store in the fridge. Put larger cuts on a rack over a plate so that the meat doesn't end up sitting in its own juices. Keep raw meat away from cooked to stop cross-contamination. To ensure the beef cooks evenly, remove it from the fridge half an hour before cooking and let it come to room temperature. Oiling small cuts of meat before storing them will help prevent the meat oxidising (turning dark). Freeze beef either vacuum-packed or well wrapped in freezer wrap. It will keep frozen for up to 1 year.

CARPACCIO

SERVES 6

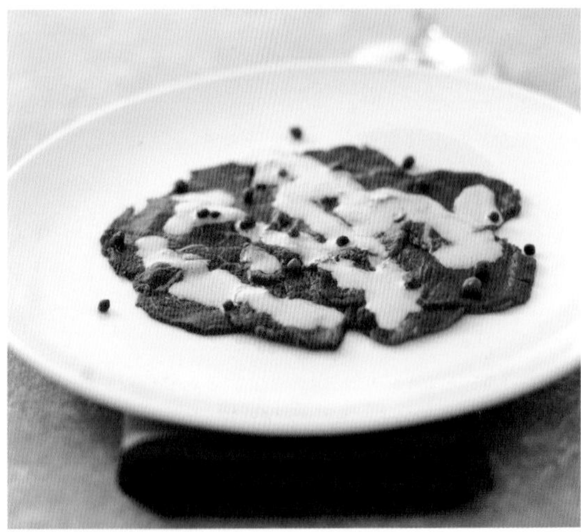

INGREDIENTS

700 g (1 lb 9 oz) beef eye fillet
1 egg yolk
3 tablespoons dijon mustard
60 ml (2 fl oz/¼ cup) lemon juice
2 drops Tabasco sauce
80 ml (2½ fl oz/⅓ cup) olive oil
1 tablespoon cream
2–3 tablespoons capers, rinsed

METHOD

1 Wrap the beef in plastic and freeze for about 30 minutes, until it's firm but not solid (this makes it easy to slice thinly).
2 Slice the beef paper-thin (don't worry if you have a few holes or tears) and arrange over six plates.
3 Whisk together the egg yolk, mustard, lemon juice and Tabasco. Add the olive oil in a thin stream, whisking or processing continuously until the mayonnaise thickens. When you've added all the oil, whisk in the cream. Season and drizzle over the beef. Sprinkle with capers.

THAI BEEF SALAD

SERVES 6

INGREDIENTS

500 g (1 lb 2 oz) lean beef fillet
2 tablespoons peanut oil
2 garlic cloves, crushed
1 tablespoon grated palm sugar (jaggery) or soft brown sugar
3 tablespoons finely chopped coriander (cilantro) roots and stems
80 ml (2½ fl oz/⅓ cup) lime juice
2 tablespoons fish sauce
¼ teaspoon ground white pepper
2 small red chillies, seeded and thinly sliced
2 red Asian shallots, thinly sliced
2 cucumbers, sliced into thin ribbons
2 large handfuls mint
90 g (3¼ oz/1 cup) bean sprouts, trimmed
40 g (1½ oz/¼ cup) chopped roasted peanuts

METHOD

1 Thinly slice the beef across the grain. Heat a wok over high heat, then add 1 tablespoon of the oil and swirl to coat. Add half the beef and cook for 1–2 minutes until medium-rare, then remove from the wok and cook the other batch of beef using the other tablespoon of oil. Put all the beef in a non-metallic bowl.
2 Mix together the garlic, palm sugar, coriander, lime juice, fish sauce, pepper and ¼ teaspoon salt, stirring until all the sugar has dissolved. Add the chilli and shallots and mix well.
3 Pour the sauce over the hot beef, mix together well, then leave to cool to room temperature.
4 Toss together the cucumber and mint, pile up on a serving platter, then top with the beef, bean sprouts and peanuts.

HAMBURGERS

SERVES 4

INGREDIENTS

- 700 g (1 lb 9 oz) minced (ground) beef
- 1 garlic clove, crushed
- 1 small onion, finely chopped
- 2 tablespoons finely chopped parsley
- 1 tablespoon tomato sauce (ketchup)
- ¼ teaspoon worcestershire sauce
- 1 tablespoon oil
- 4 bread buns, halved
- lettuce leaves
- 1 tomato, sliced
- pickles

METHOD

1. Preheat a barbecue hotplate. Mix the beef with the garlic, onion, parsley, tomato sauce and worcestershire sauce. Season and mix well, then leave to marinate.
2. Form the beef into four large patties and flatten them out to the size of the buns.
3. Heat the oil on the hotplate (or use a frying pan) and fry the burgers for 3–5 minutes on each side, or until cooked to your liking.
4. Lay a burger on each bun base, add some lettuce, tomato and pickles, and put the top on the bun.

STEAK SANDWICH

SERVES 2

INGREDIENTS

- 2 fillet steaks
- 30 g (1 oz) butter
- 1 small onion, cut into rings
- 4 thick slices bread
- 2 lettuce leaves
- 1 small tomato, sliced
- barbecue sauce

METHOD

1. Trim any fat from the steaks. Put the steaks between two sheets of plastic wrap and flatten with a meat mallet or rolling pin until 5 mm (¼ inch) thick. Nick the edges of the steak to prevent the meat curling as it cooks.
2. Melt the butter in a frying pan and fry the onion rings until soft and lightly golden.
3. Push the onion to the side of the pan. Add the steaks and cook for 1–2 minutes on each side. Keep warm.
4. Toast the bread and put some lettuce and tomato on two of the slices. Top with the steak, onions and barbecue sauce and remaining toasted bread. Serve immediately.

STEAK TARTARE

Steak tartare is a dish of finely chopped raw beef steak (not minced beef), mixed with chopped onion, herbs and often capers. This seasoned raw meat mixture is shaped into a mound on the plate, and a small hollow made in the top, into which a raw egg is broken. In restaurants, the chopping of the meat and preparation of the dish usually takes place at the table in front of the diner. Tartare is traditionally served with toast or potato chips and is particularly popular in France, Belgium and Holland.

VARIETIES OF BEEF STEAKS

SIRLOIN
A boneless steak from the sirloin, which often has the best flavour, and can be cut short or long. In America, this is not always boneless, depending on which part of the sirloin it is cut from. In Australia, a boneless sirloin with the fat removed is called a New York steak, while in America a New York steak is a cut from the loin when the fillet has been removed.

PORTERHOUSE
A steak from the sirloin and the tenderloin separated by a bone. Often cut very thick and served for two people.

T-BONE
Cut across the sirloin to include a piece of fillet.

MINUTE
A thin steak (sometimes called a frying steak) that has been tenderised so it cooks quickly (in a minute!).

CLUB STEAK (USA)
From the thin end of the loin, which includes no fillet.

RUMP
A large steak from the top of the rump.

CHATEAUBRIAND
A thick cut from the centre of the fillet. Serves two.

TOURNEDOS
The tender 'eye' or centre of the fillet cut into rounds.

MIGNON
A small round steak cut from the thin end of the fillet, sometimes called filet mignon.

ENTRECOTE
Cut from between the ribs, this is boneless and thin with a marbling of fat. It is also known as rib steak and in America is served as Delmonico or Spencer steak, which is the eye of the rib.

sirloin

T-bone

rump

filet mignon

HOW TO... TIME A PERFECT STEAK

These cooking times apply to a steak that is about 2.5 cm (1 inch) thick (the weight is irrelevant to the cooking time), has been brought to room temperature before cooking and is pan-fried in a heavy-based pan. If you want to grill your steaks, they will take about a minute longer.

For a blue steak (top), cook for 1–2 minutes per side: the steak will feel fleshy and soft when pressed. For rare, cook for 2–3 minutes per side: the steak will spring back a little when pressed. For medium, cook for 3–4 minutes per side: the steak will spring back when pressed. For well-done (bottom), cook for 4–5 minutes per side: the steak will feel very firm.

QUICK PEPPER STEAK

SERVES 4

INGREDIENTS

- 4 x 200 g (7 oz) fillet steaks
- 2 tablespoons oil
- 6 tablespoons black peppercorns, crushed
- 40 g (1½ oz) butter
- 60 ml (2 fl oz/¼ cup) Cognac or brandy
- 60 ml (2 fl oz/¼ cup) white wine
- 125 ml (4 fl oz/½ cup) cream

METHOD

1. Rub the steaks on both sides with the oil and press the crushed peppercorns into the meat.
2. Melt the butter in a large frying pan and cook the steaks for 2–4 minutes on each side, or until cooked to your liking (see left).
3. Add the Cognac or brandy and flambé by lighting the pan with your gas flame or a match (stand well back when you do this and keep a pan lid handy for emergencies). Lift the steaks out onto a warm plate. Add the wine to the pan and boil, stirring, for 1 minute to deglaze the pan. Add the cream and stir for a couple of minutes. Season with salt and pepper and pour over the steaks.

STEAK WITH GREEN PEPPERCORN SAUCE

SERVES 4

INGREDIENTS

- 4 x 200 g (7 oz) fillet steaks
- 30 g (1 oz) butter
- 2 teaspoons oil
- 250 ml (9 fl oz/1 cup) beef stock (page 11)
- 185 ml (6 fl oz/¾ cup) cream
- 2 teaspoons cornflour (cornstarch)
- 2 tablespoons green peppercorns in brine, rinsed
- 2 tablespoons brandy

METHOD

1. Put the steaks between two sheets of plastic wrap and flatten with a meat mallet or rolling pin until 1.5 cm (⅝ inch) thick. Nick the edges of the steak to prevent the meat curling as it cooks.
2. Heat the butter and oil in a large frying pan over high heat. Fry the steaks for 2–4 minutes on each side, or until cooked to your liking (see left). Transfer to a serving plate and cover with foil.
3. Add the stock to the pan juices and stir over low heat until boiling. Mix the cream and cornflour, add to the pan and stir until smooth and thick. Add the peppercorns and brandy and boil for 1 more minute before spooning over the steaks.

PEPPERCORNS

True pepper (vine pepper) is black, green or white — all three come from the same plant but are picked at various stages of ripeness. Red pepper, sichuan and cayenne are not 'true' peppers but were so called to share the kudos of this once-expensive commodity. Green peppers are picked unripe and usually preserved by artificial drying or bottling in brine, vinegar or water. Black pepper is the most pungent and flavourful variety. It's made from berries that are red but not completely ripe: when dried, they shrivel and take on a dark colour. White pepper, less aromatic but hotter than black, is made from ripe red berries that are soaked in salt water until soft, then the white seeds removed and dried.

FILLET OF BEEF WITH BEARNAISE SAUCE

SERVES 6

INGREDIENTS

1 kg (2 lb 4 oz) piece of beef fillet
1 tablespoon oil
2 garlic cloves, crushed
1 tablespoon cracked black peppercorns
2 teaspoons crushed coriander seeds

BEARNAISE SAUCE

3 spring onions (scallions), chopped
125 ml (4 fl oz/½ cup) dry white wine
2 tablespoons tarragon vinegar
1 tablespoon chopped tarragon
125 g (4½ oz) butter
4 egg yolks
1 tablespoon lemon juice

METHOD

1 Preheat the oven to 210°C (415°F/Gas 6–7). Trim the fillet and tie at regular intervals with kitchen string. Mix together the oil and garlic, brush over the fillet, then roll the fillet in the combined peppercorns and coriander seeds.
2 Put the meat on a rack in a roasting tin. Roast for 10 minutes, then reduce the oven to 180°C (350°F/Gas 4) and cook for 15–20 minutes for rare, or longer if you prefer. Cover and leave for 10–15 minutes.
3 To make the béarnaise sauce, put the spring onion, wine, vinegar and tarragon in a saucepan. Boil the mixture until only about 2 tablespoons remains in the pan. Strain the liquid.
4 Melt the butter in a small saucepan and let it settle, without stirring. Place the wine mixture in a food processor with the egg yolks and process for 30 seconds. With the motor running, add the clarified butter in a thin stream, leaving the milky white sediment in the pan. Process until thickened. Add the lemon juice and season. Carve the beef and serve with the sauce.

BEEF STROGANOFF

SERVES 6

INGREDIENTS

1 kg (2 lb 4 oz) piece rump steak
40 g (1½ oz/⅓ cup) plain (all-purpose) flour
¼ teaspoon black pepper
60 ml (2 fl oz/¼ cup) oil
1 large onion, chopped
500 g (1 lb 2 oz) baby mushrooms
1 tablespoon sweet paprika
1 tablespoon tomato paste (concentrated purée)
2 teaspoons French mustard
125 ml (4 fl oz/½ cup) dry white wine
60 ml (2 fl oz/¼ cup) chicken stock (page 11)
185 g (6½ oz/¾ cup) sour cream
1 tablespoon finely chopped parsley

METHOD

1 Trim the meat of excess fat and sinew, and slice across the grain evenly into thin strips. Mix the flour and pepper in a plastic bag, add the meat and shake to coat. Shake off the excess seasoned flour.
2 Heat 2 tablespoons of the oil in a large heavy-based frying pan. Brown the meat quickly in small batches over medium–high heat. Drain on paper towels.
3 Heat the remaining oil in the pan. Add the onion and cook over medium heat for 3 minutes, or until soft. Add the mushrooms and cook, stirring, for 5 minutes.
4 Add the paprika, tomato paste, mustard, wine, stock and meat to the pan, and bring to the boil. Reduce the heat and simmer for 5 minutes, stirring occasionally. Add the sour cream and stir until just heated through — do not boil or the sour cream may split and look curdled. Sprinkle with the parsley just before serving. Serve with rice.

BEEF WELLINGTON

SERVES 6–8

INGREDIENTS

1.2 kg (2 lb 11 oz) piece of beef fillet or rib-eye
1 tablespoon oil
125 g (4½ oz) pâté
60 g (2¼ oz) button mushrooms, sliced
375 g (13 oz) block frozen puff pastry, thawed
1 egg, lightly beaten
1 sheet ready-rolled frozen puff pastry, thawed

METHOD

1 Preheat the oven to 210°C (415°F/Gas 6–7). Trim the meat, fold the thinner part of the tail end underneath and tie securely at regular intervals with kitchen string.
2 Rub the meat with black pepper. Heat the oil over high heat in a large frying pan and brown the meat well all over. Remove from the heat and leave to cool. Remove the string.
3 Spread the pâté over the top and sides of the beef. Press the mushrooms onto the pâté. Roll out the block pastry on a lightly floured surface to make a rectangle large enough to completely wrap the beef.
4 Place the beef on the pastry, brush the edges with egg and fold up and over to wrap up the meat. Brush the pastry with egg to seal and fold in the ends to make a neat parcel. Put the parcel on a greased baking tray with the pastry seam underneath. Cut leaf shapes from the sheet of puff pastry and decorate the parcel. Cut a few slits in the top, brush the top and sides with egg, and bake for 45 minutes for rare beef, 1 hour for medium or 1½ hours for well done (cover the pastry loosely with foil if it is browning too much). Leave in a warm place for 10 minutes before carving to serve.

ROAST BEEF WITH YORKSHIRE PUDDING

SERVES 6

INGREDIENTS

2 kg (4 lb 8 oz) piece roasting beef (scotch fillet, rump or sirloin)
2 garlic cloves, crushed

YORKSHIRE PUDDINGS

90 g (3¼ oz/¾ cup) plain (all-purpose) flour
125 ml (4 fl oz/½ cup) milk
2 eggs

RED WINE GRAVY

2 tablespoons plain (all-purpose) flour
80 ml (2½ fl oz/⅓ cup) red wine
600 ml (21 fl oz) beef stock (page 11)

METHOD

1 Preheat the oven to 240°C (475°F/Gas 8). Rub the beef with the crushed garlic and some black pepper and drizzle with oil. Bake on a rack in a roasting tin for 20 minutes.

2 To make the Yorkshire puddings, sift the flour and ½ teaspoon salt into a large bowl, make a well in the centre and whisk in the milk. Whisk the eggs until fluffy, then add to the batter and mix well. Add 125 ml (4 fl oz/½ cup) water and whisk until large bubbles form on the surface. Cover the bowl with plastic wrap and refrigerate for 1 hour.

3 Reduce the oven to 180°C (350°F/Gas 4) and roast the meat for another 1 hour for rare, or longer for well done. Lift out onto a carving tray, cover with foil and leave in a warm place while making the puddings.

4 Increase the oven to 220°C (425°F/Gas 7). Spoon ½ teaspoon of the pan juices into each of twelve 80 ml (2½ fl oz/⅓ cup) patty pan or muffin holes. (Keep the rest of the pan juices for making gravy.) Heat the muffin tin in the oven until the fat is almost smoking. Whisk the batter again until bubbles form on the surface. Fill each muffin hole about three-quarters full. Bake for 20 minutes, or until puffed and lightly golden.

5 Meanwhile, make the gravy. Heat the pan juices in the roasting tin on the stovetop over low heat (you should have about 2 tablespoons of pan juices). Add the flour and stir well, scraping up all the bits from the bottom of the tin. Cook over medium heat for 1–2 minutes, stirring constantly, until the flour is well browned. Remove from the heat and gradually stir in the wine and stock. Return to the heat, stirring constantly, until the gravy boils and thickens. Simmer for 3 minutes, then season with salt and black pepper. Serve the beef with the hot Yorkshire puddings and the red wine gravy.

SILVERSIDE WITH PARSLEY SAUCE

SERVES 6

INGREDIENTS

1.5 kg (3 lb 5 oz) corned silverside
1 teaspoon black peppercorns
5 cloves
2 bay leaves, torn
2 tablespoons soft brown sugar

PARSLEY SAUCE
50 g (1¾ oz) butter
1½ tablespoons plain (all-purpose) flour
400 ml (14 fl oz) milk
125 ml (4 fl oz/½ cup) beef stock (page 11)
2 tablespoons chopped parsley

METHOD

1 Soak the beef in cold water for 45 minutes, changing the water 3–4 times (this helps eliminate some of the saltiness).
2 Put the beef in a large heavy-based saucepan with the peppercorns, cloves, bay leaves, sugar and enough cold water to just cover it. Bring to the boil, then reduce the heat to very low and simmer for 1½–1¾ hours. Turn the meat every half hour and top up the water when necessary. Don't let the water boil again or the meat will be tough. Lift out the meat and set aside for 15 minutes.
3 To make the parsley sauce, melt the butter in a saucepan over low heat, stir in the flour and cook, stirring, for 1 minute. Slowly pour in the milk and stock, whisking continuously until smooth. Cook, whisking constantly, until the sauce boils and thickens. Reduce the heat and simmer for 2 minutes before stirring in the parsley and a little salt and pepper. Serve over the sliced silverside.

MEAT LOAF

SERVES 6

INGREDIENTS

125 g (4½ oz) bacon, chopped
500 g (1 lb 2 oz) minced (ground) beef
500 g (1 lb 2 oz) minced (ground) pork
1 onion, grated
2 garlic cloves, crushed
160 g (5½ oz/2 cups) fresh breadcrumbs
2 teaspoons thyme leaves
1 egg, lightly beaten
1 tablespoon red wine vinegar
2 teaspoons soft brown sugar

METHOD

1 Preheat the oven to 180°C (350°F/Gas 4). Lightly grease a loaf (bar) tin and line with baking paper, letting it hang over the long sides.
2 Cook the bacon until crispy. Put the bacon, beef, pork, onion, garlic, breadcrumbs, thyme, egg, vinegar and sugar in a bowl. Season with salt and pepper and mix with your hands. Don't overmix or the meat loaf will be tough.
3 Spoon into the tin and press down gently. Smooth the top and bake for 1 hour 10 minutes, or until browned and cooked through, then drain off the cooking juices. Leave to stand for a few minutes before slicing. Serve with tomato relish.

BOEUF BOURGUIGNON

This classic braise from the Burgundy region of France (famous for its red wine) tastes even better if you can make it a day in advance and leave it in the fridge overnight for the flavours to blend.

SERVES 6

INGREDIENTS

- 1.5 kg (3 lb 5 oz) beef blade or chuck steak
- 750 ml (26 fl oz/3 cups) red wine (preferably burgundy)
- 3 garlic cloves, crushed
- 1 bouquet garni
- 70 g (2½ oz) butter
- 1 onion, chopped
- 1 carrot, chopped
- 2 tablespoons plain (all-purpose) flour
- 200 g (7 oz) bacon, cut into short strips
- 300 g (10½ oz) French shallots, peeled
- 200 g (7 oz) small button mushrooms

METHOD

1. Cut the meat into 4 cm (1½ inch) cubes and trim off any fat. Put the meat, wine, garlic and bouquet garni in a bowl, cover with plastic wrap and refrigerate for at least 3 hours, or overnight.
2. Preheat the oven to 160°C (315°F/Gas 2–3). Drain the meat, keeping the marinade and bouquet garni, and pat dry. Heat 30 g (1 oz) of the butter in a large flameproof casserole dish. Add the onion, carrot and bouquet garni and cook over low heat, stirring occasionally, for 10 minutes. Remove from the heat.
3. Heat another 20 g (¾ oz) of the butter in a large frying pan over high heat. Brown the meat in batches for about 5 minutes, then add to the casserole dish. Pour the marinade into the frying pan and boil, stirring, for 30 seconds to deglaze the pan. Remove from the heat.
4. Return the casserole dish to high heat and sprinkle the meat and vegetables with the flour. Cook, stirring constantly, until the meat is well coated. Pour in the marinade and stir well. Bring to the boil, stirring constantly, then cover and cook in the oven for 2 hours.
5. Heat the remaining butter in a clean frying pan and cook the bacon and shallots, stirring, for 8–10 minutes, or until the shallots are softened but not browned. Add the mushrooms and cook for 2–3 minutes until browned. Add the bacon, shallots and mushrooms to the casserole.
6. Cover the casserole dish and return to the oven for 30 minutes, or until the meat is tender. Season before serving.

BEEF PROVENCALE

SERVES 6

INGREDIENTS

- 1.5 kg (3 lb 5 oz) chuck steak, cut into cubes
- 2 tablespoons olive oil
- 1 small onion, sliced
- 375 ml (13 fl oz/1½ cups) red wine
- 2 tablespoons chopped parsley
- 1 tablespoon chopped rosemary
- 1 tablespoon chopped thyme
- 2 bay leaves
- 250 g (9 oz) speck or bacon, rind removed, cut into small pieces
- 400 g (14 oz) tin chopped tomatoes
- 250 ml (9 fl oz/1 cup) beef stock (page 11)
- 500 g (1 lb 2 oz) baby carrots
- 45 g (1½ oz/⅓ cup) pitted niçoise olives

METHOD

1. Mix the beef with 1 tablespoon of the oil, the onion, 250 ml (9 fl oz/1 cup) of the wine and half the herbs in a bowl. Cover with plastic wrap and leave to marinate in the fridge overnight. Drain the beef and onion, keeping the marinade. Heat the remaining oil in a large frying pan. Add the beef and onion and brown in batches. Remove from the pan.
2. Add the speck and cook for 3–5 minutes, or until crisp. Return the beef to the pan with the remaining wine and marinade and cook, scraping the bits from the bottom of the pan for 2 minutes, or until the wine has slightly reduced. Add the tomatoes and stock and bring to the boil. Reduce the heat and add the remaining herbs. Season, cover and simmer for 1½ hours.
3. Add the carrots and olives to the pan and cook, uncovered, for another 30 minutes, or until the meat and carrots are tender. Check the seasoning before serving.

MEATBALLS

MAKES 30

INGREDIENTS

- 4 slices white bread, crusts removed
- 150 g (5½ oz) minced (ground) pork
- 150 g (5½ oz) minced (ground) beef or veal
- 1 tablespoon chopped parsley
- 1 tablespoon chopped mint
- 1 onion, grated
- ½ teaspoon ground cumin
- 1 egg
- 25 g (1 oz/¼ cup) grated parmesan cheese
- 60 g (2¼ oz/½ cup) plain (all-purpose) flour
- olive oil, for pan-frying

METHOD

1. Cover the bread with water in a bowl, then squeeze out as much water as possible. Place in a large bowl with the pork and beef, parsley, mint, onion, cumin, egg and cheese. Season, then knead the mixture by hand for 2–3 minutes until smooth. Cover and refrigerate for 30 minutes.
2. Put the flour in a shallow dish. With wet hands, roll level tablespoons of the mixture into balls, then toss in the flour. Heat the oil over medium heat. Pan-fry in batches for 3–5 minutes, or until the meatballs are browned and cooked through. Drain on paper towels. Serve hot.

MUSAMAN BEEF CURRY

SERVES 4

INGREDIENTS

- 2 tablespoons vegetable oil
- 750 g (1 lb 10 oz) chuck steak, cut into cubes
- 500 ml (17 fl oz/2 cups) coconut milk
- 4 cardamom pods, bruised
- 500 ml (17 fl oz/2 cups) coconut cream
- 2 tablespoons musaman curry paste (page 439)
- 2 tablespoons fish sauce
- 2 tablespoons tamarind purée
- 8 small onions (see Notes)
- 8 small potatoes
- 2 tablespoons grated palm sugar (jaggery) or soft brown sugar
- 80 g (2¾ oz/½ cup) unsalted peanuts, roasted and ground

METHOD

1 Heat a non-stick wok over high heat, add the oil and swirl to coat. Add the beef in batches and cook over high heat for 5 minutes, or until browned all over. Reduce the heat, add the coconut milk and cardamom pods, and simmer for 1 hour, or until the beef is tender.

2 Remove the beef from the wok with a slotted spoon. Strain the cooking liquid into a bowl.

3 Heat the coconut cream in the clean wok and stir in the curry paste. Cook for 10 minutes, or until the oil starts to separate from the cream. Add the fish sauce, tamarind, onions, potatoes, beef, palm sugar, peanuts and the reserved cooking liquid. Simmer for 30 minutes, or until the sauce has thickened and the meat is tender. Serve with rice.

NOTES: Use small onions and potatoes that are similar in size to ensure that they cook evenly. It's important to use a non-stick or stainless steel wok for dishes containing tamarind purée — the tamarind reacts with the metal in a regular wok and will badly taint it.

TAMARIND

The tropical tamarind tree is prized for its pods, each containing a sticky, fleshy sweet-sour pulp wrapped around small hard seeds. The pulp is used to flavour Thai and Indian curries and chutneys, or in sauces such as worcestershire. Tamarind is sold as an easy-to-use purée in jars. You can also buy it in blocks or cakes that still contain the seeds. To use, cut off a little, mix with hot water and press through a sieve, then discard the fibrous leftovers and use the tamarind water. Store the purée or blocks in the fridge where they will last up to a year. Tamarind can also be sweetened into syrups and sweetmeats.

TAMARIND BEEF

SERVES 4

INGREDIENTS

- 2 tablespoons vegetable oil
- 1 kg (2 lb 4 oz) chuck steak, cut into cubes
- 2 red onions, sliced
- 3 garlic cloves, finely chopped
- 1 tablespoon julienned ginger
- 2 teaspoons ground coriander
- 2 teaspoons ground cumin
- ½ teaspoon ground fenugreek
- ½ teaspoon chilli powder
- ½ teaspoon ground cloves
- 1 cinnamon stick
- 125 g (4½ oz/½ cup) tamarind purée
- 6 fresh curry leaves
- 250 ml (9 fl oz/1 cup) coconut cream
- 100 g (3½ oz) green beans, halved
- coriander (cilantro) leaves, to garnish

METHOD

1. Heat a non-stick wok over high heat, add the oil and swirl to coat. Add the beef in batches and cook over high heat for 2–3 minutes, or until browned. Remove from the wok.
2. Add the onion and cook over medium heat for 2–3 minutes until softened, then add the garlic and ginger and cook for 2 minutes. Add the coriander, cumin, fenugreek, chilli powder, cloves and cinnamon and cook for 2 minutes.
3. Return the meat to the wok and stir to coat with the spices. Add the tamarind purée, curry leaves and 1 litre (35 fl oz/4 cups) water. Bring to the boil, then reduce the heat to very low and simmer, covered, for 1½ hours, or until the beef is tender. Stir occasionally to prevent the meat from sticking. Pour in the coconut cream and cook, uncovered, for 5–10 minutes, then add the beans and cook for 5 minutes, or until tender but still crisp. Garnish with coriander before serving.

BEEF AND BLACK BEAN SAUCE

SERVES 4–6

INGREDIENTS

- 2 tablespoons rinsed black beans, chopped
- 1 tablespoon dark soy sauce
- 1 tablespoon Chinese rice wine
- 1 garlic clove, finely chopped
- 1 teaspoon sugar
- 60 ml (2 fl oz/¼ cup) peanut oil
- 1 onion, cut into wedges
- 500 g (1 lb 2 oz) lean beef fillet, thinly sliced
- ½ teaspoon finely chopped ginger
- 1 teaspoon cornflour (cornstarch)
- 1 teaspoon sesame oil

METHOD

1. Put the beans, soy sauce, rice wine and 60 ml (2 fl oz/¼ cup) water in a small bowl and mix well. Crush the garlic and sugar to a paste using a mortar and pestle.
2. Heat a wok over high heat, add 1 teaspoon of the peanut oil and swirl to coat. Add the onion and stir-fry for 1–2 minutes, then spoon out into a bowl. Add 1 tablespoon of the peanut oil to the wok and swirl to coat, then add half the beef and stir-fry for 5–6 minutes until browned. Remove to the bowl with the onion and cook the rest of the beef.
3. Add the remaining peanut oil to the wok along with the garlic paste and ginger and stir-fry for 30 seconds, until fragrant. Add the bean mixture, onion and beef. Bring to the boil, then reduce the heat and simmer, covered, for 2 minutes.
4. Combine the cornflour with 1 tablespoon water, pour into the wok and stir until the sauce boils and thickens. Stir in the sesame oil.

BEEF AND ASPARAGUS WITH OYSTER SAUCE

SERVES 4

INGREDIENTS

1 tablespoon light soy sauce
½ teaspoon sesame oil
1 tablespoon Chinese rice wine
500 g (1 lb 2 oz) lean beef fillet, thinly sliced
2½ tablespoons vegetable oil
200 g (7 oz) asparagus spears, cut into thirds
3 garlic cloves, crushed
2 teaspoons julienned ginger
60 ml (2 fl oz/¼ cup) chicken stock (page 11)
2–3 tablespoons oyster sauce

METHOD

1. Mix the soy sauce, sesame oil and 2 teaspoons of the rice wine in a large non-metallic bowl. Add the beef, cover with plastic wrap and marinate in the fridge for at least 15 minutes.
2. Heat a wok over high heat, add 1 tablespoon of the vegetable oil and swirl to coat. Add the asparagus and stir-fry for 1–2 minutes. Remove from the wok.
3. Heat another tablespoon of oil in the wok over high heat, then stir-fry the beef in two batches for 1–2 minutes, or until cooked through. Remove from the wok and add to the asparagus.
4. Add the remaining oil to the wok, add the garlic and ginger before the oil becomes too hot and stir-fry for 1 minute, or until fragrant. Pour the stock, oyster sauce and remaining rice wine into the wok, bring to the boil and boil rapidly for 1–2 minutes, or until the sauce is slightly reduced. Return the beef and asparagus to the wok and stir-fry for a further minute, or until heated through and coated in the sauce.

LEMONGRASS

With a subtle lemon flavour and fragrance, lemongrass adds a refreshing taste to many Thai and other Southeast Asian dishes. To use it, strip off the tough outer layers and use whole in soups by lightly bruising the stems (remove before serving); finely chop and use in curry pastes; thinly slice the paler lower part of the stem and add to salads; or use whole as skewers for cooking meat, prawns and chicken. To store, wrap in plastic and keep in the fridge for 1–2 weeks. If lemongrass is unavailable, use grated lemon zest instead.

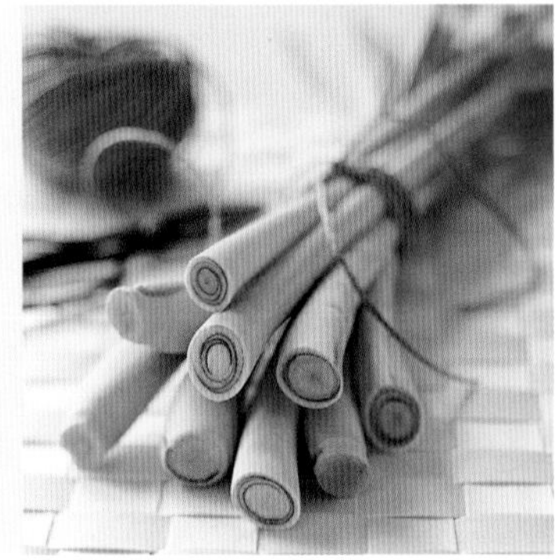

GINGER BEEF STIR-FRY

SERVES 4

INGREDIENTS

1 garlic clove, crushed
1 teaspoon grated ginger
60 ml (2 fl oz/¼ cup) kecap manis
60 ml (2 fl oz/¼ cup) Chinese rice wine
1 teaspoon sugar
pinch of Chinese five-spice
500 g (1 lb 2 oz) lean beef fillet, thinly sliced
½ teaspoon cornflour (cornstarch)
60 ml (2 fl oz/¼ cup) peanut oil
1 red onion, sliced into thin wedges
1½ tablespoons julienned ginger
400 g (14 oz) Chinese broccoli (gai larn), cut into 6 cm (2½ inch) lengths

METHOD

1 Combine the garlic, grated ginger, kecap manis, rice wine, sugar and five-spice in a large non-metallic bowl. Add the beef, toss together, then cover and marinate in the fridge for 15 minutes.
2 Mix together the cornflour with 1 tablespoon water to form a paste.
3 Heat a wok over high heat, add a little oil and swirl to coat the wok. Remove the meat from the marinade with tongs and stir-fry in two batches for 2–3 minutes, until browned and just cooked, using a little more oil for the second batch. Remove the meat from the wok.
4 Add the remaining oil to the wok and stir-fry the onion for 2–3 minutes, or until it starts to soften, then add the julienned ginger and stir-fry for another minute. Stir in the Chinese broccoli and cook for 2–3 minutes until wilted and tender.
5 Return the beef to the wok with the reserved marinade and any meat juices. Add the cornflour paste and stir well. Cook for 1–2 minutes, or until the sauce has thickened slightly and the meat is heated through.

LEMONGRASS BEEF

SERVES 4

INGREDIENTS

3 garlic cloves, finely chopped
1 tablespoon grated ginger
4 lemongrass stems, white part only, finely chopped
2½ tablespoons vegetable oil
600 g (1 lb 5 oz) lean beef fillet, thinly sliced
1 tablespoon lime juice
1–2 tablespoons fish sauce
2 tablespoons kecap manis (see Note)
1 large red onion, cut into small wedges
200 g (7 oz) green beans, sliced

METHOD

1 Mix together the garlic, ginger, lemongrass and 2 teaspoons of the oil in a large non-metallic bowl. Add the beef, toss well to coat, then cover and refrigerate for at least 10 minutes.
2 To make the stir-fry sauce, mix together the lime juice, fish sauce and kecap manis.
3 Heat the wok over high heat, add 1 tablespoon of the oil and swirl to coat. Stir-fry the beef in batches for 2–3 minutes, or until browned. Remove from the wok and set aside.
4 Heat the remaining oil in the wok over high heat. Add the onion and stir-fry for 2 minutes. Add the beans and cook for a further 2 minutes, then return the beef to the wok. Pour in the stir-fry sauce and cook until heated through.

NOTE: Kecap manis is a thick, dark sweet soy sauce used in Indonesian and Malaysian cooking. If not available, simply stir a little soft brown sugar into regular soy sauce until it dissolves.

KOREAN BEEF STIR-FRY

Koreans believe in the harmony of the Five Flavours — hot, bitter, sweet, sour and salty — and this is reflected in their use of flavourings such as chilli, spring onions, ginger, vinegar, soya bean paste and sesame oil. Colour is also important and cooks attempt to incorporate the Five Colours — red, green, yellow, white and black — into each meal. The Korean peninsula has been populated since 3000 BC and invaded repeatedly, by the Mongolians, Chinese and, most notoriously, the Japanese, who retained it as a protectorate until 1945. Both Japan and China have influenced Korea's cuisine.

SERVES 4

INGREDIENTS

- 2 garlic cloves, crushed
- 2 teaspoons grated ginger
- 3 spring onions (scallions), finely chopped
- 80 ml (2½ fl oz/⅓ cup) Japanese soy sauce
- 2 teaspoons sugar
- 1½ tablespoons sesame seeds, toasted and ground
- sesame oil, to drizzle
- 600 g (1 lb 5 oz) lean beef fillet, thinly sliced
- 1–2 tablespoons vegetable or peanut oil
- kimchi, to serve (see below)

METHOD

1. To make the marinade, mix the garlic, ginger, spring onion, soy sauce, sugar, 1 tablespoon of the ground sesame seeds and a drizzle of sesame oil in a non-metallic bowl.
2. Add the beef, season with black pepper, cover with plastic wrap and marinate in the fridge for 2 hours or overnight, if time permits.
3. Heat a wok over high heat, add the vegetable oil and swirl to coat. Remove the beef from the marinade with tongs and stir-fry in three batches for 2–3 minutes, or until well seared. Sprinkle with the remaining ground sesame seeds and drizzle with a little extra sesame oil. This is traditionally served with boiled rice and kimchi.

KIMCHI

Kimchi is a fiery condiment eaten by Koreans with practically every meal. It is made by fermenting Chinese cabbage in brine with cucumber, onion, garlic, ginger and chillies. Sometimes daikon is used instead of or with the cabbage. Kimchi's strong smell and flavour take some getting used to. It is traditionally prepared during the autumn to last through the winter months. When fermentation is complete, the kimchi is buried in the ground in jars and dug up when needed. Some kimchis are unfermented (summer kimchis) and some may use dried shrimp or fish.

TEPPANYAKI

This Japanese restaurant dish of meat or vegetables takes its name from the iron plate or sheet on which the food is cooked — the *teppan*. Patrons select their own cuts of meat, usually steak, but also chicken, pork, seafood or vegetables, and watch as the chef cooks the food on the teppan, which is set into the middle of the dining table.

TEPPANYAKI

SERVES 4

INGREDIENTS

- 350 g (12 oz) scotch fillet (rib-eye), partially frozen
- 4 small slender eggplants (aubergines)
- 100 g (3½ oz) fresh shiitake mushrooms
- 100 g (3½ oz) small green beans
- 6 yellow or green baby (pattypan) squash
- 1 red or green capsicum (pepper), seeded
- 6 spring onions (scallions)
- 200 g (7 oz) tinned bamboo shoots, drained
- 60 ml (2 fl oz/¼ cup) oil
- sesame seed sauce, to serve (see below)

METHOD

1. Slice the steak very thinly. Arrange the meat in a single layer over a large serving platter and season well with salt and black pepper.
2. Trim the ends from the eggplants and cut the flesh into long, very thin diagonal slices. Trim any hard stems from the mushrooms. Top and tail the beans. If the beans are long, cut them in half. Quarter, halve or leave the squash whole, depending on their size. Cut the capsicum into thin strips. Remove the outer layer of the spring onions and slice into 7 cm (2¾ inch) lengths, discarding the tops. Arrange the vegetables and bamboo shoots in bundles on the platter.
3. When the diners are seated, heat a portable tabletop grill or electric frying pan until very hot, then lightly brush it with the oil. Quickly fry a quarter of the meat, searing on both sides, and then push it over to the edge of the pan. Add about a quarter of the vegetables and quickly stir-fry, adding a little more oil as needed.
4. Serve a small portion of the meat and vegetables to the diners, along with the sesame seed sauce for dipping. Repeat with the remaining meat and vegetables, cooking in batches, as extra helpings are required. Serve with steamed rice.

SESAME SEED SAUCE

Dry-fry 100 g (3⅓ oz/⅔ cup) sesame seeds over medium heat for 3–4 minutes, shaking the pan gently, until the seeds are golden brown. Remove from the pan at once to prevent burning. Grind the seeds in a mortar and pestle to form a paste. Add 2 teaspoons oil, if necessary. Mix the paste with 125 ml (4 fl oz/½ cup) Japanese soy sauce, 2 tablespoons mirin, 3 teaspoons caster (superfine) sugar, ½ teaspoon dashi granules and 125 ml (4 fl oz/½ cup) warm water. Store, covered, in the refrigerator and use within 2 days.

• • VEAL • •

Veal is the meat of unweaned or recently weaned male calves. It has a delicate flavour and is finely grained, light pink to white with little marbling and fat. Veal is very popular in European cuisines, and has become the star of some areas most famous meat dishes, for example, Milan's osso buco or veal parmigiana from northern Italy, or Hungary's rich goulash stew, flavoured with paprika.

VEAL MARSALA

SERVES 4

INGREDIENTS

- 4 thin veal steaks (150 g/5½ oz each)
- seasoned flour, for dusting
- 30 g (1 oz) butter
- 1 tablespoon olive oil
- 2 tablespoons dry Marsala
- 125 ml (4 fl oz/½ cup) beef stock (page 11)
- 80 ml (2½ fl oz/⅓ cup) cream
- 1 tablespoon lemon juice
- 1 tablespoon chopped parsley

METHOD

1. Flatten each veal steak with a meat mallet or rolling pin to 5 mm (¼ inch) thick. Nick the edges to prevent curling. Lightly dust with flour.
2. Melt the butter and oil in a large heavy-based frying pan over medium–high heat and cook the veal in two batches for 2 minutes on each side, or until lightly browned. Transfer the veal to a platter and cover to keep warm.
3. Pour off any excess fat from the pan but retain any meat juices. Add the Marsala and stock to the pan, bring to the boil over high heat and cook for 1–2 minutes, or until the sauce thickens. Pour in the cream and boil for 2–3 minutes, or until thickened. Add the lemon juice, season and pour the sauce over the veal. Sprinkle with the parsley before serving.

BALSAMIC ROASTED VEAL CUTLETS WITH RED ONION

SERVES 4

INGREDIENTS

- 1½ tablespoons olive oil
- 8 veal cutlets
- 4 garlic cloves, unpeeled
- 1 red onion, cut into thin wedges
- 1 tablespoon chopped rosemary
- 250 g (9 oz) cherry tomatoes
- 60 ml (2 fl oz/¼ cup) balsamic vinegar
- 2 teaspoons soft brown sugar
- 2 tablespoons chopped parsley

METHOD

1. Preheat the oven to 200°C (400°F/Gas 6). Heat the oil in a large frying pan over medium heat. Cook the cutlets in batches for 4 minutes on both sides, or until brown.
2. Arrange the cutlets in a single layer in a large roasting tin. Add the garlic, onion, rosemary, tomatoes, vinegar and sugar. Season well with salt and black pepper.
3. Cover tightly with foil and roast for 15 minutes. Uncover and roast for a further 10–15 minutes, depending on the thickness of the veal cutlets.
4. Transfer the cutlets, garlic, onion and tomatoes to plates. Stir the pan juices and spoon over the top. Garnish with the chopped parsley and serve immediately.

SALTIMBOCCA

SERVES 4

INGREDIENTS

- 4 thin veal steaks (150 g/5½ oz each)
- 2 garlic cloves, crushed
- 4 slices prosciutto
- 4 sage leaves
- 30 g (1 oz) butter
- 170 ml (5½ fl oz/⅔ cup) dry Marsala

METHOD

1. Flatten each steak with a meat mallet or rolling pin to 5 mm (¼ inch) thick. Nick the edges to prevent curling and pat dry.
2. Combine the garlic with ¼ teaspoon salt and ½ teaspoon black pepper and rub over one side of each steak. Place a slice of prosciutto on each and top with a sage leaf. Secure with a cocktail stick.
3. Melt the butter in a large heavy-based frying pan, add the veal, prosciutto side up, and cook for 5 minutes, or until the underside is golden brown. Briefly flip the veal over and cook the other side, then turn it back over. Pour in the Marsala, then reduce the heat and simmer very gently for 5–10 minutes. Transfer the veal to warm serving plates. Boil the sauce for a further 2–3 minutes, or until it has reduced and thickened a little, then spoon it over the veal.

VEAL INVOLTINI

SERVES 4

INGREDIENTS

8 asparagus spears
4 thin veal steaks (150 g/5½ oz each)
4 thin slices mortadella
4 thin slices bel paese cheese
seasoned flour, for dusting
60 g (2¼ oz) butter
1 tablespoon olive oil
60 ml (2 fl oz/¼ cup) dry Marsala

METHOD

1 Blanch the asparagus in boiling salted water for 3 minutes. Drain, keeping 3 tablespoons water.
2 Place each veal steak between two sheets of plastic wrap and pound with a meat mallet to make a 12 x 18 cm (4½ x 7 inch) rectangle. Season lightly with salt and pepper. Trim the mortadella and cheese slices to just a little smaller than the veal.
3 Cover each piece of veal with a slice of mortadella and then a slice of cheese. Lay 2 asparagus spears down the centre, with the tips at opposite ends, overhanging the veal. Roll up tightly and tie at each end with kitchen string. Roll in the seasoned flour to coat.
4 Heat 40 g (1½ oz) of the butter with the olive oil in a frying pan. Fry the veal rolls over low heat for about 10 minutes, turning frequently, until golden and tender. Transfer to a hot serving dish and keep warm.
5 Add the Marsala, the reserved cooking water from the asparagus and the remaining butter to the pan and bring quickly to the boil. Simmer for 3–4 minutes, scraping up the bits from the base of the pan. The juices will reduce and darken. Taste for seasoning, then spoon over the veal rolls and serve immediately.

OSSO BUCO WITH TOMATOES

SERVES 4

INGREDIENTS

10 pieces veal shank
seasoned flour, for dusting
60 ml (2 fl oz/¼ cup) olive oil
60 g (2¼ oz) butter
1 garlic clove
1 small carrot, finely chopped
1 large onion, finely chopped
½ celery stalk, finely chopped
250 ml (9 fl oz/1 cup) dry white wine
375 ml (13 fl oz/1½ cups) veal or chicken stock (page 11)
400 g (14 oz) tin chopped tomatoes
bouquet garni

METHOD

1 Tie each piece of veal shank around its girth to secure the flesh, then dust with the seasoned flour. Heat the oil, butter and garlic in a large flameproof casserole dish, big enough to hold the shanks in a single layer. Add the shanks and brown for 12–15 minutes on all sides. Remove from the dish and set aside. Discard the garlic.
2 Add the carrot, onion and celery to the dish and cook over medium heat for 5–6 minutes, without browning. Increase the heat to high, add the wine and cook for 2–3 minutes. Add the stock, tomatoes and bouquet garni. Season with salt and pepper.
3 Return the shanks to the dish, standing them up in a single layer. Cover, reduce the heat and simmer for 1 hour, or until the meat is tender and you can cut it with a fork. If you prefer a thicker sauce, remove the shanks and increase the heat. Boil the sauce until reduced and thickened, then return the shanks to the casserole dish.
4 Discard the bouquet garni, and taste for salt and pepper. Serve with creamy polenta or mashed potato to soak up the juices.

OSSO BUCO MILANESE

SERVES 4

INGREDIENTS

- 12 pieces veal shank
- seasoned flour, for dusting
- 60 ml (2 fl oz/¼ cup) olive oil
- 60 g (2¼ oz) butter
- 1 garlic clove, finely chopped
- 1 onion, finely chopped
- 1 celery stalk, finely chopped
- 250 ml (9 fl oz/1 cup) dry white wine
- 1 bay leaf or lemon leaf
- pinch each of ground allspice and cinnamon
- gremolata, to serve (see recipe below)

METHOD

1. Dust the veal with seasoned flour. Heat the oil, butter, garlic, onion and celery in a flameproof casserole dish that is big enough to hold the shanks in a single layer (don't add the shanks yet). Cook for 5 minutes over low heat until softened but not browned. Add the shanks to the dish and cook for 12–15 minutes, or until well browned all over. Arrange the shanks in the dish, standing them up in a single layer. Pour in the wine and add the bay leaf, allspice and cinnamon. Bring to the boil and cover the dish. Reduce the heat to low.
2. Cook at a low simmer for 15 minutes, then add 125 ml (4 fl oz/½ cup) warm water. Cook, covered, for 45–60 minutes (the timing will depend on the age of the veal), or until tender. Check the volume of liquid during cooking time and add more warm water as needed.
3. Transfer the veal to a plate and keep warm. Discard the bay leaf. Increase the heat under the dish and stir for 1–2 minutes until the sauce has thickened, scraping up any bits off the bottom of the dish. Season to taste and return the veal shanks to the sauce. Heat through, then stir in half the gremolata. Serve sprinkled with the remaining gremolata.

GREMOLATA

This mixture of chopped lemon zest, parsley and sometimes garlic is used in Italian cooking to garnish dishes, most notably osso buco. Gremolata is sprinkled over or stirred through at the end of cooking.

To make gremolata, combine 2 teaspoons grated lemon zest, 2 tablespoons chopped flat-leaf (Italian) parsley and 1 finely chopped garlic clove. Serve straight away so the gremolata doesn't discolour.

ROAST VEAL STUFFED WITH HAM AND SPINACH

SERVES 4

INGREDIENTS

- 250 g (9 oz) spinach leaves
- 2 garlic cloves, crushed
- 2 tablespoons finely chopped parsley
- 2 teaspoons dijon mustard
- 100 g (3½ oz) ham, diced
- finely grated zest of 1 lemon
- 1 x 600 g (1 lb 5 oz) piece boneless veal loin or fillet, beaten with a meat mallet to measure 30 x 15 cm (12 x 6 inches) — ask your butcher to do this
- 4 slices bacon
- 2 tablespoons olive oil
- 50 g (1¾ oz) butter
- 16 baby carrots
- 8 small unpeeled potatoes
- 8 French shallots
- 200 ml (7 fl oz) dry Madeira

METHOD

1 Preheat the oven to 170°C (325°F/Gas 3). Wash the spinach and put in a large saucepan with just the water clinging to the leaves. Cover the pan and steam the spinach for 2 minutes, or until just wilted. Drain, cool and squeeze dry with your hands. Chop and mix with the garlic, parsley, mustard, ham and lemon zest. Season well.

2 Spread the spinach filling over the centre of the piece of veal. Starting from one of the shorter sides, roll up like a Swiss roll. Wrap the bacon around the meat and season well. Tie with string several times along the roll to secure the bacon, and to ensure the roll doesn't unravel.

3 Heat the olive oil and half the butter in a large frying pan and add the carrots, potatoes and shallots. Briefly brown the vegetables and then tip into a roasting tin. Brown the veal parcel on all sides, then place it on top of the vegetables. Add 80 ml (2½ fl oz/⅓ cup) of the Madeira to the frying pan and boil, stirring, for 30 seconds to deglaze the pan. Pour over the veal.

4 Roast the meat for 30 minutes, then cover the top with foil to prevent overbrowning. Roast for another 45–60 minutes or until the juices run clear when you pierce the thickest part of the meat with a skewer. Wrap the meat in foil and leave to rest. Test the vegetables and return to the oven for a while if they're not yet tender. When cooked, remove them from the tin.

5 Place the roasting tin over medium heat and add the rest of the Madeira. Allow it to bubble, then add the rest of the butter and season the sauce to taste. Slice the veal thickly and arrange the slices of meat on top of the vegetables. Pour over some of the Madeira sauce and serve the rest separately in a jug.

VEAL SCHNITZEL

The tenderness of veal makes it wonderful to use for schnitzels. Flatten the steaks out first with a meat mallet or rolling pin (if you put them between sheets of plastic or baking paper you'll hopefully prevent the meat tearing).

SERVES 4

INGREDIENTS

4 thin veal steaks (150 g/5½ oz each)
seasoned flour, for dusting
2 eggs, lightly beaten
100 g (3½ oz/1 cup) dry breadcrumbs
125 ml (4 fl oz/½ cup) virgin olive oil
lemon wedges, to serve

METHOD

1 Beat the veal between two sheets of plastic wrap to 5 mm (¼ inch) thickness. Coat the veal in the seasoned flour and shake off the excess. Dip the veal in the egg, then coat in breadcrumbs. Place the schnitzel on a flat tray, cover and freeze for 5 minutes.
2 Heat half the oil in a large frying pan and cook 2 pieces of veal over medium–high heat for 2–3 minutes on each side, or until golden and cooked through. Drain on crumpled paper towels. Cook the rest of the veal in the remaining oil. Serve with lemon wedges.

VEAL GOULASH

SERVES 4

INGREDIENTS

500 g (1 lb 2 oz) veal, cut into 2.5 cm (1 inch) pieces
seasoned flour, for dusting
2 tablespoons olive oil
2 onions, thinly sliced
2 garlic cloves, finely chopped
1 tablespoon sweet Hungarian paprika
1 teaspoon ground cumin
400 g (14 oz) tin chopped tomatoes
2 carrots, sliced
½ red capsicum (pepper), chopped
½ green capsicum (pepper), chopped
250 ml (9 fl oz/1 cup) beef stock (page 11)
125 ml (4 fl oz/½ cup) red wine
125 g (4½ oz/½ cup) sour cream
chopped parsley, to garnish

METHOD

1 Put the veal and flour in a plastic bag and shake to coat the veal with flour. Shake off any excess. Heat 1 tablespoon of the oil in a large, deep heavy-based saucepan over medium heat. Brown the meat well in batches, then remove the meat and set aside.
2 Add the remaining oil to the pan. Cook the onion, garlic, paprika and cumin for 5 minutes, stirring frequently. Return the meat and any juices to the pan with the tomatoes, carrot and capsicum. Cover and cook for 10 minutes.
3 Add the stock and wine, and season. Stir well, then cover and simmer over very low heat for 1½ hours. Stir in half the sour cream, season if needed and serve garnished with parsley and the remaining sour cream. Serve with buttered boiled potatoes or noodles.

VEAL PARMIGIANA

SERVES 4

INGREDIENTS

125 ml (4 fl oz/½ cup) olive oil
1 onion, finely chopped
1 kg (2 lb 4 oz) ripe tomatoes, peeled, seeded and diced (page 347)
3 garlic cloves, finely chopped
1 bouquet garni
4 thin veal steaks (150 g/5½ oz each)
seasoned flour, for dusting
2 eggs, lightly beaten
160 g (5½ oz/2 cups) fresh breadcrumbs
50 g (1¾ oz/½ cup) grated parmesan cheese
1 tablespoon chopped parsley
250 g (9 oz/1⅔ cups) grated mozzarella cheese

METHOD

1 Heat half the olive oil in a saucepan and cook the onion over low heat for 5 minutes without letting it colour. Add the tomatoes, garlic and bouquet garni, and season. Simmer for 1 hour.
2 Beat the veal between two sheets of plastic wrap to 5 mm (¼ inch) thickness. Coat the veal in the seasoned flour and shake off the excess. Dip in the beaten egg. Mix together the breadcrumbs, parmesan and parsley on a flat plate and coat the veal, pressing the crumbs in well.
3 Preheat the oven to 200°C (400°F/Gas 6). Heat half the remaining oil in a large frying pan and cook 2 pieces of veal over medium–high heat for 2–3 minutes on each side, or until golden and cooked through. Drain on paper towels. Cook the rest of the veal in the remaining oil.
4 Arrange the veal in a baking dish, cover with the mozzarella and bake for 10 minutes, or until the cheese has melted. Serve with the tomato sauce over the top.

••PORK••

There is an old saying about pork: 'every bit of the pig can be used except the squeal'. Pigs have been widely farmed for centuries and are eaten in many countries of the world. Pork can be eaten both fresh, as chops, cutlets, steaks, or cured into bacon, ham, salami and sausages. The meat takes on the flavour of the pig's diet (and pigs can be surprisingly choosy). For example, the Iberian jamon that has become so popular in recent years is produced from the Spanish pata negra pigs that have been fed on wild acorns.

CUTS OF PORK

PORK CHOPS

These come from different parts of the pig such as the loin and ribs. Chops are good for grilling (broiling), pan-frying and barbecuing.

LOIN OF PORK

This can be bought on or off the bone. Boned loin is often sold rolled up as a joint. Loin is also sold cut into chops, or off the bone and cut into cubes.

PORK FILLET

Fillet is the easiest cut to cook and is quite delicate in flavour. Sold whole or cut into medallions.

LEGS OF PORK

These are best cooked slowly as they don't have much fat. Legs are good for roasts.

PORK RIBS

Buy meatier American-style spareribs or the Chinese ones, which are bonier but barbecue and braise well. Simmer in water until tender and then cook in a sauce.

OTHER PORK PRODUCTS

MINCED (GROUND) PORK

This is paler than minced beef or lamb and can be quite fatty. It is good for making meatballs and meat loaf.

PORK SAUSAGES

These are usually flavoured with sage, parsley, garlic or even apple. The small thin sausages are chipolatas.

HAM

This is the salt-cured hind leg of a pig and is sold smoked or unsmoked. Ham has a stronger, richer flavour than fresh pork, and is often quite sweet.

BACON

Confusingly, although the word 'bacon' comes from the old German, which means 'back', bacon is English, and does not come from a pig's back. Originally it was made from the cured sides of a pig; the legs being cured separately to make ham. Now the whole side, including the back leg, is cured. Buy bacon smoked, unsmoked (green) or tendersweet (a mild cure).

PORK WITH APPLE AND PRUNE STUFFING

SERVES 8

INGREDIENTS

- 1 apple, cored and chopped
- 90 g (3¼ oz/⅓ cup) chopped pitted prunes
- 2 tablespoons port
- 1 tablespoon chopped parsley
- 2 kg (4 lb 8 oz) boned pork loin
- olive oil and salt, for rubbing

METHOD

1. Preheat the oven to 240°C (475°F/Gas 8). To make the stuffing, combine the apple, prunes, port and parsley. Lay the pork loin on a board with the rind underneath. Spread the stuffing over the meat side of the loin, roll up and secure with skewers or string at regular intervals. Score the pork rind with a sharp knife at 1 cm (½ inch) intervals (or you can ask your butcher to do this when you buy the pork) and rub generously with oil and salt.
2. Place the pork on a rack in a roasting tin. Bake for 15 minutes, then reduce the heat to 180°C (350°F/Gas 4) and bake for 1½–2 hours, or until the pork juices run clear when you poke a skewer into the thickest part of the meat. Cover and leave for 15 minutes before carving. Keep the pan juices for making gravy (page 428).

NOTE: If the pork rind doesn't crisp up to make crackling, remove it from the meat, cutting between the fat and the meat. Scrape off any fat and put the rind on a piece of foil, then place under a hot grill (broiler) until it turns to crackling.

ROAST PORK FILLET WITH APPLE AND MUSTARD SAUCE

SERVES 4

INGREDIENTS

- 750 g (1 lb 10 oz) pork fillet
- 30 g (1 oz) butter
- 1 tablespoon oil
- 1 garlic clove, crushed
- ½ teaspoon grated ginger
- 1 tablespoon seeded mustard
- 60 ml (2 fl oz/¼ cup) apple sauce
- 2 tablespoons chicken stock (page 11)
- 125 ml (4 fl oz/½ cup) cream
- 1 teaspoon cornflour (cornstarch)

GLAZED APPLES

- 50 g (1¾ oz) butter
- 2 tablespoons soft brown sugar
- 2 apples, sliced

METHOD

1. Preheat the oven to 180°C (350°F/Gas 4). Trim the pork of fat or sinew. Tie with kitchen string at intervals so the pork keeps its shape.
2. Heat the butter and oil in a frying pan and cook the pork until lightly browned all over. Lift out the pork and put on a rack in a roasting tin. (Leave the cooking oil in the frying pan.) Add ½ cupful of water to the tin, transfer to the oven and roast for 15–20 minutes. Set aside for 10 minutes before carving.
3. To make the sauce, reheat the oil in the frying pan, add the garlic and ginger and cook, stirring, for 1 minute. Stir in the mustard, apple sauce and stock. Slowly stir in the combined cream and cornflour and stir until it boils and thickens.
4. To make the glazed apples, melt the butter in a frying pan and add the sugar. Stir until the sugar dissolves. Add the apple and pan-fry, turning occasionally, until glazed and lightly browned.
5. Pour the apple and mustard sauce over the carved pork and serve with the glazed apples.

PORK WITH SAGE AND CAPERS

SERVES 4

INGREDIENTS

25 g (1 oz) butter
60 ml (2 fl oz/¼ cup) extra virgin olive oil
1 onion, finely chopped
100 g (3½ oz/1¼ cups) fresh breadcrumbs
2 teaspoons chopped sage
1 tablespoon chopped parsley
2 teaspoons finely grated lemon zest
2½ tablespoons salted capers, rinsed
1 egg, lightly beaten
2 pork fillets (about 500 g/1 lb 2 oz each)
8 thin slices bacon or prosciutto
2 teaspoons plain (all-purpose) flour
100 ml (3½ fl oz) dry vermouth
310 ml (10¾ fl oz/1¼ cups) chicken or vegetable stock (page 10–11)
sage leaves, extra to garnish

METHOD

1 Preheat the oven to 170°C (325°F/Gas 3). Heat the butter and 1 tablespoon of the oil in a frying pan, and fry the onion for 5 minutes, or until lightly golden. Mix with the breadcrumbs, sage, parsley, lemon zest, 2 teaspoons of the capers and the egg and season well.

2 Split each pork fillet in half lengthways and open out. Spread the stuffing down the length of one and cover with the other fillet. Stretch the bacon with the back of a knife and wrap, slightly overlapping around the pork to form a neat parcel. Tie with string. Put in a roasting tin and drizzle with 1 tablespoon of the oil. Bake for 1 hour, or until the juices run clear. Transfer to a carving plate and cover with foil.

3 Place the roasting tin on the stovetop and stir in the flour. Add the vermouth and allow to bubble for 1 minute. Add the stock and stir to remove any lumps. Simmer for 5 minutes, then add the remaining capers. Heat the remaining oil in a small saucepan and fry the whole sage leaves until crisp. Drain on crumpled paper towels. Carve the pork into 1 cm (½ inch) slices and serve with the sauce and crisp sage leaves.

FIGS WRAPPED IN PROSCIUTTO

With its strong salty flavour, prosciutto is a perfect partner for ripe figs. You'll need 4 skewers for this: if you're using bamboo skewers, soak them in water for 10 minutes first so they don't scorch. Cut 4 figs into quarters and wrap each quarter in a strip of prosciutto. Thread 4 fig quarters onto each skewer. Brush the figs with olive oil and barbecue or grill (broil) on both sides until browned. Serve with a cheeseboard or as part of an antipasti platter. Serves 4

PORK COOKED IN MILK

Chining the pork (detaching the backbone) before cooking makes it easier to carve between the ribs, and also looks very attractive when you serve. It's a handy skill to have, but if you find the idea daunting you can ask your butcher to do it, or just leave the pork loin as it is and start this recipe at step 4.

SERVES 6

INGREDIENTS

2.25 kg (5 lb) pork loin, on the bone
2 tablespoons olive oil
4 garlic cloves, cut in half lengthways
4 sage or rosemary sprigs
1 litre (35 fl oz/4 cups) milk
finely grated zest of 2 lemons
juice of 1 lemon

METHOD

1 To chine the pork, put the rack of ribs on a chopping board, ribs facing downwards. Using a sharp boning knife, cut down the side of the chine bone to the vertebrae. Hold the chine bone in one hand and the joint in the other and snap off the chine bone.
2 Trim the layer of fat off the back of the joint leaving just enough to act as a protective layer and to baste the joint.
3 Trim the meat away from the very end of each rib bone, exposing the bone.
4 Preheat the oven to 200°C (400°F/Gas 6). Heat the olive oil in a roasting tin. Add the pork and brown the meat on all sides. Remove the pork and pour away the fat in the roasting tin. Add the garlic and sage to the roasting tin and place the pork on top, bone side down so the ribs act as a rack. Season with salt and pepper and pour the milk over the pork. Return to the heat and bring just to the boil. Remove from the heat, add the lemon zest and drizzle with the lemon juice. The milk will be lumpy and start to curdle, but this is how the sauce is supposed to look.
5 Transfer the roasting tin to the oven and cook for about 20 minutes. Reduce the heat to 150°C (300°F/Gas 2) and cook for another 1–1¼ hours, depending on the thickness of the meat. If the milk evaporates before the end of cooking time, add a little more to keep the meat roasting in liquid. Baste the meat with the juices every 30 minutes. Do not cover, so that the juices reduce and the fat on the pork becomes crisp.
6 To test if the pork is cooked, poke a skewer into the middle of the meat, count to ten and pull it out. Quickly touch it on the inside of your wrist: if it feels very hot, the meat is cooked through. Remove the pork from the oven and leave it to rest for at least 10 minutes. Remove the herbs and garlic.
7 This is traditionally served with wet polenta or roasted potatoes, with a little of the sauce spooned over the top.

PORK NOISETTES WITH PRUNES

SERVES 4

INGREDIENTS

2 x 400 g (14 oz) pork fillets
16 pitted prunes
1 tablespoon vegetable oil
45 g (1½ oz) butter
1 onion, finely chopped
155 ml (5 fl oz) white wine
280 ml (9½ fl oz) chicken or beef stock (page 11)
1 bay leaf
2 thyme sprigs
250 ml (9 fl oz/1 cup) thick (double) cream

METHOD

1 Trim the pork, removing any membrane. Cut each fillet into 4 slices. Put the prunes in a small saucepan, cover with cold water and bring to the boil. Reduce the heat and simmer the prunes for 5 minutes. Drain well.
2 Heat the oil in a large heavy-based saucepan and add half the butter. When the butter starts foaming, add the pork, in batches if necessary, and sauté on both sides until cooked. Transfer to a warm plate, cover and keep warm.
3 Pour off the excess fat from the pan. Melt the remaining butter, add the onion and cook over low heat until softened but not browned. Add the wine, bring to the boil and simmer for 2 minutes. Add the stock, bay leaf and thyme and bring to the boil. Reduce the heat and simmer for 10 minutes or until reduced by half.
4 Strain the stock into a bowl and rinse the frying pan. Return the stock to the pan, add the cream and prunes and simmer for 8 minutes, or until the sauce thickens slightly. Return the pork to the pan and simmer until heated through.

BRAISED PORK SAUSAGES WITH PUY LENTILS

SERVES 2

INGREDIENTS

1 tablespoon olive oil
55 g (2 oz) pancetta, cubed
1 red onion, finely chopped
6 pork sausages
1 garlic clove, crushed
1 thyme sprig
150 g (5½ oz/¾ cup) puy lentils
375 ml (13 fl oz/1½ cups) tinned chicken consommé
150 g (5½ oz) English spinach leaves, chopped
2 tablespoons crème fraîche

METHOD

1 Heat the oil in a heavy-based frying pan (one with a lid) and fry the pancetta until browned. Take it out with a slotted spoon and put it in a bowl. Put the onion in the pan and cook until it is soft and only lightly browned. Add the onion to the pancetta.
2 Put the sausages in the same pan and fry until they are very brown all over. Put the pancetta and onion back in with the sausages.
3 Add the garlic and thyme to the frying pan, along with the lentils, and mix together. Add the consommé and bring to the boil. Put a lid on the pan and slowly simmer for 25 minutes. Stir in the spinach. Season with salt and pepper and stir in the crème fraîche to serve.

PORK WITH CALVADOS

SERVES 4

INGREDIENTS

- 60 g (2¼ oz) butter
- 2 apples, cored, each cut into 8 wedges
- ½ teaspoon sugar
- 1½ tablespoons oil
- 4 x 200 g (7 oz) pork chops
- 2 tablespoons Calvados
- 2 French shallots, finely chopped
- 250 ml (9 fl oz/1 cup) dry cider
- 125 ml (4 fl oz/½ cup) chicken stock (page 11)
- 150 ml (5 fl oz) thick (double) cream

METHOD

1. Melt half the butter in a frying pan, add the apple and sprinkle with the sugar. Cook over low heat, turning occasionally, until tender and glazed.
2. Heat the oil in a frying pan and sauté the pork until cooked, turning once. Pour the excess fat from the pan, add the Calvados and flambé by lighting the pan with your gas flame or a match (stand back and keep the lid handy for emergencies). Transfer the pork to a plate.
3. Add the remaining butter to the pan and cook the shallots until soft but not brown. Add the cider, stock and cream and bring to the boil. Reduce the heat and simmer for 15 minutes, or until thick enough to coat the back of a spoon.
4. Season the sauce, add the pork and simmer for 3 minutes to heat through. Serve with the apple.

SLOW-COOKED PORK BELLY

SERVES 6

INGREDIENTS

- 1 kg (2 lb 4 oz) pork belly, rind on
- 2 tablespoons oil
- 6 spring onions (scallions), sliced
- 8 slices ginger
- 100 g (3½ oz) rock sugar
- 2½ tablespoons dark soy sauce
- 2½ tablespoons light soy sauce
- 100 ml (3½ fl oz) Chinese rice wine

METHOD

1. Scrape the pork rind to make sure it is free of any bristles. Blanch the pork in a pan of boiling water for 10 minutes, then drain well and dry thoroughly with paper towels.
2. Heat a wok over high heat, add the oil and heat until very hot. Cook the pork until very well browned with a crisp brown skin (this stage is important or else the pork will become soggy). Drain the pork.
3. Put the spring onion, ginger, sugar, soy sauces, rice wine and 150 ml (5 fl oz) water in a casserole. Bring to the boil and stir until the sugar dissolves. Add the pork, cover and simmer for 2½–3 hours, or until very tender. Remove the pork and drain, straining the liquid. Slice thinly and serve with the sauce.

CIDER AND CALVADOS

Cider is made by extracting the juice from apples, which is then naturally fermented in barrels or large tanks. Calvados is a brandy made by distilling cider, and takes its name from Calvados, Normandy, where it is made. Calvados has an appellation contrôlée, requiring it to be double-distilled and matured in oak barrels. It is popular in Normandy, both as a drink and also for cooking.

HAM

The flavour of ham is attributed to many factors: the breed or age of the pig, its diet and the method of curing. Curing methods can vary, but the process is always based on salt, using either a dry-cure or brine, sometimes with added herbs, spices and treacle or molasses. The hams are then often either smoked or air-dried and possibly aged for months or even years to give the unique flavour. Hams are eaten raw or cooked according to how much they have been cured. A short curing process followed by smoking does not cure a ham to the same degree as slow-curing (dry-salting) and air-drying over time. Ham is sold either by the whole leg (for boiling or baking) or sliced.

ORANGE-GLAZED HAM

SERVES 20

INGREDIENTS

- 7 kg (15 lb 12 oz) cooked ham leg
- 1 large orange
- 6 whole cloves
- 140 g (5 oz/¾ cup) soft brown sugar
- 1 tablespoon French mustard
- 175 g (6 oz/½ cup) honey
- 2 teaspoons soy sauce
- 2 tablespoons Grand Marnier
- whole cloves, extra

MUSTARD CREAM

- 2 tablespoons French mustard
- 125 g (4½ oz/½ cup) sour cream
- 125 ml (4 fl oz/½ cup) cream

METHOD

1. Preheat the oven to 180°C (350°F/Gas 4). Remove the rind from the ham by running a thumb around the edge, under the rind. Begin pulling at the widest edge. When the rind has been removed to within 6 cm (2½ inches) of the shank end, cut through the rind around the shank. Using a sharp knife, remove some of the excess fat from the ham (but leave enough to give a good crispy skin).
2. Peel the orange, cut the white pith off the zest and cut the zest into long strips. Squeeze about 125 ml (4 fl oz/½ cup) of juice from the orange.
3. Put the ham on a rack in a deep roasting tin. Add 500 ml (17 fl oz/2 cups) water to the tin with the strips of orange zest and cloves. Cover securely with foil and cook for 2 hours.
4. Remove from the oven. Increase the heat to 210°C (415°F/Gas 6–7). Drain the meat, keeping 250 ml (9 fl oz/1 cup) of the pan juices. Using a sharp knife, score the fat into a diamond pattern.
5. Mix together the sugar, mustard, honey, soy sauce and Grand Marnier and brush over the ham. Return to the oven and cook, uncovered, for 30 minutes, glazing every 10 minutes.
6. Remove the ham from the oven again. Press a clove into each diamond. Roast, uncovered, for 1 hour, brushing with glaze every 10 minutes.
7. Meanwhile, to make the mustard cream, mix together the mustard, sour cream and cream. Cover and refrigerate.
8. Place the saved pan juices and 125 ml (4 fl oz/½ cup) of the brown sugar glaze in a small pan. Stir in the orange juice and stir over low heat until the mixture boils. Boil, without stirring, for 3 minutes. Leave the ham for 10 minutes before slicing. Serve hot or cold, with the orange glaze and mustard cream.

SPICY SALT AND PEPPER SPARERIBS

SERVES 4

INGREDIENTS

1 kg (2 lb 4 oz) Chinese-style pork spareribs
1 egg, lightly beaten
2–3 tablespoons plain (all-purpose) flour
oil, for deep-frying
2 spring onions (scallions), finely chopped
2 small red chillies, finely chopped

MARINADE

½ teaspoon ground sichuan peppercorns
½ teaspoon Chinese five-spice
½ teaspoon salt
1 tablespoon light soy sauce
1 tablespoon Chinese rice wine
¼ teaspoon sesame oil

METHOD

1 Ask the butcher to cut the slab of spare ribs crosswise into thirds that measure 4–5 cm (1½–2 inches) in length, or use a cleaver to do so yourself. Cut the ribs between the bones to separate them.
2 To make the marinade, combine the ingredients in a bowl. Add the ribs and toss lightly. Marinate in the fridge for at least 3 hours, or overnight.
3 Mix the egg, flour and a little water to form a smooth batter. Fill a wok one-quarter full of oil. Heat the oil to 180°C (350°F), or until a cube of bread dropped into the oils turns golden brown in 15 seconds. Dip the ribs in the batter and fry in batches for 5 minutes until they are crisp and golden, stirring to separate them, then remove and drain. Reheat the oil and fry the ribs for 1 minute to darken them. Remove and drain on paper towels.
4 Soak the spring onion and chilli in the hot oil (with the heat off) for 2 minutes. Remove with a wire strainer or slotted spoon and sprinkle over the ribs.

BARBECUED PORK RIBS

MAKES ABOUT 30

INGREDIENTS

½ teaspoon English mustard
½ teaspoon sweet paprika
¼ teaspoon ground oregano
¼ teaspoon ground cumin
1½ tablespoons peanut oil
1 teaspoon Tabasco sauce
1 garlic clove, crushed
125 ml (4 fl oz/½ cup) tomato sauce (ketchup)
2 tablespoons tomato paste (concentrated purée)
2 tablespoons soft brown sugar
1 tablespoon worcestershire sauce
2 teaspoons brown vinegar
1.5 kg (3 lb 5 oz) American-style pork spareribs

METHOD

1 To make the sauce, combine the mustard, paprika, oregano, cumin and peanut oil in a saucepan. Add the remaining ingredients, except the ribs. Cook, stirring, over medium heat for 3 minutes. Allow to cool, pour over the ribs, cover and marinate overnight in the fridge.
2 Heat a barbecue plate to hot and cook the ribs, turning frequently, until firm and well done. Cut into individual ribs before serving.

MEATBALLS IN SPICY TOMATO SAUCE

SERVES 6

INGREDIENTS

175 g (6 oz) minced (ground) pork
175 g (6 oz) minced (ground) veal
3 garlic cloves, crushed
35 g (1¼ oz/⅓ cup) dry breadcrumbs
1 teaspoon each ground coriander, nutmeg and cumin
pinch of ground cinnamon
1 egg, lightly beaten
2 tablespoons olive oil

SPICY TOMATO SAUCE

1 tablespoon olive oil
1 onion, chopped
1 garlic clove, crushed
125 ml (4 fl oz/½ cup) dry white wine
400 g (14 oz) tin chopped tomatoes
1 tablespoon tomato paste (concentrated purée)
125 ml (4 fl oz/½ cup) chicken stock (page 11)
½ teaspoon cayenne pepper
80 g (2¾ oz/½ cup) fresh or frozen peas

METHOD

1 Combine the pork, veal, garlic, breadcrumbs, spices and egg and mix by hand until smooth. Refrigerate, covered, for 30 minutes.
2 Roll tablespoons of the mixture into balls. Heat a little oil in a frying pan and cook the meatballs in batches over medium–high heat for 2–3 minutes, until browned. Drain on paper towels.
3 To make the tomato sauce, heat the oil in a frying pan and add the onion. Cook, stirring, for 3 minutes, or until soft and translucent. Add the garlic and cook for 1 minute. Increase the heat to high, add the wine and boil for 1 minute. Add the tomato, tomato paste and stock and simmer for 10 minutes. Stir in the cayenne, peas and meatballs and gently simmer for 5–10 minutes, or until thick. Serve hot.

SWEET AND SOUR PORK

SERVES 4

INGREDIENTS

600 g (1 lb 5 oz) centre-cut pork loin, trimmed
1 egg, lightly beaten
100 g (3½ oz) cornflour (cornstarch)
1 tablespoon oil
1 onion, cubed
1 red capsicum (pepper), cubed
300 g (10½ oz) pineapple, cubed
2 spring onions (scallions), chopped
150 g (5½ oz) Chinese pickles
250 ml (9 fl oz/1 cup) clear rice vinegar
80 ml (2½ fl oz/⅓ cup) tomato sauce (ketchup)
300 g (10½ oz) sugar
oil, for deep-frying

METHOD

1 Cut the pork into 2 cm (¾ inch) cubes. Put it in a bowl with the egg, 75 g (2½ oz) of the cornflour and 2 teaspoons water. Stir to coat the pork.
2 Heat a wok over high heat, add the oil and heat until very hot. Stir-fry the onion for 1 minute. Add the capsicum, pineapple and spring onion and cook for 1 minute. Add the pickles and toss well. Add the rice vinegar, tomato sauce and sugar and stir over low heat until the sugar dissolves. Bring to the boil, then simmer for 3 minutes.
3 Combine the remaining cornflour with 75 ml (2¼ fl oz) water, add to the sweet-and-sour mixture and simmer until thickened. Set aside.
4 Fill a deep heavy-based saucepan one-quarter full of oil. Heat the oil to 180°C (350°F), or until a cube of bread dropped into the oils turns golden brown in 15 seconds. Cook the pork in batches until golden brown and crispy. Return all of the pork to the wok, cook until crisp again, then remove with a wire sieve or slotted spoon and drain well.
5 Add the pork pieces to the sauce, stir to coat, and reheat until bubbling. Serve with rice.

PORK VINDALOO

The Portuguese first introduced this pork, garlic and vinegar stew to Goa. The locals adopted it but, finding it slightly lacking in flavour, proceeded to add spices, extra garlic and a hefty quantity of chillies. The result is vindaloo, famed (or feared) for its heat and spiciness.

SERVES 4

INGREDIENTS

- 60 ml (2 fl oz/¼ cup) oil
- 1 kg (2 lb 4 oz) pork fillet, trimmed and cubed
- 2 onions, finely chopped
- 4 garlic cloves, crushed
- 1 tablespoon finely chopped ginger
- 1 tablespoon garam masala
- 2 teaspoons brown mustard seeds
- 4 tablespoons vindaloo paste (page 439)

METHOD

1. Heat the oil in a saucepan over medium heat, add the pork in small batches and cook for 5–7 minutes until browned. Remove from the pan.
2. Add the onion, garlic, ginger, garam masala and mustard seeds to the pan, and cook, stirring, for 5 minutes, or until the onion is soft.
3. Return all the meat to the pan, add the vindaloo paste and cook, stirring, for 2 minutes. Add 625 ml (21 fl oz/2½ cups) water and bring to the boil. Reduce the heat and simmer, covered, for 1½ hours, or until the meat is tender. Serve with rice and cucumber raita (see below).

SESAME PORK STIR-FRY

SERVES 4

INGREDIENTS

- 2 tablespoons hoisin sauce
- 2 tablespoons teriyaki sauce
- 2 teaspoons cornflour (cornstarch)
- 60 ml (2 fl oz/¼ cup) peanut oil
- 600 g (1 lb 5 oz) pork loin fillet, thinly sliced
- 2 teaspoons sesame oil
- 8 spring onions (scallions), sliced
- 2 garlic cloves, crushed
- 2 teaspoons finely grated ginger
- 2 carrots, julienned
- 200 g (7 oz) snake (yard-long) beans, sliced
- 2 tablespoons sesame seeds, toasted

METHOD

1. Combine the hoisin and teriyaki sauces, cornflour and 1 tablespoon water in a bowl.
2. Heat a wok, add 1 tablespoon of the peanut oil and swirl to coat the wok. Stir-fry the pork in two batches for 3 minutes, or until browned. Remove the pork from the wok.
3. Heat the remaining peanut oil and the sesame oil in the wok. Add the spring onion, garlic and ginger and stir-fry for 1 minute. Add the carrot and beans and stir-fry for 3 minutes, or until almost cooked. Return the pork to the wok, add the stir-fry sauce and stir until the sauce thickens and the meat and vegetables are cooked. Toss in the sesame seeds and serve with rice.

RAITA

For diners eating a fiery curry, yoghurt is often a great saviour. Indian raitas are made with yoghurt mixed with grated vegetables, herbs and spices. To make a cucumber and tomato raita, put 450 g (1 lb) grated cucumber and 1 finely chopped tomato in a sieve and drain for 20 minutes. Mix with 300 g (10½ oz) Greek-style yoghurt and season with salt. Fry 1 teaspoon black mustard seeds in a little oil, then cover and shake the pan until the seeds start to pop. Pour the seeds and oil over the yoghurt and sprinkle with chopped coriander (cilantro).

••LAMB••

Lamb is traditionally a festival food and has strong associations with springtime, as well as many religious feast days in the Christian, Jewish and Muslim calendars. As a fatty meat, lamb is traditionally served with acidic accompaniments such as mint sauce and redcurrant jelly, or strong herbs like rosemary. In many dishes, fruit and sweet root vegetables are also used to complement the meat's oily richness.

BUYING LAMB

Spring lamb is usually butchered at 3–5 months and, despite the name, is now available all year round in most countries. Milk-fed lamb is very pale (and expensive). Lamb should have a healthy pink colour with waxy, dry, firm white fat. The meat from older sheep, either called hogget (up to 20 months) or mutton (30–40 months) is darker and stronger flavoured. Cheaper cuts tend to need longer, slower cooking and will not benefit from quick grilling or pan-frying.

HOW TO... TRIM A LEG OF LAMB

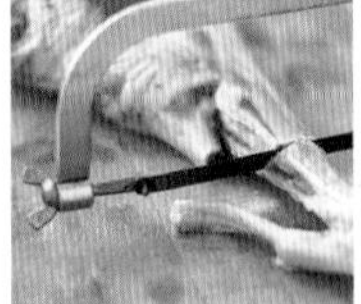
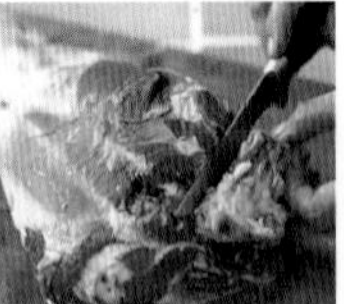

METHOD

1 Using a small knife, cut away any excess fat covering the leg. Cut through the tendon joining the meat to the knuckle and trim off any meat from the bone. Using a saw, cut off the knuckle end of the shank bone to neaten it.
2 Next, turn the leg over and, using a boning knife, cut around the edges of the pelvic bone. Following its contour down to the ball and socket joint, cut through the tendons that join the two bones and then pull out the pelvic bone.
3 Fold the flap of flesh back over the lamb and use a piece of string to tie it in place. Wind the string round the shank end and up both sides of the leg. Tie another piece of string across the joint.

HOW TO... CARVE A LEG OF LAMB

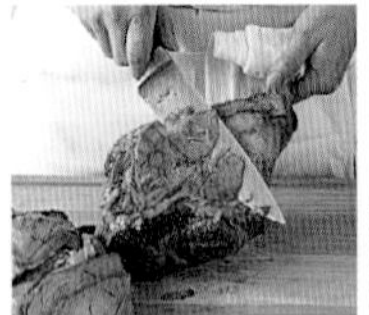
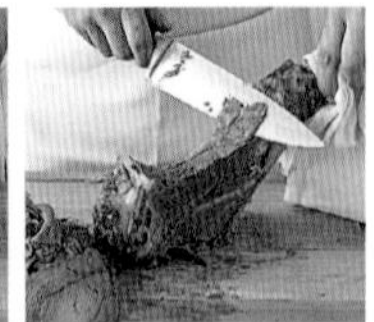

METHOD

1 Hold the bone with a napkin and start carving, parallel to the bone, cutting away from you.
2 When you reach the bone, turn the joint and carve the other side in the same way.
3 Carve the remaining meat on the shank, starting at the point where you are holding the shank.

CUTS OF LAMB

MIDDLE CUTS

Cuts include the saddle (both loins and often the tail and kidneys), the loins (on the bone), chump chops and noisettes. These cuts are good for roasting or, when off the bone, for frying and grilling.

BACK CUTS (HINDQUARTER)

The leg (gigot) as a whole is good for roasting, and the shank or knuckle end is good for slow cooking. Leg chops are cut from the top of the leg.

FRONTS CUTS (FOREQUARTER)

These range from the fatty neck or scrag end to the tender meat of the racks. Cuts include the breast, scrag end and middle neck, the shoulder (bone in or bone out), and the rack (sometimes called the 'best end of neck'), which can be bought in one piece, cut into chops and cutlets, or two racks can be joined to make a crown roast (shown above), or if inward facing, a guard of honour.

The fattier cuts are good for slow cooking and casseroles and the racks and shoulder are good for roasting, grilling and pan-frying.

MIDDLE EASTERN RICE-STUFFED LAMB

SERVES 6

INGREDIENTS

- 60 g (2¼ oz/⅓ cup) dried figs
- 1 tablespoon olive oil
- 1 onion, finely chopped
- 2 garlic cloves, crushed
- 1 teaspoon ground cinnamon
- ¼ teaspoon ground allspice
- 1 tablespoon red wine vinegar
- 65 g (2¼ oz/⅓ cup) long-grain rice
- 2 tablespoons currants
- 2 tablespoons pistachios or pine nuts, toasted
- 875 ml (30 fl oz/3½ cups) chicken stock (page 11)
- 2 tablespoons finely chopped parsley
- 1 egg, lightly beaten
- 1.5 kg (3 lb 5 oz) leg of lamb, boned and butterflied
- 60 ml (2 fl oz/¼ cup) olive oil, extra
- 2 tablespoons lemon juice
- 2–3 teaspoons finely chopped oregano
- 1 tablespoon sumac
- 250 ml (9 fl oz/1 cup) white wine

METHOD

1. Preheat the oven to 200°C (400°F/Gas 6). Soak the dried figs in warm water for 20 minutes. Drain and roughly chop.
2. To make the stuffing, heat the olive oil in a frying pan, then cook the onion for 3 minutes until softened. Add the garlic, cinnamon and allspice and cook for 30 seconds. Add the vinegar and cook over high heat until absorbed.
3. Reduce the heat to medium, then add rice, figs, currants and pistachios and stir to coat. Pour in 250 ml (9 fl oz/1 cup) of the stock, bring to the boil, then reduce the heat to low and cook, covered, for 20 minutes, or until the stock has been absorbed and the rice is tender. Season well and stir in the parsley. Leave to cool.
4. When the stuffing has cooled, mix in the beaten egg with a metal spoon until it binds together. Open out the lamb leg on a work surface and spread the stuffing over the lamb, then roll up and tie with string.
5. Combine the extra olive oil with the lemon juice, oregano and sumac, then pour onto the lamb, rubbing it in. Season with salt and pepper. Place in a roasting tin and roast for 10 minutes.
6. Remove the lamb from the oven and reduce the heat to 180°C (350°F/Gas 4). Pour the remaining stock and white wine into the roasting tin and roast for a further 1 hour, or until cooked to your liking. Add extra stock or water if the liquid is evaporating too quickly. Remove the lamb and set aside on a plate to rest.
7. Meanwhile, to make the sauce, put the roasting tin on top of the stove and simmer over medium heat for 3 minutes, or until the liquid has reduced and thickened slightly. Serve the lamb with the stuffing and sauce.

HOW TO... ROAST LAMB

* For roasting, choose joints such as saddle, rack (joined cutlets), crown roast (what the French call carré d'agneau), guard of honour, loin, shoulder or leg. A loin (6–7 chops) will feed 3 people and a chop loin (4–5 chops) will feed 2 people.
* Roast lamb is best cooked on the bone at 200°C (400°F/Gas 6). For pink meat, roast for about 20 minutes per 500 g (1 lb 2 oz), with 15 minutes extra at the end. For well-cooked lamb, cook for 25 minutes per 500 g (1 lb 2 oz) with an extra 25 minutes at the end.
* If the skin and fat are not browned or crisp enough, grill them for a few seconds. A light covering of fat will baste the meat as it cooks, but serve on hot plates as lamb fat congeals quickly.

ROAST LAMB

SERVES 4

INGREDIENTS

- 2 rosemary sprigs
- 3 garlic cloves
- 75 g (2½ oz) pancetta
- 2 kg (4 lb 8 oz) leg of lamb, shank bone cut off just above the joint, trimmed of excess fat and tied (page 160)
- 1 large onion
- 125 ml (4 fl oz/½ cup) olive oil
- 375 ml (13 fl oz/1½ cups) dry white wine

METHOD

1 Preheat the oven to 230°C (450°F/Gas 8). Strip the leaves off the rosemary sprigs and chop them with the garlic and pancetta until fine and paste-like (a food processor works well for this). Season with salt and plenty of pepper.

2 With the point of a sharp knife, make incisions about 1 cm (½ inch) deep all over the lamb. Rub the rosemary filling over the surface of the lamb, pushing it into the incisions.

3 Cut the onion into 4 thick slices and put them in the centre of a roasting tin. Place the lamb on top and gently pour the olive oil over it. Roast for 15 minutes. Reduce the temperature to 180°C (350°F/Gas 4) and pour in 250 ml (9 fl oz/1 cup) of the wine. Roast for 1½ hours for medium-rare, or longer if you prefer. Baste a couple of times and add a little water if the juices start to burn in the tin. Transfer the lamb to a carving platter and leave to rest for 10 minutes.

4 Remove the onion (if it isn't burnt, serve it with the meat) and spoon off the excess fat from the tin. Place over high heat on the stovetop, pour in the remaining wine and cook for 3–4 minutes, or until the sauce reduces and slightly thickens. Taste for seasoning. Slice the lamb and serve with the sauce spooned over the top.

MINTED RACKS OF LAMB

SERVES 4

INGREDIENTS

- 4 x 4-cutlet racks of lamb
- 300 g (10½ oz/1 cup) mint jelly
- 2 tablespoons white wine
- 3 tablespoons snipped chives

METHOD

1 Preheat the oven to 200°C (400°F/Gas 6). Trim the lamb, leaving a thin layer of fat, and clean any meat or sinew from the ends of the bones with a small sharp knife. Cover the bones with foil. Place on a rack in a roasting tin.

2 Mix the mint jelly and white wine together in a saucepan over high heat. Bring to the boil and boil for 4 minutes, or until the mixture is reduced and thickened. Cool slightly, add the chives, then brush over the racks of lamb.

3 Bake the lamb for 15–20 minutes for rare, or 35 minutes if you prefer medium-rare, brushing with glaze every 10 minutes. Remove the foil and leave the lamb to stand for 5 minutes before carving to serve.

RACK OF LAMB WITH HERB CRUST

SERVES 4

INGREDIENTS

- 2 x 6-cutlet racks of lamb, French-trimmed
- 1 tablespoon oil
- 80 g (2¾ oz/1 cup) fresh breadcrumbs
- 3 garlic cloves, crushed
- 3 tablespoons finely chopped parsley
- 2 teaspoons thyme
- ½ teaspoon finely grated lemon zest
- 60 g (2¼ oz) butter, softened
- 250 ml (9 fl oz/1 cup) beef stock (page 11)
- 1 garlic clove, extra, finely chopped
- 1 thyme sprig

METHOD

1. Preheat the oven to 250°C (500°F/Gas 9). Score the fat on the lamb in a diamond pattern. Rub with a little oil and season.
2. Heat the oil in a frying pan over high heat, add the lamb racks and brown for 4–5 minutes. Remove and set aside but do not wash the pan.
3. Mix together the breadcrumbs, garlic, parsley, thyme and lemon zest. Season, then mix in the butter to form a paste.
4. Firmly press a layer of breadcrumb mixture over the fat on the lamb racks, leaving the bones and base clean. Transfer to a roasting tin and cook for 12 minutes for medium-rare. Leave the lamb to rest on a plate while you make the jus.
5. To make the jus, add the beef stock, extra garlic and thyme sprig to the juices in the roasting tin, scraping the bits from the bottom of the tin. Pour this back into the original frying pan and simmer over high heat for 5–8 minutes, or until the sauce has reduced. Strain and serve with the lamb.

LAMB CUTLETS WITH ONION MARMALADE

SERVES 4

INGREDIENTS

- 40 g (1½ oz) butter
- 80 ml (2½ fl oz/⅓ cup) olive oil
- 4 onions, thinly sliced
- 2 teaspoons soft brown sugar
- 2 teaspoons thyme
- 2 tablespoons finely chopped parsley
- 12 lamb cutlets, French-trimmed (see Note)
- 2 tablespoons lemon juice

METHOD

1. Heat the butter and half the oil in a saucepan. Add the onion, sugar and thyme and stir well. Reduce the heat to low, cover the saucepan and cook the onion, stirring occasionally for 30–35 minutes, or until the onion is very soft and golden. Season well with salt and pepper, stir the parsley through and keep the onion warm over very low heat.
2. Heat the remaining oil in a large frying pan and, when hot, add the cutlets in a single layer. Fry for 2 minutes on each side, or until the lamb is browned on the outside but still feels springy when you press it. Add the lemon juice and season well.
3. Put a small pile of the onion marmalade on each plate and serve with the cutlets.

NOTE: To French-trim a piece of meat means to trim the meat and sinew away from the bones, leaving the bone clean. Ask your butcher to do this for you or you can buy the cutlets already trimmed.

SPICY LAMB CASSEROLE

SERVES 4

INGREDIENTS

- 60 ml (2 fl oz/¼ cup) olive oil
- 1.25 kg (2 lb 12 oz) lamb leg or shoulder, cut into 4 cm (1½ inch) cubes
- 1 small onion, finely chopped
- 1 celery stalk, finely chopped
- 3 garlic cloves, crushed
- 125 ml (4 fl oz/½ cup) dry Marsala
- ¾ teaspoon chilli flakes
- 1 tablespoon crushed juniper berries
- 2 tablespoons tomato paste (concentrated purée)
- 250 ml (9 fl oz/1 cup) chicken stock (page 11)
- 1 rosemary sprig
- 12 small onions
- 2 potatoes, cut into cubes
- 2 tablespoons finely chopped parsley

METHOD

1. Preheat the oven to 180°C (350°F/Gas 4).
2. Heat the olive oil in a large flameproof casserole dish. Add the lamb in batches, so that you don't overcrowd the dish, season with salt and pepper and brown lightly over high heat. Remove each batch from the casserole as it browns. Once all the lamb has been cooked and removed, add the onion, celery and garlic, reduce the heat and cook for 4–5 minutes until softened.
3. Return the lamb to the casserole. Pour in the Marsala and cook over high heat until it is dark brown and reduced by half. Add the chilli flakes and juniper berries and cook, stirring, for just 10–15 seconds. Add the tomato paste, stock, rosemary and about 250 ml (9 fl oz/1 cup) water, or just enough to cover.
4. Cover the casserole with a lid and bake in the oven for 45 minutes. Add the onions and potato and cook for another 45 minutes. Stir in the parsley just before serving.

LANCASHIRE HOTPOT

SERVES 8

INGREDIENTS

- 8 forequarter lamb chops, cut 2.5 cm (1 inch) thick
- 4 lamb kidneys, cut into quarters, cores removed
- 3 tablespoons seasoned flour, for dusting
- 50 g (1¾ oz) butter
- 4 potatoes, thinly sliced
- 2 large onions, sliced
- 2 celery stalks, chopped
- 1 large carrot, chopped
- 430 ml (15½ fl oz/1¾ cups) chicken or beef stock (page 11)
- 200 g (7 oz) button mushrooms, sliced
- 2 teaspoons chopped thyme
- 1 tablespoon worcestershire sauce

METHOD

1. Preheat the oven to 160°C (315°F/Gas 2–3). Lightly oil a large casserole dish. Toss the chops and kidneys in the flour, shaking off the excess.
2. Heat the butter in a large frying pan and quickly brown the chops, in batches, on both sides. Remove from the pan and brown the kidneys. Layer half the potato in the dish and place the chops and kidneys on top.
3. Add the onion, celery and carrot to the pan and cook until the carrot begins to brown. Layer on top of the chops and kidneys. Sprinkle the remaining flour over the base of the pan and cook, stirring, until brown. Stir in the stock slowly, stirring until the sauce boils and thickens.
4. Add the mushrooms, thyme and worcestershire sauce and season to taste. Reduce the heat and simmer for 10 minutes. Pour into the dish.
5. Layer the remaining potato over the top, to cover the meat and vegetables. Transfer to the oven and bake, covered, for 1¼ hours. Uncover and cook for a further 30 minutes, or until the potato is brown and cooked through.

IRISH STEW

This plain but very tasty, hearty stew was traditionally made with mutton (and the cheapest cuts of mutton at that) in northern England and Ireland.

SERVES 4

INGREDIENTS

1 kg (2 lb 4 oz) lamb neck chops
seasoned flour, for dusting
4 onions, sliced
2 kg (4 lb 8 oz) potatoes, quartered
4 large carrots, chopped
2 tablespoons chopped parsley

METHOD

1. Preheat the oven to 160°C (315°F/Gas 2–3). Trim the lamb chops of fat and sinew. Toss the chops in the flour, shaking off the excess.
2. Place the chops in a 2 litre (8 cup) casserole dish with the onion and 500 ml (17 fl oz/ 2 cups) water. Bake, covered, for 1½ hours.
3. Add the potato and carrot and bake, covered, for 1 hour, or until the meat and vegetables are tender. Stir in the parsley before serving.

SHEPHERD'S PIE

SERVES 6

INGREDIENTS

- 25 g (1 oz) butter
- 2 onions, finely chopped
- 2 tablespoons seasoned flour
- ½ teaspoon dry mustard
- 375 ml (13 fl oz/1½ cups) chicken stock (page 11)
- 750 g (1 lb 10 oz) lean cooked roast lamb, trimmed of fat and finely chopped
- 2 tablespoons worcestershire sauce
- 4 large potatoes
- 125 ml (4 fl oz/½ cup) hot milk
- 30 g (1 oz) butter, extra

METHOD

1. Lightly grease a 2 litre (8 cup) casserole dish. Preheat the oven to 210°C (415°F/Gas 6–7).
2. Melt the butter in a large frying pan over medium heat, add the onion and stir for 5–10 minutes, or until golden. Add the flour and mustard to the pan and cook for 1 minute, or until pale and foaming. Gradually stir in the stock and then keep stirring until the sauce boils and thickens. Reduce the heat and simmer for 2 minutes. Add the lamb and worcestershire sauce to the pan and stir. Season to taste. Remove from the heat and spoon into the casserole dish.
3. Meanwhile, steam or boil the potatoes for 10–15 minutes, or until just tender. Drain and mash well with the milk and extra butter. Season and mix until smooth and creamy. Spread evenly over the meat and rough up the surface with a fork. Bake for 40–45 minutes, or until the meat is heated through and the topping is golden.

NAVARIN A LA PRINTANIERE

A navarin is a hearty stew made of mutton or lamb with potatoes and other root vegetables, traditionally turnips. (The name is thought to come from the French for turnip: 'navet'.) Navarin à la printanière is traditionally made to welcome spring and the new crop of young vegetables. Of course, navarins can be made all year round, using older winter root vegetables instead.

SERVES 6

INGREDIENTS

- 1 kg (2 lb 4 oz) lean lamb shoulder
- 30 g (1 oz) butter
- 1 onion, chopped
- 1 garlic clove, crushed
- 1 tablespoon seasoned flour
- 500 ml (17 fl oz/2 cups) beef stock (page 11)
- 1 bouquet garni
- 18 baby carrots
- 8 large-bulb spring onions (scallions)
- 200 g (7 oz) baby turnips
- 175 g (6 oz) small potatoes
- 150 g (5½ oz) fresh or frozen peas

METHOD

1. Trim the lamb of any fat and sinew and then cut it into bite-sized pieces. Heat the butter over high heat in a large flameproof casserole dish. Brown the lamb in batches, then remove from the casserole.
2. Add the onion to the casserole and cook, stirring occasionally, over medium heat for 3 minutes, or until softened but not browned. Add the garlic and cook for a further minute, or until aromatic.
3. Return the meat and any juices to the casserole and sprinkle with the flour. Stir over high heat until the meat is well coated and the liquid is bubbling, then gradually stir in the stock. Add the bouquet garni and bring to the boil. Reduce the heat to low, cover the casserole and leave to simmer for 1¼ hours.
4. Trim the carrots, leaving a little bit of green stalk, and do the same with the spring onions and baby turnips. Cut the potatoes in half if they are large (you want all the vegetables to be about the same size so they cook evenly).
5. Add the vegetables to the casserole dish, bring to the boil and simmer, covered, for 15 minutes, or until the vegetables are tender. (If you are using frozen peas, add them right at the end so they just heat through.) Season with plenty of salt and pepper before serving.

LAMB AND HUMMUS WRAPS

SERVES 4

INGREDIENTS

500 g (1 lb 2 oz) minced (ground) lamb
1 onion, finely chopped
2–3 garlic cloves, chopped
1 tablespoon za'atar, plus extra for sprinkling
1 large handful coriander (cilantro)
olive oil
4 large flatbreads, to serve
hummus (page 432), to serve
75 g (2½ oz) mixed salad leaves

METHOD

1 Put the lamb, onion, garlic, za'atar and coriander leaves in a food processor and blend until smooth and pasty. Put into a bowl, cover and refrigerate for 1 hour.
2 With wet hands, form the lamb mixture into eight 12 cm (4½ inch) elongated sausage shapes. Preheat a barbecue hotplate or grill and brush with oil. Coat the lamb sausages with oil and cook for 8 minutes, turning occasionally, until cooked through.
3 Lightly brush one side of the breads with oil and sprinkle with the za'atar. Put the unoiled side on the hotplate and heat through for 2–3 minutes.
4 To serve, place the breads on serving plates and generously spread over the hummus. Top each with two of the lamb sausages and some salad leaves and roll up firmly.

LAMB SOUVLAKI

SERVES 4

INGREDIENTS

1 kg (2 lb 4 oz) lamb leg or shoulder, cut into 2 cm (¾ inch) cubes
60 ml (2 fl oz/¼ cup) olive oil
2 teaspoons finely grated lemon zest
80 ml (2½ fl oz/⅓ cup) lemon juice
125 ml (4 fl oz/½ cup) dry white wine
2 teaspoons dried oregano
2 large garlic cloves, finely chopped
2 bay leaves
250 g (9 oz/1 cup) Greek-style yoghurt
2 garlic cloves, extra, crushed

METHOD

1 Soak eight wooden skewers in water to prevent them burning, or use metal skewers.
2 Put the cubed lamb in a non-metallic bowl with 2 tablespoons of the oil, the lemon zest and juice, wine, oregano, garlic, bay leaves and some black pepper. Toss, then cover and refrigerate overnight.
3 Put the yoghurt and extra garlic in a bowl, mix well and leave for 30 minutes.
4 Drain the lamb and thread it onto the skewers. Heat a barbecue grill or chargrill pan and cook the lamb skewers, brushing with the remaining oil, for 7–8 minutes, or until done to your liking. Serve with the yoghurt.

MOUSSAKA

SERVES 6

INGREDIENTS

- 2 large tomatoes
- 1.5 kg (3 lb 5 oz) eggplant (aubergine), cut into 5 mm (¼ inch) slices
- 125 ml (4 fl oz/½ cup) olive oil
- 2 onions, finely chopped
- 2 large garlic cloves, crushed
- ½ teaspoon ground allspice
- 1 teaspoon ground cinnamon
- 750 g (1 lb 10 oz) minced (ground) lamb
- 2 tablespoons tomato paste (concentrated purée)
- 125 ml (4 fl oz/½ cup) dry white wine
- 3 tablespoons chopped parsley

CHEESE SAUCE

- 60 g (2¼ oz) butter
- 60 g (2¼ oz/½ cup) plain (all-purpose) flour
- 625 ml (21 fl oz/2½ cups) milk
- pinch of ground nutmeg
- 35 g (1¼ oz/⅓ cup) grated kefalotyri or parmesan cheese
- 2 eggs, lightly beaten

METHOD

1. Score a cross in the base of each tomato. Put in a heatproof bowl and cover with boiling water. Leave for 30 seconds, then transfer to cold water and peel the skin away from the cross. Cut each tomato in half, scoop out the seeds and finely chop the flesh. Lay the eggplant on a tray, sprinkle with salt and leave for 30 minutes. Rinse under water and pat dry.
2. Heat 2 tablespoons of the olive oil in a frying pan, add the eggplant in batches and cook for 1–2 minutes each side, or until golden and soft. Add a little more oil when needed.
3. Heat 1 tablespoon of the olive oil in a large saucepan, add the onion and cook over medium heat for 5 minutes. Add the garlic, allspice and cinnamon and cook for 30 seconds. Add the lamb and cook for 5 minutes, or until browned, breaking up any lumps with the back of a spoon. Add the tomatoes, tomato paste and wine, and simmer over low heat for 30 minutes, or until the liquid has evaporated. Stir in the chopped parsley and season to taste. Preheat the oven to 180°C (350°F/Gas 4).
4. To make the cheese sauce, melt the butter in a saucepan over low heat. Stir in the flour and cook for 1 minute, or until pale and foaming. Gradually stir in the milk and nutmeg and then stir constantly until the sauce boils and thickens. Reduce the heat and simmer for 2 minutes. Stir in 1 tablespoon of the cheese.
5. Line the base of a 25 x 30 cm (10 x 12 inch) dish with a third of the eggplant. Spoon half the meat sauce over it and cover with another layer of eggplant. Spoon the remaining meat sauce over the top and cover with the remaining eggplant. Stir the egg into the cheese sauce. Spread the sauce over the top of the eggplant and sprinkle with the remaining cheese. Bake for 1 hour. Leave for 10 minutes before slicing. Serve with a green salad.

LAMB KOFTA

SERVES 4

INGREDIENTS

- 1 kg (2 lb 4 oz) minced (ground) lamb
- 1 onion, finely chopped
- 2 garlic cloves, finely chopped
- 2 tablespoons chopped parsley
- 2 tablespoons chopped coriander (cilantro)
- 1 teaspoon paprika
- ½ teaspoon each of ground allspice, ground ginger, ground cardamom, ground cumin and cayenne pepper

SAUCE

- 2 tablespoons olive oil
- 1 onion, finely chopped
- 2 garlic cloves, finely chopped
- 2 teaspoons ground cumin
- ½ teaspoon ground cinnamon
- 1 teaspoon paprika
- 2 x 400 g (14 oz) tins chopped tomatoes
- 2 teaspoons harissa (recipe below)
- 4 tablespoons chopped coriander (cilantro)

METHOD

1. Preheat the oven to 180°C (350°F/Gas 4). Lightly grease two baking trays. Place the lamb, onion, garlic, herbs and spices in a bowl and mix well. Season with salt and pepper. Roll tablespoons of mixture into balls and place on the trays. Bake for 20 minutes, or until browned.
2. Meanwhile, to make the sauce, heat the oil in a large saucepan, add the onion and cook over medium heat for 5 minutes, or until soft. Add the garlic, cumin, cinnamon and paprika, and cook for 1 minute, or until fragrant. Stir in the tomato and harissa, and bring to the boil. Reduce the heat and simmer for 20 minutes.
3. Add the meatballs to the sauce and simmer for 10 minutes, or until the meatballs are cooked. Stir in the coriander, season and serve.

HARISSA

A North African condiment of chillies and spices, harissa is used just about anywhere aromatic fiery heat and red colour is required. It can be bought ready-made, but to make your own, soak 30 g (1 oz) dried red chillies in hot water until soft. Chop roughly, then grind with a mortar and pestle with 2 garlic cloves, 1 teaspoon each caraway and coriander seeds, ½ teaspoon cumin seeds, 1 tablespoon chopped coriander (cilantro), 3 tablespoons water, 2 tablespoons olive oil and a pinch of salt. Store in a sterilised jar.

KIBBEH

MAKES 15

INGREDIENTS

240 g (8½ oz/1⅓ cups) fine burghul (bulgur)
150 g (5½ oz) lean lamb, chopped
1 onion, grated
2 tablespoons plain (all-purpose) flour
1 teaspoon ground allspice

FILLING

2 teaspoons olive oil
1 small onion, finely chopped
100 g (3½ oz) minced (ground) lean lamb
½ teaspoon ground allspice
½ teaspoon ground cinnamon
80 ml (2½ fl oz/⅓ cup) beef stock (page 11)
2 tablespoons pine nuts, roughly chopped
2 tablespoons chopped mint
oil, for deep-frying

METHOD

1 Cover the burghul with boiling water and leave for 5 minutes. Drain in a colander, pressing well to remove the water. Spread on paper towels to absorb any moisture.
2 Process the burghul, lamb, onion, flour and allspice until a fine paste forms. Season well, then refrigerate for 1 hour.
3 To make the filling, heat the olive oil in a frying pan, add the onion and cook over low heat for 3 minutes, or until soft. Add the lamb, allspice and cinnamon and cook, stirring, over high heat for 3 minutes. Add the stock and cook, partially covered, over low heat for 6 minutes, or until the lamb is soft. Stir in the pine nuts and mint. Season, then transfer to a bowl and cool.
4 Shape 2 tablespoons of the burghul mixture at a time into a sausage 6 cm (2½ inches) long. Dip your hands in cold water and, with your index finger, make a long hole through the centre of each sausage and gently work your finger around to make a cavity for the filling. Fill each with 2 teaspoons of the filling and seal, moulding it into a torpedo shape. Smooth over any cracks with your fingers. Place on a foil-lined tray and refrigerate, uncovered, for 1 hour.
5 Fill a deep saucepan one-third full of oil. Heat the oil to 180°C (350°F), or until a cube of bread dropped into the oils turns golden in 15 seconds. Deep-fry the kibbeh in batches for 2–3 minutes, until browned. Drain on paper towels. Serve hot.

LAMB KIDNEYS WITH FENNEL

SERVES 4

INGREDIENTS

20 lamb kidneys, cut in half
90 ml (3 fl oz) vinegar
2 tablespoons olive oil
40 g (1½ oz) butter
2 large onions, thinly sliced
1 small fennel bulb, thinly sliced
3 tablespoons finely chopped parsley
4 slices day-old ciabatta, crusts removed
1 garlic clove, halved

METHOD

1 Put the kidneys in a glass bowl, cover with cold water, add the vinegar and leave for 30 minutes.
2 Meanwhile, heat the olive oil and butter in a large frying pan. Add the onion and fennel, season well and cook over very low heat without browning for 20–25 minutes. Transfer to a bowl.
3 Core the kidneys and thinly slice. Add to a dry frying pan and cook over medium heat until they release their red liquid and turn brown. Drain in a colander, rinse under cold water and drain again.
4 Wipe the pan dry, then add the cooked onion, fennel and kidneys. Add the parsley and season well. Cook over medium–high heat, stirring often, for 3–4 minutes, or until the kidneys brown.
5 Toast the bread and rub with the cut side of the garlic. Serve with the kidneys.

LAMB TAGINE WITH QUINCE

SERVES 4–6

INGREDIENTS

- 1.5 kg (3 lb 5 oz) lamb shoulder, cut into 3 cm (1¼ inch) pieces
- 2 large onions, diced
- ½ teaspoon ground ginger
- ½ teaspoon cayenne pepper
- ¼ teaspoon crushed saffron threads
- 1 teaspoon ground coriander
- 1 cinnamon stick
- 2 handfuls coriander (cilantro), chopped
- 40 g (1½ oz) butter
- 500 g (1 lb 2 oz) quinces, peeled, cored and quartered
- 100 g (3½ oz) dried apricots

METHOD

1. Place the lamb in a flameproof casserole dish or tagine. Add half the onion, the ginger, cayenne pepper, saffron, ground coriander, cinnamon stick, chopped coriander and some salt and pepper. Cover with cold water and bring to the boil. Reduce the heat and simmer, partly covered, for 1 hour.
2. Meanwhile, melt the butter in a heavy-based frying pan and cook the remaining onion and the quinces for 15 minutes over medium heat, or until lightly golden.
3. Add the quinces and apricots to the casserole and cook for another 30 minutes, until the lamb is tender. Check the seasoning before serving with couscous or rice.

BRAISED LAMB SHANKS IN RICH TOMATO SAUCE

SERVES 4

INGREDIENTS

- 2 tablespoons olive oil
- 1 large red onion, sliced
- 4 French-trimmed lamb shanks (about 250 g/9 oz each)
- 2 garlic cloves, crushed
- 400 g (14 oz) tin chopped tomatoes
- 125 ml (4 fl oz/½ cup) red wine
- 2 teaspoons chopped rosemary
- 150 g (5½ oz/1 cup) instant polenta
- 50 g (1¾ oz) butter
- 50 g (1¾ oz/½ cup) grated parmesan cheese

METHOD

1. Preheat the oven to 160°C (315°F/Gas 2–3). Heat the oil in a 4 litre (16 cup) flameproof casserole dish over medium heat and sauté the onion for 3–4 minutes, or until soft and transparent. Add the lamb shanks and cook for 2–3 minutes, or until lightly browned. Add the garlic, tomato and wine, bring to the boil and cook for 3–4 minutes. Stir in the rosemary. Season with ¼ teaspoon each of salt and pepper.
2. Cover, transfer to the oven and cook for 2 hours. Remove the lid, return to the oven and simmer for a further 15 minutes, or until the lamb just starts to fall off the bone. Check often that the sauce is not too dry, adding water if needed.
3. About 20 minutes before serving, bring 1 litre (35 fl oz/4 cups) water to the boil in a saucepan. Add the polenta in a thin stream, whisking continuously, then reduce the heat to very low. Simmer for 8–10 minutes, or until thick and coming away from the side of the saucepan. Stir in the butter and parmesan. To serve, spoon the polenta onto serving plates, top with the shanks and a little sauce from the casserole.

MONGOLIAN LAMB

SERVES 4–6

INGREDIENTS

- 2 garlic cloves, crushed
- 2 teaspoons finely grated ginger
- 60 ml (2 fl oz/¼ cup) Chinese rice wine
- 60 ml (2 fl oz/¼ cup) soy sauce
- 2 tablespoons hoisin sauce
- 1 teaspoon sesame oil
- 1 kg (2 lb 4 oz) lamb loin fillets, thinly sliced
- 80 ml (2½ fl oz/⅓ cup) peanut oil
- 6 spring onions (scallions), chopped
- 2 teaspoons chilli sauce
- 1½ tablespoons hoisin sauce, extra

METHOD

1. Combine the garlic, ginger, rice wine, soy sauce, hoisin sauce and sesame oil in a large non-metallic bowl. Add the lamb and toss well to coat in the marinade. Cover with plastic wrap and marinate in the fridge overnight.
2. Heat a wok over high heat, add 1 tablespoon of the peanut oil and swirl to coat. Stir-fry the spring onion for 1 minute, or until lightly golden. Remove, leaving the oil in the wok.
3. Lift the lamb out of the marinade with tongs, keeping the marinade.
4. Add the meat to the wok in four batches and stir-fry for 1–2 minutes, or until browned but not completely cooked through, adding more oil as needed. Make sure the wok is very hot before cooking each batch. Return all the meat to the wok and the spring onion and stir-fry for 1 minute, or until the meat is cooked through.
5. Remove the meat and spring onion from the wok with a slotted spoon, keeping the liquid in the wok. Add the saved marinade, chilli sauce and extra hoisin sauce to the wok, then bring to the boil and cook for 3–4 minutes, or until the sauce thickens and becomes slightly syrupy. Spoon over the lamb, toss together well and serve with steamed rice.

LAMB SAAG

SERVES 4–6

INGREDIENTS

- 2 teaspoons coriander seeds
- 1½ teaspoons cumin seeds
- 60 ml (2 fl oz/¼ cup) oil
- 1 kg (2 lb 4 oz) lamb leg or shoulder, cut into 2.5 cm (1 inch) cubes
- 4 onions, finely chopped
- 6 cloves
- 6 cardamom pods
- 1 cinnamon stick
- 10 black peppercorns
- 4 Indian bay (cassia) leaves
- 3 teaspoons garam masala
- ¼ teaspoon ground turmeric
- 1 teaspoon paprika
- 7 cm (2¾ inch) piece ginger, grated
- 4 garlic cloves, crushed
- 185 g (6½ oz/¾ cup) Greek-style yoghurt
- 450 g (1 lb) spinach or amaranth leaves, roughly chopped

METHOD

1. Dry-fry the coriander and cumin seeds in a frying pan over medium heat for 2–3 minutes, or until fragrant. Allow to cool. Using a mortar with a pestle, or a spice grinder, crush to a powder.
2. Heat the oil in a large heavy-based saucepan or flameproof casserole dish over low heat and fry a few pieces of meat at a time until browned. Remove from the pan. Add more oil to the pan, if needed, and fry the onion, cloves, cardamom pods, cinnamon stick, peppercorns and bay leaves until the onion is lightly browned. Add the crushed cumin and coriander, the garam masala, turmeric and paprika and fry for 30 seconds.
3. Add the meat, ginger, garlic, yoghurt and 425 ml (15 fl oz) water and bring to the boil. Reduce the heat to low. Cover and simmer for 1½–2 hours, or until the meat is very tender. At this stage, most of the water should have evaporated. If it hasn't, remove the lid, increase the heat and cook until the moisture has evaporated.
4. Cook the spinach briefly in a little simmering water until it is just wilted, then refresh in cold water. Drain thoroughly, then finely chop. Squeeze out any extra water in the spinach. Add the spinach to the lamb and cook for 3 minutes, or until the spinach and lamb are well mixed and any extra liquid has evaporated.

AMARANTH

Amaranth is a leafy vegetable cultivated for both its leaves and seeds. There are many types but the ones grown for eating are commonly known as green and red amaranth. The leaves have a slightly pungent flavour and are used in the same way as spinach, either raw in salads, in stir-fries and curries, or as an ingredient in soups. Amaranth is best used on the day of purchase as the leaves become limp quickly. Amaranth seeds, which are very high in protein, are used in soups and cereals, or ground to make a gluten-free flour.

ROGAN JOSH

SERVES 4–6

INGREDIENTS

- 8 garlic cloves, crushed
- 3 teaspoons grated ginger
- 2 teaspoons each of ground coriander, cumin and paprika
- 1 teaspoon chilli powder
- 1 kg (2 lb 4 oz) lamb leg or shoulder, cut into 3 cm (1¼ inch) cubes
- 3 tablespoons oil or ghee (page 120)
- 1 onion, finely chopped
- 6 cardamom pods, bruised
- 4 cloves
- 2 Indian bay (cassia) leaves
- 1 cinnamon stick
- 185 g (6½ oz/¾ cup) Greek-style yoghurt
- 4 saffron threads, mixed with 2 tablespoons milk
- ¼ teaspoon garam masala

METHOD

1. Mix the garlic, ginger, coriander, cumin, paprika and chilli powder in a large bowl. Stir in the meat. Cover and marinate for at least 2 hours, or overnight, in the fridge.
2. Heat the oil in a flameproof casserole dish over low heat. Cook the onion for 10 minutes, or until lightly browned. Remove from the dish.
3. Add the cardamom pods, cloves, bay leaves and cinnamon stick and fry for 1 minute. Increase the heat, add the meat and onion, then fry for 2 minutes. Stir and reduce the heat to low, cover and cook for 15 minutes. Uncover and fry for 3–5 minutes until the meat is quite dry.
4. Add 100 ml (3½ fl oz) water, cover and cook for 5–7 minutes until the water has evaporated. Fry for another 1–2 minutes, then add 250 ml (9 fl oz/1 cup) water. Cover and simmer gently for 40–50 minutes, or until the meat is tender and the sauce has reduced. Stir in the yoghurt, then the saffron and milk. Season with salt and sprinkle with the garam masala.

LAMB KORMA

SERVES 4–6

INGREDIENTS

- 1 onion, chopped, plus 1 sliced
- 2 teaspoons grated ginger
- 4 garlic cloves
- 2 teaspoons ground coriander
- 2 teaspoons ground cumin
- 1 teaspoon cardamom seeds
- ¼ teaspoon cloves
- ¼ teaspoon ground cinnamon
- 3 long green chillies, seeded, chopped
- 1 kg (2 lb 4 oz) lamb leg or shoulder, cut into 3 cm (1¼ inch) cubes
- 2 tablespoons oil or ghee (page 120)
- 2½ tablespoons tomato paste (concentrated purée)
- 125 g (4½ oz/½ cup) Greek-style yoghurt
- 125 ml (4 fl oz/½ cup) coconut cream
- 50 g (1¾ oz/½ cup) ground almonds
- toasted slivered almonds, to serve

METHOD

1. Put the chopped onion, ginger, garlic, coriander, cumin, cardamom seeds, cloves, cinnamon, chilli and ½ teaspoon salt in a food processor, or in a mortar with a pestle, and process or pound to a smooth paste.
2. Put the lamb in a bowl. Add the spice paste to the lamb and mix well. Marinate for 1 hour.
3. Heat the oil in a large saucepan over low heat, add the sliced onion and cook, stirring, for 7 minutes, or until the onion is soft. Increase the heat to medium–high and add the lamb mixture and cook, stirring constantly, for 8–10 minutes, or until the lamb changes colour.
4. Stir in the tomato paste, yoghurt, coconut cream and ground almonds. Reduce the heat and simmer, covered, stirring occasionally, for 1 hour, or until the meat is very tender. Add a little water if the mixture becomes too dry. Season well, and serve garnished with the slivered almonds.

••GAME••

Game are wild animals and birds that are hunted for food, traditionally during particular 'seasons'. When a meat is described as 'gamey', it is usually dark, lean and strong-tasting. The most popular small game animal is rabbit, with venison the favourite large game meat. The traditional venison casserole (below) features cloves, juniper and allspice — all robust flavourings in their own right to balance the strongly flavoured meat.

VENISON CASSEROLE

SERVES 4

INGREDIENTS

- 1 rosemary sprig
- 1 large onion
- 1 garlic clove
- 85 g (3 oz) prosciutto
- 100 g (3½ oz) butter
- 1 kg (2 lb 4 oz) venison, cut into large cubes
- 1 litre (35 fl oz/4 cups) beef stock (page 11)
- 75 ml (2¼ fl oz) red wine vinegar
- 100 ml (3½ fl oz) robust red wine
- 2 cloves
- 4 juniper berries
- pinch of allspice
- 1 bay leaf
- 3 tablespoons plain (all-purpose) flour
- 2 tablespoons dry Marsala or brandy
- 1½ teaspoons finely grated lemon zest
- 1½ tablespoons finely chopped parsley

METHOD

1. Strip the leaves off the rosemary sprig and chop them finely with the onion, garlic and prosciutto. Heat half the butter in a large heavy-based saucepan with a lid. Add the chopped onion mixture and soften over low heat for 5 minutes. Season with pepper.
2. Increase the heat, add the venison and cook for 10 minutes, or until brown on all sides.
3. Meanwhile, put the stock in another saucepan and bring to the boil, then reduce the heat and keep at a low simmer.
4. Increase the heat under the venison, add the vinegar and cook until the liquid becomes thick and syrupy. Pour in the red wine. When that becomes syrupy, stir in half of the simmering stock. Add the cloves, juniper berries, allspice and bay leaf and cover the pan. Simmer for 1 hour, stirring once or twice and adding a little hot water if necessary to maintain the level.
5. Meanwhile, melt the remaining butter in a saucepan. Stir in the flour and cook over moderately low heat for 1 minute. Slowly stir in the remaining stock and cook until the sauce thickens slightly.
6. Stir the sauce into the venison casserole, then add the Marsala. Uncover the pan and simmer for a further 20 minutes. Taste for salt and pepper. Mix together the lemon zest and parsley and sprinkle over the top before serving.

RABBIT FRICASSEE

A fricassée is a dish of white meat (usually chicken, veal or rabbit) in a velouté sauce of egg yolks and cream. The name comes from the old French word, *fricasser*, 'to fry'.

SERVES 4

INGREDIENTS

- 60 g (2¼ oz) clarified butter (page 120)
- 1.5 kg (3 lb 5 oz) rabbit pieces
- 200 g (7 oz) button mushrooms
- 80 ml (2½ fl oz/⅓ cup) white wine
- 170 ml (5½ fl oz/⅔ cup) chicken stock (page 11)
- 1 bouquet garni
- 80 ml (2½ fl oz/⅓ cup) oil
- leaves from a small bunch of sage
- 125 ml (4 fl oz/½ cup) thick (double) cream
- 2 egg yolks

METHOD

1. Heat half the butter in a large frying pan, season the rabbit and brown in batches, turning once. Remove from the pan. Add the remaining butter to the pan and brown the mushrooms.
2. Put the rabbit back into the pan with the mushrooms. Add the wine and boil for 2 minutes, then add the stock and bouquet garni. Cover tightly and simmer over low heat for 40 minutes.
3. Meanwhile, heat the oil in a small saucepan. Drop the sage leaves, a few at a time, into the hot oil. They will immediately start to bubble around the edges. Cook for 30 seconds, or until bright green and crispy, then drain on paper towels and sprinkle with salt.
4. Lift the rabbit and mushrooms out of the pan and keep warm. Discard the bouquet garni. Remove the pan from the heat, mix the cream with the egg yolks and stir quickly into the stock. Return to very low heat and cook, stirring, for 5 minutes to thicken slightly (don't boil or the eggs will scramble). Season and pour over the rabbit. Garnish with the sage leaves.

RABBIT CASSEROLE WITH MUSTARD SAUCE

SERVES 4–6

INGREDIENTS

- 2 tablespoons olive oil
- 1.5 kg (3 lb 5 oz) rabbit pieces
- 2 onions, sliced
- 4 slices bacon, cut into 3 cm (1¼ inch) pieces
- 2 tablespoons plain (all-purpose) flour
- 375 ml (13 fl oz/1½ cups) chicken stock (page 11)
- 125 ml (4 fl oz/½ cup) dry white wine
- 1 teaspoon thyme
- 125 ml (4 fl oz/½ cup) cream
- 2 tablespoons dijon mustard
- thyme sprigs, to garnish

METHOD

1. Preheat the oven to 180°C (350°F/Gas 4). Heat half the oil in a 2.5 litre (10 cup) flameproof casserole dish. Brown the rabbit pieces in batches, adding more oil to the dish when necessary, then remove from the dish.
2. Add the onion and bacon to the dish and cook, stirring, for 5 minutes, or until lightly browned. Sprinkle with the flour and stir well with a wooden spoon to scrape everything from the bottom of the dish. Add the stock and wine and stir until the sauce comes to the boil. Return the rabbit to the dish and add the thyme.
3. Cover and cook for 1¼–1½ hours, or until the rabbit is tender and the sauce has thickened. Stir in the combined cream and mustard. Garnish with thyme sprigs.

CHAPTER FIVE
SEAFOOD

••SASHIMI AND SUSHI••

These traditional Japanese dishes, made with only the very freshest of ingredients, are now popular throughout the world. As with all Japanese cooking, the food is beautifully and carefully presented, to appeal to the eye as well as the taste buds.

SASHIMI AND SUSHI — WHAT'S THE DIFFERENCE?

Sashimi is a Japanese delicacy made using the finest freshest fish, thinly sliced and eaten raw. It is usually served as a first course, before the palate is tainted by other foods and flavours.

The preparation of sashimi is the reserve of highly skilled chefs who train for years. Various fish and shellfish are used to make sashimi, all served raw, with the exception of octopus. So as not to overpower the delicate flavour and texture of the fish, sashimi is served with wasabi and a light dipping sauce, and often accompanied with a simple garnish of pickled ginger, finely grated daikon or shredded cucumber. Tuna (maguro) is probably the most popular fish used for sashimi, but yellowtail (hamachi), mackerel (saba), sea bream (tai), squid (ika), octopus (tako), prawns (ebi) and salmon (sake) are all used.

If buying fish for sashimi, find a supplier who sells sashimi-grade fish.

Sushi consists of sushi rice (rice prepared with sweetened vinegar), which encloses, or sits under, fillings such as sashimi, cooked prawns, vegetables, omelette or tofu. Sushi rolls, called maki sushi, are wrapped in thin sheets of seaweed (nori).

TOOLS

Very little equipment is needed to make sashimi other than a good-quality knife. Sushi, too, can be successfully made with only a few simple kitchen tools. To cook the rice, you can either use an electric rice cooker or a large, heavy-based saucepan with a lid. Once the rice is cooked, it is spread out in a tray to cool. Traditionally a fan is used to cool the rice. When the rice has cooled, the dressing is added. There are special rice paddles, usually wooden, that are designed to separate the grains without crushing them but a spatula does the same job. Lastly, you'll need a bamboo sushi mat for rolling the sushi. These are inexpensive and are sold in Asian grocery stores — there really is no substitute.

WASABI

Although often compared to horseradish, wasabi is, in fact, an unrelated herb. In Japan it grows wild near freshwater streams, but it is also cultivated widely. Although part of the plant is used as food, it is the green root that is grated and eaten with sushi and sashimi, when it is sometimes mixed with soy sauce. Most of the so-called wasabi, in powder or paste form, is actually dyed horseradish. If buying it, ask for *hon* (real) wasabi. Wasabi in tubes is the most often used for Japanese cooking and can be found in most Asian stores and large supermarkets.

MARINATED SASHIMI SALMON

SERVES 4

INGREDIENTS

MARINADE
2 tablespoons crushed green peppercorns
3 cm (1¼ inch) piece ginger, roughly chopped
2 red Asian shallots, thinly sliced
1 tablespoon soy sauce
125 ml (4 fl oz/½ cup) sake
125 ml (4 fl oz/½ cup) mirin

400 g (14 oz) piece sashimi-grade salmon, skinned and boned
Japanese soy sauce, to serve
wasabi paste, to serve
pickled ginger, to serve

METHOD

1 To make the marinade, put the peppercorns, ginger, shallots, soy sauce, sake and mirin in a blender or small processor fitted with the metal blade and process for 1 minute.
2 Slice the salmon into 3 mm (⅛ inch) slices and arrange over the base of a large, flat glass dish. Pour the marinade over the salmon, gently moving the fish around to ensure it is completely covered. Cover and refrigerate for 1½ hours.
3 Arrange the salmon on a serving platter. Serve with some soy sauce, wasabi and pickled ginger in separate dishes. Diners can mix a little wasabi into the soy sauce or smear a little wasabi onto the fish and dip into the soy sauce — don't dunk the fish or the soy sauce will overpower the delicate flavour of the raw fish. Pickled ginger will refresh the palate.

HOW TO... MAKE SUSHI RICE

The secret to making great sushi at home is the rice — get that right and you're halfway there. Sushi is made using a short-grain rice, sometimes called sticky rice. Once cooked, the rice grains stick together, making it ideal for sushi or for eating with chopsticks.

MAKES 1 QUANTITY OR 3 CUPS COOKED RICE

INGREDIENTS

210 g (7½ oz/1 cup) Japanese short-grain rice
4 cm (1½ inch) piece of kombu (kelp), wiped with a damp cloth (optional)
2 tablespoons sake or mirin (optional)

VINEGAR DRESSING
80 ml (2½ fl oz/⅓ cup) Japanese rice vinegar
1½ tablespoons caster (superfine) sugar

METHOD

1 To prepare the sushi rice, rinse the rice several times in cold water or until the water runs clear, then drain in a colander for 1 hour.
2 Put the rice in a saucepan with 375 ml (13 fl oz/ 1½ cups) cold water and, if you like, the kombu and sake or mirin. Bring to the boil, then remove the kombu. Cover with a tight-fitting lid, reduce the heat to low and simmer for 15 minutes.
3 Turn off the heat but leave the pan on the hotplate. Working quickly, remove the lid and place a clean cloth across the top (to absorb excess moisture), then put the lid on for a further 15 minutes. Alternatively, cook the rice in a rice cooker, following the manufacturer's instructions.
4 Transfer the cooked rice into a wide, shallow non-metallic container and spread it out. Combine the rice vinegar, sugar and ¼ teaspoon salt, stirring until the sugar has dissolved, then sprinkle the vinegar dressing over the warm rice. Using quick, short strokes, mix the rice and liquid together with a damp wooden rice paddle, thin wooden spoon or spatula, being careful not to mush the rice. Traditionally the rice is cooled with a hand-held fan while mixing the liquid into the rice.
5 When cooled, cover with a clean, damp tea towel. For the best results, use the rice immediately, without refrigerating it. However, if you are not making your sushi within 1–2 hours, the rice must be refrigerated or bacteria may develop.

DAIKON

A variety of white radish, daikon has a firm, crisp flesh and a mild flavour, similar to that of white turnip. Some varieties have a slight peppery taste, while others are slightly sweeter. Raw daikon can be diced and added to salads, or used like a potato or turnip and added to soups, stews or stir-fries. In Japan, grated raw daikon is formed into a small pile and is the traditional accompaniment to sashimi or tempura, and is used to make the summer version of the pungent Korean condiment kimchi. After buying, remove the green tops and store daikon wrapped in plastic in the vegetable crisper of the fridge.

NIGIRI SUSHI

MAKES 20 PIECES

INGREDIENTS

- 210 g (7½ oz/1 cup) Japanese short-grain rice
- 250 g (9 oz) sashimi-grade tuna or salmon
- lemon juice
- wasabi paste, to serve
- nori (dried seaweed), cut into strips (optional)

METHOD

1. Prepare the sushi rice (see opposite). Spread the rice out on a tray and cool to room temperature. Cover with a damp cloth.
2. Trim the tuna or salmon into a neat rectangle, removing any blood or connective tissue. Using a sharp knife, cut paper-thin slices of fish from the trimmed fillet, cleaning your knife in a bowl of water and lemon juice after cutting each slice.
3. Form 1 tablespoon of sushi rice into an oval about the same length and width as your rectangles of fish. Place a piece of fish in the open palm of one hand, then spread a small dab of wasabi over the centre of the fish. Place the rice oval on the fish and gently cup your palm to make a curve. Using the middle and index fingers of your other hand, press the rice onto the fish, firmly pushing. Turn over and repeat the shaping process, finishing with the fish on top of the rice.
4. Serve with a strip of nori tied around the centre of the rice and fish, if you like.

SUSHI

Sushi takes on many shapes and forms. One of the most popular is sushi rolls, or maki sushi, of which there are countless variations. These are made using a square of nori, spread with rice and topped with a filling such as fish, cucumber or pickles. Using a bamboo mat, the rice is rolled up into a cylinder and sliced into little rolls. This type of sushi can also be rolled by hand into a cone, in which case it is usually called temaki. Nigiri sushi consists of a pillow of rice smeared with wasabi, usually topped with a slice of raw fish or other seafood, sometimes wrapped with a thin strip of nori seaweed.

The accompaniments are just as important as the sushi itself — sharp, biting wasabi, sweet pickled ginger and salty soy sauce. Sushi can be made up to 4 hours in advance and kept on a plate, covered with plastic wrap. Keep the large rolls intact and slice just before serving. Don't refrigerate sushi or the rice will become hard.

‹ SALMON SUSHI ROLLS

MAKES 30

INGREDIENTS

210 g (7½ oz/1 cup) Japanese short-grain rice
125 g (4 oz) sashimi-grade salmon
1 small Lebanese (short) cucumber, peeled
½ small avocado
4 sheets roasted nori (dried seaweed), 20 x 18 cm (8 x 7 inches)
wasabi paste
3 tablespoons pickled ginger
Japanese soy sauce, to serve

METHOD

1 Prepare the sushi rice (page 184). Spread the rice out on a tray and cool to room temperature. Cover with a damp cloth.
2 Using a very sharp knife, cut the fish into thin strips. Cut the cucumber and avocado into thin strips 5 cm (2 inches) in length.
3 Put a nori sheet on a sushi mat, with the nori shiny side down and with the longest sides at the top and bottom. Top with a quarter of the rice, spreading it over the nori, leaving a 2 cm (¾ inch) gap at the edge furthest away from you. Spread a small amount of wasabi along the centre of the rice. Arrange a quarter of the fish, cucumber, avocado and ginger along the top of the wasabi. Starting with the end nearest to you, tightly roll up the mat and the nori, making sure you do not tuck the mat under the roll. Press along the mat to make a round roll and to seal the nori edges. Repeat with the remaining ingredients.
4 Using a sharp knife, trim the ends and cut the rolls into 2.5 cm (1 inch) rounds. Serve the sushi with small bowls of soy sauce and extra wasabi.

SUSHI HAND ROLLS

MAKES 18

INGREDIENTS

210 g (7½ oz/1 cup) Japanese short-grain rice
150 g (5½ oz) sashimi-grade fish, 2 cm (¾ inch) thick, such as tuna or salmon
9 sheets roasted nori (dried seaweed), 20 x 18 cm (8 x 7 inches)
1 small avocado
1 tablespoon lemon juice
wasabi paste
60 g (2¼ oz) pickled daikon
1 small Lebanese (short) cucumber, cut into thin strips
Japanese soy sauce, to serve
pickled ginger, to serve

METHOD

1 Prepare the sushi rice (page 184). Spread the rice out on a tray and cool to room temperature. Cover with a damp cloth.
2 Using a sharp knife, cut the fish into 12 paper-thin pieces, measuring 2 x 5 cm (¾ x 2 inches). Using scissors, cut each sheet of nori in half. Thinly slice the avocado and sprinkle with a little lemon juice.
3 Use wet hands to stop the rice sticking to your fingers as you form the sushi. Taking 1 heaped tablespoon of rice at a time, mould the rice into oval shapes — you should end up with 18 ovals.
4 Smear a little wasabi on a piece of nori. Then, holding the nori in the palm of your hand, put an oval of rice on top, then a piece of fish, avocado, daikon and cucumber. Wrap the nori around the ingredients in a cone shape, using a couple of grains of cooked rice to secure the rolls. Repeat with the remaining pieces of nori and fillings. Alternatively, put the ingredients on the table for guests to help themselves.
5 Serve with the soy sauce for dipping, and extra wasabi and pickled ginger.

SEAWEED

Seaweed is widely used in Asian cuisine, especially in Japan where it is wrapped around sushi rolls and shredded into miso soups, or processed into a powder and used as a seasoning.

TYPES OF SEAWEEDS

HIJIKI

These short, thin sticks of seaweed are usually sold dried. Soak before use — hijiki will swell to three times its size. Eat raw in salads, boil and serve with rice or in soups. Hijiki is often sautéed and then simmered in soy sauce and sugar.

KOMBU (KELP)

Kombu is a large, flat, olive-green seaweed. It is used to flavour the salty Japanese stock, dashi, cooked as a vegetable with fish, or used to flavour Japanese sushi rice. It is sold dried and often coated with a white salty mould. This gives it flavour and should not be washed off — wipe over with a damp cloth before use and cut into pieces.

NORI (LAVER)

Sold dried in paper-thin sheets, coloured from purple to green, or in flakes. Nori sheets are used for wrapping sushi, shredding into soups or crumbling onto rice. The sheets need to be crisped over a flame or under the grill (broiler) before use. Nori is the most common form of dried seaweed used in Japanese cookery and the sheets are available from Asian grocery stores and large supermarkets.

WAKAME

This dark green or brown seaweed is used in soups and to flavour salads and vegetables. Wakame is usually sold dried in pieces or flakes — soak for 2 hours before use.

HOW TO... MAKE PICKLED GINGER

Peel 500 g (1 lb 2 oz) fresh young ginger, then cut crossways into very thin slices. Put the ginger in a bowl with 1 teaspoon sea salt, toss together well and set aside for 10 minutes. Rinse under boiling water, then drain thoroughly.

Put 500 ml (17 fl oz/2 cups) rice vinegar, 170 g (6 oz/¾ cup) caster (superfine) sugar and 1½ tablespoons sea salt into a small saucepan and cook over medium heat until the sugar has dissolved. Put the ginger in a sterilised 1 litre (35 fl oz/4 cup) jar, then pour in the vinegar mixture. Cover tightly, then leave overnight before using. Note that the ginger won't be as pink as the commercial variety (pictured). The pickled ginger will keep in the fridge for 2 months.

ROE

Roe are the eggs or spawn of a female fish, also called hard roe. Caviar, the most sought after roe, is from the sturgeon. Lesser but still delicious roe can come from salmon, trout, herring, flying fish and lumpfish. Taramasalata is ideally made with the roe of the grey mullet, as is botargo, which is salted, pressed and dried roe. Roe is eaten fried in Europe, and in Japan it is used for sushi. Soft roe is the sperm (or milt) of a male fish.

CHIRASHI SUSHI

This scattered sushi is not only easy to make but its array of toppings makes it a delicious and colourful festive meal. Add other ingredients such as fresh or frozen peas and cooked or peeled prawns.

SERVES 4

INGREDIENTS

- 420 g (15 oz/2 cups) Japanese short-grain rice
- 4 dried shiitake mushrooms
- 2 tablespoons caster (superfine) sugar
- 1 tablespoon soy sauce
- 2 large eggs
- 1 tablespoon sake
- 1–2 teaspoons oil
- 1 avocado
- 1 tablespoon lemon juice
- 1 small carrot, cut into thin strips and blanched
- 300 g (10½ oz) sashimi-grade salmon fillet, cut into small chunks
- 2 spring onions (scallions), finely shredded
- 2 tablespoons crushed toasted sesame seeds or 50 g (1¾ oz) fish roe
- sliced pickled ginger, to serve
- wasabi paste, to serve
- Japanese soy sauce, to serve

METHOD

1. Prepare the sushi rice (page 184), and use the rice while it is still warm.
2. Put the mushrooms in a saucepan with 300 ml (10½ fl oz) boiling water. Add the sugar and soy sauce to the mushrooms, bring to the boil, then simmer, covered, for 15 minutes. Drain, reserving the mushrooms.
3. Beat the eggs with the sake and a pinch of salt. Heat the oil in a small frying pan, add half of the egg mixture and cook until just set. Roll the omelette to one side of the pan. Pour in the remaining egg and lift the cooked omelette so the raw egg runs underneath it. When the second omelette is cooked, roll the two together to make one roll, and allow to cool. Cut the omelette into thin slices.
4. Thinly slice the mushroom caps, discarding the stems. Peel and slice the avocado and toss in the lemon juice.
5. Arrange the omelette, mushrooms, avocado, carrot, salmon and spring onions over the rice. Scatter the sesame seeds over the top. Serve with pickled ginger, wasabi and soy sauce on the side.

••OYSTERS••

Fresh oysters served straight from the shell are one of nature's works of art. Oysters can also be cooked (they work particularly well with bacon) or topped with a creamy sauce.

BUYING

Oysters are bivalve molluscs that grow, wild or farmed, on coastlines around the world and are often named for their place of origin, for example: Breton, Colchester and Sydney. Oyster farming is a highly skilled occupation and today, when most oysters are cultivated, oyster lovers rely heavily on the farmer for both flavour and safety. Ideally, an oyster should be bought live, with the shell closed. In this state, it should be heavy and full of water. If the shell is open, it should close when lightly tapped. If buying an open oyster on the half-shell, look for plump, glossy oysters that smell fresh.

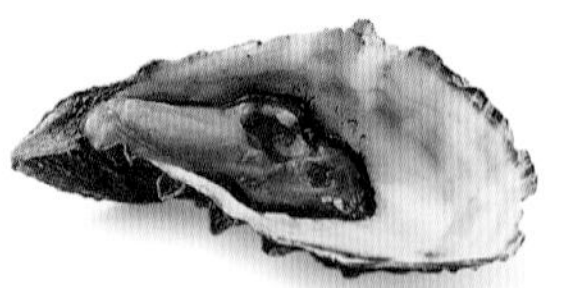

STORAGE

Unopened, oysters can be kept in the fridge for up to 1 week. If opened, store in their liquid and eat within 24 hours.

HOW TO... SHUCK AN OYSTER

This is a great skill to learn. When shucking (opening) oysters, use a proper oyster knife (an ordinary knife can break or slip). Buy one with a stainless-steel blade to avoid transferring a metallic taste to the oysters.

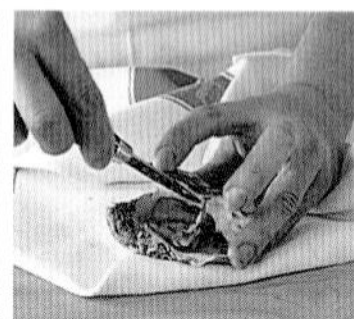

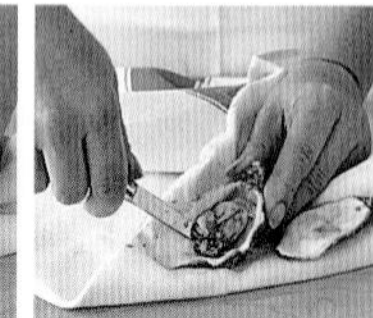

METHOD

1. Hold the oyster in a cloth, with the rounded side of the shell facing down. Insert the knife between the two shells, near the hinge.
2. Work the knife further between the two shells, then twist the knife to separate the shells. Discard the top shell.
3. Slide the blade underneath the oyster to detach it from the shell. Place the opened oyster on a platter and remove any shell fragments (washing the oyster will dilute its flavour).

BLOODY MARY OYSTER SHOTS

Into each large shot glass pour 20 ml (½ fl oz) vodka, 60 ml (2 fl oz/¼ cup) tomato juice, 2 teaspoons lime juice and 3 drops worcestershire sauce. Season with salt and pepper and a drop of Tabasco sauce. Drop a freshly shucked oyster into each glass.

The following oyster recipes each require 24 shucked oysters in the shell. Arrange the shells on a bed of rock salt on a tray (the salt helps to steady the oysters).

OYSTERS WITH GINGER AND LIME

INGREDIENTS

- ½ teaspoon finely grated ginger
- finely grated zest and juice of 2 limes
- 1 tablespoon chopped coriander (cilantro)
- 1 spring onion (scallion), very thinly sliced
- 2 teaspoons Thai fish sauce
- 2 teaspoons caster (superfine) sugar
- 1 small chilli, thinly sliced (optional)

METHOD

1. Combine the ingredients, stirring to dissolve the sugar. Drizzle a little over each oyster and serve.

OYSTERS KILPATRICK

INGREDIENTS

- worcestershire sauce
- 3 slices bacon, finely chopped

METHOD

1. Sprinkle the oysters lightly with worcestershire sauce. Top with the bacon and some pepper. Grill (broil) for 3–4 minutes.

OYSTERS MORNAY

INGREDIENTS

- 30 g (1 oz) butter
- 1 tablespoon plain (all-purpose) flour
- 170 ml (5½ fl oz/⅔ cup) hot milk
- pinch of cayenne pepper
- grated cheddar cheese

METHOD

1. Melt the butter in a small saucepan. Stir in the flour and cook for 2 minutes. Remove from the heat and slowly add the hot milk. Return the pan to medium heat and stir until the mixture boils and thickens. Season with salt, pepper and cayenne pepper. Simmer for 2 minutes, stirring occasionally. Remove from the heat.
2. Top each oyster with a teaspoon of the sauce and sprinkle with grated cheese. Grill (broil) for 2–3 minutes, or until the topping is golden.

GINGER AND SOY OYSTERS

INGREDIENTS

- 2 tablespoons soy sauce
- 2 tablespoons sweet sherry
- 3 teaspoons sesame oil
- 1 tablespoon grated ginger
- 1 spring onion (scallion), shredded

METHOD

1. Preheat the oven to 180°C (350°F/Gas 4).
2. Combine the soy sauce, sherry, sesame oil, ginger, spring onion and some freshly ground black pepper in a bowl. Drizzle the sauce over the oysters and bake for 5–10 minutes, or until they are just cooked.

NOTE: If preferred, don't bake the oysters, simply eat them raw topped with a little of the ginger and soy dressing.

••SCALLOPS••

Named for their pretty fan-shaped shells, scallops are bivalve molluscs found throughout the world's oceans. There are more than 300 species, varying in size from the large Atlantic deep-sea scallops to the smaller bay and queen scallops. The scallop enclosed within the shell, including the orange or pinky red roe (the coral or tongue), is edible.

BUYING

Scallop flesh should be pale beige to light pink, moist and glossy with a fresh sea smell. Scallops are sold either still enclosed in their shells or removed from the shell (shucked). If bought whole, discard any shells that are open and do not close when sharply tapped.

Because scallops deteriorate rapidly once out of the water, they are usually sold shucked and should be refrigerated quickly and used within 1 day. They can also be bought frozen.

COOKING

Scallops only require quick cooking, and are usually simply grilled, poached or sautéed. Add them to soups and stews but only at the last minute to avoid toughening their tender flesh. They can also be eaten raw with a little lemon juice or sliced as sashimi.

HOW TO... PREPARE SCALLOPS

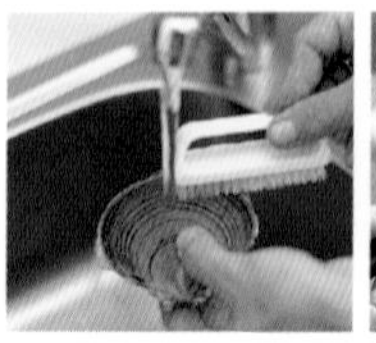
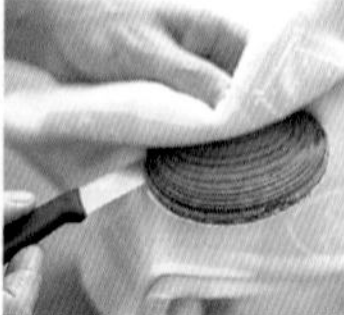

METHOD

1. Clean the closed shell by scrubbing it under running water. For easy shucking, you can put the shell under a hot grill (broiler) for 1 minute to warm, or steam them for 30 seconds.
2. Hold the scallop in a cloth with its rounded side down. Insert a sharp knife (an oyster knife is good for this) between the shells, close to the hinge. Work the knife further between the two shells and carefully prise open the shell. Lift off the top shell.
3. Loosen the scallop from the shell — you can use a spoon to scoop the scallop out. Pull off and discard any vein, membrane or hard white muscle. Retain the shells if needed.
4. Leave the orange roe (coral) intact, or remove the roe if you prefer.
5. For an attractive presentation, the scallops can be placed in their half-shells on a bed of rock salt or crushed ice on a large platter. If using the shells for serving, they should be scrubbed and rinsed in hot water.

SCALLOPS WITH AVOCADO SALSA

SERVES 4

INGREDIENTS

12 large scallops, on the half-shell
1 avocado, cut into small dice
½ green capsicum (pepper), finely chopped
1 tomato, peeled, seeded and finely chopped
½ onion, finely chopped
2 tablespoons lime juice
1½ tablespoons olive oil
coriander (cilantro) sprigs, to garnish
lime juice, to serve

METHOD

1 Remove the scallops from their shells (steps 3–4, opposite), discarding the roe. Clean and dry 4 shells and keep for serving.
2 Line a steamer with baking paper and place the scallops on top. Steam for 1–2 minutes. Reserve four of the scallops, and finely chop the remaining scallops.
3 Put the avocado, capsicum, tomato and onion in a bowl, then add the chopped scallop. Stir to combine, then add the lime juice and olive oil and season well. Divide the avocado salsa among four clean scallop shells and put one of the reserved scallops on top of each. Top with coriander and squeeze over a little lime juice.

SCALLOPS WITH LIME AND GINGER BUTTER

SERVES 4

INGREDIENTS

- 75 g (2½ oz) unsalted butter
- 6 kaffir lime leaves, finely chopped
- 1 teaspoon finely grated ginger
- 1 teaspoon finely chopped lemongrass, white part only
- 1 teaspoon fish sauce
- 16 scallops, on the half-shell

METHOD

1. Melt the butter in a small saucepan over low heat. Remove from the heat and stir in the lime leaves, ginger, lemongrass and fish sauce. Cover and keep warm.
2. Remove the scallops from their shells (steps 3–4, page 192), discarding the roe. Rinse the scallops, pat dry with paper towels and place in a bowl with half the butter mixture. Mix gently to coat the scallops.
3. Preheat a barbecue grill or hotplate. Rinse and dry the shells and put them on the edge of the barbecue to warm through. When warm, arrange the shells among four serving plates.
4. Sear the scallops for 40–60 seconds on each side, or until golden and just cooked through. Quickly transfer to the warm scallop shells and drizzle with the remaining butter mixture. Serve immediately.

SCALLOPS WITH SOY, GINGER AND SPRING ONION

SERVES 4–6

INGREDIENTS

- 24 scallops, on the half-shell
- 3 teaspoons light soy sauce
- 3 teaspoons Chinese rice wine
- 1 tablespoon chicken stock or water
- 3 spring onions (scallions), shredded
- 1½ tablespoons julienned ginger
- ½–1 tablespoon light soy sauce, extra
- ½ teaspoon sugar (optional)

METHOD

1. Remove the scallops from their shells (steps 3–4, page 192), discarding the roe. Clean and dry the shells and keep for serving.
2. Combine the soy sauce and rice wine in a non-metallic bowl with the scallops and marinate for 10 minutes.
3. Line a bamboo steamer with baking paper. Working in batches, arrange six shells in a single layer in the steamer, then return a scallop to each shell. Combine the marinade with the stock, then drizzle some over the scallops. Sprinkle with the spring onion and ginger. Cover and steam over a wok of simmering water for 2–3 minutes, or until just cooked, being careful not to overcook them.
4. Serve with some of the soy sauce (dissolve the sugar in the sauce, if using) drizzled over the top of the scallops.

ABALONE

Abalone is highly prized as a delicacy in Japan and China. This seafood has cream-coloured flesh and a mild meaty flavour, similar to that of a clam. In many countries, abalone has been over-harvested and, as it needs to be picked off the rocks by hand, it can be very expensive. Abalone clings to rock with a large muscular foot, and it is this foot that is the edible part of the creature. When using fresh abalone, you need to release the foot from its shell by running a sharp knife between the two. Abalone is also sold in tins.

COQUILLES SAINT JACQUES

SERVES 4

INGREDIENTS

- 24 scallops, on the half-shell
- 250 ml (9 fl oz/1 cup) fish stock (page 10)
- 250 ml (9 fl oz/1 cup) white wine
- 60 g (2¼ oz) butter
- 4 spring onions (scallions), chopped
- 1 slice bacon, finely chopped
- 100 g (3½ oz) button mushrooms, thinly sliced
- 30 g (1 oz/¼ cup) plain (all-purpose) flour
- 185 ml (6 fl oz/¾ cup) cream
- 1 teaspoon lemon juice
- 80 g (2¾ oz/1 cup) fresh breadcrumbs
- 30 g (1 oz) butter, melted, extra

METHOD

1. Remove the scallops from their shells (steps 3–4, page 192), leaving the roe attached. Cut in half. Heat the stock and wine in a pan and add the scallops. Cover and simmer over medium heat for 2–3 minutes, or until the scallops are opaque. Remove with a slotted spoon, cover and set aside. Bring the liquid in the pan to the boil until reduced to 375 ml (13 fl oz/1½ cups).
2. Melt the butter in a frying pan and add the spring onion, bacon and mushrooms. Cook over medium heat for 3 minutes, stirring occasionally, until the onion is soft but not brown.
3. Stir in the flour and cook for 2 minutes. Remove from the heat and gradually stir in the stock. Return to the heat and stir until the mixture boils and thickens. Reduce the heat and simmer for 2 minutes. Stir in the cream and lemon juice. Season, then cover, set aside and keep warm.
4. Combine the breadcrumbs and extra butter in a small bowl. Divide the scallops among the shells. Spoon the warm sauce over the scallops and sprinkle with the breadcrumb mixture. Place under a hot grill (broiler) until the breadcrumbs are golden brown. Serve immediately.

STIR-FRIED SCALLOPS WITH CHINESE GREENS

SERVES 6

INGREDIENTS

- 24 cleaned scallops
- 2 tablespoons Chinese rice wine
- 1 tablespoon sesame oil
- 1 teaspoon finely chopped ginger
- ½ spring onion (scallion), finely chopped
- 200 g (7 oz) Chinese broccoli (gai larn) or bok choy
- 80 ml (2½ fl oz/⅓ cup) chicken stock (page 11)
- ¼ teaspoon sugar
- ¼ teaspoon white pepper
- 1 teaspoon cornflour (cornstarch)
- 1 tablespoon oil
- 1 tablespoon finely shredded ginger
- 1 spring onion (scallion), finely shredded
- 1 garlic clove, very thinly sliced

METHOD

1. Cut the scallops in half horizontally. Put in a bowl with half the rice wine, ¼ teaspoon of the sesame oil and the chopped ginger and spring onion. Leave to marinate for 20 minutes.
2. Discard any tough stems from the broccoli and diagonally cut into 2 cm (¾ inch) pieces through the stem and leaf. Blanch in a saucepan of boiling water for 2 minutes, until just tender, then refresh in cold water and dry thoroughly.
3. Combine the stock, sugar, ½ teaspoon salt, the white pepper, cornflour and the remaining rice wine and sesame oil.
4. Heat a wok over high heat, add the oil and heat until very hot. Add the scallops and stir-fry for 30 seconds, then remove. Add the shredded ginger, spring onion and garlic and stir-fry for 10 seconds. Add the stock mixture and cook, stirring constantly, until the sauce thickens. Add the Chinese broccoli and scallops. Toss lightly to coat with the sauce. Serve with steamed rice.

••MUSSELS••

Mussels are bivalve molluscs that grow in the sea in clusters around sandbanks and rocks. A mussel holds onto rock with its byssus (beard), a mass of long silky threads found at the opening of the shell. Mussels are sold live in their shells, or the flesh can have been removed and preserved in sauce or brine.

BUYING

Mussels are filter-feeders and many harbour toxins. Most of the mussels we buy today are cultivated or farmed, making them more reliably safe to eat than wild ones. Wild or farmed, all mussels must be cleaned before cooking.

When buying mussels in the shell, allow 500–600 g (1 lb 5 oz) per person (much of the weight is in the shell) for a main course and serve with bread or French fries. Always buy mussels from a reputable source. At home, store in the fridge in a wet hessian bag or on a damp cloth (keeping them in a bowl of cold water will drown them), and cook them on the day you buy them.

COOKING

Mussels can be stuffed, baked or grilled or, when removed from their shells, added to soup, salads, paella, omelettes and stews. To open mussels and cook the meat at the same time, they are often steamed in water, stock or wine, with added flavourings such as garlic and herbs.

An easy way to eat mussels in their shells, such as Moules marinière, is to use one of the empty double shells like a pair of pinchers to pull the mussel from its shell.

HOW TO... CLEAN MUSSELS

METHOD

1 Fresh mussels must be bought live — dead mussels can be toxic. Tip the mussels into the sink and sort through them — they should all be closed. If any shells are open, tap them on the sink. If they stay open, throw them away, as they are dead. Throw away any other mussels with cracked shells. Any mussels that don't open during cooking are also dead and should also be discarded.
2 Scrub the mussels thoroughly under cold running water to remove any dirt or slime.
3 If the hairy beard is still attached, pull it off, then rinse again.

TYPES OF MUSSELS

Marine mussels are cultivated in temperate seas all over the world. Varieties include the common mussel, with dark blue to black shells (pictured right), the Mediterranean mussel, the horse mussel and the green-lipped mussel (pictured far right), sometimes called the New Zealand green mussel.

MUSSELS IN TOMATO AND HERB SAUCE

SERVES 2–4

INGREDIENTS

TOMATO AND HERB SAUCE
80 ml (2½ fl oz/⅓ cup) olive oil
3 garlic cloves, finely chopped
¼ teaspoon chilli flakes
2 x 400 g (14 oz) tins chopped tomatoes
pinch of caster (superfine) sugar, or to taste

8 slices crusty Italian bread
80 ml (2½ fl oz/⅓ cup) olive oil
2 large garlic cloves, halved
1 kg (2 lb 4 oz) mussels
1 red onion, finely chopped
6 parsley sprigs
2 thyme sprigs
2 oregano sprigs
250 ml (9 fl oz/1 cup) white wine
chopped parsley, thyme and oregano, to garnish

METHOD

1 Preheat the oven to 160°C (315°F/ Gas 2–3). To make the tomato and herb sauce, heat the oil in a saucepan, add the garlic and chilli flakes and cook over low heat for 30 seconds without browning. Add the tomatoes, sugar and 80 ml (2½ fl oz/⅓ cup) water. Season well and simmer, stirring often, for 15 minutes, or until the sauce has thickened and reduced.
2 Lightly brush the bread with olive oil, using half the oil. Place the bread in a single layer on a baking tray and bake for 10 minutes, or until crisp and golden. While still warm, rub one side of each slice with garlic.
3 Meanwhile, clean and debeard the mussels (see opposite). Discard any that are broken or that don't close when tapped on the sink. Rinse well.
4 Heat the remaining olive oil in a large saucepan, add the onion and cook for 3 minutes, or until softened but not browned. Add the parsley, thyme and oregano sprigs and the wine to the saucepan. Bring to the boil, then reduce the heat and simmer for 5 minutes.
5 Add the mussels to the pan, stir to coat in the onion and wine mixture, and cook, covered, over high heat for 3–4 minutes. Gently shake the pan often to move the mussels around. Remove the mussels as they open and discard any unopened mussels.
6 Strain the wine mixture into the tomato sauce, discarding the onion and herbs. Check the sauce for seasoning and adjust if necessary. Add the mussels and toss well to coat in the mixture. Pile into a serving bowl and garnish with the extra chopped herbs. Arrange the bread around the bowl and serve.

MUSSELS WITH LEMONGRASS

SERVES 2–4

INGREDIENTS

1 kg (2 lb 4 oz) mussels
2 tablespoons vegetable oil
2–3 garlic cloves, finely chopped
1 small onion, finely chopped
3 lemongrass stems, white part only, thinly sliced
2.5 cm (1 inch) piece galangal, cut into 7–8 slices
2 long red chillies, seeded and finely chopped
1 tablespoon fish sauce
1 tablespoon lime juice
½ teaspoon sugar
1 large handful Thai basil leaves, roughly chopped

METHOD

1 Clean and debeard the mussels (page 196). Discard any that are broken or that don't close when tapped on the sink. Rinse well.
2 Heat the oil in a wok over medium heat and stir-fry the garlic, onion, lemongrass, galangal and chilli for 1–2 minutes, or until fragrant.
3 Add the mussels and stir-fry for a few minutes. Add the fish sauce, lime juice and sugar. Cover loosely and cook for 5–7 minutes, shaking the wok frequently. Cook until the shells are open, discarding any unopened shells. Mix in the chopped basil. Taste, then adjust the seasoning if necessary with extra fish sauce, lime juice or sugar. Serve the mussels in a large bowl.

› MOULES MARINIERE

SERVES 4

INGREDIENTS

2 kg (4 lb 8 oz) mussels
40 g (1½ oz) butter
1 large onion, chopped
½ celery stalk, chopped
2 garlic cloves, crushed
400 ml (14 fl oz) white wine
1 bay leaf
2 thyme sprigs
185 ml (6 fl oz/¾ cup) thick (double) cream
2 tablespoons chopped parsley

METHOD

1 Clean and debeard the mussels (page 196). Discard any that are broken or that don't close when tapped on the sink. Rinse well.
2 Melt the butter in a large saucepan over medium heat and cook the onion, celery and garlic, stirring occasionally, until the onion is softened but not browned.
3 Add the wine, bay leaf and thyme to the pan and bring to the boil. Add the mussels, cover the pan and simmer over low heat for 2–3 minutes, shaking the pan occasionally. Use tongs to lift out the mussels as they open, putting them into a warm dish. Discard any mussels that haven't opened after 3 minutes.
4 Strain the liquid through a fine sieve into a clean saucepan, leaving behind any grit or sand. Bring to the boil and boil for 2 minutes. Add the cream and reheat the sauce without boiling. Season well. Serve the mussels in individual bowls with the liquid poured over. Sprinkle with the parsley and serve with plenty of bread.

ZARZUELA

Zarzuela is a colourful Catalan seafood stew. Its main seafood ingredients vary seasonally, but will usually include lobster, mussels, clams and monkfish. Two of the four essential Catalan sauces are used to make Zarzuela: the sofrito of onion, olive oil and tomato, and the picada of pounded fried bread, almonds and garlic. Zarzuela is named after an operetta or musical comedy, reportedly because it is a symphony of taste, colour, shape and texture.

ZARZUELA

SERVES 4–6

INGREDIENTS

SOFRITO BASE

1 tablespoon olive oil
2 onions, finely chopped
2 large tomatoes, peeled, seeded and chopped (page 347)
1 tablespoon tomato paste (concentrated purée)

PICADA SAUCE

3 slices white bread, crusts removed
1 tablespoon almonds, toasted
3 garlic cloves
1 tablespoon olive oil

1 raw lobster tail (about 400 g/14 oz)
750 g (1 lb 10 oz) skinless monkfish fillets (or use cod, warehou, flake or any firm white fish)
seasoned flour, to coat
2–3 tablespoons olive oil
125 g (4½ oz) squid, cleaned and cut into rings (page 219)
12 large prawns (shrimp), peeled and deveined, tails intact (page 204)
125 ml (4 fl oz/½ cup) dry white wine
12–15 mussels, cleaned (page 196)
125 ml (4 fl oz/½ cup) brandy
3 tablespoons chopped parsley

METHOD

1. To make the sofrito base, heat the olive oil in a large flameproof casserole dish over medium heat. Add the onion and stir for 5 minutes without browning. Add the tomatoes, tomato paste and 125 ml (4 fl oz/½ cup) water and stir for 10 minutes. Stir in another 125 ml (4 fl oz/½ cup) water, season and set the dish aside.
2. To make the picada sauce, finely chop the bread, almonds and garlic in a food processor or chop by hand. With the motor running, or continuously stirring, gradually add the oil to form a paste.
3. Preheat the oven to 180°C (350°F/Gas 4). Cut the lobster tail into rounds through the membrane that separates the shell segments, and then set aside. Cut the fish fillets into bite-sized pieces and lightly coat in the seasoned flour. Heat the olive oil in a large frying pan and fry the fish in batches over medium heat for 2–3 minutes, or until cooked and golden brown all over. Transfer to the casserole dish.
4. Add a little oil to the frying pan if necessary, add the squid and cook, stirring, for 1–2 minutes. Remove and add to the fish. Cook the lobster and prawns for 2–3 minutes, or until just pink, then add to the casserole. Add the wine to the pan and bring to the boil. Reduce the heat, add the mussels, cover the pan and steam for 4–5 minutes. Add to the fish, discarding any unopened mussels.
5. Pour the brandy into the pan, ignite and when the flames have died down, pour over the seafood. Stir all the seafood in the casserole, then cover and bake for 20 minutes. Stir in the picada sauce and cook for another 10 minutes, or until warmed through — do not overcook, or the seafood will toughen. Sprinkle with the parsley before serving.

••CLAMS••

Clams are bivalve molluscs and can be classified as either soft- or hard-shelled. Clams can be eaten raw, steamed, baked or fried. Clams must be bought live — as with all molluscs, look for ones with tightly closed shells.

HOW TO... PREPARE HARD-SHELLED CLAMS

METHOD

1. Ask your fishmonger if the clams have been purged of sand. If not, put them in a bowl or bucket of salted water for a couple of hours to ensure they expel all their grit, then rinse under cold running water. Discard any broken clams or open ones that don't close when tapped on the bench. Use the clams as directed in the recipe.
2. If the recipe asks for clam meat only, drain the clams and put them in a large pan. Heat until they just start to open, then remove from the heat.
3. Pull off the top shell and lift out the meat, collecting any juices in a bowl. Strain the juices through a piece of muslin before using.

CLAMS IN WHITE WINE

SERVES 4

INGREDIENTS

- 1 kg (2 lb 4 oz) clams
- 2 large, ripe tomatoes
- 2 tablespoons olive oil
- 1 small onion, finely chopped
- 2 garlic cloves, crushed
- 1 tablespoon chopped parsley
- pinch of ground nutmeg
- 80 ml (2½ fl oz/⅓ cup) dry white wine

METHOD

1. Prepare the clams and discard any that are broken or open (step 1, left).
2. To peel the tomatoes, score a cross in the base of each tomato. Put in a heatproof bowl and cover with boiling water. Leave for 30 seconds, then transfer to cold water and peel the skin away from the cross. Cut in half horizontally and scoop out the seeds. Roughly chop the flesh.
3. Heat the oil in a large heavy-based saucepan and cook the onion over low heat for 5 minutes. Add the garlic and tomatoes and cook for a further 5 minutes. Stir in the parsley and nutmeg and season. Add 80 ml (2½ fl oz/⅓ cup) water.
4. Add the clams and cook over low heat until they open. Discard any that don't open. Pour in the wine and cook for 3–4 minutes, moving the pan back and forth a few times, rather than stirring, so the clams stay in the shells. Transfer to a large serving bowl and serve with bread.

CLAMS IN YELLOW BEAN SAUCE

SERVES 4

INGREDIENTS

- 1.5 kg (3 lb 5 oz) clams
- 1 tablespoon oil
- 2 garlic cloves, crushed
- 1 tablespoon grated ginger
- 2 tablespoons yellow bean sauce
- 125 ml (4 fl oz/½ cup) chicken stock (page 11)
- 1 spring onion (scallion), thinly sliced

METHOD

1. Prepare the clams and discard any broken or open ones (step 1, opposite).
2. Heat a wok over high heat, add the oil and heat until very hot. Add the garlic and ginger and stir-fry for 30 seconds, then add the bean sauce and clams and toss to combine.
3. Pour in the stock and stir for 3 minutes, or until the clams have opened, discarding any that do not open after this time. Season with salt and white pepper. Transfer the clams to a large serving bowl and sprinkle with the spring onion.

••PRAWNS••

There are few meals more simple yet satisfying than fresh prawns in their shells, or perhaps marinated in garlic and chilli, thrown onto a barbecue and cooked until sweet and tender. Prawns are crustaceans found in waters all over the world. While they are called prawns in most English-speaking countries, they are referred to as shrimp in North and South America. Prawns vary in size and colour but they all become opaque and turn pink once cooked.

BUYING

Prawns perish easily, so they are often frozen on board the ships from which they are fished. They can be bought shell on or shelled, head on or off, cooked or uncooked. Avoid frozen prawns covered in frost or with freezer burn. If buying them raw (when they are sometimes called 'green'), they should have a pleasant smell and firm shells. Avoid any that smell of ammonia or with dark discolouration around the head or legs — this means they are starting to deteriorate. As a guide, 500 g (1 lb 2 oz) of prawns with their shells on will give you about 250 g (9 oz) shelled weight.

COOKING

Prawns can be steamed, boiled, fried, grilled or baked. They can be made into mousses, sauces and stuffings and can be served as salads and hors d'oeuvres. Whichever way they are cooked, they should not be overcooked or they will become tough and rubbery; 2–3 minutes is sufficient to cook medium-sized prawns. If adding cooked prawns to a dish, add them at the last minute or they will be tough.

HOW TO... PEEL AND DEVEIN PRAWNS

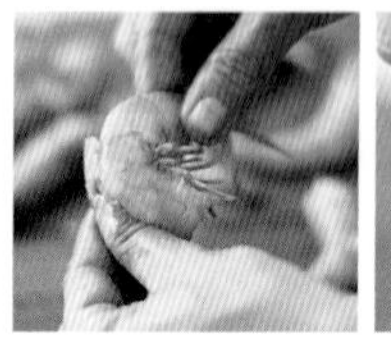

METHOD

1 Pull off the prawn head by holding the body and tugging gently at the head. Peel off the shell and legs from around the body, then (if removing) gently pull on the tail to remove it in one piece.

2 Starting at the head end, devein the prawn by removing the dark digestive tract that runs along its back. Either pull it out from one end ...

3 ... or make a very shallow cut down the back of the prawn and lift it out. If you cut too deeply, your prawns will 'butterfly' out as they cook.

PRAWN COCKTAIL

SERVES 4

INGREDIENTS

- 125 g (4½ oz/½ cup) mayonnaise
- 1 tablespoon tomato sauce (ketchup)
- 2 teaspoons lemon juice
- 1–2 drops Tabasco sauce
- 24 cooked prawns (shrimp)
- iceberg lettuce leaves
- pinch of cayenne pepper
- lemon wedges, to serve

METHOD

1. To make the cocktail sauce, combine the mayonnaise, tomato sauce, lemon juice and Tabasco sauce in a bowl. Season with salt and black pepper.
2. Peel and devein the prawns, leaving some of the prawn tails intact for presentation.
3. Arrange the lettuce in four serving glasses or bowls and divide the prawns among the glasses. Spoon over a little of the cocktail sauce and sprinkle with a pinch of cayenne pepper. Serve with lemon wedges.

PRAWN CUTLETS

SERVES 4–6

INGREDIENTS

- 1 kg (2 lb 4 oz) raw large prawns (shrimp)
- 4 eggs
- 2 tablespoons soy sauce
- cornflour (cornstarch), for coating
- 200 g (7 oz/2 cups) dry breadcrumbs
- oil, for deep-frying
- tartare sauce (page 427), to serve
- lemon wedges, to serve

METHOD

1. Peel the prawns, leaving the tails intact (page 204). Using a small knife, slit them open down the backs, remove the veins and then gently flatten them open with your fingers.
2. Beat the eggs and soy sauce in a small bowl. Coat the prawns in the cornflour, shake off the excess, dip them in the egg mixture and then press in the breadcrumbs. Refrigerate the prawns for 15 minutes.
3. Fill a deep heavy-based saucepan one-third full of oil and heat to 180°C (350°F), or until a cube of bread dropped into the oil turns golden brown in 15 seconds. Deep-fry the prawns in batches until lightly golden. Remove and drain on paper towels. Serve the prawn cutlets with the tartare sauce and lemon wedges.

› PRAWN TEMPURA

SERVES 4

INGREDIENTS

- 90 g (3¼ oz/¾ cup) tempura flour
- 170 ml (5½ fl oz/⅔ cup) ice-cold water
- oil, for deep-frying
- 12 large raw prawns (shrimp), peeled and deveined, tails intact (page 204)
- 60 ml (2 fl oz/¼ cup) mirin
- 60 ml (2 fl oz/¼ cup) soy sauce
- 10 g (¼ oz) bonito flakes
- grated daikon, to serve
- pickled ginger, to serve

METHOD

1. Put the tempura flour in a bowl with the ice-cold water and gently stir to combine — the batter may be a little lumpy.
2. Fill a deep heavy-based saucepan one-third full of oil and heat to 180°C (350°F), or until a cube of bread dropped into the oil turns golden brown in 15 seconds. Dip 3–4 prawns in the batter, allow the excess to drain off, then carefully lower into the oil and cook in batches until the prawns are crisp and golden. Remove and drain on paper towels.
3. To make a dipping sauce, put the mirin, soy sauce, 250 ml (9 fl oz/1 cup) water and the bonito flakes in a saucepan. Bring to the boil, then strain and cool.
4. Serve with the dipping sauce, a small pile of grated daikon (squeeze it dry after grating) and pickled ginger.

HOW TO... MAKE CRISP TEMPURA

Tempura is made of bite-sized pieces of vegetable or seafood, such as prawns or white fish, coated in a light batter and deep-fried until crisp and puffed. The batter is a paste made from tempura flour, water and sometimes egg. Tempura is served with a dipping sauce of dashi or bonito flakes, soy sauce and mirin. Tempura is not, as is commonly believed, a Japanese dish, but was introduced into Japan by Portuguese missionaries in the sixteenth century. The Japanese adopted their techniques and today tempura restaurants flourish throughout the country.

The secret to crisp tempura is to have the food and batter as cold as possible prior to cooking and to keep the oil maintained at 180°C (350°F) — if the temperature drops, the tempura may lose its featherlight crispness. The batter is made with ice-cold water and only whisked just enough to incorporate flavours. The lumps are not beaten out.

GARLIC PRAWNS

SERVES 4

INGREDIENTS

- 6 garlic cloves, crushed
- 1–2 small red chillies, very finely chopped
- 250 ml (9 fl oz/1 cup) olive oil
- 60 g (2¼ oz) butter
- 24 raw large prawns (shrimp), peeled and deveined, tails intact (page 204)
- 2 tablespoons chopped parsley
- crusty bread, to serve

METHOD

1. Preheat the oven to 220°C (425°F/Gas 7). Sprinkle the garlic and chilli into four cast-iron or gratin dishes. Divide the oil and butter among the dishes.
2. Put the dishes on a baking tray in the oven and heat for 6 minutes, or until the butter has melted.
3. Divide the prawns among the dishes (take care not to splash yourself with hot oil) and bake for 7 minutes, or until the prawns are pink and tender. Sprinkle with parsley and serve with crusty bread.

MARINATED PRAWNS WITH MANGO CHILLI SALSA

SERVES 4–6

INGREDIENTS

LEMON DILL MARINADE

- 80 ml (2½ fl oz/⅓ cup) lemon juice
- 80 ml (2½ fl oz/⅓ cup) olive oil
- 1 teaspoon sea salt
- 3 tablespoons chopped dill

- 1 kg (2 lb 4 oz) raw prawns (shrimp), peeled and deveined, tails intact (page 204)
- 150 g (5½ oz) rocket (arugula)

MANGO CHILLI SALSA

- 450 g (1 lb) diced mango
- 1 red onion, finely diced
- 1 small red chilli, seeded and finely chopped
- 1 tablespoon finely grated lemon zest

METHOD

1. To make the lemon dill marinade, combine the ingredients in a large non-metallic bowl and mix well. Add the prawns, toss well, then cover and refrigerate for 1 hour.
2. Preheat the barbecue hotplate. Just before you are ready to eat, prepare the mango chilli salsa by combing the ingredients in a bowl. Mix well and set aside.
3. Drain the prawns from the marinade and cook them on the hotplate for 2–4 minutes, turning once, or until they have changed colour but are still soft and fleshy to touch. Take them off the heat straight away and let them cool slightly.
4. Arrange a bed of rocket on individual serving plates. Add a generous scoop of salsa, then the prawns. Season to taste and serve.

PIRI PIRI PRAWNS

SERVES 4

INGREDIENTS

- 125 ml (4 fl oz/½ cup) olive oil
- 2 teaspoons chilli flakes
- 4 large garlic cloves, crushed
- 1 kg (2 lb 4 oz) raw large prawns (shrimp), peeled and deveined, tails intact (page 204)
- 75 g (2½ oz) butter
- 60 ml (2 fl oz/¼ cup) lemon juice

METHOD

1. Put the oil, chilli flakes, garlic and 1 teaspoon salt in a large non-metallic bowl and mix well. Add the prawns and coat them in the mixture. Refrigerate for 3 hours, stirring and turning the prawns occasionally.
2. Preheat the grill (broiler) to very hot. Put the prawns in a single layer on a baking tray and brush with the remaining oil and chilli mixture. Cook for about 5 minutes, turning once, or until the prawns turn pink.
3. Meanwhile, melt the butter with the lemon juice in a small saucepan. Serve the prawns hot, drizzled with the lemon and butter mixture. Serve with steamed rice.

INDIAN PRAWN CURRY

SERVES 4

INGREDIENTS

- 50 g (1¾ oz) ghee (page 120) or oil
- 1 onion, finely chopped
- 2 large garlic cloves, finely chopped
- ½ teaspoon grated ginger
- 2 small red chillies, seeded and finely chopped
- 1 teaspoon each ground coriander, cumin and garam masala
- 2 ripe tomatoes, peeled, seeded and chopped (page 347), juices reserved
- 2 tablespoons tomato paste (concentrated purée)
- 400 ml (14 fl oz) tin coconut milk
- 16 raw king prawns (shrimp), peeled and deveined, tails intact (page 204)
- 2 tablespoons shredded mint

METHOD

1. Melt the ghee in a saucepan and, when hot, add the onion. Cook for 8–10 minutes, then add the garlic, ginger and chilli and cook for 2 minutes.
2. Stir in the spices and cook for 1 minute. Add the tomato and juices, tomato paste and coconut milk. Bring to below boiling point and simmer for 10 minutes. Add the prawns and cook for 3–5 minutes. Season with salt and stir in the mint. Serve with naan bread, chapatis or rice.

SHRIMP AND SHRIMP PASTE

Shrimp are small crustaceans similar to prawns but belonging to a different family, except in North America, where both shrimp and prawns are encompassed under the general term 'shrimp'. Shrimp are used in seafood cocktails, canapés, potted shrimp, and can be ground, salted and dried and used in Asian cooking. In Malaysia and Indonesia ground shrimp is pressed into blocks; the Chinese version is softer and more sauce-like. Shrimp paste has a strong, salty flavour and is used sparingly as a flavouring agent. It should be fried first in a little oil to bring out the flavour. After opening, be sure to wrap the paste well and store it in an airtight container in the fridge, as it has a pungent odour.

••CRAB••

Crabs are crustaceans of which there are between 4000 and 8000 species, both saltwater and freshwater. Crabs are hard-shelled, though soft-shelled (just moulted) blue crabs are a delicacy. Crabmeat is sweet, delicate and versatile and food lovers compare it to lobster.

BUYING

Crabs are sold either live or cooked. Buy live crabs from reputable sources as they are highly perishable. Live crabs will have their front pincers tied with string, they should look fairly lively and feel heavy for their size. Never buy a dead uncooked crab.

Cooked crabs are also highly perishable, so buy with care. Make sure they smell fresh and are undamaged and their legs and feet are drawn into the body (if they were dead when cooked, their legs will be looser). Crabmeat is also available frozen and tinned.

HOW TO... HANDLE LIVE CRABS HUMANELY

METHOD

1 There are many ways to dispatch a live crab but the most humane way of handling this is to put the crab in the freezer for about 2 hours to make it lose consciousness. You can then prepare and cut up the crab following steps 3–5, or as directed in the recipe.

2 If a boiled crab is needed, prepare the crab following step 1, then drop it into a large saucepan of boiling, salted water and simmer for 15 minutes per 500 g (1 lb 2 oz), or until bright orange all over. Drain and leave to cool. If you are sautéeing crab, prepare it in the same way but cook for 2 minutes, then drain, cool under running water and cut into pieces (see below). Use as directed in the recipe.

HOW TO... PREPARE CRAB

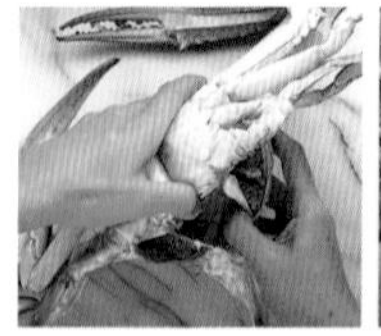

METHOD

3 Lift the 'apron', the small flap on the underside of the crab, and use your thumb as a lever to prise off the hard top shell.

4 Discard the soft stomach sac from the main body of the crab and remove the grey spongy fingers (gills). Rinse the bodies and drain well.

5 Cut the crab as directed in the recipe, or use a large sharp knife to cut the crab lengthways through the centre of the body, to form two halves with the legs attached. Cut each half of the crab in half again crossways to give you four portions, or you can cut it into smaller pieces to give you six portions. If picked crabmeat is needed, remove the meat with your fingers or a crab pick.

CHILLI CRAB

Chilli crab is best eaten with your hands, so supply finger bowls as well as special picks to help remove the meat from the crab claws.

SERVES 4

INGREDIENTS

- 4 x 250 g (9 oz) live crabs
- 60 ml (2 fl oz/¼ cup) oil
- 1 tablespoon chilli sauce
- 2 tablespoons light soy sauce
- 3 teaspoons rice vinegar
- 80 ml (2½ fl oz/⅓ cup) Chinese rice wine
- 2 tablespoons sugar
- 2 tablespoons chicken stock
- 1 tablespoon grated ginger
- 2 garlic cloves, crushed
- 2 spring onions (scallions), finely chopped

METHOD

1. To prepare the crabs humanely, freeze them for 2 hours, then cook in a large saucepan of boiling water for 2 minutes. Prepare and cut the crab into four to six portions (steps 3–5, opposite). Crack the crab claws.
2. Heat a wok over high heat, add 1 tablespoon of the oil and heat until very hot. Add half the crab and fry for several minutes to cook the meat right through (the shells will turn orange). Remove and drain. Repeat with another tablespoon of the oil and the remaining crab.
3. Combine the chilli sauce, soy sauce, vinegar, rice wine, a pinch of salt, sugar and stock.
4. Reheat the wok over high heat, add the remaining oil and heat. Stir-fry the ginger, garlic and spring onion for 10 seconds. Add the sauce mixture and cook briefly. Add the crab and toss lightly to coat with the sauce. Cook, covered, for 5 minutes, then serve.

DRESSED CRAB

This is the traditional way to enjoy fresh crab in Britain. The crab is presented in the cleaned top crab shell.

SERVES 1–2

INGREDIENTS

- 1 mud crab, about 1 kg (2 lb 4 oz), cooked (steps 1–2, page 210)
- 2 teaspoons lemon juice
- 2 tablespoons mayonnaise, plus extra to serve
- 80 g (2¾ oz/1 cup) fresh breadcrumbs
- 1 teaspoon worcestershire sauce
- 2 hard-boiled eggs, at room temperature
- 2 tablespoons chopped parsley

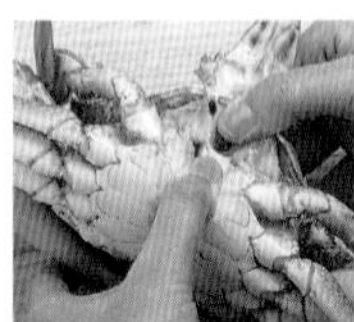

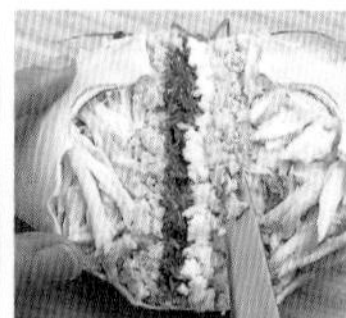

METHOD

1 Using your thumb as a lever, pull the top shell of the crab away from the bottom shell.
2 Remove the feathery gills and stomach sac, and snap off the mouth. Pick the meat out of the shells, keeping the white and dark meat separate. Remove and crack the claws and take out any meat. Wash and dry the top shell well.
3 Finely chop the dark meat and combine with the lemon juice, mayonnaise and enough breadcrumbs to combine. Add the worcestershire sauce and season with salt and pepper.
4 Press the egg whites and egg yolks separately through a sieve or chop very finely. Place the white crabmeat on both the outside edges of the shell. Spoon the brown meat into the centre of the shell and arrange the parsley, egg yolks and egg white in rows down the shell. Serve with triangles of buttered bread, lemon wedges and extra mayonnaise.

CRAB FRITTERS

MAKES ABOUT 30

INGREDIENTS

LIME AND YOGHURT MAYONNAISE

- 125 g (4½ oz/½ cup) plain yoghurt
- 125 g (4½ oz/½ cup) mayonnaise
- 2 teaspoons finely grated lime zest
- 1–2 tablespoons lime juice

FRITTERS

- 250 g (9 oz) boneless firm white fish fillets
- 1 egg white
- 60 ml (2 fl oz/¼ cup) cream
- 250 g (9 oz) cooked white crabmeat
- 2 tablespoons chopped parsley
- 240 g (8½ oz/3 cups) fresh breadcrumbs
- oil, for deep-frying

METHOD

1 To make the lime and yoghurt mayonnaise, combine the yoghurt, mayonnaise and lime zest in a bowl. Add the lime juice, to taste, then season with salt and pepper.
2 To make the fritters, put the fish in a food processor and purée. Add the egg white, season with salt and pepper and process until well blended. Using the pulse button, add the cream, being careful not to overwork the mixture or the cream will separate.
3 Transfer the mixture to a large bowl and place it inside a larger bowl filled with ice. Fold the crab and parsley into the fish mixture.
4 Shape the mixture into small balls, then roll into the breadcrumbs, being careful not to handle the mixture too much. Place on a tray lined with baking paper and refrigerate while you heat the oil.
5 Fill a deep heavy-based saucepan or deep-fryer one-third full of oil and heat to 180°C (350°F), or until a cube of bread dropped into the oil browns in 15 seconds. Deep-fry the fritters in batches for 4–6 minutes or until cooked through. Season with salt and serve with the mayonnaise on the side.

CRAB AND MANGO SALAD

SERVES 4

INGREDIENTS

DRESSING

80 ml (2½ fl oz/⅓ cup) light olive oil
60 ml (2 fl oz/¼ cup) lime juice
1 teaspoon fish sauce
½ small green chilli, finely chopped
1 tablespoon finely chopped coriander (cilantro)
2 teaspoons grated ginger

two 4 cm (1½ inch) squares fresh coconut (see Note)
1 teaspoon olive oil
60 g (2¼ oz/2 cups) watercress, trimmed
100 g (3½ oz) snow pea (mangetout) sprouts
100 g (3½ oz) cooked small prawns (shrimp), peeled and deveined, tails intact (page 204)
400 g (14 oz) cooked white crabmeat
1 firm mango, cut into thin strips
coriander (cilantro) leaves, to garnish
1 lime, cut into slices, to garnish

METHOD

1 To make the dressing, combine all the ingredients and season. Set aside.
2 Peel the coconut into wafer-thin slices with a vegetable peeler. Heat the olive oil in a frying pan and gently fry the coconut, stirring, until golden. Drain on crumpled paper towels.
3 Combine the watercress and snow pea sprouts and arrange on a platter.
4 Lightly toss the prawns, crabmeat, mango and three-quarters of the toasted coconut and dressing together. Pile in the centre of the watercress and sprout salad, scatter the remaining coconut over the top and garnish with the coriander leaves and lime slices.

NOTE: If you can't get fresh coconut, use 30 g (1 oz/½ cup) flaked coconut and toast it.

STEAMED SPICY CRAB

SERVES 4

INGREDIENTS

4 small or 2 large live crabs
2 garlic cloves, very finely chopped
2 teaspoons finely grated ginger
¼ teaspoon ground cumin
¼ teaspoon ground coriander
¼ teaspoon ground turmeric
¼ teaspoon cayenne pepper
1 tablespoon tamarind purée
1 teaspoon sugar
2 small red chillies, seeded and finely chopped
125 ml (4 fl oz/½ cup) oil
2 tablespoons chopped coriander (cilantro)

METHOD

1 To prepare the crabs humanely, freeze them for 2 hours. Prepare and cut each crab into two portions, or four portions if you are using the large crabs (steps 3–5, page 210).
2 Arrange the crabs in a single layer in a large steamer and cover with a lid. Sit the steamer over a wok or saucepan of boiling water and steam for 4–5 minutes, or until half cooked. Remove from the heat.
3 Mix together the garlic, ginger, cumin, coriander, turmeric, cayenne pepper, tamarind, sugar, chilli, half the oil and a generous pinch of salt. Heat the remaining oil in a large deep frying pan over medium heat. When the oil is hot, add the spice mixture and stir for 30 seconds.
4 Add the crab and cook, stirring, for 2 minutes, making sure the spice mix gets rubbed into the cut edges of the crab. Add ½ cupful of water, then cover and steam the crabs for a further 5–6 minutes, or until cooked. The crabs will turn pink or red when they are ready and the flesh will turn opaque. Drizzle a little of the liquid from the pan over the crabs and scatter with the coriander leaves. Serve with crab crackers, picks, finger bowls and bread.

••LOBSTER••

These large crustaceans are found in cold waters and are prized by seafood lovers the world over for their firm, delicate and slightly sweet flesh. True lobsters have eight legs and two large front pincers, which distinguish them from rock lobsters, or crayfish, which have no pincers and are found in warmer waters. Other crustaceans sometimes called 'lobsters' are the foot or slipper lobster, the smaller Norwegian lobster, and the Australian Moreton Bay bug, sometimes called a bay or flat-head lobster. Lobsters are often dark blue or almost black in colour when alive and turn red when cooked.

BUYING LIVE LOBSTERS

When buying a live lobster, make sure it's lively and has its tail tucked under its body. The shell should be hard — a soft shell indicates it has just moulted and is not in peak condition. The shell should have no holes and the lobster should have all its limbs. When picking up a lobster, make sure its claws are taped together, then pick it up just behind the head using your finger and thumb. Don't grasp it around its middle as it might close up on you suddenly.

BUYING COOKED LOBSTER

Cooked lobsters should be sweet and fresh smelling. The tail should be tightly curled (this indicates the lobster was alive when it was cooked) and spring back when you stretch it out. Discoloured meat can indicate that the lobster has been dead for too long. The meat from a cooked lobster tail can be removed in the same way as the raw tail. The claws will need to be cracked to extract the meat.

COOKING LOBSTERS

The most humane way of handling a live lobster is to freeze it for 1–2 hours to make it lose consciousness, then plunge it into a saucepan of boiling water. If the recipe calls for live lobster to be split in two, it can still be killed by this method first, then removed from the boiling water, drained and split as the recipe directs.

CRAYFISH OR LOBSTER?

The terms crayfish and lobster are often used interchangeably in Australia but the general difference is that lobsters live in the sea, while crayfish live in rivers or lakes. A lobster has a pair of large front claws, while crayfish do not. There are about 40 species of crayfish, including marrons and yabbies, freshwater species of crayfish (pictured far right), as well as another type of crayfish called, confusingly, rock lobster or spiny lobster (pictured right). In America, crayfish are called crawfish. Prepare and treat crayfish as lobsters.

HOW TO... PREPARE RAW LOBSTER

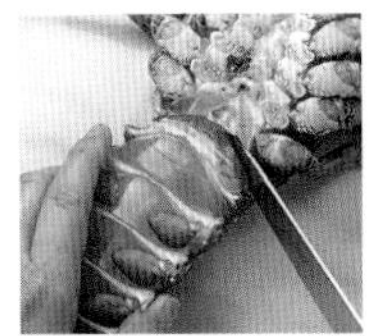
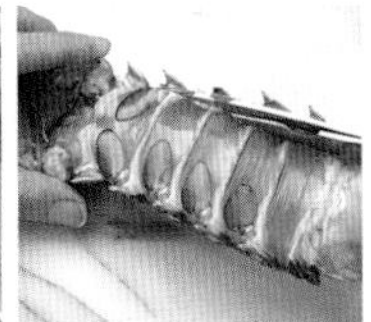
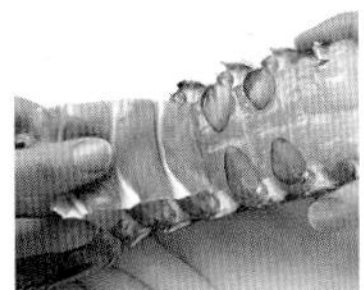

METHOD

1. Cut into the membrane on the underside of the lobster, where the head and body join, to loosen. Twist or cut off to remove the tail.
2. Cut down both sides of the shell on the underside, between the flesh and soft underside shell using a pair of scissors.
3. Peel back the soft undershell. Gently pull out the flesh in one piece. Pull out the vein from the back with your fingers or when cutting.

HOW TO... PREPARE COOKED LOBSTER

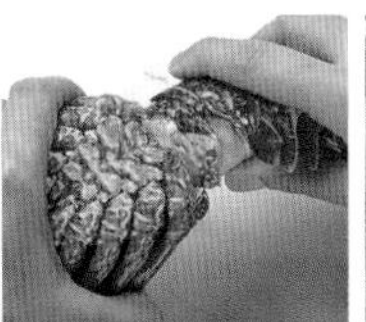

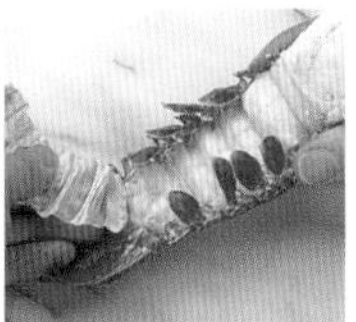

METHOD

1. Grasp the head and body with two hands and twist them firmly in opposite directions, to release the tail.
2. With scissors, cut down both sides of the shell on the underside, placing the scissors between the flesh and the soft shell.
3. Peel back the soft undershell to reveal the flesh. Gently pull out the flesh in one piece. Gently pull out the vein, starting at the head end, or remove the vein when cutting the lobster into pieces. Scrape the meat out of the claws using a lobster pick.

LOBSTER SALAD

SERVES 4

INGREDIENTS

800 g (1 lb 12 oz) live lobster
100 g (3½ oz) sugar snap peas
1 mango, flesh cut into chunks
2 spring onions (scallions), sliced
1 orange capsicum (pepper), sliced
¼ cucumber, seeded and cut into batons
juice of 2 limes
1 tablespoon fish sauce
2 tablespoons olive oil
1 teaspoon sesame oil
1 teaspoon dark soy sauce
1 red chilli, seeded and finely chopped
pinch of sugar

METHOD

1. Put the lobster in the freezer for 1–2 hours. Bring a large saucepan of water to the boil, drop the lobster into the water and return to the boil. Cook for 25 minutes, then drain and cool. Remove the cooked meat from the shell (see above). Cut into chunks and put in a large bowl.
2. Blanch the sugar snap peas, add to the lobster along with the mango, spring onion, capsicum and cucumber.
3. In a bowl, combine the lime juice, fish sauce, olive oil, sesame oil, soy sauce, chilli and sugar. Stir to combine the ingredients and to dissolve the sugar. Toss the lime dressing through the lobster mixture and serve.

STEAK WITH LOBSTER TAILS

A dish that consists of both seafood and meat is called surf 'n' turf. The seafood (surf), often prawns or lobster, is served with meat (turf), usually a steak. Surf 'n' turf is an American invention and is mostly served in restaurants. A popular Australian variation is carpetbag steak, a steak stuffed with oysters then grilled.

SERVES 4

INGREDIENTS

- 2 tablespoons oil
- 4 filet mignon steaks
- 2 raw lobster tails
- 1 tablespoon brandy
- 125 ml (4 fl oz/½ cup) cream

METHOD

1. Heat the oil in a heavy-based frying pan over high heat and cook the steaks for 2 minutes on each side (rare) and keep warm.
2. Fry the lobster tails until they turn red and the flesh inside is cooked. Cut down each side of the underneath of the tail and peel back the shell. Remove the tail meat in one piece. Slice into medallions, then return to the frying pan for 30 seconds.
3. Add the brandy, cook for 30 seconds, then add the cream. Place a steak on each plate and top with some lobster. Spoon the sauce over the top and serve.

LOBSTER MORNAY

SERVES 2

INGREDIENTS

- 1 cooked lobster
- 310 ml (10¾ fl oz/1¼ cups) milk
- 1 slice of onion
- 1 bay leaf
- 6 black peppercorns
- 30 g (1 oz) butter
- 2 tablespoons plain (all-purpose) flour
- 2 tablespoons cream
- pinch of ground nutmeg
- 60 g (2¼ oz/½ cup) grated cheddar cheese
- pinch of paprika

METHOD

1. Using a sharp knife, cut the lobster in half lengthways through the shell. Lift the meat from the tail and body. Remove the cream-coloured vein and soft body matter and discard. Cut the meat into 2 cm (¾ inch) pieces, cover and refrigerate. Wash the head and shell halves, then drain and pat dry. Set aside.
2. Heat the milk, onion, bay leaf and peppercorns in a small saucepan. Bring to the boil. Remove from the heat, cover and leave for 15 minutes, then strain.
3. Melt the butter in a large saucepan, stir in the flour and cook for 1 minute, or until pale and foaming. Remove from the heat and gradually stir in the strained milk. Return to the heat and stir constantly until the mixture boils and thickens. Reduce the heat and simmer for 1 minute. Stir in the cream. Season with the nutmeg and salt and pepper.
4. Fold the lobster meat through the sauce. Stir over low heat until the lobster is heated through. Spoon the mixture into the cleaned shells and sprinkle with the cheese. Preheat the grill (broiler) and cook the lobster for 2 minutes, or until the cheese has melted. Sprinkle with the paprika.

SHELLFISH WITH FOAMING CITRUS BUTTER

SERVES 4

INGREDIENTS

1 kg (2 lb 4 oz) live Moreton Bay bugs (see Note)
sourdough or country-style bread, to serve

FOAMING CITRUS BUTTER
50 g ($1\frac{3}{4}$ oz) butter
1 large garlic clove, crushed
1 tablespoon finely grated orange zest
1 tablespoon blood orange juice or regular orange juice
1 tablespoon lemon juice
1 tablespoon finely snipped chives

METHOD

1 Freeze the bugs for 1–2 hours before cooking. Nearer to cooking time, heat the grill (broiler) to its highest setting.
2 Plunge the bugs into a large saucepan of boiling water for 2 minutes, then drain. Using a sharp knife or cleaver, cut each bug in half from head to tail. Put the bugs on a large baking tray, cut side up. Grill (broil) for 5–6 minutes, or until the flesh turns white and opaque, turning halfway through cooking.
3 Meanwhile, make the foaming citrus butter. Melt the butter in a small saucepan and when sizzling, add the garlic. Cook over medium heat for 1 minute, stirring. Stir in the orange zest, orange juice and lemon juice and bring to the boil. Add the chives and season with salt and black pepper.
4 Divide the bugs among four serving plates, and serve the foaming citrus butter in small individual bowls for everyone to dip their shellfish and bread in. Finger bowls and napkins are also a good idea.

NOTE: Instead of Moreton Bay bugs you could use live slipper lobsters or crayfish for this recipe. You may need to boil them for a slightly longer time to cook them, and you'll need to remove the heads before slicing them down the middle.

BUGS

There are two common species of bug (a type of slipper lobster): the Moreton Bay bug (also known as the bay or flat-head lobster) and the Balmain bug (pictured right). The Balmain bug has no pincers and uses its short, wide antennae to dig into sand and mud on the ocean floor in search of food. The meat of bugs is found only in the tail and is sold frozen whole or as cleaned meat. The bugs are best prepared by poaching, steaming, barbecuing or grilling.

••OCTOPUS AND SQUID••

Octopus and squid are known as cephalopods — molluscs without shells. The octopus has eight tentacles and its curved and parrot-like mouth is found underneath its body along with an ink sac. Like its cousins the cuttlefish and squid, the octopus squirts out indelible black ink when threatened. While the ink sac should be removed during preparation, the ink can be used in cooking.

COOKING TIPS

* Larger octopus tend to be tough — tenderise them before cooking by pounding with a mallet or rolling pin. Some cooks claim that freezing octopus improves the tenderness, and in some countries it is not uncommon to see octopus being tenderised in a cement mixer. Your octopus is sufficiently tenderised when it no longer feels bouncy.
* Small or baby octopus are more tender and don't need beating or blanching before cooking. Baby octopus are perfect for barbecuing.
* Octopus can be grilled, poached, sautéed, fried or steamed. Slow cooking over low heat makes the flesh more tender. Larger octopus should be simmered gently for about 60–90 minutes.
* Fresh octopus will keep for 1–2 days in the fridge and for about 3 months in the freezer.

HOW TO... PREPARE OCTOPUS

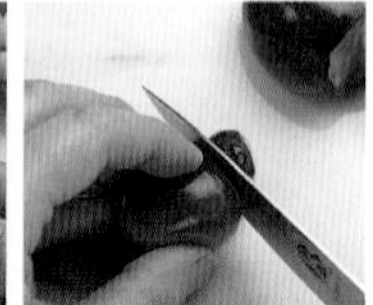

METHOD

1 Using a small knife, carefully cut between the head and tentacles of the octopus, just below the eyes.
2 Grasp the body of the octopus and push the beak up and out through the centre of the tentacles with your finger.
3 Cut the eyes from the head of the octopus by slicing off a small round, with a small sharp knife. Discard the eye section. To clean the octopus head, carefully slit through one side, avoiding the ink sac. Remove the ink sac and carefully scrape out any gut from inside the head. Rinse the head under running water to remove any remaining gut.

SQUID

These are a group of cephalopods, of which there are over 300 species, some of which can grow up to 18 metres (60 feet). The edible part of the squid is its tentacles and its long body, which can be sliced, then battered and deep-fried, stewed or left whole and stuffed. In Italy, squid are called calamari, and they are popular in the cuisines of Southeast Asia and China.

The squid has an ink sac that contains a glossy, dark ink, traditionally used to flavour and colour pasta and risotto. The ink is stored in a sac that can be removed from whole squid (and also from cuttlefish), or bought in sachets from fishmongers or at delicatessens.

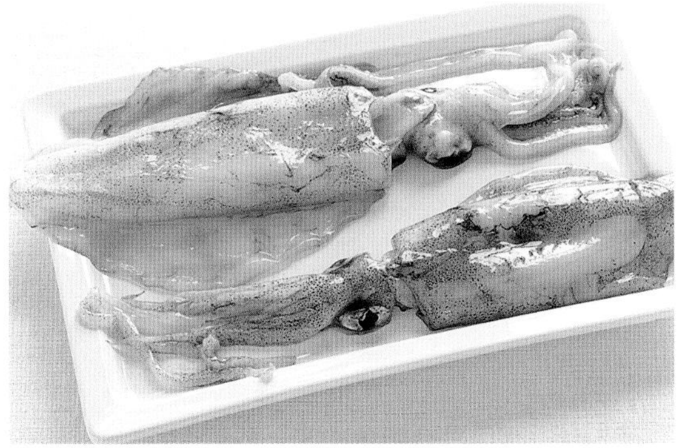

HOW TO... PREPARE SQUID

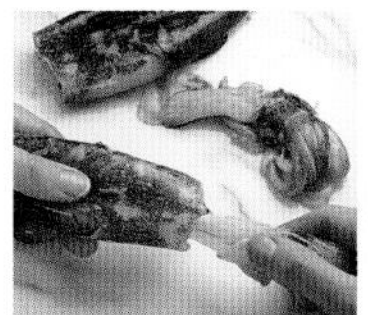

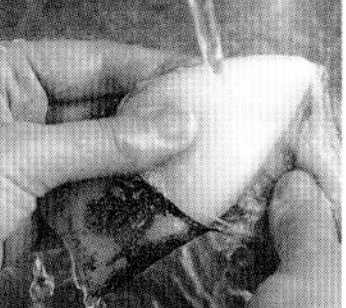

METHOD

1. Grasp the body in one hand and the head and tentacles in the other. Pull firmly to separate. If using tentacles, cut the head away and discard.
2. Pull the quill (the transparent cartilage) out from inside the body and discard it. Remove and discard any white membrane.
3. Under cold water, pull away the skin. The flaps can also be used. Use the body (tubes), flap and tentacles whole, or cut the body into rings.

SALT AND PEPPER SQUID

SERVES 6

INGREDIENTS

- 1 kg (2 lb 4 oz) cleaned squid tubes, halved lengthways
- 250 ml (9 fl oz/1 cup) lemon juice
- 250 g (9 oz/2 cups) cornflour (cornstarch)
- 1½ tablespoons salt
- 1 tablespoon ground white pepper
- 2 teaspoons caster (superfine) sugar
- 4 egg whites, lightly beaten
- oil, for deep-frying
- coriander (cilantro) leaves, to garnish
- lemon wedges, to serve

METHOD

1. Open out the squid tubes, wash and pat dry. Lay on a chopping board with the inside facing upwards. Score a fine diamond pattern on the squid, being careful not to cut all the way through. Cut the squid into 5 x 3 cm (2 x 1¼ inch) pieces. Place in a flat non-metallic dish and pour the lemon juice over. Cover and refrigerate for 15 minutes. Drain and pat dry.
2. Combine the cornflour, salt, white pepper and sugar in a bowl. Dip the squid into the egg white and dust with the flour mixture, shaking off any excess flour.
3. Fill a deep heavy-based saucepan one-third full of oil and heat to 180°C (350°F), or until a cube of bread dropped into the oil turns golden brown in 15 seconds. Deep-fry the squid in batches for 1–2 minutes, or until it turns white and curls up. Drain on paper towels. Garnish with coriander leaves and serve immediately, with lemon wedges.

CHARGRILLED OCTOPUS

SERVES 4

INGREDIENTS

16 baby octopus (about 1.5 kg/3 lb 5 oz)
170 ml (5½ fl oz/⅔ cup) extra virgin olive oil
4 thyme sprigs
2 bay leaves
2 garlic cloves, crushed
lemon wedges, to serve

METHOD

1. Prepare and clean the octopus (page 218). Skin the octopus tentacles and make small diagonal cuts along their length, cutting about a third of the way through the tentacle.
2. Put the octopus in a bowl and pour over the oil. Add the thyme, bay leaves and garlic and toss well. Cover with plastic wrap and marinate in the refrigerator overnight.
3. Soak four wooden skewers in water to prevent them burning. Heat the barbecue hotplate. Drain the oil from the octopus and thread onto the skewers. Cook for 5–7 minutes on each side, or until the octopus is golden and the tip of a knife slips through a tentacle. Season with salt and pepper and drizzle with a little of the marinade or extra virgin olive oil if you like. Leave for a few minutes and then serve with lemon wedges.

CRUMBED CALAMARI

SERVES 4

INGREDIENTS

500 g (1 lb 2 oz) squid tubes
30 g (1 oz/¼ cup) seasoned flour
1–2 eggs, lightly beaten
240 g (8½ oz/3 cups) fresh white breadcrumbs
oil, for deep-frying
tartare sauce (page 427), to serve

METHOD

1. Pat the squid with paper towels. Remove the quill and any skin. Cut into 1 cm (½ inch) rings.
2. Put the flour in a plastic bag, add the squid rings and toss to coat. Dip each ring in the beaten egg, drain off any excess, then coat in the breadcrumbs. Pat the crumbs lightly onto the rings and shake off any excess crumbs.
3. Fill a deep, heavy-based saucepan one-third full of oil and heat to 180°C (350°F), or until a cube of bread dropped into the oil turns golden brown in 15 seconds. Cook the rings in batches for 3 minutes, or until golden. Skim crumbs from the surface of the oil between batches. Drain on crumpled paper towels. Serve hot, with the tartare sauce.

CUTTLEFISH

This relation of the squid and octopus includes specimens ranging in size from 3–50 cm (1¼–20 inches) long. Like the squid, cuttlefish contain ink sacs that may be used in cooking. They have 10 large tentacles and an internal shell. To prepare, cut off the head and tentacles, then slit down one side to remove the guts and ink sac. Cut away the hard cuttleshell, cut the tentacles off the head, then discard the head. Cuttlefish can be fried briefly, steamed or barbecued. They are sold fresh, frozen or dried.

OCTOPUS SALAD

SERVES 4

INGREDIENTS

650 g (1 lb 7 oz) baby octopus
1 red chilli, seeded and finely chopped
2 tablespoons lemon juice
100 ml (3½ fl oz) olive oil
1 garlic clove, crushed
1 tablespoon chopped mint
1 tablespoon chopped parsley
1 teaspoon dijon mustard
150 g (5½ oz) mixed salad leaves
lemon wedges, to serve

METHOD

1 Prepare and clean the octopus (page 218). If the octopus seem a bit big, cut them into halves or quarters.
2 Bring a large saucepan of water to the boil, add the octopus and simmer for about 10 minutes, or until tender.
3 Make a dressing by mixing together the chilli, lemon juice, oil, garlic, mint, parsley and mustard. Season with salt and pepper.
4 Drain the octopus and put in a bowl. Pour over the dressing and cool for a few minutes before transferring to the fridge. Chill for 3 hours, then serve on a bed of salad leaves, and drizzle with dressing. Serve with lemon wedges and bread.

❮ SQUID WITH SALSA VERDE

SERVES 6

INGREDIENTS

1 kg (2 lb 4 oz) squid
250 ml (9 fl oz/1 cup) olive oil
2 tablespoons lemon juice
2 garlic cloves, crushed
2 tablespoons chopped oregano
2 tablespoons chopped flat-leaf (Italian) parsley, to serve
6 lemon wedges, to serve

SALSA VERDE

4 anchovy fillets, drained
1 tablespoon capers
1 garlic clove, crushed
3 tablespoons chopped flat-leaf (Italian) parsley
1 small handful basil
1 small handful mint
2 teaspoons red wine vinegar
60 ml (2 fl oz/¼ cup) extra virgin olive oil
1 teaspoon dijon mustard

METHOD

1 Prepare and clean the squid (page 219), reserving the tentacles. Cut the tube into 1 cm (½ inch) rings and place in a bowl with the tentacles. Add the oil, lemon juice, garlic and oregano to the bowl, and toss to coat the squid. Leave to marinate for 30 minutes.
2 To make the salsa verde, put the anchovies, capers, garlic, parsley, basil and mint in a food processor and chop in short bursts until roughly blended. Transfer to a bowl and stir in the vinegar. Slowly mix in the oil, then the mustard. Season with salt and pepper.
3 Heat a barbecue or chargrill pan until hot. Drain the squid rings and cook them in batches for 1–2 minutes each side.
4 Season the squid rings and sprinkle with parsley. Serve with the salsa verde and lemon wedges.

DEEP-FRIED SQUID WITH GINGER

SERVES 4

INGREDIENTS

500 g (1 lb 2 oz) squid tubes
1 teaspoon Chinese five-spice
1½ teaspoons sugar
3 garlic cloves, crushed
60 ml (2 fl oz/¼ cup) lime juice
60 ml (2 fl oz/¼ cup) light soy sauce
3 teaspoons sesame oil
oil, for deep-frying
20 g (¾ oz) ginger, cut into matchsticks
2 red Asian shallots, thinly sliced
1–2 red chillies, chopped
1 lime, quartered

METHOD

1 Remove the quill and any skin from the squid tubes. Cut the squid down one side to open it out, and dry with paper towels. Using a sharp knife, score into a tight diamond pattern. Combine the five-spice, 2 teaspoons salt, sugar, garlic, lime juice, soy sauce and sesame oil in a small saucepan, but don't heat it yet. Brush some of the mixture over the scored side of the squid and leave to marinate for 45 minutes. Put the squid, scored side up, on a flat surface and cut into bite-sized strips.
2 Fill a wok one-third full of oil and heat to 180°C (350°F), or until a cube of bread dropped into the oil turns golden brown in 15 seconds. Add the squid in batches and deep-fry for 50–60 seconds, or until golden brown. Drain on paper towels, then transfer to a serving bowl.
3 Add the ginger, shallots and chillies to the mixture in the saucepan and stir over medium heat for 1–2 minutes, or until fragrant. Spoon over the squid and serve at once with the lime wedges. Squeeze the juice over the squid just before eating.

FRITTO MISTO DI MARE

SERVES 4

INGREDIENTS

250 g (9 oz) baby squid
12 large prawns (shrimp)
8 baby octopus
16 scallops, cleaned
12 fresh sardines, gutted and heads removed
250 g (9 oz) firm white fish fillets, such as ling, cod or snapper, skinned and cut into large cubes

GARLIC AND ANCHOVY SAUCE

125 ml (4 fl oz/½ cup) extra virgin olive oil
2 garlic cloves, crushed
3 anchovy fillets, finely ground
2 tablespoons finely chopped parsley
pinch of chilli flakes

BATTER

200 g (7 oz) plain (all-purpose) flour
80 ml (2½ fl oz/⅓ cup) olive oil
1 large egg white

oil, for deep-frying
lemon wedges, to serve

METHOD

1 Preheat the oven to 140°C (275°F/Gas 1). Prepare and clean the squid (page 219), reserving the tentacles. Peel and devein the prawns, leaving the tails intact (page 204). Prepare and clean the octopus (page 218). If the octopus seem a bit big, cut into halves or quarters.
2 To make the garlic and anchovy sauce, warm the oil in a frying pan. Add the garlic, anchovies, parsley and chilli flakes. Cook over low heat for 1 minute, or until the garlic is soft but not brown. Serve warm or chilled.
3 To make the batter, sift the flour into a bowl and stir in ¼ teaspoon salt. Mix in the oil with a wooden spoon, then gradually add 310 ml (10¾ fl oz/1¼ cups) tepid water, changing to a whisk when the mixture becomes liquid. Continue whisking until the batter is smooth and thick. Stiffly whisk the egg white and fold into the batter.
4 Fill a deep, heavy-based saucepan one-third full of oil and heat to 190°C (375°F), or until a cube of bread dropped into the oil turns golden brown in 10 seconds.
5 Dry the seafood on paper towels so the batter will stick. Working with one type of seafood at a time, dip the pieces into the batter. Shake off the excess batter, then carefully lower into the oil. Deep-fry for 2–3 minutes, depending on the size of the pieces. Drain on paper towels, then transfer to the oven. Do not crowd the seafood. Keep warm while you fry the remaining seafood. Serve the seafood immediately with the lemon wedges and the sauce.

NOTE: In Italian, fritto misto means 'mixed fry' and refers to an assortment of small pieces of meat, fish, vegetables or cheese dipped in batter and deep-fried, or coated in egg and breadcrumbs and pan-fried. Fritto misto di mare is a platter of deep-fried fish and shellfish and is common in Italian coastal areas.

SEAFOOD ANTIPASTI

A platter of freshly prepared seafood makes a wonderful first course. The golden rule for cooking seafood is that all your ingredients must be as fresh as possible. It doesn't matter what you present on the platter but ensure that you buy fresh shellfish, or ask your fishmonger what is in season or what is the good catch of the day.

SERVES 6

INGREDIENTS

500 g (1 lb 2 oz) mussels
500 g (1 lb 2 oz) clams
250 g (9 oz) octopus
250 g (9 oz) small squid
250 g (9 oz) prawns (shrimp)
100 ml (3½ fl oz) olive oil
juice of 2 lemons
2 tablespoons finely chopped parsley
lemon wedges

METHOD

1 Clean the mussels (page 196) and clams (page 202) by scrubbing and scraping off any barnacles. Pull off the beards from the mussels and rinse well under running water. Discard any mussels or clams that are broken or open and do not close when tapped on the work surface.
2 Prepare the octopus (page 218). If the flesh is still springy and has not been tenderised, beat it with a mallet until soft. Prepare the squid (page 219), reserving the tentacles. Rinse the tubes and cut into rings. Peel and devein the prawns, leaving the tails intact (page 204).
3 Bring a large saucepan of water to the boil and add the octopus. Reduce the heat and simmer for about 20 minutes, or until tender. Add the squid and prawns. Cook for about 2 minutes, or until the prawns turn pink. Drain well.
4 Put the mussels and clams in an even layer in a steamer. Steam over boiling water for 2 minutes, or until the shells have just opened (discard any that stay closed). Pull the top shell off each mussel and clam. Arrange on a platter.
5 If you have one octopus, cut it into pieces; if you have baby ones, leave them whole. Arrange the octopus, squid and prawns on the platter and sprinkle with sea salt and black pepper. Mix the olive oil with the lemon juice and drizzle over the seafood. Cover with plastic wrap and leave to marinate in the fridge for at least 2 hours. Before serving, sprinkle with parsley. Serve with lemon wedges, and bread to mop up the juices.

SEAFOOD PLATTERS

A seafood platter makes a wonderful centrepiece for a party. For cold seafood, chill the platter or sit it on a bed of crushed ice. Serve an assortment of fresh seafood with bowls of tartare sauce (page 427) and sweet chilli sauce for dipping (page 430), lemon wedges, and finger bowls. Or make a hot seafood platter with deep-fried calamari rings, battered fish and crumbed prawn cutlets, all found in this chapter, and serve with French fries.

••FISH BASICS••

Scaling and gutting fish may seem daunting to the novice chef, but if you leave yourself enough time, and with enough practice, you will find it's not as hard as you thought. If you're still not confident, you can always ask your fishmonger to prepare your fish for you.

BUYING

It is wise to buy the best fish, whatever it is, in the shop that day, rather than an inferior fish just to fit a particular recipe. Fresh fish should smell like the sea and never smell 'fishy'. They should be firm, have shiny scales and bright, clear eyes. Really fresh fish may have gaping mouths and open gill flaps. Some fish, such as salmon and trout, are covered in a clear slime (old slime is opaque). Oily fish deteriorate faster than white fish so be particularly vigilant when buying them.

TIPS

* Allow 180–200 g (6–7 oz) fish fillet per person as a main course and 100 g (3½ oz) as a starter. If using whole fish, then buy 'plate-sized' fish.
* If buying a fish to fillet yourself, then assume it will lose half its weight in bones.

COOKING

Large fish usually benefit from being cooked in a moist heat, such as poaching or steaming, so they don't dry out. Make sure the fish is at room temperature when you cook it or the centre will stay too cold.

The most important thing when cooking fish is to cook JUST until it is done: no longer or it will be dry and fall apart. A fish is properly cooked when the flesh has turned opaque and may be more flaky in appearance (especially white fish). If the flesh is not visible, it will feel firm and flaky through the skin when you press it. If you are checking a large whole fish, you can also make a slit along the backbone and lift a little of the flesh up to check that it is opaque all the way to the bone. When cooked, the dorsal fin will pull out easily.

TIPS

* Don't salt skinned fish until just before you cook it as salt tends to draw moisture out.
* Fish cooks much faster than meat, and at a lower temperature, so keep an eye on it as you cook, especially on the barbecue.

HOW TO... SCALE AND GUT FISH

Fish need to be gutted fairly quickly as their digestive juices can break down and start to decompose the flesh. Once gutted, use the end of a teaspoon to remove any visible blood lines that run along the length of the spine, then rinse well — leaving blood in the fish may taint the flesh. For the same reason, snip out the gills. If the fins are looking ragged, trim them with scissors.

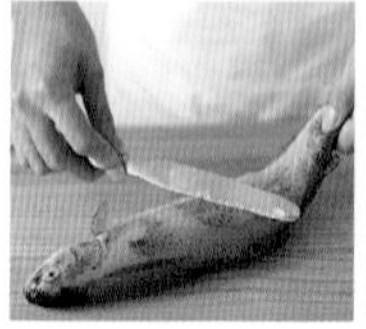

METHOD

1. To scale a fish, run the back of a knife or a fish scaler firmly across the skin against the lie of the scales.
2. With scissors, snip from the vent along to the gills, along the soft belly and then remove the guts. Snip out the gills.
3. For a smaller fish, pull the head downwards and snap the spine, then pull the guts out through the belly. Rinse and pat dry.

FILLETING

Fish can be filleted either by a fishmonger or at home (you will need a filleting knife that has a sharp flexible blade). Round fish yield two fillets, one from each side of the fish. Flat fish yield four fillets, two from each side, or two larger fillets. Depending on the size of the fish, you will need one or more fillets per person. If the fillet is very large you might just need a piece per person.

HOW TO... FILLET ROUND FISH

METHOD

1 Cut through the backbone and down the side of the head of the fish.
2 Lift the fillet by running your knife blade between the flesh and the bones until you reach the tail end.
3 Turn the fish over and remove the other fillet in the same way.

HOW TO... FILLET FLAT FISH

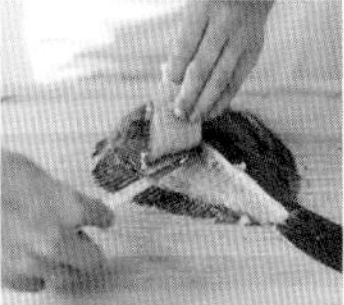
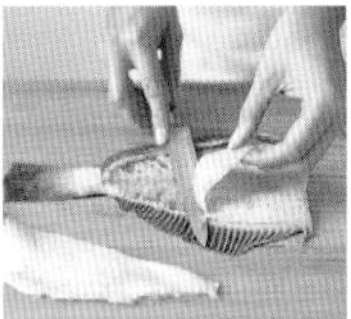

METHOD

1 Lay the fish with the dark skin side facing up. Cut behind the head, then down the centre of the spine.
2 Cut around the edge of each fillet and lift off with the knife to cut between the fillet and the bone.
3 Turn the fish over and remove the other two fillets in the same way.

SKINNING

Depending on the recipe, you may or may not need to skin your fish. If the fish is going to be covered with a sauce, it will be easier to eat the fish if it's had its skin removed. Remove the skin before cooking, or if you're cooking a whole fish, carefully peel it off after cooking.

METHOD

1 Lay the fillet, skin side down, on a chopping board, with its tail towards you. Make a small cut through the flesh to the skin.
2 Put the knife blade through the cut against the skin and slide or push the blade away from you. Hold onto the skin firmly.
3 Carry on sliding the blade up to the head. You may need to move the blade from side to side as the fillet gets thicker.

HOW TO... POCKET BONE A FISH

Fish can also be boned, leaving a whole fish with no bones and a pocket in the flesh which can be stuffed. Pocket boning is suitable for trout and mackerel.

METHOD

1 Slit an ungutted fish along its spine from the head to the tail.
2 Ease the flesh away from the bone on both sides of the fish with a sharp knife.
3 Snip though the spine and pull it out, along with the guts, and rinse well.

••OILY FISH••

There are a staggering number of fish swimming in our oceans, and myriad ways in which to cook them. Although there are many species of fish, we have divided them into two families: oily and white. Oily fish have oils throughout the fillet and in the belly cavity, rather than only in the liver like white fish. Oily fish are rich in omega-3 fatty acids and are a good source of vitamins A and D. Oily fish include salmon, fresh tuna, trout, mackerel, sardines, anchovies, whitebait, kipper, swordfish and orange roughy. Tinned tuna loses much of its oils in the canning process and so is not strictly classified as 'oily', however we have included recipes for tinned tuna in this chapter. Oily fish have a stronger flavour than white fish, and can usually cope with being teamed with more robust flavours and marinades or 'harsher' cooking methods, such as barbecuing or smoking.

GRILLED SARDINES WITH BASIL AND LEMON

SERVES 2

INGREDIENTS

- 1 lemon, cut into thin slices
- 8 large fresh sardines, scaled and gutted (page 226)
- coarse sea salt
- 80 ml (2½ fl oz/⅓ cup) olive oil
- 3 tablespoons small basil leaves

METHOD

1. Preheat a grill (broiler) or barbecue grill to very hot. Put a couple of slices of lemon inside each sardine and season both sides with sea salt and some black pepper. Drizzle with half the olive oil.
2. Put the sardines on a tray and grill (broil) for 3 minutes on each side, or place the fish directly onto the barbecue. Check to see if the fish is cooked by lifting the top side to check the inside. The flesh should look opaque.
3. Place in a shallow serving dish, scatter with basil and drizzle with the remaining olive oil. Serve warm or at room temperature.

SARDINES

These tiny oily-fleshed fish have a distinctive strong flavour and vary considerably in size. Superb summer fish, sardines are often barbecued outdoors over coals, which allows the skin to develop a wonderful crispness. Sardines are best eaten fresh as their flesh deteriorates quickly, but they can also be salt-cured and packed in oil in tins or jars.

MOROCCAN-STYLE STUFFED SARDINES

SERVES 4

INGREDIENTS

16 large fresh sardines
16 large fresh or preserved vine leaves
lemon wedges, to serve
Greek-style yoghurt, to serve

COUSCOUS STUFFING

75 g (2½ oz) instant couscous
2 tablespoons olive oil
2 tablespoons finely chopped dried apricots
3 tablespoons raisins
1 tablespoon flaked toasted almonds
1 tablespoon chopped parsley
1 tablespoon chopped mint
finely grated zest of 1 orange
2 tablespoons orange juice
1 teaspoon finely chopped preserved lemon zest (page 668)
1 teaspoon ground cinnamon
½ teaspoon harissa (page 172)

METHOD

1. Butterfly the sardines. To butterfly a sardine, cut off the head, slit open the belly with a sharp knife and remove the guts. Open out the stomach gently and place each down on its opened stomach — press lightly but firmly to open it out. Turn the fish over the other way and gently pull out the backbone. Cut the bone off at the tail end, leaving the tail attached for presentation. Rinse and pat dry with paper towels.
2. To make the stuffing, put the couscous in a bowl and add half of the oil and 50 ml (1¾ fl oz) boiling water. Stir and leave for 10 minutes to let the couscous absorb the liquid. Fluff up the grains with a fork and add the remaining oil and stuffing ingredients. Season to taste and mix well.
3. Preheat a barbecue hotplate. If you are using fresh vine leaves, bring a saucepan of water to the boil and blanch the leaves in batches for 30 seconds, then remove and pat dry with paper towels. If you are using preserved vine leaves, simply rinse and pat them dry.
4. Divide the couscous stuffing between the sardines, saving any leftover couscous for serving. Fold the sardine fillets back together to enclose the stuffing, then gently wrap a vine leaf around each sardine. Secure with a toothpick.
5. Lightly brush the hotplate with oil and cook the sardines for 6 minutes, turning halfway through the cooking time. Serve hot with lemon wedges and yoghurt.

FRIED WHITEBAIT

SERVES 4

INGREDIENTS

- 500 g (1 lb 2 oz) whitebait
- 2 teaspoons sea salt
- 2 tablespoons plain (all-purpose) flour
- 1½ tablespoons cornflour (cornstarch)
- 2 teaspoons finely chopped parsley
- oil, for deep-frying
- lemon wedges, to serve

METHOD

1. Combine the whitebait and sea salt in a bowl and mix well. Cover and refrigerate until needed.
2. Combine the sifted flours and parsley in a bowl and season well with black pepper. Fill a large heavy-based saucepan one-third full of oil and heat to 180°C (350°F), or until a cube of bread dropped into the oil browns in 15 seconds. Toss a third of the whitebait in the flour mixture, shake off the excess flour, and deep-fry for 1½ minutes, or until pale and crisp. Drain well on paper towels. Repeat with the remaining whitebait.
3. Just before you are ready to serve, reheat the oil to 190°C (375°C), or until a cube of bread browns in 10 seconds, and fry the whitebait a second time, in batches, for 1 minute, or until lightly browned. Drain on paper towels and salt lightly (this will help absorb any excess oil). Serve while hot with lemon wedges.

MARINATED FRESH ANCHOVIES

SERVES 4

INGREDIENTS

- 400 g (14 oz) fresh anchovies
- 80 ml (2½ fl oz/⅓ cup) extra virgin olive oil
- 60 ml (2 fl oz/¼ cup) lemon juice
- 2 garlic cloves, crushed
- 2 tablespoons finely chopped parsley
- 2 tablespoons finely chopped basil
- 1 small red chilli, seeded and chopped

METHOD

1. To fillet the anchovies, run your thumbnail or a sharp knife along each side of the backbone through the skin, then pull the head upwards. The head, bones and guts should all come away together, leaving you with the fillets. Carefully wash under cold water and pat dry with paper towels. Put the fillets in a single layer in a shallow serving dish.
2. Mix the remaining ingredients together with some salt and pepper and pour evenly over the anchovies. Cover the dish with plastic wrap and leave the anchovies to marinate in the fridge for at least 3 hours.
3. Before serving, bring the anchovies back to room temperature so they regain their full flavour. Serve with bread as a starter or part of an antipasti platter.

ANCHOVIES

Fresh anchovies can come as a surprise to many of us who thought anchovies only existed in tins and jars. These tiny Mediterranean fish, like sardines and whitebait, belong to the herring family and can be found at your local fishmonger. Some recipes ask for tinned anchovies and they can add a wonderful flavour to many dishes — they have been salt-cured and packed in oil. Because of their saltiness, some recipes specify for them to be soaked in water or milk for a while before cooking.

OCEAN TROUT WITH LEEK AND CAPER SAUCE

SERVES 4

INGREDIENTS

45 g (1½ oz) butter, melted
4 thick skinless ocean trout fillets (about 150 g/5½ oz each)

LEEK AND CAPER SAUCE

50 g (1¾ oz) butter
1 leek, white part only, chopped
250 ml (9 fl oz/1 cup) white wine
2 tablespoons capers, drained
1 tablespoon chopped parsley

METHOD

1 Brush a baking tray with the melted butter, put the trout on the tray and brush with a little more melted butter. Preheat the grill (broiler) to hot and place the trout under the grill. Cook, without turning, until the fish is just cooked and flakes easily when tested with a fork.
2 To make the leek and caper sauce, melt the butter in a small saucepan over low heat, add the leek and cook until soft, but not brown. Add the wine and simmer for 3–4 minutes. Stir in the capers and parsley and season with salt and black pepper.
3 Spoon the hot sauce over the fish and serve immediately with steamed baby potatoes.

NOTE: You can use salmon fillets or cutlets instead of trout.

TROUT WITH ALMONDS

SERVES 2

INGREDIENTS

2 rainbow trout, scaled and gutted (page 226)
plain (all-purpose) flour, for coating
60 g (2¼ oz) butter
1 tablespoon oil
25 g (1 oz/¼ cup) flaked almonds
2 tablespoons lemon juice
1 tablespoon finely chopped parsley, plus extra leaves to garnish
lemon wedges, to serve

METHOD

1 Wash the fish and pat dry with paper towels. Coat the fish with flour and season well on each side, as well as inside.
2 Heat half the butter and all of the oil in a large frying pan until it is very hot, then add the fish. Cook for 4 minutes on each side, or until golden brown and cooked through. Lift up one side of the fish to check if the flesh on the inside is opaque and cooked through. If cooked, the dorsal fin should pull out easily. Remove the fish and place on heated serving plates. Cover very loosely with foil and place in a warm oven.
3 Heat the remaining butter in the frying pan, add the almonds and stir over low heat until the almonds turn light golden. Add the lemon juice and parsley and season with salt and pepper. Stir until the sauce is heated through. Pour the sauce over the fish, garnish with parsley, then serve with lemon wedges.

TUNA MORNAY

SERVES 4

INGREDIENTS

- 375 ml (13 fl oz/1½ cups) milk
- 1 bay leaf
- 1 slice of onion plus 1 finely chopped onion
- 5 whole black peppercorns
- 60 g (2¼ oz) butter
- 1 celery stalk, finely chopped
- 30 g (1 oz/¼ cup) plain (all-purpose) flour
- 425 g (15 oz) tin tuna in brine, drained, flaked, brine reserved
- ¼ teaspoon ground nutmeg
- 80 ml (2½ fl oz/⅓ cup) cream
- 1 handful parsley, finely chopped
- 125 g (4½ oz/1 cup) grated cheddar cheese
- 2 hard-boiled eggs, chopped
- 40 g (1½ oz/½ cup) fresh breadcrumbs

METHOD

1. Heat the milk, bay leaf, slice of onion and peppercorns in a small saucepan. Bring to the boil, then remove from the heat, cover and set aside for 15 minutes. Strain and reserve the milk.
2. Preheat the oven to 180°C (350°F/Gas 4). Heat the butter in a saucepan and add the chopped onion and celery. Cook, stirring, for 5 minutes, until soft. Add the flour and stir for 1 minute, until the mixture is bubbly. Remove from the heat and gradually stir in the combined reserved milk and tuna brine. Stir until smooth. Return to the heat, stirring until the mixture almost boils, then simmer for 5 minutes, until thickened.
3. Add the nutmeg, cream, parsley and half the cheese. Stir until the cheese has melted. Remove from the heat, add the tuna and eggs and season. Stir to combine. Spoon the mixture into a 750 ml (26 fl oz/3 cup) greased ovenproof dish or into four ramekins. Sprinkle the top with the breadcrumbs and remaining cheese. Bake for 15–20 minutes, then place the dish under a hot grill (broiler) to brown the breadcrumb topping.

FISH CAKES

MAKES 8

INGREDIENTS

- 3 floury potatoes, quartered
- 30 g (1 oz) butter
- 1 onion, finely chopped
- 1 garlic clove, crushed
- 1 red capsicum (pepper), finely chopped
- 415 g (15 oz) tin tuna or salmon, drained
- 1 egg, lightly beaten
- 2 tablespoons lemon juice
- 3 tablespoons chopped parsley
- 30 g (1 oz/¼ cup) plain (all-purpose) flour
- 100 g (3½ oz/1 cup) dry breadcrumbs
- 1 egg, lightly beaten, extra
- 2 tablespoons milk
- oil, for shallow-frying

METHOD

1. Steam or boil the potatoes for 8–10 minutes, or until tender when pierced with the point of a knife. Drain and return to the pan. Stir over medium heat, then mash. Set aside to cool.
2. Melt the butter in a frying pan, add the onion and garlic and stir over medium heat for 5 minutes, or until soft. Add the capsicum and cook, stirring, for 5 minutes, or until soft.
3. Put the tuna in a bowl and flake with a fork. Mix in the potato, egg, onion mixture, lemon juice and parsley.
4. Place the flour on a shallow plate and the breadcrumbs on another plate. Combine the extra egg and milk in a shallow dish or bowl. Form the mixture into eight patties, coat lightly in flour, then in the egg and milk. Finally, coat with the breadcrumbs and place on a plate or baking tray. Cover and chill for 30 minutes.
5. Heat 80 ml (2½ fl oz/⅓ cup) of the oil in a heavy-based frying pan over medium heat. Add the fish cakes in batches and cook for 2–3 minutes on each side, until golden brown. Drain and serve hot.

MOROCCAN TUNA SKEWERS WITH CHERMOULA

SERVES 4

INGREDIENTS

800 g (1 lb 12 oz) tuna steaks, cut into 3 cm (1¼ inch) cubes
2 tablespoons olive oil
½ teaspoon ground cumin
2 teaspoons finely grated lemon zest

CHERMOULA

½ teaspoon ground coriander
3 teaspoons ground cumin
2 teaspoons paprika
pinch of cayenne pepper
4 garlic cloves, crushed
1 large handful parsley, chopped
2 large handfuls coriander (cilantro), chopped
80 ml (2½ fl oz/⅓ cup) lemon juice
125 ml (4 fl oz/½ cup) olive oil

METHOD

1. Soak eight wooden skewers in water for about 30 minutes to prevent them burning during cooking, or use metal skewers.
2. Put the tuna in a shallow non-metallic dish. Combine the oil, cumin and lemon zest and pour over the tuna. Toss to coat, then cover and marinate in the fridge for 10 minutes.
3. Meanwhile, to make the chermoula, put the ground coriander, cumin, paprika and cayenne pepper in a small frying pan and cook over medium heat for 30 seconds, or until fragrant. Combine with the garlic, herbs, lemon juice and olive oil and set aside.
4. Thread the tuna onto the skewers. Lightly oil a chargrill pan or barbecue grill and cook the skewers for 1 minute on each side for rare, or 2 minutes for medium. Serve the tuna skewers with rice or on a bed of couscous, with the chermoula drizzled over the tuna.

CHERMOULA

This Moroccan marinade and sauce is a wonderful pairing with fish (recipe above). The recipe varies from region to region, but usually includes fresh herbs such as parsley, basil or coriander; spices such as cumin, coriander, paprika and cayenne pepper; onions or garlic; preserved lemon or lemon juice and oil — it all depends on the cook's preferences. The fish, either whole or in pieces, is left to marinate, then fried, grilled or baked. Chermoula can also be used as a relish or dressing and served with fish, meat and vegetables. It makes a great marinade for olives as well.

ROSEMARY TUNA KEBABS WITH CHICKPEA SALSA

SERVES 4

INGREDIENTS

CHICKPEA SALSA

1 tablespoon olive oil
2–3 small red chillies, seeded and chopped
3–4 garlic cloves, crushed
1 red onion, finely chopped
3 tomatoes, seeded and chopped
60 ml (2 fl oz/¼ cup) white wine or water
400 g (14 oz) tin chickpeas, rinsed
3 tablespoons chopped oregano
4 tablespoons chopped parsley

TUNA KEBABS

1 kg (2 lb 4 oz) piece of tuna, cut into 4 cm (1½ inch) cubes
8 rosemary stems, about 20 cm (8 inches) long, with the leaves on the stem thinned out a little
lemon wedges, to serve

METHOD

1. To make the chickpea salsa, heat the olive oil in a large non-stick frying pan. Add the chilli, garlic and onion and stir over medium heat for 5 minutes, or until softened. Add the tomatoes and wine. Cook over low heat for 10 minutes, or until the mixture is soft and most of the liquid has evaporated. Stir in the chickpeas, oregano and parsley. Season with salt and freshly ground black pepper.
2. Preheat a grill (broiler) or barbecue hotplate. Thread the tuna onto the rosemary stems, lightly brush with oil, then cook, turning, for 3 minutes, or until lightly browned on the outside but still a little pink in the centre.
3. Serve the tuna with the chickpea salsa and lemon wedges.

NOTE: This recipe also works well with swordfish and salmon.

SWORDFISH WITH CAPER AND ANCHOVY SAUCE

SERVES 4

INGREDIENTS

CAPER AND ANCHOVY SAUCE

1 large garlic clove
1 tablespoon capers, rinsed and finely chopped
50 g (1¾ oz) anchovy fillets, finely chopped
1 tablespoon finely chopped rosemary or 2 teaspoons dried oregano
finely grated zest and juice of ½ lemon
80 ml (2½ fl oz/⅓ cup) extra virgin olive oil
1 large tomato, finely chopped

4 swordfish steaks
1 tablespoon extra virgin olive oil
crusty Italian bread, to serve

METHOD

1. Using a mortar and pestle, crush the garlic with a little salt. To make the caper and anchovy sauce, mix together the garlic, capers, anchovies, rosemary, lemon zest and juice, oil and tomato. Set aside for 10 minutes.
2. Preheat a barbecue grill or chargrill pan to very hot. Pat the fish dry with paper towels and lightly brush with olive oil. Sear the swordfish over high heat for 2 minutes on each side, depending on the thickness of the fish, or until just cooked. To check if the fish is cooked, use the tip of a knife to pull the flesh apart — it should be opaque.
3. If the cooked swordfish is a little oily, drain it on paper towels, then place on serving plates and drizzle with the sauce. Serve with crusty bread.

GRAVLAX

This Swedish speciality consists of raw salmon cured with salt, sugar, a spirit such as vodka and flavoured with dill. The salmon is sliced thinly and served on pumpernickel or rye bread. Gravlax means 'buried salmon', referring to the classic method of burying the salmon in the ground to cure it. It is traditionally served on 30 April in Sweden to celebrate the arrival of spring.

SERVES 24

INGREDIENTS

2 x 1 kg (2 lb 4 oz) salmon fillets
3 tablespoons sugar
1 teaspoon freshly ground black pepper
1½ tablespoons salt
1 tablespoon vodka or brandy
4 tablespoons finely chopped dill
mustard and dill sauce (page 424), to serve

METHOD

1 Freeze and then defrost the salmon to kill any bacteria or nematodes. Remove the small bones using your fingers or tweezers. Dry the fillets with paper towels and lay one fillet, skin side down, on a tray.
2 Combine the sugar, pepper and salt. Sprinkle the fillet on the tray with vodka, then rub in half the sugar mixture. Sprinkle with half of the dill. Rub the remaining sugar mixture into the other fillet and lay it, flesh side down, on top of the first fillet. Cover with plastic wrap, put a heavy board on top and weigh the salmon down with heavy tins or a foil-covered brick. Put in the fridge for 24 hours, turning it over after 12 hours.
3 Tip off any liquid. Brush off the dill and any seasoning mixture with a stiff pastry brush. Sprinkle with the dill and press onto the flesh. Shake off any excess. Serve as a whole fillet or slice it thinly on an angle towards the tail. Serve with the mustard and dill sauce.

HOW TO... PIN BONE

To pin bone a fish, you need to locate any small bones by running your fingers over the flesh. Once you've found them, pull them out with your fingers or a pair of tweezers. Wipe the fish dry with paper towels and your fish is ready for cooking.

COULIBIAC

SERVES 4–6

INGREDIENTS

- 60 g (2¼ oz) butter
- 1 onion, finely chopped
- 200 g (7 oz) button mushrooms, sliced
- 2 tablespoons lemon juice
- 220 g (7¾ oz) salmon fillet, skinned (page 227) and pin boned, cut into 2 cm (¾ inch) pieces
- 2 hard-boiled eggs, chopped
- 2 tablespoons chopped dill
- 2 tablespoons chopped parsley
- 185 g (6½ oz/1 cup) cold, cooked rice (see Notes)
- 60 ml (2 fl oz/¼ cup) cream
- 375 g (13 oz) block frozen puff pastry, thawed
- 1 egg, lightly beaten

METHOD

1. Lightly grease a baking tray. Melt half the butter in a frying pan. Add the onion and cook over medium heat for 5 minutes, or until soft but not browned. Add the mushrooms and cook for 5 minutes. Add the lemon juice to the pan and stir to combine. Transfer the mixture to a bowl.
2. Melt the remaining butter in the pan, add the salmon and cook for 2 minutes. Transfer to a separate bowl, cool slightly and add the egg, dill and parsley and season with salt and pepper. Combine gently and set aside. Combine the rice and cream in another bowl and season with salt and pepper.
3. Roll out half the pastry to a rectangle measuring 18 x 30 cm (7 x 12 inches) and place on the prepared tray. Spread half the rice mixture onto the pastry, leaving a 3 cm (1¼ inch) border all the way around. Top with the salmon mixture, then the mushroom mixture, and finish with the remaining rice.
4. Roll out the remaining pastry to 20 x 32 cm (8 x 13 inches) and place over the filling. Press the pastry edges together, then crimp to seal. Decorate with pastry offcuts if you like. Refrigerate for 30 minutes.
5. Meanwhile preheat the oven to 210°C (415°F/Gas 6–7). Brush the pastry with the beaten egg and bake for 15 minutes. Reduce the oven to 180°C (350°F/Gas 4) and bake for another 15–20 minutes, or until the top is golden brown. Serve with a green salad.

NOTES: Use ocean trout instead of the salmon if preferred.
You will need 65 g (2½ oz/⅓ cup) raw rice to give you 1 cup of cooked rice.

BAKED SALMON

SERVES 8

INGREDIENTS

- 2 kg (4 lb 8 oz) whole salmon, scaled and gutted (page 226)
- 2 spring onions (scallions), roughly chopped
- 3 dill sprigs
- ½ lemon, thinly sliced
- 6 black peppercorns
- 60 ml (2 fl oz/¼ cup) dry white wine
- 3 bay leaves

METHOD

1 Preheat the oven to 180°C (350°F/Gas 4). Rinse the salmon under cold running water and pat dry inside and out with paper towels. Stuff the cavity of the fish with the spring onion, dill, lemon slices and peppercorns.

2 Brush a large double-layered piece of foil with oil and lay the salmon on the foil. Sprinkle with wine and arrange the bay leaves over the top. Fold the foil over and wrap up, enclosing the salmon tightly.

3 Place the salmon in a shallow baking tin and bake for 30 minutes. Turn the oven off and leave the salmon in the oven for 45 minutes with the door closed.

4 Undo the foil and carefully peel away the skin of the salmon on the top side. Carefully flip the salmon onto the serving plate and remove the skin from the other side. Pull out the fins and any visible bones. Serve at room temperature. The baked salmon can be served with a sauce of your choice.

SAKE-GLAZED SALMON

SERVES 4

INGREDIENTS

- 4 x 175 g (6 oz) salmon fillets
- 1 tablespoon vegetable oil
- 1 teaspoon sesame oil
- 40 g (1½ oz) butter
- 60 ml (2 fl oz/¼ cup) sake
- 1½ tablespoons Japanese soy sauce
- 1 tablespoon mirin
- 2 teaspoons caster (superfine) sugar
- ¼ teaspoon finely grated ginger

METHOD

1 Check the salmon carefully for bones, pulling out any you find with clean tweezers. Season lightly with salt.

2 Heat the oils in a large heavy-based frying pan over medium–high heat. Add the salmon pieces, skin side down, and cook for 3 minutes, or until the skin is golden. Reduce the heat to medium, turn the fish over and cook for a further 2–3 minutes, or until almost cooked through. Remove the salmon from the pan, cover and set aside.

3 Remove any excess oil from the pan, then add the butter, sake, soy sauce, mirin, sugar and ginger to the pan. Increase the heat to high and stir to dissolve the sugar. Bring to the boil and cook, stirring, for 2 minutes, or until slightly thickened. Drizzle the glaze over the salmon. Serve with a vegetable side dish and a bowl of steamed rice.

SMOKED FISH

The technique of smoking as a means of preserving meat and fish has been in use for thousands of years. Commercially smoked fish may be salted first or immersed in brine, then exposed to smoke from hardwoods such as oak, beech or hickory, which not only preserves, but adds flavour. At home you can smoke your own fish using a kettle barbecue or a barbecue with a lid. Special woodchips (sold in barbecue and outdoor stores) give off a wonderfully scented smoke and infuse food with their aroma. Don't use wood that isn't specifically intended for smoking food.

SMOKED TROUT SALAD

SERVES 4

INGREDIENTS

6 hickory woodchips, soaked overnight
2 whole rainbow trout
1 tablespoon oil
750 g (1 lb 10 oz) kipfler (fingerling) potatoes
3 baby fennel bulbs, cut into wedges
2 tablespoons olive oil
40 g (1½ oz/1⅓ cups) watercress sprigs

DILL AND CAPER DRESSING

125 g (4½ oz/½ cup) egg mayonnaise
2 garlic cloves, crushed
1 tablespoon chopped dill
1 tablespoon baby capers, rinsed and chopped
1 tablespoon lemon juice

METHOD

1. Preheat a kettle or covered barbecue to low indirect heat. Let the coals burn down to ash, then add three woodchips to each pile of coals. When the chips begin to smoke, brush the trout with the oil, place in the middle of the barbecue, then lower the lid and cook for 10–15 minutes.
2. Combine the dill and caper dressing ingredients in a small bowl and refrigerate until needed.
3. Cook the peeled potatoes in boiling water for 5 minutes, until almost tender. Drain and cool slightly, then slice on the diagonal. Combine with the fennel and olive oil, season and toss to coat.
4. Cook the potatoes on the barbecue grill for 5 minutes on each side. Grill the fennel for 2–3 minutes on each side, or until golden. Put the potato and fennel in a serving bowl.
5. Remove the skin from the smoked trout and gently pull the flesh off the bones, flaking it into pieces. Add to the potato with the watercress and fennel. Pour on the dressing and serve.

SMOKED TROUT PATE

SERVES 6

INGREDIENTS

2 whole smoked trout or 4 smoked trout fillets, skinned, flesh flaked
200 g (7 oz) cream cheese, softened
2 tablespoons finely chopped dill
juice of ½ lemon
pinch of cayenne pepper
melba toast (page 95), to serve
lemon wedges, to serve

METHOD

1. Put the flaked trout in a bowl or food processor. Mash the flesh with a fork or briefly process until it is broken up, but still with plenty of texture.
2. Beat the cream cheese with a wooden spoon until soft. Add the smoked trout and mix together. Stir in the dill and lemon juice, then season with salt, pepper and cayenne pepper.
3. Chill the pâté until you need it but bring it to room temperature before serving or it will be too firm. Serve with melba or brown toast. Provide lemon wedges to squeeze over the pâté.

TYPES OF SMOKED FISH

SALMON
Salmon fillets are first dry-cured, then cold-smoked over chips of wood from an old oak whisky barrel or other hardwoods.

TROUT
Whole trout can be hot- or cold-smoked and are sold either as whole fish or fillets. Trout is cured and smoked like salmon to which it is similar in texture and flavour.

COD
Used like smoked haddock but often hard to find in its undyed form.

HERRINGS
The most famous smoked herring is the kipper. Real kippers are oak-smoked and pale yellow. They are sold under several names: bloaters are whole herrings brined and cold-smoked, and bucklings are hot-smoked.

MACKEREL
True smoked mackerel are beheaded and gutted before being hot-smoked. The fillets that are sold vacuum-packed may be artificially coloured and flavoured.

EEL
Sold as hot-smoked whole eel or as thin strips of fillet.

HADDOCK
Usually cold-smoked and sold as fillets under various names. Arbroath smokies (pinwiddies) are haddock that are dry-salted, hung, then smoked. Finnan haddie are oak-smoked, and Glasgow pales are lightly smoked. Buy undyed pale yellow smoked haddock if possible.

HALIBUT
This fish has a very pale whitish flesh and a slightly darker yellow skin. It is eaten cold without being recooked.

MONKFISH
This is the tail fillet that has been cured, then cold-smoked. It is eaten cold without further cooking.

salmon

trout

cod

herrings (kippers)

mackerel

eel

••WHITE FISH••

'White' is a fisheries term referring to several species of fish with fins. White fish are divided into round fish (cod, coley), which live near the sea bed, and flat fish such as plaice, which live on the sea bed. Unlike oily fish, white fish contain oil only in their livers and their flesh is firm, dry and white, often forming thick flakes when cooked. The subtle flavour of white fish is usually best suited to quick cooking methods, such as pan-frying, poaching or steaming. Some examples of firm white fish include cod, blue-eye, pike, haddock, whiting, sole, skate, dory, ling, monkfish, red and grey mullet, snapper, sea bass, sea bream and shark.

FISH TERRINE

This terrine has a soft texture and is delicately flavoured with dill and chives. It makes an elegant first course. Serve in slices sprinkled with a little caviar. The refreshing cucumber and watercress salad offsets the richness of the terrine.

SERVES 4

INGREDIENTS

- 400 g (14 oz) pike fillet, skinned (page 227) (or use trout or carp)
- 110 g (3¾ oz) salmon fillet, skinned (page 227)
- 2 large egg whites
- 250 ml (9 fl oz/1 cup) thick (double) cream
- 1 tablespoon lemon juice
- 1 tablespoon chopped dill
- 1 teaspoon chopped chives
- pinch of white pepper
- pinch of ground nutmeg
- salmon roe, to garnish
- 1 Lebanese (short) cucumber, thinly sliced lengthways
- 1 handful watercress leaves
- dill sprigs, to garnish

METHOD

1. Cut the pike into bite-sized pieces and chill well. Cut the salmon into short, thin strips.
2. Prepare a 22 x 7 x 7 cm (8½ x 2¾ x 2¾ inch) loaf (bar) tin by lining it with baking paper and lightly oiling the paper.
3. Using a food processor, blend the pike to a smooth paste. Add the egg whites, cream, lemon juice, dill and chives, and process briefly using the pulse. Season with salt, white pepper and nutmeg. Alternatively, chop the fish very finely by hand and mix with the other ingredients.
4. Preheat the oven to 180°C (350°F/Gas 4). Transfer half of the pike mixture to the loaf tin. Lay the salmon strips on top, all facing the same direction so the terrine will cut easily. Season with salt and white pepper and cover with the remaining pike mixture. Cover with foil and place the loaf tin in a roasting tin. Add boiling water to the roasting tin until one-third of the loaf tin is immersed in water. You may find it easier to add the boiling water to the tin once it is in the oven.
5. Bake for 40–45 minutes, or until firm to the touch. Remove the tin from the water and leave until cold. Refrigerate overnight. Invert the terrine out onto a serving plate. Peel off the paper and serve in slices, garnished with the salmon roe, cucumber, watercress and dill.

PAN-FRIED FISH

SERVES 4

INGREDIENTS

2–3 tablespoons plain (all-purpose) flour
4 firm white fish fillets
olive oil, for shallow-frying

METHOD

1 Sift the flour with a little salt and pepper onto a plate. Pat the fish dry and coat both sides with the flour, shaking off any excess.

2 Heat about 3 mm (⅛ inch) of oil in a large frying pan until very hot. Put the fish into the hot oil and cook for 3 minutes on one side, then turn and cook the other side for 2 minutes, or until the coating is crisp and well browned. Reduce the heat to low and cook for another 2–3 minutes, or until the flesh flakes easily when tested with a fork.

3 Remove the fish from the pan and drain briefly on paper towels. If you are cooking in batches, keep warm while cooking the remaining fish. Serve immediately with a salad or steamed vegetables.

COATING AND BATTER FOR FISH

Batter provides a protective coating for the fish, which not only seals in the juices but also adds flavour. Most firm white fish are suitable to be battered and deep-fried. Each of the following batters will coat four fish fillets (we used snapper), but the egg white batter is enough for six fillets. You can use the mixtures for other seafood too.

To prepare for the deep-fried recipes, fill a deep heavy-based saucepan or deep-fryer one-third full of oil and heat to 180°C (350°F), or until a cube of bread dropped into the oil turns golden brown in 15 seconds. Pat the fish dry with paper towel, dust lightly with flour, then dip in the batter, in batches, allowing the excess to drain off. Lower the fish in batches into the oil and deep-fry until golden brown. Drain on crumpled paper towels.

BASIC BATTER

INGREDIENTS

- 125 g (4½ oz/1 cup) self-raising flour
- 1 egg
- 250 ml (9 fl oz/1 cup) milk
- 1 tablespoon oil

METHOD

1. Sift the flour into a large bowl and make a well in the centre. Beat the egg with the milk and oil in a large jug. Gradually pour into the well, whisking to make a smooth batter.
2. Cover and leave to stand for 10 minutes. The mixture should be the consistency of thick cream. Thin with a little extra milk if necessary.

BEER BATTER

INGREDIENTS

- 30 g (1 oz/¼ cup) self-raising flour
- 30 g (1 oz/¼ cup) cornflour (cornstarch)
- 60 g (2¼ oz/½ cup) plain (all-purpose) flour
- 250 ml (9 fl oz/1 cup) chilled beer

METHOD

1. Sift the self-raising flour, cornflour and plain flour into a large bowl and make a well in the centre.
2. Gradually whisk in the beer to make a smooth batter. Cover and set aside.

NOTE: You can use soda water instead of beer, or vary the beer for a different flavour.

EGG WHITE BATTER

INGREDIENTS

- 125 g (4½ oz/1 cup) self-raising flour
- 250 ml (9 fl oz/1 cup) water
- 2 egg whites

METHOD

1. Sift the flour into a large bowl, make a well in the centre and gradually whisk in the water to make a smooth batter. Leave to stand for 5 minutes.
2. Beat the egg whites in a small clean bowl with electric beaters until stiff peaks form, then fold into the batter in two batches. Use immediately.

OTHER BATTER AND COATING IDEAS

* Add a little oil or melted butter to the basic batter to enrich the flavour.
* Flavour the flour used for coating the fish with spices such as cayenne pepper, chilli flakes or curry powder. Or add snipped chives and finely grated lemon or lime zest to the flour.
* Finely chop a mixture of herbs such as parsley and dill and mix with spices such as crushed fennel or cumin seeds. Press the herb and spice mixture onto the fish and pan-fry in a little hot oil in a non-stick frying pan.

NORI AND CRUMB COATING

INGREDIENTS

90 g (3¼ oz/1½ cups) Japanese breadcrumbs (panko)
1 sheet nori (dried seaweed), cut into small pieces
seasoned flour, for coating
1 egg

METHOD

1 Combine the breadcrumbs with the torn nori.
2 Put the flour in a shallow bowl. Lightly beat the egg in a separate bowl.
3 Pat the fish dry with paper towel and dust lightly with flour. Dip in the egg, allowing the excess to drain off, then coat in the breadcrumbs and nori.

CHIVE AND LEMON COATING

INGREDIENTS

100 g (3½ oz/1¼ cups) fresh breadcrumbs
6 tablespoons finely snipped chives
1 teaspoon finely grated lemon zest
seasoned flour, for coating
1 egg
30 g (1 oz) butter
2 tablespoons oil

METHOD

1 Combine the breadcrumbs, chives and lemon zest in a shallow bowl. Put the flour in another shallow bowl and lightly beat the egg in a separate bowl.
2 Pat the fish dry with paper towel, dust lightly with the flour, then dip into the egg, allowing the excess to drain off. Coat in the breadcrumbs, pressing on the fish to adhere.
3 Melt the butter and oil in a large frying pan, add the fish in batches and cook over medium heat until golden brown. Turn and cook the other side, adding butter and oil if required.

BEER-BATTERED FISH AND CHIPS

SERVES 4

INGREDIENTS

oil, for deep-frying
4 large all-purpose potatoes, such as pontiacs, cut into finger-sized chips
1 quantity beer batter (see opposite)
4 firm white fish fillets (about 200 g/7 oz each), skinned and pin boned (page 236)
seasoned flour, for coating
2 lemons, cut into wedges

METHOD

1 Preheat the oven to 180°C (350°F/Gas 4).
2 Fill a large heavy-based saucepan one-third full of oil and heat to 180°C (350°F), or until a cube of bread dropped into the oil turns golden brown in 15 seconds. Deep-fry the potato chips in batches for 2–4 minutes, or until pale golden. Remove with a slotted spoon and drain on paper towels. Deep-fry again for 3 minutes, or until golden and cooked through. Keep hot in the oven while you cook the fish.
3 Reheat the oil to 180°C (350°F). Stir the batter, then coat the fish fillets in the seasoned flour, shaking off the excess. Dip the fillets into the batter, allowing the excess to drip off a little. Slowly ease the fillets into the hot oil, holding the tail out for a few seconds — turn with tongs if necessary. Cook for 4–5 minutes, or until golden brown and the fish is cooked through. Remove with a slotted spoon and drain on paper towels. Serve with the chips and lemon wedges.

NOTE: Use any type of white fish (flathead, ling, snapper, blue-eye or john dory are all good).

THAI FISH CAKES

MAKES 30

INGREDIENTS

450 g (1 lb) firm white fish fillets
1 tablespoon Thai red curry paste (page 438)
1 tablespoon fish sauce
1 egg
50 g (1¾ oz) snake (yard-long) beans, thinly sliced
5 kaffir lime leaves, finely shredded
oil, for deep-frying
sweet chilli sauce, to serve
chopped peanuts, to serve
finely diced cucumber, to serve

METHOD

1 Remove any skin and bone from the fish and roughly chop the flesh. In a food processor or a blender, mince the fish fillets until smooth.
2 Add the curry paste, fish sauce and egg, then blend briefly until smooth. Spoon into a bowl and mix in the beans and lime leaves.
3 Use wet hands to shape the fish paste into thin, flat cakes, about 5 cm (2 inches) across, using about a tablespoon of mixture for each.
4 Heat 5 cm (2 inches) of oil in a wok or deep frying pan over medium heat. When the oil is just starting to smoke, drop a small piece of fish cake into the oil. If it sizzles immediately, the oil is ready.
5 Lower five or six of the fish cakes into the oil and deep-fry them until they are golden brown on both sides and very puffy. Remove with a slotted spoon and drain on paper towels. Keep the cooked fish cakes warm while deep-frying the rest. Serve hot with sweet chilli sauce. Garnish with chopped peanuts and cucumber.

NOTE: For a variation, make up another batch of the fish mixture but leave out the curry paste. Cook as above and serve both types together.

SKATE WITH BROWN BUTTER

This is considered by many as the classic way in which to prepare skate. Black or brown butter (beurre noire or beurre noisette) is the classic accompaniment to many French dishes, and in this recipe the butter works well with the sweet flavour of the skate.

SERVES 4

INGREDIENTS

COURT BOUILLON
250 ml (9 fl oz/1 cup) white wine
1 onion, sliced
1 carrot, sliced
1 bay leaf
4 black peppercorns

4 x 250 g (9 oz) skate wings, skinned
100 g (3½ oz) butter
1 tablespoon chopped parsley
1 tablespoon capers, rinsed and chopped

METHOD

1 To make the court bouillon, put the wine, onion, carrot, bay leaf, peppercorns and 1 litre (35 fl oz/4 cups) water into a large frying pan. Bring to the boil and simmer for 20 minutes. Strain the court bouillon and return the liquid to the cleaned pan.
2 Add the skate, making sure that it is completely covered with the liquid. Simmer for 5–10 minutes (depending on the thickness of the wing), or until the flesh is opaque and flakes when tested with the point of a knife. Lift out the fish, drain, then cover and keep warm.
3 Heat the butter in a frying pan and cook over medium heat for about 2 minutes, or until it turns brown to make a beurre noisette. Do not let it get too brown or it will taste burnt. Remove from the heat and stir in the parsley and capers. Season with salt and black pepper. Pour the sauce over the fish and serve immediately with steamed potatoes and lemon wedges.

FISH PIE

SERVES 4

INGREDIENTS

- 800 g (1 lb 12 oz) firm white fish fillets
- 375 ml (13 fl oz/1½ cups) milk
- 1 onion, roughly chopped
- 2 cloves
- 50 g (1¾ oz) butter
- 2 tablespoons plain (all-purpose) flour
- pinch of ground nutmeg
- 2 tablespoons chopped parsley
- 155 g (5½ oz/1 cup) peas
- 750 g (1 lb 10 oz) floury potatoes, peeled and quartered
- 2 tablespoons hot milk
- 30 g (1 oz/¼ cup) grated cheddar cheese

METHOD

1 Put the fish in a frying pan and cover with the milk. Add the onion and cloves and bring to the boil. Reduce the heat and simmer for about 5 minutes, or until the fish is cooked — the flesh should be opaque and flake easily with a fork.

2 Preheat the oven to 180°C (350°F/Gas 4). Remove the fish from the pan, reserving the milk and onion mixture. Discard the cloves. Allow the fish to cool, then remove any skin and bones and flake into bite-sized pieces.

3 Heat half the butter in a saucepan, stir in the flour and cook, stirring, for a minute. Remove from the heat, add the reserved milk mixture and stir until smooth. Return to the heat and cook, stirring until the sauce comes to the boil and thickens. Cook for 1 minute. Remove from the heat, allow to cool slightly, then add the nutmeg, parsley and peas. Season well with salt and freshly ground black pepper, and gently fold in the fish. Spoon into a 1.25 litre (5 cup) ovenproof dish.

4 Cook the potatoes in boiling water until tender. Drain and add the hot milk and remaining butter. Mash until very smooth, then add the cheese. If the mash is very stiff you may need to add a little more milk — only add a little bit at a time, as the mash should be fairly firm.

5 Spoon the mashed potato into a piping bag and pipe it over the filling. Rough up the surface with a fork. Transfer to the oven and bake for 30 minutes, or until heated through and the potato is golden.

CEVICHE

Popular in Spanish-speaking South American countries, ceviche consists of thinly sliced raw fish, left to marinate overnight in a mixture of lime juice, chilli, onion, coriander and garlic. The acid from the lime juice partially cooks the fish and turns the flesh opaque. Ceviche was traditionally made with white fish, but today scallops, prawns and even salmon are used. Ceviche is served cold as an appetiser and sometimes mixed with tomatoes, capsicum, onions and avocado and presented in a lettuce leaf.

SALT COD FRITTERS

MAKES 35

INGREDIENTS

- 500 g (1 lb 2 oz) salt cod
- 1 large potato (200 g/7 oz), unpeeled
- 2 tablespoons milk
- 60 ml (2 fl oz/¼ cup) olive oil
- 1 small onion, finely chopped
- 2 garlic cloves, crushed
- 30 g (1 oz/¼ cup) self-raising flour
- 2 eggs, separated
- 1 tablespoon chopped parsley
- olive oil, for deep-frying

METHOD

1. Soak the cod in cold water for 24–48 hours, changing the water regularly to remove as much salt as possible (see box below).
2. Cook the potato in a saucepan of boiling water for 20 minutes, or until soft. When cool, peel and mash with the milk and 2 tablespoons of the oil.
3. Drain the cod, cut into large pieces and place in a saucepan. Cover with water, bring to the boil over high heat, then reduce the heat to medium and cook for 10 minutes, or until soft and there is a froth on the surface. Drain. When cool enough to handle, remove the skin and any bones, then mash well with a fork until flaky.
4. Heat the remaining oil in a small frying pan and cook the onion over medium heat for 5 minutes, or until softened and starting to brown. Add the garlic and cook for 1 minute. Remove from the heat.
5. Combine the potato, cod, onion, flour, egg yolks and parsley in a bowl and season. Whisk the egg whites until stiff, then fold into the mixture. Fill a large heavy-based saucepan one-third full of oil and heat to 190°C (375°F), or until a cube of bread dropped into the oil turns golden brown in 10 seconds. Drop heaped tablespoons of mixture into the oil and cook for 2 minutes, or until puffed and golden. Drain and serve.

HOW TO... PREPARE SALT COD

Salt cod, also known as baccala, bacalao or bacalhau, is made by coating whole gutted fish or fillets with a coarse salt to dry and preserve it. When buying salt cod, look for centre cuts of fillet, as these are fatter and more meaty.

To prepare the cod, soak it in cold water for 24–48 hours. After every 3 hours, drain the cod and add fresh water. The salt cod is ready when the fish has plumped up and the water is no longer very salty — test the water by dipping your finger in and tasting it. The cod is now ready to be cooked.

COD BRANDADE

This rich garlicky purée is traditionally made with *morue*, the French word for salt cod. Salt cod is also sold as *bacalao*, its Spanish name. Serve warm or cold with toasted slices of baguette.

SERVES 6

INGREDIENTS

- 450 g (1 lb) salt cod
- 200 g (7 oz) roasting potatoes, cut into 3 cm (1¼ inch) chunks
- 150 ml (5 fl oz) olive oil
- 250 ml (9 fl oz/1 cup) milk
- 4 garlic cloves, crushed
- 2 tablespoons lemon juice
- olive oil, extra, to drizzle

METHOD

1 Soak the cod in cold water for 24–48 hours, changing the water regularly to remove as much salt as possible (see box, opposite).

2 Drain the cod and place in a large saucepan of clean water. Bring to the boil over medium heat, reduce the heat and simmer for 30 minutes. Drain, then cool for 15 minutes.

3 Cook the potatoes in boiling, salted water for 15 minutes, until tender. Drain and keep warm.

4 Remove the skin from the fish and break the flesh into large flaky pieces, discarding any bones. Put the flesh in a food processor. Using two separate pans, gently warm the oil in one, and the milk and garlic in another.

5 Start the food processor and, with the motor running, alternately add small amounts of milk and oil until you have a thick, paste-like mixture. Add the potato and process this in short bursts until combined, being careful not to overwork the mixture once the potato has been added.

6 Transfer to a bowl and gradually add the lemon juice, to taste, and plenty of freshly ground black pepper. Gently lighten the mixture by fluffing it up with a fork. Drizzle with the oil before serving.

GRILLED RED MULLET WITH HERB SAUCE

SERVES 4

INGREDIENTS

- 4 x 200 g (7 oz) whole red mullet
- 60 ml (2 fl oz/¼ cup) lemon juice
- 60 ml (2 fl oz/¼ cup) olive oil

HERB SAUCE

- 100 g (3½ oz) English spinach
- 60 ml (2 fl oz/¼ cup) olive oil
- 1 tablespoon white wine vinegar
- 1 tablespoon chopped parsley
- 1 tablespoon chopped chervil
- 1 tablespoon chopped chives
- 1 tablespoon finely chopped capers
- 2 anchovy fillets, finely chopped
- 1 hard-boiled egg, finely chopped

METHOD

1 Preheat a barbecue grill or hotplate. Make a couple of deep slashes in the thickest part of each fish. Pat the fish dry with paper towel and sprinkle inside and out with salt and pepper. Drizzle with a little of the combined lemon juice and olive oil. Transfer to the barbecue and cook for 4–5 minutes on each side, or until the fish flakes when tested with the tip of a knife. Baste with the lemon juice and oil during cooking.

2 To make the herb sauce, wash the spinach and put it in a large saucepan with just the water clinging to the leaves. Cover the pan and steam the spinach for 2 minutes, or until just wilted. Drain, cool and squeeze with your hands to get rid of the excess liquid. Finely chop. Mix the spinach with the oil, vinegar, herbs, capers, anchovy and egg in a food processor, or pound to a thick paste using a mortar and pestle.

3 Spoon the sauce onto a plate and place the fish on top to serve.

❮ SOLE VERONIQUE

SERVES 4

INGREDIENTS

- 12 sole fillets
- 250 ml (9 fl oz/1 cup) fish stock (page 10)
- 60 ml (2 fl oz/¼ cup) white wine
- 1 French shallot, thinly sliced
- 1 bay leaf
- 6 black peppercorns
- 2 parsley sprigs
- 3 teaspoons butter
- 3 teaspoons plain (all-purpose) flour
- 125 ml (4 fl oz/½ cup) milk
- 60 ml (2 fl oz/¼ cup) cream
- 125 g (4½ oz) seedless white grapes, peeled

METHOD

1. Preheat the oven to 180°C (350°F/Gas 4). Put the fish in a greased shallow ovenproof dish.
2. Combine the stock, wine, shallot, bay leaf, peppercorns and parsley in a jug and pour over the fish. Cover with greased foil and bake for 15 minutes, or until the fish flakes when tested with a fork. Carefully lift the fish out of the liquid and transfer to another dish. Cover with foil and keep warm.
3. Pour the cooking liquid into a saucepan and boil for about 2 minutes, or until reduced by half, then strain through a fine sieve.
4. In a clean saucepan, melt the butter, add the flour and stir for 1 minute, or until pale and foaming. Remove from the heat and gradually stir in the combined milk, cream and reduced cooking liquid. Return to the heat and stir until the mixture boils and thickens. Season with salt and pepper, add the grapes and then stir until heated through. Serve the sauce over the fish.

NOTE: You can substitute flounder for the sole.

SOLE MEUNIERE

This classic recipe, served in some of the world's top restaurants, is actually a quick and easy staple supper in France. Meunière means 'millers' style', probably referring to the flour for dusting.

SERVES 4

INGREDIENTS

- 4 Dover sole, gutted and dark skin removed
- 3 tablespoons plain (all-purpose) flour
- 200 g (7 oz) clarified butter (page 120)
- 2 tablespoons lemon juice
- 4 tablespoons chopped parsley
- lemon wedges, to serve

METHOD

1. Pat the fish dry with paper towels and then dust lightly with the flour and season. Heat 150 g (5½ oz) of the butter in a frying pan large enough to fit all four fish, or use half the butter and cook the fish in two batches.
2. Put the fish in the pan, skin side up, and cook for 4 minutes on each side, until golden. Lift the fish out onto warm plates and drizzle with the lemon juice and sprinkle with parsley. Add the remaining butter to the pan and heat until it browns to make a beurre noisette. Pour over the fish (it will foam as it mixes with the lemon juice) and serve with lemon wedges.

QUENELLES

Quenelles are small oval balls of chopped fish or meat, usually cooked by poaching. Originally quenelles were made from chopped fish, meat or poultry, but today the term more widely refers to their shape, and quenelles can be made of anything from fish to thickened cream, mousse or sorbet. Quenelles can be a little tricky to make — the key lies in keeping the mixture chilled.

PIKE QUENELLES

SERVES 6

INGREDIENTS

- 450 g (1 lb) pike fillet, bones and skin removed
- 2 tablespoons finely chopped parsley
- 200 ml (7 fl oz) milk
- 80 g (2¾ oz/⅔ cup) plain (all-purpose) flour
- 2 large eggs, lightly beaten
- 150 g (5½ oz) butter, softened and cubed
- 2 large egg whites
- 200 ml (7 fl oz) thick (double) cream
- 1 litre (35 fl oz/4 cups) fish stock (page 10)

SAUCE

- 50 g (1¾ oz) butter
- 40 g (1½ oz/⅓ cup) plain (all-purpose) flour
- 400 ml (14 fl oz) milk
- 80 ml (2½ fl oz/⅓ cup) thick (double) cream
- large pinch of ground nutmeg
- 65 g (2¼ oz/½ cup) grated gruyère cheese

METHOD

1. Pound the fish to a paste using a mortar and pestle, or purée in a food processor. Transfer to a mixing bowl, stir in the parsley, then cover and refrigerate.
2. Put the milk in a saucepan and bring just to boiling point. Take the pan off the heat and add all the flour. Return to gentle heat and beat in the flour, then take the pan off the heat and leave to cool. Using electric beaters or a wooden spoon, gradually add the eggs, beating after each addition. Add the butter, piece by piece, then stir the mixture into the fish purée, cover and chill.
3. When the mixture is very cold, put the bowl inside a larger bowl filled with ice cubes. Gradually and alternately add the egg whites and cream, beating after each addition. Season generously, cover and chill again.
4. To make the sauce, melt the butter in a saucepan, then stir in the flour to make a roux. Cook, stirring constantly, for 2 minutes without allowing the roux to brown. Remove from the heat and gradually add the milk, stirring after each addition until smooth. Return to the heat and bring to the boil. Simmer for 2 minutes, add the cream and season with nutmeg, salt and pepper.
5. Using two tablespoons, mould the fish mixture into 30 quenelles. (Hold the bowl ends of the spoons opposite each other and round off the sides of the quenelles with one of the spoons.) Place them on a buttered baking tray in the fridge for 20 minutes.
6. Heat the stock in a large frying pan until barely simmering and gently lower the quenelles into the liquid in batches. Poach, without boiling, for 5–7 minutes, or until the quenelles rise to the surface and feel firm to the touch. Use a slotted spoon to gently lift the quenelles into six lightly buttered gratin dishes or one large dish.
7. Preheat the grill (broiler). Pour the sauce over the quenelles and scatter with the cheese. Grill until golden brown and bubbling. Serve with steamed potatoes and green beans

NOTE: Use sole or salmon if pike is not available.

SPICY WHOLE SNAPPER WITH A WINE BUTTER SAUCE

SERVES 4

INGREDIENTS

- 1 kg (2 lb 4 oz) whole snapper, cleaned and scaled (page 226)
- 2 celery stalks, sliced on the diagonal
- 2 red capsicums (peppers), sliced on the diagonal
- 3 spring onions (scallions), thinly sliced
- 125 ml (4 fl oz/½ cup) white wine
- 1 tablespoon Japanese seven-spice powder (shichimi togarashi) (page 419)
- 1 lemon, halved lengthways and thinly sliced
- 40 g (1½ oz) unsalted butter, chopped

METHOD

1. Preheat a kettle or covered barbecue to medium indirect heat.
2. Trim the snapper fins using a pair of kitchen scissors. Wash the fish well and pat dry with paper towels. Take two sheets of foil large enough to encase the fish and lay them on a flat surface. Top with the same amount of baking paper. Fold the edges into a tight, secure seam to form a large waterproof casing for the fish.
3. Spread the celery, capsicum and spring onion in the centre of the baking paper, then lay the fish lengthways over the vegetables. Pour the wine over and around the fish and sprinkle generously with salt, freshly ground black pepper and the seven-spice powder. Overlap the lemon slices along the centre of the fish, then dot with butter and enclose the paper over the fish. Fold the ends in several times to seal in the liquid.
4. Put the fish parcel on the barbecue grill, then lower the lid and cook for about 15 minutes, or until the fish flakes when tested in the thickest part with a fork. Serve hot, with rice and steamed green vegetables.

FISH BAKED IN SALT

SERVES 4–6

INGREDIENTS

- 1.8 kg (4 lb) whole white fish, such as blue-eye or sea bass, scaled and gutted (page 226)
- 2 lemons, sliced
- 4 thyme sprigs
- 1 fennel bulb, thinly sliced
- 3 kg (6 lb 12 oz) rock salt

METHOD

1. Preheat the oven to 200°C (400°F/Gas 6). Rinse the fish and pat dry inside and out with paper towels. Place the lemon, thyme and fennel inside the cavity.
2. Pack half the salt into a large baking tin and place the fish on top. Cover with the remaining salt, pressing down until the salt is packed firmly around the fish.
3. Bake the fish for 30–40 minutes, or until a skewer inserted into the centre of the fish comes out hot. Carefully remove the salt from the top of the fish to one side of the tin. Peel the skin away, ensuring that no salt remains on the flesh. Serve hot or cold with aïoli (page 422) or your choice of accompaniment.

STEAMING

Steaming is a popular and gentle way to cook fish fillets, parcels of fish and whole fish. Use a bamboo steamer and put the fish on a piece of baking paper or a plate. If you are using flavourings such as herbs, put the herbs in the bottom of the steamer, then lay the fish on top of them. When steaming, choose pieces of fish that will hold their shape and not become too fragile. Banana leaves can also be used when steaming. Use them for wrapping the fish — they will protect it from direct heat, as well as add a subtle extra flavour. The leaves will char as they cook. You can find banana leaves in Asian supermarkets, often in the freezer cabinets.

JASMINE TEA-STEAMED FISH

SERVES 4

INGREDIENTS

- 200 g (7 oz) jasmine tea leaves
- 100 g (3½ oz) ginger, thinly sliced
- 4 spring onions (scallions), cut into 5 cm (2 inch) lengths
- 4 x 200 g (7 oz) skinless firm white fish fillets

SPRING ONION SAUCE

- 125 ml (4 fl oz/½ cup) fish stock (page 10)
- 60 ml (2 fl oz/¼ cup) light soy sauce
- 3 spring onions (scallions), thinly sliced
- 1 tablespoon grated ginger
- 2 teaspoons sugar
- 1 large red chilli, sliced

METHOD

1. Line a double bamboo steamer with baking paper. Place the tea, ginger and spring onion in a layer on the bottom steamer basket. Cover and steam over a wok of simmering water for 10 minutes, or until the tea is moist and fragrant.
2. Lay the fish in a single layer in the top steamer basket and steam for 5–10 minutes, or until the fish flakes easily when tested with a fork.
3. To make the sauce, combine all the ingredients in a small saucepan with 125 ml (4 fl oz/½ cup) water. Heat over low heat for 5 minutes, or until the sugar has dissolved. Drizzle the fish with the sauce and serve with rice.

› STEAMED SNAPPER WITH ASIAN FLAVOURS

SERVES 2

INGREDIENTS

- 800 g (1 lb 12 oz) whole snapper, scaled and gutted (page 226)
- 3 lemongrass stems
- 1 handful coriander (cilantro)
- small knob of ginger, cut into thin matchsticks
- 1 large garlic clove, cut into thin slivers
- 2 tablespoons soy sauce
- 60 ml (2 fl oz/¼ cup) oil
- 1 tablespoon fish sauce
- 1 small red chilli, seeded and finely chopped

METHOD

1. Score the fish with diagonal cuts on both sides. Cut each stem of lemongrass into three and lightly squash each piece with the end of the handle of a large knife. Put half the lemongrass in the middle of a piece of foil large enough to cover the fish. Lay the fish on top. Put the remaining lemongrass and half of the coriander leaves inside the cavity of the fish.
2. Mix the ginger, garlic, soy sauce, oil, fish sauce and chilli together. Drizzle the mixture over the fish and scatter with the remaining coriander.
3. Enclose the fish in the foil and sit in a large bamboo or metal steamer over a pan or wok of simmering water. Steam for 25 minutes, or until the flesh of the fish is opaque and white. Serve with stir-fried Asian greens and rice.

GREEN CURRY WITH FISH BALLS

This is a Thai classic curry using fish balls rather than slices of fish but, if time is short, use the fish slices. To make the fish balls, the fish is processed, then pounded to give it more texture.

SERVES 4

INGREDIENTS

- 350 g (12 oz) firm white fish fillets, roughly cut into pieces
- 60 ml (2 fl oz/¼ cup) coconut cream
- 2 tablespoons Thai green curry paste (page 438)
- 400 ml (14 fl oz) coconut milk
- 350 g (12 oz) mixed Thai eggplants (aubergines), quartered, and pea eggplants
- 2 tablespoons fish sauce
- 2 tablespoons grated palm sugar (jaggery)
- 50 g (1¾ oz) galangal, thinly sliced
- 3 kaffir lime leaves, torn in half
- 1 handful Thai basil, to garnish
- ½ long red chilli, seeded and thinly sliced, to garnish

METHOD

1 In a food processor or a blender, chop the fish fillets into a smooth paste. If you have a mortar and pestle, pound the fish paste for another 10 minutes to give it a chewy texture.

2 Put the coconut cream in a wok or saucepan and simmer over medium heat for 5 minutes, or until the cream separates and a layer of oil forms on the surface. Stir the cream if it starts to brown around the edges. Add the curry paste, stir well to combine and cook until fragrant. Add nearly all of the coconut milk and mix well.

3 Use a spoon or wet hands to shape the fish paste into small balls or discs, about 2 cm (¾ inch) across, and drop them into the coconut milk. Add the eggplants, fish sauce and sugar to the wok and cook for 12–15 minutes, stirring occasionally, until the fish balls and eggplants are cooked through.

4 Stir in the galangal and lime leaves. Taste, then adjust the seasoning if necessary. Spoon into a serving bowl and sprinkle with the last bit of coconut milk, basil leaves and sliced chilli.

FISH SAUCE

Popular throughout Southeast Asia, particularly in Thailand and Vietnam, fish sauce is a pungent, salty liquid used as a condiment and flavouring. The liquid is clear amber to dark brown in colour and is used in much the same way as soy sauce. In Vietnam, fish sauce is served with most meals as a dipping sauce. It's made from salted and fermented dried fish or shrimp, which are layered into large wooden barrels and left to ferment. After 3 months or so, the liquid is drained off to produce a high-quality sauce, normally reserved for table use. Subsequent drainings yield a fish sauce of lower quality that is used for cooking. Fish sauce is called *nam pla* in Thailand and *nuoc mam* in Vietnam.

FISH TIKKA

Tikka is the Hindi word for chunk. Here, fish chunks are marinated in a blend of spices and yoghurt and cooked. In India, a tandoor, a charcoal-fired clay oven is used but the home barbecue is a good substitute.

SERVES 8

INGREDIENTS

MARINADE
- 500 g (1 lb 2 oz/2 cups) Greek-style yoghurt
- ½ onion, finely chopped
- 2 cm (¾ inch) piece ginger, grated
- 4 garlic cloves, crushed
- 1 teaspoon ground coriander
- 2 tablespoons lemon juice
- 1½ tablespoons garam masala
- 1 teaspoon paprika
- 1 teaspoon chilli powder
- 2 tablespoons tomato paste (concentrated purée)
- 1 teaspoon salt

- 500 g (1 lb 2 oz) firm white fish fillets
- 2 onions, each cut into 8 chunks
- 2 small green or red capsicums (peppers), each cut into 8 chunks
- 50 g (1¾ oz) cucumber, peeled and diced
- 1 tablespoon chopped coriander (cilantro)
- lemon wedges, to serve

METHOD

1. To make the marinade, mix half the yoghurt with the remaining marinade ingredients in a shallow dish large enough to take the prepared skewers. You will need eight metal skewers.
2. Cut the fish into 24–32 bite-sized chunks. On each skewer, thread three or four pieces of fish and chunks of onion and capsicum, alternating them. Put the skewers in the marinade and turn them so that all the fish and vegetables are well coated. Cover and marinate in the fridge for at least 1 hour, or until you are ready to cook.
3. Preheat the barbecue hotplate. Lift the skewers out of the marinade and cook for 5–6 minutes, turning once, or until the fish is cooked and the fish and the vegetables are slightly charred.
4. Meanwhile, stir the cucumber and coriander into the other half of the yoghurt. Serve the fish with the yoghurt and lemon wedges.

MILD INDIAN MOLEE

SERVES 6

INGREDIENTS
- 1 tablespoon oil
- 1 large onion, thinly sliced
- 3 garlic cloves, crushed
- 2 small green chillies, finely chopped
- 2 teaspoons ground turmeric
- 1 teaspoon ground coriander
- 1 teaspoon ground cumin
- 4 cloves
- 6 curry leaves
- 400 ml (14 fl oz) tin coconut milk
- 600 g (1 lb 5 oz) firm white fish fillets, cut into large pieces
- 1 tablespoon chopped coriander (cilantro)

METHOD

1. Heat the oil in a deep, heavy-based frying pan, add the onion and cook for 5 minutes. Add the garlic and chilli and cook for 5 minutes, or until the onion is soft. Add the turmeric, coriander, cumin and cloves and stir-fry for 2 minutes.
2. Stir in the curry leaves, ½ teaspoon salt and the coconut milk and bring to just below boiling point. Reduce the heat and simmer for 20 minutes.
3. Add the fish pieces to the sauce. Bring the sauce back to a simmer and cook for 5 minutes, or until the fish is cooked through and flakes easily. Check the seasoning, add more salt if necessary, then stir in the coriander.

CHAPTER SIX

PASTA, RICE AND NOODLES

••PASTA••

There can be no ingredient more instantly connected with Italian cooking than pasta. Marco Polo used to be credited with its discovery during his travels in medieval China and, while it is undoubtedly true that both countries have a long history of noodle-making, it has now been proved that pasta existed in the Mediterranean world long before Marco Polo.

FRESH EGG PASTA

Fresh egg pasta is made from eggs and doppio zero (00) flour, a soft wheat flour, sometimes with a little semolina flour added. This mixture gives a soft pliable pasta that can be easily shaped by hand. It is used to make lasagne sheets, folded into shapes such as tortellini or cut into ribbons. You can buy fresh pasta from the refrigerated section of most supermarkets or you can make your own at home.

DRIED PASTA

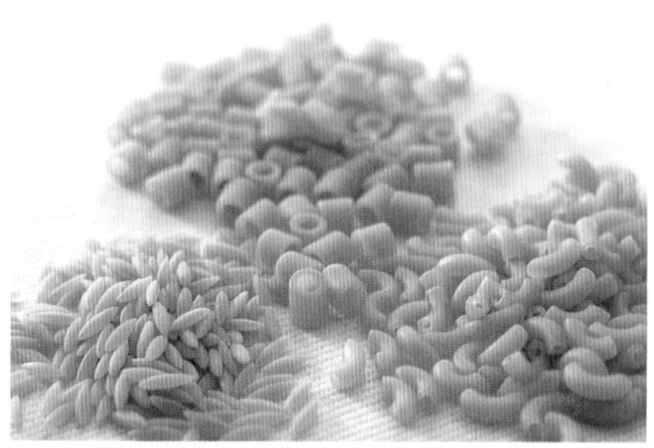

Dried pasta is made with high-gluten durum wheat flour and water. It is a tough dough that can be easily forced through machines known as dies to be shaped and cut, then dried. Dried pasta includes short pastas such as penne and macaroni and lengths such as spaghetti and tagliatelle. Dried pasta can also be made with flour and eggs; this is usually shaped into filled pasta such as ravioli or cut as ribbons and dried as nests.

HOW TO... COOK PASTA

* Always cook pasta in lots of boiling salted water — about 1 litre (35 fl oz/4 cups) per 100 g/3½ oz pasta. The Italians say that water for cooking pasta should be as salty as the sea.
* Keep the water at a rolling boil and stir the pasta only once or twice to stop it clumping together. Adding a little oil to the water may prevent the pasta from sticking, but this will make it slippery and harder for the sauce to stick.
* Cook pasta until it is *al dente* (to the tooth) — the pasta should retain a little bite.
* Taste the pasta until it is right, following the cooking instructions on the packet as a guide. When the pasta is cooked, add cold water to the saucepan to stop it cooking, then drain — do not rinse it.
* Drained pasta should still have a little water clinging to it to stop it sticking.

HOME-MADE FRESH PASTA

Although there are so many varieties of commercially made pasta available, making pasta by hand is a satisfying experience, and it isn't as hard as you think.

INGREDIENTS

500 g (1 lb 2 oz/4 cups) doppio zero (00) or plain (all-purpose) flour
4 eggs
chilled water

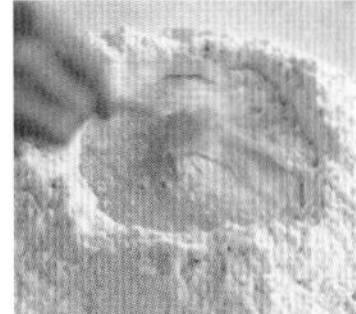

MAKES 700 G (1 LB 9 OZ)

METHOD

1. Mound the flour on a work surface or in a large bowl. Make a well in the centre.
2. Break the eggs into the well and whisk with a fork, incorporating the flour as you whisk. You may need to add chilled water (¼ teaspoon at a time) to make a loosely massed dough.
3. Turn the dough onto a lightly floured surface — the dough should be soft, pliable and dry to the touch. Knead for 6–8 minutes, or until smooth and elastic with a slightly glossy appearance. Cover with a tea towel and leave for 30 minutes. The dough is then ready to roll out.

HOW TO... ROLL OUT THE DOUGH

Divide the dough into two or three portions. Work with one portion at a time, keeping the rest covered. Flatten the dough onto a lightly floured surface and roll out from the centre to the outer edge, rotating the dough often. When you have a 5 mm (¼ inch) thick circle of dough, fold it in half and roll it out again. Do this four times to give a smooth circle of pasta, then roll to a thickness of 2.5 mm (⅛ inch), mending any tears with a little pasta from the edge of the circle and a little water. Transfer to a lightly floured tea towel.

If the pasta is to be filled, keep it covered so it doesn't dry out. If the sheets are to be cut into lengths or shapes, leave them uncovered while you roll out the other portions, so that the surface will dry out.

If you have a pasta machine, divide the dough into six to eight flattened rectangular pieces and cover with plastic wrap. Work the dough through the rollers three times, making the setting smaller each time.

HOW TO... CUT BY MACHINE

METHOD

1. Attach the blades to your machine: the wide one for tagliatelle, the narrower one for linguine.
2. Feed a sheet of pasta into the machine and carefully collect the cut pasta as it comes out at the other end.
3. Hang the pasta to dry on a floured broomhandle or on a pasta dryer, or coil it into nests. Toss the nests in a little semolina to stop them sticking.

HOW TO... CUT BY HAND

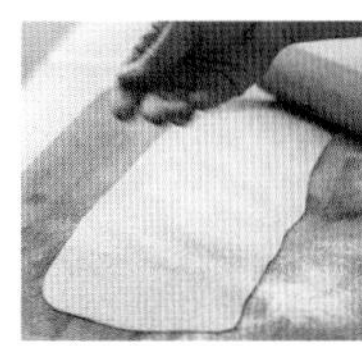

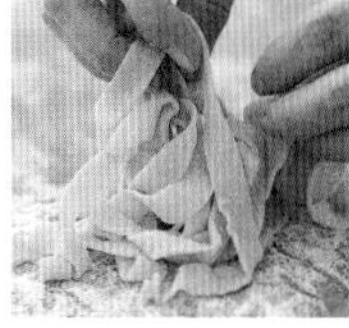

METHOD

1. Roll out the pasta into long flat sheets of the width you want and dust them with semolina.
2. Roll up each sheet loosely and cut into slices of whatever width you want. (The thicker widths are easier to handle when they are unrolled.)
3. Toss the strips in more semolina to keep them separate or hang them up to dry, as above.

SPAGHETTI WITH GARLIC AND CHILLI

SERVES 4

INGREDIENTS

- 500 g (1 lb 2 oz) spaghetti
- 125 ml (4 fl oz/½ cup) extra virgin olive oil
- 2–3 garlic cloves, finely chopped
- 1–2 red chillies, seeded and finely chopped
- 3 tablespoons chopped parsley
- grated parmesan cheese, to serve

METHOD

1. Cook the spaghetti in a large saucepan of rapidly boiling salted water until *al dente*. Drain and return to the pan.
2. Meanwhile, heat the extra virgin olive oil in a large frying pan. Add the garlic and chilli, and cook over very low heat for 2–3 minutes, or until the garlic is golden. Take care not to burn the garlic or chilli as this will make the sauce bitter.
3. Toss the parsley and the warmed oil, garlic and chilli mixture through the pasta. Season with salt and pepper. Serve with the parmesan.

SPAGHETTI PUTTANESCA

SERVES 4

INGREDIENTS

- 80 ml (2½ fl oz/⅓ cup) olive oil
- 2 onions, finely chopped
- 3 garlic cloves, finely chopped
- ½ teaspoon chilli flakes
- 6 large ripe tomatoes, diced
- 4 tablespoons salted capers, rinsed
- 8 anchovy fillets in oil, drained and chopped
- 150 g (5½ oz) kalamata olives
- 3 tablespoons chopped parsley
- 500 g (1 lb 2 oz) spaghetti

METHOD

1. Heat the olive oil in a saucepan, add the onion and cook over medium heat for 5 minutes. Add the garlic and chilli flakes to the saucepan and cook for 30 seconds. Add the tomato, capers and anchovies. Simmer over low heat for 10–15 minutes, or until the sauce is thick and pulpy. Stir in the olives and parsley.
2. While the sauce is cooking, cook the spaghetti in a large saucepan of rapidly boiling salted water until *al dente*. Drain and return to the pan.
3. Add the sauce to the pasta and stir it through. Season to taste and serve immediately.

ORECCHIETTE WITH BROCCOLI

SERVES 4

INGREDIENTS

- 750 g (1 lb 10 oz) broccoli, cut into florets
- 500 g (1 lb 2 oz) orecchiette
- 60 ml (2 fl oz/¼ cup) extra virgin olive oil
- 8 anchovy fillets
- ½ teaspoon chilli flakes
- 30 g (1 oz/⅓ cup) grated pecorino or parmesan cheese

METHOD

1. Blanch the broccoli in a large saucepan of boiling salted water for 5 minutes, or until just tender. Remove with a slotted spoon, drain well and return the water to the boil. Cook the pasta in the boiling water until *al dente*, then drain well and return to the pan.
2. Meanwhile, heat the oil in a heavy-based frying pan and cook the anchovies over very low heat for 1 minute. Add the chilli flakes and broccoli. Increase the heat to medium and cook, stirring, for 5 minutes, or until the broccoli is well coated and beginning to break apart. Season. Add to the pasta, add the cheese and toss.

FETTUCINE PRIMAVERA

SERVES 6

INGREDIENTS

- 500 g (1 lb 2 oz) fettucine or tagliatelle
- 150 g (5½ oz) asparagus spears, cut into short lengths
- 155 g (5½ oz/1 cup) frozen or fresh broad (fava) beans
- 30 g (1 oz) butter
- 1 celery stalk, sliced
- 155 g (5½ oz/1 cup) fresh peas
- 310 ml (10¾ fl oz/1¼ cups) cream
- 50 g (1¾ oz/½ cup) grated parmesan cheese

METHOD

1. Cook the pasta in a large saucepan of rapidly boiling salted water until *al dente*. Drain and return to the pan.
2. Meanwhile, cook the asparagus in boiling water for 2 minutes, then lift out and drop into a bowl of iced water.
3. Add the frozen broad beans to the boiling water. Remove immediately and cool in cold water. Drain, then peel. If you're using fresh broad beans, cook them for 2–5 minutes, or until tender. If the beans are young, the skin can be left on, but old beans should be peeled.
4. Heat the butter in a heavy-based frying pan. Add the celery and stir for 2 minutes. Add the peas and cream and cook gently for 3 minutes. Add the asparagus, broad beans, parmesan, and season to taste. Bring to the boil and cook for 1 minute. Add the cooked pasta and toss well.

BUCATINI ALLA NORMA

SERVES 4–6

INGREDIENTS

- 1 large eggplant (aubergine), cut into 1 cm (½ inch) slices
- 185 ml (6 fl oz/¾ cup) olive oil
- 1 onion, finely chopped
- 2 garlic cloves, crushed
- 800 g (1 lb 12 oz) tin chopped tomatoes
- 1 handful basil, torn
- 500 g (1 lb 2 oz) bucatini
- 60 g (2¼ oz/¼ cup) fresh ricotta cheese, crumbled
- 50 g (1¾ oz/½ cup) grated pecorino or parmesan cheese

METHOD

1. Put the eggplant slices in a bowl of salted water for 10 minutes. Drain and dry thoroughly with a tea towel.
2. Heat 2 tablespoons of the oil in a heavy-based frying pan and cook the onion over medium heat for 5 minutes, or until softened. Add the garlic to the pan and cook for a further 30 seconds. Add the tomatoes and season to taste. Reduce the heat and cook for 20–25 minutes, or until the sauce has thickened and reduced.
3. Heat the remaining olive oil in a large frying pan. When the oil is hot, add the eggplant slices a few at a time and cook for 3–5 minutes, or until lightly browned on both sides. Drain well on paper towels. Cut each slice of eggplant into three pieces and add to the tomato sauce with the torn basil. Stir and keep warm over low heat.
4. Cook the pasta in a large saucepan of rapidly boiling salted water until *al dente*. Drain well and add to the tomato sauce along with the ricotta and pecorino. Toss well and serve.

PENNE WITH FRESH TOMATO SAUCE

SERVES 4

INGREDIENTS

- 2 tablespoons extra virgin olive oil
- 2 garlic cloves, thinly sliced
- 1 tablespoon chopped herbs, such as thyme, rosemary or basil
- 800 g (1 lb 12 oz) tomatoes, chopped
- 500 g (1 lb 2 oz) penne
- grated parmesan cheese, to serve

METHOD

1. Heat the olive oil in a saucepan and add the garlic and herbs, except the basil, which should be added at the end or it will become bitter. Cook until the garlic just browns, then add the tomatoes. Season and break up the tomatoes with the edge of a spoon.
2. Simmer for 20–30 minutes, or until the sauce thickens. Stir occasionally to stop it sticking to the saucepan.
3. Cook the pasta in a large saucepan of rapidly boiling salted water until *al dente*. Drain. Stir the basil into the sauce and taste for seasoning. Serve the sauce over the pasta and sprinkle with the grated parmesan.

SPAGHETTI VONGOLE

SERVES 4

INGREDIENTS

- 500 g (1 lb 2 oz) spaghetti or linguine
- 80 ml (2½ fl oz/⅓ cup) olive oil
- 2 garlic cloves, crushed
- pinch of chilli flakes
- 500 g (1 lb 2 oz) clams (vongole), cleaned (page 202)
- 150 ml (5 fl oz) white wine
- 3 tablespoons chopped parsley

METHOD

1 Cook the pasta in a large saucepan of rapidly boiling salted water until *al dente*.

2 While the pasta is cooking, heat the oil in a large saucepan over low heat. Add the garlic and chilli and sauté for 1 minute.

3 Add the clams and wine. Bring to the boil and cook until the wine has evaporated, stirring occasionally. Cover and cook for 3 minutes. Remove the lid and discard any clams that remain closed. Stir in the parsley.

4 Drain the pasta and stir in the clams. Serve with crusty bread.

RIGATONI WITH OXTAIL SAUCE

SERVES 4

INGREDIENTS

- 2 tablespoons olive oil
- 1.5 kg (3 lb 5 oz) oxtail, jointed
- 2 large onions, sliced
- 4 garlic cloves, chopped
- 2 celery stalks, sliced
- 2 carrots, thinly sliced
- 60 ml (2 fl oz/¼ cup) red wine
- 2 large rosemary sprigs
- 3 tablespoons tomato paste (concentrated purée)
- 4 tomatoes, peeled and chopped (page 347)
- 1.5 litres (6 cups) beef stock (page 11)
- 500 g (1 lb 2 oz) rigatoni

METHOD

1 Heat the oil in a large heavy-based saucepan. Brown the oxtail, remove from the pan and set aside. Add the onion, garlic, celery and carrot to the pan and stir for 3–4 minutes, or until the onion is lightly browned.

2 Return the oxtail to the pan and add the wine and rosemary. Cover and cook for 10 minutes, shaking the pan occasionally to prevent the meat from sticking to the bottom. Add the tomato paste, tomatoes and 500 ml (17 fl oz/2 cups) of the stock and simmer, uncovered, for 30 minutes, stirring the mixture occasionally.

3 Add another 500 ml (17 fl oz/2 cups) of the stock and cook for 30 minutes, then add another 250 ml (9 fl oz/1 cup) of stock and cook for a further 30 minutes. Finally, add the remaining stock and cook until the oxtail is tender and the meat is falling from the bone. The liquid should have reduced to a thick sauce.

4 Just before the meat is cooked, cook the pasta in a large saucepan of rapidly boiling salted water until *al dente*. Serve the meat and sauce over the hot pasta.

SPAGHETTI CARBONARA

SERVES 6

INGREDIENTS

500 g (1 lb 2 oz) spaghetti
8 slices bacon
4 eggs
50 g (1¾ oz/½ cup) grated parmesan cheese
310 ml (10¾ fl oz/1¼ cups) cream

METHOD

1. Cook the spaghetti in a large saucepan of rapidly boiling salted water until *al dente*. Drain and return to the pan.
2. While the pasta is cooking, discard the bacon rind and cut the bacon into thin strips. Fry over medium heat until crisp. Drain on paper towels.
3. Beat the eggs, parmesan and cream until well combined. Add the bacon and pour over the warm pasta. Toss gently to coat the pasta.
4. Return the pan to the heat and cook over low heat for 1 minute, or until slightly thickened. Season with black pepper before serving

LINGUINE PESTO

SERVES 4–6

INGREDIENTS

PESTO
100 g (3½ oz) basil
2 garlic cloves, crushed
40 g (1½ oz/¼ cup) pine nuts, toasted
185 ml (6 fl oz/¾ cup) olive oil
50 g (1¾ oz/½ cup) grated parmesan cheese, plus extra to serve

500 g (1 lb 2 oz) linguine

METHOD

1. Process the basil, garlic and pine nuts together in a food processor. With the motor running, add the oil in a steady stream until mixed to a smooth paste. Transfer to a bowl, stir in the parmesan and season to taste.
2. Cook the pasta in a large saucepan of rapidly boiling salted water until *al dente*. Drain and return to the pan. Toss enough of the pesto through the pasta to coat it well. Serve sprinkled with parmesan.

NOTE: Refrigerate any leftover pesto in an airtight jar for up to a week. Cover the surface with a layer of oil. Freeze for up to 1 month.

PESTO

Originating in Genoa, pesto is an uncooked sauce of basil, pine nuts, garlic, olive oil and either parmesan or pecorino sardo cheese, with basil being the prominent flavour (see recipe above). Pesto is usually served as a pasta sauce, but it also works well with chicken and fish. Traditionally it is made using a mortar and pestle but can also be made in a food processor — turn the machine off and on as you make it so the blade does not heat up and spoil the basil leaves. Use a sweet rather than peppery olive oil such as a Ligurian olive oil, so that it doesn't overpower the flavour.

SPAGHETTI BOLOGNESE

SERVES 4–6

INGREDIENTS

- 2 tablespoons olive oil
- 2 garlic cloves, crushed
- 1 large onion, chopped
- 1 carrot, chopped
- 1 celery stalk, chopped
- 500 g (1 lb 2 oz) minced (ground) beef
- 500 ml (17 fl oz/2 cups) beef stock (page 11)
- 375 ml (13 fl oz/1½ cups) red wine
- 850 g (1 lb 14 oz) tin chopped tomatoes
- 1 teaspoon sugar
- 3 tablespoons chopped parsley
- 500 g (1 lb 2 oz) spaghetti
- grated parmesan cheese, to serve

METHOD

1. Heat the olive oil in a large deep frying pan. Add the garlic, onion, carrot and celery and stir for 5 minutes over low heat until the vegetables are golden.
2. Increase the heat, add the beef and brown well, stirring and breaking up any lumps with a fork as it cooks. Add the stock, wine, tomatoes, sugar and parsley.
3. Bring the mixture to the boil, reduce the heat and simmer for 1½ hours, stirring occasionally. Season to taste.
4. While the sauce is cooking and shortly before serving, cook the pasta in a large saucepan of rapidly boiling salted water until *al dente*. Drain and then divide among serving bowls. Serve the sauce over the top of the pasta and sprinkle with parmesan.

SPAGHETTI MARINARA

SERVES 6

INGREDIENTS

- 60 ml (2 fl oz/¼ cup) white wine
- 60 ml (2 fl oz/¼ cup) fish stock (page 10)
- 1 garlic clove, crushed
- 500 g (1 lb 2 oz) clams, cleaned (page 202)
- 12 mussels, cleaned (page 196)
- 500 g (1 lb 2 oz) spaghetti
- 30 g (1 oz) butter
- 125 g (4½ oz) small squid tubes, sliced into rings
- 125 g (4½ oz) firm white fish fillets, cubed
- 200 g (7 oz) raw prawns (shrimp), peeled and deveined
- 1 large handful parsley, chopped

TOMATO SAUCE

- 2 tablespoons olive oil
- 1 onion, finely diced
- 1 carrot, sliced
- 1 red chilli, seeded and chopped
- 2 garlic cloves, crushed
- 425 g (15 oz) tin chopped tomatoes
- 125 ml (4 fl oz/½ cup) dry white wine
- 1 teaspoon sugar
- pinch of cayenne pepper

METHOD

1. To make the tomato sauce, heat the oil in a saucepan, add the onion and carrot and stir over medium heat for 10 minutes, until the vegetables are lightly browned. Add the chilli, garlic, tomatoes, wine, sugar and cayenne pepper. Simmer for 30 minutes, stirring occasionally.
2. Meanwhile, heat the wine, stock and garlic in a large saucepan and add the clams. Cover the pan and shake it over high heat for 1–2 minutes. Remove the clams as they open and discard any that remain stubbornly closed. Once you have removed all the clams, add the mussels to the pan, cover and steam for 3–5 minutes. After 3 minutes start lifting out the opened mussels. After 5 minutes discard any unopened mussels. Strain and keep the cooking liquid.
3. Cook the pasta in a large saucepan of rapidly boiling salted water until *al dente*. Drain and keep warm. Meanwhile, melt the butter in a frying pan, add the squid, fish and prawns and stir-fry for 2 minutes. Remove the seafood from the pan.
4. Add the cooking liquid, clams, mussels, squid, fish, prawns and parsley to the tomato sauce and reheat gently. Gently toss with the pasta.

CREAMY PRAWNS WITH FETTUCINE

SERVES 4

INGREDIENTS

- 500 g (1 lb 2 oz) fettucine
- 30 g (1 oz) butter
- 1 tablespoon olive oil
- 6 spring onions (scallions), chopped
- 1 garlic clove, crushed
- 500 g (1 lb 2 oz) raw prawns (shrimp), peeled and deveined
- 250 ml (9 fl oz/1 cup) cream
- 2 tablespoons chopped parsley

METHOD

1. Cook the pasta in a large pan of boiling salted water until *al dente*. Drain and return to the pan.
2. Heat the butter and oil in a frying pan, add the spring onion and garlic and stir over low heat for 1 minute. Add the prawns and cook for 2–3 minutes, or until the flesh changes colour. Remove the prawns from the pan and set aside.
3. Add the cream to the pan and bring to the boil. Reduce the heat and simmer until the sauce begins to thicken. Return the prawns to the pan, season to taste, and simmer for 1 minute. Add the pasta and toss together well to coat. Sprinkle with parsley and serve.

RAVIOLI

This Italian dish is made of small pasta parcels enclosing a variety of fillings. Ravioli are cooked in boiling water and served with a sauce or with butter or olive oil and seasoning. Fillings for ravioli vary, from the simplest spinach and ricotta to elaborate veal, sweetbread, lambs' brains, pork, parmesan and breadcrumbs.

SERVES 4

INGREDIENTS

FILLING

30 g (1 oz) butter
½ small onion, finely chopped
2 garlic cloves, crushed
90 g (3¼ oz) prosciutto, finely chopped
125 g (4½ oz) minced (ground) pork
125 g (4½ oz) minced (ground) veal
½ teaspoon finely chopped fresh oregano, or ⅛ teaspoon dried oregano
1 teaspoon paprika
2 teaspoons tomato paste (concentrated purée)
125 ml (4 fl oz/½ cup) chicken stock (page 11)
2 egg yolks

1 quantity fresh pasta dough (page 259), rolled out
1 egg, lightly beaten

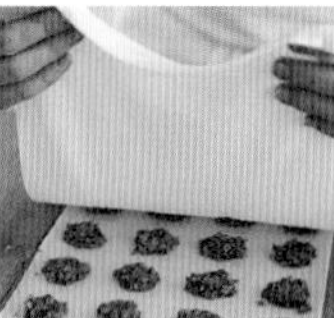

METHOD

1 To make the filling, heat the butter in a frying pan. Cook the onion, garlic and prosciutto over low heat for 5–6 minutes without browning. Add the pork and veal, increase the heat and lightly brown, breaking up the lumps. Add the oregano and paprika, season well and stir in the tomato paste and stock.
2 Cover the pan and cook for 50 minutes. Uncover, increase the heat and cook for 10 minutes, until the filling is quite dry. Cool, then chop to get rid of any lumps. Stir in the egg yolks.
3 To make the ravioli, divide the pasta sheets into four: two 20 x 30 cm (8 x 12 inch) sheets and two slightly larger. Dust the surface with semolina and lay out one of the smaller sheets (cover the rest of the pasta with a damp tea towel). Lightly score the sheet into 24 squares. Place a scant teaspoon of filling in the centre and flatten it slightly with the back of the spoon.
4 Brush beaten egg along the score lines around the filling. Take one of the larger pasta sheets and cover the first, starting at one end. Match the edges and press the top sheet onto the beaten egg as you go (avoid stretching the top sheet). Run your finger around the filling and along the cutting lines to seal. Use a pastry wheel or sharp knife to cut into 24 squares. Repeat with the remaining sheets and filling. (If you are not using the ravioli immediately, place them on baking paper dusted with semolina and cover with a tea towel — don't refrigerate or they will become damp.)
5 Cook the ravioli, in small batches, in a large saucepan of boiling salted water until *al dente*. Remove and drain with a slotted spoon. Serve on their own or with melted butter and snipped chives, a drizzle of olive oil or grated parmesan.

TORTELLINI FILLED WITH PUMPKIN AND SAGE

According to legend, it was Venus' navel glanced through a keyhole that provided the inspiration for the shape of this small filled pasta. Tortellini are often served in a broth or with sage-flavoured butter or, as here, simply with a drizzle of oil and a sprinkling of parmesan.

SERVES 6

INGREDIENTS

FILLING

- 900 g (2 lb) pumpkin or butternut pumpkin (squash), peeled and cubed
- 125 ml (4 fl oz/½ cup) olive oil
- 1 small red onion, finely chopped
- 100 g (3½ oz) ricotta cheese
- 1 egg yolk, beaten
- 25 g (1 oz/¼ cup) grated parmesan cheese
- 1 teaspoon ground nutmeg
- 2 tablespoons chopped sage

- 1 quantity fresh pasta dough (page 259), rolled out
- 1 egg
- 2 teaspoons milk
- extra virgin olive oil, to serve
- grated parmesan cheese, to serve

METHOD

1. Preheat the oven to 190°C (375°F/Gas 5). To make the filling, put the pumpkin in a roasting tin with half the olive oil and lots of salt and pepper. Bake in the oven for 40 minutes, or until it is completely soft.
2. Meanwhile, heat the remaining olive oil in a saucepan and gently cook the onion until soft. Put the onion and pumpkin in a bowl, draining off any excess oil, and mash well. Leave to cool, then crumble in the ricotta. Mix in the egg yolk, parmesan, nutmeg and sage. Season well.
3. To make the tortellini, roll out the pasta to the thinnest setting on the machine or with a large rolling pin. Cut the pasta into 8 cm (3¼ inch) squares. Mix together the egg and milk to make an egg wash and brush lightly over the pasta just before you fill each one. To fill the pasta, put a small teaspoon of filling in the middle of each square and fold it over diagonally to make a triangle, pressing down the corners. Pinch together the two corners on the longer side. (If you are not cooking the tortellini immediately, place them, well spaced out, on baking paper dusted with semolina and cover with a tea towel. They can be left for 1–2 hours, but don't refrigerate or they will become damp.)
4. Cook the tortellini in small batches in a large saucepan of rapidly boiling salted water until *al dente*. Remove with a slotted spoon and allow to drain. Serve with a drizzle of olive oil and sprinkle with the parmesan.

HOW TO... SHAPE TORTELLINI

Tortellini look impressive and are really quite simple to make. Start with a square of pasta, brush with the egg wash, put the filling in the centre and then fold the square into a triangle. Now just pinch the two corners together. The egg wash will make the pasta stick together.

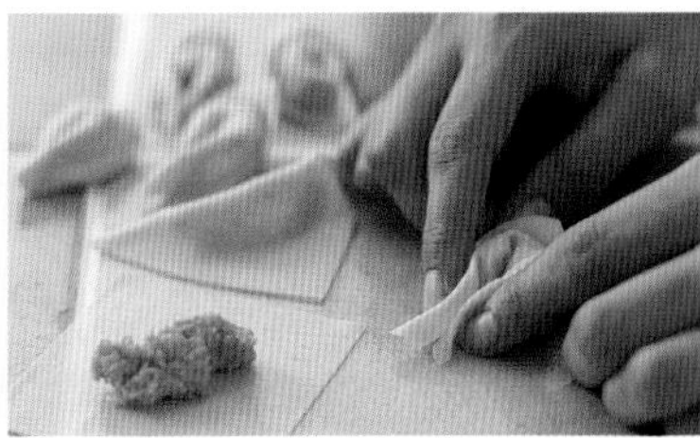

LASAGNE

SERVES 4

INGREDIENTS

- 2 tablespoons oil
- 30 g (1 oz) butter
- 1 large onion, finely chopped
- 1 carrot, finely chopped
- 1 celery stalk, finely chopped
- 500 g (1 lb 2 oz) minced (ground) beef
- 150 g (5½ oz) chicken livers, finely chopped (see Notes)
- 250 ml (9 fl oz/1 cup) tomato passata (puréed tomatoes)
- 250 ml (9 fl oz/1 cup) red wine
- 2 tablespoons chopped parsley
- 375 g (13 oz) fresh lasagne sheets (page 259) (see Notes)
- 100 g (3½ oz/1 cup) grated parmesan cheese

BECHAMEL SAUCE

- 60 g (2¼ oz) butter
- 40 g (1½ oz/⅓ cup) plain (all-purpose) flour
- 560 ml (19¼ fl oz/2¼ cups) milk
- ½ teaspoon ground nutmeg

METHOD

1. Heat the oil and butter in a heavy-based frying pan and cook the onion, carrot and celery over medium heat until softened, stirring constantly. Increase the heat, add the beef and brown well, breaking up any lumps with a fork. Add the chicken livers and cook until they change colour. Add the tomato passata, wine and parsley, and season with salt and pepper. Bring to the boil, reduce the heat and simmer for 45 minutes, then set aside.
2. To make the béchamel sauce, melt the butter in a saucepan over low heat. Add the flour and stir for 1 minute until pale and foaming. Gradually stir in the milk, stirring constantly until the sauce boils and begins to thicken. Simmer for another minute. Add the nutmeg and season to taste. Lay plastic wrap on the surface of the sauce to prevent a skin forming, and set aside.
3. Cut the lasagne sheets to fit a deep, rectangular ovenproof dish.
4. Preheat the oven to 180°C (350°F/Gas 4). Grease the ovenproof dish. To assemble the lasagne, spread a thin layer of the meat sauce over the base of the dish and follow with a thin layer of béchamel. If the béchamel has cooled and become too thick, warm it gently to make spreading easier. Lay the lasagne sheets on top, gently pressing to push out any air. Continue the layers, finishing with the béchamel. Sprinkle with parmesan and bake for 35–40 minutes, or until golden brown. Cool for 15 minutes before cutting and serving.

NOTES: You can use instant lasagne instead of fresh lasagne.

If you prefer, leave out the chicken livers and increase the amount of mince accordingly.

CANNELLONI

SERVES 4

INGREDIENTS

MEAT SAUCE
- 60 ml (2 fl oz/¼ cup) olive oil
- 1 onion, finely chopped
- 2 garlic cloves, crushed
- 120 g (4¼ oz) bacon, finely chopped
- 60 g (2¼ oz) button mushrooms, finely chopped
- ¼ teaspoon dried basil
- 220 g (7¾ oz) minced (ground) pork
- 220 g (7¾ oz) minced (ground) veal
- 1 tablespoon finely chopped parsley
- 200 g (7 oz) tin chopped tomatoes
- 250 ml (9 fl oz/1 cup) beef stock (page 11)
- 3 tablespoons dried breadcrumbs
- 1 egg

TOMATO SAUCE
- 2 tablespoons olive oil
- 1 small onion, finely chopped
- 2 garlic cloves, crushed
- 2 x 400 g (14 oz) tins chopped tomatoes
- 1 teaspoon chopped basil

- 10 fresh lasagne sheets (page 259), about 17 x 12 cm (6½ x 4½ inches)
- 4 large slices prosciutto, cut in half
- 60 g (2¼ oz/½ cup) grated fontina cheese
- 200 ml (7 fl oz) thick (double) cream
- 60 g (2¼ oz/⅔ cup) grated parmesan cheese

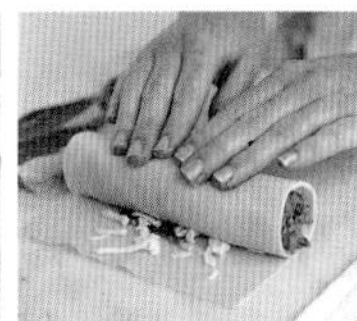
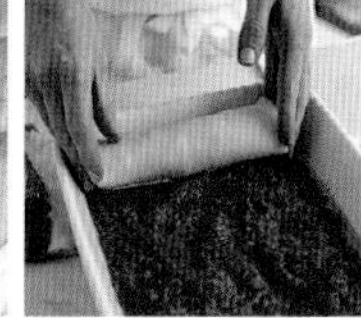

METHOD

1 To make the meat sauce, heat the oil in a frying pan and cook the onion, garlic and bacon over medium heat for 6 minutes, or until the onion is soft and golden. Stir in the mushrooms and basil, cook for 2–3 minutes, then add the pork and veal. Cook, stirring often to break up the lumps, until the mince has changed colour. Season well, add the parsley, tomatoes and stock, partially cover and simmer for 1 hour. Uncover and simmer for another 30 minutes to reduce the liquid. Cool slightly then stir in the breadcrumbs, then the egg.

2 To make the tomato sauce, heat the oil in a pan and cook the onion and garlic for 6 minutes, or until the onion has softened but not browned. Stir in the tomatoes and basil. Add 250 ml (9 fl oz/1 cup) water and season well. Simmer for 30 minutes, or until you have a thick sauce.

3 Cook the lasagne in batches in a large saucepan of boiling salted water until *al dente*. Scoop out each batch with a slotted spoon and drop into a bowl of cold water. Spread the sheets out in a single layer on a tea towel, turning them over once to blot dry each side. Trim away any torn edges. (We have allowed two extra sheets in case of tearing.) The grain of the pasta should run with the width, not the length, or the pasta will split when you roll it up.

4 Preheat the oven to 190°C (375°F/Gas 5). Grease a shallow 30 x 18 cm (12 x 7 inch) ovenproof dish and spoon the tomato sauce over the base.

5 Place a half slice of prosciutto over each pasta sheet. Top with a sprinkling of fontina cheese. Spoon an eighth of the meat sauce across one end of the pasta sheet. Starting from this end, roll the pasta up tightly to enclose the filling. Repeat with the remaining lasagne sheets and meat sauce. Place the filled rolls, seam side down, in a row in the dish.

6 Beat together the cream and parmesan and season. Spoon over the cannelloni and bake for 20 minutes, or until lightly browned on top. Leave to rest for 10 minutes before serving.

PASTITSIO

SERVES 6

INGREDIENTS

150 g (5½ oz) elbow macaroni (see Note)
40 g (1½ oz) butter
¼ teaspoon ground nutmeg
60 g (2¼ oz) kefalotyri or parmesan cheese, grated
1 egg, lightly beaten

MEAT SAUCE

2 tablespoons oil
1 onion, finely chopped
2 garlic cloves, crushed
500 g (1 lb 2 oz) minced (ground) beef
125 ml (4 fl oz/½ cup) red wine
250 ml (9 fl oz/1 cup) beef stock (page 11)
3 tablespoons tomato paste (concentrated purée)
1 teaspoon chopped oregano

BECHAMEL SAUCE

40 g (1½ oz) butter
1½ tablespoons plain (all-purpose) flour
375 ml (13 fl oz/1½ cups) milk
pinch of ground nutmeg
1 egg, lightly beaten

METHOD

1 Cook the macaroni in a large saucepan of boiling salted water for 10 minutes, or until *al dente*. Drain and return to the pan. Melt the butter in a small saucepan until golden, then pour it over the macaroni. Stir in the nutmeg and half the cheese and season, to taste. Leave until cool, then mix in the egg and set aside.

2 To make the meat sauce, heat the oil in a large frying pan, add the onion and garlic and cook over medium heat for 6 minutes, or until the onion is soft. Increase the heat, add the beef and cook, stirring, for 5 minutes or until the meat is browned. Add the wine and cook over high heat for 1 minute, or until evaporated. Add the stock, tomato paste, oregano and season with salt and pepper. Reduce the heat, cover and simmer for 20 minutes. Preheat the oven to 180°C (350°F/Gas 4). Lightly grease a 1.5 litre (6 cup) ovenproof dish.

3 To make the béchamel sauce, melt the butter in a small saucepan over low heat. Stir in the flour and cook for 1 minute, or until pale and foaming. Gradually stir in the milk, stirring constantly until the sauce boils and thickens. Reduce the heat and simmer for 2 minutes. Add the nutmeg and some salt and pepper. Cool a little before stirring in the egg. Stir 3 tablespoons of the béchamel into the meat sauce.

4 Spread half the meat sauce in the dish, then layer half the pasta over it. Layer with the remaining meat sauce and then the remaining pasta. Press down firmly with the back of a spoon. Spread the béchamel sauce over the pasta and sprinkle the remaining cheese on top. Bake for 45–50 minutes, or until golden. Let it stand for 15 minutes before serving.

NOTE: Tubular bucatini, which is available in varying thicknesses, makes a good substitute for the elbow macaroni in pastitsio. Choose one that is a little thicker than spaghetti.

MACARONI CHEESE

SERVES 4

INGREDIENTS

- 225 g (8 oz) macaroni
- 80 g (2¾ oz) butter
- 1 onion, finely chopped
- 3 tablespoons plain (all-purpose) flour
- 500 ml (17 fl oz/2 cups) milk
- 2 teaspoons wholegrain mustard
- 250 g (9 oz/2 cups) grated cheddar cheese
- 30 g (1 oz) fresh breadcrumbs

METHOD

1. Cook the pasta in rapidly boiling salted water until *al dente*. Drain. Preheat the oven to 180°C (350°F/Gas 4) and grease a casserole dish.
2. Melt the butter in a large saucepan over low heat and cook the onion for 5 minutes, or until softened. Stir in the flour and cook for a minute, or until pale and foaming. Gradually stir in the milk, stirring constantly until the sauce boils and thickens. Reduce the heat and simmer for 2 minutes. Stir in the mustard and most of the cheese. Season to taste.
3. Mix the pasta with the cheese sauce. Spoon into the dish and sprinkle the breadcrumbs and remaining cheese over the top. Bake for 15 minutes, or until golden and bubbling.

••RICE BASICS••

One of the most versatile grains in the world, rice is eaten daily by more than 300 billion people. Rice grows in all conditions on nearly every continent. Most rice eaten is white rice, that is with the husks (hulls) removed and milled, because it stores better and is more highly esteemed. Many different cultures have embraced rice — thus we have dishes as diverse as the Italian risotto, American gumbos, Indian pulaos, Middle Eastern pilaffs and Southeast Asian rice noodle stir-fries, to name just a few.

WHAT RICE IS THAT?

Rice can be classified according to its culinary use (pudding rice), its method of processing (easy-cook), its grain shape (long-grain), its country or place of origin (Dhera Dun) or its degree of stickiness (glutinous).

LONG-GRAIN

Long-grain rice is not a strain of rice, but a descriptive term for the size of the rice grains — the grains are three to five times as long as they are wide. Long-grain rice has slender grains that stay separate and fluffy after cooking, so this is the best choice if you want to serve rice as a side dish, or as a bed for sauces. A good all-purpose rice, it may also be sold as Texmati, Calrose and Patna.

JASMINE

This is a fragrant rice, usually long grained. It is named after the sweet-smelling jasmine flower of Southeast Asia because, on cooking, it releases a similar floral aroma. Jasmine rice cooks to a soft, slightly sticky grain. It is also served plain as it needs no seasoning. Serve with Indian and Thai food.

BASMATI

This is a long-grained, needle-shaped rice used in Indian cooking. It has a light, dry texture and is lightly perfumed. The grains are fluffy and stay separate when cooked, as well as elongating. These are ideal rices for Middle Eastern pilaffs, and north Indian pulaos and biryani. Basmati is sold as Punni, Dehra Dun, Jeera-Sali or Delhi.

EASY-COOK

This rice may be either white or brown, short or long grained. It is parboiled before milling and is a non-sticky all-purpose rice. Because it is milled and has no bran or germ oil to go rancid, parboiled rice has better storage qualities. It can generally handle a wider range of cooking methods and still emerge intact. Not all cooking methods are recommended for parboiled rice, as it does not absorb water easily. It is less suitable for dishes where flavour absorption is important, such as risotto or paella.

SHORT-GRAIN
This is often sold as round or pudding rice. When cooked, the grains swell without disintegrating and its high starch content makes it sticky and good for puddings, moulds and stuffings. The rices used for making risotto are short grained.

BROWN
The grains of brown rice have had their husks removed, but the outer bran layer is left intact, not milled and polished like white rice. It is the most nutritious rice and has a pronounced nutty flavour. It takes longer to cook than most other varieties of rice. Brown rice is available both as a short- and medium-grain rice.

PAELLA
Varieties of short-grained Spanish rice include bahia, Calasparra, sequia and the firm-grained bomba. Valencia is the most prized Spanish grain for paella as it cooks up tender, moist and clingy due to its high starch content. Paella rices can absorb a lot of water and they soak up a lot of the delicious flavours from the paella; they are also suitable for puddings. Paella rice can be difficult to find; risotto rice (page 286) makes a good substitute, if necessary.

GLUTINOUS
This is also called sticky rice or sold as Japanese sushi rice, Korean rice or black sweet rice and may be either white or black. It is a sticky, short-grained rice used in Asian cooking. Its name is purely a description of texture as rice does not contain gluten. Once cooked, the grains stick together, making it suitable for using in sushi or for eating with chopsticks. Use for sweet and savoury dishes.

CAMARGUE RED
Also sold as Griotto rice, this has a distinctive nutty flavour and chewy texture. It is good with duck and game. It is a medium- to short-grain rice grown in the Camargue region of southern France. Other red rices include Thai and Bhutanese red rice and Vietnamese red cargo.

WILD RICE
Wild rice is not technically rice, but actually the seed of an aquatic grass. It grows mainly in central and northern parts of America and southern Canada, but also in parts of Africa, Southeast Asia and China. Wild rice grows in lake and river marshes and was the principal foodstuff for the North American Indians who gathered it from their canoes by hand.

Unlike rice, which is 'pearled' to remove the outer coat, wild rice is brown to green in colour as it retains its seed coat. It has a rich, nutty flavour and chewy texture and, because it is quite expensive, it is often extended with brown or white rice — this also gives it added texture, colour and flavour. Wild rice is good served in salads or as an accompaniment to meats and makes a particularly good stuffing, especially for chicken or turkey.

HOW TO... COOK RICE

Rice can be cooked in a number of different ways. Some rices lend themselves to being cooked using more than one method, but others are suitable for only one style of cooking. Individual recipes will guide you.

If you're reheating cooked rice, make sure it is all piping hot to destroy any bacteria.

WASHING RICE

Traditionally, rice had to be picked over and any stones or rubble discarded. Most modern-day rice is clean enough to not require checking, but rice bought in sacks may still need picking over. Some rice cooks better if it has been soaked first — basmati and sushi rice being two examples. Soaking makes the rice less brittle. But most rice can be cooked without being soaked. One point to remember: if you do wash or soak your rice before cooking it, remember to drain it thoroughly, particularly when cooking by the absorption method, or you will have too much liquid to cook the rice properly.

RICE-COOKERS

The electric rice-cooker is designed to cook rice by the absorption method. Sold in Asian stores, many kitchen stores and some department stores, they have markings on the inside to show the amount of water needed for the amount of rice. The rice-cooker automatically switches off when the grains are cooked, so the rice is then steam-dried. Usually, though, it is only the portion closest to the surface that is steamed — the rice at the bottom of the cooker is boiled. The rice-cooker then keeps the rice warm until you're ready to eat.

STORAGE

Store white rice in a cool, dry place. An unopened box will keep for up to a year. Cooked rice should be cooled quickly and will store for up to 2 days in the fridge. Brown rice has a higher fat content than white, so can only be kept for a much shorter time. It is best stored in the fridge or in a cool place to prevent it going rancid.

ABSORPTION METHOD

Probably the most familiar method of cooking rice, the absorption method is an efficient and nutritious way to cook rice, as nutrients are not discarded with the cooking water. Generally, long-grain rices suit this method.

METHOD

1 Put the rice in a saucepan, stick your finger into the top of the rice, then add enough cold water to come up to the first finger joint.
2 Cover the pan with a tight-fitting lid and bring to the boil. Reduce the heat to a simmer so the rice at the bottom of the pan doesn't burn, and cook until little steam holes appear in the rice. The rice is cooked by the hot water and by the remaining steam once the water has been absorbed.
3 Remove the lid to allow the steam to escape. Fluff up the grains with a fork and serve.

STEAMING METHOD

This method is preferred for sticky rice. Soak the rice overnight, then drain. Spread out the grains in a steamer, and put the steamer over a wok or saucepan of boiling water. The rice does not touch the water — it is cooked only by the steam.

RAPID BOILING METHOD

Many rices, from arborio to parboiled types, cook well in plenty of water, just like pasta. Bring a large saucepan of water to the boil. Sprinkle in the rice and boil, uncovered, keeping an eye on it so it does not stick or overcook. Drain the rice in a sieve (if you're using jasmine or Japanese rice, rinse it with a little tepid water to prevent further cooking).

SAFFRON RICE

SERVES 6 AS AN ACCOMPANIMENT

INGREDIENTS

400 g (14 oz/2 cups) basmati rice
25 g (1 oz) butter
3 bay leaves
¼ teaspoon saffron threads
500 ml (17 fl oz/2 cups) hot vegetable stock (page 10)

METHOD

1 Wash the rice thoroughly, cover with cold water and soak for 30 minutes. Drain.
2 Heat the butter in a frying pan over low heat until it melts. Add the bay leaves and washed rice, and cook, stirring, for 6 minutes, or until all the moisture has evaporated.
3 Soak the saffron in 2 tablespoons hot water for a few minutes. Add the saffron and its soaking liquid to the rice with the vegetable stock and 375 ml (13 fl oz/1½ cups) boiling water. Season with salt. Bring to the boil, then reduce the heat and cook, covered, for 12–15 minutes, or until all the water has absorbed and the rice is cooked.

MINT RICE

SERVES 6 AS AN ACCOMPANIMENT

INGREDIENTS

1 tablespoon olive oil
1 onion, finely chopped
400 g (14 oz/2 cups) basmati rice
875 ml (30 fl oz/3½ cups) hot chicken stock (page 11)
1 handful mint, chopped

METHOD

1 Heat the oil in a large saucepan and add the onion. Cook for 5–6 minutes over medium heat, or until soft.
2 Add the rice and cook for 2 minutes, then add the stock and bring to the boil. Reduce the heat, cover and simmer for 15 minutes, or until all the liquid has absorbed and the rice is cooked. Stir in the mint and season with salt and pepper.

SAFFRON

It is often pointed out that saffron is one of the most expensive commodities in the world, and is literally worth more than its own weight in gold. However, it's so light and so little is usually needed that it's not an expensive item to buy. Saffron strands are the stigmas of a type of crocus and are harvested by hand. They can be bought in small packets or as a ground powder (the whole stigmas are preferable). The best-quality saffron comes from Spain and a tiny amount is also grown in Abruzzi in Italy. Cheaper saffron is inferior in aroma and flavour. Saffron is very strongly flavoured and can be overpowering, so don't be tempted to use more than the recipe specifies.

••RICE SALADS AND STARTERS••

Rice is so versatile and popular in so many cuisines that it can be combined with just about any flavours to make a light meal: whether it's the hint of Indian curry combined with smoked fish in kedgeree, the Asian flavours of this salad (below) or traditional Greek dolmades.

WILD RICE AND ASIAN CHICKEN SALAD

SERVES 8

INGREDIENTS

- 190 g (6¾ oz/1 cup) wild rice
- 200 g (7 oz/1 cup) jasmine rice
- 1 Chinese barbecued chicken (see Note)
- 3 tablespoons chopped mint
- 3 tablespoons chopped coriander (cilantro)
- 1 large Lebanese (short) cucumber
- 6 spring onions (scallions)
- 85 g (3 oz/½ cup) roasted peanuts, roughly chopped
- 80 ml (2½ fl oz/⅓ cup) mirin
- 2 tablespoons Chinese rice wine
- 1 tablespoon soy sauce
- 1 tablespoon lime juice
- 2 tablespoons sweet chilli sauce, plus extra to serve

METHOD

1. Bring a large saucepan of water to the boil and add the wild rice and 1 teaspoon salt. Cook for 30 minutes, then add the jasmine rice and cook for a further 10 minutes, or until tender. Drain the rice, refresh under cold water and drain again.
2. Shred the chicken (both the skin and flesh) into bite-sized pieces, place in a large bowl and add the mint and coriander. Cut the cucumber lengthways through the centre (do not peel) and slice thinly on the diagonal. Slice the spring onions on the diagonal. Add the cucumber, spring onion, rice and peanuts to the bowl.
3. Mix together the mirin, rice wine, soy sauce, lime juice and sweet chilli sauce in a small jug, pour over the salad and toss to combine. Pile the salad onto a serving platter and serve with a little extra chilli sauce.

NOTE: Chinese barbecued chicken is sold in Asian barbecue shops. The flavours of five-spice and soy used to cook it will add to the flavour of the salad.

HOW TO... COOK WILD RICE

* Wild rice absorbs up to four times its own volume in liquid, so a little rice will go a long way.
* Like brown rice, wild rice can take 40–60 minutes to cook, depending on whether you prefer a tender or more chewy texture. Test the rice after the specified cooking time — it may need a few more minutes cooking time.
* Soaking wild rice overnight in cold water reduces the cooking time. Then just boil for about 20 minutes.

WILD RICE SALAD

SERVES 4

INGREDIENTS

- 95 g (3¼ oz/½ cup) wild rice
- 250 ml (9 fl oz/1 cup) chicken stock (page 11)
- 20 g (¾ oz) butter
- 100 g (3½ oz/½ cup) basmati rice
- 60 g (2¼ oz/½ cup) slivered almonds
- 1 tablespoon olive oil
- 2 slices bacon, chopped
- 125 g (4½ oz) currants
- 30 g (1 oz) chopped parsley
- 6 spring onions (scallions), thinly sliced
- finely grated zest and juice of 1 lemon
- olive oil, to drizzle
- lemon wedges, to serve

METHOD

1. Put the wild rice and stock in a saucepan, add the butter, bring to the boil, then cook, covered, over low heat for 1 hour. Drain.
2. Put the basmati rice in a separate saucepan with cold water and bring to the boil. Cook at a simmer for 12 minutes, then drain. Mix the rices together in a bowl and leave to cool to room temperature.
3. Lightly toast the almonds in a dry frying pan for a few minutes, or until lightly golden, watching carefully to make sure they don't burn. Heat the oil in the same pan and cook the bacon for 5 minutes, or until cooked. Remove from the pan and cool.
4. Combine the rice with the bacon, currants, almonds, parsley, spring onion and lemon zest and juice. Season, then drizzle with olive oil and serve with lemon wedges.

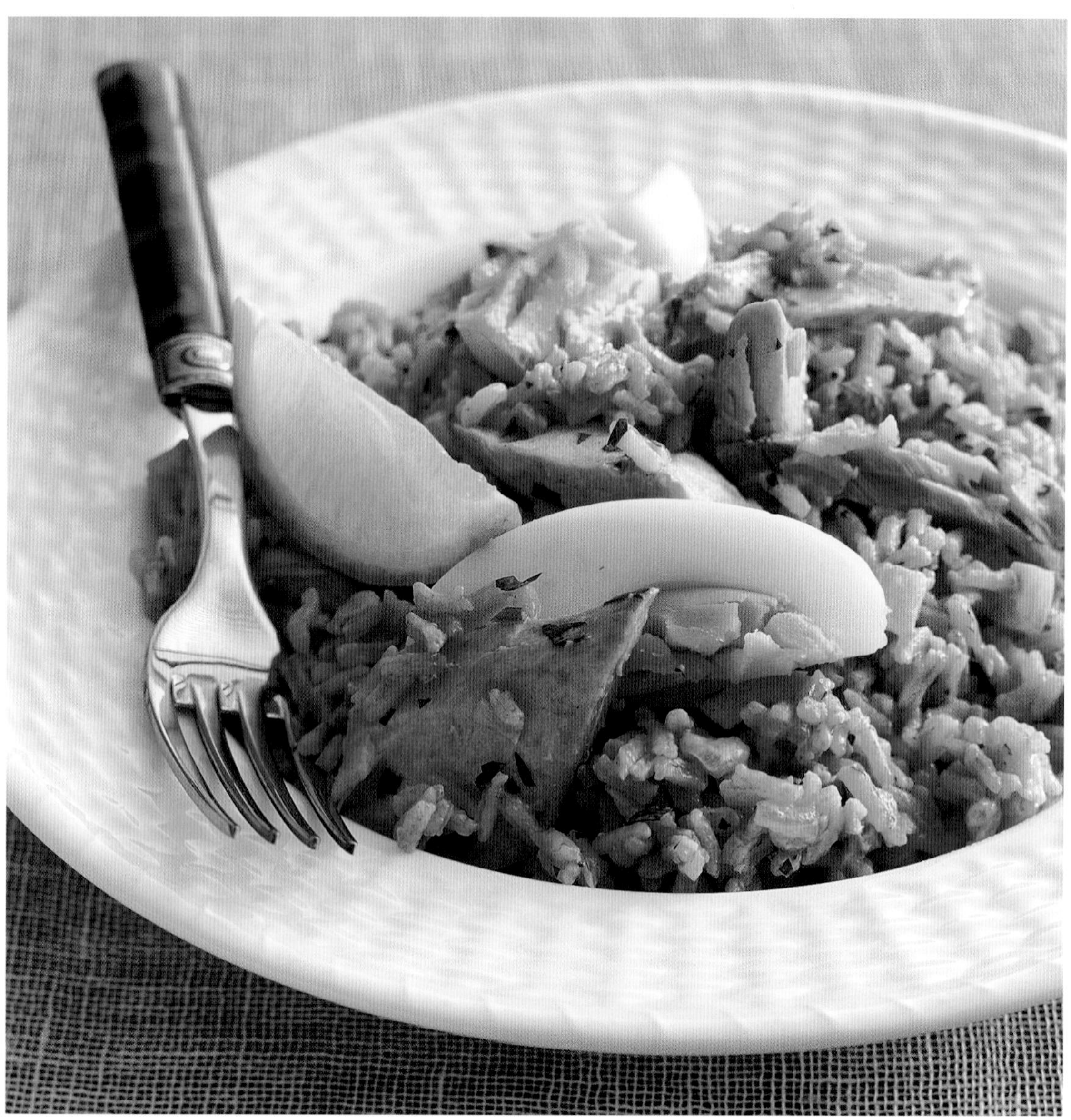

KEDGEREE

Kedgeree is a popular English brunch dish made with smoked fish, boiled eggs, curry powder and cream mixed into rice. The dish evolved from the breakfast dish called khichri, made with boiled rice, lentils and spices, which was enjoyed in colonial India. Kedgeree is traditionally made with smoked haddock, although any white or smoked fish will do, and many modern recipes use salmon.

❮ KEDGEREE

SERVES 4

INGREDIENTS

- 350 g (12 oz) undyed smoked haddock or smoked cod fillets
- 3 lemon slices
- 1 bay leaf
- 300 ml (10½ fl oz) milk
- 175 g (6 oz) long-grain rice
- 60 g (2¼ oz) butter
- 1 small onion, finely chopped
- 2 teaspoons mild curry powder
- 1 tablespoon finely chopped parsley
- 3 hard-boiled eggs, cut into wedges or roughly chopped
- 170 ml (5½ fl oz/⅔ cup) thick (double) cream
- mango chutney, to serve

METHOD

1. Put the smoked fish in a deep frying pan with the lemon slices and bay leaf, cover with the milk and simmer for 6 minutes, or until cooked through. Remove the fish with a slotted spoon and break into large flakes, discarding any bones. Discard the poaching liquid.
2. Put the rice in a saucepan along with 350 ml (12 fl oz) water, bring to the boil, cover and cook for 10 minutes, or until the rice is just cooked — there should be steam holes in the rice. Drain any excess water and fork through to fluff up the rice.
3. Melt the butter in a frying pan over medium heat. Add the onion and cook for 3 minutes, or until soft. Add the curry powder and cook for another 2 minutes. Carefully stir in the rice and cook for 2–3 minutes to heat through.
4. Add the fish, parsley, egg and cream and stir until heated through. Season well with pepper. Serve immediately with mango chutney.

RED RICE AND CHICKEN SALAD

SERVES 4

INGREDIENTS

- 225 g (8 oz/1 cup) Camargue red rice
- 1 red capsicum (pepper)
- 1 yellow capsicum (pepper)
- 80 ml (2½ fl oz/⅓ cup) olive oil
- 1 red onion, cut into slivers
- 2 zucchini (courgettes), diced
- 20 g (¾ oz) butter
- 1 garlic clove, crushed
- 1 boneless chicken breast, with skin
- 2 tablespoons lemon juice
- 2 tablespoons chopped basil
- 2 tablespoons chopped parsley

METHOD

1. Put the rice in a saucepan with plenty of boiling water and cook for 30 minutes, or until tender. Drain well, then cool.
2. Cut the capsicums in half lengthways. Remove the seeds and membrane, then cut into large, flattish pieces. Grill (broil) or hold over a gas flame until the skin blackens and blisters. Place on a cutting board, cover with a tea towel and cool. Peel the skin off and cut the flesh into smaller pieces. Add the capsicum to the rice.
3. Heat most of the oil in a frying pan, then cook the onion and zucchini until lightly charred around the edges, adding more oil if necessary. Add the onion and zucchini to the rice.
4. Mix the butter with the garlic. Push the mixture under the skin of the chicken so it is evenly distributed. Grill (broil) the chicken on both sides until the skin is crisp and the breast is cooked through. Leave the chicken to rest for 2 minutes, then slice into strips.
5. Add the chicken slices to the rice with any juices. Add the lemon juice, any remaining olive oil and the herbs, and toss together. Season well and serve immediately.

RICE-STUFFED TOMATOES

MAKES 8

INGREDIENTS

- 8 tomatoes
- 110 g (3½ oz/½ cup) short-grain rice
- 2 tablespoons olive oil
- 1 red onion, chopped
- 1 garlic clove, crushed
- 1 teaspoon dried oregano
- 40 g (1½ oz/¼ cup) pine nuts
- 35 g (1¼ oz/¼ cup) currants
- 30 g (1 oz) finely chopped basil
- 2 tablespoons finely chopped parsley
- 1 tablespoon finely chopped dill
- olive oil, to brush

METHOD

1. Preheat the oven to 160°C (315°F/Gas 2–3). Lightly grease a large ovenproof dish.
2. Cut the tops off the tomatoes and keep. Spoon out the tomato flesh into a sieve set over a bowl. Strain the juice into the bowl. Finely dice the flesh and keep in a separate bowl. Drain the tomato shells upside down on a rack.
3. Boil the rice in salted water for 10–12 minutes, or until just tender. Drain and cool.
4. Heat the oil in a frying pan. Fry the onion, garlic and oregano for 8 minutes, or until the onion is soft. Add the pine nuts and currants and cook for 5 minutes, stirring frequently. Remove from the heat and stir in the herbs. Season.
5. Add the onion mixture and the reserved diced tomato to the rice and mix well. Fill the tomato shells with the rice mixture, piling it up over the top. Spoon 1 tablespoon of the reserved tomato juice over the filling in each tomato and replace the tops.
6. Lightly brush the tomatoes with the oil. Arrange them in the ovenproof dish. Bake for 30 minutes, or until heated through.

STUFFED CAPSICUMS

You can use the same rice filling (above) for stuffed capsicums (peppers). Bring a large saucepan of water to the boil, cut the tops off the capsicums and keep them on one side. Carefully cut out and remove the membrane and seeds from inside the capsicums and then blanch them (not the lids) in boiling water for 2 minutes. Drain them on paper towels. Preheat the oven to 180°C (350°F/Gas 4). Fill the capsicums with the rice stuffing, put the tops back on and sit the capsicums snugly in an ovenproof dish. Pour 100 ml (3½ fl oz) of water into the dish and drizzle oil over the capsicums. Bake for 40 minutes, or until they are cooked through and tender.

DOLMADES

MAKES 24

INGREDIENTS

- 200 g (7 oz) packet vine leaves in brine
- 200 g (9 oz/1 cup) long- or medium-grain rice
- 1 small onion, finely chopped
- 1 tablespoon olive oil
- 60 g (2¼ oz) pine nuts, toasted
- 2 tablespoons currants
- 2 tablespoons finely chopped dill
- 1 tablespoon finely chopped mint
- 1 tablespoon finely chopped parsley
- 80 ml (2½ fl oz/⅓ cup) olive oil, extra
- 2 tablespoons lemon juice
- 500 ml (17 fl oz/2 cups) chicken stock (page 11)
- lemon wedges, to serve

METHOD

1. Soak the leaves in cold water for 15 minutes, then pat dry. Cut off any stems. Keep some leaves to line the pan. Discard any with holes.
2. Meanwhile, soak the rice in boiling water for 10 minutes to soften, then drain. Mix together the rice, onion, olive oil, pine nuts, currants, herbs and add salt and pepper to taste.
3. Lay some leaves, vein side down, on a flat surface. Place 1 tablespoon of filling in the centre of each, fold in the stalk end over the filling, then the sides. Roll up firmly.
4. Line the base of a large heavy-based saucepan with the vine leaves you have kept. Drizzle with 1 tablespoon olive oil. Pack the dolmades tightly in one layer, then pour the lemon juice and remaining oil over them.
5. Pour the stock over the dolmades and cover with an upside-down plate to stop them moving around. Bring to the boil, then reduce the heat and simmer, covered, for 45 minutes. Serve warm or cold, with lemon wedges.

••FRIED RICE••

If you have any leftover rice, don't throw it away — most cultures have developed recipes specifically to use up leftover rice, from Italian suppli, which uses up leftover risotto, to the fried rice of China and Southeast Asia. Cooked rice should be quickly cooled and then stored in an airtight container in the fridge. It should be eaten within 2 days.

NASI GORENG

In Malay, nasi means 'cooked rice' and goreng means 'fried', but there is much more to this dish than just rice. It is a Dutch-Indonesian recipe in which a selection of ingredients, including any type of meat and seafood, is added to the rice, along with slices of omelette.

SERVES 4

INGREDIENTS

- 2 eggs
- 80 ml (2½ fl oz/⅓ cup) oil
- 3 garlic cloves, finely chopped
- 1 onion, finely chopped
- 2 red chillies, seeded and very finely chopped
- 1 teaspoon shrimp paste
- 1 teaspoon coriander seeds
- ½ teaspoon sugar
- 400 g (14 oz) raw prawns (shrimp), peeled and deveined
- 200 g (7 oz) rump steak, thinly sliced
- 550 g (1 lb 4 oz/3 cups) cold cooked long-grain rice (see Note)
- 2 teaspoons kecap manis
- 1 tablespoon soy sauce
- 4 spring onions (scallions), finely chopped
- 1 cucumber, thinly sliced
- 3 tablespoons crisp fried onions

METHOD

1. Beat the eggs and ¼ teaspoon salt until foamy. Heat a frying pan and lightly brush with a little of the oil. Pour about one-quarter of the egg into the pan and cook for 1–2 minutes over medium heat, or until the omelette sets. Turn the omelette over and cook the other side for 30 seconds. Lift out of the pan and cook another 3 omelettes. Allow to cool, then roll them up, cut into strips and set aside.
2. Combine the garlic, onion, chilli, shrimp paste, coriander seeds and sugar in a food processor to make a paste. Alternatively, pound the ingredients to a paste using a mortar and pestle.
3. Heat 1–2 tablespoons of the oil in a wok or large, deep frying pan; add the paste and cook over high heat for 1 minute, or until fragrant. Add the prawns and steak, and stir-fry for 2–3 minutes, or until they change colour.
4. Add the remaining oil and the cold rice to the wok. Stir-fry, breaking up any lumps, until the rice is heated through. Add the kecap manis, soy sauce and spring onion, and stir-fry for 1 minute. Serve immediately with the omelette, cucumber slices and fried onion.

NOTE: You'll need to cook 200 g (7 oz/1 cup) rice to get 3 cups of cooked rice.

EGG FRIED RICE

SERVES 4

INGREDIENTS

- 4 eggs
- 1 spring onion (scallion), chopped
- 50 g (1¾ oz/⅓ cup) fresh or frozen peas
- 60 ml (2 fl oz/¼ cup) oil
- 550 g (1 lb 4 oz/3 cups) cold cooked long-grain rice (see Note)

METHOD

1. Beat the eggs with 1 teaspoon of the spring onion and a pinch of salt. Cook the peas in simmering water for 3–4 minutes for fresh or 1 minute for frozen.
2. Heat a wok over high heat, add the oil and heat until very hot. Reduce the heat, add the egg and lightly scramble. Add the rice before the egg is set too hard, increase the heat and stir to separate the rice grains and break the egg into small bits. Add the peas and the remaining spring onion and season with salt. Stir-fry for 1 minute before serving.

NOTE: You'll need to cook 200 g (7 oz/1 cup) rice to get 3 cups of cooked rice.

FRIED RICE WITH CHINESE BARBECUED PORK

SERVES 4

INGREDIENTS

- 6 spring onions (scallions)
- 150 g (5½ oz) snow peas (mangetout)
- 200 g (7 oz) Chinese barbecued pork (char siu)
- 3 teaspoons sesame oil
- 2 eggs, lightly beaten
- 2 garlic cloves, finely chopped
- 550 g (1 lb 4 oz/3 cups) cold cooked long-grain rice (see Note)
- 2 tablespoons soy sauce

METHOD

1. Thinly slice the spring onions and snow peas. Cut the pork into thin slices.
2. Heat a wok until hot, add 1 teaspoon of the oil and swirl to coat the base of the wok. Add the egg and swirl over the base until it has just set. Turn the egg over and cook for 30 seconds, or until lightly browned, then remove from the wok. Allow the egg to cool slightly, then roll up and cut into 1 cm (½ inch) thick slices.
3. While the wok is still very hot, add the remaining oil, then the garlic, spring onion and snow peas and stir-fry for 1–2 minutes, or until softened. Add the pork, rice, soy sauce and omelette strips and toss until heated through — the sauce should turn the rice brown. Serve immediately.

NOTE: You'll need to cook 200 g (7 oz/1 cup) rice to get 3 cups of cooked rice.

••RISOTTO••

Risotto originated in the rice-growing areas of northern Italy. A 'sofrito' is prepared by sautéeing finely chopped flavourings such as onion and garlic in oil. The rice is then coated in the oil and then cooked with stock. Many cooks have strong opinions on how to cook risotto: most say the stock must be stirred in a ladleful at a time and the rice stirred constantly so it releases its creaminess. Others add all the stock, put a lid on the pan, turn the heat as low as it will go and walk away for 15 minutes.

RISOTTO RICE

Risotto rices are high in starch, which means they can absorb large quantities of liquid without breaking up. This gives the risotto its classic creaminess. There are three well-known varieties of risotto rice that are widely available today.

ARBORIO RICE

This rice has a large plump grain that is rich in amylopectin, the starch that dissolves in cooking to produce a stickier risotto.

VIALONE NANO

This rice has a stubby small grain with more of another starch, amylose, which does not soften easily in cooking. It gives the risotto a looser consistency but keeps more of a bite in the middle.

CARNAROLI

A new variety developed in 1945 by a Milanese rice grower, carnaroli is a cross between vialone and a Japanese strain. Small-scale production makes this grain more expensive. The outer skin has enough soft starch to dissolve and make the risotto creamy but it also contains more tough starch than any of the other risotto rices and so keeps a firm consistency.

HOW TO... MAKE PERFECT RISOTTO

* Use a large deep frying pan or shallow saucepan with a heavy base that will distribute the heat evenly and prevent the rice burning.
* Make sure the stock or liquid you are using is hot so that you don't cool the risotto down every time you add a little. Keep the stock at a low simmer on the stovetop.
* Cook the rice in the oil or butter first. This creates a seal around the rice grains, trapping the starch. Stir frequently to prevent the rice sticking to the bottom of the pan and to ensure all the grains are cooked evenly.
* Add the liquid a little at a time so you don't swamp the rice. Stir constantly so the rice cooks evenly and releases some of the starch, giving the risotto its creaminess. If you cook the rice too slowly, it will become gluey; too fast and the liquid will evaporate — keep it at a fast simmer.
* Season the rice early on while it is absorbing flavour. Once it is cooked and the grains saturated, it won't soak up the seasoning as well. Taste the liquid around the rice to check the seasoning.
* It is impossible to gauge the exact amount of stock you will need. Once you have added nearly all the stock, start tasting the rice to prevent overcooking. The rice should be creamy but still with a little texture in the middle of the grain. The risotto should be rich and thick like porridge, not too wet or dry.

RISOTTO MILANESE

SERVES 6 AS AN ACCOMPANIMENT

INGREDIENTS

200 ml (7 fl oz) dry white vermouth or wine
large pinch of saffron threads
1.5 litres (6 cups) chicken stock (page 11)
100 g (3½ oz) butter
70 g (2½ oz) beef marrow (see Note)
1 large onion, finely chopped
1 garlic clove, crushed
360 g (12¾ oz/1⅔ cups) risotto rice
50 g (1¾ oz/½ cup) grated parmesan cheese

METHOD

1 Put the vermouth in a bowl, add the saffron and leave to soak. Pour the stock into a saucepan and keep at a low simmer.

2 Melt the butter and beef marrow in a saucepan. Add the onion and garlic and cook, stirring, until softened. Add the rice and stir until well coated. Add the vermouth and saffron to the rice and stir until absorbed.

3 Add a ladleful of the hot stock to the rice and stir until absorbed. Continue stirring and adding the stock, a ladleful at a time, for about 25 minutes, until the stock has all been absorbed and the rice is creamy. Remove from the heat and stir in the parmesan.

NOTE: Risotto Milanese is the traditional accompaniment to osso buco (page 145). Beef marrow gives the risotto its rich flavour. If your butcher doesn't have marrow, use a fatty piece of prosciutto or pancetta, finely chopped.

ASPARAGUS RISOTTO

This risotto has an intensity of flavour from cooking and blending the asparagus stems to use as stock. You could try the same method with other vegetables such as broccoli and peas. This recipe is best made when asparagus is in season and has a good flavour.

SERVES 4

INGREDIENTS

- 450 g (1 lb) asparagus
- 100 g (3½ oz) butter
- 1 onion, finely chopped
- 1 large garlic clove, finely chopped
- 1 tablespoon chopped thyme
- 220 g (7¾ oz/1 cup) risotto rice
- 150 ml (5½ fl oz) dry white vermouth or wine
- 25 g (1 oz/¼ cup) grated parmesan cheese

METHOD

1. To make the asparagus stock, wash the asparagus and snap off the woody ends but don't throw them away. Cut the delicate tips off the asparagus and set aside. Finely chop the asparagus stems.
2. Pour 750 ml (26 fl oz/3 cups) water into a small saucepan, add a pinch of salt and bring to the boil. Cook the woody asparagus ends in the water for about 10 minutes, pressing them with the back of a slotted spoon to release their flavour. Remove the ends with the spoon and throw them away. In the same water, cook the asparagus tips for 2 minutes, then remove, drain and set aside. Finally, cook the chopped asparagus stems for 3 minutes.
3. Pour the water and asparagus stems into a blender and mix until smooth. Pour into a measuring jug — you should have 750 ml (26 fl oz/3 cups) of liquid. If you don't, top up with water. Pour the stock back into the saucepan and maintain at a low simmer.
4. Heat 75 g (2½ oz) of the butter in a deep heavy-based frying pan and gently cook the onion until soft but not browned. Add the garlic and thyme and stir briefly. Add the rice and reduce the heat to low. Season and stir to coat the grains of rice in the butter. Add the vermouth to the rice and increase the heat to medium. Cook, stirring, until all the liquid has been absorbed.
5. Stir in a ladleful of the stock and cook at a fast simmer, stirring constantly. When the stock has been absorbed, stir in another ladleful. Continue like this for about 25 minutes, or until the rice is creamy but still has a little bite in the centre. When you have one ladleful of stock left, add the asparagus tips and the remaining stock and cook until the liquid is absorbed. Adding the delicate asparagus tips at the end of cooking prevents them breaking up and helps them maintain their bright green colour.
6. Stir in the remaining butter and the parmesan. Leave the risotto in the pan for 1–2 minutes to allow the flavours to infuse before serving.

MUSHROOM RISOTTO

SERVES 4–6

INGREDIENTS

- 20 g (¾ oz) dried porcini mushrooms
- 1 litre (35 fl oz/4 cups) chicken or vegetable stock (page 10–11)
- 2 tablespoons olive oil
- 100 g (3½ oz) butter
- 650 g (1 lb 7 oz) small cap or Swiss brown mushrooms, stems trimmed, sliced
- 3 garlic cloves, crushed
- 80 ml (2½ fl oz/⅓ cup) dry white vermouth or wine
- 1 onion, finely chopped
- 440 g (15½ oz/2 cups) risotto rice
- 150 g (5½ oz/1½ cups) grated parmesan cheese

METHOD

1. Soak the porcini in 500 ml (17 fl oz/2 cups) hot water for 30 minutes. Drain, keeping the liquid. Chop, then pour the liquid through a fine sieve lined with paper towel.
2. Put the stock and the mushroom liquid together in a saucepan. Bring to the boil, then reduce the heat and keep at a low simmer.
3. Heat half the oil and half the butter in a large heavy-based saucepan over high heat. Add all the mushrooms and the garlic to the pan. Cook, stirring, for 10 minutes, or until soft. Reduce the heat to low and cook for a further 5 minutes. Increase the heat, add the vermouth and cook for 2–3 minutes, until evaporated.
4. Heat the remaining oil and a little butter in a large heavy-based frying pan. Add the onion and cook for 10 minutes, or until soft. Add the rice and stir for 1–2 minutes. Add a ladleful of stock and stir over medium heat until it is absorbed. Continue adding the stock, a ladleful at a time, for about 25 minutes, or until the rice is tender but still has a little bite. Remove from the heat and stir in the mushrooms, parmesan and the remaining butter. Season to taste.

RISI E BISI

Risi e bisi (rice and peas) is served much wetter than most other risottos. The consistency should be more like a thick soup than a risotto.

SERVES 4

INGREDIENTS

- 1.5 litres (6 cups) chicken or vegetable stock (page 10–11)
- 2 teaspoons olive oil
- 40 g (1½ oz) butter
- 1 small onion, finely chopped
- 80 g (2¾ oz) pancetta, cubed
- 2 tablespoons chopped parsley
- 375 g (13 oz) peas
- 220 g (7¾ oz/1 cup) risotto rice
- 50 g (1¾ oz/½ cup) grated parmesan cheese

METHOD

1. Pour the stock into a saucepan. Bring to the boil, then reduce the heat and keep at a low simmer.
2. Heat the oil and half the butter in a large wide heavy-based saucepan and cook the onion and pancetta over low heat for 5 minutes, or until softened. Stir in the parsley and peas and add two ladlefuls of the hot stock. Simmer for 6–8 minutes.
3. Add the rice and the remaining stock. Simmer until the rice is tender but still has a little bite, and most of the stock has been absorbed. Stir in the remaining butter and the parmesan, season and serve.

SUPPLI

The full name for this recipe is *suppli al telefono*. Serve hot so that, when bitten into, the cheese filling pulls out into long thin strands, like telephone wires.

MAKES 30

INGREDIENTS

- 750 ml (26 fl oz/3 cups) chicken stock (page 11)
- 60 g (2¼ oz) butter
- 1 small onion, finely chopped
- 440 g (14 oz/2 cups) risotto rice
- 125 ml (4 fl oz/½ cup) dry white wine
- pinch of powdered saffron
- 50 g (1¾ oz/½ cup) grated parmesan cheese
- 2 eggs, lightly beaten
- 100 g (3½ oz) mozzarella, cut into 30 cubes
- 30 small basil leaves
- 100 g (3½ oz/1 cup) dry breadcrumbs
- oil, for deep-frying

METHOD

1. Put the stock in a pan and keep at simmering point. Heat the butter in a large heavy-based pan. Cook the onion for 2–3 minutes, until softened but not browned, then add the rice and stir for 2–3 minutes to coat.
2. Add the wine and saffron to the rice and stir until absorbed. Stir in a ladleful of stock and stir until absorbed, then add another ladleful. Continue for about 15 minutes until you add the last of the stock, then cover the pan. Reduce the heat to very low and cook for 10–15 minutes. Allow to cool.
3. Stir in the parmesan and eggs. With wet hands, roll into 30 walnut-sized balls. Push a cube of mozzarella and a basil leaf into the centre of each and mould the rice around it.
4. Coat the balls with breadcrumbs and chill for at least 1 hour. Fill a deep pan one-third full of oil and heat to 180°C (350°F). Fry a few balls at a time for 4–5 minutes, or until golden brown.

SEAFOOD RISOTTO

SERVES 4–6

INGREDIENTS

- 1.75 litres (7 cups) fish stock (page 10)
- 2 tablespoons olive oil
- 2 onions, finely chopped
- 2 garlic cloves, finely chopped
- 1 celery stalk, finely chopped
- 440 g (14 oz/2 cups) risotto rice
- 8–10 mussels, cleaned (page 196)
- 150 g (5½ oz) firm white fish fillets, cubed
- 8 raw prawns (shrimp), peeled and deveined
- 2 tablespoons chopped parsley
- 1 tablespoon chopped oregano
- 1 tablespoon chopped thyme

METHOD

1. Pour the stock into a saucepan. Bring to the boil, then reduce the heat and keep at a low simmer.
2. Heat the oil in a deep heavy-based frying pan over medium heat. Cook the onion, garlic and celery for 2–3 minutes, until softened but not browned, then add the rice to the pan and stir for 2–3 minutes until well coated.
3. Stir in a ladleful of the stock and cook at a fast simmer, stirring constantly. When the stock has been absorbed, stir in another ladleful. Continue like this for about 25 minutes until you have just a little stock left.
4. Meanwhile, bring 60 ml (2 fl oz/¼ cup) water to the boil in a saucepan. Add the mussels, cover with a lid and cook for 3–5 minutes, shaking the pan occasionally, until the mussels have opened. Drain off the water, and discard any mussels that remain closed.
5. Add the fish, prawns and remaining stock to the rice and stir well. Cook for 5–10 minutes, or until the seafood is just cooked and the rice is tender and creamy. Remove from the heat, add the mussels, cover and set aside for 5 minutes. Stir in the parsley, oregano and thyme, and season to taste with salt and pepper.

BAKED CHICKEN AND LEEK RISOTTO

Though risottos are traditionally prepared on the stove, they can also be made in the oven in a casserole dish. The result may not be quite as creamy as a stovetop risotto, but the method is much kinder on your wrists.

SERVES 4–6

INGREDIENTS

- 60 g (2¼ oz) butter
- 1 leek, thinly sliced
- 2 boneless, skinless chicken breasts, cubed
- 440 g (14 oz/2 cups) risotto rice
- 60 ml (2 fl oz/¼ cup) white wine
- 1.25 litres (5 cups) chicken stock (page 11)
- 35 g (1¼ oz/⅓ cup) grated parmesan cheese
- 2 tablespoons thyme

METHOD

1. Preheat the oven to 150°C (300°F/Gas 2) and put a large casserole dish with a lid in the oven to warm.
2. Heat the butter in a saucepan over medium heat, add the leek and cook for 2 minutes, or until softened but not browned.
3. Add the chicken to the pan and cook, stirring, for 2–3 minutes, or until lightly coloured. Add the rice and stir so that it is well coated with butter. Cook for 1 minute. Add the wine and stock and bring to the boil.
4. Pour into the warm dish and cover. Transfer to the oven and bake for 30 minutes, stirring halfway through cooking time. Stir in the parmesan and thyme, season well and serve.

TIMBALLO OF LEEK, ZUCCHINI AND BASIL

SERVES 4

INGREDIENTS

pinch of saffron threads
125 ml (4 fl oz/½ cup) dry white wine
750 ml (26 fl oz/3 cups) chicken stock (page 11)
50 g (1¾ oz) butter
1 onion, finely chopped
2 garlic cloves, crushed
440 g (14 oz/2 cups) risotto rice
leaves from 2 thyme sprigs
50 g (1¾ oz/½ cup) grated parmesan cheese
2 tablespoons olive oil
2 leeks, thinly sliced
400 g (14 oz) thin zucchini (courgettes), thinly sliced on the diagonal
¼ teaspoon ground nutmeg
10 basil leaves, shredded
70 g (2½ oz) thinly sliced prosciutto, cut into strips
90 g (3¼ oz/⅓ cup) sour cream

METHOD

1 Soak the saffron in the wine. Pour the stock and 125 ml (4 fl oz/½ cup) water into a saucepan and keep at a low simmer.
2 Melt half the butter in a large heavy-based saucepan. Add the onion and garlic and cook over low heat for about 5 minutes, or until softened but not browned. Add the rice and stir until well coated. Stir in the thyme and season well. Stir in the saffron-infused wine, then increase the heat and cook, stirring constantly, until it is absorbed.
3 Stir in a ladleful of the stock and cook at a fast simmer, stirring constantly. When the stock has been absorbed, stir in another ladleful. Continue like this for about 25 minutes, or until the rice is creamy and tender. Remove from the heat and stir in the remaining butter and the parmesan.
4 Heat the oil in a frying pan and cook the leek, without browning, over low heat for 5 minutes. Add the zucchini and cook for about 5 minutes, or until softened. Add the nutmeg and season well. Stir in the basil, prosciutto and sour cream. Cook, stirring, for 2–3 minutes, or until the sauce thickens.
5 Preheat the oven to 180°C (350°F/Gas 4) and grease a 1.5 litre (6 cup) pudding basin or rounded ovenproof bowl. Cut out a piece of baking paper the size of the basin's base and line the base. Cover with half the rice, pressing it down firmly. Spoon in two-thirds of the zucchini mixture, keeping the remaining third warm in the pan. Press in the last of the rice mixture. Cover with foil and transfer to the oven.
6 Bake for 20 minutes. Remove from the oven and rest for 5 minutes. Carefully unmould the timballo onto a serving plate. Serve the remaining zucchini on the side.

NOTE: You can easily make a vegetarian version of this by using vegetable stock instead of chicken and not adding the prosciutto.

••PAELLA••

Paella is a rice dish brought to Spain by the Arabs. Traditionally, paellas were reserved for celebrations and were cooked outdoors over hot coals by men, and this tradition of men being responsible for the cooking of the paella still continues today. The ingredients, strictly adhered to in and around Valencia (where the definitive paella is made), include chicken, rabbit or pork, butterbeans, snails, tomatoes, paprika and saffron. Today, with seafood replacing most of the meat (except chicken), paella has become the emblematic dish of Spain.

MEXICAN PAELLA

This dish of rice with shellfish is the Mexican version of Spanish paella. It includes firm-fleshed fish and a unique, delicious flavour derived from roasting the base ingredients before adding them to the sauce.

SERVES 4

INGREDIENTS

- 1 large garlic clove, peeled
- 1 onion, quartered
- 2 firm tomatoes
- 1 red capsicum (pepper), seeded and quartered
- 60 ml (2 fl oz/¼ cup) olive oil
- 55 g (2 oz) bacon, chopped
- 265 g (9¼ oz/1⅓ cups) long-grain rice
- 625 ml (21½ fl oz/2½ cups) hot fish stock (page 10)
- 2 tinned and drained, or fresh, poblano chillies, finely shredded
- 16 raw prawns (shrimp), peeled and deveined, tails intact
- 250 g (9 oz) firm white fish, such as snapper, cut into chunks
- 2 tablespoons chopped coriander (cilantro)
- lime wedges, to serve

METHOD

1. Dry-roast the garlic, onion, tomatoes and capsicum in a heavy-based frying pan over low heat, turning often, for about 45 minutes, or until the ingredients are browned all over.
2. When cool enough to handle, peel the tomato and capsicum, and roughly chop the flesh. Put the flesh in a food processor with the garlic and onion, and blend to a purée. Alternatively, finely chop the ingredients by hand.
3. Heat the olive oil in a deep frying pan. Add the bacon and cook until crisp. Add the rice and cook for 1 minute, stirring the grains to make sure they are completely coated in oil.
4. Add the puréed tomato mixture and cook for 3 minutes. Add the stock and 1 teaspoon salt. Bring to the boil and stir once. Reduce the heat to low and cover with a lid. Cook gently for 15 minutes.
5. Add the chillies, prawns and fish to the frying pan, and cook for another 5 minutes. Add a little hot water to the rice if it is becoming too dry. Check the seasoning, sprinkle with coriander and serve with lime wedges.

JAMBALAYA

A New Orleans dish of Spanish origin, and a Cajun speciality, jambalaya is based on long-grain rice, green capsicum (peppers), celery and onion, mixed with ingredients such as chicken, prawns, ham or even alligator. A red jambalaya uses tomatoes and tomato sauce; a brown one uses chicken or beef stock. The name is thought to be a jumbling of jamón, Spanish for ham, and paella.

CHICKEN AND PRAWN JAMBALAYA

SERVES 4–6

INGREDIENTS

- ½ teaspoon dried oregano
- ¾ teaspoon dried thyme
- ¾ teaspoon garlic powder
- ¾ teaspoon onion powder
- 1 teaspoon paprika
- ½ teaspoon ground white pepper
- ¼ teaspoon cayenne pepper
- 500 g (1 lb 2 oz) boneless, skinless chicken thighs, cut into quarters
- 2 tablespoons oil
- 250 g (9 oz) chorizo, cut into 1 cm (½ inch) slices
- 1 large onion, chopped
- 2 celery stalks, sliced
- 1 large green capsicum (pepper), cubed
- 4 garlic cloves, crushed
- 2 teaspoons thyme
- 400 g (14 oz) tin chopped tomatoes
- 2 bay leaves
- ¼ teaspoon Tabasco sauce
- 200 g (7 oz/1 cup) long-grain rice
- 875 ml (30 fl oz/3½ cups) hot chicken stock (page 11)
- 450 g (1 lb) raw prawns (shrimp), peeled and deveined
- 5 spring onions (scallions), thinly sliced
- 3 tablespoons chopped parsley

METHOD

1. Combine the oregano, thyme, garlic powder, onion powder, paprika, white pepper, cayenne, ¾ teaspoon salt and ½ teaspoon black pepper in a bowl. Add the chicken and mix to coat well.
2. Heat the oil in a wide, heavy-based frying pan over medium heat and cook the chorizo for 5–6 minutes, or until lightly browned. Remove with a slotted spoon, leaving as much oil in the pan as possible. Add the chicken in batches and cook over medium heat for 6–8 minutes, until lightly browned, adding a little more oil if necessary. Remove the chicken from the pan with a slotted spoon, leaving as much oil in the pan as possible.
3. Add the onion, celery, capsicum, garlic and thyme to the pan and cook over medium heat for 6–8 minutes, stirring often with a wooden spoon to lift any sediment from the base of the pan. When the vegetables begin to brown, add the tomatoes, bay leaves and Tabasco sauce and simmer for 2–3 minutes.
4. Return the chorizo and chicken to the pan. Add the rice, stir briefly, then pour in the stock. Don't stir at this point. Reduce the heat and simmer, uncovered, for 25–30 minutes, or until all the liquid has been absorbed and the rice is tender. Remove from the heat and add the prawns. Cover and leave for 10 minutes, then fluff the rice with a fork, season well and stir in the spring onion and parsley.

CHICKEN AND CHORIZO PAELLA

SERVES 6

INGREDIENTS

- 60 ml (2 fl oz/¼ cup) olive oil
- 1 large red capsicum (pepper), seeded and cut into strips
- 600 g (1 lb 5 oz) boneless, skinless chicken thighs, cubed
- 200 g (7 oz) chorizo, thickly sliced
- 200 g (7 oz) flat mushrooms, thinly sliced
- 3 garlic cloves, crushed
- 1 tablespoon finely grated lemon zest
- 700 g (1 lb 9 oz) ripe tomatoes, roughly chopped
- 200 g (7 oz) green beans, cut into short lengths
- 1 tablespoon chopped rosemary
- 2 tablespoons chopped parsley
- ¼ teaspoon saffron threads soaked in 60 ml (2 fl oz/¼ cup) hot water
- 440 g (14 oz/2 cups) paella rice
- 750 ml (26 fl oz/3 cups) hot chicken stock (page 11)
- lemon wedges, to serve

METHOD

1 Heat the olive oil in a paella pan, or in a large, deep heavy-based frying pan over medium heat. Add the capsicum and cook, stirring, for about 5 minutes. Remove from the pan. Stir in the chicken and cook for 10 minutes, or until browned all over. Remove from the pan. Add the chorizo to the pan and cook for 5 minutes. Remove from the pan. Add the mushrooms, garlic and lemon zest, cover and cook over medium heat for about 5 minutes.

2 Stir in the tomato and capsicum and cook for another 5 minutes, or until the tomato is soft. Add the beans, rosemary, parsley, saffron mixture, rice, chicken and chorizo. Stir briefly and add the stock. Do not stir at this point.

3 Reduce the heat and simmer for 30 minutes. Remove from the heat, cover loosely with foil and leave to stand for 10 minutes. Season to taste with salt and black pepper, then serve with lemon wedges.

HOW TO... MAKE PERFECT PAELLA

* There are several key ingredients that distinguish an excellent paella. Saffron threads are arguably the most important; these tiny strands possess a deep, earthy, musky flavour and merely a pinch will promote intense colour and flavour. Sweet paprika adds a little smokiness; tomatoes contribute sweetness and depth.
* Calasparra or bomba rice will give the perfect paella texture — this firm, round, medium-grain rice cooks to a slightly sticky yet dry finish without being glutinous. Look for rice labelled 'Valencia rice' or 'rice for paella'. Arborio or another risotto rice can be substituted but the result will be a little stickier.
* Stir the rice as little as possible to discourage the starches from being released or the rice will end up mushy.
* Paella derives its name from the special pan (doubling as a serving vessel) in which it is cooked. The paella pan, or *paellera*, is a wide, shallow pan most often made from cast iron, but also seen in earthenware. The pans have no lid, but usually have a round handle on one or both sides. Paella pans are now widely available at cookware stores or special Spanish food stores.

CLASSIC SPANISH PAELLA

SERVES 4

INGREDIENTS

- 12 black mussels, cleaned (page 196)
- 125 ml (4 fl oz/½ cup) dry white wine
- 12 raw prawns (shrimp), peeled and deveined (heads and shells reserved)
- 500 ml (17 fl oz/2 cups) chicken stock (page 11)
- 60 ml (2 fl oz/¼ cup) olive oil
- 600 g (1 lb 5 oz) boneless, skinless chicken thighs, halved
- 3 tomatoes
- 1 large red onion, chopped
- 1 red capsicum (pepper), cut into large cubes
- 1 green capsicum (pepper), cut into large cubes
- 3 garlic cloves, crushed
- 2 teaspoons sweet Spanish paprika
- ¼ teaspoon saffron threads, soaked in 60 ml (2 fl oz/¼ cup) hot water
- 300 g (10½ oz/1⅓ cups) paella rice
- 300 g (10½ oz) firm white fish, such as snapper, cubed
- 150 g (5½ oz) peas
- lemon wedges, to serve

METHOD

1. Put the mussels in a saucepan with the wine, cover and cook for 2–3 minutes, or until they have opened. Lift the mussels out of the liquid with a slotted spoon and set them aside on a plate, discarding any that have not opened.
2. Put the prawn heads and shells in the pan with the mussel liquid, add 500 ml (17 fl oz/2 cups) water and simmer for 5 minutes. Strain the liquid into a bowl, then pour the liquid back into the pan and add the stock. Bring to the boil, then reduce the heat and keep at a low simmer.
3. Heat 2 tablespoons of the oil in a paella pan or large, heavy-based frying pan. Add the chicken and cook over medium heat for 10 minutes, or until browned all over, then remove from the pan.
4. To peel the tomatoes, score a cross in the base of each tomato. Put in a heatproof bowl and cover with boiling water. Leave for 30 seconds, then transfer to cold water and peel the skin away from the cross. Cut the tomatoes in half horizontally and scoop out the seeds with a teaspoon. Roughly chop the flesh.
5. Add the remaining oil to the pan and cook the onion and tomato over low heat for 4–5 minutes, or until softened but not browned. Add the red and green capsicum and cook for 1 minute, then stir in the garlic, paprika and saffron with its soaking water, and cook for 30 seconds. Return the chicken to the pan, arranging it around the edge and stir to coat with the tomato mixture.
6. Pour in the stock and bring it to simmering point, then add the rice. Do not stir the rice, instead use the spatula to gently move it down into the liquid. Arrange the capsicum on top of the rice. Bring back to the boil, then reduce the heat and simmer for 8–10 minutes, or until the rice is becoming tender. The paella should not be stirred after it has come to the boil.
7. Arrange the fish, mussels, prawns and peas evenly over the rice, taking care not to stir through to the bottom. Reduce the heat to very low and simmer without stirring for 15 minutes, or until the rice is tender and the prawns and fish are cooked through. Shake the pan from time to time to prevent the rice from burning, but do not stir to the bottom. This will allow a crust to form across the bottom. Pour in a little hot water if the mixture seems dry towards the end of cooking. Remove the pan from the heat, cover loosely with foil and leave to rest for 5–10 minutes. Season and serve, straight from the pan, with lemon wedges.

••PILAFF••

A pilaff is essentially a rice dish in which each grain of rice, when cooked, remains separate and fluffy. Though the cooking method originated in the Middle East, you will find many versions of pilaff around the world: polo in Iran, pilav in Russia, pulao in India, pilaff in Turkey and purloo in the deep south of America. And it is not only rice that is used as a base — pilaff can be based on other grains, such as burghul, barley, buckwheat, quinoa or even lentils.

WHICH RICE?

In general pilaff is made with a long, thin rice grain with little starch, though this does depend on the particular region in which the pilaff originated. For instance, the pilaffs of Central Asia are unique in using short-grain rice but for most types, basmati or long-grain rice gives a good result.

STOVETOP OR BAKED?

If cooking on a stovetop, you'll need a large heavy-based saucepan or a deep frying pan with a lid. Heavy-based pans allow even heat distribution, and prevent the rice catching and burning on the bottom of the pan. Ideally, the pan should be made from copper, stainless steel or cast iron.

Oven-baked pilaffs should be cooked in a sturdy ceramic or cast-iron casserole dish with a lid — some can be started off on the stove and then transferred to the oven.

Every pilaff aficionado has their own secret technique for the best results. Some cooks soak the rice first to wash out as much starch as possible. Some start by pouring boiling water over the top to soften the grains. Some pilaffs are stirred for a little while and then left; most are covered but a few are not; and some are cooked on the stovetop and some are baked (for example, the traditional Indian biryani).

TOMATO AND HERB PILAFF

Peel 1 kg (2 lb 4 oz) tomatoes by scoring a cross in the base of each tomato. Put in a heatproof bowl and cover with boiling water. Leave for 30 seconds, then transfer to cold water and peel the skin away from the cross. Cut the tomatoes in half horizontally and scoop out the seeds with a teaspoon. Roughly chop the flesh. Fry 200 g (7 oz) chopped onion and 1 crushed garlic clove in olive oil. Add the tomatoes and fry. Add 200 ml (7 fl oz) water and simmer for 30 minutes. Add 500 g (1 lb 2 oz/2½ cups) basmati rice and enough water to cover the rice. Simmer, covered, until the rice is cooked, then season and stir in some chopped parsley. Serves 8

PULAO

SERVES 6

INGREDIENTS

- 500 g (1 lb 2 oz/2½ cups) basmati rice
- 1 teaspoon cumin seeds
- 4 tablespoons ghee (page 120) or oil
- 2 tablespoons chopped almonds
- 2 tablespoons raisins or sultanas
- 2 onions, thinly sliced
- 2 cinnamon sticks
- 5 cardamom pods
- 1 teaspoon sugar
- 2 teaspoons finely grated ginger
- 15 saffron threads, soaked in 1 tablespoon warm milk
- 2 Indian bay leaves (cassia leaves)
- 250 ml (9 fl oz/1 cup) coconut milk
- 2 tablespoons fresh or frozen peas
- rosewater (optional)

METHOD

1. Wash the rice under running water until the water runs clear. Put in a saucepan, cover with water and soak for 30 minutes. Drain.
2. Place a small frying pan over low heat and dry-fry the cumin seeds until aromatic.
3. Heat the ghee in a heavy-based frying pan and fry the almonds and raisins until browned. Remove from the pan. Add the onion to the pan and fry until dark golden brown, then remove from the pan.
4. Add the rice, cumin, cinnamon, cardamom, sugar, ginger, saffron and a pinch of salt to the pan and fry for 2 minutes, until aromatic.
5. Add the bay leaves and coconut milk, then add water to come about 5 cm (2 inches) above the rice. Bring to the boil, cover and cook for 8 minutes, or until most of the water has evaporated. Stir in the peas.
6. Reduce the heat to very low and cook until the rice is cooked through. Stir in the almonds, raisins and onion. Drizzle with a few drops of rosewater for perfume if you like.

CHICKEN AND ALMOND PILAFF

SERVES 4–6

INGREDIENTS

- 700 g (1 lb 9 oz) boneless, skinless chicken thighs, cut into strips
- 1 tablespoon baharat (page 418)
- 400 g (14 oz/2 cups) basmati rice
- 750 ml (26 fl oz/3 cups) chicken stock (page 11)
- 2 tablespoons ghee (page 120) or oil
- 1 large onion, chopped
- 1 garlic clove, finely chopped
- 1 teaspoon ground turmeric
- 400 g (14 oz) tin chopped tomatoes
- 1 cinnamon stick
- 4 cardamom pods, bruised
- 4 cloves
- ½ teaspoon finely grated lemon zest
- 3 tablespoons chopped coriander (cilantro)
- 2 teaspoons lemon juice
- 40 g (1½ oz/⅓ cup) slivered almonds, toasted

METHOD

1. Combine the chicken and baharat in a large bowl, cover with plastic wrap and refrigerate for 1 hour. Meanwhile, put the rice in a large bowl, cover with cold water and soak for at least 30 minutes. Rinse under cold running water until the water runs clear, then drain and set aside.
2. Bring the stock to the boil in a saucepan. Reduce the heat, cover and keep at a low simmer. Meanwhile, heat the ghee in a large heavy-based saucepan over medium heat. Add the onion and garlic and cook for 5 minutes, or until soft and golden. Add the chicken and turmeric and cook for 5 minutes, or until browned, then add the rice and cook, stirring, for 2 minutes.
3. Add the tomatoes, hot stock, cinnamon stick, cardamom pods, cloves, lemon zest and 1 teaspoon salt to the pan. Stir well and bring to the boil, then reduce the heat to low and cover the saucepan with a tight-fitting lid. Simmer for 20 minutes, or until the stock has been absorbed and the rice is cooked. Remove from the heat and set aside, covered, for 10 minutes.
4. Stir in the coriander, lemon juice and almonds. Season to taste.

SAFFRON CHICKEN PULAO

SERVES 6

INGREDIENTS

- ½ teaspoon saffron threads
- 400 g (14 oz/2 cups) basmati rice
- 4 tablespoons ghee (page 120) or oil
- 1 cinnamon stick, broken
- 3 cloves
- 2 cardamom pods, lightly crushed
- 2 tablespoons sultanas
- 2 tablespoons blanched almonds
- 300 g (10½ oz) boneless, skinless chicken breasts, diced

METHOD

1. Soak the saffron in 60 ml (2 fl oz/¼ cup) water. Put the rice and half the ghee in a large heavy-based saucepan and stir until the rice grains are well coated with ghee. Add the saffron and its soaking water, cinnamon stick, cloves, cardamom pods and 625 ml (21 fl oz/2½ cups) water. Cover and bring to the boil, then reduce the heat to as low as possible and cook without removing the lid for 20 minutes.
2. Heat the remaining ghee in a frying pan, add the sultanas, almonds and chicken and cook for about 5 minutes, or until the chicken is cooked through. Season to taste with salt.
3. Stir the chicken mixture into the rice and leave to stand for 5 minutes before serving.

CHICKEN BIRYANI

Biryani is the Southeast Asian version of a pilau. This aromatic dish is often cooked with chicken or lamb.

SERVES 8

INGREDIENTS

3 onions, sliced
125 ml (4 fl oz/½ cup) oil
180 g (6½ oz) ghee (page 120) or unsalted butter
4 cm (1½ inch) piece cinnamon stick
2 cardamom pods
3 cloves
2 star anise
2 stalks of curry leaves
2 cm (¾ inch) piece ginger, grated
6 garlic cloves, crushed
1.3 kg (3 lb) chicken pieces
4–6 green chillies, slit lengthways
500 ml (17 fl oz/2 cups) buttermilk
4 ripe tomatoes, diced
185 ml (6 fl oz/¾ cup) coconut milk
1 litre (35 fl oz/4 cups) chicken stock (page 11)
800 g (1 lb 12 oz/4 cups) basmati rice, rinsed
lemon wedges, to serve

METHOD

1 Put the onion in a sieve, sprinkle with ½ teaspoon salt and leave for 10 minutes to drain. Rinse and pat dry.
2 Heat the oil and ghee in a flameproof casserole dish. Add the cinnamon, cardamom and cloves and heat until they begin to crackle. Reduce the heat to low and add the star anise and the curry leaves from one stalk. Stir in the onion and cook for a few minutes until golden. Toss in the ginger and garlic and cook until golden.
3 Mix in the chicken, increase the heat and brown the pieces on all sides. Add the chillies, remaining curry leaves, buttermilk and some salt. Cook for 12 minutes, or until the chicken is cooked through and the liquid is reduced by half. Stir in the tomato and coconut milk. Cook until the tomato is tender, then pour in the stock and bring to the boil. Preheat the oven to 220°C (425°F/Gas 7).
4 Add the rice to the chicken and stir well. Season, then cook for 10 minutes, until most of the liquid is absorbed. Remove the casserole from the heat, cover with a clean wet cloth, then the lid, and transfer to the oven for 15 minutes, or until the rice is cooked. Serve with lemon wedges.

BURGHUL

Burghul is made by boiling wheat until soft, drying and then grinding it. To use burghul, cover with boiling water and allow the liquid to absorb. Burghul has a slightly nutty flavour and is used widely in Middle Eastern cuisines, in tabouleh, kibbeh, pilaffs, stews or soups. Cracked wheat is sometimes erroneously called burghul or bulgar.

To make a burghul pilaff, fry a chopped onion in oil until soft. Add 6 chopped tomatoes and 1 crushed garlic clove. Bring to the boil, add 1 drained tin of chickpeas, 6 tablespoons soaked burghul, some chopped coriander and seasoning. Heat through and serve with yoghurt or sour cream. Serves 4

••POLENTA AND COUSCOUS••

Grains such as polenta and couscous lend themselves to many dishes, and endless preparation possibilities, both as accompaniments and as main-course meals. Polenta and couscous, like rice, have a fairly neutral flavour, so are often prepared with lots of herbs and spices or served as accompaniments to rich stews and braised meat dishes.

POLENTA

Polenta is the name of the dish — the raw ingredient is actually cornmeal or ground corn kernels — and it is a staple of northern Italy, where it's more widely eaten than pasta. Polenta can be served soft, sometimes mixed with cheese, and served with meat or vegetables, or it can be left to set, cut into pieces and grilled.

HOW TO... MAKE POLENTA

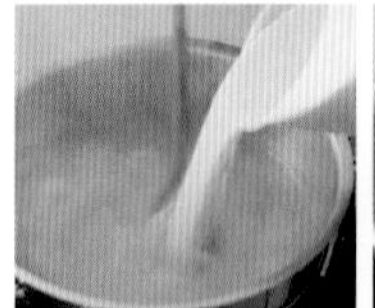

METHOD

1 Put the specified amount of cold water and salt in a deep heavy-based saucepan and bring to the boil. Add the polenta in a steady stream, stirring vigorously with a wooden spoon.
2 As soon as you've added all the polenta, reduce the heat so the water is just simmering and keep stirring for the first 30 seconds to prevent lumps.
3 The finished texture of the polenta will improve the more you stir it. Leave it to bubble away for about 40 minutes, stirring every few minutes to prevent sticking. When cooked, it should be thick enough to fall from the spoon in lumps.
4 The polenta can be flavoured with grated cheese or fried vegetables, stirred in at the end, or herbs or chillies, added at the beginning. You can also use stock or milk to cook rather than water.

HOW TO... GRILL POLENTA

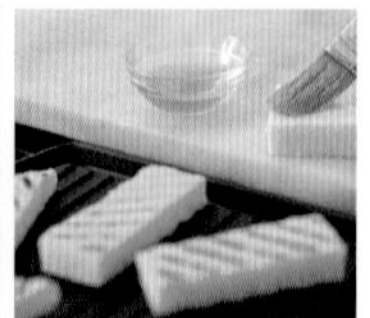

METHOD

1 Pour the cooked polenta onto a flat plate or serving dish and leave to cool. Do not put it in the fridge or condensation will form and make the polenta stick when grilled.
2 Cut the polenta into triangles or strips.
3 Brush the pieces with olive oil and grill or chargrill for 3 minutes on each side. Use the grilled polenta for canapé bases as well as an accompaniment to stews and sauces.
4 The wet polenta can also be moulded into shapes for layering with sauce. Pour into a serving dish (no more than 2.5 cm (1 inch) thick or it will be too stodgy). Cool, then turn it out of the dish onto a board. Slice horizontally through the polenta slab. The two slices can then be layered with sauce and reformed in the dish.

BAKED POLENTA WITH FOUR CHEESES

SERVES 6

INGREDIENTS

POLENTA
300 g (10½ oz) polenta
75 g (2½ oz) butter

TOMATO SAUCE
2 rosemary or thyme sprigs
60 ml (2 fl oz/¼ cup) extra virgin olive oil
2 garlic cloves, thinly sliced
800 g (1 lb 12 oz) tin tomatoes or 350 g (12 oz) ripe tomatoes, peeled (page 347) and chopped

200 g (7 oz) gorgonzola cheese, cubed
250 g (9 oz) taleggio cheese, cubed
250 g (9 oz) mascarpone cheese
100 g (3½ oz) parmesan cheese, grated

METHOD

1 Bring 1.5 litres (6 cups) water to the boil in a deep heavy-based saucepan and add 1 tablespoon salt. Add the polenta in a gentle stream, whisking or stirring vigorously as you pour. Reduce the heat immediately so the water is simmering and keep stirring for the first 30 seconds to prevent lumps appearing — the more you stir, the better the finished texture of the polenta. Leave the polenta to gently bubble away for about 40 minutes, stirring it every few minutes to stop it sticking to the pan. The finished polenta should drop from the spoon in thick lumps. Stir in the butter.

2 Pour the polenta into a large 2.25 litre (9 cup) oiled gratin or casserole dish that is about 5.5 cm (2¼ inches) deep. The polenta should reach no further than halfway up the side of the dish or the filling will overflow. Set aside to cool completely.

3 To make the tomato sauce, first strip the leaves off the rosemary or thyme. Heat the olive oil in a saucepan over low heat and cook the garlic gently until light brown. Add half the rosemary or thyme and then the tomatoes. Season with salt and pepper and cook gently, stirring occasionally, until reduced to a thick sauce.

4 Preheat the oven to 180°C (350°F/Gas 4). Carefully turn the polenta out of the dish onto a board, then slice it horizontally in two. Pour half of the tomato sauce into the bottom of the dish, place the bottom slice of the polenta on top of the sauce and season with salt and pepper. Scatter the gorgonzola and taleggio over the top. Using a teaspoon, dot the mascarpone over the polenta and then sprinkle with half of the parmesan and the remaining rosemary or thyme. Put the other slice of polenta on top and pour over the last of the tomato sauce. Sprinkle with the remaining parmesan. Transfer to the oven and bake for 40 minutes. Leave to rest for at least 10 minutes before serving.

NOTE: This dish is very rich so try serving it with a simple rocket (arugula) salad.

COUSCOUS

A food generally associated with North African cuisine, couscous is usually made from semolina flour. In the traditional method of preparing it, the flour is laid out on a large round mesh frame, sprinkled with water, and laboriously rolled into tiny balls of grain. Couscous is also the name of the dish that is cooked in a couscoussier. A stew cooks in the lower half while the couscous steams in the perforated upper section. As well as being a staple food in North Africa, couscous is also popular in parts of Italy, Egypt and the Middle East.

HOW TO... PREPARE COUSCOUS

Couscous and packets of instant couscous both require steaming for the grains to swell and become light. This is the traditional way to prepare it and gives the best results. The microwave method below will give a similar result — couscous with light, fluffy grains. For quicker preparation, simply follow the directions on the packet, or as directed in the recipe.

SERVES 4–5

INGREDIENTS

- 325 g (11½ oz/1¾ cups) couscous
- 30 g (1 oz) butter, chopped

MICROWAVE METHOD

1. Put the couscous in a large, shallow bowl and cover with water. Stir and pour the water off through a strainer, returning the grains to the bowl. Leave for 15 minutes to swell, then rake with your fingers to separate the grains. Put the couscous in a 3 litre (12 cup) ceramic dish.
2. Stir ½ teaspoon salt into 250 ml (9 fl oz/1 cup) water. Sprinkle a third of the water over the couscous, cover and microwave on full power for 3 minutes. Add the butter and fluff up with a fork. Repeat twice more with the remaining water and fluff with the fork each time. Uncover and fluff up again before serving.

PISTACHIO COUSCOUS

SERVES 4

INGREDIENTS

- 125 ml (4 fl oz/½ cup) orange juice
- 2 tablespoons lemon juice
- ½ teaspoon ground cinnamon
- 250 g (9 oz/1⅓ cups) couscous
- 50 g (1¾ oz) butter
- 35 g (1¼ oz/¼ cup) currants
- 45 g (1½ oz) chopped pistachio nuts
- 425 g (15 oz) tin chickpeas, rinsed
- 3 tablespoons chopped parsley

METHOD

1. Combine the orange juice and lemon juice in a bowl, then add 125 ml (4 fl oz/½ cup) water. Pour into a saucepan and add the cinnamon. Bring to the boil, then remove from the heat. Pour in the couscous, cover and set aside for 5 minutes.
2. Add the butter and fluff up the grains with a fork, raking out any lumps, then fold in the currants, pistachios, chickpeas and parsley. Serve with vegetable tagines, lamb salads or stews.

MOROCCAN CHICKEN WITH COUSCOUS SALAD

SERVES 4

INGREDIENTS

COUSCOUS SALAD
¼ preserved lemon (page 668)
500 ml (17 fl oz/2 cups) apple juice
370 g (13 oz/2 cups) couscous
½ small red onion, halved and thinly sliced
50 g (1¾ oz/⅓ cup) pistachio nuts, toasted
8 dried apricots, chopped
60 g (2¼ oz/⅓ cup) green olives, pitted and chopped
1 small handful mint, roughly chopped
1 small handful parsley, roughly chopped

2 tablespoons plain (all-purpose) flour
1 tablespoon ras el hanout (page 419)
12 chicken tenderloins, trimmed
2–3 tablespoons olive oil
250 g (9 oz/1 cup) plain yoghurt
2 tablespoons chopped mint
2 teaspoons ras el hanout, extra
1 teaspoon honey

METHOD

1 To make the couscous salad, remove and discard the salty flesh from the preserved lemon and rinse the zest thoroughly under running water. Chop the zest finely: you will need about 1 tablespoon.
2 Heat the apple juice in a saucepan until hot but not boiling. Put the couscous in a bowl, pour over the apple juice, cover and set aside for 5 minutes. Fluff up the grains with a fork. Toss the onion, pistachios, apricots, olives and herbs through the couscous.
3 Meanwhile, combine the flour and ras el hanout on a flat plate. Coat the chicken in the mixture and shake off the excess flour. Heat the oil in a large non-stick frying pan. Cook the chicken for 2–3 minutes on each side, or until cooked and golden. Add a little more oil as needed. Slice the chicken.
4 To make the yoghurt dressing, combine the yoghurt, mint, extra ras el hanout and honey in a bowl. To serve, pile the couscous salad onto serving plates, top with the chicken slices and spoon over the yoghurt dressing.

QUINOA

Pronounced keen wa, this tiny seed has been used as a cereal for over 5000 years, and regarded as a sacred food by the Incas who called it 'the mother seed'. The quinoa plant produces masses of small seeds, usually pink or white. Quinoa provides one of the best sources of vegetable protein and an essential amino acid balance. It has a very delicate flavour, comparable to couscous and is often a good substitute for rice. The seeds can be made into flour and the spinach-like leaves of the plant are also edible. Quinoa takes about 15 minutes to cook and needs to be rinsed well before cooking. Add 200 g (7 oz) to 500 ml (17 fl oz/2 cups) water, bring to the boil, then reduce to a simmer, just like rice. Serves 4 as an accompaniment

••NOODLES••

The term 'noodles' (a type of pasta made from flour, water and sometimes egg) can be used to describe hundreds of different varieties used around the world. Noodles are important to Asian cuisine, especially to China and Japan, and long egg noodles are eaten with stews in Eastern Europe. In Asia, noodles can be served at main meals along with other dishes or eaten as a snack, especially served in soupy broths. Short noodles can be cooked in soup or the pasta can be filled to make won tons, which was most likely the original form taken by noodles.

CHICKEN CHOW MEIN

SERVES 4

INGREDIENTS

- 250 g (9 oz) fresh thin egg noodles
- 2 teaspoons sesame oil
- 125 ml (4 fl oz/½ cup) peanut oil
- 1 tablespoon Chinese rice wine
- 1½ tablespoons light soy sauce
- 3 teaspoons cornflour (cornstarch)
- 400 g (14 oz) boneless, skinless chicken breasts, cut into thin strips
- 1 garlic clove, crushed
- 1 tablespoon finely chopped ginger
- 100 g (3½ oz) sugar snap peas, trimmed
- 250 g (9 oz) Chinese cabbage (wom bok), finely shredded
- 4 spring onions (scallions), chopped
- 100 ml (3½ fl oz) chicken stock (page 11)
- 1½ tablespoons oyster sauce
- 100 g (3½ oz) bean sprouts, trimmed

METHOD

1. Cook the noodles in a saucepan of boiling water for 1 minute, or until tender. Drain well. Add the sesame oil and 1 tablespoon of the peanut oil and toss. Place on a baking tray and spread out in a thin layer. Leave in a dry place for 1 hour.
2. Meanwhile, combine the rice wine, 1 tablespoon of the soy sauce and 1 teaspoon of the cornflour in a large non-metallic bowl. Add the chicken and toss well. Cover with plastic wrap and marinate for 10 minutes.
3. Heat 1 tablespoon of the peanut oil in a small non-stick frying pan over high heat. Add a quarter of the noodles and shape into a pancake. Lower the heat and cook for 4 minutes on each side, or until crisp and golden. Drain on crumpled paper towels and keep warm. Repeat to make four noodle cakes in total.
4. Heat a wok over high heat, add the remaining peanut oil and swirl to coat the side of the wok. Stir-fry the garlic and ginger for 30 seconds, then add the chicken and stir-fry for 3–4 minutes, or until golden. Add the sugar snap peas, Chinese cabbage and spring onion to the wok and stir-fry for 2 minutes, or until the cabbage has wilted. Stir in the stock, oyster sauce and bean sprouts and bring to the boil.
5. Mix the remaining cornflour with 2 teaspoons cold water. Stir it into the wok with the remaining soy sauce and cook for 1–2 minutes, or until the sauce thickens.
6. To assemble, place a noodle cake on each serving plate, then spoon the chicken and vegetable mixture on top.

ROAST DUCK, HERB AND NOODLE SALAD

SERVES 4

INGREDIENTS

DRESSING

60 ml (2 fl oz/¼ cup) fish sauce
2 tablespoons lime juice
1 tablespoon grated palm sugar (jaggery) or soft brown sugar
1 small red chilli, finely chopped

250 g (9 oz) dried flat rice stick noodles
1 Chinese roast duck (see Note)
1 tablespoon julienned ginger
90 g (3¼ oz/1 cup) bean sprouts, tailed
1 small red onion, thinly sliced
3 tablespoons chopped coriander (cilantro)
3 tablespoons chopped Thai basil or basil
1 lime, cut into wedges

METHOD

1 To make the dressing, mix the fish sauce, lime juice, palm sugar and chilli.
2 Cover the noodles with warm water and soak for about 20 minutes, or until soft and pliable. Drain, then return to the bowl.
3 Preheat the oven to 180°C (350°F/Gas 4). Remove the flesh and skin from the duck in large pieces, then cut into thin strips, trying to keep some skin on every piece. Put the duck pieces on a baking tray and heat in the oven for 10 minutes, or until warmed through.
4 Add the ginger, bean sprouts, onion, herbs and dressing to the noodles and toss well. Serve the salad on a platter, or on individual serving plates or bowls, and arrange the duck strips on top. Serve with lime wedges.

NOTE: Chinese roast duck is sold ready to eat from Asian barbecue shops or restaurants. If the skin on your duck has become limp, cook under the grill (broiler), skin side up, under high heat for 1 minute, or until crisp.

BEEF AND NOODLE SALAD

SERVES 4

INGREDIENTS

500 g (1 lb 2 oz) beef fillet, 5 cm (2 inches) in diameter
1½ tablespoons vegetable oil
1 teaspoon dried shrimp
1 teaspoon jasmine rice
1 lemongrass stem, white part only, chopped
1 small red chilli, seeded and finely chopped
2 coriander (cilantro) roots, finely chopped
2 kaffir lime leaves, finely shredded
1–2 tablespoons lime juice
2 teaspoons finely chopped ginger
1 Lebanese (short) cucumber
1 vine-ripened tomato
1 red onion
300 g (10½ oz) dried rice vermicelli
2 handfuls Thai basil and Vietnamese mint, torn
1 tablespoon crisp fried shallots
coriander (cilantro) leaves, to garnish

DRESSING

80 ml (2½ fl oz/⅓ cup) lime juice
2 tablespoons grated palm sugar (jaggery)
1 tablespoon fish sauce
1 small red chilli, seeded and finely chopped
1 teaspoon sesame oil

METHOD

1 Heat a barbecue grill or chargrill pan over high heat. Brush the beef with the oil and season generously with salt and black pepper. Sear the beef on all sides for 3–4 minutes, keeping the meat rare in the centre. Remove to a plate and leave to rest.
2 Dry-fry the dried shrimp and rice in a clean frying pan for 1–2 minutes, or until fragrant. Grind to a fine powder with a spice grinder or mortar and pestle. Mix the powder with the lemongrass, chilli, coriander roots, lime leaves, lime juice and ginger in a non-metallic bowl. Add the beef and turn to coat well. Cover with plastic wrap and marinate for at least 5 minutes, then cut into 1 cm (½ inch) thick slices across the grain.
3 To make the dressing, mix all the ingredients in a small bowl, stirring to dissolve the sugar.
4 Peel the cucumber, cut it in half lengthways and slice into 1 cm (½ inch) pieces. Cut the tomato into wedges and the onion into thin wedges.
5 Put the vermicelli in a heatproof bowl, cover with boiling water and soak for 6–7 minutes, or until softened. Drain, rinse under cold water and drain again. Transfer the noodles to a large bowl, then add the beef, cucumber, tomato, onion, basil, mint and dressing and toss well. Serve garnished with the crisp fried shallots and coriander leaves.

KAFFIR LIME

These small, fragrant citrus fruit are characterised by their knobbly dark-green skins and uniquely double-shaped glossy leaves. The juice and flesh of the kaffir lime are quite bitter, so it's only the zest and leaves that are used in cooking, finely grated or shredded and added to Asian-style soups, curries and salads, to give them a wonderful tangy flavour. Kaffir limes and leaves are sold in Asian food stores. If unavailable, use lime zest and young lime leaves. Kaffir limes are also known as makrut limes.

CHILLED SOBA NOODLES

SERVES 4

INGREDIENTS

250 g (9 oz) dried soba (buckwheat) noodles
4 cm (1½ inch) piece ginger, cut into thin matchsticks
1 carrot, cut into thin matchsticks
4 spring onions (scallions), thinly sliced
1 sheet roasted nori (dried seaweed), cut into strips
pickled ginger, to garnish
thinly sliced pickled daikon, to garnish

DIPPING SAUCE

3 tablespoons dashi granules
125 ml (4 fl oz/½ cup) Japanese soy sauce
80 ml (2½ fl oz/⅓ cup) mirin

METHOD

1. Put the noodles in a large saucepan of boiling water. When the water returns to the boil, pour in 250 ml (9 fl oz/1 cup) cold water. Bring the water back to the boil and cook the noodles for 2–3 minutes, or until just tender — take care not to overcook them. Drain the noodles, then cool under cold running water. Drain and set aside.
2. Bring a small saucepan of water to the boil, add the ginger, carrot and spring onion and blanch for 30 seconds. Drain and put in a bowl of iced water to cool, then drain.
3. To make the dipping sauce, combine 375 ml (13 fl oz/1½ cups) water, the dashi granules, soy sauce, mirin and a good pinch each of salt and pepper in a small saucepan. Bring to the boil, then cool completely. When ready to serve, pour the sauce into four small dipping bowls.
4. Gently toss the cooled noodles and vegetables to combine. Arrange in four individual serving bowls. Scatter the nori strips over the noodles. Place a little pickled ginger and daikon on the side of each bowl. Serve the noodles with the dipping sauce.

VIETNAMESE RICE PAPER ROLLS

MAKES 20

INGREDIENTS

100 g (3½ oz) dried rice vermicelli
20 x 16 cm (6¼ inch) round rice paper wrappers
40 mint leaves
20 cooked prawns (shrimp), peeled and deveined, cut in half through the back
3 spring onions (scallions), sliced

DIPPING SAUCE

60 ml (2 fl oz/¼ cup) hoisin sauce
2 tablespoons soy sauce
1 tablespoon sweet chilli sauce
1 small red chilli, finely chopped
1 tablespoon chopped roasted peanuts

METHOD

1. Soak the noodles in boiling water for 15 minutes, or until tender. Drain, pat dry and cut into shorter lengths with scissors.
2. To make the dipping sauce, mix the ingredients in a bowl and top with the chopped peanuts.
3. Dip one rice wrapper at a time into a bowl of warm water and soak for 30 seconds, until soft.
4. Place the wrappers onto a dry surface, spoon one heaped tablespoon of the noodles along the bottom third of each one, top with two mint leaves and two prawn halves.
5. Fold in the sides and roll up firmly, enclosing a spring onion. Lay the rolls, seam side down, on a plate and cover with a damp tea towel. Serve with the dipping sauce.

PHAD THAI

SERVES 4–6

INGREDIENTS

- 250 g (9 oz) dried rice stick noodles
- 1 tablespoon tamarind purée
- 1 small red chilli, chopped
- 2 garlic cloves, chopped
- 2 spring onions (scallions), sliced
- 1½ tablespoons sugar
- 2 tablespoons fish sauce
- 2 tablespoons lime juice
- 2 tablespoons oil
- 2 eggs, beaten
- 150 g (5½ oz) pork fillet, thinly sliced
- 8 large raw prawns (shrimp), peeled and deveined
- 100 g (3½ oz) fried tofu puffs, cut into thin strips
- 90 g (3¼ oz/1 cup) bean sprouts
- 40 g (1½ oz/¼ cup) chopped roasted peanuts
- 3 tablespoons coriander (cilantro) leaves
- 1 lime, cut into wedges

METHOD

1. Put the noodles in a heatproof bowl, cover with warm water and soak for 15–20 minutes, or until soft and pliable. Drain well.
2. Combine the tamarind purée with 1 tablespoon water. Put the chilli, garlic and spring onion in a spice grinder or use a mortar and pestle and grind to a smooth paste. Transfer the mixture to a bowl. Stir in the tamarind mixture along with the sugar, fish sauce and lime juice.
3. Heat a wok until very hot, add 1 tablespoon of the oil and swirl to coat. Add the egg, swirl to coat and cook for 1–2 minutes, or until set. Remove, roll up and cut into thin slices.
4. Heat the remaining oil in the wok, add the chilli mixture and stir-fry for 30 seconds. Add the pork and stir-fry for 2 minutes. Add the prawns and stir-fry for 1 minute, or until pink and curled.
5. Stir in the noodles, egg, tofu and bean sprouts and toss together. Serve immediately topped with the peanuts, coriander and lime wedges.

VEGETABLE WON TONS

MAKES 24

INGREDIENTS

- 8 dried shiitake mushrooms
- 1 tablespoon vegetable oil
- 2 teaspoons finely chopped ginger
- 2 garlic cloves, crushed
- pinch of white pepper
- 100 g (3½ oz) garlic chives, chopped
- 100 g (3½ oz) water spinach (ong choy), cut into 1 cm (½ inch) lengths
- 60 ml (2 fl oz/¼ cup) chicken stock (page 11)
- 2 tablespoons oyster sauce
- 1 tablespoon cornflour (cornstarch)
- 1 teaspoon soy sauce
- 1 teaspoon Chinese rice wine
- 45 g (1½ oz/¼ cup) tinned water chestnuts, chopped
- 24 square won ton wrappers
- chilli sauce, to serve

METHOD

1. Soak the dried mushrooms in boiling water for 20 minutes. Squeeze dry, discard the stems and finely chop the caps.
2. Heat a wok over high heat, add the oil and swirl to coat. Add the ginger, garlic, white pepper and a pinch of salt and cook for 30 seconds. Add the chives and water spinach and cook for 1 minute.
3. Combine the stock, oyster sauce, cornflour, soy sauce and rice wine. Add to the spinach mixture along with the water chestnuts and mushrooms. Cook for 1–2 minutes, until the mixture thickens, then remove from the heat and cool completely.
4. Put 1 tablespoon of the filling in the centre of each wrapper. Pinch the edges of the wrapper together to seal.
5. Line a bamboo steamer with baking paper. Place the won tons in a single layer in the steamer. Cover and steam each batch over a wok of simmering water for 7–8 minutes. Serve with chilli sauce.

PORK AND PRAWN WON TONS

MAKES ABOUT 35

INGREDIENTS

- 300 g (10½ oz) minced (ground) pork
- 300 g (10½ oz) minced (ground) prawn (shrimp)
- 3 spring onions (scallions), thinly sliced
- 60 g (2¼ oz/⅓ cup) chopped tinned water chestnuts
- 1½ teaspoons finely chopped ginger
- 1 tablespoon light soy sauce, plus extra to serve
- 1 teaspoon caster (superfine) sugar
- 250 g (9 oz) packet square won ton wrappers
- chilli sauce, to serve

METHOD

1. To make the filling, put the pork and prawn meat, spring onion, water chestnuts, ginger, soy sauce and sugar in a large non-metallic bowl and combine well.
2. Working with one wrapper at a time, place a heaped teaspoon of the filling in the centre of the wrapper. Bring the corners up to meet in the middle and pinch the top and sides to seal. Cover with a damp cloth. Repeat with the remaining wrappers and filling to make about 35 won tons.
3. Line a large double bamboo steamer with baking paper. Place the won tons in the steamer in a single layer, leaving a gap between each one. (Depending on the size of your steamer, you may need to cook the won tons in batches.) Cover and steam over a wok of simmering water for 10 minutes, or until cooked through. Serve with the soy and chilli sauces, for dipping.

NOTE: The prepared won tons can also be deep-fried in hot oil for 3–4 minutes, or until brown and crisp.

WON TONS

A Chinese speciality, won tons are made from dough wrappers stuffed with a filling of minced meat, vegetables or seafood. They can be boiled and served in a broth, either with or without noodles, or steamed or deep-fried and served as an appetiser with a dipping sauce. The name won ton (or huntun) means 'swallowing clouds'. Won tons are traditionally served on the winter solstice (December 22) in northern China, the day on which winter arrives and ancestors are remembered. Originally a food for emperors, won tons are now a roadside snack to be enjoyed by everyone.

Won ton wrappers or skins are thinly rolled sheets of dough made from flour and eggs — the same dough used to make egg noodles. They are cut into squares. Both ready-made wrappers and won tons are available from Asian supermarkets. Store in their packets in the freezer for several months and defrost as needed.

MEE GROB

SERVES 4–6

INGREDIENTS

4 dried Chinese mushrooms
oil, for deep-frying
100 g (3½ oz) dried rice vermicelli
100 g (3½ oz) fried tofu puffs, julienned
4 garlic cloves, crushed
1 onion, chopped
1 boneless, skinless chicken breast, thinly sliced
8 green beans, sliced on the diagonal
6 spring onions (scallions), thinly sliced
8 raw prawns (shrimp), peeled and deveined, tails intact
30 g (1 oz/⅓ cup) bean sprouts, trimmed
coriander (cilantro) leaves, to garnish

SAUCE

1 tablespoon light soy sauce
60 ml (2 fl oz/¼ cup) white vinegar
80 g (2¾ oz/⅓ cup) caster (superfine) sugar
60 ml (2 fl oz/¼ cup) fish sauce
1 tablespoon sweet chilli sauce

METHOD

1 Put the mushrooms in a heatproof bowl, cover with boiling water and soak for 20 minutes. Drain and squeeze dry, discard the stems and thinly slice the caps.
2 Fill a wok or deep fryer one-third full of oil and heat to 180°C (350°F), or until a cube of bread dropped into the oil turns golden brown in 15 seconds. Cook the vermicelli in batches for 5 seconds, or until puffed and crispy. Drain on paper towels.
3 Add the tofu to the wok in batches and deep-fry for 1 minute, or until crisp. Drain on paper towels. Cool the oil slightly and carefully remove all but 2 tablespoons of the oil.
4 Reheat the wok over high heat until very hot. Add the garlic and onion, and stir-fry for 1 minute. Add the chicken slices, mushrooms, green beans and half the spring onion and stir-fry for 2 minutes, or until the chicken has almost cooked through. Add the prawns and stir-fry for a further 2 minutes, or until the prawns just turn pink.
5 To make the sauce, combine the soy sauce, vinegar, sugar, fish sauce and sweet chilli sauce, stirring to dissolve the sugar. Add to the wok and stir-fry for 2 minutes, or until the meat and prawns are tender and the sauce is syrupy. Remove the wok from the heat and stir in the vermicelli, tofu and bean sprouts. Garnish with the coriander and the remaining spring onion and serve.

WATER CHESTNUTS

The walnut-sized corm of an aquatic plant native to Southeast Asia, water chestnuts have dark-brown skin and a crisp, white, mildly sweet flesh, eaten raw or cooked. Bought fresh or in tins, water chestnuts add texture to Asian cooking, especially in minced meat dishes, stir-fries, won tons or sweet dishes. They are usually cooked quickly to retain their crisp texture, for which they are prized. Tinned chestnuts keep in a jar covered with water for up to 1 week (change the water daily), or can be frozen.

SPRING ROLLS

MAKES 20

INGREDIENTS

4 dried Chinese mushrooms
80 g (2¾ oz) dried rice vermicelli
1 tablespoon peanut oil
2 garlic cloves, chopped
2 teaspoons grated ginger
250 g (9 oz) minced (ground) pork
250 g (9 oz) raw prawns (shrimp), peeled and deveined, finely chopped
1 tablespoon light soy sauce
1 tablespoon oyster sauce
1 tablespoon Chinese rice wine
1 carrot, grated
8 tinned water chestnuts, finely chopped
4 spring onions (scallions), thinly sliced
200 g (7 oz) Chinese cabbage (wom bok), finely shredded
1 tablespoon sweet chilli sauce
2 teaspoons cornflour (cornstarch)
20 large spring roll wrappers
oil, for deep-frying

METHOD

1 Put the mushrooms in a heatproof bowl, cover with boiling water and soak for 20 minutes. Drain and squeeze dry, discard the stems and thinly slice the caps. Soak the vermicelli in boiling water for 6–7 minutes, until soft. Drain and cut into 5 cm (2 inch) lengths.
2 Heat the oil in a wok over high heat. Add the garlic and ginger and cook for 1 minute. Add the pork and cook for 3 minutes, stirring. Add the prawn meat and cook for 1 minute, then stir in the soy sauce, oyster sauce, rice wine, carrot, water chestnuts, spring onion, Chinese cabbage and sweet chilli sauce and cook for 2 minutes. Season with salt and pepper. Stir in the mushrooms and vermicelli.
3 Mix the cornflour and 2 tablespoons water in a small bowl until smooth.
4 Lay the spring roll wrappers under a damp tea towel. Working with one at a time, place a wrapper on the work surface with one corner facing you. Place 2 tablespoons of the filling along the centre of each spring roll wrapper. Brush the edges with the cornflour paste and roll up firmly, tucking in the ends as you go, and sealing with the cornflour paste. Continue, covering the completed rolls with a damp tea towel to prevent them drying out.
5 Fill a wok one-third full of oil and heat to 180°C (350°F), or until a cube of bread dropped into the oil turns golden brown in 15 seconds. Cook the spring rolls in batches of two to three rolls, turning gently to brown evenly, for 2 minutes, or until golden. Drain on paper towels.
6 Serve the spring rolls with soy sauce or your favourite dipping sauce. If the rolls are too big, serve cut in half on the diagonal.

CHAPTER SEVEN

VEGETABLES

ROOT VEGETABLES

Root vegetables are the fleshy edible roots or tubers of plants that grow underground or just above the ground. Potatoes, sweet potatoes and yams are starchy roots that provide an important source of food for millions of people, while others such as carrots, turnips and beetroot provide more sweetness than starch.

CARROTS

Carrots are an essential ingredient in many of the world's cuisines. This versatile root vegetable is used in stocks, soups, in dishes as varied as cakes and casseroles, and, unlike many other root vegetables, they are delicious raw in salads and as a juice.

New crop or baby carrots (sometimes called Dutch carrots) are best for eating raw in salads and only need to be cleaned with a stiff brush before use. They are usually sold in bunches with their green, feathery tops attached. Remove these before storing, as they drain the carrots of moisture and nutrients. The larger, older carrots are best peeled and cooked. They can be steamed and served with butter, roasted and served with a garlicky mayonnaise, used in soups, puréed, or added to sweet dishes such as cakes and muffins.

Don't store carrots near apples, pears or potatoes as the ethylene gas produced by these fruit and vegetables causes carrots to turn bitter.

ROASTING CARROTS

Everybody knows how to boil a carrot but we don't often think of roasting them. In fact, carrots are delicious when roasted, as the dry heat of the oven concentrates and caramelises their sugars.

To roast carrots, peel them, then cut into quarters lengthways. Put in a roasting tin with olive oil and a pinch of salt. (You can add some lightly smashed unpeeled garlic cloves if you like.) Roast the carrots in a 180°C (350°F/Gas 4) oven for 35 minutes, turning once, until golden and tender. Serve drizzled with a little balsamic vinegar and olive oil and sprinkled with sea salt.

VICHY CARROTS

SERVES 6

INGREDIENTS

- 500 g (1 lb 2 oz) carrots
- 1½ teaspoons sugar
- 40 g (1½ oz) butter
- 1½ tablespoons chopped parsley

METHOD

1. Slice the carrots quite thinly, then put them in a deep frying pan. Cover with cold water and add ½ teaspoon salt, the sugar and butter. Simmer until the water has evaporated. Shake the pan occasionally to glaze the carrots, then add the parsley, toss together and serve.

CARROT AND WATERCRESS TIMBALES

SERVES 4

INGREDIENTS

300 g (10½ oz) carrots, chopped
400 g (14 oz) watercress, trimmed
125 ml (4 fl oz/½ cup) cream
6 egg yolks
pinch of ground nutmeg

METHOD

1. Preheat the oven to 160°C (315°F/Gas 2–3). Steam the carrot until soft. Wash the watercress and put in a saucepan with just the water clinging to the leaves. Cover the pan and steam the watercress for 2 minutes, or until just wilted. Drain, cool and squeeze dry with your hands.
2. Purée each vegetable individually in a food processor. Squeeze out any liquid, then put each purée in its own bowl to cool, adding half the cream to each.
3. Stir 2 egg yolks into the watercress purée and the remaining 4 egg yolks into the carrot purée. Season with salt, pepper and nutmeg.
4. Grease four 125 ml (4 fl oz/½ cup) timbale moulds and divide the carrot purée equally among them. Smooth the surface. Spoon the watercress purée on top and smooth the surface. Put the moulds in a roasting tin and pour in hot water to come halfway up the sides of the timbales. Cook for 1 hour. Remove the timbales to a wire rack and stand for a few minutes before turning out.
5. To serve, hold a plate on top of each timbale and then turn it upside down. Give the plate and timbale one sharp shake and the timbale will release itself onto the plate. Serve with a salad and baguette.

MOROCCAN CARROT SALAD

SERVES 4

INGREDIENTS

HARISSA DRESSING
1½ teaspoons cumin seeds
½ teaspoon coriander seeds
1 tablespoon red wine vinegar
2 tablespoons olive oil
1 garlic clove, crushed
2 teaspoons harissa (page 172)
¼ teaspoon orange flower water

600 g (1 lb 5 oz) baby carrots, tops trimmed, well scrubbed
8 large green olives, pitted and thinly sliced
2 tablespoons shredded mint
30 g (1 oz/1 cup) picked watercress leaves

METHOD

1. To make the harissa dressing, dry-fry the cumin and coriander seeds in a small frying pan over medium heat for 30 seconds, or until fragrant. Cool and then grind using a mortar and pestle or spice grinder. Place into a large mixing bowl with the vinegar, olive oil, garlic, harissa and orange flower water. Whisk to combine.
2. Blanch the carrots in boiling salted water for 5 minutes, or until almost tender. Drain into a colander and set aside for a few minutes until they dry. While still hot, add to the harissa dressing, and toss gently to coat. Cool to room temperature, for the dressing to infuse into the carrots. Add the olives and mint. Season well and toss gently to combine. Serve on the watercress leaves.

(pictured page 316)

BEETROOT

For those who know beetroot (beets) only from tins, trying the fresh variety will open your eyes to a whole new world. This delicious, suede-skinned, deep-red vegetable can be used in all manner of ways: grate it raw and add to salads; roast whole beets with garlic; boil or steam them; purée with oil and spices to make a dip; or as in Eastern European kitchens, use to make the soup, borscht.

Cook and use beetroot leaves as you would spinach: blanch and add to soups or salads. Store beetroot in the crisper drawer of the fridge for up to 2 weeks.

HOW TO... COOK BEETROOT

PREPARATION

To prepare the beetroot, cut off the leaves, leaving 3 cm (1¼ inches) of stalk above the bulb. Wash thoroughly, but don't peel it: the skin and root must be intact when cooked or the beetroot will 'bleed' and lose its colour. When the cooked beetroot are cool enough to handle, peel off the skins (wearing rubber gloves will prevent purple-stained hands).

BOILING

Cook medium to large beetroot in simmering, salted water for up to 1½ hours, or until tender when tested with a knife. Baby beetroot will take 20–30 minutes to cook. Drain well and when cool, slip the skins off.

ROASTING

Put the beetroot in a roasting tin in a single layer and brush with olive oil. Cook in a 180°C (350°F/Gas 4) oven for 1½–2 hours, depending on size, or until tender when tested with a knife or a skewer — the tip of the knife should easily slip through the beetroot. When the beetroot are cool enough to handle, peel off the skins. Beetroot can also be wrapped tightly in foil before baking. Serve roasted beetroot with horseradish cream (see opposite).

STEAMING

Cook the beetroot over boiling water in a bamboo or metal steamer. Medium to large beetroot will take 1¼ hours to cook (watch the water level in the steamer), and baby beetroot will take about 20 minutes.

BEETROOT MASH

Prepare the beetroot, as explained above. Cook the beetroot in simmering water for 1½–2 hours, or until tender when tested with a knife. When cool enough to handle, rub off the skins and mash with an equal quantity of cooked potatoes. Season with salt and pepper. Add chopped chives and a knob of butter. Serve with fish, chicken or meat. Serves 4

FRESH BEETROOT AND GOAT'S CHEESE SALAD

SERVES 4

INGREDIENTS

- 4 fresh beetroot (beets), with leaves
- 200 g (7 oz) green beans, trimmed
- 1 tablespoon red wine vinegar
- 2 tablespoons extra virgin olive oil
- 1 garlic clove, crushed
- 1 tablespoon capers, rinsed and squeezed dry, roughly chopped
- 100 g (3½ oz) goat's cheese

METHOD

1. Trim the leaves from the beetroot, scrub the bulbs and wash the leaves. Boil the beetroot until tender (see opposite).
2. Bring a saucepan of water to the boil, add the beans and cook for 3 minutes. Remove with a slotted spoon and plunge into a bowl of cold water. Drain well. Add the beetroot leaves to the boiling water and cook for 3–5 minutes, or until the leaves and stems are tender. Drain, plunge into cold water, then drain. Drain and cool the beetroot, peel the skins off and cut into wedges.
3. To make the dressing, mix the vinegar, oil, garlic, capers and ½ teaspoon each of salt and pepper. Divide the beans, beetroot wedges and leaves among four plates. Crumble the goat's cheese over the top and drizzle with the dressing.

ROASTED BEET SALAD

SERVES 4

INGREDIENTS

- 2 tablespoons red wine vinegar
- 80 ml (2½ fl oz/⅓ cup) walnut oil
- 1 garlic clove, crushed
- 1 teaspoon dijon mustard
- 6 fresh beetroot (beets), plus 70 g (2½ oz) small beetroot leaves
- 12 French shallots, unpeeled
- 12 garlic cloves, unpeeled
- 1 tablespoon vegetable oil
- 50 g (1¾ oz/½ cup) walnuts, toasted

METHOD

1. Preheat the oven to 200°C (400°F/Gas 6). In a small bowl, whisk together the vinegar, walnut oil, garlic and mustard. Season well and set aside.
2. Scrub the beetroot, then put in a roasting tin with the shallots, garlic and vegetable oil. Roast in the oven for 1 hour, then remove the shallots and garlic. Continue to roast the beetroot for 30 minutes, or until tender.
3. Slip the shallots and garlic from their skin, and cut the beetroot into wedges. Add the dressing, toss together, and cool to room temperature.
4. Place the beetroot leaves, walnuts and vegetables in a bowl, season well with sea salt and pepper and gently toss together. Arrange on a serving platter, or individual plates.

HORSERADISH CREAM

Horseradish belongs to the mustard family, and it is cultivated mainly for its pungent, spicy root. The root is generally grated and used as a condiment or in sauces. When not available fresh, it can be bought bottled or dried.

To make horseradish cream, lightly whip 150 ml (5 fl oz) cream until it starts to thicken a little. Fold in 2 tablespoons grated fresh or bottled horseradish, 2 teaspoons lemon juice, a pinch of salt and sugar. Don't overwhip the cream, as the acid from the lemon juice and horseradish will act as a thickener. Serve with beetroot, smoked salmon or roast beef dishes. Makes 185 ml (6 fl oz/¾ cup)

HONEY-ROASTED ROOT VEGETABLES

SERVES 4

INGREDIENTS

- 60 g (2¼ oz) butter
- 2 tablespoons honey
- 4 thyme sprigs
- 3 carrots, peeled and cut into chunks
- 2 parsnips, peeled and cut into chunks
- 1 orange sweet potato, peeled and cut into chunks
- 1 white sweet potato, peeled and cut into chunks
- 8 small onions, peeled
- 8 jerusalem artichokes, peeled
- 1 whole garlic bulb

METHOD

1. Preheat the oven to 200°C (400°F/Gas 6). Melt the butter in a large roasting tin over medium heat. Add the honey and thyme and stir. Remove from the heat and add the carrot, parsnip, orange and white sweet potato, onions and jerusalem artichokes. Season well with salt and pepper and toss gently so the vegetables are coated with the honey butter.
2. Trim the base of the garlic and wrap in foil. Add to the tin and transfer to the oven for 1 hour, turning the vegetables occasionally so they caramelise evenly. When cooked, remove the foil from the garlic and pop the cloves from their skin. Add to the other vegetables and serve.

PARSNIP CHIPS

SERVES 4

INGREDIENTS

- 4 parsnips
- vegetable oil, for deep-frying
- ¼ teaspoon ground cumin

METHOD

1. Trim and peel the parsnips. Using a vegetable peeler, cut them into long, thick strips.
2. Fill a deep heavy-based saucepan or deep-fryer one-third full of oil and heat to 180°C (350°F), or until a cube of bread dropped into the oil turns golden brown in 15 seconds. Deep-fry the parsnip strips in batches for 1 minute, or until they are golden and crisp. Remove from the oil and drain on paper towels.
3. Mix 2 teaspoons of salt with the cumin in a small bowl. Put the hot parsnip chips in a large bowl and season with the cumin and salt mixture. Serve immediately.

PARSNIPS

Parsnip is a root vegetable from the same family as carrots. Their distinctive flavour relies on the icy snap of winter. After the first frosts they become sweeter, as the cold causes them to convert their starch into sugar. Parsnips have creamy white flesh and can be served roasted, mashed or added to casseroles and soups. Roasting in butter or oil or puréeing with cream in soups, often with curry or spices, brings out their silky texture and sweet, nutty flavour. When buying parsnips, choose firm, smooth vegetables. Leave the skin on for cooking, then peel once cooked. If peeled before cooking, store in water with a squeeze of lemon or vinegar (acidulated water), as their flesh darkens on contact with the air.

CELERIAC

Celeriac, as its name suggests, is a member of the celery family, and has a taste similar to both celery and parsley. Celeriac is a winter vegetable and it is cultivated for its knobbly root. Unlike celery, only the root and not the leaves or stalk is eaten.

To prepare, peel and cut into cubes or strips. The flesh discolours on contact with air, so soak or cook in water with a squeeze of lemon juice. Celeriac can be eaten raw in salads, or used in soups and stews. Cooked and mashed with garlic and potatoes, it's perfect served with game or meat. When buying celeriac, choose smoother roots as these will be easier to peel. If sold with its leaves, remove them and store the root in the crisper drawer of the fridge for up to 1 week.

CELERIAC REMOULADE

A classic French mayonnaise, rémoulade can be served with all manner of dishes — cold meat, fish and shellfish, but probably the most classic is this combination, with grated celeriac. Serve as a starter with a fresh baguette.

SERVES 4

INGREDIENTS

REMOULADE
2 egg yolks
1 tablespoon white wine vinegar or lemon juice
1 tablespoon dijon mustard
150 ml (5 fl oz) light olive oil

juice of 1 lemon
2 celeriac, trimmed and peeled
2 tablespoons capers, rinsed and squeezed dry
5 gherkins (cornichons), chopped
2 tablespoons finely chopped parsley
baguette, to serve

METHOD

1 To make the rémoulade, whisk the egg yolks, vinegar and mustard together. Add the oil, drop by drop from the tip of a teaspoon, whisking constantly until it begins to thicken, then add the oil in a very thin stream. (You can also make the mayonnaise using a food processor. Put the egg yolks, vinegar and mustard in the small bowl of a food processor and combine. With the motor running, pour the oil in a thin stream, to form a thick mayonnaise.) Season with sea salt and freshly ground black pepper and, if necessary, thin with a little warm water. Cover and set aside.

2 Put 1 litre (35 fl oz/4 cups) cold water in a large bowl and add half the lemon juice. Roughly grate the celeriac and place in the acidulated water. Bring a saucepan of water to the boil over high heat and add the remaining lemon juice. Drain the celeriac and add to the saucepan. After 1 minute, drain again and cool under running water. Pat dry with paper towels. Toss with the rémoulade, capers, gherkins and parsley. Serve with a baguette.

TURNIPS

For centuries a European staple, turnips fell from favour once potatoes were introduced from South America. According to type, turnips may have white, green or purplish skin. The flesh is usually white. They can be eaten raw or cooked, but are best young, when their flavour is delicate.

SPICED BABY TURNIPS

SERVES 4

INGREDIENTS

- 400 g (14 oz) small roma (plum) tomatoes, peeled (page 347)
- 60 ml (2 fl oz/¼ cup) olive oil
- 3 small onions, sliced
- 3 teaspoons ground coriander
- 1 teaspoon sweet paprika
- 350 g (12 oz) baby turnips, trimmed
- 1 teaspoon soft brown sugar
- 600 g (1 lb 5 oz) silverbeet (Swiss chard)
- 1 handful parsley

METHOD

1. Cut the tomatoes in half and gently squeeze out most of the juice and seeds, then cut into 1.5 cm (⅝ inch) slices.
2. Heat the oil in a large frying pan over medium heat and fry the onion for 5–6 minutes, or until soft. Stir in the coriander and paprika, cook for 1 minute, then add the tomato, turnips, sugar and 80 ml (2½ fl oz/⅓ cup) hot water. Season well and cook for another 5 minutes.
3. Cover the pan, reduce the heat to low and cook for 4–5 minutes, or until the turnips are tender.
4. Strip the silverbeet leaves off the stalks, to give about 250 g (9 oz) of leaves. Rinse under cold water and shake off the excess.
5. Stir the parsley and silverbeet into the pan, check the seasoning and then cook, covered, for 4 minutes, until wilted. Serve hot.

RADISH, CUCUMBER AND TOMATO SALAD

SERVES 4–6

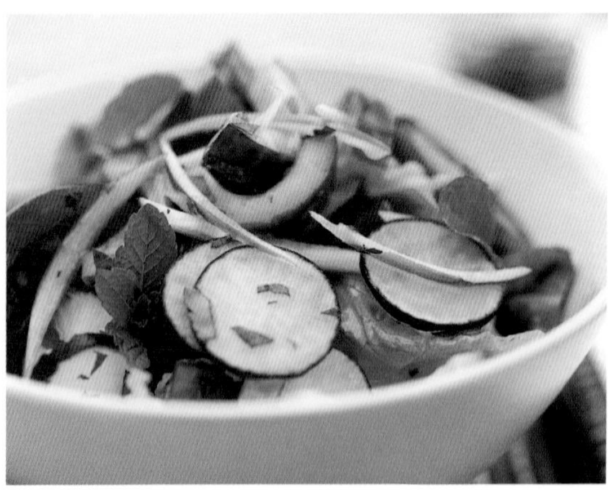

INGREDIENTS

- 2 tablespoons extra virgin olive oil
- 2 tablespoons lemon juice
- 1 cos (romaine) lettuce, torn into bite-sized pieces
- 3 ripe tomatoes, each cut into 8 pieces
- 1 green pepper (capsicum), cut into bite-sized pieces
- 1 telegraph (long) cucumber, seeded and chopped
- 6 radishes, thinly sliced
- 1 small salad or red onion, thinly sliced (see Note)
- 2 tablespoons chopped parsley
- 2 tablespoons chopped mint

METHOD

1. In a bowl, whisk together the olive oil and lemon juice. Season well with salt and pepper.
2. Combine the remaining ingredients in a large serving bowl and toss well. Add the dressing and toss to combine.

NOTE: Salad onions are sweeter than normal onions and are readily available from supermarkets and greengrocers.

SALMON WITH RADISH AND CUCUMBER SALAD

SERVES 4

INGREDIENTS

SALAD

1 Lebanese (short) cucumber
2 celery stalks, thinly sliced
1 French shallot, diced
1 avocado, diced
20 red or white radishes, halved
1 small handful coriander (cilantro)

DRESSING

80 ml (2½ fl oz/⅓ cup) olive oil
2 tablespoons lime juice
1 teaspoon finely grated lime zest
1 garlic clove, crushed
1 teaspoon honey

4 small salmon fillets, skin on
2–3 tablespoons olive oil

METHOD

1 To make the salad, peel the cucumber and cut in half lengthways. Using a teaspoon, scoop out and discard the seeds. Slice very thinly and put in a large bowl. Add the celery, shallot, avocado, radish and coriander.
2 To make the dressing, put the oil, lime juice, lime zest, garlic and honey in a small bowl and mix well. Season with sea salt and freshly ground black pepper. Set aside until ready to serve.
3 Brush the salmon fillets lightly with olive oil and sprinkle the skin with a little salt. Heat the remaining oil in a large frying pan over high heat. When hot, add the salmon, skin side down, and then hold a spatula on top of the fillets to keep them flat. Fry for 1–2 minutes, or until the skin is crisp and brown all over. Reduce the heat to medium and turn the salmon over. Cook for 2–3 minutes, or until just opaque, depending on the thickness. Drain on paper towels.
4 When cool enough to handle, use kitchen scissors to cut each salmon fillet across the grain into 3 strips. Break each strip into bite-sized pieces. Add to the salad with the dressing. Toss gently to coat, and serve.

RADISHES

A peppery root vegetable related to the mustard plant, whose many varieties are grouped under red, black or white (see daikon radish, page 184). Red are the mildest and are crisp and juicy, and are usually eaten raw in salads. Black radishes have a stronger flavour and are often peeled before use to reduce their pungency.

Buy smooth, firm radishes that are not too large, as they may be tough. Store without leaves, as these will accelerate moisture loss.

POTATOES

Native to South America, the potato is now a staple across the world. Potatoes are the world's fourth largest food crop, after rice, wheat and corn. They are cheap, hardy and easy to grow, and are high in starch, protein and vitamins. Almost all nationalities have a traditional dish based on potatoes, such as gratin dauphinois, rösti and Irish stew. Potatoes can be divided into new crop (early) potatoes and old (main crop) potatoes and their texture can be floury or waxy. Potatoes are never eaten raw as they contain 20 per cent indigestible starch — when cooked this converts into sugar.

TYPES OF POTATOES

russet (idaho)

FLOURY

These have a low moisture and sugar content and are high in starch. They are good for baking, roasting, mashing and fries, gnocchi and in bread, but disintegrate when boiled. They include russet (idaho), spunta, coliban, pentland squire and king edward.

king edward

WAXY

These have a high moisture content and are low in starch. They hold their shape when boiled or roasted but don't mash well. Use in salads or stews. These include roseval, charlotte, pink fir apple, kipfler (fingerling) and cara.

pink fir apple

SALAD

These are waxy, have a distinct flavour and are not usually peeled. They are best for boiling or roasting. These include kipfler (fingerling), pink fir apple, jersey royal and la ratte.

desiree

ALL-PURPOSE

Use these in recipes that don't specify the type of potato needed. These include desiree, sebago, nicola, kennebecs, maris piper, romano, wilja, bintje (yellow fin), spunta, pontiac and pink eye.

bintje

STORAGE

Store potatoes in paper bags to allow moisture to escape and to keep light out. Keep in a cool and dry, dark, well-ventilated place to prevent them from sprouting. If exposed to light, potatoes turn green — these will be bitter and indigestible and can be poisonous. Ready-washed potatoes have a shorter storage life, as washing removes their protective coating of earth. Older potatoes keep for 2 weeks or so, but new potatoes are best eaten soon after purchase.

pontiac

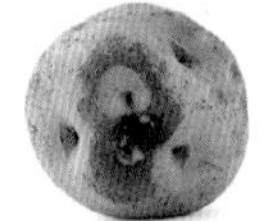

pink eye

HOW TO... MAKE PERFECT CHIPS

The best potatoes to use are floury or all-purpose varieties, such as king edward, maris piper, sebago, spunta and russet (idaho), as they give a fluffy inside and a crisp outside. The chips need to be blanched at a low temperature to cook the inside, then cooked at a high temperature to brown the outside.

METHOD

1 Wash and peel the potatoes, then cut into 1 cm (½ inch) wide sticks. Soak in water for 10 minutes to wash off the starch. This will stop them sticking and will make the outside crispy. Dry thoroughly on paper towel or the water will make the oil spit.
2 For cooking the chips, use a heavy-based saucepan, deeper than it is wide. A removable deep-frying basket is useful, but isn't necessary.
3 Half-fill the saucepan with oil. You need an oil that won't smoke or burn at temperatures of 190°C (375°F) or more. Most vegetable oils fit the bill, and peanut oil is an excellent choice, as its smoking point is well above the temperatures required and it has a mild, pleasant flavour.
4 Heat the oil to 160°C (315°F). If you don't have a thermometer, dip in a wooden spoon — the oil is hot enough if bubbles rise from the spoon. Alternatively, a cube of bread dropped into the oil will turn golden brown in 30–35 seconds.
5 Fry the potatoes in batches, for 4–5 minutes initially; they will have just a touch of colour. Drain on paper towels, and increase the heat to 190°C (375°F), or until a cube of bread browns in 10 seconds. Return the chips to the oil and cook for 1 minute, or until golden brown.
6 Drain on paper towels. Sprinkle the chips with salt — this will help absorb excess oil so they stay crisp. Serve immediately.

POTATO WEDGES

SERVES 4

INGREDIENTS

8 floury potatoes, unpeeled
olive oil, to brush
sweet paprika, to dust
sweet chilli sauce (page 430) or aïoli (page 422)

METHOD

1 Preheat the oven to 220°C (425°F/Gas 7). Scrub and pat dry the potatoes and cut into thick wedges. Put in a single layer on a baking tray.
2 Brush the wedges lightly with oil, and sprinkle with sea salt and paprika (or chilli powder for a spicier flavour). Cook for 35–40 minutes, until crisp and golden. Serve with sweet chilli sauce or aïoli.

POTATO CRISPS

SERVES 4

INGREDIENTS

6 large all-purpose potatoes, peeled
oil, for deep-frying

METHOD

1 Wash the potatoes and pat dry. Slice the potatoes very thinly using a mandolin or knife.
2 Fill a deep heavy-based saucepan or deep-fryer one-third full of oil and heat to 180°C (350°F), or until a cube of bread dropped into the oil turns golden brown in 15 seconds. Deep-fry the potato in batches for 3–4 minutes, or until golden and crisp. Drain on paper towels and season with salt.

NOTE: Don't stack just-cooked crisps or they'll go soggy. Keep them in a warm oven in one layer.

MASHED POTATOES

SERVES 4

INGREDIENTS

4 large floury potatoes
3–4 tablespoons milk
60 g (2¼ oz) butter

METHOD

1 Peel and chop the potatoes and cook in a saucepan of boiling salted water until just tender, then drain.
2 Return the potato to the pan over low heat. Add the milk and quickly mash, adding more milk, if necessary, for fluffy potatoes. Beat in the butter and season well.

VARIATIONS

* For herbed mash, add 2 tablespoons finely chopped chives or parsley.
* For creamy parsnip mash, cook equal quantities of potato and parsnip. Mash with milk, butter and 2 tablespoons sour cream.
* For cheesy potato mash, add 2 tablespoons sour cream instead of the butter. Add 2–3 tablespoons finely grated cheddar cheese and 1 teaspoon dijon mustard.

BAKED POTATOES WITH ROSEMARY

SERVES 4

INGREDIENTS

750 g (1 lb 10 oz) all-purpose potatoes, such as pontiac or sebago, or waxy potatoes, such as pink fir apple or kipfler (fingerling)
1½ tablespoons olive oil
8 large garlic cloves, unpeeled
2 tablespoons rosemary leaves

METHOD

1 Preheat the oven to 200°C (400°F/Gas 6). Peel and cut the potatoes in half lengthways and pat dry. Heat the oil in a large roasting tin, add the potato and garlic and toss for a minute to coat in the hot oil. Remove from the heat and turn all the potato cut side up. Sprinkle with rosemary.
2 Bake for 30 minutes, or until the potatoes are cooked and golden. The garlic will be creamy and soft — squeeze the flesh out of the papery skins over the potatoes. Serve immediately.

COLCANNON

Irish in origin, colcannon is a dish made with chopped cooked cabbage, finely chopped onions (or spring onions or leeks) and mashed potato mixed with butter and hot milk or cream.

To make colcannon, steam 500 g (1 lb 2 oz) cabbage or curly kale, then chop it finely. Add the cabbage to 500 g (1 lb 2 oz) cooked, mashed potatoes and 1 chopped, fried onion. Mix the ingredients together and season. Pile the mixture into individual bowls and make a well in the centre. Divide 100 g (3½ oz) melted butter among them. Dip each forkful of the colcannon in the butter as you eat it. Serves 4

JACKET POTATOES

SERVES 4

INGREDIENTS

4 even-sized potatoes
oil, for brushing

METHOD

1 Preheat the oven to 220°C (425°F/Gas 7). Scrub the potatoes clean, dry and prick all over for even cooking. For crisp skins, brush the potatoes with oil and sprinkle with salt. Bake directly on the oven rack for 1–1½ hours, or until tender when tested with a skewer.
2 Cut a cross in the top of the cooked potato and squeeze from the base to open. Top with butter, or one of the following topping ideas:

TOPPINGS

* Mix drained tuna with tinned mixed beans. Add some chopped parsley and a squeeze of lemon juice and spoon into the potato. Drizzle with a little olive oil.
* Fry some thinly sliced mushrooms in olive oil with a crushed garlic clove and a little chopped parsley. Season and top with a teaspoon of sour cream.
* Finely chop a tomato and add to plain yoghurt with grated cucumber, chopped mint and spring onion. Season and mix well.
* Put a small wedge of camembert, brie or creamy blue cheese in the potato and return to the oven for 2–3 minutes to soften the cheese.
* Mash 1 small avocado with 1 teaspoon lemon juice and a dash of Tabasco sauce to make guacamole. Top with sour cream, or mix in chopped bacon and snipped chives.
* Fill the potato with a large spoonful of herbed cream cheese and return to the oven for 2 minutes. Toast a few pine nuts and scatter over the melted cream cheese.
* Mix some butter with ½ teaspoon finely grated lemon zest, 1 teaspoon lemon juice and some chopped dill. Chill before spooning onto the potato.

DUCHESS POTATOES

SERVES 6

INGREDIENTS

850 g (1 lb 14 oz) floury potatoes, quartered
2 eggs
60 ml (2 fl oz/¼ cup) cream
2 tablespoons grated parmesan cheese
¼ teaspoon ground nutmeg
1 egg yolk, for glazing

METHOD

1 Boil the potato for 10 minutes, until just tender. Drain, then return the potatoes to the pan over very low heat for 1–2 minutes to dry out the potato. Transfer to a bowl and mash well.
2 Beat together the eggs, cream, parmesan and nutmeg. Season well, then add to the potato and mash well. Cover and leave for 20 minutes. Preheat the oven to 180°C (350°F/Gas 4).
3 Put the just-warm potato mixture in a piping bag with a 1.5 cm (⅝ inch) star nozzle. Pipe the mixture in swirls, not too close together, onto greased baking trays. Brush lightly all over with the extra egg yolk. Bake for 15–20 minutes, or until the potatoes are crisp and golden.

HASSELBACK POTATOES

SERVES 4

INGREDIENTS

60 g (2¼ oz) butter, melted
4 potatoes
2 tablespoons fresh white breadcrumbs
3 tablespoons grated parmesan cheese
½ teaspoon paprika

METHOD

1. Preheat the oven to 200°C (400°F/Gas 6). Brush a shallow baking tray with a little melted butter.
2. Peel the potatoes and cut in half. Put the potatoes, cut side down, on a board. Make thin evenly spaced cuts about two-thirds of the way through, then place, flat side down, on the tray. Brush liberally with melted butter and bake for 30 minutes, brushing occasionally with butter.
3. Combine the breadcrumbs and parmesan and sprinkle over the potatoes. Sprinkle with paprika and bake for 15 minutes, or until golden brown.

HASH BROWNS

SERVES 4

INGREDIENTS

2 large potatoes, peeled and halved
oil, for shallow-frying

METHOD

1. Boil the potato for 10 minutes, until just tender. Drain and cool, then grate into a bowl. Season well, then shape the potato into patties about 10 cm (4 inches) round. The starchiness of the potato will hold the patties together.
2. Pour enough oil into a frying pan to cover the base. Heat the oil and cook the patties over medium heat for 2–3 minutes on each side, or until golden and crispy. Drain on paper towels.

BACON AND ONION ROSTI

SERVES 4

INGREDIENTS

850 g (1 lb 14 oz) waxy potatoes, halved
60 g (2¼ oz) butter
6 thin slices bacon, rind removed, chopped
1 small red onion, chopped
2 garlic cloves, crushed
2 tablespoons chopped parsley
1 teaspoon chopped oregano
1 teaspoon chopped thyme

METHOD

1. Boil or steam the unpeeled potato until just tender. Drain, cover and refrigerate for 1 hour. Peel the potato and grate into a bowl.
2. Heat half the butter in a 23 cm (9 inch) heavy-based, non-stick frying pan. Add the bacon, onion and garlic and stir for 2 minutes, until soft but not brown. Add to the potato with the herbs.
3. Add a little butter to the pan, spread the potato mixture over the base and press with a spatula. Cook over medium heat for 8 minutes, or until a crust forms on the base. Shake the pan occasionally to stop the potato sticking.
4. Slide the rösti onto a greased plate, add the remaining butter to the pan and when melted, flip the rösti back into the pan on its uncooked side. Cook for 6 minutes, or until the base is crusty.

JANSSON'S TEMPTATION

A gratin of grated potato, anchovies, butter, onions and cream, Jansson's temptation is supposedly served at the end of a party to make the guests stay longer. The debate of how it acquired its interesting name is ongoing — some say the dish was thought to have tempted a religious fanatic who had vowed to give up all earthly pleasures, while other theories suggest it came from the Swedish opera singer Pelle Janzon or from the title of a 1928 film.

SERVES 4

INGREDIENTS

15 tinned anchovy fillets
80 ml (2½ fl oz/⅓ cup) milk
60 g (2¼ oz) butter
2 large onions, thinly sliced
5 floury potatoes, peeled, cut into 5 mm (¼ inch) slices, then cut into matchsticks
500 ml (17 fl oz/2 cups) cream

METHOD

1 Preheat the oven to 200°C (400°F/Gas 6). Soak the anchovies in the milk for 5 minutes to lessen their saltiness. Drain and rinse.
2 Melt half the butter in a frying pan and cook the onion over medium heat for 5 minutes, or until golden and tender. Chop the remaining butter into small cubes and set aside.
3 Spread half the potato over the base of an ovenproof dish, top with the anchovies and onion and finish with the remaining potato.
4 Pour half the cream over the potato and scatter the butter cubes on top. Bake for 20 minutes, or until golden. Pour the remaining cream over the top and cook for another 40 minutes, or until the potato feels tender when tested with a knife.

POTATO CROQUETTES

MAKES 12

INGREDIENTS

750 g (1 lb 10 oz) floury potatoes, roughly chopped
2 tablespoons cream or melted butter
3 eggs, lightly beaten
¼ teaspoon ground nutmeg
plain (all-purpose) flour, for coating
150 g (5½ oz/1½ cups) dry breadcrumbs
oil, for deep-frying

METHOD

1 Cook the potato in a saucepan of boiling salted water for 8–10 minutes, or until tender. Drain and return the potato to the hot pan and mash with a fork. Stir in the cream, a third of the beaten egg and the nutmeg. Season with salt and pepper. Spread the potato mixture on a baking tray, cover and refrigerate for 30 minutes.
2 Divide the mixture into 12 portions and roll each into a sausage shape. Roll in the flour, shaking off the excess. Dip each croquette in the beaten egg, coat in the breadcrumbs, shaking off any excess. Cover and refrigerate for at least 2 hours.
3 Half-fill a deep heavy-based saucepan one-third full of oil and heat to 180°C (350°F), or until a cube of bread dropped into the oil turns golden brown in 15 seconds. Cook the croquettes in batches for 5 minutes each, or until golden. Drain on paper towels and serve.

GRATIN DAUPHINOIS

SERVES 6

INGREDIENTS

- 1 kg (2 lb 4 oz) all-purpose potatoes, peeled
- 2 garlic cloves, crushed
- 65 g (2¼ oz/½ cup) grated gruyère cheese
- pinch of ground nutmeg
- 310 ml (10¾ fl oz/1¼ cups) cream
- 125 ml (4 fl oz/½ cup) milk

METHOD

1. Preheat the oven to 170°C (325°F/Gas 3). Thinly slice the potatoes with a mandolin or sharp knife.
2. Butter a 23 x 16 cm (9 x 6¼ inch) baking or gratin dish and layer the potatoes, sprinkling the garlic, cheese, nutmeg and salt and pepper between the layers, leaving a bit of cheese for the top. Pour the cream and milk over the top and sprinkle with the remaining cheese.
3. Bake for 50–60 minutes, or until the potatoes are completely cooked and the liquid absorbed. If the top browns too much, cover loosely with foil. Leave to rest for 10 minutes before serving.

POMMES ANNA

SERVES 4

INGREDIENTS

- 850 g (1 lb 14 oz) waxy potatoes
- 125 g (4½ oz) clarified butter (page 120), melted

METHOD

1. Preheat the oven to 210°C (415°F/Gas 6–7). Grease a deep 20 cm (8 inch) round cake tin or ovenproof dish with melted butter.
2. Peel the potatoes and cut into very thin slices with a mandolin or sharp knife. Lay the potato slices on paper towels and pat dry. Starting from the centre of the dish, overlap one-fifth of the potato over the base. Drizzle one-fifth of the butter over the top. Season well. Repeat the layers four more times, finishing with the butter over the top.
3. Cut a circle of baking paper to fit over the top of the potato. Bake for 1 hour, or until the potato is golden and cooked through. Remove from the oven and leave for 5 minutes, then pour off any excess butter. Run a knife around the edge, then turn out onto a serving plate.

JERUSALEM ARTICHOKE

Neither from Jerusalem nor an artichoke, this winter root is a relative of the sunflower (in Spanish, 'girasol', mispronounced in English as 'Jerusalem'). They have a mildly sweet, smoky flavour. Thinly slice and add raw to salads, boil or roast like potatoes or use to make wonderful velvety soups and mashes. When cut, drop into acidulated water to stop them going brown. Jerusalem artichokes have a reputation for causing flatulence. This can be countered with a pinch of asafoetida.

To roast jerusalem artichokes, first scrub 750 g (1 lb 10 oz) jerusalem artichokes, then toss in 2 tablespoons olive oil with plenty of seasoning. Put in a roasting tin and roast in a 200°C (400°F/Gas 6) oven for about 40 minutes, or until tender, then drizzle with a little hazelnut or walnut oil. Serve as a side dish, or to use in a salad, toss with rocket (arugula) leaves and fried cubes of bacon. Serves 4

HOT POTATO SALAD

SERVES 6–8

INGREDIENTS

4 slices bacon
1.5 kg (3 lb 5 oz) small all-purpose potatoes, such as desiree or other red-skinned potatoes
4 spring onions (scallions), sliced
2 tablespoons chopped parsley

DRESSING

170 ml (5½ fl oz/⅔ cup) extra virgin olive oil
1 tablespoon dijon mustard
80 ml (2½ fl oz/⅓ cup) white wine vinegar

METHOD

1 Trim the rind and fat from the bacon and cook under a hot grill (broiler) until crisp. Cool, then chop into small pieces.
2 Simmer the potatoes in a large saucepan of water until just tender, trying not to let the skins break away too much. Drain and cool.
3 To make the dressing, whisk together the oil, mustard and vinegar.
4 Cut the potatoes into quarters and put in a bowl with half the bacon, the spring onion, parsley, ½ teaspoon salt and some black pepper. Pour in the dressing and toss gently. Serve sprinkled with the remaining bacon.

COLD POTATO SALAD

SERVES 8

INGREDIENTS

1.2 kg (2 lb 10 oz) all-purpose potatoes, such as desiree, unpeeled and cubed
2 onions, finely chopped
2 green capsicums (peppers), finely chopped
4–5 celery stalks, finely chopped
6 tablespoons finely chopped parsley

DRESSING

375 g (13 oz/1½ cups) egg mayonnaise
90 g (3¼ oz/⅓ cup) sour cream
about 80 ml (2½ fl oz/⅓ cup) white wine vinegar or lemon juice

METHOD

1 Steam or boil the potato for 5–10 minutes, or until the potato feels tender when tested with the point of a knife. Don't let the skins break away. Drain and cool completely.
2 Combine the onion, capsicum, celery and parsley with the potato in a large bowl, reserving some parsley for garnish.
3 To make the dressing, combine the mayonnaise, sour cream and vinegar in a bowl (you may not need all the vinegar). Season with salt and pepper. Pour over the potato salad and toss gently. Garnish with the reserved parsley.

NOTE: If you overcook the potatoes, drain them carefully and spread out on a large flat tray and cool completely. Most of the potatoes will firm up if you do this. In this case, you should also take a little extra care when stirring in the dressing.

POTATO GNOCCHI WITH PANCETTA AND BASIL

SERVES 4

INGREDIENTS

POTATO GNOCCHI

1 kg (2 lb 4 oz) floury potatoes, unpeeled
2 egg yolks
2 tablespoons grated parmesan cheese
125–185 g (4½–6½ oz) plain (all-purpose) flour

SAUCE

75 g (2½ oz) pancetta
50 g (1¾ oz) butter
1 handful basil leaves, torn

METHOD

1. Preheat the oven to 180°C (350°F/Gas 4). Prick the potatoes all over and bake for 1 hour, or until tender. Cool for 15 minutes, then peel and mash (do not use a food processor or the potatoes will become gluey).
2. Mix in the egg yolks and parmesan, then gradually stir in the flour. When the mixture gets too dry to use a spoon, use your hands. Once a loose dough forms, transfer to a lightly floured surface and knead gently. Work in enough extra flour to give a very soft, light, pliable dough.
3. Divide the dough into six portions. Dust your hands lightly in flour, then, working with one portion at a time, roll out on a floured surface to make a rope about 1.5 cm (⅝ inch) thick. Cut into 1.5 cm (⅝ inch) lengths. Take each piece of dough and press your finger into it to form a concave shape, then, holding the piece at each end, roll the outer surface over the tines of a fork to make deep ridges. At this point the gnocchi will look like little blocks. Fold the outer edges in towards each other to make a hollow in the middle. These will open as the gnocchi cook. Place on a lightly floured tray and leave to rest, ideally for 10 minutes or more.
4. To make the sauce, fry the pancetta in the butter until crisp, then set aside.
5. Bring a large saucepan of salted water to the boil, then reduce the heat a little. Add the gnocchi in batches, stir gently and return to the boil. Cook until they rise to the surface. Remove with a slotted spoon and drain. Add the basil to the pancetta and toss together, season well and sprinkle over the gnocchi before serving.

BAKED SWEET POTATO AND WATERCRESS GNOCCHI

SERVES 6

INGREDIENTS

- 700 g (1 lb 9 oz) orange sweet potato
- 300 g (10½ oz) all-purpose potatoes, such as desiree
- 350 g (12 oz/2¾ cups) plain (all-purpose) flour
- 35 g (1¼ oz/⅓ cup) grated parmesan cheese
- 30 g (1 oz/1 cup) watercress leaves, finely chopped
- 1 garlic clove, crushed
- 60 g (2¼ oz) butter
- grated parmesan cheese, to serve
- 2 tablespoons chopped parsley

METHOD

1. Boil the sweet potato and potatoes in their skins until tender when tested with the point of a knife. Drain, and when cool enough to handle, peel and press the sweet potato and potato through a potato ricer or mouli into a large bowl.
2. Add the flour, parmesan, watercress and garlic and season well. Gently bring together with your hands until a soft dough forms. It is important not to overwork the dough to keep the gnocchi tender. Portion the dough into walnut-sized pieces and shape using the back of a fork to create the traditional 'gnocchi' shape.
3. Melt the butter in a large baking tray. Preheat the grill (broiler) to medium–high heat.
4. Meanwhile, bring a large saucepan of salted water to the boil, then reduce the heat a little. Add the gnocchi in batches, stir gently and return to the boil. Cook for about 2 minutes, or until they rise to the surface. Remove with a slotted spoon and drain well.
5. Arrange the gnocchi in the baking tray, tossing gently in the butter, and grill (broil) for 5 minutes, or until lightly golden. Sprinkle with the parmesan and chopped parsley and serve.

SWEET POTATO, SPINACH AND ORANGE SALAD

SERVES 4

INGREDIENTS

- 1 pitta bread
- 60 ml (2 fl oz/¼ cup) olive oil
- 500 g (1 lb 2 oz) orange sweet potato, unpeeled, cut into 1 cm (½ inch) thick slices
- 1 small orange
- 150 g (5½ oz) baby spinach

ORANGE SESAME DRESSING

- 60 ml (2 fl oz/¼ cup) olive oil
- 1 teaspoon sesame oil
- 2 tablespoons orange juice
- 1 teaspoon lemon juice
- 1 teaspoon finely grated orange zest
- 1 garlic clove, crushed
- 2 teaspoons dijon mustard

METHOD

1. Preheat a grill (broiler) to high. Cut off and discard the edge of the pitta bread, split the bread into 2 thin halves, and lightly brush all over with some of the oil. Place under the grill and toast until crisp and lightly browned.
2. Toss the sweet potato in the remaining oil and grill for 8–10 minutes, until soft and golden on both sides. Transfer to a salad bowl.
3. Peel the orange, removing all the pith. To segment the orange, hold the orange over a bowl and use a sharp knife to cut down either side of the membranes. Put the segments in the bowl and add the spinach. Break up the pitta crisps into small shards and put into the bowl. Toss lightly.
4. To make the dressing, put all the ingredients in a small bowl and whisk to blend. Season with salt and freshly ground black pepper. Pour over the salad just before serving.

SWEET POTATO

Not a relation of the potato at all, the sweet potato is a member of the morning glory family. There are several varieties of sweet potato, and their flesh, which may be white, orange or yellow, ranges from mealy to moist and watery, and their skins may be white, yellow, red, purple or brown. Orange-fleshed sweet potatoes are softer than the other varieties when cooked.

Sweet potatoes can be cooked as you would a potato — roasted, boiled, mashed or fried, but their soft, slightly sweet flesh makes them an ideal ingredient in cakes or sweet dishes, as well as in breads, soups and casseroles. Sprinkle them with brown sugar, dot with butter and roast them. Sweet potatoes don't store for as long as potatoes but will last for 1 week if kept in a cool, dry place.

BAKED SWEDES WITH BLUE CHEESE AND RICOTTA

When buying swedes, choose those with a purplish top and fresh green stalks for the finest flavour. Store in the fridge for up to 10 days, though they will soften and their flavour strengthen. Should you find the flavour too strong, simply blanch them for 10 minutes, then discard the cooking water and resume cooking in fresh water.

SERVES 4

INGREDIENTS

- 4 swedes (rutabaga), scrubbed
- 1½ tablespoons olive oil
- 40 g (1½ oz) butter
- 55 g (2 oz) creamy blue vein cheese, crumbled
- 125 g (4½ oz/½ cup) ricotta cheese (see Note)
- 12 sage leaves
- 1 garlic clove, crushed

METHOD

1. Preheat the oven to 180°C (350°F/Gas 4). Rub the swedes with one-third of the oil. Place each in the centre of a 30 cm (12 inch) square of foil, season lightly with salt and pepper and dot with the butter. Fold up the foil to enclose the swedes. Arrange, root down, in a small baking tin and bake for 1 hour, or until tender.
2. Mix the blue cheese and ricotta together in a small saucepan and heat over low heat until soft. Keep warm. Heat the remaining olive oil in a small frying pan until hot. Fry the sage leaves for a few seconds until crisp, then remove and drain on paper towels.
3. Add the garlic to the pan, reduce the heat to low and fry until just beginning to colour. Transfer to the cheese mixture and add 4 of the sage leaves. Season to taste with salt and black pepper and stir to combine.
4. Remove the foil from the swedes and cut them diagonally into 2–3 cm (¾–1¼ inch) slices. Reassemble to serve, with the sauce spooned over the top. Top with the remaining sage leaves.

NOTE: Use bulk ricotta from the delicatessen rather than ricotta in tubs, which is wetter and grainier.

OTHER ROOT VEGETABLES

TARO

The general name for a family of tropical tubers, taro is a staple in Asia, the Pacific Islands and the West Indies. Brown skinned, their flesh ranges from white and pink to purple. Taro cannot be eaten raw as it contains indigestible substances, but these are neutralised after cooking. Like potato, taro can be boiled, steamed or used in soups and stews. Taro starch used in Asian cooking is similar to arrowroot.

YAM

These are the edible tubers of a tropical and subtropical plant, and the staple food of many regions, particularly South and Central America, the West Indies, Africa and the Pacific Islands. Strictly speaking, yams are the tubers of one family, but the word is often used loosely to encompass a range of other tropical roots such as sweet potato, taro and cassava. In the United States, sweet potatoes are called yams. There are many varieties, some have a coarse skin, others smooth, while some may be pale brown or purple in colour. The flesh colour also varies, from white to cream, yellow, pink or purple.

Yams are cooked as for potatoes, which they resemble in flavour, though they are more starchy and mealy. Yams must be cooked before eating to destroy the bitter toxic substance (dioscorine) that they contain. They can be boiled, puréed, baked, added to soups and stews, and deep-fried. Store in a cool, dark and well-ventilated place.

CASSAVA

A native of South and Central America, this starchy, tuberous root has thick, bark-like skin and creamy white flesh. There are two varieties, bitter and sweet. Both contain toxic hydrocyanic acid in the roots (the bitter variety containing most), which is removed by steaming or boiling it thoroughly before use. Tapioca is a refined starch derived from cassava. Sweet cassava can be cooked, mashed or fried just like a potato, and the young, tender leaves can be cooked like spinach. Dried cassava is processed to make a flour used in bread and cakes.

SWEDE

Swedes, or rutabaga as they are also known, resemble turnips, but have a more mellow flavour and a creamier texture, and are best suited to roasting, soups, stews and mashing. They are not a true root vegetable, but a vegetable with a swollen base at the stem. Older swedes are better for mashing, and also hold their shape when added to stews and pies. In Scotland, swedes (neeps) are mashed (or bashed) as a traditional accompaniment to haggis.

To make clapshot, a traditional Scottish side dish, cut 500 g (1 lb 2 oz) swedes (rutabaga) and 500 g (1 lb 2 oz) potatoes into even-sized pieces. Put 1 finely chopped onion, the chopped swede and potato in a saucepan and cover with boiling water. Cook until the vegetables are tender, then drain and mash with 1 tablespoon each of butter, milk and chopped chives. Season well. Serves 4

••STEMS AND BULBS••

This group of vegetables includes those with edible stems, such as asparagus, celery and fennel, as well as the lower part, or bulb, of some vegetables. The bulb is the underground structure where the plant stores its nutrients, and common bulb vegetables include onion, shallots, garlic and leek.

ASPARAGUS

A member of the lily family, these delicately flavoured shoots are best eaten in spring, just after harvesting, when they will be in peak condition. Asparagus is traditionally boiled or steamed, then served as an accompaniment, or cooled and used in salads or other dishes. Serve asparagus with melted butter and parmesan, or add to risottos, quiches, stir-fries or salads. When buying asparagus, choose firm, bright-green spears with tight tips. Check the cut ends are not split or dried out. Asparagus does not keep for long and ideally should be cooked on the day of purchase.

TYPES OF ASPARAGUS

GREEN

This is the most common type of asparagus and is cut above ground when the shoots are 15 cm (6 inches) long. Snap off the woody ends before cooking.

WHITE

White asparagus is cut while the asparagus is below the ground (the lack of light prevents it from producing chlorophyll and turning green). It is more tender than the green variety and is popular in parts of Europe. Before cooking, white asparagus needs to be peeled up to the tip as the skin is tough.

PURPLE

Purple when fresh, this type of asparagus turns green when it is cooked.

HOW TO... COOK ASPARAGUS

METHOD

1. Snap off the woody bottom of the asparagus spear at its natural breaking point. Peel any thick, woody stems.
2. Lay the asparagus flat in a frying pan filled with simmering water. Cook until tender when pierced with the tip of a knife.
3. A well-cooked spear of asparagus should be tender and bend when you pick it up with a fork; it should not droop over.

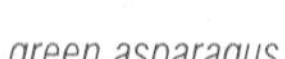

green asparagus

white asparagus

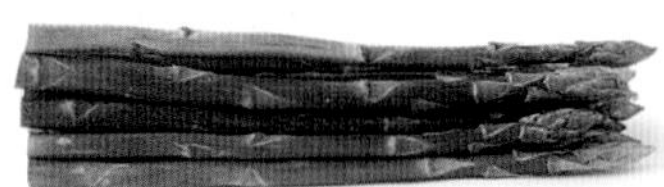

purple asparagus

ASPARAGUS AND ORANGE SALAD

SERVES 4

INGREDIENTS

- 16 thin asparagus spears, trimmed
- 45 g (1½ oz/1½ cups) watercress, trimmed
- ½ small red onion, very thinly sliced
- 1 orange, cut into 12 segments (page 601)
- 60 g (2¼ oz) soft goat's cheese

DRESSING

- 1 tablespoon orange juice
- 1 teaspoon finely grated orange zest
- 1 teaspoon sugar
- 1 tablespoon red wine vinegar
- 2 teaspoons poppy seeds
- 2 tablespoons olive oil

METHOD

1. Snap off the woody ends of the asparagus, then cook in a frying pan filled with simmering water until just tender (see opposite). Rinse under cold water, then combine with the watercress, red onion and orange segments in a serving dish.
2. To make the dressing, combine the orange juice, zest, sugar, vinegar and poppy seeds in a bowl. Whisk in the oil with a fork until combined, then drizzle the dressing over the salad. Crumble the goat's cheese over the top and season with salt and pepper.

WARM ASPARAGUS WITH CREAMY LEMON DRESSING

SERVES 4

INGREDIENTS

- 80 ml (2½ fl oz/⅓ cup) extra virgin olive oil
- 2 tablespoons lemon juice
- 60 g (2¼ oz/¼ cup) crème fraîche, softened
- 20 asparagus spears

METHOD

1. Preheat a barbecue grill or hotplate to medium. In a small bowl, combine the oil and lemon juice and season well with salt and freshly ground black pepper. Pour half the mixture into a shallow dish for coating the asparagus. Stir the crème fraîche through the remaining mixture in the bowl, then season and set aside.
2. Snap off the woody ends of the asparagus. Put the spears in the dish with the oil and lemon juice mixture and roll them around to coat.
3. Cook the asparagus on the barbecue, turning frequently with tongs, for 4–5 minutes, or until just tender and lightly charred. If any spears begin to brown too quickly, move them to the outside of the barbecue.
4. Put the asparagus on a serving platter and pour the reserved crème fraîche dressing over the spears. Serve immediately.

ASPARAGUS STEAMERS

For the true lover of asparagus, there is a purpose-built asparagus steamer, available in specialist cookware shops. This steamer is a tall slender pot that cooks the asparagus without damaging the fragile tips. The asparagus stands upright in the steamer basket (pictured), which is then lowered into boiling water in the pot. The spears cook in water while the tips cook in steam.

BRAISED FENNEL

SERVES 4

INGREDIENTS

- 4 baby fennel bulbs
- 40 g (1½ oz) butter
- 1 teaspoon soft brown sugar
- 1 tablespoon white wine vinegar
- 125 ml (4 fl oz/½ cup) chicken stock (page 11)
- 2 tablespoons cream

METHOD

1. Cut the fennel bulbs into quarters and blanch them in boiling water for 5 minutes. Drain well.
2. Melt the butter in a frying pan over medium heat, add the fennel and fry until browned, then add the brown sugar and caramelise. Add the vinegar and stock, then cover and simmer until the bulbs are tender. Remove the lid and boil until the liquid is reduced, then stir in the cream.

FENNEL, TOMATO AND GARLIC GRATIN

SERVES 4

INGREDIENTS

- 1 kg (2 lb 4 oz) fennel bulbs
- 80 ml (2½ fl oz/⅓ cup) olive oil
- 1 large red onion, halved and thinly sliced
- 2 garlic cloves, crushed
- 500 g (1 lb 2 oz) tomatoes

GRATIN TOPPING

- 60 g (2¼ oz) white bread, broken into coarse crumbs
- 65 g (2¼ oz/⅔ cup) grated parmesan cheese
- 2 teaspoons finely grated lemon zest
- 1 garlic clove, crushed

METHOD

1. Preheat the oven to 200°C (400°F/Gas 6). Grease a baking dish with melted butter or oil. Cut the fennel in half lengthways, then thinly slice.
2. Heat the oil in a large frying pan. Cook the onion for 3–4 minutes, until softened but not browned. Add the garlic and cook for 2 minutes. Add the fennel and cook, stirring, for 7 minutes, or until softened and lightly golden brown.
3. Peel the tomatoes by scoring a cross in the base of each tomato. Put in a heatproof bowl and cover with boiling water. Leave for 30 seconds, then transfer to cold water and peel the skin away from the cross. Cut the tomatoes in half horizontally and scoop out the seeds with a teaspoon. Roughly chop the flesh and add to the fennel. Cook, stirring, for 5 minutes, or until the tomato is softened. Season well and pour the mixture into the dish.
4. To make the gratin topping, mix together all the topping ingredients, sprinkle over the vegetables and bake for 15 minutes, or until golden brown and crisp. Serve immediately.

BRAISED CELERY

SERVES 4

INGREDIENTS

- 30 g (1 oz) butter
- 1 bunch celery, trimmed and cut into 5 cm (2 inch) lengths
- 500 ml (17 fl oz/2 cups) chicken or vegetable stock (page 10–11)
- 2 teaspoons finely grated lemon zest
- 60 ml (2 fl oz/¼ cup) lemon juice
- 60 ml (2 fl oz/¼ cup) cream
- 2 egg yolks
- 1 tablespoon cornflour (cornstarch)
- 1 small handful chopped parsley
- ½ teaspoon ground mace

METHOD

1. Preheat the oven to 180°C (350°F/Gas 4). Grease a shallow baking dish.
2. Melt the butter in a large frying pan. Add the celery and toss to coat in the butter. Cover and cook for 2 minutes. Add the stock, lemon zest and juice, then cover and simmer for 10 minutes. Remove the celery with a slotted spoon and place into the prepared dish. Reserve 60 ml (2 fl oz/¼ cup) of the cooking liquid in the pan.
3. Blend the cream, egg yolks and cornflour in a bowl. Whisk in the reserved cooking liquid. Pour into the pan and return to the heat. Cook until the mixture boils and thickens. Add the parsley and mace and season well.
4. Pour the sauce over the celery in the dish. Cook in the oven for 15–20 minutes, or until the celery softens. Serve warm with poached chicken breast, chargrilled lamb or slices of corned beef.

LEEKS

Leeks, like onions, are a vegetable usually relegated to a supporting role as a flavour base in stews, stocks and sauces. But they can also be used as a vegetable in their own right, as evident in French cooking, with dishes such as vichyssoise, leek and potato soup; flamiche, leek pie; and leeks à la grecque, a recipe that pays homage to the Greek method of preparing vegetables in a wine-based stock.

The thick white stems of cultivated leeks are blanched by piling up dirt around them as they grow. Some recipes ask for just the white part, but most of the leek can be used if it is young and the green leaves are not too tough, otherwise, discard the coarse green tops. Like onions, they need to be cooked for a reasonable amount of time or they will be crunchy rather than tender and sweet; however, if overcooked, they will go slimy.

HOW TO... PREPARE LEEKS

Leeks often contain earth and dirt between their layers and need to be washed thoroughly. Trim off the roots, remove any coarse outer leaves, then wash in a colander under running water. You can also wash the cut leeks in lots of water to rinse away any dirt. If you are planning to serve the leeks whole, make a deep, crossways slit through the leafy end of the leeks, then soak them in a bowl of water, shaking them well to dislodge any dirt.

SPRING ONIONS

This onion has a confusing number of names — green onion, shallot and scallion — depending on where you live or what term you prefer. Spring onions are an immature onion that, if left in the ground, would grow to full size. Depending on when it is picked, it has a small, white bulb of varying size, and long green tops. Spring onions have a mild, delicate flavour and both the green tops and white stem can be sliced and added to salads or omelettes, tossed into stir-fries or finely shredded and used as a garnish. Spring onions are sold in bunches — look for ones that have firm white bases and undamaged green tops.

LEEKS A LA GRECQUE

SERVES 4

INGREDIENTS

- 60 ml (2 fl oz/¼ cup) extra virgin olive oil
- 2 tablespoons white wine
- 1 tablespoon tomato paste (concentrated purée)
- ¼ teaspoon sugar
- 1 bay leaf
- 1 thyme sprig
- 1 garlic clove, crushed
- 4 coriander seeds, crushed
- 4 peppercorns
- 8 small leeks, trimmed
- 1 teaspoon lemon juice
- 1 tablespoon chopped parsley

METHOD

1. Put the oil, wine, tomato paste, sugar, bay leaf, thyme, garlic, coriander seeds, peppercorns and 250 ml (9 fl oz/1 cup) water in a large non-aluminium frying pan. Bring to the boil, then cover and simmer for 5 minutes.
2. Add the leeks in a single layer and bring to simmering point. Reduce the heat, cover the pan again and cook for 20–30 minutes, or until the leeks are tender. Transfer to a serving dish.
3. Add the lemon juice to the cooking liquid and boil rapidly until the liquid is slightly syrupy. Remove the bay leaf, thyme and peppercorns. Season with salt and pour over the leeks. Serve the leeks cold, sprinkled with the parsley.

MINI LEEK PIES

MAKES 32

INGREDIENTS

- 80 g (2¾ oz) butter
- 2 tablespoons olive oil
- 1 onion, finely chopped
- 3 leeks, thinly sliced
- 1 garlic clove, chopped
- 1 tablespoon plain (all-purpose) flour
- 2 tablespoons sour cream
- 100 g (3½ oz/1 cup) grated parmesan cheese
- 1 teaspoon chopped thyme
- 4 sheets frozen puff pastry, thawed
- 1 egg, lightly beaten

METHOD

1. Heat the butter and oil in a frying pan over medium heat. Add the onion and cook, stirring occasionally, for 2 minutes. Add the leek and garlic and cook for 5 minutes, or until the leek is softened and lightly browned.
2. Add the flour to the mixture and stir for 1 minute. Add the sour cream and stir until thickened a little. Transfer to a bowl and add the parmesan and thyme. Season with salt and pepper and set aside to cool.
3. Preheat the oven to 200°C (400°F/Gas 6). Place two lightly greased baking trays in the oven to heat up. Using a 6 cm (2½ inch) round cutter, cut the puff pastry into 64 circles. Place 2 heaped tablespoons of leek filling on half of the pastry circles, leaving a small border. Lightly brush the edges with the beaten egg, then place another pastry circle on top. Seal the edges with a fork and lightly brush the tops with the egg.
4. Place the pies on the heated trays and bake for 25 minutes, or until the pies are puffed and golden brown.

SPRING ONION PANCAKES

MAKES 24

INGREDIENTS

- 250 g (9 oz/2 cups) plain (all-purpose) flour
- 1 tablespoon oil
- 60 ml (2 fl oz/¼ cup) sesame oil
- 2 spring onions (scallions), green part only, finely chopped
- oil, for frying

METHOD

1. Put the flour and ½ teaspoon salt in a bowl and stir to combine. Add the oil and 220 ml (7¾ fl oz) water and mix into a rough dough using a wooden spoon. Turn the dough out onto a lightly floured surface and knead for 5 minutes, or until smooth and elastic. Cover the dough with a cloth and let it rest for 20 minutes.
2. On a lightly floured surface, roll the dough into a long roll. Divide the dough into 24 portions. Working with one portion at a time, place the dough, cut edge down, on the work surface. Using a small rolling pin, roll it out to a 10 cm (4 inch) circle. Brush the surface with sesame oil and sprinkle on some spring onion. Starting with the edge closest to you, roll up the dough into a log and pinch the ends to seal. Lightly flatten the roll, then roll it up lengthways to form a snail, pinching the ends to seal. Repeat with the remaining dough, sesame oil and spring onion. Let the rolls rest for 20 minutes.
3. Place each roll flat on the work surface and press down with the palm of your hand. Roll out to a 10 cm (4 inch) circle and place on a lightly floured tray. Stack the pancakes between floured sheets of baking paper; rest for 20 minutes.
4. Heat a frying pan over medium heat, brush the surface of the pan with oil and add two or three pancakes at a time. Cook for 2–3 minutes on each side, turning once, until the pancakes are light golden and crisp. Remove and drain on paper towels. Serve immediately.

ONIONS

One of the most important ingredients in the kitchen, onions are used in just about every nation's cuisine, adding a depth of flavour to dishes, although they are a delicious vegetable in their own right.

Most of the onions we use in cooking are the brown or yellow-skinned variety, available year round. Baby onions, small white- or brown-skinned onions, are good for pickling but can also be added whole to stews and casseroles. They are sometimes called pearl or pickling onions. The Spanish onion, or yellow Spanish onion, is a large variety, popular for use in salads because of its juicy, mild-flavoured flesh. Red onions are good in salads, adding both flavour and colour. When cooked, red onions have less flavour than other varieties, although they can be slightly sweeter. Confusingly, in Australia, red onions are sometimes called Spanish onions.

HOW TO... CARAMELISE ONIONS

Thinly slice 6–8 onions, then cook in olive oil in a large saucepan over medium heat for 45–60 minutes, stirring often, or until golden and very soft. You can add a dash of sugar, some red wine vinegar or balsamic vinegar near the end of cooking if you like. The onions will be thick and jammy, and make an excellent accompaniment for roast meats.

HOW TO... DICE AN ONION

METHOD

1 Using a sharp knife, cut the peeled onion in half from top to bottom. Lay one half, cut surface down, on the chopping board with the root end away from you. Cut lengthways into slices, keeping the slices attached at the root.
2 Now slice horizontally back towards the root, being careful not to cut through it.
3 Next, starting at the far end and working towards the root, slice down through the previous cuts, giving diced pieces. Discard the root.

COOKING TIPS

* Slicing onions causes the cell walls to rupture, releasing the sulphurous contents. When mixed with air, these turn into allyl sulphate, which irritates the eyes. Try one of these steps to overcome the discomfort: soak the onions in water for 30 minutes or chill them before peeling; peel them under an open window or exhaust fan; or breathe with your mouth open.
* To peel baby onions, or any that are to be used whole or in wedges, do not trim them. Keeping the root intact will prevent the layers from falling apart during cooking, while retaining the top gives an attractive shape. Peel off the outer leaves one or two at a time from the top down towards the root.
* To remove the smell of onions from your hands, rub them with lemon juice or vinegar.
* If frying onions, don't chop them in the food processor as they release too much liquid and will steam rather than fry. To bring out their sweet flavour, sweat them gently over low heat without letting them brown.

ROASTED RED ONION AND TOMATOES

SERVES 4

INGREDIENTS

- oil, to brush
- 8 roma (plum) tomatoes
- 2 red onions
- 2 garlic cloves
- 1½ tablespoons balsamic vinegar
- 1 teaspoon French mustard
- 60 ml (2 fl oz/¼ cup) extra virgin olive oil

METHOD

1. Preheat the oven to 150°C (300°F/Gas 2) and lightly brush a baking tray with oil.
2. Cut the tomatoes into quarters and put on the tray. Remove the tops of the onion and peel. Cut each onion into 8 wedges and place on the tray with the tomatoes. Place the garlic in the middle of the tray, spaced apart and season the vegetables well. Roast for 1 hour.
3. Arrange the tomatoes and onions on a serving plate. Peel the garlic and crush in a small bowl. Add the balsamic vinegar and mustard to the garlic and, using a small whisk, beat in the olive oil, adding it slowly in a thin stream. Season the dressing well and drizzle over the onions and tomatoes. Serve immediately.

SHALLOTS

Shallots, sometimes called eschalotes, are a close relative of the onion, but have a milder, delicate flavour. Shallots grow in clusters and are joined with a common root end. There are several varieties including the grey or common shallot; the Jersey shallot, a round bulb with pink skin; the French shallot, which has golden copper-coloured skin and an elongated bulb; and red Asian shallots, which are a light pink colour. In some countries, spring onions are erroneously called shallots.

Shallots feature in delicate sauces such as beurre blanc; they can be used as a garnish; thinly sliced and eaten raw in salads; or peeled and cooked whole as a vegetable. In France, shallots are used in sauces, as the flesh dissolves well when cooked. Store shallots in a cool, well-ventilated place for up to 1 month.

COOKING TIPS

- If using shallots in large quantities, the skins can be hard to peel. Pour boiling water over shallots in a bowl, weight them with a plate to submerge, then set aside for 5 minutes. Drain well, and cool slightly. To peel, slice across the skin from the top of each bulb. Then, using a small knife, pull a section of skin away from the flesh, then pull it down to the root end.
- If leaving shallots whole, only trim the root or they will fall apart.
- When browning shallots, make sure they are well browned all over, as the colour will wash off if they are added to a liquid such as stock.

Asian shallot

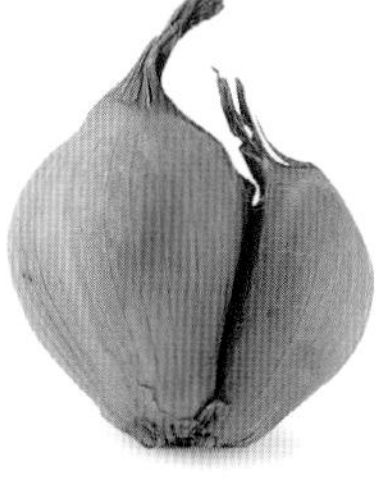

French shallot

••FRUITING VEGETABLES••

Although botanically classed as fruit, this group, which includes tomatoes, capsicums, eggplants, cucumbers, avocado and pumpkin, are used in cooking as vegetables.

TOMATOES

Most varieties of tomatoes are red, although others are yellow or pink. Unripe green tomatoes are used in pickles and chutneys. The best flavoured are those that are vine-ripened. Buy tomatoes that are firm and bright coloured, with no wrinkles and a strong tomato smell. Buy only in small quantities (unless making sauce), or buy some greener than others. For salads and pasta sauces, buy only the reddest, ripest tomatoes — uniformity of shape or colour has no relation to their flavour. Pale red tomatoes can be left to ripen naturally on your kitchen windowsill but won't ripen if left in the fridge.

TYPES OF TOMATOES

cherry tomato

CHERRY

These come in various sizes but essentially are a tiny variety of tomato. Some are red, others are yellow and some are pear-shaped. They are good in salads or use whole or halved in stews and pasta sauces.

roma (plum) tomato

ROMA (PLUM)

Also called egg tomatoes, these are commercially used for canning and drying. They have few seeds and a dry flesh, which makes them ideal in sauces and purées.

beef steak tomato

BEEF STEAK

These are large tomatoes, either smooth and rounded or more irregular and ridged. Because of their size they can be stuffed with various fillings, or used in salads.

round tomato

ROUND

These are a good all-purpose tomato. These are commercially bred to be round and red. They can be bought vine-ripened or on the vine, in different varieties such as the striped tigerella, or may be yellow or orange coloured.

HOW TO... PEEL AND SEED TOMATOES

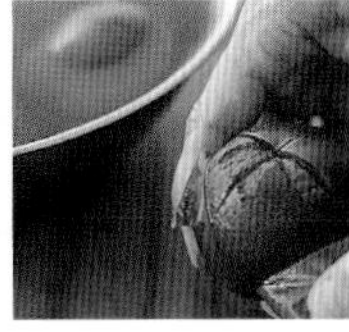

METHOD

1 Remove the stems of the tomatoes and score a cross in the base of each one with a knife, cutting just through the skin. Put in a bowl and cover with boiling water. Leave for 20 seconds, or so.
2 Test one tomato to see if the skin will come off easily, otherwise leave them to soak for a few seconds more. Don't leave them for too long or they might start to cook.
3 Transfer the tomatoes to a bowl of cold water and then peel the skin away from the cross — it should slip off very easily. If the recipe asks for the seeds to be removed, cut the peeled tomato in half horizontally and squeeze out the seeds with your hands or scoop them out with a teaspoon. You can also remove the seeds from an unpeeled tomato the same way. Cut or dice as directed.

SLOW-ROASTED BALSAMIC TOMATOES

MAKES 40

INGREDIENTS

10 firm roma (plum) tomatoes
8 garlic cloves, crushed
80 g (2¾ oz/⅓ cup) caster (superfine) sugar
4 tablespoons torn basil
1 tablespoon chopped oregano
few drops of balsamic vinegar

METHOD

1 Preheat the oven to 140°C (275°F/Gas 1). Line two baking trays with baking paper. Cut each tomato lengthways into quarters and put the quarters in rows on the trays.
2 Mix the garlic with the sugar, basil, oregano and balsamic vinegar. Using clean fingers, put a little of the mixture onto the sides of each tomato quarter and season with sea salt and freshly ground black pepper.
3 Roast in the oven for 2½ hours. The tomatoes are ready when they are slightly shrivelled at the edge and semi-dried (they should still be soft in the middle). Eat them warm or cold, served with barbecued lamb chops, beef steak or as part of an antipasti selection. Store in the fridge.

SUN-DRIED AND SEMI-DRIED TOMATOES

Sun-dried tomatoes (pictured far right) have been halved, sprinkled with salt and left to dry in the sun. They are also commercially available in jars. These are soaked in a solution of vinegar and water, then drained, dried and covered in olive oil, sometimes with other flavours. Semi-dried, or sun-blushed, tomatoes are partially dried in a dehydrator. They need to be immersed in oil to preserve them for any length of time.

PANZANELLA

SERVES 6–8

INGREDIENTS

- 1 small red onion, thinly sliced
- 250 g (9 oz) day-old Italian bread, crusts removed
- 4 tomatoes
- 6 tinned anchovy fillets, rinsed and finely chopped
- 1 small garlic clove, crushed
- 1 tablespoon baby capers, rinsed and chopped
- 2 tablespoons red wine vinegar
- 125 ml (4 fl oz/½ cup) extra virgin olive oil
- 2 small Lebanese (short) cucumbers, sliced
- 1 small handful basil, torn

METHOD

1. Put the onion in a small bowl, cover with cold water and leave for 5 minutes. Squeeze the onion rings in your hand, closing tightly and letting go and repeating that process about five times. This removes the acid from the onion. Repeat the whole process twice more, using fresh water each time.
2. Tear the bread into 3 cm (1¼ inch) squares and toast lightly under a grill (broiler) for 4 minutes, or until the bread is crisp but not browned. Cool and set aside.
3. To peel the tomatoes, score a cross in the base of each tomato. Put in a heatproof bowl and cover with boiling water. Leave for 30 seconds, then transfer to cold water and peel the skin away from the cross. Cut the tomatoes in half horizontally and scoop out the seeds with a teaspoon. Roughly chop two of the tomatoes and purée the other two.
4. Combine the anchovies, garlic and capers in a bowl. Add the vinegar and olive oil and whisk to combine. Season, then transfer to a large bowl and add the bread, onion, puréed and chopped tomato, cucumber and basil. Toss well and season to taste. Leave to stand for at least 15 minutes to allow the flavours to develop. Serve at room temperature.

ZUCCHINI

Zucchini (courgettes) are baby marrows, usually dark green in colour, but there are also yellow and so-called 'white' varieties, which are actually light green in colour. Young zucchini can be sliced thinly, dressed in oil and lemon juice and eaten raw in salads. Use larger ones in stir-fries, steam or boil them, coat slices in batter and deep-fry, or hollow out, stuff and bake them. If using in fritters or frying, salt them first to degorge them so they soak up less oil. Buy and eat quickly as storage in the fridge makes the texture deteriorate. Zucchini flowers are edible too, available in the male (the flower has a stalk) or female (the flower has a baby zucchini attached) form. They are sold at speciality fruit and vegetable shops. Wash before use and make sure there are no insects hidden inside.

green zucchini

white zucchini

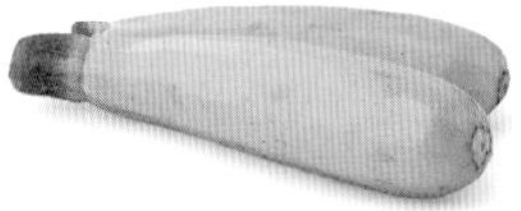
yellow zucchini

zucchini flowers

ZUCCHINI FRITTERS

MAKES 16

INGREDIENTS

300 g (10½ oz) (about 3) zucchini (courgettes), grated
1 small onion, finely chopped
30 g (1 oz/¼ cup) self-raising flour
35 g (1¼ oz/⅓ cup) grated parmesan cheese
1 tablespoon chopped mint
2 teaspoons chopped parsley
pinch of ground nutmeg
25 g (1 oz/¼ cup) dry breadcrumbs
1 egg, lightly beaten
olive oil, for shallow-frying
lemon wedges, to serve
tzatziki (page 351), to serve

METHOD

1 Put the zucchini and onion in the centre of a clean tea towel, gather the corners together and twist as tightly as possible to remove all the juices. Combine the zucchini, onion, flour, parmesan, mint, parsley, nutmeg, breadcrumbs and egg in a large bowl. Season with salt and freshly ground black pepper, then mix with your hands to a stiff mixture that clumps together.

2 Heat the oil in a large frying pan over medium heat. When hot, drop tablespoons of the zucchini mixture into the pan and shallow-fry for 2–3 minutes, or until well browned all over. Drain well on paper towels and serve hot with lemon wedges and tzatziki.

FRIED ZUCCHINI FLOWERS

SERVES 4

INGREDIENTS

BATTER
50 g (1¾ oz) plain (all-purpose) flour
2 teaspoons olive oil
3 egg whites

8–12 zucchini (courgette) flowers
oil, for deep-frying
lemon wedges, to serve

METHOD

1 To make the batter, sift the flour into a bowl and stir in ¼ teaspoon salt. Mix in the oil with a wooden spoon, then slowly add 75–100 ml (2¼–3½ fl oz) warm water, changing to a whisk when the mixture becomes liquid. Continue whisking until the batter is smooth and thick. Whisk the egg whites until stiff peaks form, then gently fold them into the batter.

2 Check the zucchini flowers are clean and aren't hiding any stray insects. Trim the stem of each flower to about 2 cm (¾ inch) — this gives you something to hold on to when dipping.

3 Fill a deep frying pan (large enough to fit the zucchini) or a deep heavy-based saucepan one-third full of oil and heat to 180°C (350°F), or until a cube of bread dropped into the oil turns golden brown in 15 seconds. If the oil starts to smoke it is too hot.

4 Dip the zucchini flowers into the batter, coating both sides, then lower them in batches into the oil and cook until golden brown, turning once to cook on both sides. Drain on paper towels, sprinkle with salt and serve with lemon wedges. Serve and eat them immediately.

FATTOUSH

SERVES 6

INGREDIENTS

- 2 pitta breads
- 6 cos (romaine) lettuce leaves, shredded
- 1 large Lebanese (short) cucumber, cubed
- 4 tomatoes, cubed
- 8 spring onions (scallions), chopped
- 4 tablespoons chopped parsley
- 1 tablespoon chopped mint
- 2 tablespoons chopped coriander (cilantro)

DRESSING

- 2 garlic cloves, crushed
- 100 ml (3½ fl oz) extra virgin olive oil
- 100 ml (3½ fl oz) lemon juice

METHOD

1. Preheat the oven to 180°C (350°F/Gas 4). Split the bread into two through the centre and bake on a baking tray for about 8 minutes, or until golden and crisp, turning halfway through. Break the bread into small pieces.
2. To make the dressing, whisk all the ingredients together in a bowl until combined.
3. Place the bread pieces and remaining salad ingredients in a bowl and toss. Pour on the dressing and toss well. Season with salt and black pepper. Serve immediately.

TABOULEH

SERVES 6–8

INGREDIENTS

- 130 g (4½ oz/¾ cup) burghul (bulgur)
- 3 tomatoes
- 1 telegraph (long) cucumber
- 4 spring onions (scallions), sliced
- 120 g (4¼ oz) flat-leaf (Italian) parsley, chopped
- 2 large handfuls mint, chopped

DRESSING

- 80 ml (2½ fl oz/⅓ cup) lemon juice
- 60 ml (2 fl oz/¼ cup) olive oil
- 1 tablespoon extra virgin olive oil

METHOD

1. Put the burghul in a bowl, cover with 500 ml (17 fl oz/2 cups) water and leave for 1 hour.
2. Cut the tomatoes in half, squeeze to remove the seeds and cut into 1 cm (½ inch) cubes. Cut the cucumber in half lengthways, scoop out the seeds with a teaspoon and cut the flesh into 1 cm (½ inch) cubes.
3. To make the dressing, put the lemon juice and 1½ teaspoons salt in a bowl and whisk until well combined. Season well with freshly ground black pepper and slowly whisk in the olive oil and extra virgin olive oil.
4. Drain the burghul and squeeze out any excess water. Spread the burghul out on a clean tea towel or paper towels and leave to dry for about 30 minutes. Put the burghul in a large serving bowl, add the tomato, cucumber, spring onion, parsley and mint and toss to combine. Pour the dressing over the salad and toss well.

GREEK SALAD

SERVES 4

INGREDIENTS

- 1 large tomato
- 1 Lebanese (short) cucumber
- 2 radishes
- 1 small onion
- 100 g (3½ oz) feta cheese
- 45 g (1½ oz/⅓ cup) pitted black olives
- 2 tablespoons lemon juice
- 60 ml (2 fl oz/¼ cup) olive oil
- ½ teaspoon oregano

METHOD

1 Chop the tomato and cut the cucumber into rounds. Thinly slice the radishes and onion, and cut the feta cheese into small cubes.

2 Combine the prepared tomato, cucumber, radishes, onion, feta and olives in a serving bowl. Drizzle with the combined lemon juice, olive oil and oregano. Serve on a bed of coral lettuce if you like.

TZATZIKI

MAKES 500 G (1 LB 2 OZ/2 CUPS)

INGREDIENTS

- 2 Lebanese (short) cucumbers
- 400 g (14 oz/1⅔ cups) Greek-style yoghurt
- 4 garlic cloves, crushed
- 3 tablespoons finely chopped mint
- 1 tablespoon lemon juice
- chopped mint, extra to garnish

METHOD

1 Cut the cucumbers in half lengthways, scoop out the seeds with a teaspoon and discard (see below). Leave the skin on and coarsely grate the cucumber into a small colander. Sprinkle with a little salt and leave to stand over a large bowl for 20 minutes to drain off any bitter juices.

2 Combine the yoghurt, garlic, mint and lemon juice in a bowl. Rinse the cucumber under cold water then, taking small handfuls, squeeze out any excess moisture. Combine the cucumber with the yoghurt mixture and season. Serve immediately or refrigerate until ready to serve. Garnish with mint. Serve as a dip with flatbread or as a sauce for seafood and meat dishes.

HOW TO... PEEL AND SEED CUCUMBERS

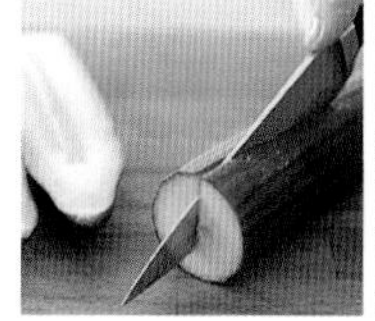
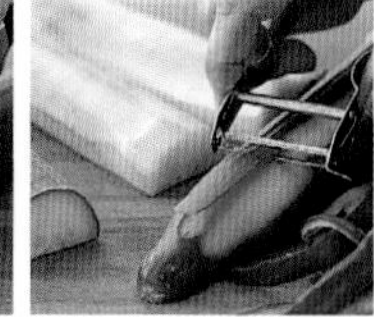
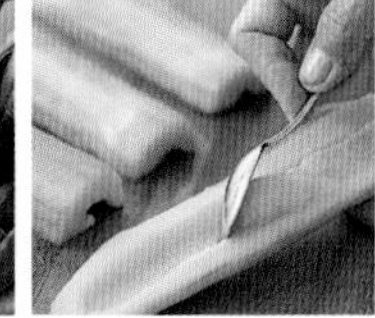

METHOD

1 Halve the cucumber horizontally. If your cucumber is long, cut it in half first as long pieces are difficult to cut evenly.

2 Peel both halves with a potato peeler or a small sharp knife. A swivel peeler is the easiest thing to use as it removes the least amount of flesh with the skin.

3 Scrape out the seeds with a teaspoon and then allow the cucumber pieces to drain with the seeded side down. Then cut or use as directed by the recipe.

4 Some recipes ask for the cucumbers to be salted to remove any bitterness. To do this, sprinkle the cut cucumber with salt, then put in a colander and leave to drain for 20–30 minutes. Rinse well and pat dry with paper towel.

EGGPLANT

The eggplant (aubergine) is an extremely versatile fruit, used in Italian, French, Middle Eastern and Asian cuisines. Eggplants can be served hot or cold, puréed, fried, stuffed or battered, and they are the main ingredient of many famous dishes such as moussaka, baba ghanoush and ratatouille. Recipes sometimes ask for the eggplant to be degorged (salted and drained). This can help reduce their bitterness, as well as reduce the amount of oil they absorb as they cook. Eggplants vary in size and shape and some of the most commonly grown varieties are listed below.

TYPES OF EGGPLANT

Eggplants vary greatly in size and shape: from the small pea-shaped eggplant to the classic large, purple egg-shaped variety, which can weigh up to 500 g (1 lb). Japanese eggplants are long, slender eggplants, perfect for stuffing or baking. Other kinds of eggplants, used mainly in Thai and other Asian cooking, include the bitter-tasting pea eggplants, which grow in clusters and may be red, green or purple, and Thai eggplants, small, round eggplants, usually pale purple in colour with green markings, or green and cream.

HOW TO... DEGORGE EGGPLANTS

METHOD

1. Cut the eggplants into pieces and layer in a colander, sprinkling each layer with salt. This helps draw out any bitter juices. It also stops the flesh from soaking up too much oil if you are frying them. Always cut eggplant with a stainless steel knife to stop them discolouring.
2. Leave for about 20 minutes to let the eggplants degorge their bitter juices, then rinse thoroughly under cold running water. You can weigh the eggplant down with a plate to speed up the removal of liquid.
3. Squeeze each piece of eggplant dry, making sure you have got rid of most of the water, then pat dry with paper towels.

RATATOUILLE

SERVES 4

INGREDIENTS

- 2 tablespoons olive oil
- 1 large onion, diced
- 1 red and 1 yellow capsicum (pepper), diced
- 1 eggplant (aubergine), diced
- 2 zucchini (courgettes), diced
- 1 teaspoon tomato paste (concentrated purée)
- 4 tomatoes, peeled and seeded (page 347), roughly chopped
- ½ teaspoon sugar
- 1 bay leaf
- 3 thyme sprigs
- 2 basil sprigs
- 1 garlic clove, crushed
- 1 tablespoon chopped parsley

METHOD

1. Heat the oil in a frying pan. Add the onion and cook over low heat for 5 minutes. Add the capsicum and cook, stirring, for 4 minutes. Remove from the pan and set aside.
2. Fry the eggplant until lightly browned and remove from the pan. Fry the zucchini until browned and then return the onion, capsicum and eggplant to the pan. Add the tomato paste, stir and cook for 2 minutes. Add the tomato, sugar, bay leaf, thyme and basil. Stir, then cover and cook for 15 minutes. Remove the bay leaf, thyme and basil.
3. Mix together the garlic and parsley and add to the ratatouille at the last minute. Stir to combine.

CAPONATA

SERVES 4–6

INGREDIENTS

2 large eggplants (aubergines), cut into 3 cm (1¼ inch) cubes
3 large celery stalks, finely chopped
60 ml (2 fl oz/¼ cup) extra virgin olive oil
1 large onion, finely chopped
50 g (1¾ oz) pine nuts
4 garlic cloves, thinly sliced
400 g (14 oz) tomatoes, peeled (page 347) and chopped, or 400 g (14 oz) tin chopped tomatoes
olive oil, for shallow-frying
1 teaspoon dried oregano
3 tablespoons capers, rinsed and squeezed dry
80 ml (2½ fl oz/⅓ cup) red wine vinegar
12 green olives, pitted and chopped

METHOD

1 Put the eggplant cubes in layers in a colander, sprinkling salt on each layer. Leave the eggplant for about 20 minutes to degorge, then rinse well and dry (see opposite). Put the eggplant in a large bowl.
2 Blanch the celery in boiling water for 1 minute then plunge into cold water, drain and set aside. (Blanching dilutes the flavour of the celery a little, as it can be quite overpowering.)
3 Heat the extra virgin olive oil in a saucepan over low heat and cook the onion and pine nuts until the onion is soft and the pine nuts are light brown. Add the garlic and cook for another minute. Add the celery and tomatoes and cook until the sauce has thickened.
4 Pour a generous amount of olive oil into a deep frying pan. To test the oil is deep enough, hold a teaspoon upright in the pan: the oil should reach a quarter of the way up the spoon. Add enough eggplant to just cover the base of the pan and cook over medium heat until golden brown and soft on both sides. Remove from the pan and place in a colander to drain off any oil. Repeat until all the eggplant is cooked.
5 Add the oregano, capers and vinegar to the tomato sauce. Bring to the boil and simmer gently until thickened. Remove from the heat and add the eggplant and olives. Stir briefly and season with salt and pepper. Leave to rest for at least 15 minutes before serving.

NOTE: This Italian dish is often served warm or at room temperature as part of an antipasti platter or to accompany meat. The dish can be prepared in advance — the flavours will only improve.

IMAM BAYILDI

A classic Turkish dish, imam bayildi is made with eggplants hollowed out or slit down one side and cooked, then stuffed with onions, garlic, tomatoes and parsley. Translated from the Turkish, imam bayildi means 'the imam (priest) fainted' — perhaps because the dish was so wonderful. This dish is usually served cold, but it can be served warm, either as an entrée or with salad as a light meal.

❮ IMAM BAYILDI

SERVES 4–6

INGREDIENTS

- 185 ml (6 fl oz/¾ cup) olive oil
- 1 kg (2 lb 4 oz) eggplants (aubergines), cut in half lengthways
- 3 onions, thinly sliced
- 3 garlic cloves, finely chopped
- 400 g (14 oz) roma (plum) tomatoes, peeled (page 347) and chopped, or 400 g (14 oz) tin chopped tomatoes
- 2 teaspoons dried oregano
- 4 tablespoons chopped parsley
- 35 g (1¼ oz/¼ cup) currants
- ¼ teaspoon ground cinnamon
- 2 tablespoons lemon juice
- pinch of sugar
- 125 ml (4 fl oz/½ cup) tomato juice

METHOD

1. Preheat the oven to 180°C (350°F/Gas 4). Heat half the olive oil in a large heavy-based frying pan and cook the eggplants on all sides for 8–10 minutes, until the cut sides are golden. Remove from the pan and scoop out some of the flesh, leaving the skins intact and some flesh lining the skins. Finely chop the scooped-out flesh and set aside.
2. Heat the remaining olive oil in the same frying pan and cook the onion over medium heat for 8–10 minutes, until transparent. Add the garlic and cook for another minute. Add the tomatoes, oregano, parsley, currants, cinnamon, reserved eggplant flesh and season with salt and pepper.
3. Place the eggplant shells in a large ovenproof dish and fill each with the tomato mixture.
4. Mix the lemon juice, sugar, tomato juice and some salt and pour over the eggplants.
5. Cover and bake for 30 minutes, then uncover and cook for another 10 minutes. To serve, place the eggplants on a serving platter and lightly drizzle with any remaining juice.

TUNISIAN EGGPLANT SALAD WITH PRESERVED LEMON

SERVES 4

INGREDIENTS

- 2 large eggplants (aubergines), cut into 2 cm (¾ inch) cubes
- 125 ml (4 fl oz/½ cup) olive oil
- 1 teaspoon cumin seeds
- 2 garlic cloves, very thinly sliced
- 1 tablespoon currants
- 1 tablespoon slivered almonds
- 6 small roma (plum) tomatoes, quartered
- 1 teaspoon dried oregano
- 4 red bird's eye chillies, halved and seeded
- 2 tablespoons lemon juice
- 4 tablespoons chopped parsley
- ½ preserved lemon (page 668), rinsed, pith and flesh removed, zest thinly sliced
- extra virgin olive oil, to serve

METHOD

1. Put the eggplant in layers in a colander, sprinkling salt on each layer. Leave the eggplant for 1 hour to degorge, then rinse and dry. (The eggplant is left to degorge for 1 hour, so that less oil is needed for frying.)
2. Heat half the oil in a large flameproof casserole dish over medium–high heat. Fry the eggplant in batches for 5–6 minutes, until golden, adding more oil as required. Drain on paper towels.
3. Reduce the heat and add any remaining oil to the dish, along with the cumin, garlic, currants and almonds. Fry for 20–30 seconds, until the garlic starts to colour. Add the tomatoes and oregano and cook for 1 minute. Remove from the heat. Return the eggplant to the dish and add the chilli, lemon juice, parsley and preserved lemon zest. Toss gently and season with pepper.
4. Set aside at room temperature for 1 hour before serving, or longer if possible to allow the flavours to develop. Check the seasoning, then drizzle with extra virgin olive oil.

CAPSICUM

Also known as pepper, bell pepper and sweet pepper, these colourful fruit come in a variety of colours but are all basically smooth, shiny and hollow, and contain thin white membranes and seeds. Most sweet capsicums (bell peppers) are green at first, they then turn red, yellow or orange or even purple–black, depending on the variety.

Capsicums can be prepared in many ways. Simply cut into slices, chunks or quarters, and eat raw in salads; stuff or fry; or roasted skinned capsicums can be sliced and added to salads, or drizzled with olive oil and added to an antipasti platter. To make capsicum sauces, grill and remove the skins, then purée or push the flesh through a sieve.

HOW TO... GRILL AND PEEL CAPSICUMS

METHOD

1 Cut the capsicums in half, trim off the membrane and scrape out the seeds. Put the capsicums, cut side down, under a very hot grill (broiler). Alternatively, cook them whole (this gives an even softer result as they steam from the inside).

2 Cook until the skin is completely black and blistered. You may need to move them around a bit to make sure all the skin gets cooked.

3 Remove the capsicums from the grill and stack them up on top of each other or put them in a plastic bag — this will help the steam loosen the charred skin. Peel off the skin. Scrape off any stubborn bits with a knife. Peeled, seeded capsicums can be kept covered in oil in the fridge for 1 week.

CAPSICUM PUREE

MAKES 300 ML (10 FL OZ/$1^1/_4$ CUPS)

INGREDIENTS

- 3 large red capsicums (peppers)
- 4 spring onions (scallions), chopped
- 2 garlic cloves, crushed
- 2 small red chillies, finely chopped
- 2 tablespoons lime juice
- 2 tablespoons chopped coriander (cilantro)

METHOD

1 Grill (broil) the capsicums under high heat for 10 minutes, turning often, until the skin blisters and blackens. When cool, peel then remove the seeds and roughly chop (see left).

2 Put the capsicums into a food processor and add the spring onion, garlic and chilli. Process until smooth. Transfer to a saucepan and stir in the lime juice and coriander. Cook over medium heat until slightly thickened. Serve the capsicum purée as a dip with an antipasti selection or as a pasta sauce.

CAPSICUM CROSTINI

Crostini are thin slices of bread, cut into pieces and brushed with oil or butter, then toasted or baked. The crostini are then topped with various mixtures such as capsicum, pâté, puréed eggplants (aubergines), artichoke hearts, chopped mushrooms or olive tapenade (page 436).

MAKES 16–20

INGREDIENTS

BASIC CROSTINI

- 1 day-old ciabatta bread
- 80 ml (2½ fl oz/⅓ cup) extra virgin olive oil

CAPSICUM TOPPING

- 60 ml (2 fl oz/¼ cup) extra virgin olive oil
- 1 onion, finely chopped
- 2 red capsicums (peppers), thinly sliced
- 2 garlic cloves, crushed
- 1 tablespoon capers, drained and chopped
- 2 tablespoons balsamic vinegar
- 1 tablespoon chopped parsley

METHOD

1. To make the crostini, preheat the oven to 180°C (350°F/Gas 4). Thinly slice the bread, cut each piece into quarters and drizzle the olive oil over both sides. Place on a baking tray and lightly toast in the oven until just crisp. (The crostini will keep in an airtight container for 2–3 days and then crisp them in a 180°C (350°F/Gas 4) oven for 10 minutes before you use them.)
2. To make the capsicum topping, heat the olive oil in a frying pan and cook the onion for a few minutes until soft. Add the capsicum and cook for 15 minutes, stirring frequently. Season, then add the garlic and cook for another minute. Add the capers and vinegar and simmer gently for a few minutes to reduce the liquid. Add the parsley just before spreading onto the crostini.

CHARGRILLED VEGETABLE SALAD

SERVES 4

INGREDIENTS

- 4 long thin eggplants (aubergines)
- 4 zucchini (courgettes)
- 4 roma (plum) tomatoes
- 1 small red capsicum (pepper)
- 1 small green capsicum (pepper)
- 1 small yellow capsicum (pepper)
- 60 ml (2 fl oz/¼ cup) olive oil
- 2 garlic cloves, halved

DRESSING

- 60 ml (2 fl oz/¼ cup) extra virgin olive oil
- 1 tablespoon balsamic vinegar
- 1 garlic clove, crushed
- 3 tablespoons chopped parsley
- ¼ teaspoon caster (superfine) sugar

METHOD

1. Slice the eggplants and zucchini diagonally into 1 cm (¾ inch) thick pieces. Halve the tomatoes lengthways and slice the capsicums into short strips. Place all the vegetables in a bowl and add the olive oil and garlic. Toss well.
2. Preheat a barbecue grill or chargrill pan and brush with oil. Cook the eggplants and zucchini for 2–4 minutes on each side, or until browned. Transfer to a shallow serving dish. Cook the tomatoes and capsicum slices for 1–2 minutes on each side, or until the capsicums start to smell sweet and their skins blister. Transfer to the serving dish and set aside to cool.
3. To make the dressing, mix together all the ingredients and season with salt and pepper. Drizzle the dressing over the vegetables and toss lightly. Serve at room temperature.

CHILLIES

Chillies belong to the *Capsicum* family and are native to South and Central America. Not all chillies provide that distinctive blast of 'heat' — each has its own flavour and varies in its degree of 'hotness'. In countries that use a lot of chilli in their cooking, it is important to have the right chilli for each dish. Generally, red chillies are hotter than green or yellow chillies, and small chillies tend to be hotter than larger ones.

TYPES OF CHILLIES

BANANA (2)
These are mild and sweet large, long chillies, creamy yellow or orange-red in colour. Use split in half and grilled.

ANCHO (3)
This is a dried poblano chilli, dark red and mildly sweet. It is used widely in Mexican cuisine, often with mulato and pasilla to form the 'Holy Trinity' of chillies used in mole sauces.

JALAPENO (5)
This oval-shaped chilli has thick, juicy flesh and a wheel shape when sliced. They are red or green and are very hot if the seeds and septa (membrane) are used. When dried it is called a chipotle.

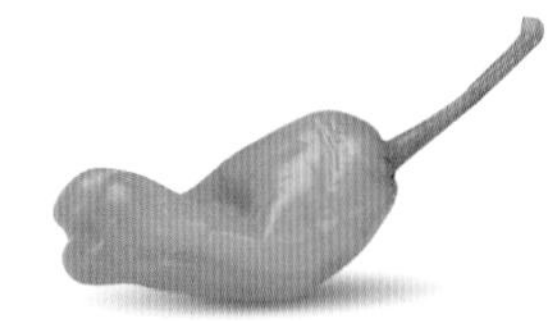

SERRANO (7)
A common Mexican chilli, cylindrical in shape, red or green, and often used in salsas or pickled.

BIRD'S EYE CHILLI (8)
Also called Thai chillies, these are tiny, either red or green, and very hot. Use in Thai curries or sliced raw onto Asian salads.

HABANERO (10)
These lantern-shaped chillies can be green, red or orange. They are very, very hot but with a good, slightly acidic flavour. Use in salsas and marinades.

COOKING TIPS

* Buy chillies that are uniform in colour and unbroken or the essential oils will be lost.
* If you do get chilli burn, run your hands under cold water and rub them against a stainless steel surface (the sink) or soak in milk. If you burn your mouth, eat dairy products or starchy foods.
* Roasting chillies gives a smoky flavour to the flesh. Drying them intensifies the flavour.
* Cooking a whole chilli in a dish rather than chopping it will contain the heat somewhat. If in doubt about how hot your chilli is, use less than the recipe specifies: you can always add more. If the dish is too hot, add yoghurt, coconut milk or cream.

HOW TO... CHOP CHILLIES

METHOD

1 When you chop a chilli, you expose your flesh to the part of the chilli (the membrane) that holds the capsaicin. Because of this you may want to wear rubber gloves to stop the volatile oils getting on your fingers. Don't put your hands near your face and wash your hands after handling them. Chilli oil remains on your skin for some time.
2 Cut the chilli in half lengthways with a sharp knife. Cut out the membrane and scrape out any seeds. Cut off the stalk.
3 Lay each chilli half, cut side down, on the chopping board and make cuts lengthways (quite close together), reaching almost as far as the stalk end, then cut across the other way to give little squares, or as your recipe directs.

THE HEAT SCALE

Various methods can be used for measuring the heat in chillies including the Scoville scale, which ranges from grade 0 (sweet pepper) to 300,000 (habanero), or a simple 1–10 used by many supermarkets (and used opposite). None are completely accurate, as chillies vary quite considerably, even those on the same bush.

CAPSAICIN

Chillies are hot because they contain an irritant alkaloid, a chemical that acts directly on the pain receptors in the mouth to produce a burning sensation. The body reacts by secreting endorphins — these are natural painkillers that cause a physical 'high', thought to account for the addictiveness of eating chillies. Capsaicin is primarily found in the membrane and seeds of the chilli. It is not very soluble in water (water does little to extinguish the heat) but is soluble in oil and alcohol (this is why milk, yoghurt and beer help relieve the heat of curries).

CHILLI CON CARNE

SERVES 2

INGREDIENTS

115 g (4 oz) dried kidney beans
2 tablespoons oil
1 red onion, finely chopped
1 garlic clove, crushed
1 handful coriander (cilantro), chopped
1 or 2 chillies, seeded and finely chopped
800 g (1 lb 12 oz) chuck steak, cut into cubes
400 g (14 oz) tin chopped tomatoes
1 tablespoon tomato paste (concentrated purée)
250 ml (9 fl oz/1 cup) beef stock (page 11)
1 red capsicum (pepper), cut into squares
1 ripe tomato, chopped
½ avocado, diced
juice of 1 lime
2 tablespoons sour cream

METHOD

1 Soak the beans in cold water overnight, or put them in a pan, cover with cold water, bring to the boil and cook for 10 minutes, then reduce the heat and simmer for 10 minutes. Turn off the heat and leave for 2 hours. Drain and rinse the beans.
2 Heat half the oil in a flameproof casserole dish and cook three-quarters of the onion, the garlic, half the coriander, and the chilli for 5 minutes.
3 Increase the heat, push the onion to one side and add the remaining oil. Add the steak and cook for 3 minutes, or until well browned. Add the beans, tinned tomatoes, tomato paste and stock and stir well. Bring to the boil, then reduce to a simmer, cover and cook for 1 hour. Add the capsicum and cook for another 30 minutes.
4 To make the topping, combine half the remaining coriander, the tomato, avocado and remaining onion. Season and add half the lime juice.
5 When the meat is tender, add the remaining coriander and lime juice and season well. Serve with some of the avocado topping, a dollop of sour cream and with rice or flour tortillas.

AVOCADO

Avocados have soft, buttery flesh and a mild, slightly nutty flavour, and are the only fruit that contains fat (monounsaturated fat). Because of their pear shape, avocados are sometimes called 'avocado pear' or 'alligator pear', referring to the rough skin texture of some varieties, such as Sharwill and Hass. Other varieties have thin, smooth skin, such as Fuerte, and the small, stoneless cocktail avocado.

Avocados are best eaten raw — cut in half and serve with a vinaigrette; slice and add to salads; purée for use in dips or guacamole; or use as a base for sweet dishes such as ice cream. Cut avocado turns brown, so cut it just before use or brush with lemon juice to stop it discolouring.

HOW TO... RIPEN AVOCADOS

Avocados don't ripen well on the tree, but firm, unripe avocados will ripen at room temperature after 3–4 days. To speed this up, put them in a bowl or in a paper bag with fruit that give off ethylene gas (such as a ripe apple or banana), which speeds up the ripening process. Avocados should feel tender or give slightly at the stem end when ripe.

BEEF NACHOS WITH GUACAMOLE

SERVES 4

INGREDIENTS

- oil, for cooking
- 400 g (14 oz) lean minced (ground) beef
- 1 onion, chopped
- 1–2 teaspoons chopped chilli
- 1 tablespoon ground cumin
- 3 teaspoons ground coriander
- 3 tablespoons tomato paste (concentrated purée)
- 125 g (4½ oz/½ cup) bottled tomato pasta sauce or salsa
- 115 g (4 oz/½ cup) refried beans or 425 g (15 oz) tin red kidney beans, rinsed
- corn chips, grated cheddar cheese and sour cream, to serve
- 1 quantity guacamole (see opposite)
- chilli powder, to sprinkle

METHOD

1. Heat a little oil in a frying pan and brown the beef in batches, stirring and breaking up any lumps with a fork or wooden spoon. Transfer to a bowl and set aside.
2. Add a little more oil to the pan and stir in the onion, chilli, cumin and coriander. Cook over medium heat for 2–3 minutes. Return the meat to the frying pan and stir in the tomato paste, pasta sauce and beans. Simmer for 5–10 minutes.
3. Spoon the beef into a large ovenproof dish. Arrange the corn chips around the mixture and sprinkle with the cheese. Place under a hot grill (broiler) or in a 180°C (350°F/Gas 4) oven for 5–10 minutes, or until the cheese has melted. Top with the guacamole, a spoonful of sour cream and a dash of chilli powder.

AVOCADO, BACON AND TOMATO SALAD

SERVES 2

INGREDIENTS

3 garlic cloves, unpeeled
2 tablespoons olive oil
3 teaspoons balsamic vinegar
1 teaspoon dijon mustard
125 g (4½ oz) bacon slices
50 g (1¾ oz) mixed green salad leaves
½ small red onion, thinly sliced
1 avocado, cut into chunks
2 small tomatoes, cut into chunks

METHOD

1 Preheat the oven to 180°C (350°F/Gas 4). Put the garlic cloves on a baking tray and roast for 30 minutes. Remove, allow to cool, then squeeze the flesh out of the skins and mash in a small bowl. Add the oil, vinegar and mustard, then whisk to combine well.
2 Chop the bacon into bite-sized pieces, then cook under a hot grill (broiler) or dry-fry in a frying pan over medium heat for 3–5 minutes, or until crisp. Gently toss the bacon, salad leaves, onion, avocado and tomato in a bowl. Drizzle the garlic mixture over the salad just before serving.

AVOCADO, PRAWN AND MANGO SALAD

SERVES 2

INGREDIENTS

80 ml (2½ fl oz/⅓ cup) olive oil
1 tablespoon white wine vinegar
1 tablespoon dijon mustard
1 teaspoon finely grated orange zest
24 raw prawns (shrimp), peeled and deveined, tails intact
1 small red onion, thinly sliced
2 avocados, sliced into wedges
2 mangoes, flesh cut into wedges
mixed salad leaves, such as cos (romaine), red oakleaf and butter lettuce

METHOD

1 To make the dressing combine the oil, vinegar, mustard and orange zest. Season with salt and freshly ground black pepper.
2 Preheat a barbecue grill or chargrill pan, brush the prawns with a little of the dressing and cook for 5 minutes. Transfer to a large bowl with the onion, avocado and mango.
3 Tear the lettuce into small pieces if necessary and add to the bowl. Pour in the dressing and toss lightly before serving.

GUACAMOLE

Guacamole is a Mexican dish made from ripe, mashed avocado, traditionally served as a dip with nachos, as a side dish or a sauce for tacos.

To make the guacamole, peel 1 ripe avocado and mash the flesh in a bowl. Add 1 chopped small onion, 1 finely chopped tomato, 2 tablespoons chopped coriander (cilantro), 2–3 tablespoons sour cream and 3–4 teaspoons lemon juice. Mix well with a fork. Add some salt, freshly ground black pepper and Tabasco sauce, to taste.

BABY SQUASH BAKED ON THE BARBECUE

SERVES 4

INGREDIENTS

- 12 yellow baby (pattypan) or 12 scallop squash
- 60 ml (2 fl oz/¼ cup) olive oil
- 1½ tablespoons crème fraîche
- 1 tablespoon orange juice
- ½ teaspoon finely grated orange zest
- 1 teaspoon chopped mint, plus 1 small handful mint leaves
- 1 small handful baby English spinach
- 1 small handful rocket (arugula)

METHOD

1. Preheat one burner of a covered barbecue to medium heat. Put the squash in a foil baking tray and toss with half the olive oil. Season with salt and pepper. Place the tray on a rack over the unlit burner in the barbecue, close the lid and bake by indirect heat for 30–35 minutes, or until tender. Alternatively, you can cook the squash in a preheated 180°C (350°F/Gas 4) oven.
2. Put the remaining oil, crème fraîche, orange juice, zest and chopped mint in a small bowl and mix until smooth. Season with salt and pepper.
3. Cut the squash in half and put in a bowl with the mint leaves, spinach and rocket. Toss with the dressing and serve immediately, while warm.

YELLOW CURRY WITH PUMPKIN AND BEANS

SERVES 4

INGREDIENTS

- 500 ml (17 fl oz/2 cups) tin coconut cream (do not shake the tin)
- 3 teaspoons yellow curry paste
- 125 ml (4 fl oz/½ cup) vegetable or chicken stock (page 10–11)
- 500 g (1 lb 2 oz) jap or kent pumpkin (squash), peeled and diced
- 300 g (10½ oz) green beans, halved
- 2 tablespoons soy sauce
- 2 tablespoons lime juice
- 1 tablespoon grated palm sugar (jaggery)
- 1 handful coriander (cilantro)
- 40 g (1½ oz/¼ cup) cashew nuts, toasted

METHOD

1. Spoon the thick coconut cream from the top of the tin into a wok, and heat until boiling. Add the curry paste, then reduce the heat and simmer, stirring, for 5 minutes, until the oil begins to separate. Add the remaining coconut cream, stock and pumpkin and simmer for 10 minutes. Add the beans and cook for a further 8 minutes, or until the vegetables are tender.
2. Gently stir in the soy sauce, lime juice and palm sugar. Garnish with the coriander and cashews.

SQUASH

Baby (pattypan) squash belong to the marrow family, which also includes pumpkins (winter squash), cucumbers, melons and gourds. Although they can be eaten raw, they are best enjoyed when cooked, as this makes their flesh soft and luscious. Abundant throughout summer, baby squash may be green or yellow and, like all summer squash, the skin is edible, which makes them good for baking and stewing.

PUMPKIN

This vegetable is a member of the gourd family classified as a winter squash, often with orange flesh and used in Halloween lanterns. Their flesh has a pronounced sweet flavour and is used in both sweet and savoury dishes. Pumpkins can be boiled, steamed, roasted or mashed. In some countries, all squashes are referred to as pumpkins; in others, only large round segmented ones (pictured).

If boiling pumpkin, remove the skin and seeds. If roasting larger pieces, the skin can be left intact for cooking. Choose pumpkins that are heavy for their size and have unblemished skins. Store whole at room temperature for around 1 month. Cover cut pumpkin with plastic wrap and store in the fridge.

POTATO AND PUMPKIN GRATIN

SERVES 4

INGREDIENTS

450 g (1 lb) all-purpose potatoes, peeled and thinly sliced
leaves from 3 large thyme or rosemary sprigs, finely chopped
700 g (1 lb 9 oz) pumpkin (winter squash), thinly sliced
1 large garlic clove, crushed
500 ml (17 fl oz/2 cups) cream

METHOD

1 Preheat the oven to 180°C (350°F/Gas 4). Lightly grease a 25 x 23 cm (10 x 9 inch) baking or gratin dish with a little butter. Arrange a layer of potato in the dish, season with salt, pepper and some of the herbs, then top with a layer of pumpkin. Continue the layers, finishing with pumpkin. Mix the garlic with the cream and pour over the top. Cover the dish with buttered foil and bake in the oven for about 45 minutes.

2 Test to see if the gratin is cooked by inserting a knife into the centre. If the slices seem soft, it is cooked. Remove the foil and increase the oven to 190°C (375°F/Gas 5). Cook for a further 15 minutes, or until golden on top. Leave to rest for 10 minutes before serving. Serve with grilled meats or on its own with a green salad.

ROAST PUMPKIN WITH SAGE

SERVES 4

INGREDIENTS

1 kg (2 lb 4 oz) pumpkin (winter squash), peeled and seeded
olive oil, to coat
2 tablespoons chopped sage, plus extra to garnish

METHOD

1 Preheat the oven to 220°C (425°C/Gas 7). Cut the pumpkin into small cubes and toss well in olive oil. Transfer to a baking dish, sprinkle the sage over the top and season well.

2 Bake for 20 minutes, or until lightly browned. Serve scattered with extra sage.

❮ STUFFED PUMPKINS

SERVES 4

INGREDIENTS

- 4 large golden nugget pumpkins (squash)
- 1 tablespoon olive oil
- 140 g (5 oz/⅔ cup) wild rice blend
- 30 g (1 oz) butter
- 1 onion, finely chopped
- 250 g (9 oz) orange sweet potato, peeled and cubed
- 4 spring onions (scallions), chopped
- 2 teaspoons ground cumin
- ½ teaspoon ground ginger
- 1 teaspoon ground coriander
- 1 teaspoon ground turmeric
- 1 teaspoon garam masala
- 2 tablespoons currants, soaked in hot water and drained
- 40 g (1½ oz/⅓ cup) grated cheddar cheese

METHOD

1. Preheat the oven to 180°C (350°F/Gas 4). Slice the top third off each pumpkin. Scoop out the seeds, leaving a deep cavity. Brush the pumpkins lightly with oil. Stand the pumpkins in an ovenproof dish. Pour in enough water to come halfway up the sides of the pumpkins. Put the lid on each, then bake for 20 minutes. Remove from the water bath and allow to cool.
2. Meanwhile, cook the rice in a large saucepan of boiling water for 25 minutes, or until tender. Drain and allow to cool.
3. Melt the butter in a frying pan over medium heat, then add the onion and sweet potato and cook, covered, for 5 minutes. Add the spring onion and cook, uncovered, for 1 minute. Stir in the spices and cook for 2 minutes, or until fragrant. Remove from the heat. Fold in the rice and currants.
4. Spoon the filling into the pumpkin cavities, then sprinkle with cheese. Put the lids on at an angle. Cover with foil, then put on a baking tray and bake for 20 minutes. Serve hot.

VEGETABLE TAGINE

SERVES 4–6

INGREDIENTS

- 2 tablespoons oil
- 2 onions, chopped
- 1 teaspoon ground ginger
- 2 teaspoons ground paprika
- 2 teaspoons ground cumin
- 1 cinnamon stick
- pinch of saffron threads
- 1.3 kg (3 lb) mixed vegetables (such as pumpkin, orange sweet potato, carrot, parsnip and potato), peeled and cut into large chunks
- ½ preserved lemon (page 668), rinsed, pith and flesh removed, zest thinly sliced
- 400 g (14 oz) tin peeled tomatoes
- 250 ml (9 fl oz/1 cup) vegetable stock (page 10)
- 100 g (3½ oz) dried pears, halved
- 50 g (1¾ oz) pitted prunes
- 2 zucchini (courgettes), cut into large chunks
- 300 g (10½ oz) couscous
- 1 handful parsley, chopped
- 50 g (1¾ oz/⅓ cup) almonds

METHOD

1. Preheat the oven to 180°C (350°F/Gas 4). Heat the oil in a large flameproof casserole dish or tagine, add the onion and cook for 5 minutes, until soft. Add the spices and cook for 3 minutes.
2. Add the vegetables and cook, stirring, until coated with the spices and until they begin to soften. Add the preserved lemon zest, tomatoes, stock, pears and prunes. Cover, transfer to the oven and cook for 30 minutes. Add the zucchini and cook for 15–20 minutes, until the vegetables are tender.
3. Prepare the couscous following the packet instructions (or see page 306).
4. Remove the cinnamon stick from the vegetables, then stir in the parsley. Serve on a platter with the couscous formed into a ring and the vegetable tagine in the centre, sprinkled with the almonds.

••FLOWERING VEGETABLES••

The most important edible flowers in cooking aren't what you may first think. Love them or loathe them, broccoli and cauliflower are actually immature flowers, and the artichoke is the large flower bud of a thistle, eaten before the flower has opened. Of course, some plants do produce edible flowers, such as geranium and rose, but these are not covered here.

CAULIFLOWER

Cauliflower is at its best in autumn. Choose those with compact, creamy white heads (known as curds) with no discolouration. They should smell fresh and have crispy green leaves with no sign of yellowing. Remove the leaves and store in the vegetable crisper in the fridge. Cauliflowers are usually creamy white, but there are also green and purple varieties, as well as miniature ones. Cauliflower can be eaten raw as crudités or steamed, boiled, stir-fried, pickled or used in soups.

COOKING TIPS

* Prepare florets or the whole cauliflower by soaking it in salted water to get rid of any bugs.
* Cook in a non-aluminium saucepan (aluminium reacts with cauliflower and can turn it yellow).
* Cauliflower can be steamed or boiled, but steaming keeps the florets intact. Cauliflower can also be roasted in a 180°C (350°F/Gas 4) oven. Lay the florets in a roasting tin, drizzle with olive oil and cook for 30 minutes, turning the cauliflower often, until cooked and golden.
* If cooking a whole cauliflower, cut a cross in the base of the stalk or cut out the core to help it cook evenly.
* Cauliflower contains a natural chemical that breaks down into a sulphur compound when cooked. To prevent this, add a bay leaf to the water and cook until just tender — the longer it cooks, the stronger the smell will become.

ACIDULATED WATER

White or pale-coloured vegetables and fruit, such as cauliflower, artichokes and apples, tend to darken when cut and exposed to air. To prevent this, put the cut vegetable or fruit in a bowl of water and add 1 tablespoon of lemon juice or white wine vinegar. This acidulates the water and prevents this from occurring.

VEGETABLE PAKORAS

MAKES ABOUT 20

INGREDIENTS

YOGHURT MINT DIP

250 g (9 oz/1 cup) Greek-style yoghurt
2 teaspoons ground cumin
2 teaspoons honey
3 tablespoons chopped mint

BESAN BATTER

120 g (4¼ oz) besan (chickpea flour)
85 g (3 oz/⅔ cup) self-raising flour
1½ teaspoons ground coriander
1 teaspoon chilli powder
1 teaspoon garam masala
1 teaspoon ground cumin
1 garlic clove, crushed
1 potato, peeled and diced
125 g (4½ oz) cauliflower, cut into small florets
125 g (4½ oz) broccoli, cut into small florets
125 g (4½ oz) slender eggplants (aubergines), diced
80 g (2¾ oz/½ cup) frozen peas, thawed
vegetable oil, for deep-frying

METHOD

1 To make the yoghurt mint dip, combine all the ingredients in a small bowl.
2 To make the batter, sift the flours and spices into a large bowl. Make a well in the centre, then gradually whisk in 310 ml (10¾ fl oz/1¼ cups) water along with the garlic. Season with salt. Set the batter aside while preparing the vegetables.
3 Par-boil the potato in boiling water for 3 minutes, or until half cooked. Drain and cool. Mix the potato, cauliflower, broccoli, eggplant and peas into the batter.
4 Fill a wok one-third full of oil and heat to 180°C (350°F), or until a cube of bread dropped into the oil turns golden brown in 15 seconds. Drop a few heaped tablespoonfuls of the batter mixture into the oil at a time, and cook until the pakoras are golden brown. Drain on paper towels. Serve hot with the yoghurt mint dip.

CAULIFLOWER CHEESE

SERVES 4–6

INGREDIENTS

500 g (1 lb 2 oz) cauliflower
30 g (1 oz) butter
3 teaspoons plain (all-purpose) flour
125 ml (4 fl oz/½ cup) milk
60 ml (2 fl oz/¼ cup) cream
40 g (1½ oz/⅓ cup) grated cheddar cheese
¼ teaspoon paprika
snipped chives, to serve

METHOD

1 Cut the cauliflower into large florets and steam or boil until just tender.
2 Meanwhile, melt the butter in a saucepan. Stir in the flour and cook for 1 minute. Remove from the heat and gradually stir in the combined milk and cream. Return to the heat and stir until the mixture boils and thickens. Remove from the heat and stir in half the grated cheese. Season with salt and pepper.
3 Put the drained cauliflower in a heatproof serving dish, spoon the cheese sauce over the top and sprinkle with the remaining cheese. Brown under a hot grill (broiler) for 3 minutes. Sprinkle with the paprika and chives before serving.

BROCCOLI

Broccoli and cauliflower are both good sources of vitamin C and minerals but broccoli is particularly high in many nutrients. It contains high levels of vitamin A as well as folate and potassium. Broccoli is also rich in carotene, and high intakes may provide protection against cancer and heart disease.

There are many varieties of broccoli, but the most common is the calabrese with green, densely packed heads. Other varieties may be purple, lime-green and white. Hybrid varieties such as broccolini are also available. Drain well before serving as the florets hold lots of water.

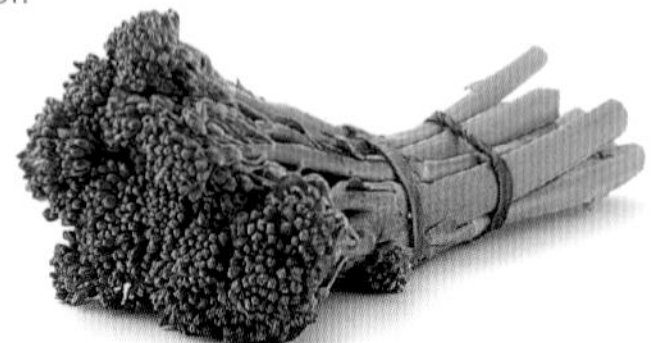

broccolini

common broccoli

BROCCOLI AND MUSHROOM STIR-FRY

SERVES 4

INGREDIENTS

- 1 tablespoon vegetable or peanut oil
- 1 red onion, cut into thin wedges
- 2 garlic cloves, crushed
- 1 tablespoon chilli jam (page 430)
- 150 g (5½ oz) snow peas (mangetout), topped and tailed, halved on the diagonal
- 200 g (7 oz) small broccoli florets
- 150 g (5½ oz) oyster mushrooms, larger ones halved
- 1 teaspoon sesame oil
- 2 tablespoons oyster sauce
- 2 tablespoons soya bean sauce
- 1 tablespoon Chinese rice wine

METHOD

1. Heat a wok over high heat, add the oil and swirl to coat. Stir-fry the onion for 2 minutes, or until softened. Add the garlic and chilli jam and cook for 30 seconds. Add the vegetables and stir-fry for a further 2 minutes.
2. Combine the sesame oil, oyster sauce, soya bean sauce and rice wine, add to the wok and stir-fry for 1–2 minutes to coat the vegetables in the sauce. Serve with rice or as a side dish.

ROASTED SPICY BROCCOLI

In a bowl, combine 1 tablespoon ground cumin, 1 tablespoon ground coriander, 5 crushed garlic cloves, 2 teaspoons chilli powder and 80 ml (2½ fl oz/⅓ cup) oil. Toss 800 g (1 lb 12 oz) broccoli florets through the oil. Spread out on a baking tray and roast in a 200°C (400°F/Gas 6) oven for 20 minutes, or until cooked through.

CAULIFLOWER, TOMATO AND GREEN PEA CURRY

SERVES 4–6

INGREDIENTS

- 1 small cauliflower
- 200 g (7 oz) broccoli
- 1 onion
- 2 large tomatoes
- 235 g (8½ oz/1½ cups) peas
- 60 ml (2 fl oz/¼ cup) ghee (page 120) or oil
- 1 teaspoon crushed garlic
- 1 teaspoon grated ginger
- ¾ teaspoon ground turmeric
- 1 tablespoon ground coriander
- 1 tablespoon vindaloo paste (page 439)
- 2 teaspoons sugar
- 2 cardamom pods, lightly crushed
- 185 g (6½ oz/¾ cup) plain yoghurt

METHOD

1. Cut the cauliflower and broccoli into small florets. Thinly slice the onion and cut the tomatoes into thin wedges. Steam the cauliflower, broccoli and peas until just tender.
2. Heat the ghee in a large saucepan and cook the onion, garlic and ginger over medium heat until soft and golden. Add the turmeric, coriander, vindaloo paste, sugar, cardamom pods and yoghurt and cook for 3–4 minutes. Add the tomatoes and cook for 3–4 minutes.
3. Add the cauliflower, broccoli and peas and simmer for 3–4 minutes. Serve with rice.

STIR-FRIED VEGETABLES

SERVES 4

INGREDIENTS

- 4 thin asparagus spears
- 4 baby sweet corn
- 50 g (1¾ oz) snake (yard-long) beans
- 115 g (4 oz) mixed red and yellow capsicums (peppers)
- ½ small carrot
- 50 g (1¾ oz) broccoli florets
- 25 g (1 oz) snow peas (mangetout), topped and tailed
- 2 cm (¾ inch) piece of ginger, thinly sliced
- 1 tablespoon fish sauce
- 1½ tablespoons oyster sauce
- 2 tablespoons vegetable stock or water
- ½ teaspoon sugar
- 1½ tablespoons vegetable oil
- 3–4 garlic cloves, finely chopped
- 2 spring onions (scallions), sliced

METHOD

1. Cut off the tips of the asparagus and slice each spear into 5 cm (2 inch) lengths. Cut the sweet corn into halves lengthways and the beans into 2.5 cm (1 inch) lengths. Cut both on an angle. Halve the capsicums and remove the seeds, then cut into bite-sized pieces. Peel the carrot and cut into batons.
2. Blanch the asparagus stalks, corn, beans and broccoli in boiling salted water for 30 seconds. Remove and place in a bowl of iced water. Drain and place in a bowl with the capsicum, carrot, snow peas, asparagus tips and ginger.
3. Mix the fish sauce, oyster sauce, stock and sugar in a small bowl.
4. Heat the oil in a wok and stir-fry the garlic over medium heat until light brown. Add the mixed vegetables and the sauce mixture, then stir-fry over high heat for 2–3 minutes. Taste, then adjust the seasoning if necessary. Add the spring onions and toss.

ARTICHOKES

The globe artichoke is a member of the thistle family. When young, it may be eaten whole, even raw in salads; a more mature bud may be stuffed, quartered, boiled or fried; and the large artichokes may be boiled and eaten one leaf at a time (suck or scrape the flesh off the fibrous base with your teeth), dipped into vinaigrette or hollandaise sauce. In all but the baby artichoke, you need to discard the prickly choke, above the fleshy (and delicious) base, known also as the heart. Choose heavy artichokes with firm heads and stems, and leaves that are tightly overlapping.

HOW TO... PREPARE ARTICHOKES

METHOD

1 Hold the artichoke head in one hand, snap off the stem and remove any tough fibres. Trim any spiky tops on the leaves with scissors. Using a stainless steel knife, cut away the top one-third of the globe.

2 Snap off the tough outer leaves until you reach the paler, tender ones. If you want to serve the artichoke whole and sitting flat, trim around the base of the artichoke; otherwise, trim the stems to about 4 cm (1½ inches) long and lightly peel them. Rub the cut surfaces with half a lemon to stop them turning brown. If the artichokes are to be served halved or quartered, slice them now and cut away the hairy choke with a knife.

3 If you aren't using the artichokes immediately, prepare a bowl of acidulated water by squeezing the juice from 1 lemon into a large glass bowl of cold water. As you finish preparing each artichoke, drop it into the acidulated water and put a plate on top to keep it submerged. Set aside for 10 minutes.

COOKING TIPS

* Rub the cut surfaces with lemon or vinegar and cut with a stainless steel knife to avoid staining the flesh.
* Wash your hands after handling the stem as it gives off a bitter flavour.
* Cook in stainless steel, glass or enamel pots, as aluminium pots can impart a metallic flavour and will discolour the artichoke.
* If serving cold, plunge artichokes in iced water for 3 minutes to stop the cooking process, then drain them upside down.
* If frying artichokes, first boil them in a blanc (boiling water with a little flour and lemon juice mixed in) so they keep their colour.
* Artichokes contain cynarin, which makes everything you eat or drink with, or after, them taste sweet. This makes artichokes difficult to match with wine.

ARTICHOKES VINAIGRETTE

SERVES 4

INGREDIENTS

4 globe artichokes
juice of 1 lemon

VINAIGRETTE

100 ml (3½ fl oz) olive oil
2 spring onions (scallions), finely chopped
2 tablespoons white wine
2 tablespoons white wine vinegar
¼ teaspoon dijon mustard
pinch of sugar
1 tablespoon finely chopped parsley

METHOD

1 Prepare the artichokes, leaving them whole (steps 1–2, opposite). Bring a large pan of salted water to the boil and add the lemon juice. Add the artichokes and put a small plate on top of them to keep them submerged. Cook at a simmer for 20–25 minutes, or until a leaf from the base comes away easily. (The base will be tender when pierced with a skewer.) Cool quickly under cold running water, then drain upside down.
2 To make the vinaigrette, heat 1 tablespoon of the oil in a small saucepan, add the spring onion and cook over low heat for 2 minutes. Leave to cool a little, then add the wine, vinegar, mustard and sugar and gradually whisk in the remaining oil. Season with sea salt and freshly ground black pepper and stir in half the parsley.
3 Put an artichoke on each plate and gently prise it open a little. Spoon some dressing over the top and pour the rest into a small bowl. Sprinkle each artichoke with a little parsley.
4 Eat the leaves one by one, dipping them in the vinaigrette and scraping the flesh off the leaves between your teeth. When you reach the middle, pull off any small leaves and then use a teaspoon to remove the furry choke — you can eat the tender base or 'heart' of the artichoke.

WARM ARTICHOKE SALAD

SERVES 4

INGREDIENTS

8 young globe artichokes (200 g/7 oz each)
1 lemon
25 g (1 oz/½ cup) shredded basil
50 g (1¾ oz/½ cup) shaved parmesan cheese

DRESSING

1 garlic clove, finely chopped
½ teaspoon sugar
1 teaspoon dijon mustard
2 teaspoons finely chopped lemon zest
60 ml (2 fl oz/¼ cup) lemon juice
80 ml (2½ fl oz/⅓ cup) extra virgin olive oil

METHOD

1 Prepare the artichokes, trimming the stems to about 4 cm (1½ inches) long. Cut each artichoke in half lengthways and remove the hairy choke. Rub the artichokes with lemon while you work and place the prepared artichokes in a bowl of acidulated water to prevent them turning brown (steps 1–3 opposite).
2 Bring a large saucepan of salted water to the boil. Add the artichokes and put a small plate on top of them to keep them submerged. Cook at a simmer for 20–25 minutes, or until a leaf from the base comes away easily. (The base will be tender when pierced with a skewer.) Drain and cut in half again to serve.
3 To make the dressing, mix the garlic, sugar, mustard, lemon zest and juice in a jug. Season with salt and freshly ground black pepper, then whisk in the oil until combined. Pour the dressing over the artichokes and sprinkle with the basil and parmesan.

••LEAFY VEGETABLES••

No summer salad would be complete without a bowl brimming with fresh, crisp salad leaves, dressed simply with a vinaigrette or served with an array of other vegetables. We usually eat them raw in salads or use them as wrappers or containers for fillings, but some leafy greens are usually cooked, such as cabbage and brussels sprouts.

LETTUCE

Lettuce is mainly used fresh in salads or sandwiches but can also be cooked. In a green salad, lettuces are generally interchangeable, but when adding other ingredients, pick a leaf type that will suit them — floppy leaves won't go well with heavy ingredients like potatoes, and crisp firm leaves need a fairly robust dressing. For a mixed salad, you need a good combination of textures and flavours.

There are many varieties now available, and they can be divided into four categories.

CRISPHEAD OR ROUND

Generally round lettuces, consisting of tightly packed layers of crisp leaves, including the iceberg — so named because the heads were packed in boxes and covered with ice for transport and said to resemble icebergs. Other varieties include the webb, imperial, western and vanguard lettuces.

BUTTERHEAD

This has a mild buttery flavour, with smaller, looser heads than crisphead lettuces. Other varieties include: butter lettuce, with its soft, pale green leaves; mignonette, with curly, reddish–purple tinged dark green leaves; and the bibbs and boston, popular in the United States.

COS (ROMAINE)

Named after the Greek island of Cos, this lettuce has narrow, upright, elongated, deep green leaves and a sweet, crisp, almost nutty flavour. Very young, tender-hearted versions, sold as 'baby cos' or 'little gems', are also available.

LOOSE-LEAF

Distinguished by the fact that they do not form a distinct heart or head, this group includes the slightly bitter lollo rosso (red leaves), lollo biondo (frilly leaves) and the oakleaf (feuille de chêne).

MESCLUN

A mixture of young salad leaves and herbs, a typical mesclun may include rocket (arugula) and dandelion leaves, curly endive and chervil. It is seasoned with a vinaigrette of olive oil, fines herbes and garlic. The aim of a mesclun salad is to provide a contrast of both flavour and textures by combining mild and bitter tastes and soft and crunchy textures. In Provence, mesclun is served with small baked goat's milk cheeses, pieces of bacon, croutons, or chicken livers fried in butter. The word 'mesclun' is derived from the Nice dialect *mesclumo*, meaning 'mixture'.

WALDORF SALAD

SERVES 4

INGREDIENTS

lettuce leaves, to serve
2 red apples, quartered and cored
1 large green apple, quartered and cored
1½ celery stalks, sliced
25 g (1 oz/¼ cup) halved walnuts
2 tablespoons egg mayonnaise
1 tablespoon sour cream

METHOD

1 Line a serving bowl with lettuce leaves. Cut the apples into 2 cm (¾ inch) chunks and place in a large mixing bowl with the celery and walnuts.
2 In a small bowl, combine the mayonnaise and sour cream and mix well. Fold the dressing through the apple, celery and walnut mixture, then transfer to the lettuce-lined serving bowl and serve immediately.

SALAD LYONNAISE

SERVES 4

INGREDIENTS

- 1 garlic clove, cut in half
- oil, for shallow-frying
- 4 slices white bread, crusts removed, cut into cubes
- 60 ml (2 fl oz/¼ cup) olive oil
- 2 spring onions (scallions), chopped
- 3 slices bacon, cut into short strips
- 80 ml (2½ fl oz/⅓ cup) red wine vinegar
- 3 teaspoons wholegrain mustard
- 225 g (8 oz) frisée (endive), lamb's lettuce (corn salad) and dandelion leaves
- 4 poached eggs

METHOD

1. Rub the cut garlic over the base of a frying pan. Pour about 1 cm (½ inch) of oil into the pan and fry the bread cubes for 1–2 minutes, until golden. Drain on paper towels. Wipe out the pan.
2. Heat the olive oil in the frying pan and cook the spring onion and bacon for 2 minutes. Add the vinegar and mustard and boil for 2 minutes to reduce by a third. Pour over the salad leaves and toss to wilt a little. Arrange on plates.
3. Place the poached eggs on the leaves and sprinkle with the croutons. Serve immediately.

SALAD NICOISE

SERVES 4

INGREDIENTS

- 2 vine-ripened tomatoes
- 175 g (6 oz) baby green beans, trimmed
- 125 ml (4 fl oz/½ cup) olive oil
- 2 tablespoons white wine vinegar
- 1 large garlic clove, halved
- 325 g (11½ oz) iceberg lettuce heart, cut into 8 wedges
- 3 hard-boiled eggs
- 1 small red capsicum (pepper), thinly sliced
- 1 Lebanese (short) cucumber, cut into thin 5 cm (2 inch) lengths
- 1 celery stalk, cut into thin 5 cm (2 inch) lengths
- ¼ large red onion, thinly sliced
- 375 g (13 oz) tin tuna, drained and broken into chunks
- 12 kalamata olives
- 45 g (1½ oz) tinned anchovy fillets, drained
- 2 teaspoons capers, rinsed and squeezed dry
- 12 small basil leaves

METHOD

1. To peel the tomatoes, score a cross in the base of each tomato. Plunge into boiling water for 20 seconds, then drain and peel the skin away from the cross. Cut each tomato into eight pieces. Cook the beans in a saucepan of boiling water for 2 minutes, or until just tender. Rinse under cold water, then drain.
2. To make the dressing, whisk together the olive oil and vinegar.
3. Rub the garlic over the base of a platter. Arrange the lettuce wedges over the platter. Cut each egg into quarters and layer the egg, tomato, beans, capsicum, cucumber and celery over the lettuce. Scatter the onion and tuna over them, then the olives, anchovies, capers and basil. Drizzle with the dressing and serve.

WATERCRESS AND WALNUT SALAD

SERVES 4–6

INGREDIENTS

500 g (1 lb 2 oz) watercress, leaves picked
3 celery stalks
1 cucumber
3 oranges
1 red onion, thinly sliced and separated into rings
35 g (1¼ oz/¾ cup) snipped chives
60 g (2¼ oz/½ cup) chopped walnuts or pecans

DRESSING

60 ml (2 fl oz/¼ cup) olive oil
60 ml (2 fl oz/¼ cup) lemon juice
2 teaspoons finely grated orange zest
1 teaspoon wholegrain mustard
1 tablespoon honey

METHOD

1. To make the salad, wash and drain all the vegetables. Break the watercress into small sprigs, discarding the coarser stems. Cut the celery into thin 5 cm (2 inch) long sticks. Peel, halve and seed the cucumber and cut into thin slices. Peel the oranges, remove all the white pith and cut the oranges into segments between the membrane. Refrigerate until needed.
2. To make the dressing, combine the olive oil, lemon juice, orange zest, mustard and honey in a screw-top jar. Season with freshly ground black pepper. Shake vigorously to combine well.
3. Combine all the salad ingredients, except the nuts, in a serving bowl. Pour the dressing over and toss. Sprinkle with the nuts and serve.

CAESAR SALAD

SERVES 4

INGREDIENTS

4 slices white bread, crusts removed, cubed
3 slices bacon, chopped
1 cos (romaine) lettuce
60 g (2¼ oz) shaved parmesan cheese, plus extra to serve

DRESSING

2–4 tinned anchovies, chopped
1 egg
2 tablespoons lemon juice
1 garlic clove, crushed
125 ml (4 fl oz/½ cup) olive oil

METHOD

1. Preheat the oven to 190°C (375°F/Gas 5). Spread the bread cubes on a baking tray in a single layer and bake for 15 minutes, or until golden. Fry the bacon in a frying pan until crisp, then drain on paper towels.
2. Tear the lettuce leaves into pieces and put in a bowl with the croutons, bacon and parmesan.
3. To make the dressing, whisk together the anchovies, egg, lemon juice and garlic until smooth. Start whisking in the oil, drop by drop at first, then in a thin stream, until the dressing is thick and creamy. Drizzle over the salad, sprinkle with extra parmesan and serve.

SAN CHOY BAU

SERVES 6

INGREDIENTS

- 12 soft lettuce leaves, such as iceberg lettuce
- 250 g (9 oz) boneless, skinless chicken breasts
- 450 g (1 lb) centre-cut pork loin, trimmed
- 80 ml (2½ fl oz/⅓ cup) light soy sauce
- 60 ml (2 fl oz/¼ cup) Chinese rice wine
- 2 teaspoons sesame oil
- 8 dried Chinese mushrooms
- 240 g (8½ oz) peeled water chestnuts
- 125 ml (4 fl oz/½ cup) oil
- 1 celery stalk, thinly sliced
- 2 spring onions (scallions), finely chopped
- 2 tablespoons finely chopped ginger
- 1 teaspoon sugar
- 1 teaspoon cornflour (cornstarch)

METHOD

1. Rinse the lettuce and separate the leaves. Drain thoroughly, then arrange the leaves in a basket or on a platter.
2. Put the chicken in a food processor and process until minced (ground), or chop very finely with a sharp knife. Mince the pork to the same size as the chicken. Put the chicken and pork in a bowl with 2 tablespoons of the soy sauce, 1½ tablespoons of the rice wine and 1 teaspoon of the sesame oil, and toss lightly. Marinate in the fridge for 20 minutes.
3. Soak the dried mushrooms in boiling water for 30 minutes, then drain and squeeze out the water. Discard the stems and chop the caps. Blanch the water chestnuts in a pan of boiling water for 1 minute, then refresh in cold water. Drain, pat dry and roughly chop them.
4. Heat a wok over high heat, add half the oil and heat until very hot. Stir-fry the meat mixture, mashing and separating the pieces, until browned. Remove and drain. Reheat the wok, add the remaining oil and heat until very hot. Stir-fry the celery, spring onion and ginger for 10 seconds, until fragrant. Add the mushrooms and stir-fry for 5 seconds, then add the water chestnuts and stir-fry for 15 seconds, or until heated through. Add the remaining soy sauce, rice wine and sesame oil with 1 teaspoon salt, sugar, cornflour and 125 ml (4 fl oz/½ cup) water. Stir-fry, stirring constantly, until thickened. Add the cooked meat mixture and toss lightly.
5. To serve, place some of the stir-fried meat in a lettuce leaf, roll up and eat.

NOTE: Traditionally, this Chinese recipe is made using squab or pigeon breast meat.

CHINESE RICE WINE

Made from rice, millet and yeast in the Chinese province of Shaoxing, this is a fermented rice wine with a rich, sweetish taste, similar to sherry. Chinese rice wine, or Shaoxing rice wine as it is also known, is used in Asian cooking in stir-fries and meat dishes. In China, good-quality rice wine is served warm as a drink in small cups. If Chinese rice wine is unavailable, dry sherry is the best substitute.

GADO GADO

SERVES 4

INGREDIENTS

- 4 small potatoes
- 2 small carrots, thinly sliced
- 100 g (3½ oz) cauliflower, cut into small florets
- 60 g (2¼ oz) snow peas (mangetout), trimmed
- 100 g (3½ oz) bean sprouts
- 8 well-shaped iceberg lettuce leaves
- 1 Lebanese (short) cucumber, thinly sliced
- 2 hard-boiled eggs, cut into quarters
- 2 tomatoes, cut into wedges

PEANUT SAUCE

- 1 tablespoon oil
- 1 small onion, finely chopped
- 125 g (4½ oz/½ cup) crunchy peanut butter
- 185 ml (6 fl oz/¾ cup) coconut milk
- 1 teaspoon sambal oelek (see Note)
- 1 tablespoon lemon juice
- 1 tablespoon kecap manis

METHOD

1. Boil or steam the potato until just tender. Drain and leave to cool, then cut into thin slices. Boil the carrots and cauliflower for 3 minutes, or until nearly tender. Add the snow peas and cook for 2 minutes, then add the bean sprouts and cook for a further 1 minute. Drain and leave the vegetables to cool.
2. To make the peanut sauce, heat the oil in a saucepan over low heat and cook the onion for 5 minutes, or until soft and lightly golden. Add the peanut butter, coconut milk, sambal oelek, lemon juice, kecap manis and 60 ml (2 fl oz/¼ cup) water and stir well. Bring to the boil, stirring constantly, then reduce the heat and simmer for 5 minutes, or until the sauce has reduced and thickened. Remove from the heat.
3. Place two lettuce leaves together (one inside the other) to make 4 lettuce cups.
4. In each lettuce cup, arrange a quarter of the potato, carrot, cauliflower, snow peas, bean sprouts and cucumber. Top with some of the peanut sauce, and garnish with the egg quarters and tomato.

NOTE: Hot chilli paste, sambal oelek, is used as a relish in Malaysian and Indonesian cooking. It is made with chillies ground with salt and either vinegar or tamarind. For vegetarian cooking, check the brand you buy does not contain shrimp paste.

RADICCHIO WITH FIGS AND GINGER VINAIGRETTE

SERVES 4

INGREDIENTS

1 head radicchio
1 baby frisée (curly endive)
3 oranges or mandarins
½ small red onion, thinly sliced into rings
8 small green figs, cut into quarters
60 ml (2 fl oz/¼ cup) extra virgin olive oil
1 teaspoon red wine vinegar
pinch of ground cinnamon
2 tablespoons orange juice
2 tablespoons very finely chopped glacé ginger, plus 2 teaspoons syrup

METHOD

1 Wash the radicchio and frisée leaves thoroughly and drain well. Tear any large leaves into bite-sized pieces and toss in a salad bowl.
2 Peel and segment the oranges, discarding all the bitter white pith. Add to the salad leaves with the onion and 8 of the fig quarters, reserving the remaining fig quarters.
3 Whisk the oil, vinegar, cinnamon, orange juice, ginger and ginger syrup in a small jug. Season well, pour over the salad and toss. Arrange the reserved figs in pairs over the salad and serve.

BAKED RADICCHIO

SERVES 4

INGREDIENTS

1 kg (2 lb 4 oz) radicchio
2 tablespoons olive oil
100 g (3½ oz) bacon, thinly sliced

METHOD

1 Preheat the oven to 180°C (350°F/Gas 4). Remove the outer leaves of the radicchio and split the heads into four wedges.
2 Heat the olive oil in a flameproof casserole dish large enough to fit all the radicchio in a single layer (but do not add the radicchio yet). Add the bacon to the dish and cook over medium heat until the fat has just melted but the meat is not crisp. Add the radicchio to the dish and turn it over to coat it well.
3 Transfer to the oven and bake, covered, for 25–30 minutes, or until the radicchio are tender when pierced with a knife, turning them occasionally. Season and transfer to a warm dish with all the liquid. Serve immediately.

ROCKET

Called *rucola* in Italian, *roquette* in French, or arugula in America, rocket is a slightly bitter salad leaf with a nutty, peppery flavour. Younger leaves are milder than the mature, which can get quite hot. Rocket is used mainly as a salad ingredient, most notably in the Italian dish that simply combines rocket and shaved parmesan cheese. It can be used as a pizza topping or added to soups. Rocket is best used on the day of purchase, as it wilts quickly but will keep in the fridge wrapped in plastic for up to 2 days.

To make a rocket and parmesan salad, put 2 bunches of washed and dried rocket in a serving dish. Mix 80 ml (2½ fl oz/⅓ cup) olive oil with 1 tablespoon balsamic vinegar. Pour over the rocket and mix well. Scatter shaved parmesan cheese over the rocket and sprinkle with a little coarse salt and pepper. Serves 4

CHICORY

Not one but a group of leafy vegetables cultivated from European wild chicory, all of which share differing degrees of bitterness. They vary from long-leafed varieties through the various radicchios to the witlof types, which are tightly curled and usually blanched (grown in the dark) to control the bitterness.

TYPES OF CHICORY

CHICORY

Also known as Belgian endive, Brussels chicory or witlof, this is a blanched, tightly furled spear-shaped chicon (chicory head). It is slightly bitter and eaten raw or cooked. Buy pale chicory as green chicory will be bitter. Chicory is sensitive to light, which turns them bitter when exposed to it.

RADICCHIO

This is the Italian name for red chicory. There are several varieties, but two of the most common are rosso di Verona, a pink, flower-like chicory that looks similar to a round cabbage and is usually called radicchio in other countries, and rossa di Treviso, deep red and creamy streaked and usually called red chicory elsewhere.

FRISEE

Also called curly endive, frisée has loose, feathery leaves and a slightly bitter flavour. Frisée bulks up salads well.

ESCAROLE

Escarole has a head of loose or red-tinged leaves. It is the least bitter tasting type of chicory.

FRISEE AND GARLIC CROUTON SALAD

SERVES 4–6

INGREDIENTS

VINAIGRETTE

1 French shallot, finely chopped
1 tablespoon dijon mustard
60 ml (2 fl oz/¼ cup) tarragon vinegar
170 ml (5½ fl oz/⅔ cup) extra virgin olive oil

1 tablespoon olive oil
½ bread stick, sliced
4 whole garlic cloves
1 baby frisée (curly endive), washed and dried
100 g (3½ oz/1 cup) walnuts, toasted
100 g (3½ oz/⅔ cup) crumbled feta cheese

METHOD

1. To make the vinaigrette, whisk together the shallot, mustard and vinegar. Slowly add the oil, whisking constantly until thickened. Set aside.
2. Heat the olive oil in a large frying pan, add the bread and garlic cloves and cook over medium–high heat for 5–8 minutes, until the bread is crisp. Remove the garlic from the pan. Once the bread is cool, break into small pieces.
3. Place the frisée, croutons, walnuts, feta cheese and vinaigrette in a large bowl. Toss together well and serve.

SPINACH

Spinach is a green leafy plant with slender stems. The young leaves are used in salads; the older ones are cooked. Use within 1 to 2 days and store with the roots attached in the fridge in a plastic bag. Spinach contains iron and vitamins A and C, but also oxalic acid, which is responsible for its slightly bitter taste, and which acts as an inhibitor to the body's ability to absorb calcium and iron. This knowledge has somewhat diminished its famous 'Popeye' reputation.

New Zealand spinach (or Warrigal greens), though not botanically related, is an Australian and New Zealand native, fleshy leaved vegetable with tough leaves that looks and tastes similar. Silverbeet, or Swiss chard or chard, has large, thick leaves that are crinkled, with pronounced white veins and thick white stems. It is actually a form of beet leaf.

COOKING TIPS

* Cook spinach in the minimum of water — the water that is left on the leaves after washing is often enough to cook them.
* Steam or cook spinach in a covered saucepan.
* Spinach that is to be added to dishes needs to be squeezed dry. This is best done by pressing it between two plates.

SORREL

Sorrel is a leafy green plant that grows wild in northern Asia and Europe. There are many species, including common sorrel and the round-leaved (French) sorrel. Sorrel has large, spinach-like leaves that have a lemony acidic, slightly bitter taste, due to the presence of oxalic acid. Use sorrel in a mixed green salad or cook it like spinach. Sorrel is also made into soups or used as a flavouring herb in omelettes.

BUBBLE AND SQUEAK

SERVES 4

INGREDIENTS

- 750 g (1 lb 10 oz) floury potatoes
- 125 ml (4 fl oz/½ cup) milk
- 90 g (3¼ oz) butter
- 450 g (1 lb) green vegetables, such as English spinach, cabbage, leek or brussels sprouts, thinly sliced

METHOD

1 Cut the potatoes into even-sized pieces and put them in a saucepan of cold water. Bring to the boil, then lower the heat and simmer until tender — do not boil or the potatoes may break up and absorb water before they cook. Drain thoroughly.

2 Heat the milk in the pan. Return the potatoes to the pan and half the butter, then mash with a fork until the potato is smooth and creamy.

3 Melt half of the remaining butter in a large heavy-based frying pan with a heatproof handle, and cook the green vegetables until they are tender and cooked through. Add them to the potato and mix together. Season with salt and freshly ground black pepper.

4 Melt the remaining butter in the frying pan and spoon in the potato mixture, smoothing off the top. Cook until the bottom is browned and crispy. Remove the pan from the heat and place it under a preheated grill (broiler) and cook until the top is browned and golden. If you prefer, you can turn the bubble and squeak over in the pan and cook it on the other side, but grilling is easier. Serve as a meal by itself or as an accompaniment to poached eggs.

VEGETABLE TORTE

SERVES 4

INGREDIENTS

- 150 g (5½ oz) asparagus
- 80 ml (2½ fl oz/⅓ cup) olive oil
- 1 onion, chopped
- 1 zucchini (courgette), halved lengthways and thinly sliced
- 2 garlic cloves, chopped
- 100 g (3½ oz) English spinach or silverbeet, stalks removed if necessary, roughly chopped
- 2 tablespoons chopped basil
- 75 g (2½ oz/¾ cup) grated parmesan cheese
- 250 g (9 oz) ricotta cheese
- 250 g (9 oz) mascarpone cheese
- 6 eggs

METHOD

1. Wash the asparagus and remove the woody ends (hold each spear at both ends and bend it gently — it will snap at its natural breaking point). Remove the spear tips of the asparagus and slice the remaining stems. Bring a small saucepan of salted water to the boil and cook the asparagus stems for about 2 minutes. Add the tips and cook for a further 1 minute. Drain the asparagus and set aside.
2. Preheat the oven to 180°C (350°F/Gas 4). Heat the olive oil in a saucepan over medium heat and cook the onion until soft. Increase the heat and add the zucchini. Cook until the zucchini is soft and a little golden brown, stirring occasionally. Add the garlic and cook for 1 minute. Add the spinach and mix briefly until just wilted and cooked.
3. Remove the pan from the heat, add the asparagus and basil, season with salt and pepper and set aside to cool.
4. Grease a 20 cm (8 inch) spring-form cake tin with butter and dust with a tablespoon of the parmesan. Mix the ricotta, mascarpone, eggs and most of the parmesan into the cooled vegetables, and taste for seasoning.
5. Spoon into the tin and scatter with the remaining parmesan. Place the tin on a tray (to catch any drips) and bake for 50–60 minutes. The top should be a light golden brown and the mixture should still wobble slightly in the centre. Cool for 30 minutes, then chill in the fridge for 3 hours, or until the torte has set.

NOTE: The torte needs to be refrigerated for 3 hours before serving, to give it time to firm up, so it is easy enough to prepare it a day in advance and serve chilled. If so, use only 4 eggs and reduce the cooking time to about 40 minutes.

CREAMED SPINACH

SERVES 4–6

INGREDIENTS

- 1.5 kg (3 lb 5 oz) English spinach
- 10 g (¼ oz) butter
- 1 garlic clove, crushed
- ¼ teaspoon ground nutmeg
- 80 ml (2½ fl oz/⅓ cup) cream
- 1 tablespoon grated parmesan cheese

METHOD

1. Remove the tough ends from the spinach stalks and wash the leaves well. Shake to remove any excess water from the leaves, but do not dry.
2. Melt the butter in a large frying pan. Add the garlic and spinach, season with nutmeg, salt and pepper, and cook over medium heat until the spinach is just wilted. Remove from the heat and place the spinach in a sieve. Press down to squeeze out all of the excess moisture. Transfer the drained spinach to a chopping board and finely chop.
3. Pour the cream into the frying pan and heat gently. Add the spinach to the pan and stir until warmed through. Arrange the spinach on a serving dish and sprinkle with the parmesan.

CABBAGE ROLLS

MAKES 12 LARGE ROLLS

INGREDIENTS

1 tablespoon olive oil
1 onion, finely chopped
large pinch of allspice
1 teaspoon ground cumin
large pinch of ground nutmeg
2 bay leaves
1 large head of cabbage
500 g (1 lb 2 oz) minced (ground) lamb
250 g (9 oz) short-grain white rice
4 garlic cloves, crushed
50 g (1¾ oz/⅓ cup) pine nuts, toasted
2 tablespoons chopped mint
2 tablespoons chopped parsley
1 tablespoon chopped currants
250 ml (9 fl oz/1 cup) olive oil, extra
80 ml (2½ fl oz/⅓ cup) lemon juice
extra virgin olive oil, to drizzle
lemon wedges, to serve

METHOD

1 Heat the oil in a saucepan, add the onion and cook over medium heat for 10 minutes, or until golden. Add the allspice, cumin and nutmeg, and cook for 2 minutes, or until fragrant. Remove from the pan.

2 Bring a very large saucepan of water to the boil and add the bay leaves. Cut the tough outer leaves and about 5 cm (2 inches) of the core from the cabbage, then carefully add the cabbage to the boiling water. Cook it for 5 minutes, then carefully loosen a whole leaf with tongs and remove. Continue to cook and remove the leaves until you reach the core. Drain, reserving the cooking liquid and set aside to cool.

3 Take 12 leaves of equal size and cut a small 'V' from the core end of each to remove the thickest part. Trim the firm central veins so the leaf is as flat as possible. Place three-quarters of the remaining leaves on the base of a very large saucepan to prevent the rolls catching.

4 Combine the lamb, onion mixture, rice, garlic, pine nuts, mint, parsley and currants in a bowl and season well. With the core end of the leaf closest to you, form 2 tablespoons of the mixture into an oval and place in the centre of the leaf. Roll up, tucking in the sides. Repeat with the remaining 11 leaves and filling. Place tightly, in a single layer, in the lined saucepan, seam side down.

5 Combine 625 ml (21 fl oz/2½ cups) of the cooking liquid with the extra olive oil, lemon juice and 1 teaspoon salt, and pour over the rolls (the liquid should just come to the top of the rolls). Lay the remaining cabbage leaves over the top. Cover and bring to the boil over high heat, then reduce the heat and simmer for 1¼ hours, or until the lamb and rice are cooked. Carefully remove from the pan with a slotted spoon, place on serving plates and drizzle with extra virgin olive oil. Serve with lemon wedges.

CLASSIC COLESLAW

SERVES 4

INGREDIENTS

½ small green cabbage
¼ small red cabbage
2 carrots, coarsely grated
4 radishes, coarsely grated
½ red capsicum (pepper), chopped
3 spring onions (scallions), sliced
3 tablespoons chopped parsley
160 g (5½ oz/⅔ cup) egg mayonnaise

METHOD

1 Remove the hard core from the cabbages and shred the leaves with a sharp knife. Toss in a large bowl and add the carrot, radish, capsicum, spring onion and parsley. Refrigerate until ready to serve.
2 Just before serving, add the mayonnaise, season to taste with sea salt and freshly ground black pepper, and toss until well combined.

BRUSSELS SPROUTS AND CHESTNUTS

SERVES 8

INGREDIENTS

500 g (1 lb 2 oz) fresh chestnuts or
240 g (8½ oz) tinned chestnuts
1 kg (2 lb 4 oz) brussels sprouts
30 g (1 oz) butter
pinch of ground nutmeg

METHOD

1 To prepare the fresh chestnuts, make slits in the skins and put them in a saucepan. Cover with cold water and bring to the boil over high heat. Reduce the heat and simmer for 10 minutes. Drain and leave until cool enough to handle. Peel off the skins.
2 Trim the sprouts and cut a cross in the base of each. Bring a saucepan of water to the boil, add the sprouts and simmer for 5–8 minutes, or until just tender. Melt the butter in a large frying pan and add the chestnuts. Cook until they begin to brown, then add the sprouts and toss together until heated through. Season well with salt, pepper and nutmeg.

BRUSSELS SPROUTS

A member of the cabbage family, brussels sprouts were first cultivated in Flanders, near Brussels. When buying sprouts, choose smaller ones as they are more tender and tastier. Brussels sprouts can be steamed or boiled, or shredded and used in a stir-fry. To boil them, remove the outer leaves and soak in salted water for a few minutes to remove any bugs. Cooking in lots of boiling water with the lid off helps them to stay green.

For a quick side dish, fry 400 g (14 oz) shredded brussels sprouts in a little oil until tender. Add 4 finely chopped bacon slices and fry together until crisp. To serve, season with pepper and sprinkle a few chopped almonds over the top. Serves 4

••SEEDS AND PODS••

Springtime heralds the arrival of a bounty of vegetables — plump pods of sweet green beans and peas, and cobs of sweet corn wrapped in their papery husks. Left to linger in the fridge, most will lose their sweetness, so buy a day or two before you want to use them.

TYPES OF BEANS

broad beans

BROAD (FAVA) BEANS

Very young broad beans can be eaten in their pods like snow peas, but as they get older, the pods become tougher and the beans inside develop a grey, leathery skin. Generally though, broad beans need to be removed from their pods before cooking and should also be double podded to remove the grey skins. To do this, blanch them for a couple of minutes, drain and cool under cold running water, then slip off the skins. When buying fresh broad beans, remember that most of the weight is the pods, which you will be throwing away. (1 kg/2 lb broad beans will give you about 300 g/10½ oz of podded beans.) Frozen broad beans are also available.

runner beans

RUNNER BEANS

These flat beans should snap crisply when fresh, and most need to be stringed down each side unless they are very young. Though it is common to chop or slice the beans before cooking, this will cause most of the nutrients to leach out during cooking.

snake beans

SNAKE (YARD-LONG) BEANS

These long beans are like green beans and are generally sold in bundles. Make sure any swellings in the pods are small — this will mean the beans are young and fresh.

green beans

GREEN BEANS (FRENCH BEANS OR STRING BEANS)

These are usually fine, thin green beans, but they are also available in yellow waxy pods, purple or cream pods, and green and purple pods. Make sure the pods snap crisply when you buy them.

borlotti beans

BORLOTTI (CRANBERRY) BEANS

Available dried or fresh, borlotti beans have distinguishable cream and red pods with beans the same colour. Borlotti beans are popular in Italy, where they are mainly used in soups or stewed with olive oil and garlic as a side dish.

BROAD BEANS WITH HAM

SERVES 4

INGREDIENTS

- 20 g (¾ oz) butter
- 1 onion, chopped
- 180 g (6½ oz) serrano ham, roughly chopped (see Note)
- 2 garlic cloves, crushed
- 500 g (1 lb 2 oz) broad (fava) beans, fresh or frozen
- 125 ml (4 fl oz/½ cup) dry white wine
- 185 ml (6 fl oz/¾ cup) chicken stock (page 11)

METHOD

1 Melt the butter in a large saucepan and add the onion, ham and garlic. Cook over medium heat for about 5 minutes, stirring often, until the onion is soft.

2 Add the broad beans and wine and cook over high heat until reduced by half. Add the stock, reduce the heat, then cover and cook for 10 minutes. Uncover and simmer for another 10 minutes. Serve hot as a vegetable accompaniment to meat, or warm as a snack with crusty bread.

NOTE: Instead of serrano ham, you can use thickly sliced prosciutto.

STIR-FRIED SNAKE BEANS WITH BASIL AND CHILLI

SERVES 4

INGREDIENTS

- 60 ml (2 fl oz/¼ cup) soy sauce
- 60 ml (2 fl oz/¼ cup) vegetable or chicken stock (page 10–11)
- 2 tablespoons vegetable oil
- 1 teaspoon red curry paste
- 1 red Asian shallot, finely chopped
- 3 garlic cloves, thinly sliced
- 1 small red chilli, seeded and sliced
- 500 g (1 lb 2 oz) snake (yard-long) beans, cut into 8 cm (3¼ inch) lengths on the diagonal
- 1 large handful Thai basil

METHOD

1 Combine the soy sauce, stock and 60 ml (2 fl oz/¼ cup) water and set aside.

2 Heat a wok over high heat, add the oil, red curry paste, shallot, garlic and chilli and stir-fry until fragrant. Add the snake beans and cook for 5 minutes. Stir in the sauce and cook, tossing gently, until the beans are tender. Remove from the heat and season well. Stir in half the basil and scatter the rest on top. Serve immediately.

QUICK BRAISED GREEN BEANS

Heat 60 ml (2 fl oz/¼ cup) olive oil in a frying pan over medium heat. Add 1 chopped onion and 1 crushed garlic clove, and stir-fry for 7 minutes, or until the onion is soft. Add 500 g (1 lb 2 oz) green beans and fry for a few minutes, then add 400 g (14 oz) tin chopped tomatoes and simmer until the beans are tender. Season well. Serves 4

VEGETABLE SAMOSAS

MAKES 32

- 500 g (1 lb 2 oz/4 cups) plain (all-purpose) flour
- 80 ml (2½ fl oz/⅓ cup) vegetable oil
- 1 onion, chopped
- 2 garlic cloves, finely chopped
- 2 tablespoons grated ginger
- 2 tablespoons mild curry powder
- 600 g (1 lb 5 oz) waxy potatoes, cooked and finely diced
- 185 g (6½ oz) cauliflower florets, cooked and finely diced
- 100 g (3½ oz/⅔ cup) frozen peas
- 2 tablespoons lemon juice
- oil, for deep-frying

METHOD

1. Put the flour and 1 teaspoon salt in a food processor and process for 5 seconds. Combine half the oil with 250 ml (9 fl oz/1 cup) warm water. Add to the flour and process in short bursts until the mixture just comes together. Turn out onto a floured surface and gather the dough into a ball. Cover with plastic wrap and refrigerate for 20 minutes.
2. Heat the remaining oil in a large frying pan and cook the onion for 5 minutes, or until soft. Add the garlic, ginger and curry powder and cook for 2 minutes. Stir in the potato, cauliflower, peas and lemon juice. Remove from the heat and cool.
3. Divide the dough into 16 portions. On a floured surface, roll each portion into a 15 cm (6 inch) round, cut in half and put a tablespoon of the mixture in the middle of each semicircle. Brush the edge with a little water and fold the pastry over the mixture, pressing the edges to seal.
4. Fill a deep heavy-based saucepan one-third full of oil and heat to 180°C (350°F), or until a cube of bread fries golden brown in 15 seconds. Deep-fry the samosas in batches for 1 minute, or until golden. Drain and serve hot with mango chutney, sweet chilli sauce or plain yoghurt.

SNOW PEA SALAD WITH JAPANESE DRESSING

SERVES 4–6

INGREDIENTS

- 250 g (9 oz) snow peas (mangetout), trimmed
- 50 g (1¾ oz) snow pea (mangetout) sprouts
- 1 small red capsicum (pepper), julienned
- ½ teaspoon dashi granules
- 1 tablespoon soy sauce
- 1 tablespoon mirin
- 1 teaspoon soft brown sugar
- 1 garlic clove, crushed
- 1 teaspoon very finely chopped ginger
- ¼ teaspoon sesame oil
- 1 tablespoon vegetable oil
- 1 tablespoon sesame seeds, toasted

METHOD

1. Cook the snow peas in a saucepan of boiling water for 1 minute. Drain, then put into a bowl of iced water for 2 minutes. Drain well and combine with the sprouts and capsicum in a serving bowl.
2. Dissolve the dashi granules in 1½ tablespoons of hot water. Whisk in the soy sauce, mirin, sugar, garlic, ginger, oils and half of the sesame seeds. Pour over the salad and toss to combine. Season, and serve sprinkled with the remaining sesame seeds.

SUGARSNAP PEAS AND CARROTS IN LIME BUTTER

SERVES 4

INGREDIENTS

- 125 g (4½ oz) carrots
- 125 g (4½ oz) sugarsnap peas or snow peas (mangetout)
- 60 g (2¼ oz) butter
- 2 garlic cloves, crushed
- 1 tablespoon lime juice
- ½ teaspoon soft brown sugar
- finely grated zest of 1 lime

METHOD

1. Peel the carrots and cut into thin diagonal slices. Wash and string the sugarsnap peas.
2. Heat the butter in a large heavy-based frying pan. Add the garlic and cook over low heat for 1 minute. Add the lime juice and sugar and cook until the sugar has completely dissolved. Add the carrots and peas and cook over medium heat for 2–3 minutes, or until just cooked. Serve hot, garnished with lime zest.

MINTED PEAS

SERVES 4

INGREDIENTS

- 625 g (1 lb 6 oz/4 cups) fresh or frozen peas
- 4 mint sprigs
- 30 g (1 oz) butter
- 2 tablespoons shredded mint

METHOD

1. Place the peas in a saucepan and pour in water to just cover the peas. Add the mint sprigs.
2. Bring to the boil and simmer for 5 minutes, or until the peas are just tender. Drain and discard the mint sprigs. Return to the saucepan, add the butter and shredded mint and stir over low heat until the butter has melted. Season with salt and freshly ground black pepper.

PEAS

Peas should be bought at their optimum time — if harvested too late, they become dry and less sweet as their sugar converts into starch. Look for bright, shiny, green pods that feel firm and taut. In some cases, frozen peas are actually fresher than freshly podded peas because fresh peas deteriorate so quickly. Peas should be cooked quickly in boiling water or a little butter. They are usually served hot as a vegetable or added to soups and risottos.

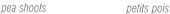

Snow peas (mangetout) are a variety of garden pea, eaten pod and all (top and tail before eating). There are two types, those with a flat, thin pod (snow peas) and those with a more rounded pod (sugarsnap or snap peas). Snow peas are eaten raw in salads or used in stir-fries. Sugarsnap peas are more developed than snow peas. Use whole, in stir-fries or noodle dishes.

pea shoots

petits pois

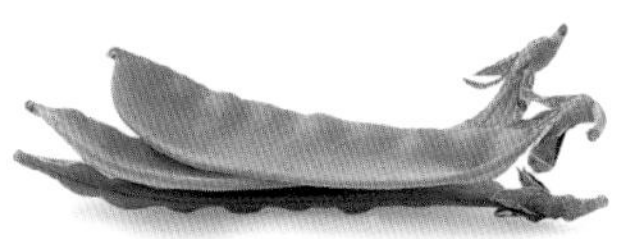

snow peas (mangetout)

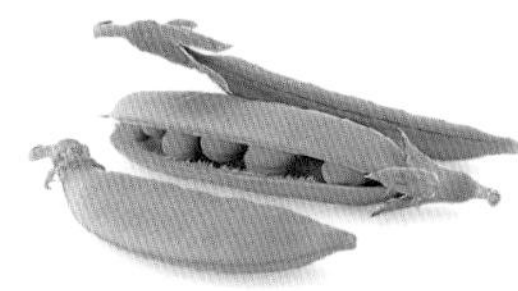

sugarsnap peas

CORN

No food is more emblematic of summer than sweet corn. With its bright yellow kernels and sweet juice, sweet corn (also called corn on the cob) is used in all manner of ways — boiled and eaten straight off the cob, drizzled with butter, or the kernels may be sliced off the cob and used to make hearty corn chowders or fritters.

When buying sweet corn, choose the freshest possible — still in its husk, with a fresh-looking silk and kernels that are not shrivelled or discoloured. Use it as soon as possible, as it loses its sweetness and nutritional benefits quickly. Sweet corn should therefore be refrigerated.

In Europe, the word 'corn' is a general term used to refer to any type of grain, but in America it refers to maize. Now the word 'corn' is usually accepted as meaning maize, and other grains are called by their own names. Dent corn, named for the dent in its top, is ground to make maize meal and flour. Ground corn is used for polenta in Italy, and grits and corn bread in America. Finely ground corn is used for Mexican tortillas and other breads, and as a staple in Africa where it is made into a porridge (mealies). Corn is also made into cornflakes and other breakfast cereals.

COOKING TIPS FOR SWEET CORN

* Do not salt the water as the salt stops the kernels softening as quickly. Cook in slightly sweetened water or add a little milk to retain flavour and softness.
* To remove the kernels from sweet corn, stand the cob on one end and slice downwards, as close to the cob as possible.
* To barbecue cobs of sweet corn, strip back the husk and remove the silk, then replace the husk and soak it briefly in water. The husk will burn off as it cooks. This will stop the corn from burning.

CORN FRITTERS

SERVES 4

INGREDIENTS

90 g (3¼ oz/¾ cup) self-raising flour
110 g (3¾ oz/¾ cup) fine polenta
250 ml (9 fl oz/1 cup) milk
310 g (11 oz/1½ cups) sweet corn kernels (about 3 cobs)
oil, for frying

METHOD

1. Sift the flour into a bowl and stir in the polenta. Add the milk and corn kernels and stir until just combined, adding more milk if the batter is too dry. Season with sea salt and black pepper.
2. Heat the oil in a large frying pan and spoon half the batter into the pan in batches, making four 9 cm (3½ inch) pancakes. Cook for 2 minutes each side, or until golden. Repeat with the remaining batter.
3. Serve the corn fritters with fried thickly sliced tomatoes, or with fried bacon, drizzled with maple syrup.

CORN SPOONBREAD

SERVES 4

INGREDIENTS

- 250 g (9 oz/1 cup) crème fraîche
- 1 egg
- 25 g (1 oz/¼ cup) grated parmesan cheese
- 30 g (1 oz/¼ cup) self-raising flour
- 3 sweet corn cobs
- pinch of cayenne pepper
- 2 tablespoons grated parmesan cheese, extra
- 40 g (1½ oz) butter

METHOD

1. Preheat the oven to 190°C (375°F/Gas 5). Lightly grease an 18 cm (7 inch) square baking dish.
2. Combine the crème fraîche, egg, parmesan and flour in a large bowl. Slice the kernels off the corn cobs and add to the bowl. Add the cayenne pepper and season with salt and freshly ground black pepper.
3. Spoon the corn mixture into the prepared dish. Sprinkle with the extra parmesan and dot with the butter. Bake for 30–35 minutes, or until the mixture is set and the top is golden brown. Serve hot, as a side dish or with a salad and bread.

SWEET SPICED CORN

SERVES 4

INGREDIENTS

- 4 sweet corn cobs
- 50 g (1¾ oz) butter
- 2 tablespoons olive oil
- 1 lemongrass stem, bruised and cut in half
- 3 small bird's eye chillies, seeded and finely chopped
- 2 tablespoons finely grated lime zest
- 2 tablespoons lime juice
- 2 tablespoons finely chopped coriander (cilantro)

METHOD

1. Remove the husks and silky threads from the corn cobs. Wash well, then, using a sharp knife cut each cob into 2 cm (¾ inch) thick chunks.
2. Heat the butter and oil in a large saucepan over low heat. Add the lemongrass and heat gently for 5 minutes, then remove the lemongrass from the pan. Add the chilli and cook for 2 minutes. Stir in the lime zest, juice, 60 ml (2 fl oz/¼ cup) water and the corn. Cover and cook, shaking the pan frequently, for 5–8 minutes, or until the corn is tender. Season, stir in the coriander and serve.

OKRA

When young, okra is eaten as a vegetable; the older pods are usually dried, then powdered and used as a flavouring. Okra is characterised by the sticky, gelatinous substance it releases when cooked, which serves to thicken stews and soups such as the Cajun and Creole dish, gumbo. Okra is also used in the cooking of India, the Caribbean, Southeast Asia and the Middle East. Buy pods that are tender and healthy green in colour; if too ripe the pod will feel sticky. To prepare okra, gently scrub with paper towel, rinse and drain. If using as a thickener, first blanch, then slice and add to the dish about 10 minutes before the end of cooking. In some recipes, the pod is used whole, thus preventing the release of the sticky substances within it.

SOYA BEAN

The most nutritious and versatile of all beans, soya beans have been cultivated in their native China for thousands of years. Soya beans (or soybeans) contain a higher proportion of protein than any other legume, even higher than that of red meat, making them an important part of vegetarian diets and in Japanese, Chinese and Southeast Asian cooking where little meat is used.

Soya beans are eaten fresh or dried but are also used as a source of oil, milk, curd, pastes, sauces and flavourings. They may also be cracked, sprouted and even roasted and ground as a coffee substitute.

TOFU

Probably one of the most well known soya bean products is tofu, or bean curd, as it's also called. This white, cheese-like curd was first made by the Chinese about 2000 years ago. The Chinese call it doufu, meaning 'rotten beans', and the Japanese name is tofu. To make it, soya beans are liquidised to form soya milk. A coagulating agent is added, causing the whey and protein to separate. The whey is drained off and the curd is pressed into blocks. Tofu is bland in taste, but its soft, silken texture absorbs the flavour of the ingredients it's cooked with. Tofu is usually sold in blocks, either fresh, vacuum-packed or in small tubs or cartons of water.

Store fresh tofu covered in water in the fridge for up to 5 days and change the water daily. Dry tofu before use by sitting it on paper towels, but don't squeeze the water out as this will make it chewy.

TYPES OF TOFU

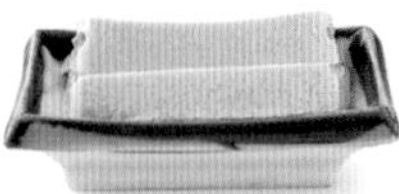

SOFT (SILKEN)

Soft tofu needs to be handled carefully. It can be added to soups (at the end of cooking), gently steamed or scrambled and piled on top of noodles. Use it as a dairy substitute in ice cream or cheesecakes.

FIRM AND SILKEN FIRM

This is more robust and can be stir-fried or deep-fried without it breaking up, added to miso soup, or eaten as a side dish. Dust cubes of tofu in rice flour before frying to give them a crisp coating. Firm tofu can also be flavoured, preserved in rice wine, chilli or brine.

SHEETS

Sheets can be bought dried, frozen or vacuum-packed. If dried, they need to be softened before use with a little water. Fill them with rice (inari sushi), use to wrap food parcels, or cut into strips and use as a garnish. They can be fried, braised or steamed.

DEEP-FRIED (PUFFS)

Sold as large cubes, usually in plastic bags, and used in stir-fries and soups. If using in soup, such as laksa, prick the skin a few times to help them to absorb the flavours. Add at the last minute or they will soak up all the soup.

EDAMAME

Fresh soya beans in the pod, known as *edamame* in Japan, where the dish originated, are available fresh when in season or can be found in your local Asian grocery store in frozen form. Serve as a snack with a cold beer or glass of wine.

SERVES 4–6

INGREDIENTS

- 500 g (1 lb 2 oz) fresh or frozen soya beans in pods
- 1–2 teaspoons instant dashi granules

METHOD

1. Rub the fresh soya beans with salt between your hands to rub off the fine hairy fibres. Rinse the pods. If you are using frozen soya beans, this step is not necessary.
2. Combine the dashi with 1.25 litres (5 cups) water in a saucepan and bring to the boil over high heat, stirring to dissolve the granules. Add the soya beans and cook for 6–8 minutes if using fresh or 3–4 minutes if using frozen, or until tender but still bright green. Drain well. You can serve the edamame either warm, at room temperature or chilled.
3. Sprinkle with lots of salt. To eat, simply suck the beans out of the pods and throw the pods away. Supply a bowl to collect the empty pods.

TOFU, SNOW PEA AND MUSHROOM STIR-FRY

SERVES 4

INGREDIENTS

- 250 g (9 oz/1¼ cups) jasmine rice
- 60 ml (2 fl oz/¼ cup) peanut oil
- 600 g (1 lb 5 oz) firm tofu, drained and cubed
- 2 garlic cloves, finely chopped
- 2 teaspoons sambal oelek or chilli paste
- 400 g (14 oz) fresh Asian mushrooms (shiitake, oyster or black fungus), sliced
- 300 g (10½ oz) snow peas (mangetout), trimmed
- 60 ml (2 fl oz/¼ cup) kecap manis

METHOD

1. Bring a large saucepan of water to the boil. Add the rice and cook for 12 minutes, stirring occasionally. Drain well.
2. Meanwhile, heat a wok until very hot. Add 2 tablespoons of the peanut oil and swirl to coat. Add the tofu in two batches and stir-fry on all sides for 2–3 minutes, or until lightly browned. Transfer to a plate.
3. Heat the remaining oil in the wok, add the garlic, sambal oelek, mushrooms, snow peas and 1 tablespoon water and stir-fry for 1–2 minutes, or until the vegetables are almost cooked but still crunchy. Return the tofu to the wok, add the kecap manis and stir-fry for 1 minute, or until heated through. Serve with the rice.

AGEDASHI TOFU

Put 2 teaspoons dashi granules, 1 tablespoon light soy sauce and 400 ml (14 fl oz) water in a saucepan and bring to the boil. Cut 600 g (1 lb 5 oz) firm tofu into cubes and dust with cornflour (cornstarch) or rice flour. Deep-fry in batches until golden, then drain well. Divide the tofu among four bowls and add chopped spring onions (scallions) and grated ginger. Pour over a little of the hot dashi liquid and garnish with bonito flakes. Serves 4

••ASIAN GREENS••

The curious cook will discover new and fascinating vegetables in Asian markets and greengrocers. There are countless varieties, too many to list here, so below is a guide to some of the most common. As with all vegetables, choose crisp-leaved, firm-stemmed healthy specimens. At home, wash and store in a cool place or wrap in foil and store in the vegetable crisper.

SOME COMMON ASIAN GREENS

bok choy

BOK CHOY (PAK CHOY)

Bok choy is a member of the cabbage family. Separate the leaves and wash well and use both leaf and stem in soups and stir-fries. A smaller type is Shanghai bok choy, or baby bok choy (pictured).

Chinese broccoli

CHINESE BROCCOLI (GAI LARN)

Chinese broccoli is distinguished by its small white flowers. It can be steamed whole and served with oyster sauce, or cut up the leaves and stems and add to soups and stir-fries. The young stalks are crisp and mild; thicker stalks need to be peeled and then halved.

Chinese cabbage

CHINESE CABBAGE (WONG BOK)

A versatile vegetable with a mild, sweet flavour. It can be shredded and eaten raw, steamed, used in stir-fries, soups and curries, or used to make cabbage rolls. Chinese cabbage is also used to make Korean kimchi.

choy sum

CHOY SUM (CHINESE FLOWERING CABBAGE)

Related to bok choy, choy sum has mild mustard-flavoured leaves and small, yellow flowers. Steam or stir-fry whole and serve with oil and garlic and oyster sauce, or chop and add the leaves to soups.

water spinach

WATER SPINACH (ONG CHOY)

An aquatic plant popular in Southeast Asia, water spinach is cooked like spinach and used in soups, curries and stir-fries. It is sometimes steamed and served as a side dish.

tatsoi

TATSOI (ROSETTE PAK CHOY)

This vegetable has small, dark green, shiny leaves with a white stem. The leaves need to be thoroughly washed and can be steamed or stir-fried and often used in soups. Baby tatsoi can be used raw in salads.

STIR-FRIED TOFU WITH ASIAN GREENS

SERVES 4

INGREDIENTS

- 2 tablespoons lime juice
- 60 ml (2 fl oz/¼ cup) vegetable oil
- 1½ tablespoons fish sauce
- 1 teaspoon sambal oelek
- ½ teaspoon soft brown sugar
- 200 g (7 oz) smoked tofu
- 400 g (14 oz) choy sum (Chinese flowering cabbage), trimmed
- 150 g (5½ oz) torn English spinach leaves
- 2 teaspoons sesame seeds, toasted
- 1 small handful coriander (cilantro)

METHOD

1. To make the dressing, put the lime juice and 2 tablespoons of the oil, the fish sauce, sambal oelek and sugar in a bowl and whisk well.
2. Cut the tofu into 2 cm (¾ inch) cubes. Trim the choy sum and cut into 8 cm (3¼ inch) lengths. Heat 1 tablespoon of the oil in a large wok over medium heat and gently stir-fry the tofu for 2–3 minutes, or until golden brown. Add half the dressing and toss to coat. Remove from the wok and set aside.
3. Add the choy sum to the wok and stir-fry for 1 minute. Add the spinach leaves and stir-fry for 1 minute. Return the tofu to the wok, add the sesame seeds and the remaining dressing and toss lightly. Serve with the coriander leaves piled on top.

CHINESE BROCCOLI AND SESAME STIR-FRY

SERVES 4

INGREDIENTS

- 1 tablespoon vegetable or peanut oil
- 3 garlic cloves, crushed
- 1.5 kg (3 lb 5 oz) Chinese broccoli (gai larn), cut into thirds
- 2 teaspoons sesame oil
- 60 ml (2 fl oz/¼ cup) oyster sauce
- 2 tablespoons sesame seeds, toasted

METHOD

1. Heat a wok over high heat, add the oil and swirl to coat. Cook the garlic for about 30 seconds. Add the Chinese broccoli and 2 tablespoons of water and stir-fry for 3–4 minutes, or until wilted and the water has evaporated.
2. Add the sesame oil and oyster sauce and stir-fry for 1 minute, or until the Chinese broccoli is coated in the sauce. Serve sprinkled with sesame seeds.

••MUSHROOMS••

Mushrooms are not technically vegetables — they are the fleshy, fruiting body of a form of fungus, which grows in soil or decaying matter. There are countless varieties of mushrooms, some cultivated, others gathered from the wild, but only some of these are edible. Wild mushrooms are generally in season during autumn, with the exception of morels, which are picked in spring, and cultivated mushrooms are available year round.

HOW TO... PREPARE MUSHROOMS

Cultivated mushrooms don't need to be washed before use — simply wipe over them with paper towel. To prepare wild mushrooms, wipe them with a damp cloth or paper towel. Remove the gritty base of the stem and brush the caps with a soft brush to remove earth or grit. If necessary, quickly run them under cold water, then pat dry with a paper towel.

HOW TO... PREPARE DRIED MUSHROOMS

The flavour of some mushrooms intensifies when dried, so mushrooms such as shiitake (also called Chinese black mushroom) and Italian porcini (cep) are often bought dried, then reconstituted.

Soak in hot water for 30 minutes, or simmer with a little sugar for 15 minutes. Drain and squeeze out the water. Cut off the stems and chop the caps. The soaking water will be flavourful, so strain it and add to stock or a sauce. Dried mushrooms reconstitute up to six or eight times their original weight.

STORAGE

Store mushrooms in the fridge in a paper bag to allow them to breathe. Don't leave them in plastic as this makes them sweat. Wild mushrooms are best eaten on the day they are picked and will last no longer than 1 day in the fridge; cultivated mushrooms will last up to 3 days.

TYPES OF MUSHROOMS

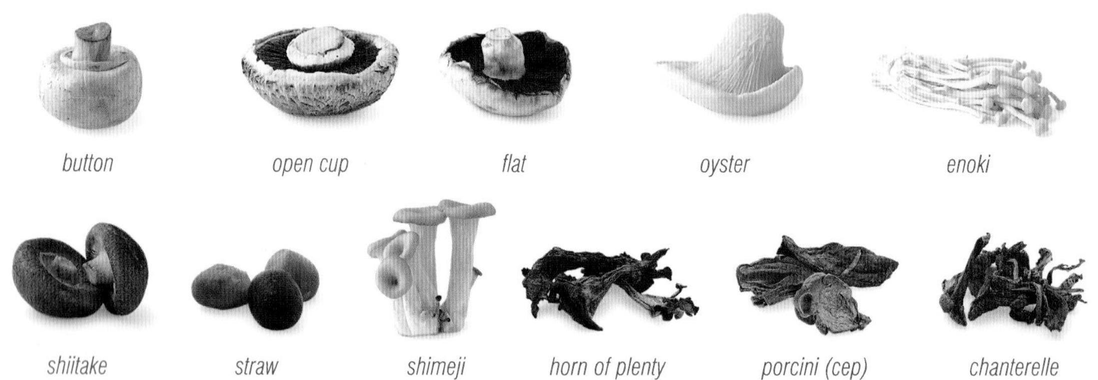

button *open cup* *flat* *oyster* *enoki*

shiitake *straw* *shimeji* *horn of plenty* *porcini (cep)* *chanterelle*

WARNING

Some innocuous-looking mushrooms are highly poisonous. Never eat a mushroom unless you are certain that it is edible, especially if picking them in the wild. Always ask a professional to identify any suspect mushrooms before eating them.

STUFFED FIELD MUSHROOMS

SERVES 4

INGREDIENTS

- 4 field mushrooms
- 60 ml (2 fl oz/¼ cup) olive oil
- 50 g (1¾ oz) bacon, finely chopped
- 3 garlic cloves, crushed
- 2 tablespoons chopped parsley
- 1 tablespoon chopped mint
- 1 teaspoon finely grated lemon zest
- 25 g (1 oz/¼ cup) toasted pistachio nuts, finely chopped
- 2 tablespoons fresh breadcrumbs
- pinch of ground nutmeg
- 90 g (3¼ oz/⅓ cup) crème fraîche

METHOD

1. Preheat the oven to 200°C (400°F/Gas 6). Lightly oil a shallow baking dish. Remove and finely chop the mushroom stems. Wipe the mushroom caps with a dry paper towel to get rid of any residual grit. Only use a lightly moistened paper towel if the mushrooms have dirt on them. Brush the outside of the caps with some of the olive oil. Arrange in the prepared dish, gills upwards.
2. Heat ½ teaspoon of the olive oil in a small frying pan over high heat. Add the bacon and fry for 1 minute, or until it is crisp and the bacon fat has melted. Add the chopped mushroom stems and fry for 1 minute. Add the garlic and fry for 15–20 seconds, until aromatic but not browned.
3. Remove the pan from the heat and set aside to cool for 2–3 minutes. Stir in the parsley, mint, lemon zest, pistachios, breadcrumbs and nutmeg. Season with salt and freshly ground black pepper.
4. Scatter the bacon and breadcrumb mixture into the mushroom caps, covering the gills. Drizzle any remaining olive oil over the top. Transfer to the oven and bake for 12–15 minutes, or until the crumbs are golden and the mushrooms are soft. Serve hot with crème fraîche.

MIXED MUSHROOM STIR-FRY

Trim 500 g (1 lb 2 oz) mixed mushrooms, slicing any larger ones. Heat 25 g (1 oz) butter and 1 tablespoon olive oil in a frying pan. Add 1 finely chopped chilli, 1 finely chopped shallot and 1 finely chopped garlic clove and fry briefly. Add the mushrooms and toss over high heat until starting to brown (if using shimeji or enoki, add them at the end). Add 1 tablespoon chopped coriander (cilantro), 1 tablespoon soy sauce, season and drizzle with sesame oil. Serve tossed through noodles or pasta, or on bruschetta. Makes enough for 12 bruschetta or 4 entrée noodle or pasta serves.

TRUFFLE AND ROCKET SALAD

SERVES 6

INGREDIENTS

BRUSCHETTA

6 slices sourdough bread
1 garlic clove
2 tablespoons extra virgin olive oil

180 g (6½ oz) rocket (arugula)
1 tablespoon lemon juice
about 80 ml (2½ fl oz/⅓ cup) extra virgin olive oil
1 small black or white truffle
shaved parmesan cheese, to serve

METHOD

1 To make the bruschetta, toast the bread until it is crisp. Cut the garlic clove in half and rub the cut edge over both sides of the bread, then drizzle a little olive oil over each slice.
2 Put the rocket in a bowl and dress with the lemon juice, most of the olive oil and salt and freshly ground black pepper. Toss together and divide among six plates.
3 Thinly slice the truffle, ideally using a truffle slicer or sharp mandolin. Slice the truffle over each plate — the pieces should be as thin as possible and will break up easily if touched by hand.
4 Arrange the shaved parmesan around the truffle (you won't need much parmesan: you don't want to overwhelm the truffle) and drizzle with a little olive oil. Serve with the pieces of bruschetta.

MUSHROOMS WITH WET POLENTA

SERVES 6

INGREDIENTS

- 300 g (10½ oz/2 cups) fine polenta
- 60 ml (2 fl oz/¼ cup) olive oil
- 400 g (14 oz) wild mushrooms, such as fresh porcini (cep), sliced if large
- 2 garlic cloves, crushed
- 1 tablespoon chopped thyme
- 150 g (5½ oz) mascarpone cheese
- 50 g (1¾ oz) butter
- 50 g (1¾ oz/½ cup) grated parmesan cheese, plus extra to serve

METHOD

1. Bring 1.5 litres (6 cups) water and 1 tablespoon salt to the boil in a deep heavy-based saucepan. Add the polenta in a gentle stream, whisking or stirring vigorously as you pour. Reduce the heat immediately so the water is simmering and keep stirring for the first 30 seconds to prevent lumps appearing — the more you stir, the better the finished texture of the polenta. Leave the polenta to gently bubble away for about 40 minutes, stirring it every few minutes to stop it sticking. The finished polenta should drop from the spoon in thick lumps.
2. Meanwhile, heat the olive oil in a large frying pan, then add enough mushrooms to cover the base of the pan. Cook over high heat, stirring frequently, until any liquid given off by the mushrooms has evaporated. Add the garlic and thyme and cook briefly. Remove the mushrooms from the pan and cook the next batch. Return all mushrooms to the pan and season well.
3. When the polenta is almost cooked, reheat the mushrooms, add the mascarpone and let it melt.
4. Add the butter and parmesan to the cooked polenta and season with pepper. Spoon the polenta onto plates and top with the mushroom mixture. Sprinkle with extra parmesan to serve.

MUSHROOMS WITH STICKY BALSAMIC SYRUP

SERVES 4

INGREDIENTS

- 80 ml (2½ fl oz/⅓ cup) olive oil
- 750 g (1 lb 10 oz) baby button mushrooms
- 2 large garlic cloves, finely chopped
- 3 tablespoons soft brown sugar, firmly packed
- 60 ml (2 fl oz/¼ cup) balsamic vinegar
- 3 teaspoons thyme

METHOD

1. Heat the oil in a large, heavy-based frying pan. Add the mushrooms and cook over high heat for 5 minutes, or until slightly softened and golden. Season the mushrooms with salt while they are cooking. Add the garlic and cook for 1 minute. Stir in the sugar, vinegar and 1 tablespoon water, and boil for 5 minutes, or until reduced by one-third. Season with pepper.
2. Arrange the mushrooms on a serving plate. Reduce the remaining liquid for 1 minute, or until thick and syrupy. Pour over the mushrooms and garnish with the thyme.

••PULSES••

There are thousands of plants whose seed pods split open down both seams when ripe, and it is these seed pods that are known as legumes. Some are eaten fresh, such as green beans and peas, but most are eaten when dried, such as lentils and split peas, and these are referred to as pulses. Pulses are an important source of protein and are a staple food in many countries where little or no meat is eaten.

LENTILS

These tiny, flat pulses grow in pods worldwide in warm countries, and vary in colour and size. The most common lentils are green, brown and red. Some of the rarer varieties are named after the area in which they are grown.

Lentils have a high food value (they are high in protein, fibre and B vitamins) and are considered adequate protein to replace meat. They must be cooked and can then be puréed and used in soups and curries or added to stews and salads. But choose your lentils accordingly: some lentils, such as the red and brown ones, will cook to a mush and are good for purées; others, like puy lentils, will hold their shape no matter how much you cook them.

PREPARATION

Lentils don't need to be soaked overnight before cooking, but you do need to pick them over to remove any discoloured ones or pieces of grit, then rinse well and discard any lentils that float (these may have been partially eaten by bugs).

TYPES OF LENTILS

RED

Also called Egyptian lentils, these break down when cooked and can be used for making soups and purées. They are often used in Indian dishes such as dhals.

GREEN AND BROWN

The largest of the lentils, these keep their shape when cooked. They are good in casseroles, soups and dishes where you want texture. Green and brown vary in size and colour and aren't always easy to differentiate from each other — treat in the same way.

PUY

This tiny, grey-green lentil is considered a delicacy in France and is relatively expensive. Unlike most other lentils, puy lentils keep their shape and have a firm texture after cooking. They are used mostly for making salads and side dishes.

CASTELLUCCIO

From Umbria in Italy, these are small, brownish-green lentils. They cook quickly (about 30 minutes) and retain their shape when cooked. They are often served with game.

LENTIL AND BURGHUL FRITTERS

MAKES 35

INGREDIENTS

- 140 g (5 oz/¾ cup) brown lentils, rinsed
- 90 g (3¼ oz/½ cup) burghul (bulgur)
- 80 ml (2½ fl oz/⅓ cup) olive oil
- 1 onion, finely chopped
- 2 garlic cloves, finely chopped
- 3 teaspoons ground cumin
- 2 teaspoons ground coriander
- 3 tablespoons finely chopped mint
- 4 eggs, lightly beaten
- 60 g (2¼ oz/¼ cup) plain (all-purpose) flour
- 1 teaspoon sea salt

YOGHURT SAUCE

- 1 small Lebanese (short) cucumber, peeled and seeded
- 250 g (9 oz/1 cup) Greek-style yoghurt
- 1–2 garlic cloves, crushed

METHOD

1. Place the lentils in a saucepan with 625 ml (21 fl oz/2½ cups) water. Bring to the boil over high heat, then reduce the heat and simmer for 30 minutes, or until tender. Remove from the heat and top up with enough water to just cover. Pour in the burghul, cover and leave for 1½ hours, or until the burghul has expanded.
2. To make the yoghurt sauce, grate the cucumber flesh into a bowl and mix with the yoghurt and garlic.
3. Heat half the oil in a large frying pan over medium heat and cook the onion and garlic for 5 minutes, or until soft. Stir in the cumin and coriander. Add the onion mixture, mint, eggs, flour and sea salt to the lentil mixture and mix well. The mixture should hold together; if it is too wet, add flour to bind.
4. Heat the remaining oil in the cleaned frying pan. Drop heaped tablespoons of mixture into the pan and cook for 3 minutes each side, or until browned. Drain, season with salt and serve with the yoghurt sauce.

EGGPLANT LENTIL SALAD

SERVES 4–6

INGREDIENTS

60 ml (2 fl oz/¼ cup) olive oil
300 g (10½ oz) eggplant (aubergine), finely diced
1 small red onion, finely diced
¼ teaspoon ground cumin
3 garlic cloves, chopped
185 g (6½ oz) puy lentils
375 ml (13 fl oz/1½ cups) vegetable stock (page 10)
2 tablespoons chopped parsley
1 tablespoon red wine vinegar
1 tablespoon extra virgin olive oil

METHOD

1 Heat 2 tablespoons of the oil in a large frying pan over medium heat. Add the eggplant and cook, stirring, for 5 minutes, until soft. Add the onion and cumin and cook for 3 minutes, or until the onion is soft. Transfer to a bowl and season.
2 Heat the remaining oil in the pan over medium heat. Cook the garlic for 1 minute, then add the lentils and stock and cook, stirring regularly, over low heat for 40 minutes, or until the liquid has evaporated and the lentils are tender.
3 Add the lentils to the bowl with the eggplant and stir in the parsley and vinegar. Season well with salt and black pepper, drizzle with the extra virgin olive oil and serve warm.

INDIAN DHAL

SERVES 4–6

INGREDIENTS

2 tablespoons oil or ghee (page 120)
1 onion, finely chopped
2 garlic cloves, crushed
1 teaspoon grated ginger
1 teaspoon ground turmeric
1 teaspoon garam masala
300 g (10½ oz/1¼ cups) red lentils, rinsed
4 pitta breads
2–3 tablespoons olive oil

METHOD

1 Heat the oil or ghee in a frying pan, add the onion and fry for about 5 minutes, or until soft. Add the garlic, ginger and spices and cook, stirring, for another minute.
2 Add the lentils and 500 ml (17 fl oz/2 cups) water and bring to the boil. Lower the heat and simmer, stirring occasionally, for 15 minutes, or until all the water has absorbed. Watch carefully towards the end of cooking time, as the mixture could burn on the bottom of the pan.
3 To make pitta toasts, preheat the oven to 180°C (350°F/Gas 4). Cut the pitta bread into wedges and brush lightly with the oil. Place on a baking tray and cook for 5–7 minutes, until crisp.
4 Transfer the dhal to a serving bowl. Serve warm or at room temperature with the pitta toasts.

SAUSAGES AND LENTILS

Fry 4 chopped bacon slices and 8 large pork sausages until brown. Add 200 g (7 oz) puy lentils, 1 chopped garlic clove and a thyme sprig, then pour over 400 ml (14 fl oz) beef stock (page 11). Simmer for 30–40 minutes, or until the lentils are tender. Stir in 1 tablespoon redcurrant jelly and 1 tablespoon cream. Season with black pepper. Serves 4

LENTIL AND BROWN RICE SALAD

SERVES 6–8

INGREDIENTS

- 200 g (7 oz/1 cup) brown rice
- 2 tomatoes
- 100 ml (3½ fl oz) extra virgin olive oil
- 1 red onion, diced
- 2 garlic cloves, crushed
- 1 carrot, diced
- 2 celery stalks, diced
- 185 g (6½ oz) puy lentils
- 3 tablespoons chopped coriander (cilantro)
- 3 tablespoons chopped mint
- 2 tablespoons balsamic vinegar
- 1 tablespoon lemon juice
- 2 tablespoons pine nuts, toasted
- 90 g (3¼ oz) baby English spinach leaves, washed

METHOD

1. Bring a large saucepan of water to the boil. Add 1 teaspoon salt and the rice, and cook for 20 minutes, or until tender. Drain and refresh under cold water.
2. Meanwhile, cut the tomatoes in half horizontally and squeeze out the seeds or scoop them out with a teaspoon. Cut the flesh into small dice.
3. Heat 2 tablespoons of the oil in a saucepan. Add the onion, garlic, carrot and celery. Cook over low heat for 5 minutes, or until the vegetables are softened, then add the lentils and 375 ml (13 fl oz/1½ cups) water. Bring to the boil and simmer for 15 minutes, or until tender. Drain well, but do not rinse. Combine with the rice, tomato, coriander and mint in a large bowl.
4. Whisk the remaining oil with the vinegar and lemon juice, and season well with salt and pepper. Pour over the salad, add the pine nuts and spinach and toss well to combine.

SPICED PUMPKIN AND LENTIL TAGINE

SERVES 4–6

INGREDIENTS

- 275 g (9¾ oz/1½ cups) brown lentils
- 2 tomatoes
- 600 g (1 lb 5 oz) pumpkin (winter squash)
- 60 ml (2 fl oz/¼ cup) olive oil
- 1 onion, finely chopped
- 3 garlic cloves, finely chopped
- ½ teaspoon ground cumin
- ½ teaspoon ground turmeric
- ⅛ teaspoon cayenne pepper
- 1 teaspoon paprika
- 3 teaspoons tomato paste (concentrated purée)
- ½ teaspoon sugar
- 1 tablespoon finely chopped parsley
- 2 tablespoons chopped coriander (cilantro)

METHOD

1. Rinse the lentils in a sieve. Tip into a saucepan and add 1 litre (35 fl oz/4 cups) cold water. Bring to the boil, then cover and simmer over low heat for 20 minutes, or until tender.
2. Meanwhile, cut the tomatoes in half horizontally and squeeze out the seeds. Coarsely grate the tomatoes into a bowl down to the skin. Set the tomato aside. Peel and seed the pumpkin and cut into 3 cm (1¼ inch) cubes. Set aside.
3. Heat the oil in a large saucepan, add the onion and cook over low heat until softened. Add the garlic, cook for a few seconds, then stir in the cumin, turmeric and cayenne pepper. Cook for 30 seconds, then add the grated tomatoes, paprika, tomato paste, sugar, half the parsley and coriander. Season with sea salt and freshly ground black pepper.
4. Add the drained lentils and chopped pumpkin, stir well, then cover and simmer for 20 minutes, or until the pumpkin and lentils are tender. Adjust the seasoning and sprinkle with the remaining parsley and coriander. Serve hot or warm.

DRIED BEANS

This group of pulses includes hundreds of varieties and many are called different things depending on where you live.

Adzuki beans are a small reddish-brown bean. These are sweet and are ground to make flour or used in desserts in Japan. Haricot beans, including flageolet, cannellini and navy beans, are used widely in Europe and America, where they are known as white beans. Butter, or lima, beans are large white beans, which break down to a purée when cooked. Red and black kidney beans are a staple of South and Central America and are used in soups and stews or refried as a paste. Borlotti, also called a cranberry bean, and pinto beans have speckled skins. Pintos are used in Central and South America and borlotti in Italy. Black-eyed beans are eaten in the American south.

Broad beans, or fava beans, are large brownish beans with a thick skin, and ful medames are a staple of Egypt and are also known as Egyptian brown beans. Split dried broad beans, which are already skinned, are available from specialist stores. If whole broad beans are used, they will need to be skinned after soaking. To do this, squeeze each broad bean to allow the skin to pop off, or pierce each skin with your fingernail, then peel it off.

This group also includes chickpeas, or garbanzos, which are not peas but beans (see opposite).

HOW TO... COOK DRIED BEANS

Most dried beans need to be soaked overnight, with the exception of adzuki and mung beans, which only need soaking for 1–2 hours, and broad (fava) beans, which are soaked for 48 hours. After soaking, discard the water, cover the beans with plenty of fresh water and bring to the boil, then reduce to a simmer and cook for 1–2 hours, or until tender. Do not salt the beans during cooking or this will cause their skins to become tough.

Kidney beans must be boiled for 15 minutes and then rinsed well before cooking to get rid of the toxins on their skins. Soya beans must be properly cooked to inactivate their anti-nutrients and to make them digestible.

WARM CHICKPEA AND SPINACH SALAD

SERVES 4

INGREDIENTS

- 250 g (9 oz) dried chickpeas
- 125 ml (4 fl oz/½ cup) olive oil
- 1 onion, cut into thin wedges
- 2 tomatoes
- 1 teaspoon sugar
- ¼ teaspoon ground cinnamon
- 2 garlic cloves, chopped
- 1 kg (2 lb 4 oz) English spinach
- 3 tablespoons chopped mint
- 2–3 tablespoons lemon juice
- 1½ tablespoons ground sumac (see Note)

METHOD

1. Place the chickpeas in a large bowl, cover with water and leave to soak overnight. Drain and place in a large saucepan. Cover with water and bring to the boil, then simmer for 1¾ hours, or until tender. Drain thoroughly.
2. Heat the oil in a heavy-based frying pan, add the onion and cook over low heat for 5 minutes, or until softened and just starting to brown.
3. Cut the tomatoes in half horizontally and squeeze out the seeds. Cut the flesh into small dice. Add the tomato to the pan with the sugar, cinnamon and garlic and cook for 2–3 minutes, or until softened.
4. Thoroughly wash the spinach and pat dry with paper towels. Trim the stems and finely shred the leaves. Add to the tomato mixture with the chickpeas and cook for 3–4 minutes, or until the spinach wilts. Add the mint, lemon juice and sumac, season, and cook for 1 minute. Serve immediately.

NOTE: Sumac is a deep-red powder ground from berries. It adds colour and a fruity, lemony flavour to dishes. Sumac is available from Middle Eastern speciality stores.

CHICKPEAS WITH CHORIZO

This combination of two emblematic ingredients of Spanish cooking — chorizo sausage and chickpeas — provides a simple but satisfying hearty tapas dish.

SERVES 6

INGREDIENTS

170 g (6 oz/¾ cup) dried chickpeas
1 bay leaf
4 cloves
1 cinnamon stick
750 ml (26 fl oz/3 cups) chicken stock (page 11)
2 tablespoons olive oil
1 onion, finely chopped
1 garlic clove, crushed
a pinch of dried thyme
375 g (13 oz) chorizo sausage, chopped into cubes slightly larger than the chickpeas
1 tablespoon chopped parsley

METHOD

1. Put the chickpeas in a large bowl, cover with water and soak overnight. Drain, then put in a large saucepan with the bay leaf, cloves, cinnamon stick and stock. Cover completely with water, bring to the boil, then reduce the heat and simmer for 1 hour, or until the chickpeas are tender. If they need more time, add a little more water. There should be just a little liquid left in the pan. Drain and remove the bay leaf, cloves and cinnamon stick.
2. Heat the oil in a large frying pan, add the onion and cook over medium heat for 3 minutes, or until translucent. Add the garlic and thyme and cook, stirring, for 1 minute. Increase the heat to medium–high, add the chorizo and cook for 3 minutes.
3. Add the chickpeas to the frying pan, mix well, then stir over medium heat until they are heated through. Remove from the heat and mix through the parsley. Taste before seasoning with salt and freshly ground black pepper. This dish is equally delicious served hot or at room temperature.

CHICKPEAS

Chickpeas (garbanzos) are not peas but beans and are eaten all over Europe, India and the Middle East. There are two kinds of chickpea, the large white garbanzo and the smaller brown dessi. They are sometimes eaten green but usually dried. Chickpeas have a wonderful nutty flavour and are used in soups and stews, to make the dip, hummus, and ground to make a flour, called besan. Dried chickpeas need to be soaked overnight, then cooked in fresh water for about 2 hours, or until tender, then leave in their cooking water to cool. Tinned chickpeas have already been cooked.

BESAN TEMPURA

SERVES 2–4

INGREDIENTS

- 145 g (5 oz/1⅓ cups) besan (chickpea flour)
- 75 g (2½ oz) rice flour
- 1 teaspoon turmeric
- 1 teaspoon chilli powder
- ½ teaspoon nigella seeds
- oil, for deep-frying
- vegetables such as thinly sliced pumpkin, carrots or snowpeas (mangetout) cut into sticks, small florets of broccoli or cauliflower, or baby spinach leaves

METHOD

1. Sift the besan, rice flour and a pinch of salt into a bowl. Add the turmeric, chilli powder and nigella seeds and stir to combine. Gradually add 250 ml (9 fl oz/1 cup) water, stirring to make a smooth batter. Leave to stand for 10 minutes.
2. Fill a deep heavy-based saucepan or deep-fryer one-third full of oil and heat to 180°C (350°F), or until a cube of bread dropped into the oil turns golden brown in 15 seconds. Dip the vegetables into the batter, drain off the excess, and carefully lower into the oil. Deep-fry in batches until lightly golden and cooked through. Remove and drain on paper towels. Serve the vegetable tempura with a chilli sauce or chutney.

› FALAFEL

MAKES 30

INGREDIENTS

- 150 g (5½ oz/1 cup) dried split broad (fava) beans (see Note)
- 220 g (7¾ oz/1 cup) dried chickpeas
- 1 onion, roughly chopped
- 6 garlic cloves, roughly chopped
- 2 teaspoons ground coriander
- 1 tablespoon ground cumin
- 1 large handful parsley, chopped
- ¼ teaspoon chilli powder
- ½ teaspoon bicarbonate of soda (baking soda)
- 3 tablespoons chopped coriander (cilantro)
- oil, for deep-frying

METHOD

1. Place the broad beans in a large bowl, cover well with water and soak for 48 hours. Drain, then rinse several times in fresh water. Place the chickpeas in a large bowl, cover well with water and soak for 12 hours.
2. Drain the broad beans and chickpeas, then process in a food processor with the onion and garlic until smooth. Add the ground coriander, cumin, parsley, chilli powder, bicarbonate of soda and fresh coriander. Season, and mix until well combined. Transfer to a large bowl and set aside for 30 minutes.
3. Shape tablespoons of mixture into balls, flatten slightly to 4 cm (1½ inch) rounds, place on a tray and refrigerate for 20 minutes.
4. Fill a deep heavy-based saucepan one-third full of oil and heat to 180°C (350°F), or until a cube of bread dropped into the oil turns golden brown in 15 seconds. Cook the falafel in batches for 1–2 minutes until golden. Drain on paper towels. Serve with hummus, tabouleh and pitta bread.

NOTE: Split broad beans, which are already skinned, are available from specialist Middle Eastern stores.

BOSTON-STYLE BAKED BEANS WITH HAM

SERVES 6

INGREDIENTS

400 g (14 oz/2 cups) dried cannellini beans
2 teaspoons vegetable oil
1 large onion, finely chopped
1.5 kg (3 lb 5 oz) ham hock
1 bay leaf
60 ml (2 fl oz/¼ cup) molasses
80 g (2¾ oz/⅓ cup) soft brown sugar
160 g (5½ oz/⅔ cup) tomato paste (concentrated purée)
2 tablespoons worcestershire sauce
1 teaspoon mustard powder
1 garlic clove

METHOD

1 Soak the beans in a large saucepan of water overnight. Drain well, rinse and drain again.
2 Heat the oil in a large saucepan and brown the onion for 5 minutes, or until golden. Add the beans, ham hock, bay leaf and 3 litres (12 cups) water and bring to the boil. Reduce the heat and simmer for 1 hour, stirring occasionally. Drain, reserving the liquid. Put the beans and hock mixture into a large flameproof casserole dish.
3 Combine 750 ml (26 fl oz/3 cups) of the reserved bean liquid with the molasses, brown sugar, tomato paste, worcestershire sauce, mustard, garlic and 1 teaspoon salt and pour into the dish. Add enough of the remaining cooking liquid to cover the beans. Cover and cook over low heat for 3 hours, stirring occasionally and turning the hock halfway through cooking time, until the meat is tender and starting to fall off the bone.
4 Remove the hock and cut the meat from the bone. Cut the meat into smallish chunks, then return to the dish and stir to combine. Cook, uncovered, for 30 minutes, or until the sauce is thick and syrupy. Serve with thick buttered toast or cornbread to mop up the juices.

TUNA AND CANNELLINI BEAN SALAD

SERVES 4–6

INGREDIENTS

400 g (14 oz) tuna steaks
1 tablespoon olive oil
1 small red onion, thinly sliced
1 tomato, seeded and chopped
1 small red capsicum (pepper), thinly sliced
2 x 400 g (14 oz) tins cannellini beans
2 garlic cloves, crushed
1 teaspoon chopped thyme
4 tablespoons chopped parsley
1½ tablespoons lemon juice
80 ml (2½ fl oz/⅓ cup) extra virgin olive oil
1 teaspoon honey
100 g (3½ oz) rocket (arugula)
1 teaspoon finely grated lemon zest

METHOD

1 Place the tuna steaks on a plate, brush with the oil and sprinkle with freshly ground black pepper on both sides. Cover with plastic wrap and refrigerate until needed.
2 Combine the onion, tomato and capsicum in a large bowl. Rinse the cannellini beans under cold running water for 30 seconds, drain and add to the bowl with the garlic, thyme and 3 tablespoons of the parsley.
3 Place the lemon juice, oil and honey in a small saucepan, bring to the boil, then reduce the heat to low and simmer, stirring, for 1 minute, or until the honey dissolves. Remove from the heat.
4 Heat the barbecue hotplate or grill. Sear the tuna for 1 minute on each side. The meat should still be pink in the middle. Slice into 3 cm (1½ inch) cubes and combine with the salad. Pour on the warm dressing and toss well.
5 Place the rocket on a large platter. Top with the salad, season and garnish with the lemon zest and remaining parsley. Serve immediately.

CAPSICUM AND BEAN STEW

SERVES 4–6

INGREDIENTS

- 200 g (7 oz/1 cup) dried haricot beans (see Note)
- 2 tablespoons olive oil
- 2 large garlic cloves, crushed
- 1 red onion, halved and cut into thin wedges
- 1 red capsicum (pepper), cut into large cubes
- 1 green capsicum (pepper), cut into large cubes
- 2 x 400 g (14 oz) tins chopped tomatoes
- 2 tablespoons tomato paste (concentrated purée)
- 500 ml (17 fl oz/2 cups) vegetable stock (page 10)
- 2 tablespoons chopped basil
- 115 g (4 oz/¾ cup) pitted kalamata olives
- 1–2 teaspoons soft brown sugar

METHOD

1 Put the beans in a large bowl, cover with cold water and soak overnight. Rinse well, then transfer to a saucepan, cover with cold water, bring to the boil and simmer for 45 minutes, or until just tender. Drain and set aside.

2 Heat the oil in a large saucepan. Cook the garlic and onion over medium heat for 2–3 minutes, or until the onion is soft. Add the capsicum and cook for a further 5 minutes.

3 Stir in the tomatoes, tomato paste, stock and beans. Simmer, covered, for 40 minutes, or until the beans are cooked through. Stir in the basil, olives and sugar. Season with sea salt and freshly ground black pepper. Serve hot with crusty bread.

NOTE: 1 cup of dried haricot beans yields about 2½ cups cooked beans. Use 2½ cups of drained tinned haricot or borlotti beans instead if you prefer, but add these at the end with the basil, olives and sugar, and just heat through.

BORLOTTI BEANS WITH TOMATOES

This bean salad can be made with dried, fresh or tinned borlotti beans. As the beans are cooking, a little olive oil is added — this not only gives flavour to the beans but also softens their skins.

INGREDIENTS

- 200 g (7 oz/1 cup) dried borlotti (cranberry) beans, or 250 g (9 oz) fresh borlotti beans, or 800 g (1 lb 12 oz) tin borlotti beans
- 3 garlic cloves, unpeeled
- 1 bay leaf
- 80 ml (2½ fl oz/⅓ cup) extra virgin olive oil
- 60 ml (2 fl oz/¼ cup) red wine vinegar or balsamic vinegar
- 2 tomatoes, peeled (page 347) and finely chopped
- ½ large mild red chilli, finely chopped
- 3 tablespoons roughly chopped mint
- 3 tablespoons roughly chopped parsley

METHOD

1 If using dried beans, soak them in cold water for at least 6 hours, or overnight. Drain the beans, put them in a saucepan, cover with water and bring to the boil. Drain again, rinsing away any foam on the surface. If using fresh beans, there is no need to soak and precook them. If using tinned beans, simply rinse well and drain before mixing with the olive oil and vinegar below.

2 To cook the dried or fresh beans, cover with water and bring to the boil, add the garlic, bay leaf and 1 tablespoon of the olive oil. Reduce the heat and simmer gently for 20–30 minutes for fresh beans and 40 minutes for dried, or until tender. Do not salt the beans during cooking, as this will toughen the skins. Drain the beans, keeping the garlic.

3 Remove the skin from the garlic and mash with a fork. While the beans are still hot, mix in the rest of the oil, the vinegar and salt and pepper. Stir in the tomatoes, chilli and herbs before serving.

CHAPTER EIGHT

HERBS AND SPICES

••HERBS••

Herbs are the leaves, flowers and sometimes stems of a group of aromatic non-woody plants used in cooking. The word is derived from the Latin *herba*, which means grass. Culinary herbs are used to impart an aromatic quality to food, either individually or in a mixture. The flavour comes from the oil stored in the leaves, which is released when the herb is crushed, chopped or heated. Particular herbs suit different styles of cooking and every cuisine has its favourites — the Middle East and Greece favour oregano, mint and dill; Thai cuisine uses coriander and lemongrass; in Italy, basil, parsley and oregano are commonly used; and in France, tarragon, chervil and fennel.

HOW TO... STORE AND PREPARE HERBS

* Herbs that are sold in plastic boxes or cellophane bags keep well in them. Put loose herbs in plastic bags and store in the vegetable crisper of the fridge. Herbs with more robust leaves will keep longer.
* Big bunches of mint, parsley and coriander will keep in a jug of water for a few days.
* Coarse robust herbs such as rosemary and parsley can be finely chopped in a food processor. For other herbs, use scissors, a flat knife or a mezzaluna. The blades of the mezzaluna must always be sharp enough to cut without tearing.
* Fine herbs such as tarragon or chives can be left large, shredded or snipped. For most recipes, basil leaves will be torn rather than chopped. This prevents the edges from blackening. Basil should be torn at the last minute, just before use, as it loses its flavour quickly. Herbs should be kept as dry as possible to help them keep their colour when torn or chopped.
* Flavour vinaigrette or mayonnaise by finely chopping or pounding the herbs using a mortar and pestle, then adding the rest of the ingredients.
* Whole leaves of mint or basil can be steeped in boiling water to make 'tea'. Crush them gently in your hand first to release the aromatic oils.
* If fresh herbs are unavailable, use dried, but remember that they are often more concentrated in flavour (unless stale) and you only need to use half or less of the quantity specified for fresh herbs.

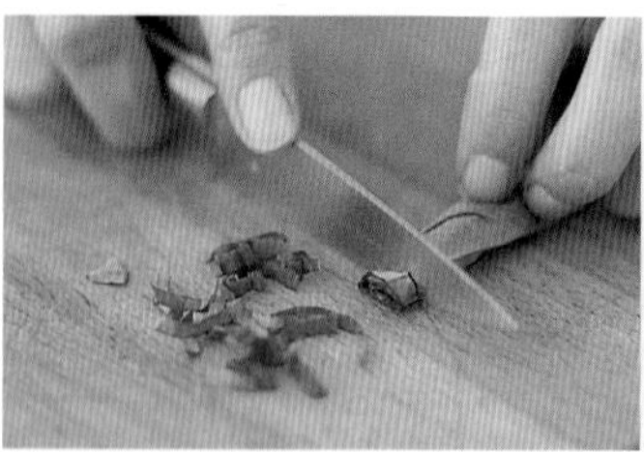

HOW TO... CHIFFONADE BASIL LEAVES

To neatly shred (chiffonade) larger leaves such as basil, lay the leaves on top of each other in a pile, then roll up the pile into a fat cigar. Slice thinly with a very sharp knife to prevent the basil bruising. Prepare fragile leaves such as basil at the last minute before adding to a dish so they don't discolour.

ANISE

Anise are liquorice-flavoured leaves used in salads and to flavour fish and vegetables, especially in Eastern European cuisine.

BALM

Balm leaves can be used in salads and stuffings and to scent custards. Balm's strong lemon flavour is lost when the herb is dried. It is also brewed as a tea and is a good substitute for lemongrass. Also known as lemon balm.

BASIL

The several types of basil all have different flavours. Genoa or sweet basil is the best known. It has a spicy smell and is used extensively in Italian cooking. Opal basil has purple leaves, Greek basil has smaller leaves and a pungent flavour, and Thai sweet basil and holy basil complement Thai and Southeast Asian dishes. Basil should be torn rather than chopped (or large quantities can be chiffonaded) and added to hot food at the last moment. It doesn't dry well.

BAY LEAVES

These glossy green leaves are used to add a strong, slightly peppery flavour to many dishes. Bay leaves were probably introduced into Europe by the Romans (who used it to make laurel wreaths). The berries of the tree are poisonous. Bay leaves can be used fresh or dried and are usually removed before serving. Fresh bay leaves have a stronger flavour. Wash fresh leaves well and store in the fridge for up to 3 days. Dried will keep in an airtight container for 6 months.

BORAGE

Borage flowers are small, bright blue or violet and star-shaped and are used in salads or to garnish drinks — the most famous being Pimm's. The youngest, least hairy leaves can be finely chopped and used in salads. They are similar to cucumber in flavour.

CHERVIL

This herb has delicate, lacy, pale-green leaves that deteriorate quickly and should be added to hot dishes just before serving. Chervil is one of the classic fines herbes. Use in salads or with creamy dishes, or use with tarragon to make béarnaise sauce. Chervil has a subtle parsley flavour with a hint of aniseed and goes particularly well with fish.

CHIVES

Related to the onion and leek, these herbs have long, thin, hollow leaves with a mild onion flavour. Chives can be snipped to length with scissors and used to garnish soup and stews. Best picked and used very fresh but can be stored in the vegetable crisper for 2 days. Garlic chives have flat dark leaves and a mild garlic taste and are also known as Chinese chives.

COMFREY

Comfrey belongs to the same family as borage and is similar in that the smaller leaves can be eaten as a vegetable. They are especially good dipped in batter and fried. The plant's white, yellow or pinkish bell-shaped flowers can be used for decoration in salads.

CORIANDER

The leaves, stem and root can all be used and each has its own purpose. The roots are used in curry pastes, the stems are used when a strong flavour is needed, and the leaves are added at the end of cooking, both as a flavouring and a garnish. Coriander is used extensively in Asian, South American, Mexican, Middle Eastern and Mediterranean cuisines. It goes very well with chilli, lime juice and meat dishes. Coriander is known as cilantro in the United States.

CURRY LEAVES

These dark, shiny green leaves look like bay leaves but have a distinctive curry flavour. Used widely in southern Indian and Malay cooking, the leaves are added to dishes during cooking or can be used as a garnish.

DILL

Dill has feathery leaves with a strong aniseed flavour. This is a delicate herb that should be chopped and added at the end of cooking. Dill is common in Scandinavian dishes such as gravlax and goes well with fish, chicken, creamy sauces and in salads.

LAVENDER

Lavender has a strong flavour and needs to be used sparingly. Use the dried, chopped flowers in shortbread, cakes, sorbets and custards or add to roasting lamb for extra flavour. Crystallised lavender flowers can be used as decoration on cakes.

LOVAGE

Lovage has a strong celery flavour and grows well in pots. Both the leaves and stems can be used in soups and sauces and to marinate meat and poultry.

MARJORAM AND OREGANO

Traditionally used to flavour tomato sauces in Italian and Greek cooking, these are usually used dried, and in sausages and stuffings. Both herbs come from the same family, of which there are several varieties. These herbs have a strong flavour and should be used sparingly.

MINT

Traditionally used in British cooking to go with lamb as mint sauce and on new potatoes. Mint also goes well in salads and with steamed fish. There are lots of varieties, including applemint, peppermint and spearmint.

PARSLEY

Available as flat-leaf (Italian) or curly-leaf parsley. Flat-leaf parsley tends to be stronger in flavour but the two can be used interchangeably. Parsley is used as an ingredient in dishes such as tabouleh as well as a garnish, and is used extensively in European cooking.

ROSEMARY

This strong-flavoured herb needs to be used judiciously. If you're using rosemary in food, chop it very finely; if using it as a flavouring, use small sprigs and remove them before serving. Rosemary goes well with roast lamb and pork and in breads. Sprigs can be used as skewers for flavouring meat, fish or chicken as it cooks on the barbecue.

SAGE

Sage leaves are traditionally used with onion to stuff goose, and in Italian cuisine to flavour butter served with pasta. Sage also works well with pork, veal and liver dishes. The whole leaves can be deep-fried and used as a garnish. Use sparingly as the flavour can be strong.

SALAD BURNET

Used in French and Italian cooking, the young leaves can be added to salads, soups and casseroles and to flavour vinegar. Salad burnet is similar in taste to cucumber and can be used as a lovely garnish for iced drinks.

SAVORY

This pungent herb is similar in flavour to thyme and mint. It is customarily used in bean dishes but also in pâtés, meat and fish, such as trout. Its name is a German word, meaning 'bean herb'. Savory dries very well.

TARRAGON

Tarragon has a hint of aniseed to its flavour and is used in many classic French dishes. It makes good aromatic sauces for poultry and can be used to flavour vinegar. It is important to use French tarragon in French dishes and not Russian, which has a coarser flavour.

THYME

There are many varieties and all have small leaves that can be used as a flavouring in casseroles and soups. Thyme gives a rich, aromatic flavour to slow-cooked food and roasts.

VIETNAMESE MINT

Not a member of the mint family. The leaves are served as a garnish for laksa, beef pho and with spring rolls and dipping sauce. It can be used in salads to give a spicy flavour. Also known as hot mint and laksa leaf.

HOW TO... MAKE A BOUQUET GARNI

A bouquet garni is a bundle of herbs tied together with string. It is used for flavouring stews and soups and then removed at the end of cooking. To make a bouquet garni, wrap the green part of a leek around a bay leaf, a thyme sprig, a parsley sprig and some young celery leaves. Tie the stems with string. You can tie this to the pan handle so you can find it easily when the dish is cooked.

••SPICES••

Spices are aromatic seasonings obtained from tropical plants and trees, including the seeds and pods, stems, bark, roots, buds, berries and fruits. Spices such as nutmeg and cloves were once so highly sought after that wars were fought over the medieval spice trading routes. Use spices sparingly so as not to overpower the other flavours in a dish.

ALLSPICE

These are the dried berries of the pimento tree indigenous to the West Indies, where it is used for 'jerk seasoning'. Allspice is used whole or ground. The taste is a combination of nutmeg, cinnamon, cloves and black pepper. It is used to flavour curries, relishes, preserves and marinades, and to give a mild spiciness to cakes and biscuits. Grind the berries prior to use. Not to be confused with mixed spice. Also known as Jamaica pepper and pimento.

ANISE

These liquorice-like flavoured seeds are from the bush of the hemlock family. Anise features in cooking of the Mediterranean, where it is a native. Anise has a sweet flavour and is used in both sweet and savoury cooking — in cakes, breads and confectionery, as well as with seafood and meat. It is also used to flavour the alcoholic drinks pernod and ouzo. Buy the seeds whole as the powder quickly loses its flavour. Also known as aniseed and sweet cumin.

ASAFOETIDA

This spice comes from the creamy sap from the root of a giant plant of the fennel family, and dries to a hard resin. Used in powder form as a flavour enhancer in Middle Eastern and Indian cooking, in curries, fish and vegetable stews, and pickles. Use in very small quantities as it has a strong sulphurous odour and taste. It is an effective anti-flatulent. Store in an airtight container for up to 1 year. Also known as devil's dung, giant fennel, heeng and stinking gum.

CARAWAY

Native to Europe and western Asia and related to anise, caraway has an aromatic, pungent flavour. Popular in German and Austrian cooking, as well as in Tunisia, where it is essential for harissa. The elongated seeds are used in breads, especially rye breads, seed cakes, cheeses and savoury dishes such as goulashes and cabbage dishes. It is available as seeds or ground.

CARDAMOM

Of the many varieties, the green cardamom from South India and Sri Lanka is superior. Use the whole pod or the seeds whole or ground to flavour both sweet and savoury Indian food from curries and rice dishes to sweet milk desserts. The seeds have a sweet, mild flavour. Also flavours tea, coffee, cakes and breads. Also known as cardamon.

CASSIA

This is dried bark used as small pieces or ground. It has a similar taste to cinnamon but has less flavour and is harder and coarser. Cassia is used in curries, rice and vegetable dishes and is an ingredient of Chinese five-spice. Cassia also has buds that are sold dried with the stalk attached, used in pickles and 'paan', a betel leaf parcel filled with nuts, seeds and spices. Dried cassia leaves, also called Indian bay leaves, are used in Indian curry and rice dishes.

CAYENNE PEPPER

A powder made from dried red chillies, native to South America. This is very pungent and should be used sparingly. Used in curry powder, chilli sauce and Tabasco sauce. Cayenne pepper is common in Indian and Latin American cuisines.

CELERY SEEDS

The seeds of a wild celery called lovage. They have a slightly bitter, strong concentrated celery taste. Use whole or crushed to flavour soups, in stuffings, sauces, stews and pickles.

CINNAMON

Cinnamon is a member of the laurel family native to Sri Lanka. The inner bark is dried and sold as quills or sticks. Used whole to flavour milk puddings, curries, pilau rice, in pickles and mulled wine. Ground or powdered cinnamon is used in baking and desserts and is sometimes added to savoury dishes such as curries and stews.

CLOVES

The dried aromatic unopened flower buds of an evergreen tree native to the Moluccas (Indonesia). Used whole to flavour stews, game dishes and traditionally to decorate whole ham. Also added to blended spice mixtures. The bud head is ground and used in sweet and savoury dishes, spiced wines, and liqueurs. Available whole and ground.

CORIANDER SEEDS

Native to southern Europe and the Mediterranean, the dried seeds are left whole or ground. Crushed they form a basis for curry pastes and powder. The whole seeds are enhanced if they are lightly dry-roasted before crushing. Use in curries.

CUMIN

A herb indigenous to the East Mediterranean. The fruits of the seeds are used whole or ground in many cuisines, particularly North African, Indian, Mexican and Japanese. It has a hot pungent taste. Light dry-roasting of the seeds releases their aroma. Use in couscous, rice, kebabs, stews, curries and yoghurt.

DILL SEEDS

Native to western Asia and today grown worldwide, especially in Europe and North America. The leaves are used dried and the seeds whole or ground. Used to flavour dill pickles, meat and egg dishes, breads and in soups, salads and sauces. Also known as dill weed.

FENNEL SEEDS

Originally from southern Europe but now grown worldwide, fennel seeds have a slightly liquorice or aniseed taste, and are used whole or ground. Use in stuffing, salads, fish and seafood dishes, or add to curries, pickles and chutneys in Indian cuisine. Often offered after an Indian meal as a palate cleanser.

FENUGREEK

Pods containing seeds of a native plant from western Asia. The flavour of the dried seeds is enhanced by lightly roasting before using the seeds or grinding to a powder. The flavour is mild and aromatic. Fenugreek is a popular flavouring in Indian cooking.

JUNIPER BERRIES

These hard berries are blue to purple in colour when ripened, and are used to flavour gin, game, pork and pâtés. Juniper is popular in German dishes such as sauerkraut and preserves. The flavour is slightly pine scented. Crush the berries lightly before use.

MACE

Mace is the outer lace-like covering of nutmeg. It has a similar but more delicate flavour. It is sold as fragments known as blades and may also be ground into a powder. Mace is used to flavour delicate dishes, such as soups, sauces and milk puddings, and is traditionally used in English potted meats.

NIGELLA

These small black seeds have a slight peppery taste. Nigella is used in Indian and Middle Eastern cooking, especially vegetable and fish dishes. It is also sprinkled over salads and breads. The aromatic flavour is enhanced if the seeds are heated. Also known as black cumin, black onion seed and kalonji.

NUTMEG

Nutmeg is the hard kernel or nut of an evergreen plant native to the Moluccas (Indonesia). The best flavour, described as warm and spicy, comes from using a whole nutmeg, freshly grated just prior to use. Nutmeg is also available ground. It is used to enhance the flavour of savoury dishes but is particularly good with milk-based desserts and sauces.

PAPRIKA

The national spice of Hungary, which is famous for its goulash flavoured with paprika. This is made from the dried and ground fruits of sweet red capsicums (peppers). Paprika varies in flavour from hot to mild (also called sweet) depending on the type of capsicum used and whether the seeds have been added.

SICHUAN PEPPERCORNS

This Chinese spice native to the province of Sichuan is made from the red berries of the prickly ash tree and sold whole or ground. Although not related to the peppercorn, the Sichuan berry resembles the black peppercorn in appearance but has enclosed seeds. The flavour and fragrance has a distinctive woody–spicy smell and a strong, hot, numbing aftertaste. Widely used in Chinese everyday cooking (often in very large amounts) and as one of the components of Chinese five-spice. It is sometimes crushed and dry-fried to bring out the flavour. Also known as anise pepper, Chinese aromatic pepper, Szechuan pepper and xanthoxylum.

STAR ANISE

A native Chinese tree, related to the magnolia, that has a star-shaped fruit containing a seed. Star anise is similar to anise but stronger and more liquorice-like in flavour. Star anise is an ingredient of Chinese five-spice, and is used in Arabic and Asian cooking, especially Chinese cuisine with pork and duck. Use whole or powdered. Also known as badian.

TURMERIC

A relative of ginger, turmeric is from the underground root of a tropical plant. It has a musky, faintly peppery aroma and flavour and is used in curry powders, rice, lentil and potato dishes, and commercially to colour drinks, butter, cheese and mustards. It is sometimes called 'poor man's saffron' — its vivid yellow colouring certainly resembles that of the expensive spice but the two are not interchangeable.

For other spices, see saffron (page 277) and vanilla (page 636).

HOW TO... STORE SPICES

* Most spices are available whole, ground and powdered. Ground spices lose their flavour and aroma quickly so buy them in small quantities and store in airtight containers in a cool, dark place for up to 6 months only.
* Similarly, spice mixes will only keep for a short time and the individual spices may have different rates of staling, which can upset the balance of flavour.
* Where possible, buy spices whole and use your own spice grinder or mortar and pestle to grind them as needed.
* Buy good-quality spice mixes — those that contain whole spices should be in good condition and not just a way of using up broken spices; powdered mixes should be freshly ground, if possible.

SPICE MIXES

There are many established mixtures of spices, usually dried or powdered, which are used specifically for certain cooking methods or are peculiar to a local region or country. In some instances, spice mixes can refer to a paste such as tandoori or masala. Although each spice mixture is usually made in a certain way, the amount and type of spice used can vary, depending on local preferences, the spices at hand, or the desires of an individual cook.

BAHARAT

An aromatic spice blend used in Arabic cuisine to add depth of flavour to a variety of dishes from soups to curries. This is a mix of black pepper, cassia, cloves, cumin, nutmeg, paprika, cardamom and coriander with loomi (dried Omani limes).

BEBERE

A complex Ethiopian blend of spices, of which chillies, ginger and cloves form the basis.

CHAAT MASALA

An Indian mix that includes cumin, salt, fennel seed, amchur, garam masala, asafoetida and chilli. Used in Indian dishes to season potato and vegetables.

CHINESE FIVE-SPICE

Of Chinese origin, this consists of equal parts of sichuan pepper, cassia or cinnamon, fennel seed, star anise and cloves. Typically used in stir-fries and pork and beef dishes.

GARAM MASALA

This means 'hot mixture' and is the most commonly used of the Indian masalas. It can be bought ready-made, or make your own by dry-frying for 2–3 minutes separately 2 tablespoons coriander seeds, 1–2 tablespoons cardamom pods, 1 tablespoon cumin seeds, 2 teaspoons whole black peppercorns, 1 teaspoon cloves and 3 cinnamon sticks. Put in a spice grinder or grind using a mortar and pestle with 1 grated nutmeg. Store in an airtight container.

INDIAN CURRY POWDER

Indian curry powders can include up to nine ingredients, with the spices used varying regionally. Versions include Madras, rendang, Ceylon, tandoori and vindaloo. To make your own Indian curry powder, dry-fry separately 2 teaspoons cumin seeds, 2 teaspoons coriander seeds, 2 teaspoons fenugreek seeds, 1 teaspoon yellow mustard seeds, 1 teaspoon black peppercorns and 1 teaspoon cloves, then grind to a fine powder using a mortar and pestle or spice grinder. Mix with 1 teaspoon chilli powder, 2 teaspoons ground turmeric, ½ teaspoon ground cinnamon and ½ teaspoon ground cardamom. Store in an airtight container.

LA KAMA

A Moroccan mixture of five spices — cinnamon, pepper, ginger, turmeric and nutmeg, used to flavour stews, soups and lamb dishes.

MASALA

An Indian spice mixture of which there are many regional specialities and spice combinations: garam masala, chaat masala (both opposite) and goda masala (pictured) are common, but every family has their own version. Masala (meaning 'mixture') may be dry or a wet paste, strong, mild or aromatic in flavour. In northern India, masala is generally made with dry spices, freshly roasted and ground. In southern India, the spices are usually ground when green with liquid such as coconut milk, lime or vinegar for dishes such as chicken tikka masala.

MIXED SPICE

A mixture of cinnamon, allspice, cloves, coriander, mace and nutmeg. It is often added to sweet puddings, desserts, mince pies, yeasted buns and biscuits.

PANCH PHORAN

An aromatic Indian blend of equal quantities of seeds: cumin, fennel, fenugreek, brown mustard and nigella. This may be used whole or ground and has a bittersweet flavour. Usually added to hot oil to bring out the flavour before adding to lentils, pulses and vegetables.

PICKLING SPICES

A mixture of spices used in chutneys, pickles and vinegar. The quantities and number of ingredients vary depending on personal taste and the recipe but usually consist of allspice, bay leaves, cardamom, chilli, cinnamon, cloves, coriander, mustard seeds and peppercorns. The spices are tied into a muslin bag which can be lifted out at the end of cooking.

QUATRE EPICES

The French name means 'four spices', although this mixture may consist of more. The main ingredients are black pepper, nutmeg, ginger and cloves and possibly cayenne pepper and cinnamon. The spices are tied in muslin, then either lifted out after cooking or left in the dish. This is often added to casseroles as a flavour enhancer.

RAS EL HANOUT

Meaning 'top of the shop', this Moroccan spice mixture can include many ingredients, sometimes up to 50 or 100. Typically it includes aniseed, allspice, cloves, cayenne pepper, cinnamon, cardamom, cumin, dried rose buds or petals, galangal, ginger, mace, nutmeg, orris root and various peppers. Some versions may include green Spanish fly, believed to be an aphrodisiac. It is used to flavour rice and couscous, meat and game dishes.

SEVEN-SPICE POWDER (SHICHIMI TOGARASHI)

A Japanese mixture of seven ground spices, seeds and flavourings, which varies from city to city. It may consist of, for example, two hot and five aromatic flavours — red pepper, sansho pepper, sesame seeds, flax seeds, poppy seeds, ground nori (seaweed) and dried tangerine or orange peel. Used as a seasoning in noodles and on cooked and grilled meats and fish.

CHAPTER NINE

SAUCES AND DIPS

••DRESSINGS••

Dressings, mayonnaise and vinaigrettes are really very simple to make, so there should be no excuse for reaching for the bottled varieties. Dress your salads in style at home.

MAYONNAISE

MAKES ABOUT 250 ML (9 FL OZ/1 CUP)

INGREDIENTS

2 egg yolks
2 tablespoons lemon juice
1 teaspoon dijon mustard
185 ml (6 fl oz/¾ cup) olive oil

METHOD

1 Start with the ingredients at room temperature. Beat the egg yolks with 1 tablespoon lemon juice and the mustard in a deep bowl.
2 Add a drop of oil to the egg mixture and blend with a whisk until light and creamy. Repeat, then continue to add the oil, drop by drop, until an emulsion is formed.
3 As the mixture thickens and becomes pale and glossy, add the oil faster, in a steady stream.
4 When all the oil has been added, add the rest of the lemon juice (and thin with 1 tablespoon water if preferred). Season with salt and white pepper. Store covered in the fridge for up to 4 days.
5 Alternatively, mix the egg yolks, mustard and lemon juice in a food processor for 10 seconds. With the motor running, add the oil in a slow, thin stream. Season to taste.

TIPS

* Mayonnaise can be made with a whisk, an electric whisk or in a blender. Add the oil very slowly. If you pour it in too quickly, the mayonnaise will curdle.
* If it does curdle, try adding 1–2 teaspoons hot water. If it still won't emulsify, start again with a new egg yolk and add the curdled mixture very slowly.
* Use good-quality extra virgin olive oil. For light-flavoured mayonnaise use vegetable oil.
* Commercially made mayonnaise has a 'softer' texture as it has water added — add a tablespoon of water to your mayonnaise if you like that effect.
* TO MAKE GREEN GODDESS SAUCE to serve with seafood, stir 4 finely chopped spring onions, 1 crushed garlic clove, 4 mashed anchovies, a handful of chopped parsley, a handful of snipped chives and 1 teaspoon of tarragon vinegar into 1 quantity of mayonnaise (left).

AIOLI

MAKES ABOUT 250 ML (9 FL OZ/1 CUP)

INGREDIENTS

2 egg yolks
4 garlic cloves, crushed
1 tablespoon lemon juice
250 ml (9 fl oz/1 cup) olive oil

METHOD

1 Beat the egg yolks with the garlic and lemon juice, then whisk in the oil, drop by drop, following the method for mayonnaise (see left).

THOUSAND ISLAND DRESSING

MAKES 125 ML (4 FL OZ/½ CUP)

INGREDIENTS
- 125 ml (4 fl oz/½ cup) mayonnaise (see opposite)
- 1 tablespoon tomato paste (concentrated purée)
- 1 teaspoon worcestershire sauce
- 1 teaspoon French or dijon mustard
- 2 teaspoons chilli sauce

METHOD
1 Mix together all the ingredients.

ITALIAN DRESSING

MAKES ABOUT 125 ML (4 FL OZ/½ CUP)

INGREDIENTS
- 60 ml (2 fl oz/¼ cup) white wine vinegar
- 60 ml (2 fl oz/¼ cup) olive oil
- ½ teaspoon sugar
- 1 tablespoon torn basil

METHOD
1 Whisk together all the ingredients until the sugar has dissolved. Add the basil leaves.

BALSAMIC DRESSING

MAKES ABOUT 125 ML (4 FL OZ/½ CUP)

INGREDIENTS
- 2 tablespoons balsamic vinegar
- 1 teaspoon French or dijon mustard
- 80 ml (2½ fl oz/⅓ cup) extra virgin olive oil
- 1 small garlic clove, halved

METHOD
1 Whisk the vinegar, mustard and oil. Season. Add the garlic and leave to infuse for at least 1 hour.

CITRUS VINAIGRETTE

MAKES 250 ML (9 FL OZ/1 CUP)

INGREDIENTS
- 170 ml (5½ fl oz/⅔ cup) light olive oil
- 80 ml (2½ fl oz/⅓ cup) lime juice
- 2 tablespoons lemon thyme
- 1 teaspoon honey

METHOD
1 Whisk together all the ingredients and season with salt and black pepper.

BASIC VINAIGRETTE

MAKES ABOUT 170 ML (5½ FL OZ/⅔ CUP)

INGREDIENTS
- 125 ml (4 fl oz/½ cup) extra virgin olive oil
- 2 tablespoons white wine vinegar
- 1 teaspoon sugar

METHOD
1 Whisk together the oil, vinegar and sugar until well blended. Season with salt and black pepper.

RASPBERRY VINAIGRETTE

MAKES ABOUT 125 ML (4 FL OZ/½ CUP)

INGREDIENTS
- 80 ml (2½ fl oz/⅓ cup) hazelnut oil
- 2 tablespoons raspberry vinegar
- 5 raspberries, finely chopped
- ½ teaspoon sugar

METHOD
1 Whisk together all the ingredients and season.

••SAVOURY SAUCES••

Hot or cold sauces can raise the most everyday dishes to great heights. Savoury sauces are worth taking the time to make, and can make a wonderful meal of simply cooked meat, chicken, seafood, vegetables and even eggs.

BECHAMEL SAUCE

This classic sauce is made by adding milk to a roux. Unlike a basic white sauce, the milk is infused with flavourings such as onions, cloves, bay leaves and nutmeg, with many variations on the theme. Use béchamel as a topping for lasagne, cannelloni and gratin, and as a pouring sauce for vegetables, fish or chicken. A white sauce is made in exactly the same way, using just flour, butter and milk, and without any flavourings. When the sauce is cooling, cover the surface with plastic wrap to stop a skin forming.

MAKES ABOUT 250 ML (9 FL OZ/1 CUP)

INGREDIENTS

- 250 ml (9 fl oz/1 cup) milk
- 1 onion, sliced
- 3 peppercorns
- 1 bay leaf
- 20 g (¾ oz) butter
- 1 tablespoon plain (all-purpose) flour
- pinch of ground nutmeg

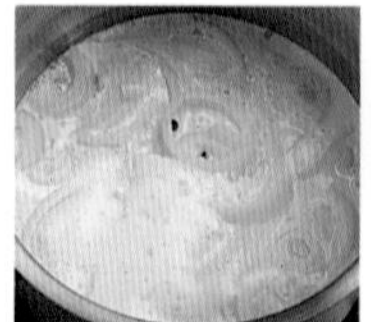

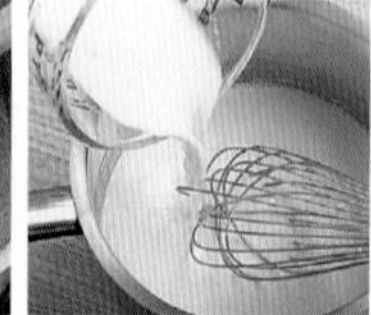

METHOD

1. Bring the milk, onion, peppercorns and bay leaf just to boiling point then remove from the heat (this is 'scalding') and leave to infuse.
2. To make a roux, melt the butter, then add the flour and cook, stirring, for 2 minutes over low heat until golden and foaming.
3. Strain the scalded milk, then slowly whisk in to the roux (if you are nervous about lumps you can do this off the heat). Bring to the boil, whisking constantly until thick. Season with salt, pepper and nutmeg and simmer for 20 minutes.

TIPS

* For a smooth sauce, whisk the milk gradually into the flour. If the sauce does becomes lumpy, pass it through a sieve, then reheat it.
* To prevent a raw, floury taste, it is important to cook the flour for 1–2 minutes in the butter before adding the milk, so the starch grains burst.

MUSTARD AND DILL SAUCE

Mustard and dill sauce is traditionally served with gravlax (page 235). In a small bowl, whisk together 3 tablespoons dijon mustard, 3 tablespoons wholegrain mustard, 150 ml (5 fl oz) olive oil, 2 teaspoons cider vinegar and 2 tablespoons finely chopped dill. Season to taste. Cover and refrigerate until needed. Makes 250 ml (9 fl oz/1 cup)

BEARNAISE SAUCE

Named after the French province of Béarn, béarnaise is a thick, creamy pungent sauce made with butter, egg yolks, vinegar and tarragon. Use a non-reactive saucepan so there is no danger of the sauce discolouring or being tainted with a metallic flavour. Serve this with pan-fried steak, roast beef or lamb, or poached salmon, or try it with vegetables and eggs.

MAKES 250 ML (9 FL OZ/1 CUP)

INGREDIENTS

- 80 ml (2½ fl oz/⅓ cup) white wine vinegar
- 2 spring onions (scallions), roughly chopped
- 2 teaspoons chopped tarragon
- 2 egg yolks
- 125 g (4½ oz) butter, cubed

METHOD

1. Put the white wine vinegar, spring onion and tarragon in a small saucepan. Bring to the boil, then reduce the heat slightly and simmer until reduced by a third. Allow to cool completely, then strain the vinegar into a heatproof bowl.
2. Add the egg yolks to the bowl, then place the bowl over a saucepan of barely simmering water. Whisk until the mixture is thick and pale. Add the butter, a cube at a time, whisking between each addition until the mixture is thick and smooth. Season to taste with salt and pepper.

HOLLANDAISE SAUCE

One of the classic French sauces, hollandaise is made traditionally over a double boiler or, quickly, in a food processor. It can't be reheated, but can be kept warm over a bain-marie. Serve with asparagus or artichoke, with poached eggs and English muffins to make Eggs Benedict, and with poultry and seafood. You can add freshly chopped herbs at the end of cooking.

MAKES 250 ML (9 FL OZ/1 CUP)

INGREDIENTS

- 175 g (6 oz) butter
- 4 egg yolks
- 1 tablespoon lemon juice

METHOD

1. Melt the butter until boiling. Mix the egg yolks, lemon juice and 1 tablespoon water in a food processor for 10 seconds. With the motor running, add the hot butter in a thin stream. The mixture will thicken as the hot butter cooks the yolks. Season well.

* To make hollandaise in the microwave, melt the butter on high for 1 minute. Beat the egg yolks, water and lemon juice together and whisk in the butter. Cook for 1 minute 20 seconds on medium, whisking every 20 seconds.
* For foaming hollandaise, whisk 2 egg whites until soft peaks form and fold into the sauce.

MORNAY SAUCE

This is a white béchamel sauce to which grated cheese is added. Other ingredients such as egg yolks, mustard, cream or stock may also be added. Food served with mornay sauce is usually coated in the sauce, sprinkled with additional grated cheese and/or breadcrumbs, then grilled. Serve with fish, shellfish such as oysters and lobster, eggs, vegetables and chicken.

SERVES 4

INGREDIENTS

330 ml (11¼ fl oz/1⅓ cups) milk
1 slice of onion
1 bay leaf
6 peppercorns
30 g (1 oz) butter
1 tablespoon plain (all-purpose) flour
60 g (2¼ oz/½ cup) finely grated cheddar cheese
¼ teaspoon mustard powder

METHOD

1 Put the milk, onion, bay leaf and peppercorns in a small saucepan. Bring just to the boil, remove from the heat and leave to infuse for 10 minutes. Strain the milk, discarding the flavourings.
2 Melt the butter in a small saucepan and add the flour. Cook, stirring, for 2 minutes until the roux is golden and foaming. Add the scalded milk, a little at a time, stirring until completely smooth. Continue stirring until the mixture boils and thickens. Boil for 1 minute more and then remove from the heat. Stir in the cheese and mustard and season well.

VELOUTE SAUCE

One of the basic French white sauces, velouté is made with a butter and flour roux that is cooked until pale (blonde), then blended with a white stock, either veal, chicken or fish. The mixture is slow cooked until velvety in texture and sometimes further enriched with a liaison of egg yolks and cream. Velouté may also have other added flavourings such as saffron, tomato and fish stock. Serve with chicken, seafood or veal.

SERVES 4

INGREDIENTS

30 g (1 oz) butter
3 tablespoons plain (all-purpose) flour
375 ml (13 fl oz/1½ cups) chicken, fish (page 10–11) or veal stock
lemon juice, to taste
1 tablespoon cream

METHOD

1 Melt the butter in a small saucepan and add the flour. Cook, stirring, for 2 minutes until the roux is golden and foaming. (Be careful not to brown the roux or it will colour your sauce.)
2 Whisk in the stock a little at a time to prevent the sauce becoming lumpy. Cook, whisking continuously, for 3–5 minutes, until the sauce is quite thick.
3 Season with salt, pepper and lemon juice, adding a little at a time. Finally, stir in the cream. Serve immediately — the sauce will quickly thicken if left to stand. If necessary, add a little extra stock to thin it down.

BUTTER SAUCES

Butter can be used to enhance the flavour of a sauce or make it shiny (to 'monter au beurre'). To do this, remove the sauce from the heat and vigorously whisk in a tablespoon of butter. For browned butter (beurre noisette), gently heat butter until it turns golden and nutty. Use as is, or stir in lemon juice and chopped parsley.

BEURRE BLANC

This classic French sauce is made by beating butter into a reduction of wine and vinegar. It is traditionally served with fish, but also good with chicken, eggs, asparagus or artichokes. When making the sauce, form an emulsion quickly so you can add the butter with less risk of the sauce separating. Prepare just before serving and keep warm in a bain-marie (or in a heatproof bowl over a pan of gently simmering water), as reheating will cause the sauce to split. You can enhance the flavour with finely snipped chives or citrus zest.

SERVES 4

INGREDIENTS

- 2 French shallots, chopped
- 60 ml (2 fl oz/¼ cup) white wine vinegar
- 125 ml (4 fl oz/½ cup) white wine
- 250 g (9 oz) unsalted butter, cubed

METHOD

1. Put the shallots, vinegar and wine in a saucepan and bring to the boil. Reduce the heat and simmer until reduced to 3 tablespoons. Remove from the heat, strain into a clean saucepan and return to low heat.
2. Whisk in the butter, a few cubes at a time, over low heat. The sauce will thicken as the butter is added, until it is the same consistency as cream. Season with salt and pepper.

ROMESCO

This classic sauce from Tarragona in Catalonia, Spain, traditionally contains dried nyora peppers. Today, there are many versions, but it is typically made with tomatoes, garlic, nyora peppers, parsley, hazelnuts, almonds, chilli and bread. We've used roasted capsicum here, as nyora peppers can be hard to find. Serve with grilled fish.

SERVES 4–6

INGREDIENTS

- 2 tomatoes, halved
- 1 red capsicum (pepper), halved and seeded
- 4 garlic cloves, peeled
- 4 tablespoons fresh breadcrumbs
- 100 g (3½ oz) hazelnuts
- 50 g (1¾ oz/⅓ cup) almonds
- ½ teaspoon chilli powder
- 1 tablespoon red wine vinegar
- 1 tablespoon olive oil

METHOD

1. Preheat the oven to 200°C (400°F/Gas 6). Put the tomatoes, capsicum and garlic cloves on a baking tray and roast for 20 minutes. Peel the capsicum (page 356).
2. Fry the breadcrumbs with the hazelnuts and almonds until lightly golden. Crush or process them using a mortar and pestle or food processor to form a paste, adding the roasted tomatoes, capsicum and garlic as you go. Add the chilli powder, vinegar, olive oil and season.

TARTARE SAUCE

Tartare is a French word, dating back to the thirteenth century and the ferocious Mongolian Tartars (who also gave their name to Steak Tartare). Mix 250 ml (9 fl oz/1 cup) mayonnaise (page 422), 2 tablespoons chopped capers, 2 tablespoons chopped parsley, 2 chopped cornichons, 1 finely chopped French shallot and 1 finely chopped hard-boiled egg. Season with salt and pepper and serve with fish. Serves 4

BREAD SAUCE

SERVES 4

INGREDIENTS

- 2 cloves
- 1 onion
- 250 ml (9 fl oz/1 cup) milk
- 1 bay leaf
- 50 g (1¾ oz) fresh breadcrumbs (made using about 3 slices of day-old bread)
- 60 ml (2 fl oz/¼ cup) cream

METHOD

1. Push the cloves into the onion and put in a saucepan with the milk and bay leaf. Bring just to the boil, then remove from the heat, cover and leave for 10 minutes for the flavour to infuse the milk. Remove the onion and bay leaf.
2. Add the breadcrumbs to the milk and season. Return to the heat, cover and simmer gently for 10 minutes, stirring occasionally. Stir in the cream. Serve warm with roast chicken, turkey, goose or game.

GRAVY

SERVES 8

INGREDIENTS

- pan juices from the roast
- 2 tablespoons plain (all-purpose) flour
- 500 ml (17 fl oz/2 cups) beef or chicken stock (page 11)

METHOD

1. Pour off any excess fat from the roasting tin. Sprinkle the flour over the pan juices and stir well, scraping any bits from the bottom. Cook over medium heat, stirring, for 1–2 minutes.
2. Add the stock a little at a time, stirring after each addition. Bring to the boil and stir for 1 minute, or until thickened a little. Season to taste.

CUMBERLAND SAUCE

SERVES 8

INGREDIENTS

- 2 oranges
- 1 lemon
- 225 g (8 oz) redcurrant jelly
- 2 teaspoons dijon mustard
- 2 tablespoons red wine vinegar
- 250 ml (9 fl oz/1 cup) port

METHOD

1. Grate the zest from the oranges and lemon and put in a small pan with 250 ml (9 fl oz/1 cup) water and bring to the boil. Cook for 5 minutes, then strain the liquid, keeping the zest.
2. Squeeze the juice from the oranges and lemon into the pan. Add the jelly, mustard, vinegar, port and zest. Slowly bring to the boil, stirring as the jelly melts. Reduce the heat and simmer gently for 15 minutes. Season with salt and pepper. Serve at room temperature with ham.

DEMI-GLACE

SERVES 8

INGREDIENTS

- 2 tablespoons oil
- 2 carrots, finely chopped
- 1 onion, finely chopped
- 1 celery stalk, finely chopped
- 1 tablespoon plain (all-purpose) flour
- 1 litre (35 fl oz/4 cups) beef stock (page 11)
- ½ teaspoon tomato paste (concentrated purée)
- 1 bouquet garni

METHOD

1. Heat the oil in a frying pan and brown the carrot, onion and celery over medium heat. Add the flour and cook, stirring, until browned.
2. Add 625 ml (21 fl oz/2½ cups) of the stock to the pan, along with the tomato paste and bouquet garni and bring to the boil. Reduce the heat, half-cover the pan and simmer, skimming off any scum from the surface, for 30 minutes, or until reduced to 250 ml (9 fl oz/1 cup). Strain and leave to cool. This is called an espagnole.
3. To make the demi-glace, put the espagnole and the remaining stock in a saucepan and simmer until reduced by half. Strain thoroughly through a fine mesh sieve or muslin. Serve with roast beef or steaks.

TOMATO PASTA SAUCE

SERVES 4

INGREDIENTS

- 125 ml (4 fl oz/½ cup) olive oil
- 2 garlic cloves, crushed
- 400 g (14 oz) tin chopped tomatoes
- 3 basil leaves

METHOD

1. Heat the olive oil in a heavy-based saucepan, add the garlic and cook very gently until you can smell the garlic.
2. Add the tomatoes and 250 ml (9 fl oz/1 cup) water and season well. Simmer for about 30 minutes, then allow to cool a little. Add the basil and then purée with a hand-held mixer or blender. Use the tomato sauce on pizzas or toss through pasta.

BARBECUE SAUCE

MAKES ABOUT 125 ML (4 FL OZ/½ CUP)

INGREDIENTS

- 2 teaspoons oil
- 1 small onion, finely chopped
- 1 tablespoon malt vinegar
- 1 tablespoon soft brown sugar
- 80 ml (2½ fl oz/⅓ cup) tomato sauce (ketchup)
- 1 tablespoon worcestershire sauce

METHOD

1. Heat the oil in a small saucepan and cook the onion over low heat for 3 minutes, or until soft, stirring now and then.
2. Add the remaining ingredients and bring to the boil. Reduce the heat and simmer for 3 minutes, stirring occasionally. Serve warm or at room temperature. Barbecue sauce can be kept, covered and refrigerated, for up to 1 week.

APPLE SAUCE

SERVES 6–8

INGREDIENTS

- 4 green apples, cored, peeled and chopped
- 2 teaspoons caster (superfine) sugar
- 2 cloves
- 1 cinnamon stick
- 1–2 teaspoons lemon juice

METHOD

1. Put the apple, sugar, cloves, cinnamon stick and 125 ml (4 fl oz/½ cup) water in a saucepan, cover and simmer over low heat for 10 minutes, or until the apple is soft. Remove the cloves and cinnamon. Mash the apples (or purée them for a finer sauce). Stir in the lemon juice.

MINT SAUCE

SERVES 4

INGREDIENTS

- 90 g (3¼ oz) sugar
- 2 tablespoons malt vinegar
- 1 handful mint leaves, finely chopped

METHOD

1. Put the sugar in a pan with 60 ml (2 fl oz/¼ cup) water. Stir over low heat, without boiling, until dissolved. Bring to the boil, then simmer for 3 minutes without stirring. Remove from the heat.
2. Mix the sugar mixture with the vinegar and mint. Cover and leave for 10 minutes for the flavours to develop.

CHILLI JAM

SERVES 6–8

INGREDIENTS

- oil, for frying
- 20 red Asian shallots, sliced
- 10 garlic cloves, sliced
- 3 tablespoons dried shrimp
- 7 dried long red chillies, chopped
- 3 tablespoons tamarind purée or lime juice
- 90 g (3¼ oz/½ cup) grated palm sugar (jaggery)
- 1 teaspoon shrimp paste

METHOD

1. Heat the oil in a frying pan. Fry the shallots and garlic until golden, then transfer to a blender.
2. Fry the shrimp and chillies for 1–2 minutes, then add to the blender with the remaining ingredients. Mix, adding as much of the frying oil as necessary to make a pourable paste.
3. Put the mixture in a saucepan and bring to the boil. Reduce the heat and simmer until the sauce is thick. (Don't overcook or it will caramelise into a lump.) Season with salt or fish sauce.

SWEET CHILLI SAUCE

MAKES ABOUT 60 ML (2 FL OZ/¼ CUP)

INGREDIENTS

- 7 long red chillies, seeded and roughly chopped
- 185 ml (6 fl oz/¾ cup) white vinegar
- 140 g (5 oz/⅔ cup) sugar

METHOD

1. Pound or blend the chillies to a rough paste.
2. Put the vinegar, sugar and ½ teaspoon salt in a saucepan over high heat. Bring to the boil, stirring, then simmer for 15–20 minutes, or until the mixture forms a thick syrup. Add the chilli paste and cook for a further 1–2 minutes.

SALSAS

Salsa means 'sauce' in Italian and Spanish, but it is also the South and Central American cooking term for the mixture of chopped vegetables that falls somewhere between a sauce and a salad. This is illustrated by the fact that traditional Italian salsa verde (page 223) is made with parsley, capers, anchovies, oil and vinegar, while the Mexican version is made with chopped green tomatoes, chillies, onion and coriander.

ROCKET SALSA VERDE

SERVES 4

INGREDIENTS

- 20 g (¾ oz/¼ cup) fresh breadcrumbs (made using 1 slice of day-old bread)
- 125 ml (4 fl oz/½ cup) olive oil
- 2 tablespoons lemon juice
- 1 garlic clove, crushed
- 4 anchovy fillets, finely chopped
- 2 handfuls rocket (arugula), finely chopped
- 1 handful flat-leaf (Italian) parsley, finely chopped
- 1 tablespoon capers, finely chopped

1. Put all the ingredients in a bowl, mix together and season well with black pepper. Cover with plastic wrap and leave at room temperature for 4 hours. Stir well just before serving.

PEACH SALSA

SERVES 6

- 6 peaches (or nectarines), finely diced
- 1 red onion, finely diced
- juice of 4 limes
- 2 handfuls coriander (cilantro), finely chopped
- 2 red chillies, finely chopped

1. Put all the ingredients in a bowl, mix together gently and season well with black pepper.

CORN, AVOCADO AND OLIVE SALSA

SERVES 6

INGREDIENTS

- 2 sweet corn cobs
- 1 avocado
- 90 g (3¼ oz) stuffed green olives, chopped
- 2 tablespoons finely chopped parsley
- 3 spring onions (scallions), shredded
- 1 tablespoon olive oil
- 2 tablespoons lemon juice

METHOD

1. Cook the corn in boiling water for 5 minutes, or until just soft. Drain, cool and pat dry with paper towels. Using a large sharp knife, cut the kernels from the cobs and place in a single layer on a foil-lined baking tray. Grill (broil) for 10 minutes, or until the corn is golden brown, turning the kernels once. Allow to cool.
2. Chop the avocado into small dice. Combine the corn, avocado, olives, parsley, spring onion, oil and lemon juice, and season with salt and pepper. Toss well to make sure the avocado is coated with the dressing. Cover and chill for 15 minutes before serving. Serve the salsa with pan-fried salmon or chicken, lamb or beef.

• • DIPS • •

Dips are easy enough to buy at supermarkets and delis, but once you've made your own with fresh ingredients you'll probably never buy them again. Most of these can be made in less time than it takes to get to the shops and taste far better than any commercial variety.

HUMMUS

SERVES 6

INGREDIENTS

- 225 g (8 oz/1 cup) dried chickpeas
- 2 tablespoons tahini
- 4 garlic cloves, crushed
- 2 teaspoons ground cumin
- 80 ml (2½ fl oz/⅓ cup) lemon juice
- 60 ml (2 fl oz/¼ cup) olive oil
- large pinch of cayenne pepper
- extra lemon juice (optional)
- extra olive oil, to garnish
- paprika, to garnish
- finely chopped parsley, to garnish

METHOD

1. Soak the chickpeas in 1 litre (35 fl oz/4 cups) water overnight. Drain and put in a large saucepan with 2 litres (8 cups) fresh water (enough to cover the chickpeas by a few centimetres). Bring to the boil, then reduce the heat and simmer for 1¼ hours, or until the chickpeas are very tender. Skim any scum from the surface. Drain well, keeping the cooking liquid, and leave the chickpeas until cool enough to handle. Pick over to remove any loose skins.
2. Process the chickpeas, tahini, garlic, cumin, lemon juice, olive oil, cayenne pepper and 1½ teaspoons salt in a food processor until thick and smooth. With the motor still running, gradually add enough cooking liquid — about 185 ml (6 fl oz/¾ cup) — to form a smooth creamy purée. Taste and season with salt or extra lemon juice.
3. Spread onto a flat bowl or plate, drizzle with oil, sprinkle with paprika and scatter the parsley over the top. Serve with pitta bread or pide.

TAHINI

Tahini is a thick oily paste extracted from white sesame seeds. The seeds are husked by crushing and soaking, then dried and lightly roasted before being ground into a thick paste or cream. Tahini is used in dips or blended with garlic and lemon and used as a dressing for roast vegetables. It can be made by grinding seeds in a blender or using a mortar and pestle until smooth, or can be bought both as light and dark pastes.

BABA GHANOUSH

SERVES 6–8

INGREDIENTS

2 eggplants (aubergines)
3–4 garlic cloves, crushed
2 tablespoons lemon juice
2 tablespoons tahini
1 tablespoon olive oil

METHOD

1 Halve the eggplants lengthways and put in a colander. Sprinkle with salt and leave over a bowl for 15–20 minutes. Rinse and pat dry. Preheat the oven to 180°C (350°F/Gas 4).
2 Bake the eggplants for 35 minutes, or until soft. Peel off the skin and process the flesh with the garlic, lemon juice, tahini and oil. Season and process for 20–30 seconds. Serve with bread.

ARTICHOKE DIP

SERVES 8

INGREDIENTS

2 x 400 g (14 oz) tins artichoke hearts in brine, drained well and chopped
250 g (9 oz/1 cup) mayonnaise
100 g (3½ oz/1 cup) grated parmesan cheese
2 teaspoons onion flakes
1–2 red chillies, seeded and finely chopped (optional)
paprika, to sprinkle

METHOD

1 Preheat the oven to 180°C (350°F/Gas 4). Mix the artichokes, mayonnaise, parmesan, onion flakes and chillies (if you want your dip spicy).
2 Spread into a shallow ovenproof dish, sprinkle with paprika and bake for 15 minutes, or until lightly browned on top. Serve with crusty bread.

MUSHROOM DIP

SERVES 4

INGREDIENTS

60 g (2¼ oz) butter
1 small onion
3 garlic cloves
375 g (13 oz) button mushrooms, quartered
125 g (4½ oz/1 cup) slivered almonds, toasted
2 tablespoons cream
2 tablespoons finely chopped thyme
3 tablespoons finely chopped parsley
melba toast (page 95) or crusty bread, to serve

METHOD

1 Heat the butter in a large frying pan over medium heat and cook the onion and garlic for 2 minutes, or until soft. Increase the heat, add the mushrooms and cook for 5 minutes, or until the mushrooms are soft and most of the liquid has evaporated. Cool for 10 minutes.
2 Put the almonds in a food processor and chop roughly. Add the mushrooms and process until smooth. With the motor running, gradually pour in the cream. Stir in the herbs and season. Spoon into individual ramekins or one large serving bowl and refrigerate for 5 hours for the flavours to develop. Serve with melba toast or bread.

SKORDALIA

This traditional Greek garlic dip is served cold with raw vegetables and bread. It is also served as a sauce with grilled or fried vegetables, especially eggplant, or meat, poultry and fish such as salt cod fritters.

SERVES 6

INGREDIENTS

- 2 large floury potatoes (about 500 g/1 lb 2 oz in total), chopped
- 5 garlic cloves, crushed
- 60 g (2¼ oz) ground almonds
- 170 ml (5½ fl oz/⅔ cup) olive oil
- 2 tablespoons white wine vinegar

METHOD

1. Boil the potatoes until tender, drain then mash. Mash the garlic and almonds into the potato.
2. Add the oil gradually, mashing until smooth. Add the vinegar and season to taste. Continue to mash, adding a tablespoon of water at a time (you will need 3–4 tablespoons), until thick and creamy. Serve cold or keep, covered, in the fridge for up to 1 day.

CHILLI CON QUESO

SERVES 6–8

INGREDIENTS

- 30 g (1 oz) butter
- ½ red onion, finely chopped
- 2 large green chillies, seeded and finely chopped
- 2 small red chillies, seeded and finely chopped
- 1 garlic clove, crushed
- ½ teaspoon sweet paprika
- 1½ tablespoons beer
- 125 g (4½ oz/½ cup) sour cream
- 200 g (7 oz) cheddar cheese, grated
- 1 tablespoon chopped coriander (cilantro)
- 1 tablespoon sliced jalapeño chilli
- corn or tortilla chips, to serve

METHOD

1. Melt the butter in a saucepan over medium heat. Add the onion and green and red chillies and cook for 5 minutes, or until softened. Increase the heat to high, add the garlic and paprika, and cook for 1 minute, or until fragrant.
2. Add the beer, bring to the boil and cook until almost evaporated. Reduce the heat to low and add the sour cream, stirring until smooth. Add the cheese and stir until just melted and smooth. Remove from the heat, stir in the coriander and jalapeño, and season to taste. Serve with corn or tortilla chips for dipping.

ROASTED VEGETABLE DIP

SERVES 8

INGREDIENTS

- 1 small eggplant (aubergine), sliced
- 2 zucchini (courgettes), sliced
- 3 red capsicums (peppers)
- 125 ml (4 fl oz/½ cup) extra virgin olive oil
- 2 garlic cloves, sliced
- 2 roma (plum) tomatoes
- 200 g (7 oz) tinned, drained artichoke hearts
- 3 tablespoons oregano leaves
- 250 g (9 oz/1 cup) ricotta cheese
- 40 g (1½ oz/¼ cup) sliced black olives

METHOD

1. Put the eggplant and zucchini in a colander and sprinkle with 1–2 tablespoons salt. Leave over a bowl for 15–20 minutes to drain. Meanwhile, cut the capsicums into large flat pieces, removing the seeds and membrane. Brush the capsicum pieces with a little oil and put them, skin side up, under a very hot grill (broiler). Cook until the skin blackens and blisters. Leave to cool in a plastic bag, then peel off the skin. Put the peeled capsicum in a large non-metallic bowl.
2. Place half the olive oil in another bowl, along with half the garlic and a pinch of salt, and mix together. Rinse the eggplant and zucchini and pat dry. Put the eggplant on a non-stick or foil-lined tray and brush with the garlic oil. Cook under a very hot grill for 4–6 minutes each side, or until golden brown, brushing both sides with the oil during cooking. The eggplant will burn easily, so keep a close watch. Grill the zucchini in the same way. Add both to the capsicum.
3. Slice the tomatoes lengthways, place on the tray and brush with the garlic oil. Reduce the grill temperature slightly and cook for 10–15 minutes, or until soft. Put the tomatoes in the bowl with the other vegetables.
4. Cut the artichokes into quarters and add to the bowl. Mix in any remaining garlic oil and the remaining olive oil. Stir in the oregano and remaining garlic. Cover with a tight-fitting lid or plastic wrap and refrigerate for at least 2 hours.
5. Drain the vegetables and transfer to a food processor. Add the ricotta and process for 20 seconds, or until smooth. Add the olives and process in a couple of short bursts, then transfer to a bowl and cover with plastic wrap. Chill for 2 hours before serving.

BROAD BEAN DIP

SERVES 6

INGREDIENTS

- 200 g (7 oz/1⅓ cups) dried broad (fava) beans
- 2 garlic cloves, crushed
- ¼ teaspoon ground cumin
- 1½ tablespoons lemon juice
- 70 ml (2¼ fl oz) olive oil
- 2 tablespoons chopped parsley

METHOD

1. Rinse the beans, then put them in a bowl and cover with 750 ml (26 fl oz/3 cups) water. Leave to soak for 48 hours, changing the water once. Drain the beans, then remove the skins by slitting the skin with the point of a knife. Slip the beans out of the skins.
2. Put the beans in a large saucepan, cover with water and bring to the boil. Cover and simmer for 1 hour, then remove the lid and simmer for 15 minutes, or until the beans are tender and the liquid has almost evaporated, taking care the beans don't catch on the base of the pan. Leave to cool slightly, then transfer to a food processor and purée.
3. Transfer to a bowl and stir in the garlic, cumin and lemon juice. Gradually stir in enough oil to give a dipping consistency. As the mixture cools it may become thick — add a little warm water. Spread into a dish and serve with flatbread.

TARAMASALATA

Tarama is the salted, dried roe, traditionally from the grey mullet, but now usually from cod or carp. Tarama is best known as the main ingredient of taramasalata, this creamy dip, popular in Greek and Turkish meze. Shop-bought taramasalata is usually bright pink, as it has usually been dyed. Your home-made version will only have a hint of colour, but the pinkness will depend on the type of roe you buy. Tarama is available from most delicatessens and fishmongers and also Greek food stores.

SERVES 8

INGREDIENTS

- 4 slices white bread, crusts removed
- 60 ml (2 fl oz/¼ cup) milk
- 100 g (3½ oz) smoked cod's roe (tarama)
- 1 egg yolk
- 1 garlic clove, crushed
- 1 tablespoon grated onion
- 60 ml (2 fl oz/¼ cup) olive oil
- 80 ml (2½ fl oz/⅓ cup) lemon juice

METHOD

1. Soak the bread slices in the milk for 5 minutes, then squeeze out the milk.
2. Process the cod's roe and egg yolk in a food processor for 10 seconds. Add the bread, garlic and onion and process for 20 seconds, or until well combined and smooth.
3. With the motor running, gradually add the olive oil in a thin stream. Process until all the oil has been absorbed. Add the lemon juice in small amounts, to taste. Transfer to a bowl and serve with bread and black olives. Refrigerate in an airtight container for up to 1 week and bring to room temperature before serving.

OLIVE TAPENADE

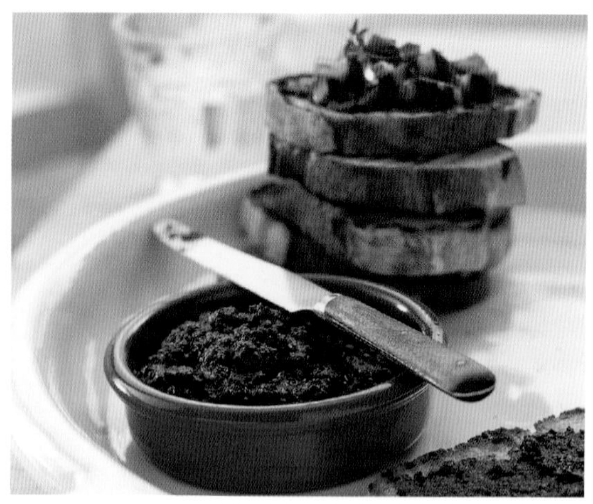

MAKES 375 ML (13 FL OZ/1½ CUPS)

INGREDIENTS

- 400 g (14 oz) kalamata olives, pitted
- 2 garlic cloves, crushed
- 2 anchovy fillets in oil, drained
- 2 tablespoons capers in brine, rinsed and squeezed dry
- 2 teaspoons chopped thyme
- 2 teaspoons dijon mustard
- 1 tablespoon lemon juice
- 60 ml (2 fl oz/¼ cup) olive oil
- 1 tablespoon brandy (optional)

METHOD

1. Process all the ingredients together in a food processor until the tapenade has a smooth consistency. Season with freshly ground black pepper and serve with crostini (page 357). Spoon into a warm, sterilised jar, seal and refrigerate for up to 2 weeks.

NOTE: When your tapenade is chilled in the fridge the olive oil will solidify, making it turn white. This will not affect the flavour of the dish. Bring it to room temperature for 30 minutes before serving and the oil will return to its liquid state.

BAGNA CAODA

A speciality of Piedmont in northern Italy, bagna caôda (meaning 'hot bath') is a dip made with olive oil, butter, anchovies and garlic. It is served warm over a burner or spirit stove, accompanied by strong red wine. Vegetables in season (celery, cardoons, fennel, endives, spring onions and artichokes) are dipped and then lifted to the mouth over a piece of bread.

SERVES 4

INGREDIENTS

200 ml (7 fl oz) olive oil
6 garlic cloves, crushed
125 g (4½ oz) anchovy fillets, finely minced
90 g (3¼ oz) butter
assorted raw vegetables (carrot, celery, spring onion, fennel, cauliflower florets), cut into strips
ciabatta, or other Italian bread, to serve

METHOD

1 Put the oil, garlic and anchovies in a saucepan and cook, stirring occasionally, over low heat until the anchovies have dissolved. Add the butter and leave over low heat until melted.
2 Transfer the sauce to a bowl or fondue pot and keep warm on the table. Serve with the vegetables and bread.

CRAB AND LEMON DIP

MAKES 625 ML (21 FL OZ/2½ CUPS)

INGREDIENTS

85 g (3 oz) butter
2 garlic cloves, crushed
3 French shallots, thinly sliced
1 teaspoon mustard powder
½ teaspoon cayenne pepper
125 ml (4 fl oz/½ cup) cream
150 g (5½ oz) cream cheese
60 g (2¼ oz/½ cup) grated cheddar cheese
350 g (12 oz) tin crabmeat, drained
2 tablespoons lemon juice
2 teaspoons worcestershire sauce
3 teaspoons chopped tarragon
40 g (1½ oz/½ cup) fresh breadcrumbs
1 tablespoon chopped parsley

METHOD

1 Preheat the oven to 170°C (325°F/Gas 3). Melt half the butter in a saucepan and cook the garlic and shallots for 2–3 minutes, or until just softened. Add the mustard powder, cayenne pepper and cream. Bring to a simmer and slowly whisk in the cream cheese, a little at a time. When the cream cheese is completely incorporated, whisk in the cheddar and cook, stirring, over very low heat for 1–2 minutes until smooth.
2 Remove the pan from the heat and add the crabmeat, lemon juice, worcestershire sauce and 2 teaspoons of the tarragon. Season to taste with salt and black pepper. Mix, then transfer to a small baking dish.
3 Melt the remaining butter in a small saucepan, add the breadcrumbs, chopped parsley and remaining tarragon and stir until just combined. Sprinkle over the crab mixture and bake for 15 minutes, or until golden. Serve warm.

••CURRY PASTES••

You can make your own curry pastes in a few simple steps. Most of these pastes will keep in a sterilised jar in the fridge for up to 2 weeks or in the freezer for up to 2 months, and will give you enough paste to make at least two curries.

THAI GREEN CURRY PASTE

MAKES 125 G ($4^{1}/_{2}$ OZ/$^{1}/_{2}$ CUP)

INGREDIENTS

- 1 teaspoon ground coriander
- 1 teaspoon ground cumin
- 8–10 small green chillies, seeded
- 2 lemongrass stems, white part only, finely sliced
- 2.5 cm (1 inch) piece of galangal, finely chopped
- 1 teaspoon very finely chopped kaffir lime skin or leaves (about half the skin from a kaffir lime or 4–5 leaves)
- 4–5 garlic cloves, finely chopped
- 3–4 red Asian shallots, chopped
- 5–6 coriander (cilantro) roots, finely chopped
- 1 handful holy basil leaves, finely chopped
- 2 teaspoons shrimp paste

METHOD

1. Dry-roast the coriander in a small frying pan for 1 minute until fragrant, then remove and dry-fry the cumin.
2. Using a mortar and pestle, pound the chillies, lemongrass, galangal and lime skin or leaves into a paste. Add the garlic, shallots and coriander roots and pound together. Add the remaining ingredients and dry-roasted spices one at a time, and pound until you have a smooth paste.
3. Alternatively, use a food processor or blender to mix all the ingredients into a smooth paste. Add cooking oil as needed to assist the blending. Store in a sterilised jar in the fridge for 2 weeks, or 2 months in the freezer.

THAI RED CURRY PASTE

MAKES 125 G ($4^{1}/_{2}$ OZ/$^{1}/_{2}$ CUP)

INGREDIENTS

- 3–4 dried long red chillies
- 8–10 dried small red chillies
- 2 lemongrass stems, white part only, finely sliced
- 2.5 cm (1 inch) piece of galangal, finely sliced
- 1 teaspoon very finely chopped kaffir lime skin or lime leaves (about half the skin from a kaffir lime or 4–5 leaves)
- 4–5 garlic cloves, finely chopped
- 3–4 red Asian shallots, finely chopped
- 5–6 coriander (cilantro) roots, finely chopped
- 2 teaspoons shrimp paste
- 1 teaspoon ground coriander, dry-roasted

METHOD

1. Remove the stems from the dried chillies and slit the chillies lengthways with a sharp knife. Discard the seeds and soak the chillies in hot water for 1–2 minutes, or until soft. Drain and roughly chop.
2. Using a mortar and pestle, pound the chillies, lemongrass, galangal and lime skin or leaves into a paste. Add the remaining ingredients and pound together until you have a smooth paste.
3. Alternatively, use a food processor or blender to mix all the ingredients into a smooth paste. Add cooking oil as needed to assist the blending. Store in a sterilised jar in the fridge for 2 weeks, or 2 months in the freezer.

VINDALOO PASTE

MAKES 125 G (4½ OZ/½ CUP)

INGREDIENTS

- 2 tablespoons grated ginger
- 4 garlic cloves, chopped
- 4 red chillies, chopped
- 2 teaspoons ground turmeric
- 2 teaspoons ground cardamom
- 4 cloves
- 6 peppercorns
- 1 teaspoon ground cinnamon
- 1 tablespoon ground coriander
- 1 tablespoon cumin seeds
- 125 ml (4 fl oz/½ cup) cider vinegar

METHOD

1 Mix all the ingredients in a food processor for 20 seconds, or until well combined and smooth.

MADRAS CURRY PASTE

MAKES 125 G (4½ OZ/½ CUP)

INGREDIENTS

- 2½ tablespoons coriander seeds, dry-roasted and ground
- 1 tablespoon cumin seeds, dry-roasted and ground
- 1 teaspoon brown mustard seeds
- ½ teaspoon cracked black peppercorns
- 1 teaspoon chilli powder
- 1 teaspoon ground turmeric
- 2 garlic cloves, crushed
- 2 teaspoons grated ginger
- about 80 ml (2½ fl oz/⅓ cup) white vinegar

METHOD

1 Mix together the spices, garlic, ginger and 1 teaspoon salt. Mix in enough of the vinegar to form a smooth paste.

MUSAMAN CURRY PASTE

MAKES 250 G (9 OZ/1 CUP)

INGREDIENTS

- 2 dried long red chillies
- 1 lemongrass stem, white part only, finely sliced
- 2.5 cm (1 inch) piece of galangal, finely chopped
- 5 cloves
- 10 cm (4 inch) piece of cinnamon stick, crushed
- 10 cardamom seeds
- ½ teaspoon ground nutmeg
- 6 garlic cloves, finely chopped
- 4 red Asian shallots, finely chopped
- 4–5 coriander (cilantro) roots, finely chopped
- 1 teaspoon shrimp paste

METHOD

1 Slit the chillies lengthways with a sharp knife. Discard the seeds and soak the chillies in hot water for 1–2 minutes, or until soft. Drain and roughly chop.

2 Using a mortar and pestle, pound the chillies, lemongrass, galangal, cloves, cinnamon stick, cardamom seeds and nutmeg into a paste. Add the garlic, shallots and coriander roots. Pound together. Add the shrimp paste and pound until you have a smooth paste.

3 Alternatively, use a food processor or blender to mix all the ingredients into a smooth paste. Add cooking oil as needed to assist the blending. Store in a sterilised jar in the fridge for 2 weeks, or 2 months in the freezer.

CHAPTER TEN
BAKING

••BREAD••

There is nothing better than good bread fresh from the oven, with its heady aroma, crisp golden crust and soft, light crumb. Bread is a staple food made from flour, salt and water. Some breads are leavened, that is, they use a raising agent such as yeast to give them a lighter texture, and others such as flatbreads use no leavening. Once you understand some of the bread basics, such as working with yeast and kneading techniques, you'll find that delicious bread is simple and rewarding to make.

MAIN INGREDIENTS IN BREAD

YEAST

Working with yeast is not as difficult as you may think. Yeast is available dried or fresh. Dried yeast generally comes in a box containing 7 g (¼ oz) sachets, one of which is enough for a standard loaf. Dried yeast will keep for about 1 year in a cool, dark place.

Fresh yeast is available at some health food stores and bakeries. Store fresh yeast in the fridge for up to 1 week or freeze for several months.

FLOUR

Different flours produce breads with different flavours and textures. Strong flour, or bread flour, is made from hard wheat. This is high in protein and will form gluten, which helps the bread rise well and bake into a light airy loaf with a good crust. Ordinary plain flour will create a denser bread, more authentic in texture to the country-style loaves found in Italy.

SALT

Controls the rate of fermentation, which strengthens the gluten, as well as adds flavour. If used on its own, salt will kill the yeast, so mix it with flour first.

LIQUID

Activates the yeast. Water is usually used — it strengthens gluten, resulting in a chewy bread and crisp crust. Milk gives a softer crumb and beer gives a malty flavour.

SUGAR

A source of food for yeast. Too much sugar will slow the fermentation process. Sweet dough takes longer to rise.

FAT

Gives bread dough a softer crumb, but has to be used carefully as fats inhibit fermentation. If large amounts of fat are used, they are usually added after the first rising.

DRIED YEAST

Dried yeast has twice the potency of fresh yeast — 15 g (½ oz) of fresh yeast is equivalent to a 7 g (¼ oz) sachet of dried. Sprinkle into a small glass bowl containing a little tepid water and leave to dissolve.

HOW TO... ACTIVATE FRESH YEAST

METHOD

1 Mix the yeast with tepid water and 1 tablespoon flour until smooth.
2 Set aside for 5 minutes, or until the yeast is frothy (sponged). If your yeast doesn't foam, it is dead, so discard it and start again.

HOW TO... MAKE BREAD

To make leavened bread you need flour (preferably high-gluten 'strong flour'), a liquid and a leavening agent such as yeast. After the dough is made, it is left to rise, preferably at room temperature. The dough is then knocked back (deflated) to rid it of any large or irregular air bubbles, then shaped and left to prove until it doubles in size — don't over-prove or your bread will collapse when cooked.

Baking gives bread its final rise as the moisture in the dough turns to steam and expands. As soon as the bread gets hot enough, the yeast dies and the bread crust forms.

KNEADING THE DOUGH

Kneading firstly distributes the yeast evenly throughout the dough and, secondly, allows the flour's protein to develop into gluten. Don't be tempted to cut short the kneading time as it affects the texture of the finished bread. Gluten gives the dough elasticity, strength and the ability to expand, as it traps the carbon dioxide gas created by the yeast and this allows the bread to rise.

The kneading action is simple and it is quite easy to get into a rhythm. Hold one end of the dough down with one hand, and stretch it away from you with the other hand. Fold the dough back together, make a quarter turn and repeat the action. Knead for 10 minutes, or until smooth and elastic. When you have finished, gather the dough into a ball.

PROVING

Shape the dough into a ball and put it in a large, lightly oiled bowl, turning to coat the surface of the dough in the oil. Cover the bowl with plastic wrap and leave to rise in a draught-free place for 1–2 hours, or until the dough has doubled in size. Heavier or enriched doughs will take longer to rise.

Ambient room temperature is the perfect environment for the bread to rise, rather than in a room that is too hot — a slower, unforced rise gives a better flavoured bread. You can also allow bread to rise overnight in the refrigerator; the cold doesn't kill the yeast, it merely retards it. If leaving bread to rise in the refrigerator, remove and leave at room temperature for about 2 hours before shaping it.

PUNCHING DOWN

Knock back the dough by punching it gently (this will knock out the air to reduce the volume) and turn out onto a lightly floured surface. If making bread rolls or buns, use a knife to cut the dough into even-sized pieces.

Using your hands, work the dough into the specified shape. The dough can be either pressed into a tin or placed on a lightly floured baking tray. The dough is then usually left to prove again before baking.

FINISHES ON BREAD

You can finish the tops of loaves in many different ways. A dusting of flour will give a rustic look, a wash of milk or milk and egg produces a shinier finish, and a pure egg glaze will turn the top dark shiny brown, as will a sugar and water glaze. Sesame seeds and poppy seeds can be added to a glazed surface. Scoring a cross in the top of the loaf with a sharp knife also looks attractive.

HOW TO... STORE FRESH BREAD

Most breads will keep for a couple of days and those with fat in them will keep longer. Always cool bread thoroughly before putting it in a plastic bag — the steam will give it a stale texture and cause it to go mouldy quicker. Store bread in a bag or wrapped in a cloth at room temperature — putting it in the fridge will dehydrate it and make it go stale.

BASIC WHITE BREAD

These steps show how to make a basic loaf of bread. The dough is mixed and kneaded by hand but bread can also be made with an electric mixer, using the dough hook attachment.

METHOD

1. Sprinkle 2 teaspoons dried yeast and 1 teaspoon sugar over 150 ml (5 fl oz) warm water in a small bowl. Stir to dissolve the sugar, then set aside until the yeast sponges (foams).
2. Sift 450 g (1 lb) white strong flour and 1½ teaspoons salt into a bowl and make a well in the centre.
3. Pour the yeast mixture into the well in the flour and add another 150 ml (5 fl oz) warm water. Use a wooden spoon to bring the ingredients together to form a sticky dough. (The moisture content of flour can vary greatly between brands, so add extra water or flour, 1 tablespoon at a time, if the dough is too dry or too sticky. Do not add too much flour because the dough will absorb more flour during kneading.)
4. Knead the dough for 10 minutes, stretching it away from you with the heel of your hand, then turn the dough 45 degrees and draw it back into the centre. Repeat this process.
5. The dough will now be smooth and a finger indent will pop out quickly. Place in an oiled bowl and brush the dough with oil. Cover with plastic wrap and leave in a draught-free place to rise.
6. The dough is ready when it has doubled in size. A finger indent will pop out slowly.
7. Knock back the dough by punching it down gently. Turn out onto a floured surface. Knead out any air pockets for 3–4 minutes.
8. Knead the dough into an oval shape, then roll it into a tight sausage shape.
9. Put the dough, seam side down, in a lightly oiled tin. Leave to prove until the dough doubles in size. Preheat the oven to 220°C (425°F/Gas 7).
10. Bake the bread for 45 minutes, or until golden and it sounds hollow when tapped on the base.

SOURDOUGH

This bread is traditionally made with a fermented starter as leavener, rather than a manufactured yeast. It was made like this, thousands of years before yeast was available in convenient packets. The starter can be a paste of flour and water, which is left to ferment for several days, allowing it to absorb the naturally occurring yeasts from the air, or it can be a ferment of potato or fruit. The fermentation process produces the distinctive sour taste that is characteristic of these breads. The starter is then mixed with more liquid and flour and left to 'sponge'. It is traditional to save a quarter of the starter dough to mix in with the next batch. In France, some starter doughs have been kept alive for more than a hundred years, passed down through the generations. As the starter ages, it picks up the yeasts and develops its own characteristics and flavours. Today, for convenience, it is often made using a yeast starter.

SOURDOUGH RYE BREAD

MAKES 2 LOAVES

INGREDIENTS

SOURDOUGH STARTER
2 teaspoons dried yeast
1 teaspoon caster (superfine) sugar
200 g (7 oz/2 cups) rye flour

BREAD DOUGH
100 g (3½ oz/1 cup) rye flour
550 g (1 lb 4 oz/4½ cups) unbleached plain (all-purpose) flour
45 g (1½ oz/¼ cup) soft brown sugar
3 teaspoons caraway seeds
2 teaspoons dried yeast, extra
60 ml (2 fl oz/¼ cup) oil
rye flour, extra, to sprinkle

METHOD

1 To make the starter, combine the yeast, sugar, rye flour and 435 ml (15¼ fl oz/1¾ cups) warm water in a bowl. Cover with plastic wrap and set aside overnight at room temperature to sour. For a stronger flavour, leave for up to 3 days.
2 Brush a large baking tray with oil or melted butter. To make the bread dough, combine the rye flour, 440 g (15½ oz/3½ cups) of the plain flour, sugar, caraway seeds and 2 teaspoons salt in a large bowl. Dissolve the yeast in 250 ml (9 fl oz/1 cup) warm water. Make a well in the centre of the dry ingredients and add the sourdough starter, dissolved yeast and oil. Mix, using a wooden spoon then your hands, until the dough forms a rough, slightly sticky ball, which leaves the side of the bowl. Add some of the remaining flour, if necessary — you may not need to use it all.
3 Turn onto a lightly floured work surface. Knead for 10 minutes, or until smooth and elastic. Incorporate the remaining flour, if needed. Place the dough in a large, lightly oiled bowl. Cover with plastic wrap or a damp tea towel and leave in a draught-free place for 45 minutes, or until well risen. Punch down and knead for 1 minute.
4 Divide the dough into two even-sized portions. Shape into round or oblong loaves and place on the baking tray. Sprinkle with rye flour and use the end of a wooden spoon handle to press holes 2 cm (¾ inch) deep in the top, or make three slashes. Cover the dough and leave in a draught-free place for 45 minutes, or until the dough is well risen.
5 Preheat the oven to 180°C (350°F/Gas 4). Sprinkle the loaves with a little extra flour. Bake for 40 minutes, or until golden and the bread sounds hollow when tapped on the base. Cool on a wire rack.

RYE

Rye is a strongly flavoured cereal grain, similar to wheat. Because it grows well in cold conditions it is widely used in Northern and Eastern European and Russian cooking. When milled, rye grains produce a dark flour, which is used to make black breads like pumpernickel. These breads are denser than those made with wheat because rye flour has a low gluten content, so, for this reason, rye flour is often mixed with wheat flour.

SOY, LINSEED AND BARLEY LOAF

MAKES 1 LOAF

INGREDIENTS

- 110 g (3¾ oz/½ cup) pearl barley
- 2 teaspoons dried yeast
- 1 teaspoon caster (superfine) sugar
- 1 tablespoon linseeds (flax seeds)
- 2 tablespoons soy flour
- 2 tablespoons gluten flour
- 150 g (5½ oz/1 cup) wholemeal strong flour
- 310 g (11 oz/2½ cups) white strong flour
- 2 tablespoons olive oil

METHOD

1. Brush a 10 x 26 cm (4 x 10½ inch) bread tin with oil. Put the barley in a saucepan with 500 ml (17 fl oz/2 cups) water, bring to the boil and boil for 20 minutes, or until softened. Drain.
2. Put the yeast, sugar and 150 ml (5 fl oz) warm water in a small bowl and mix well. Leave in a draught-free place for 10 minutes, or until bubbles appear on the surface. The mixture should be frothy and slightly increased in volume. If your yeast doesn't foam, it is dead, so you will have to discard it and start again.
3. Put the barley, linseeds, soy and gluten flours, wholemeal flour, 250 g (9 oz/2 cups) of the plain flour and 1 teaspoon salt in a large bowl. Make a well in the centre and add the yeast mixture, oil and 150 ml (5 fl oz) warm water. Mix with a wooden spoon to a soft dough. Turn out onto a floured surface and knead for 10 minutes, or until smooth and elastic. Incorporate enough of the remaining flour until the dough is no longer sticky.
4. Place the dough in a lightly oiled bowl. Cover with plastic wrap or a damp tea towel and leave in a draught-free place for 45 minutes, or until doubled in size. Punch down and knead the dough for 2–3 minutes.
5. Pat the dough into a 20 x 24 cm (8 x 9½ inch) rectangle. Roll up firmly from the long side and place, seam side down, in the bread tin. Cover the dough and leave in a draught-free place for 1 hour, or until risen to the top of the tin. Preheat the oven to 200°C (400°F/Gas 6).
6. Brush the dough with water and make two slits on top. Bake for 30 minutes, or until golden and the bread sounds hollow when tapped on the base. Remove from the tin and cool on a wire rack.

BARLEY

Barley is the earliest known cultivated cereal and in the past was often mixed with wheat to make a nutritious bread. Barley contains little gluten, so it is rarely used alone in bread making. Barley has a slightly nutty flavour and is a popular substitute for rice in risotto or pilaff dishes.

Pearl barley has been processed to remove both the husk and germ. Pearl barley is particularly good in meat stews and soups. Pot barley has only had the outer husk removed. It is used in the same way as pearl barley, but requires longer cooking to soften it. Scotch barley is unhusked. Barley flakes are partially cooked barley that has been flattened and dried. It can be used like rolled oats in muesli or to make porridge.

WHOLEMEAL MINI LOAVES

MAKES 4 SMALL LOAVES

INGREDIENTS

- 2 teaspoons dried yeast
- 1 tablespoon caster (superfine) sugar
- 125 ml (4 fl oz/½ cup) warm milk
- 600 g (1 lb 5 oz/4 cups) wholemeal strong flour
- 60 ml (2 fl oz/¼ cup) oil
- 1 egg, lightly beaten

METHOD

1. Grease four 13 x 6½ x 5 cm (5 x 2¾ x 2 inch) baking tins. Put the yeast, sugar and milk in a small bowl and mix well. Leave in a draught-free place for 10 minutes, or until bubbles appear on the surface. The mixture should be frothy and increased in volume.
2. Put the flour and 1 teaspoon salt in a large bowl, make a well in the centre and add the yeast mixture, the oil and 250 ml (9 fl oz/1 cup) warm water. Mix to a soft dough and gather into a ball. Turn out onto a floured surface and knead for 10 minutes. Add a little extra flour if the dough is too sticky.
3. Place the dough in a lightly oiled bowl. Cover with plastic wrap or a damp tea towel and leave in a draught-free place for 1 hour, or until well risen. Punch down the dough, turn out onto a floured surface and knead for 1 minute, or until smooth. Divide into four portions, knead into shape and put in the tins. Cover and leave in a draught-free place for 45 minutes, or until risen.
4. Preheat the oven to 210°C (415°F/Gas 6–7). Brush the loaf tops with the beaten egg. Bake for 10 minutes, then reduce the oven to 180°C (350°F/Gas 4) and bake for a further 30–35 minutes, or until golden and the bread sounds hollow when tapped on the base. Cover with foil if the tops become too brown.

TRADITIONAL CORN BREAD

MAKES 1 LOAF

INGREDIENTS

- 150 g (5½ oz/1 cup) polenta
- 2 tablespoons caster (superfine) sugar
- 125 g (4½ oz/1 cup) plain (all-purpose) flour
- 2 teaspoons baking powder
- ½ teaspoon bicarbonate of soda (baking soda)
- 1 egg, lightly beaten
- 250 ml (9 fl oz/1 cup) buttermilk
- 60 g (2¼ oz) butter, melted

METHOD

1. Preheat the oven to 210°C (415°F/Gas 6–7). Brush a 20 cm (8 inch) square cake tin with oil or melted butter. Line the base with baking paper.
2. Put the polenta and sugar in a large bowl. Add the sifted flour, baking powder, bicarbonate of soda and ½ teaspoon salt and mix thoroughly.
3. In a separate bowl, combine the egg, buttermilk and butter. Stir the mixture quickly into the dry ingredients, stirring only until the ingredients are moistened. Pour the mixture into the prepared tin and smooth the surface. Bake for 20–25 minutes, or until a skewer inserted in the centre of the bread comes out clean.
4. Place on a wire rack and leave for 10 minutes to cool before turning out. Cut into squares and serve warm.

BEER BREAD ROLLS

MAKES 4

INGREDIENTS

400 g (14 oz/3¼ cups) plain (all-purpose) flour
3 teaspoons baking powder
1 tablespoon sugar
50 g (1¾ oz) butter, chopped
375 ml (13 fl oz/1½ cups) beer

METHOD

1 Process the flour, baking powder, sugar, butter and 1 teaspoon salt in a food processor until crumbly. Add the beer and process in bursts to form a soft dough.
2 Preheat the oven to 210°C (415°F/Gas 6–7). Turn the dough out onto a well-floured surface and knead until smooth, adding extra flour if needed. Divide the dough into four balls, place on greased oven trays and flatten slightly. Brush with a little water and slash the tops with a knife.
3 Transfer to the oven and bake for 10 minutes. Reduce the oven to 180°C (350°F/Gas 4) and bake for 10 minutes, or until cooked. Cool on a wire rack and serve with butter.

BANANA BREAD

MAKES 1 LOAF

INGREDIENTS

250 g (9 oz/2 cups) self-raising flour
1 teaspoon mixed spice
½ teaspoon bicarbonate of soda (baking soda)
115 g (4 oz/½ cup) soft brown sugar
2 eggs, lightly beaten
50 g (1¾ oz) unsalted butter, melted and cooled
250 ml (9 fl oz/1 cup) milk
235 g (8½ oz/1 cup) mashed ripe bananas (about 2 bananas)
60 g (2¼ oz/½ cup) sultanas or raisins (optional)

METHOD

1 Preheat the oven to 180°C (350°F/Gas 4). Grease and line the base of a 6 x 13 x 23 cm (2½ x 5 x 9 inch) loaf (bar) tin.
2 Sift together the flour, mixed spice, bicarbonate of soda and ¼ teaspoon salt into a large bowl. Stir in the sugar and make a well in the centre.
3 Combine the eggs, butter, milk and banana. Add the banana mixture and sultanas, if using, to the flour well and stir until just combined. Pour into the tin and smooth the top. Bake for 45 minutes, or until the top is nicely coloured and a skewer inserted into the centre of the bread comes out clean. Cool in the tin for 10 minutes, then turn out onto a wire rack. Dust with icing sugar.

BAKING POWDER AND BICARBONATE OF SODA

Baking powder is a mixture of cream of tartar and sodium bicarbonate. In baking, when liquid is added, cream of tartar (an acid) reacts with sodium bicarbonate (an alkali), and releases bubbles of carbon dioxide, causing the cake or bread to rise. Most commercial brands are double-acting: they produce bubbles when activated first by liquid, then by heat. Don't be too heavy-handed when using it as too much will taint the cake with a slight soapy flavour. Replace every 6 months — to see if it's still active, stir some into hot water — it should bubble vigorously. Bicarbonate of soda (baking soda) is also a rising agent, but needs an acid such as buttermilk or sour cream to activate it. Bicarbonate of soda starts acting as soon as liquid is added, so cook the mixture quickly.

DAMPER

Damper is a simple bread of flour and water eaten by early Australian settlers and bushmen, although modern versions add milk and butter for flavour. The dough may be wrapped around a stick and cooked over camp-fire coals or cooked in a camp oven. Damper is so called because it was said to 'dampen' the appetite.

MAKES 1 LOAF

INGREDIENTS

- 375 g (13 oz/3 cups) self-raising flour
- 90 g (3¼ oz) butter, melted
- 125 ml (4 fl oz/½ cup) milk
- milk, for glazing
- flour, for dusting

METHOD

1. Preheat the oven to 210°C (415°F/Gas 6–7). Lightly grease a baking tray. Sift the flour and 2 teaspoons salt into a bowl and make a well in the centre. Combine the butter, milk and 125 ml (4 fl oz/½ cup) water and pour into the well. Stir with a knife until just combined.
2. Turn the dough onto a lightly floured surface and knead for 20 seconds, or until smooth. Place the dough on the baking tray and press out to a 20 cm (8 inch) circle.
3. Using a sharp pointed knife, score the dough into eight sections, about 1 cm (½ inch) deep. Brush with milk, then dust with flour. Bake for 10 minutes, then reduce the oven to 180°C (350°F/Gas 4) and bake the damper for another 15 minutes, or until the top is golden and the bread sounds hollow when the surface is tapped. Serve with butter.

BAGUETTE

As their French name suggests, these long, thin loaves of bread do look like 'little rods'. The French have such a fondness for their baguette, with its crunchy golden-brown crust and snow-white crumb, that it appears daily or twice daily on every table throughout France. Traditionally, baguettes were not baked in a tin but shaped into a thin loaf and left to rise between the folds of a cloth. Before baking, the loaf is slashed in its characteristic diagonal pattern.

MINI BAGUETTES

MAKES 3 LOAVES

INGREDIENTS

- 2 teaspoons dried yeast
- 1 teaspoon sugar
- 90 g (3¼ oz/¾ cup) plain (all-purpose) flour
- 375 g (13 oz/3 cups) white strong flour
- 2 tablespoons polenta, to sprinkle

METHOD

1. Put the yeast, sugar and 310 ml (10¾ fl oz/1¼ cups) warm water in a small bowl and mix well. Leave in a warm, draught-free place for 10 minutes, or until bubbles appear on the surface. The mixture should be frothy and slightly increased in volume.
2. Mix together the flours and ½ teaspoon salt. Transfer half the combined flour to a large bowl. Make a well in the centre and add the yeast mixture. Using a large metal spoon fold the flour into the yeast mixture. This should form a soft dough. Cover the bowl with plastic wrap or a damp tea towel and set aside for 30–35 minutes, or until frothy and risen by about one-third of its original size.
3. Mix in the remaining combined flour and add up to 60 ml (2 fl oz/¼ cup) warm water, enough to form a soft, but slightly sticky dough. Knead the dough on a lightly floured surface for about 10 minutes, or until smooth and elastic. If the dough sticks to the work surface while kneading, flour the surface sparingly, but try to avoid adding too much flour. Shape the dough into a ball and place in a lightly oiled bowl. Cover and leave in a draught-free place for 1 hour, or until the dough has doubled in size.
4. Lightly grease two large baking trays and sprinkle with polenta. Punch down the dough and knead for 2–3 minutes. Divide the dough into three portions and press or roll each into a rectangle about 20 x 40 cm (8 x 16 inches). Roll each up firmly into a long sausage shape and place, seam side down, well spaced on the prepared trays. Cover loosely and set aside in a draught-free place for 40 minutes, or until doubled in size.
5. Preheat the oven to 220°C (425°F/Gas 7). Lightly brush the loaves with water and make diagonal slashes across the top at 6 cm (2½ inch) intervals. Place the trays in the oven and spray the oven with water.
6. Bake the bread for 20 minutes, spraying inside the oven with water twice during this time. Lower the temperature to 180°C (350°F/Gas 4) and bake for another 5–10 minutes, or until the crust is golden and firm and the bread sounds hollow when tapped on the base. Cool on a wire rack. Baguettes are best eaten within a few hours of baking them.

BRIOCHE

Brioche is made from a light yeast dough enriched with butter and eggs, which gives the bread a cake-like texture. Brioche dough can be shaped into a loaf, ring, plait or small buns, but the most classic is brioche à tête, with its distinctive small knot of dough on the top, resembling the 'head'. Brioche is so buttery that you can serve it for breakfast with nothing more fancy than a little good-quality jam or curd. If you have one, use a fluted brioche tin; if not, an ordinary loaf tin will be fine.

MAKES 6 SMALL AND 1 MEDIUM BRIOCHE

INGREDIENTS

- 2 teaspoons dried yeast
- 1 teaspoon caster (superfine) sugar
- 125 ml (4 fl oz/½ cup) warm milk
- 540 g (1 lb 3 oz/4⅓ cups) plain (all-purpose) flour
- 2 tablespoons caster (superfine) sugar, extra
- 4 eggs, at room temperature, lightly beaten
- 175 g (6 oz) butter, softened
- 1 egg yolk
- 1 tablespoon cream

METHOD

1. Grease six small brioche moulds and an 11 x 21 cm (4¼ x 8¼ inch) bread or loaf (bar) tin (if brioche moulds are not available, bake as two loaves). Put the yeast, sugar and warm milk in a small bowl and stir well. Leave in a draught-free place for 10 minutes, or until bubbles appear on the surface. The mixture should be frothy and slightly increased in volume. If your yeast doesn't foam, it is dead, so you will have to discard it and start again.
2. Sift 500 g (1 lb 2 oz/4 cups) of the flour, add 1 teaspoon salt and the extra sugar into a large bowl. Make a well in the centre and pour in the yeast mixture and beaten egg. Beat the mixture with a wooden spoon until well combined and the mixture forms a rough ball. Turn out onto a lightly floured surface and knead for 5 minutes, or until the dough is smooth and firm. Gradually incorporate small amounts of the butter into the dough. This will take about 10 minutes and the dough will be very sticky.
3. Sprinkle a clean work surface, your hands and the dough with a small amount of the remaining flour. Knead the dough lightly for 10 minutes, or until smooth and elastic. Place the dough in a large buttered bowl and brush the surface with oil. Cover with plastic wrap or a damp tea towel and leave in a draught-free place for 1½–2 hours, or until well risen.
4. Punch down the dough and divide in half. Cover one half with plastic wrap and set aside. Divide the other half into six even-sized pieces. Remove a quarter of the dough from each piece. Mould the larger pieces into even rounds and place into the brioche moulds. Combine the egg yolk and cream to make a glaze and brush the surface of the dough. Shape the small pieces into small even-sized balls and place on top of each roll. Push a floured wooden skewer through the centre of the top ball to the base of the roll, then remove — this will secure the ball to the roll. Brush again with the glaze, then cover and leave in a draught-free place for 45 minutes, or until well risen.
5. Meanwhile, place the remaining dough in the bread tin and brush with glaze. Cover and set aside for 1 hour, or until well risen.
6. Preheat the oven to 210°C (415°F/Gas 6–7). Bake the small brioche for 10 minutes, then reduce the oven to 180°C (350°F/Gas 4) and bake for 10 minutes, or until golden and cooked. Turn out immediately onto a wire rack to cool. Increase the oven to 210°C (415°F/Gas 6–7). Bake the medium loaf for 15 minutes. Reduce the oven to 180°C (350°F/Gas 4) and bake for 15 minutes, or until golden and cooked. Turn out onto a wire rack to cool.

GRISSINI

Grissini are crisp Italian bread sticks made with flour, water, yeast and often olive oil. The bread sticks were once eaten for breakfast but are now usually served with antipasto or eaten as a snack with a piece of prosciutto wrapped around them. The bread is made either by hand by stretching out the dough to form a long, thin stick, or commercially to form a more uniform shape. Handmade grissini vary in thickness, look somewhat knobbly and are usually the length of their baker's arms.

PARMESAN GRISSINI

MAKES 32

INGREDIENTS

- 1 teaspoon dried yeast
- pinch of caster (superfine) sugar
- 1 tablespoon extra virgin olive oil
- 250 g (9 oz/2 cups) white strong flour
- 60 g (2¼ oz/⅔ cup) grated parmesan cheese

METHOD

1. Sprinkle the yeast and sugar over 170 ml (5½ fl oz/⅔ cup) warm water in a small bowl. Stir to dissolve the sugar, then leave in a draught-free place for 10 minutes, or until the yeast is foamy. Stir in the olive oil.
2. Put the flour in a large bowl, add the parmesan and 1 teaspoon salt and stir to combine well. Pour in the yeast mixture and stir until a dough forms. Turn the dough out onto a lightly floured work surface and knead for 5 minutes, or until the dough is smooth and elastic.
3. Place the dough in a lightly oiled bowl, turning the dough to coat in the oil. Cover with plastic wrap or a damp tea towel and leave in a draught-free place for 1 hour, or until the dough has doubled in size.
4. Preheat the oven to 200°C (400°F/Gas 6). Lightly grease two baking trays. Knock back the dough by punching it gently, then turn out onto a floured work surface and cut in half. Roll out one piece of dough to form a rectangle measuring 20 x 16 cm (8 x 6¼ inches), then cut into sixteen 1 cm (½ inch) wide strips. Using your hands, roll each strip to form a 22–24 cm (8½–9½ inch) long stick, then place on one of the baking trays. Repeat for the second piece of dough.
5. Bake for 17–20 minutes, until golden and crisp, swapping the trays halfway through to ensure even cooking. Transfer to a wire rack to cool.

NOTE: Grissini will keep, stored in an airtight container, for up to 7 days. If they become soft, re-crisp in a 180°C (350°F/Gas 4) oven.

FLATBREADS

The most basic of all breads, flatbreads are the ancestors of the modern loaf. Flatbreads are produced in virtually every cuisine in the world from Mexican tortillas, Middle Eastern pitta and lavash breads to the Indian naan. They can be cooked on hearths, griddles, on the sides of ovens and over open fires and can be made from low-gluten grains like buckwheat, corn and barley, which can't be used for ordinary bread. Flatbreads not only add carbohydrate to a meal but also often act as the dish or cutlery — chapatis are used to pick up food in India, tortillas are used to wrap Mexican food and pitta bread are the universal pocket stuffed with all kinds of fillings.

FLATBREAD WITH ZA'ATAR

MAKES 10

INGREDIENTS

- 1 tablespoon dried yeast
- 1 teaspoon sugar
- 400 g (14 oz/3¼ cups) plain (all-purpose) flour
- 125 ml (4 fl oz/½ cup) olive oil
- 20 g (¾ oz/⅓ cup) za'atar (see Note)
- 1 tablespoon sea salt flakes

METHOD

1. Put the yeast and sugar in a small bowl with 60 ml (2 fl oz/¼ cup) warm water and stir until dissolved. Leave in a draught-free place for 10 minutes, or until bubbles appear on the surface. The mixture should be frothy and slightly increased in volume.
2. Sift the flour and ½ teaspoon salt into a large bowl. Make a well in the centre and pour in the yeast mixture and 310 ml (10¾ fl oz/1¼ cups) warm water. Beat with a wooden spoon to form a dough, then knead on a lightly floured surface for 10–15 minutes, or until smooth and elastic, gradually adding 1 tablespoon of the olive oil as you knead, until all the oil has been used. Cover with plastic wrap or a damp tea towel and leave in a draught-free place for 1 hour, or until risen.
3. Punch down the dough and then knead again. Set aside and leave to rise for 30 minutes. Knead again briefly and divide the dough into 10 portions. Roll each portion to a smooth circle about 5 mm (¼ inch) thick. Set aside, covered, for 20 minutes.
4. Preheat the oven to 220°C (425°F/Gas 7). Grease two baking trays. Place the dough circles on the trays and gently press the surface with your fingers to create a dimpled effect. Brush with the remaining oil and sprinkle with za'atar and sea salt flakes. Bake for 12–15 minutes, or until golden brown. Serve warm.

NOTE: Za'atar is a Middle Eastern spice blend of toasted sesame seeds, dried thyme, dried marjoram and sumac. It is available from speciality food stores.

PITTA BREAD

MAKES 12

INGREDIENTS

2 teaspoons dried yeast
1 teaspoon caster (superfine) sugar
440 g (15½ oz/3½ cups) plain (all-purpose) flour
2 tablespoons olive oil

METHOD

1. In a bowl, combine the yeast, sugar and 375 ml (13 fl oz/1½ cups) warm water and stir until dissolved. Leave in a draught-free place for 10 minutes, or until bubbles appear on the surface. The mixture should be frothy and slightly increased in volume. If your yeast doesn't foam, it is dead, so you will have to discard it and start again. Process the flour, yeast mixture and oil in a food processor for 30 seconds, or until the mixture forms a ball.
2. Turn the dough onto a well-floured surface and knead until smooth and elastic. Place the dough in a lightly oiled bowl. Cover with plastic wrap and then a damp tea towel and leave in a draught-free place for 20 minutes, or until almost doubled in size. Punch down the dough and divide into 12 equal portions. Roll each portion into a 5 mm (¼ inch) thick round. Place on greased baking trays and brush well with water. Set aside to rise for 20 minutes.
3. Preheat the oven to 250°C (500°F/Gas 9). If the dough has dried, brush it again with water. Bake for 4–5 minutes. The pitta bread should be soft and pale, slightly swollen, and hollow inside.

LAVASH

MAKES 4

INGREDIENTS

125 g (4½ oz/1 cup) plain (all-purpose) flour
½ teaspoon sugar
20 g (¾ oz) chilled butter, chopped
80 ml (2½ fl oz/⅓ cup) milk
sesame and poppy seeds, to sprinkle

METHOD

1. Put the flour, sugar, butter and ½ teaspoon salt in a food processor. Process in short bursts until the butter is incorporated. With the machine running, gradually pour in the milk and process until the dough comes together — you may need to add an extra 1 tablespoon milk. Turn out onto a lightly floured surface and knead briefly until smooth. Cover with plastic wrap and refrigerate for 1 hour.
2. Preheat the oven to 190°C (375°F/Gas 5). Lightly grease a large baking tray. Cut the dough into four portions. Working with one portion at a time, roll until very thin, into a rough square, measuring about 20 cm (8 inches) along the sides. Place a dough square on the greased tray, brush the top lightly with water and sprinkle with the sesame and poppy seeds. Roll a rolling pin lightly over the surface of the dough to press in the seeds.
3. Bake for 6–8 minutes, or until golden brown and dry. Repeat the process with the remaining dough. Transfer to a wire rack until cool and crisp. Break into large pieces.

MATZO

This unleavened Jewish flatbread is traditionally eaten during Passover. While usually made with only flour and water, some add flavourings such as onion. Matzo (matzoh) can be ground into a meal, which is used as an ingredient in a variety of foods such as matzo balls and pancakes. It is used to thicken soups and as a substitute for leavened breadcrumbs to coat food during Passover.

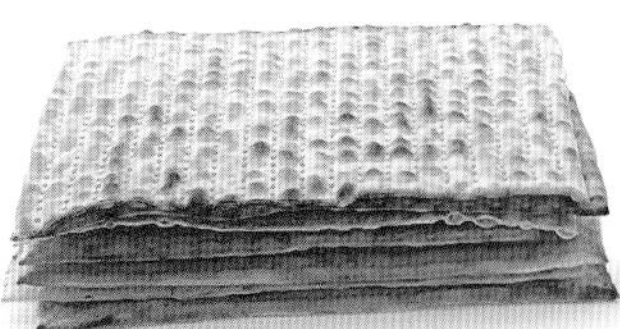

FOCACCIA

An Italian flatbread made from yeasted dough, the basic focaccia is made by rolling the dough into a flat rectangular shape and dimpling with fingermarks. It is then drizzled with oil and sprinkled with salt. Other versions may use toppings such as olives, onions or tomatoes. Originally, the bread was cooked over an open fire, which provided the inspiration for its name, derived from the Latin, *focus*, meaning 'fireplace'.

MAKES 1 FLAT LOAF

INGREDIENTS

- 2 teaspoons dried yeast
- 1 teaspoon caster (superfine) sugar
- 2 tablespoons olive oil
- 400 g (14 oz/3¼ cups) white strong flour
- 1 tablespoon full-cream milk powder
- 1 tablespoon olive oil
- 1–2 garlic cloves, crushed
- 1–2 teaspoons coarse sea salt

TOPPING SUGGESTIONS

- black olives
- rosemary sprigs or leaves
- pine nuts
- dried oregano

METHOD

1 Lightly grease an 18 x 28 cm (7 x 11¼ inch) baking tin. Put the yeast, sugar and 250 ml (9 fl oz/1 cup) warm water in a small bowl and stir well. Leave in a draught-free place for 10 minutes, or until bubbles appear on the surface. The mixture should be frothy and slightly increased in volume. Add the oil.

2 Sift 375 g (13 oz/3 cups) of the flour, the milk powder and ½ teaspoon salt into a large bowl. Make a well in the centre and add the yeast mixture. Beat with a wooden spoon until the mixture is well combined. Add enough of the remaining flour to form a soft dough, and then turn onto a lightly floured surface.

3 Knead for 10 minutes, or until the dough is smooth and elastic. Place the dough in a large, lightly oiled bowl and brush the surface with oil. Cover with plastic wrap and leave in a draught-free place for 1 hour, or until well risen. Punch down the dough, then knead for 1 minute.

4 Roll into a rectangle, 18 x 28 cm (7 x 11¼ inches) and place in the prepared tin. Cover with plastic wrap and leave to rise for 20 minutes. Using your fingertips or the handle of a wooden spoon, form indents 1 cm (½ inch) deep all over the dough at regular intervals. Cover and set aside for 30 minutes, or until the dough is well risen. Preheat the oven to 180°C (350°F/Gas 4).

5 Brush the combined olive oil and garlic over the surface of the dough. Choose your topping and scatter over the top. Sprinkle with sea salt.

6 Bake for 20–25 minutes, or until golden and crisp. Cut into large squares and serve warm.

FLAVOURED OR ENRICHED BREADS

These are usually not an everyday bread, but eaten as part of a celebration or religious meal, and are often given as gifts during these times. Challah, the plaited Jewish bread is eaten on the Sabbath, stollen and panettone are eaten at Christmas in Germany and Italy, and fougasse is made with candied peel and is an Easter bread in the south of France. Rich breads are usually soft in texture, flavoured with spices or with dried and candied fruit, then glazed to a shine.

CHALLAH

MAKES 1 LOAF

INGREDIENTS

- 270 g (9½ oz) boiling potatoes, cubed
- 2 teaspoons dried yeast
- 80 ml (2½ fl oz/⅓ cup) oil
- 2 large eggs
- 2 large egg yolks
- 2 tablespoons honey
- 550 g (1 lb 4 oz/4½ cups) white strong flour
- 1 egg yolk, extra
- sesame seeds or poppy seeds

METHOD

1. Boil the potato in 625 ml (21 fl oz/2½ cups) water for 10 minutes, or until very soft. Drain well, reserving the potato water. Cool for 5 minutes, then mash the potato until very smooth.
2. Grease and lightly flour a baking tray. Put the yeast and 125 ml (4 fl oz/½ cup) warm water in a small bowl and stir well. Set aside for 10 minutes.
3. Put the oil, eggs, yolks, honey, 125 ml (4 fl oz/½ cup) reserved potato water, mashed potato and 1½ teaspoons salt in a large bowl and beat with a wooden spoon until smooth. Leave to cool. Add the yeast mixture and gradually mix in 250 g (9 oz/2 cups) of the flour, beating until smooth. Add another 185 g (6½ oz/1½ cups) flour and mix until a rough soft dough is formed. Knead the dough for 10 minutes, incorporating the remaining flour as required, to keep the dough from sticking. Place the dough in an oiled bowl and brush the surface with oil. Cover with plastic wrap and leave in a draught-free place for 1½ hours, or until doubled in size.
4. Turn the dough out onto a floured work surface and knead for 4 minutes. Divide into two, a one-third portion and a two-thirds portion, then divide each portion into three equal parts. Leave to rest for 10 minutes. Roll each part into ropes about 35 cm (14 inches) long, with the centre slightly thicker than the ends. Braid the three thicker ropes, pinching the ends together, and place on the tray. Whisk the extra egg yolk and 1 tablespoon water and brush over the challah. Repeat with the remaining three ropes and place on top of the first braid, making sure the ends of the braids overlap. Secure tightly and brush with some of the egg glaze. Cover with plastic wrap and leave in a draught-free place for 30 minutes, or until doubled in size. Preheat the oven to 180°C (350°F/Gas 4).
5. Brush the dough with the remaining glaze and sprinkle with the seeds. Bake for 50–55 minutes, or until golden brown. Cool on a wire rack.

PANETTONE

A speciality bread-like cake from Milan, now eaten all over Italy during Christmas and Easter. Easily recognised by its tall, large cylindrical shape (panettone means 'big bread'), it is made from a raised dough enriched with eggs and contains sultanas or raisins, and candied orange and lemon peel. Panettone can be made in individual portions or in one large cake. It can be eaten for breakfast with coffee or it may be served as a dessert with liqueur wine.

MAKES 1

INGREDIENTS

- 90 g (3¼ oz/½ cup) mixed peel
- 60 g (2¼ oz/½ cup) sultanas
- 1 teaspoon finely grated lemon zest
- 1 teaspoon finely grated orange zest
- 1 teaspoon brandy or rum
- 2 teaspoons dried yeast
- 220 ml (7½ fl oz) warm milk
- 60 g (2¼ oz/¼ cup) caster (superfine) sugar
- 400 g (14 oz/3¼ cups) white strong flour
- 2 eggs
- 1 teaspoon vanilla extract
- 150 g (5½ oz) unsalted butter, softened
- 20 g (¾ oz) unsalted butter, melted, to glaze

METHOD

1. Put the mixed peel, sultanas and grated lemon and orange zest in a small bowl. Add the brandy, mix well and set aside.
2. Put the yeast, milk and 1 teaspoon of the sugar in a small bowl and stir well. Leave in a draught-free place for 10–15 minutes, or until foamy.
3. Sift 200 g (7 oz) of the flour and ½ teaspoon salt into a large bowl, make a well in the centre and add the yeast mixture. Mix together with a large spoon to form a soft dough. Cover the bowl with plastic wrap and leave to 'sponge' and rise in a draught-free place for 45 minutes, or until bubbles appear on the surface.
4. Add the eggs, remaining sugar and vanilla and mix. Add the butter and stir until well combined. Stir in the remaining flour and mix well. Knead well on a floured surface until the dough is smooth and elastic. You may need to add up to 60 g (2¼ oz/½ cup) more flour to the dough as you knead. Place the dough in a lightly oiled bowl. Cover with plastic wrap or a damp tea towel and leave in a draught-free place for 1½–2 hours, or until doubled in size.
5. Lightly grease a 15 cm (6 inch) round cake tin and line the base and side with a double thickness of baking paper, ensuring the collar extends above the rim of the tin by 10 cm (4 inches). (See page 530.)
6. Knock back the dough and turn out onto a floured work surface. Roll into a 30 x 20 cm (12 x 8 inch) rectangle. Drain the fruit mixture and spread half the fruit over the surface of the dough. Fold over the short edges like an envelope to cover the fruit. Roll again and repeat the process to incorporate all the fruit. Gently knead the dough for 2–3 minutes and shape into a neat ball. Place in the tin, brush with the melted butter, then slash a cross on the top with a sharp knife and leave to rise again in a draught-free place for 45 minutes, or until doubled in size.
7. Preheat the oven to 190°C (375°F/Gas 5). Bake for 50 minutes, or until golden brown and a skewer inserted into the centre comes out clean. Leave in the tin for 5 minutes, then transfer to a wire rack to cool.

STOLLEN

Stollen is a sweet yeasted bread, eaten at Christmas time (and sometimes called Christstollen), originally from the German city of Dresden. The dough is enriched with egg, sugar, butter, dried fruits and almonds and sometimes marzipan is placed along the centre, before it is folded into an oval and baked. The shape is said to represent the baby Jesus wrapped in swaddling cloths.

MAKES 1

INGREDIENTS

- 80 ml (2½ fl oz/⅓ cup) warm milk
- 2 teaspoons sugar
- 2 teaspoons dried yeast
- 125 g (4½ oz) unsalted butter, softened
- 85 g (3 oz/⅓ cup) caster (superfine) sugar
- 1 egg
- 1 teaspoon vanilla extract
- ½ teaspoon ground cinnamon
- 375 g (12 oz/3 cups) white strong flour
- 80 g (2¾ oz/⅔ cup) raisins
- 75 g (2½ oz/½ cup) currants
- 95 g (3¼ oz/½ cup) mixed peel
- 60 g (2¼ oz/½ cup) slivered almonds
- 30 g (1 oz) butter, melted
- icing (confectioners') sugar, for dusting

METHOD

1. Combine the milk, sugar and yeast with 80 ml (2½ fl oz/⅓ cup) warm water in a bowl and leave for 10 minutes, or until bubbles appear on the surface. The mixture should be frothy and slightly increased in volume.
2. Beat the butter and sugar with electric beaters until creamy, then add the egg and vanilla. Add the yeast mixture, cinnamon and almost all the flour and mix to a soft dough. Turn out onto a floured surface and knead for 10 minutes, or until smooth. Place the dough in a lightly oiled bowl. Cover with plastic wrap or a damp tea towel and leave in a draught-free place for 1¾ hours, or until doubled in size.
3. Lightly grease a baking tray. Punch down the dough and turn it out onto a floured work surface. Press it out to a thickness of 1.5 cm (⅝ inch). Sprinkle over the dried fruit and almonds, then knead to mix them through the dough. Shape the dough into an oval, 18 cm (7 inches) wide and 30 cm (12 inches) long, then fold in half lengthways. Press down to flatten, with the fold slightly off centre on top of the loaf.
4. Place on the tray, cover and leave in a draught-free place for 1 hour, or until doubled in size. Preheat the oven to 180°C (350°F/Gas 4).
5. Bake for 40 minutes, or until golden. As soon as the stollen comes out of the oven, brush with the melted butter, allowing each brushing to be absorbed, until you have used all the butter. Cool on a wire rack. Dust with icing sugar.

HOT CROSS BUNS

Traditionally eaten on Good Friday, hot cross buns are small yeast buns flavoured with spices and raisins or sultanas. The custom of eating the buns on Good Friday was popularised in Tudor England when a law was introduced that forbade the sale of the spiced buns except on Good Friday, Christmas and at burials.

MAKES 12 BUNS

INGREDIENTS

1 tablespoon dried yeast or 30 g (1 oz) fresh yeast
500 g (1 lb 2 oz/4 cups) white strong flour
2 tablespoons caster (superfine) sugar
1 teaspoon mixed spice
1 teaspoon ground cinnamon
40 g (1½ oz) butter
150 g (5½ oz/1¼ cups) sultanas

PASTE FOR CROSSES

30 g (1 oz/¼ cup) plain (all-purpose) flour
¼ teaspoon caster (superfine) sugar

GLAZE

1½ tablespoons caster (superfine) sugar
1 teaspoon powdered gelatine

METHOD

1 In a small bowl, put the yeast, 2 teaspoons of the flour, 1 teaspoon of the sugar and 125 ml (4 fl oz/½ cup) warm water and stir well. Leave in a draught-free place for 10 minutes, or until bubbles appear on the surface. The mixture should be frothy and slightly increased in volume. If your yeast doesn't foam, it is dead, so you will have to discard it and start again.

2 Sift the remaining flour and spices into a large bowl and stir in the sugar. Using your fingertips, rub in the butter. Stir in the sultanas. Make a well in the centre, stir in the yeast mixture and up to 185 ml (6 fl oz/¾ cup) water to make a soft dough. Turn the dough out onto a lightly floured surface and knead for 5 minutes, or until smooth, adding more flour if necessary, to prevent sticking. Place the dough in a large floured bowl, cover with plastic wrap or a damp tea towel and leave in a draught-free place for 30–40 minutes, or until doubled in size.

3 Preheat the oven to 200°C (400°F/Gas 6). Lightly grease a baking tray. Turn the dough out onto a lightly floured surface and knead gently to deflate. Divide into 12 portions and roll each into a ball. Place the balls on the tray, just touching each other, in a rectangle three rolls wide and four rolls long. Cover loosely with plastic wrap and leave in a draught-free place for 20 minutes, or until nearly doubled in size.

4 To make the crosses, mix the flour, sugar and 2½ tablespoons water into a paste. Spoon into a piping (icing) bag and pipe crosses on top of the buns. Bake for 20 minutes, or until golden brown. To make the glaze, put the sugar, gelatine and 1 tablespoon water in a small saucepan and stir over medium heat until dissolved. Brush over the hot buns and leave to cool.

••PIZZA••

The most famous of all the flatbreads, Italian pizza is loved the world over. There are countless variations but it is the pizza of Naples in southern Italy that is considered to be the true pizza. The first pizza was pizza bianca (white) and the topping was garlic, lard, salt and anchovies. The arrival of the tomato from South America gave rise to pizzas topped with tomato.

PIZZA BASE

METHOD

1 Mix 2 teaspoons (7 g/¼ oz sachet) dried yeast with 2 teaspoons sugar and 90 ml (3 fl oz) warm water and leave until the mixture bubbles.

2 Sift 450 g (1 lb) plain (all-purpose) flour into a bowl with a pinch of salt, add the yeast and 185 ml (6 fl oz/¾ cup) water and mix to a soft dough.

3 Knead the dough until smooth and springy — at least 5 minutes. Place the dough in an oiled bowl. Cover with plastic wrap and leave in a draught-free place for 1½ hours, or until doubled in size.

4 Gently punch the air out of the dough with your fist and divide it into two equal pieces.

5 Flatten each piece of dough into a circle, then, working from the centre out, make the circle bigger using the heel of your hand.

6 Leave a slightly raised rim around the edge and place each onto a 30 cm (12 inch) pizza tray, dusted with polenta. Use as directed in the recipe. Makes 2 x 30 cm (12 inch) pizza bases.

TOMATO SAUCE

Remove the cores from 375 g (13 oz) ripe roma (plum) tomatoes, then chop them finely by hand or in a food processor. Add 10 finely chopped basil leaves, 4 crushed garlic cloves, 4 tablespoons tomato passata and 1 tablespoon olive oil. Mix well and leave to stand for 30 minutes to allow the flavours to infuse. Season with salt and pepper. This makes enough sauce for two 30 cm (12 inch) pizzas.

MARGHERITA PIZZA

This classic pizza was supposedly created in 1889 in honour of Queen Margherita. The queen had heard so much of the fabled pizzas of Naples that she requested one to eat when she visited the city.

MAKES 1 PIZZA

INGREDIENTS

- 1 x 30 cm (12 inch) pizza base (opposite)
- ½ quantity tomato sauce (opposite)
- 150 g (5½ oz) mozzarella cheese, chopped
- 9 small basil leaves (optional)
- 1 tablespoon olive oil

METHOD

1. Preheat the oven to 240°C (475°F/Gas 8). Place the pizza base on a baking tray dusted with polenta and spoon the tomato sauce onto the base, spreading it up to the rim. Scatter with the mozzarella and basil, if using. Drizzle with the oil.
2. Bake for 12–15 minutes, or until golden and puffed. Remove from the oven and brush the rim with a little extra olive oil before serving.

Each of the following pizzas will require one pizza base (page 464)

QUATTRO STAGIONI

Preheat the oven to 240°C (475°F/Gas 8). Place the pizza base on a baking tray dusted with polenta and spoon the tomato sauce (page 464) onto the base, spreading it up to the rim. Scatter 60 g (2¼ oz) chopped mozzarella cheese over the pizza. Visually divide the pizza into quarters. Put 30 g (1 oz) sliced prosciutto on one quarter, 4 quartered artichoke hearts on another, 4 sliced mushrooms on the next and 1 sliced tomato on the last quarter. Bake for 12 minutes, or until the crust is browned and the centre is bubbling.

ROMANA

Preheat the oven to 240°C (475°F/Gas 8). Place the pizza base on a baking tray dusted with polenta and spoon the tomato sauce (page 464) onto the base, spreading it up to the rim. Scatter 60 g (2¼ oz) chopped mozzarella cheese, a pinch of dried oregano and 6 chopped anchovy fillets over the pizza. Drizzle with some oil and bake for 12 minutes, or until the crust is browned and the centre is bubbling. Drizzle with a little more oil and serve.

SPINACHI

Preheat the oven to 240°C (475°F/Gas 8). Spread the prepared pizza base with 1 kg (2 lb 4 oz) chopped, cooked spinach, then drizzle with olive oil and season well. Scatter 150 g (5½ oz) chopped mozzarella cheese and 15 small pitted black olives over the pizza. Bake for 12 minutes, or until the crust is browned and the centre is bubbling. Drizzle with a little more oil and serve.

CALZONE

A speciality of Naples and meaning 'trousers' (originally its shape was long and baggy), calzone is a pizza shaped into a half-moon. The dough is rolled into a thin oval, one half filled, then the dough is folded and sealed. Calzone are usually brushed with oil and baked; some are also brushed with tomato sauce or herbs.

SERVES 1–2

Each one of the following fillings makes one 25 cm (10 inch) calzone — enough for one or two people.

INGREDIENTS

- polenta, for dusting
- ½ quantity pizza dough (page 464), for each calzone
- 1½ tablespoons olive oil

MOZZARELLA AND PROSCIUTTO

- 170 g (6 oz) mozzarella cheese, cut into 2 cm (¾ inch) cubes
- 2 thin slices prosciutto, cut in half
- 1 artichoke heart, marinated in oil, drained and cut into 3 slices from top to bottom

POTATO, ONION AND SALAMI

- 2 tablespoons vegetable oil
- 1 small onion, very thinly sliced
- 75 g (2½ oz) small red potatoes, unpeeled, very thinly sliced
- 75 g (2½ oz) mozzarella cheese, chopped
- 60 g (2¼ oz) sliced salami
- 2 tablespoons grated parmesan cheese

METHOD

1. Preheat the oven to 230°C (450°F/Gas 8). Lightly oil a baking tray and dust with polenta.
2. On a lightly floured surface roll out the dough into an 18 cm (7 inch) circle. Using the heels of your hands and working from the centre outwards, press the circle out to a diameter of about 30 cm (12 inches). Transfer to the baking tray. Brush the entire surface lightly with the oil.
3. To make the mozzarella and prosciutto calzone, spread the mozzarella cheese over one half of the pizza base, leaving a narrow border around the edge. Roll the half slices of prosciutto into little tubes and place on top of the cheese. Top with the artichoke slices, then season well.
4. To make the potato, onion and salami calzone, heat the oil in a frying pan and add the onion slices. Cook for 1 minute, then scatter the potato on top. Cook, stirring, for 3–4 minutes, until beginning to brown. Season with salt and pepper. Spread over one half of the pizza base, leaving a narrow border around the edge. Scatter the mozzarella on top, followed by the salami slices and parmesan.
5. Whichever calzone you are making, now fold the plain side of the base over the filling to make a half-moon shape. Match the cut edges and press them firmly together to seal. Fold them over and press into a scrolled pattern to thoroughly seal in the filling. Brush the surface with a little extra olive oil, then transfer to the oven. Bake for about 20 minutes, or until the crust is golden.

PISSALADIERE

A speciality of Nice in southern France and similar to an Italian pizza, a pissaladière is an open tart made with either a bread dough or pastry base topped with onions and garnished in a chequerboard pattern with anchovy fillets and black olives. Traditionally, the top was spread with *pissala* (from which the dish takes its name), a paste of anchovy purée, herbs and olive oil, and then baked. Some versions include tomatoes.

SERVES 6

INGREDIENTS

BREAD DOUGH
2 teaspoons dried yeast
250 g (9 oz/2 cups) plain (all-purpose) flour
60 ml (2 fl oz/¼ cup) olive oil

40 g (1½ oz) butter
1 tablespoon olive oil
1.5 kg (3 lb 5 oz) onions, thinly sliced
2 tablespoons thyme
olive oil, for brushing
16 anchovy fillets, halved lengthways
24 pitted black olives

METHOD

1 To make the bread dough, mix the yeast with 125 ml (4 fl oz/½ cup) warm water. Leave in a draught-free place for 10 minutes, or until bubbles appear on the surface.
2 Sift the flour into a large bowl, add ½ teaspoon salt, the olive oil and the yeast mixture. Mix until the dough clumps together and forms a ball. Turn out onto a lightly floured work surface. Knead the dough, adding a little more flour or a few drops of warm water if necessary, until you have a soft dough that is not sticky but dry to the touch. Knead for 10 minutes, or until smooth, and the impression made by a finger springs back immediately.
3 Rub the inside of a large bowl with olive oil. Roll the ball of dough around in the bowl to coat it with oil, then cut a shallow cross on the top of the ball with a knife. Place the dough in the bowl, cover with plastic wrap or a damp tea towel and leave in a draught-free place for 1–1½ hours, or until the dough has doubled in size.
4 Gently knock back the dough by punching it with your fist and then knead it again for a couple of minutes. (At this stage the dough can be stored in the fridge for 4 hours, or frozen. Bring back to room temperature before continuing.) Leave in a draught-free place to rise until doubled in size.
5 Melt the butter with the olive oil in a saucepan and add the onion and half the thyme. Cover the saucepan and cook over low heat for about 45 minutes, stirring, until the onion has softened but not browned. Season and cool. Preheat the oven to 200°C (400°F/Gas 6).
6 Roll out the dough to roughly fit a greased 34 x 26 cm (13½ x 10½ inch) shallow baking tray. Brush the dough with the oil, then spread with the onion.
7 Lay the anchovies in a lattice pattern over the onion and arrange the olives in the lattice diamonds. Bake for 20 minutes, or until the dough is cooked and lightly browned. Sprinkle with the remaining thyme and cut into squares. Serve hot or warm.

••QUICHES AND TARTS••

A quiche is a savoury dish originating in the Alsace Lorraine region of France. The classic is quiche Lorraine, an open tart with a pastry base filled with eggs, cream and bacon and served hot or cold, but variations today can include almost anything, including onion, cheese, fish and herbs.

QUICHE LORRAINE

SERVES 8

INGREDIENTS

SHORTCRUST PASTRY

220 g (7¾ oz/1¾ cups) plain (all-purpose) flour
150 g (5½ oz) unsalted butter, chilled and diced

FILLING

25 g (1 oz) butter
300 g (10½ oz) bacon, rind and fat removed, diced
250 ml (9 fl oz/1 cup) thick (double) cream
3 eggs, lightly beaten
ground nutmeg, to season

METHOD

1 To make the pastry, sift the flour and a pinch of salt into a large bowl, add the butter and rub in with your fingertips until the mixture resembles breadcrumbs. Add 4–5 tablespoons of chilled water and mix with a flat-bladed knife until the dough just starts to come together. Bring the dough together with your hands, kneading it lightly if necessary, and shape into a ball. Cover with plastic wrap and refrigerate for at least 30 minutes.
2 Preheat the oven to 200°C (400°F/Gas 6). Roll out the pastry on a lightly floured surface to fit the base and side of a 25 cm (10 inch) fluted loose-based tart tin.
3 Line the pastry shell with a piece of baking paper and fill with baking beads or uncooked rice. Blind bake the pastry for 10 minutes, remove the paper and beads and bake for a further 5 minutes, or until the pastry is just cooked but still very pale. Remove the pastry shell from the oven. Reduce the oven to 180°C (350°F/Gas 4).
4 Melt the butter in a small frying pan and cook the bacon until golden. Remove and drain on paper towels.
5 Whisk together the cream and eggs and season with salt, pepper and nutmeg. Scatter the bacon over the pastry shell and then pour in the egg mixture. Bake for 30 minutes, or until the filling is set. Leave in the tin for 5 minutes before serving.

COOKING TIPS

* A preheated baking tray placed under your quiche tin will help crisp the bottom crust. Metal tins are best for making quiche as ceramic quiche plates do not conduct heat as well and the pastry will not crisp up properly.
* Blind baking the pastry until it is very dry will help stop it going soggy when you add a liquid filling. Brush the pastry while it is still hot with a beaten egg first. This will fill in any holes that may leak during cooking.
* The easiest way to fill a quiche is to put the case on the oven shelf and then pour in the mixture.

SALMON AND SPINACH QUICHE

SERVES 8

INGREDIENTS

1 quantity shortcrust pastry (see Quiche Lorraine, page 470)

FILLING

250 g (9 oz) packet frozen chopped spinach, thawed
210 g (7½ oz) tin salmon, drained
3 eggs, lightly beaten
300 ml (10½ fl oz) cream
pinch of ground nutmeg

METHOD

1 Preheat the oven to 200°C (400°F/Gas 6). Following steps 2–3 on page 470, roll out and line a 25 cm (10 inch) fluted loose-based tart tin with the pastry. Blind bake the pastry shell, then remove it from the oven. Reduce the oven to 180°C (350°F/Gas 4).

2 Put the spinach into a sieve and squeeze out the water. Transfer the spinach to a bowl and combine with the salmon and eggs. Beat in the cream, then season with salt and pepper and a pinch of nutmeg. Pour into the pastry shell and bake for 30 minutes, or until the filling is just set. Leave in the tin for 5 minutes before serving.

ROCKET, BASIL AND LEEK QUICHE

SERVES 8

INGREDIENTS

1 quantity shortcrust pastry (see Quiche Lorraine, page 470)

FILLING

1 tablespoon oil
1 large leek, white part only, thinly sliced
2 garlic cloves, crushed
100 g (3½ oz) rocket (arugula) leaves
3 eggs
125 ml (4 fl oz/½ cup) milk
125 ml (4 fl oz/½ cup) cream
basil leaves, to garnish
parmesan cheese shavings, to garnish

METHOD

1 Preheat the oven to 200°C (400°F/Gas 6). Following steps 2–3 on page 470, roll out and line a 25 cm (10 inch) fluted loose-based tart tin with the pastry. Blind bake the pastry shell, then remove it from the oven. Reduce the oven to 180°C (350°F/Gas 4).
2 To make the filling, heat the oil in a frying pan, add the leek and garlic and stir over low heat for 5 minutes, or until the leek is soft.
3 Meanwhile, roughly chop the rocket leaves. Add the rocket to the pan and stir over low heat for 1 minute. Remove from the heat and allow to cool. Spread the mixture over the base of the pastry shell.
4 Combine the eggs, milk and cream and whisk until smooth. Pour into the pastry shell. Bake for 30 minutes, or until the filling is set and golden. Serve the quiche topped with the basil leaves and shaved parmesan.

BLUE CHEESE AND WALNUT QUICHE

SERVES 8

INGREDIENTS

1 quantity shortcrust pastry (see Quiche Lorraine, page 470)

FILLING

90 g (3¼ oz) walnuts
200 g (7 oz) blue cheese, mashed
100 ml (3½ fl oz) milk
3 eggs
2 egg yolks
250 ml (9 fl oz/1 cup) thick (double) cream

METHOD

1 Preheat the oven to 200°C (400°F/Gas 6). Toast the walnuts on a baking tray for 5 minutes, then chop them.
2 Following steps 2–3 on page 470, roll out and line a 25 cm (10 inch) fluted loose-based tart tin with the pastry. Blind bake the pastry shell, then remove it from the oven. Reduce the oven to 180°C (350°F/Gas 4).
3 To make the filling, mix together the blue cheese, milk, eggs, egg yolks and cream and season. Pour into the pastry shell and scatter with the chopped walnuts. Bake for 25–30 minutes, or until the filling is just set. Leave in the tin for 5 minutes before serving.

FLAMICHE

A speciality of the Picardie region in France, flamiche is made as an open tart and a closed pie. It is usually made with leeks but sometimes with onion or pumpkin.

SERVES 6

INGREDIENTS

TART PASTRY

220 g (7¾ oz/1¾ cups) plain (all-purpose) flour
150 g (5½ oz) unsalted butter, chilled and diced
1 egg yolk

500 g (1 lb 2 oz) leeks, white part only, thinly sliced
50 g (1¾ oz) butter
180 g (6½ oz) soft cheese such as maroilles, or use livarot or port salut
2 eggs, 1 lightly beaten
1 egg yolk
60 ml (2 fl oz/¼ cup) thick (double) cream

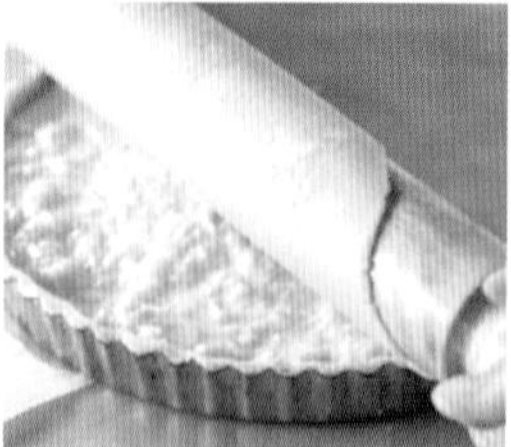

METHOD

1 To make the tart pastry, sift the flour and a pinch of salt into a large bowl. Add the butter and rub in with your fingertips until the mixture resembles breadcrumbs. Add the egg yolk, 2–3 teaspoons of chilled water and mix with a flat-bladed knife until the dough just starts to come together. Bring the dough together with your hands and shape into a ball. Cover with plastic wrap and refrigerate for at least 30 minutes.
2 Preheat the oven to 180°C (350°F/Gas 4) and put a baking tray on the top shelf. Roll out the pastry on a lightly floured surface. Use three-quarters of the pastry to line the base and side of a 23 cm (9 inch) fluted loose-based tart tin.
3 Cook the leek for 10 minutes in a saucepan of boiling salted water, then drain. Heat the butter in a frying pan, add the leek and cook, stirring, for 5 minutes. Stir in the cheese. Tip into a bowl and add the unbeaten egg, egg yolk and cream. Season and mix well.
4 Pour the filling into the pastry shell and smooth. Roll out the remaining pastry into a round large enough to cover the pie. Pinch the edges together and trim. Cut a hole in the centre and brush the top with the beaten egg. Bake for 35–40 minutes on the baking tray until browned. Leave in the tin for 5 minutes before serving. Serve warm or at room temperature. The flamiche is best eaten on the day it is made.

SWEET ONION TARTLETS

MAKES 20

INGREDIENTS

125 g (4½ oz/1 cup) plain (all-purpose) flour
80 g (2¾ oz) butter, chopped
1 tablespoon bottled green peppercorns, rinsed
1 egg yolk
1 teaspoon dijon mustard
1 tablespoon olive paste
80 g (2¾ oz) feta cheese

SWEET ONION FILLING
2 tablespoons olive oil
3 onions, sliced
1 garlic clove, sliced
2 teaspoons sugar
2 tablespoons balsamic vinegar
40 g (1½ oz/⅓ cup) raisins

METHOD

1 Grease 20 holes in two 12-hole patty pans or mini muffin tins.
2 To make the pastry, sift the flour and ¼ teaspoon salt into a bowl. Add the butter and rub in with your fingertips until the mixture resembles fine breadcrumbs. Make a well in the centre. Crush the peppercorns with a knife and chop finely. Add to the flour with the egg yolk, mustard and 2 teaspoons chilled water. Mix with a flat-bladed knife, using a cutting action, until the mixture comes together in beads. Turn onto a lightly floured work surface and press together into a ball. Cover with plastic wrap and refrigerate for 30 minutes.
3 Preheat the oven to 200°C (400°F/Gas 6). Roll the dough out on a floured surface to 3 mm (⅛ inch). Cut out 20 rounds with an 8 cm (3¼ inch) cutter. Put in the patty pans and prick with a fork. Bake for 8 minutes, or until golden.
4 To make the filling, heat the oil in a heavy-based saucepan. Cook the onion and garlic over low heat for 30 minutes, or until the onion is very soft and beginning to brown. Increase the heat to medium, add the sugar and vinegar and cook, stirring, until most of the liquid has evaporated and the onion is glossy. Stir in the raisins.
5 Spread a little olive paste into the base of each pastry case. Spoon the onion mixture over it and crumble the feta on top. Serve warm.

PUMPKIN TARTS

MAKES 6

INGREDIENTS

250 g (9 oz/2 cups) plain (all-purpose) flour
125 g (4½ oz) chilled butter, cubed
80 ml (2½ fl oz/⅓ cup) chilled water

PUMPKIN FILLING
1.25 kg (2 lb 12 oz) pumpkin (winter squash), cut into 6 cm (2½ inch) pieces
125 g (4½ oz/½ cup) sour cream or cream cheese
sweet chilli sauce

METHOD

1 Make the pastry following step 1 on page 470. Cover the dough with plastic wrap and refrigerate for 30 minutes.
2 Preheat the oven to 200°C (400°F/Gas 6). Divide the pastry into six portions, roll each one out and fit into six 10 cm (4 inch) pie tins. Trim the edge and prick the bases all over with a fork. Bake on a baking tray for 15 minutes, or until lightly golden, pressing down any pastry that puffs up. Cool, then remove from the tins.
3 Meanwhile, to make the filling, steam the pumpkin for 15 minutes, or until tender.
4 Place a tablespoon of sour cream in the middle of each pastry case and top with the pumpkin. Season with salt and pepper and drizzle with sweet chilli sauce. Return to the oven for a few minutes to heat through. Serve immediately.

••SAVOURY PASTRIES AND PIES••

Puff pastry, filo pastry or savoury shortcrust — these flaky, melt-in-the-mouth pastries are used to encase all manner of fillings — from rich, hearty meats to lighter fillings such as vegetables or seafood, sometimes mixed with cheese.

PUFF PASTRY

A delicate, crisp pastry made up of many layers, puff is made with butter and dough, which is rolled and folded so that the butter becomes trapped between the layers, causing it to puff up as the layers separate. Making your own pastry is very rewarding, but you can substitute ready-made block or sheets of puff pastry if preferred.

MAKES ABOUT 1 KG (2 LB 4 OZ)

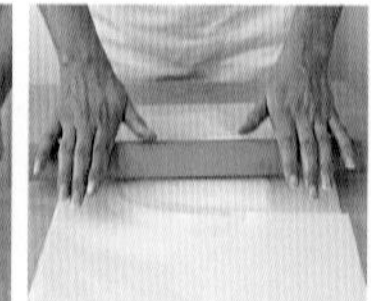

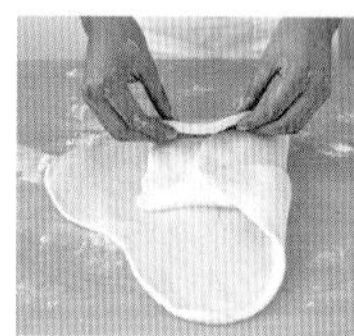

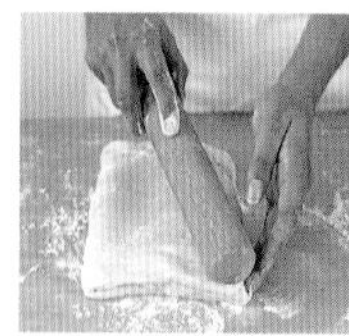
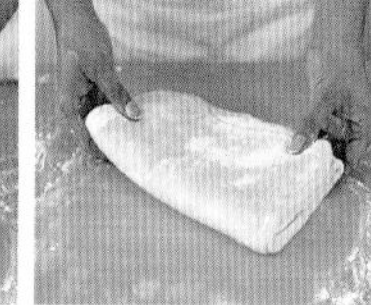

METHOD

1. Mix 500 g (1 lb 2 oz/2 cups) plain (all-purpose) flour, 250 ml (9 fl oz/1 cup) chilled water, 75 g (2½ oz) butter, melted, and 2 teaspoons salt to a rough dough and chill for 30 minutes.
2. Put 300 g (10½ oz) butter between two sheets of baking paper and flatten with a rolling pin to a 20 cm (8 inch) square.
3. Roll out the dough on a floured surface to form a cross shape, with a 20 cm (8 inch) centre.
4. Put the butter in the centre and fold in the sides. Seal the pastry edges with your fingers to completely enclose the butter. The butter and dough should be the same consistency.
5. Roll out the dough to form a 20 x 45 cm (8 x 18 inch) rectangle.
6. Fold the bottom third of the dough up towards the middle, then bring the top third of the dough over the folded thirds.
7. Turn the dough through a quarter turn, gently seal the edges and roll out to a 20 x 45 cm (8 x 18 inch) rectangle.
8. Fold in thirds again, keeping the edges straight, then chill.
9. Repeat the rolling, folding and chilling a total of six times. Mark the side of the dough each time so you remember how many you have done. After the final roll and fold, leave it folded. It is now ready.

NOTES: Try to keep the pastry rectangular as you make it and roll it out — every layer must be exactly the same or it will rise.
Freeze any leftover pastry for next time.

MUSHROOM AND CHEESE PIES

MAKES 6

INGREDIENTS

- 40 g (1½ oz) butter
- 2 garlic cloves, crushed
- 500 g (1 lb 2 oz) button mushrooms, sliced
- 1 small red capsicum (pepper), seeded, membrane removed and finely chopped
- 165 g (5¾ oz/⅔ cup) sour cream
- 3 teaspoons wholegrain mustard
- 70 g (2½ oz/½ cup) finely grated gruyère or cheddar cheese
- 6 sheets ready-rolled puff pastry
- 70 g (2½ oz/½ cup) finely grated gruyère or cheddar cheese, extra
- 1 egg, lightly beaten

METHOD

1. Preheat the oven to 190°C (375°F/Gas 5). Lightly grease two baking trays with melted butter or oil. Heat the butter in a large frying pan. Add the garlic and mushrooms and cook over medium heat, stirring occasionally, until the mushrooms are tender and the liquid has evaporated. Remove from the heat and cool. Stir in the capsicum.
2. Combine the sour cream, mustard and cheese. Cut out twelve circles with a 14 cm (5½ inch) diameter from the pastry. Spread the cream mixture over six of the circles, leaving a 1 cm (½ inch) border. Top each with some of the mushroom mixture. Sprinkle with 2 teaspoons of the extra cheese.
3. Brush the outer edges with the beaten egg then place the reserved pastry rounds on top of the filling, sealing the edges with a fork. Brush the tops of the pastry with egg and sprinkle the remaining cheese over the pastry. Place the pies on the prepared trays and bake for 20 minutes, or until lightly browned and puffed.

HAM AND OLIVE EMPANADILLAS

MAKES ABOUT 15

INGREDIENTS

- 2 hard-boiled eggs, roughly chopped
- 40 g (1½ oz) stuffed green olives, chopped
- 100 g (3½ oz) ham, finely chopped
- 30 g (1 oz) cheddar cheese, grated
- 3 sheets ready-rolled puff pastry
- 1 egg yolk, lightly beaten

METHOD

1. Preheat the oven to 220°C (425°F/Gas 7). Lightly grease two baking trays. Combine the egg with the olives, ham and cheddar in a bowl.
2. Cut the puff pastry sheets into 10 cm (4 inch) rounds (about five rounds from each sheet). Spoon a tablespoon of the egg mixture into the centre of each round, fold over the pastry to enclose the filling and crimp the edges to seal.
3. Place the pastries on the trays 2 cm (¾ inch) apart. Brush the tops with egg yolk and bake for 15 minutes, or until brown and puffed. Swap the trays around after 10 minutes. Cover loosely with foil if browning too much. Serve hot.

VOL AU VENTS

MAKES 4

INGREDIENTS

250 g (9 oz) block ready-made puff pastry, thawed
1 egg, lightly beaten

SAUCE AND FILLING
40 g (1½ oz) butter
2 spring onions (scallions), finely chopped
2 tablespoons plain (all-purpose) flour
375 ml (13 fl oz/1½ cups) milk
your choice of filling (see Note)

METHOD

1 Preheat the oven to 220°C (425°F/Gas 7). Line a baking tray with baking paper. Roll out the pastry to a 20 cm (8 inch) square. Cut four circles of pastry with a 10 cm (4 inch) cutter. Place the rounds onto the tray and cut 6 cm (2½ inch) circles into the centre of the rounds with a cutter, taking care not to cut right through the pastry. Place the baking tray in the refrigerator for 15 minutes.

2 Using a floured knife blade, 'knock up' the sides of each pastry round by making even indentations about 1 cm (½ inch) apart around the circumference. This should allow even rising of the pastry as it cooks. The dough can be made ahead of time up to this stage and frozen until needed. Carefully brush the pastry with the egg, avoiding the 'knocked up' edge, as any egg glaze spilt on the sides will stop the pastry from rising.

3 Bake for 15–20 minutes, or until the pastry has risen and is golden brown and crisp. Cool on a wire rack. Remove the centre from each pastry circle and pull out and discard any partially cooked pastry from the centre. The pastry can be returned to the oven for 2 minutes to dry out if the centre is undercooked. The pastry cases are now ready to be filled with a hot filling before serving.

4 To make the sauce, melt the butter in a saucepan, add the spring onion and stir over low heat for 2 minutes, or until soft. Add the flour and stir for 2 minutes, or until lightly golden. Gradually add the milk, stirring until smooth. Stir constantly over medium heat for 4 minutes, or until the mixture boils and thickens. Season well. Remove and stir in your choice of filling.

NOTE: Add 350 g (12 oz) of any of the following to your white sauce: sliced, cooked mushrooms; peeled, deveined and cooked prawns (shrimp); chopped, cooked chicken breast; smoked salmon; cooked and dressed crabmeat; or steamed asparagus spears.

SAUSAGE ROLLS

MAKES 36

INGREDIENTS

- 3 sheets ready-rolled puff pastry, thawed (see Note)
- 2 eggs, lightly beaten
- 750 g (1 lb 10 oz) sausage mince
- 1 onion, finely chopped
- 1 garlic clove, crushed
- 80 g (2¾ oz/1 cup) fresh breadcrumbs
- 3 tablespoons chopped parsley
- 3 tablespoons chopped thyme
- ½ teaspoon each of ground sage, nutmeg, black pepper and cloves

METHOD

1. Preheat the oven to 200°C (400°F/Gas 6). Lightly grease two baking trays.
2. Cut the pastry sheets in half and lightly brush the edges with some of the beaten egg.
3. Mix half the remaining egg with the remaining ingredients in a large bowl, then divide into six even portions. Pipe or spoon the filling down the centre of each piece of pastry, then brush the edges with some of the egg. Fold the pastry over the filling, overlapping the edges and placing the join underneath. Brush the rolls with more egg, then cut each into six short pieces.
4. Cut two small slashes on top of each roll, place on the baking trays and bake for 15 minutes. Reduce the oven temperature to 180°C (350°F/Gas 4) and bake for another 15 minutes, or until puffed and golden.

NOTE: If using home-made pastry, divide 500 g (1 lb 2 oz) puff pastry into thirds and roll each piece between two sheets of baking paper to form a 30 cm (12 inch) square, about 3 mm (⅛ inch) thick. Cut each sheet in half.

CHUTNEY CHICKEN SAUSAGE ROLLS

MAKES 36

INGREDIENTS

- 3 sheets ready-rolled puff pastry, thawed
- 2 eggs, lightly beaten
- 750 g (1 lb 10 oz) minced (ground) chicken
- 4 spring onions (scallions), finely chopped
- 80 g (2¾ oz/1 cup) fresh breadcrumbs
- 1 carrot, finely grated
- 2 tablespoons fruit chutney
- 1 tablespoon sweet chilli sauce
- 1 tablespoon grated ginger
- sesame seeds, to sprinkle

METHOD

1. Preheat the oven to 200°C (400°F/Gas 6). Lightly grease two baking trays.
2. Cut the pastry sheets in half and lightly brush the edges with some of the beaten egg. Mix half the remaining egg with the remaining ingredients (except the sesame seeds) in a large bowl, then divide the mixture into six even portions.
3. Pipe or spoon the filling down the centre of each piece of pastry, then brush the edges with some of the egg. Fold the pastry over the filling, overlapping the edges and placing the join underneath. Brush the rolls with more egg, then cut each into six short pieces. Sprinkle with sesame seeds.
4. Cut two small slashes on top of each roll and place on the trays. Bake for 15 minutes. Reduce the oven to 180°C (350°F/Gas 4) and bake for another 15 minutes, or until puffed and golden.

PIROZHKI

Russian for pie, these semicircular pastries are made from various pastries or yeasted doughs. They are either baked or deep-fried and fillings include rice, fish, game, poultry, vegetables or cream. Pirozhki are served as an accompaniment to soup, especially borscht, with sour cream, or as a snack or hot starter.

FISH AND MUSHROOM PIROZHKI

SERVES 4

INGREDIENTS

PASTRY

300 g (10½ oz/2⅓ cups) plain (all-purpose) flour
175 g (6 oz) butter, chilled and cubed
3 large egg yolks

50 g (1¾ oz) long-grain rice
450 g (1 lb) skinless firm white fish
50 g (1¾ oz) butter
200 g (7 oz) mushrooms, sliced
200 g (7 oz) sour cream
1 tablespoon lemon juice
3 tablespoons chopped parsley

METHOD

1 To make the pastry, sift the flour with a generous pinch of salt into a large bowl. Rub the butter into the flour until fine crumbs form. Lightly beat 2 of the egg yolks and stir into the flour mixture with a little chilled water. Mix together, adding more water if necessary to bring the dough together. Cover the dough with plastic wrap and refrigerate for at least 30 minutes.
2 To make the filling, put the rice in a small saucepan with 100 ml (3½ fl oz) boiling water and a pinch of salt. Bring to the boil, then reduce the heat to medium–low and cook, covered with a tight-fitting lid, for 15 minutes. Add a further 1–2 tablespoons boiling water if the rice begins to dry out. Allow to cool.
3 Chop the fish coarsely. Melt the butter in a large frying pan and when hot, add the mushrooms. Cook for 4–5 minutes, or until soft. Add the fish and cook, stirring occasionally, for 4–5 minutes, or until the fish is opaque. Remove the pan from the heat and stir in the cooked rice, sour cream, lemon juice and parsley. Season with salt and pepper and set aside until cold.
4 Preheat the oven to 190°C (375°F/Gas 5). Lightly grease and flour a large baking tray.
5 Roll the pastry out on a floured work surface to a thickness of 3 mm (⅛ inch). Cut out eight or ten circles, each 12 cm (4½ inches) in diameter. Put a tablespoon of filling on each circle, leaving a border around the edges. Mix the remaining egg yolk with a teaspoon of water and use to brush around the edges of the pastry. Fold the pastry in half, seal the parcel and brush the outside with the egg yolk. Make two small cuts in the top for steam holes. Transfer the pies to the prepared baking tray. Bake for 30–35 minutes, or until the pastry is golden.

CORNISH PASTIES

MAKES 6

INGREDIENTS

SHORTCRUST PASTRY

310 g (11 oz/2½ cups) plain (all-purpose) flour
125 g (4½ oz) chilled butter, cubed
80–100 ml (2½–3½ fl oz) chilled water

165 g (5¾ oz) round steak, finely chopped
1 small potato, finely chopped
1 small onion, finely chopped
1 small carrot, finely chopped
1–2 teaspoons worcestershire sauce
2 tablespoons beef stock
1 egg, lightly beaten

METHOD

1. Lightly grease a baking tray. Sift the flour and a pinch of salt into a large bowl. Using your fingertips, rub in the butter until the mixture resembles fine breadcrumbs. Make a well in the centre and add almost all the water. Mix together with a flat-bladed knife, using a cutting action, until the mixture comes together in beads. Add a little more water if the dough is too dry. Turn out onto a lightly floured work surface and form into a ball. Cover with plastic wrap and refrigerate for 20 minutes.
2. Preheat the oven to 210°C (415°F/Gas 6–7). Mix together the steak, potato, onion, carrot, worcestershire sauce and stock in a bowl and season well.
3. Divide the dough into six portions. Roll out each portion to 3 mm (⅛ inch) thick. Using a 16 cm (6¼ inch) diameter plate as a guide, cut six circles. Divide the filling among the circles.
4. Brush the edges with beaten egg and bring the pastry together to form a semicircle. Pinch the edges into a frill and place on the tray. Brush the pastry with beaten egg and bake for 15 minutes. Reduce the oven to 180°C (350°F/Gas 4) and cook for 25–30 minutes, or until golden.

TUNISIAN TUNA BRIK

MAKES 2

INGREDIENTS

30 g (1 oz) butter
1 small onion, finely chopped
200 g (7 oz) tin tuna in oil, drained
1 tablespoon baby capers, rinsed and chopped
2 tablespoons finely chopped parsley
2 tablespoons grated parmesan cheese
6 sheets filo pastry
30 g (1 oz) butter, extra, melted
2 small eggs

METHOD

1. Preheat the oven to 200°C (400°F/Gas 6). Lightly grease a baking tray.
2. Melt the butter in a small frying pan and cook the onion over low heat for 5 minutes, or until soft but not brown. Combine the onion, tuna, capers, parsley and parmesan in a bowl and season with salt and pepper.
3. Cut the filo pastry sheets in half widthways. Layer four of the half sheets together, brushing each with melted butter. Keep the remaining pastry covered with a damp tea towel. Spoon half the tuna mixture onto one end of the buttered pastry, leaving a border. Make a well in the centre of the mixture and break an egg into the well, being careful to leave it whole.
4. Layer two more sheets of filo together, brushing with melted butter, and place on top of the tuna and egg. Fold in the pastry sides, then carefully roll into a firm parcel, keeping the egg whole. Place on the prepared tray and brush with melted butter. Repeat with the remaining pastry, filling and egg. Bake for 15 minutes, or until the pastry is golden brown. Serve warm or at room temperature with a green salad.

SPINACH AND FETA TRIANGLES

MAKES 8

INGREDIENTS

1 kg (2 lb 4 oz) English spinach
60 ml (2 fl oz/¼ cup) olive oil
1 onion, chopped
10 spring onions (scallions), sliced
4 tablespoons chopped parsley
1 tablespoon chopped dill
large pinch of ground nutmeg
35 g (1¼ oz/⅓ cup) grated parmesan cheese
150 g (5½ oz/1 cup) crumbled feta cheese
90 g (3¼ oz/⅓ cup) ricotta cheese
4 eggs, lightly beaten
40 g (1½ oz) butter, melted
1 tablespoon olive oil, extra
12 sheets filo pastry

METHOD

1. Trim any coarse stems from the spinach, then wash the leaves thoroughly, roughly chop them and place in a large saucepan with just a little water clinging to the leaves. Cover and cook over low heat for 5 minutes, or until the leaves have wilted. Drain well and allow to cool slightly. Squeeze tightly to remove the excess water.
2. Heat the oil in a heavy-based frying pan. Add the onion and cook over low heat for 10 minutes, or until tender and golden. Add the spring onion and cook for 3 minutes. Remove from the heat. Stir in the spinach, parsley, dill, nutmeg, parmesan, feta, ricotta and egg. Season well.
3. Preheat the oven to 180°C (350°F/Gas 4). Lightly grease two baking trays. Combine the butter with the extra oil. Work with three sheets of pastry at a time, keeping the rest covered with a damp tea towel. Brush each sheet with butter mixture and layer them and cut in half lengthways.
4. Place 4 tablespoons of the filling on an angle at the end of each strip. Fold the pastry over to enclose the filling and form a triangle. Continue folding the triangle over until you reach the end of the pastry. Put the triangles on the baking trays and brush with the remaining butter mixture. Bake for 20–25 minutes, or until the pastry is golden brown.

FILO PASTRY

Filo is a paper-thin pastry made with flour and water. Filo means 'leaf' in Greek, and is used widely in the Middle East, Turkey, Greece and Europe for making a variety of pastries and pies such as spanakopita and baklava, or it may be used to wrap seafood or vegetable fillings. The dough for filo is easy enough to make, but stretching it until it is tissue-thin requires great skill and patience. For this reason, commercially made filo, which is available fresh or frozen, is often used. If using frozen filo, thaw it in the packet, then take out the sheets and stack them on a cloth. Cover with a damp cloth and use one at a time as they dry out quickly when exposed to air.

SPANAKOPITA

SERVES 4–6

INGREDIENTS

- 1.5 kg (3 lb 5 oz) silverbeet (Swiss chard)
- 60 ml (2 fl oz/¼ cup) olive oil
- 1 onion, finely chopped
- 10 spring onions (scallions), chopped (include some of the green part)
- 1½ tablespoons chopped dill
- 200 g (7 oz/1⅓ cups) crumbled Greek feta cheese
- 125 g (4½ oz/½ cup) cottage cheese
- 3 tablespoons finely grated kefalotyri or pecorino cheese
- ¼ teaspoon ground nutmeg
- 4 eggs, lightly beaten
- 10 sheets filo pastry
- 80 g (2¾ oz) butter, melted

METHOD

1. Rinse and drain the silverbeet thoroughly. Discard the stems and shred the leaves. Heat the olive oil in a large frying pan, add the onion and cook, stirring, over a medium heat for 5 minutes, or until softened. Add the spring onion and silverbeet and cook, covered, over medium heat for 5 minutes. Add the dill and cook, uncovered, for 3–4 minutes, or until most of the liquid has evaporated. Remove from the heat and cool to room temperature.
2. Preheat the oven to 180°C (350°F/Gas 4) and lightly grease a 20 x 25 cm (8 x 10 inch) 2.5 litre (10 cup) baking dish. Place the feta, cottage and kefalotyri cheeses in a large bowl. Stir in the silverbeet mixture and add the nutmeg. Gradually add the eggs and combine well. Season, to taste.
3. Line the base and sides of the baking dish with a sheet of filo pastry. (Keep the rest covered with a damp tea towel to prevent them drying out.) Brush with butter and cover with another sheet of filo. Butter the sheet and repeat in this way, using five sheets of pastry. Spoon the filling into the dish and level the surface. Fold the exposed pastry up and over to cover the top of the filling. Cover with a sheet of pastry, brush with butter and continue until all the sheets are used. Roughly trim the pastry with kitchen scissors then tuck the excess inside the wall of the dish.
4. Brush the top with butter. Using a sharp knife, score the surface into squares. Sprinkle a few drops of cold water on top to discourage the pastry from curling. Bake for 45 minutes, or until puffed and golden. Rest at room temperature for 10 minutes before serving.

CURRIED CHICKEN PIES

MAKES 24

INGREDIENTS

PASTRY
375 g (13 oz/3 cups) plain (all-purpose) flour
1 teaspoon ground cumin
1 teaspoon ground turmeric
200 g (7 oz) butter, chopped
2 egg yolks, lightly beaten
100–115 ml (3½–3¾ fl oz) chilled water
milk, to glaze

FILLING
50 g (1¾ oz) butter
1 onion, chopped
350 g (12 oz) chicken tenderloins, trimmed and finely diced
1 tablespoon curry powder
1 teaspoon cumin seeds
1 tablespoon plain (all-purpose) flour
250 ml (9 fl oz/1 cup) chicken stock (page 11)
2 tablespoons mango chutney (see Note)
3 tablespoons chopped coriander (cilantro)

METHOD

1 To make the pastry, sift the flour, cumin and turmeric into a bowl. Using your fingertips, rub in the butter until the mixture resembles fine breadcrumbs. Make a well in the centre and add the egg yolks and the chilled water. Mix with a flat-bladed knife, using a cutting action, until the mixture comes together in beads. Lift onto a lightly floured work surface and gently gather into a ball. Cover with plastic wrap and refrigerate for 30 minutes.

2 Lightly grease two deep 12-hole patty pans or mini muffin tins. Roll out two-thirds of the pastry to about 2 mm (1/16 inch) thick, and cut 8 cm (3¼ inch) rounds to fit the tins. Place the pastry in the holes. Roll out the remaining pastry and cut 24 tops with a 5.5 cm (2¼ inch) cutter. Chill the pastry.

3 To make the filling, heat the butter in a large saucepan and cook the onion until soft. Add the chicken and, when browned, stir in the curry powder and cumin seeds for 2 minutes. Add the flour and stir for 30 seconds. Remove from the heat and gradually stir in the stock. Return to the heat and stir until the sauce boils and thickens. Reduce the heat and simmer for 2–3 minutes, or until reduced and very thick. Stir in the mango chutney and coriander. Season and cool.

4 Preheat the oven to 180°C (350°F/Gas 4). Divide the filling equally among the pastry cases and brush the edges with water. Lay the pastry tops over the pies and press around the edges with the tip of a sharp knife. Slash each top to allow steam to escape. Brush with milk and bake for 30 minutes. Cool slightly before removing from the tins. Serve warm.

NOTE: If the mango pieces in the chutney are quite large, chop them.

BEEF AND RED WINE PIES

MAKES 6

INGREDIENTS

- 60 ml (2 fl oz/¼ cup) oil
- 1.5 kg (3 lb 5 oz) chuck steak, cubed
- 2 onions, chopped
- 1 garlic clove, crushed
- 30 g (1 oz/¼ cup) plain (all-purpose) flour
- 310 ml (10¾ fl oz/1¼ cups) dry red wine
- 500 ml (17 fl oz/2 cups) beef stock (page 11)
- 2 bay leaves
- 2 thyme sprigs
- 2 carrots, chopped
- 400 g (14 oz) shortcrust pastry (page 533)
- 400 g (14 oz) block ready-made puff pastry, thawed
- 1 egg, lightly beaten

METHOD

1. Lightly grease six metal pie tins measuring 9 cm (3½ inches) along the base and 3 cm (1¼ inches) deep.
2. Heat 2 tablespoons of the oil in a large frying pan and brown the steak in batches. Remove from the pan. Heat the remaining oil in the same pan, add the onion and garlic and stir over medium heat until golden brown. Add the flour and stir over medium heat for 2 minutes, or until well browned. Remove from the heat and gradually stir in the combined wine and stock.
3. Return to the heat and stir until the mixture boils and thickens. Return the meat to the pan, add the bay leaves and thyme and simmer for 1 hour. Add the carrot and simmer for another 45 minutes, or until the meat and carrot are tender and the sauce has thickened. Season, then remove the bay leaves and thyme. Allow to cool.
4. Preheat the oven to 200°C (400°F/Gas 6). Divide the shortcrust pastry into six portions and roll out each piece between two sheets of baking paper to a 25 cm (10 inch) square, 3 mm (⅛ inch) thick. Cut a circle from each shortcrust sheet big enough to line the base and side of each pie tin. Place in the tins and trim the edges. Line each pastry shell with baking paper and fill with baking beads or uncooked rice. Place on a baking tray and bake for 8 minutes. Remove the paper and beads and bake for another 8 minutes, or until the pastry is lightly browned. Allow to cool.
5. Divide the puff pastry into six portions and roll each piece between two sheets of baking paper to a square. Cut circles from the squares of dough, to fit the tops of the pie tins. Divide the filling evenly among the pastry cases and brush the edges with some of the beaten egg. Cover with a puff pastry round and trim any excess pastry, pressing the edges with a fork to seal. Cut a slit in the top of each pie. Brush the pie tops with the remaining beaten egg and bake for 20–25 minutes, or until the pastry is cooked and golden brown.

NOTE: You can make a family-sized pie using the same ingredients, but substituting a 23 cm (9 inch) metal pie tin. Bake in a 200°C (400°F/Gas 6) oven for 30–35 minutes. Any remaining pastry can be rolled and used to decorate the pie.

••TEA TIME••

From warm, freshly baked scones served with homemade strawberry jam or delicate, soft madeleines to more traditional favourites such as lamingtons, rich chocolate brownies, caramel slices and sticky finger buns, there's something in this chapter to suit every mood and any occasion.

SCONES

Originating in Scotland, the scone is a flat cake, soft and light on the inside and golden and crisp on the outside. Scones are at their best when served fresh and warm from the oven, most famously with butter, or jam and whipped cream.

MAKES ABOUT 18

INGREDIENTS

- 250 g (9 oz/2 cups) self-raising flour
- ½ teaspoon bicarbonate of soda (baking soda)
- 50 g (1¾ oz) unsalted butter, chopped
- 150 ml (5 fl oz) milk or buttermilk

METHOD

1. Preheat the oven to 200°C (400°F/Gas 6). Sift the flour, bicarbonate of soda and a pinch of salt into a bowl.
2. Rub in the butter with your fingertips until the mixture is crumbly.
3. Make a well in the centre, then add the milk. Add a little more milk if needed.
4. Cut the liquid into the flour using a knife and mix to form a soft rough dough.
5. Turn the dough out onto a floured surface and pat to an even 2 cm (¾ inch) thick round.
6. Using a floured 4 cm (1½ inch) cutter, cut the dough into rounds. Put the rounds close together on a baking tray. Transfer to the oven and bake for 12–15 minutes, or until the scones are well risen. Serve warm with jam and cream.

NOTE: To make fruit scones, add 75 g (2½ oz/ ½ cup) currants or 95 g (3¼ oz) chopped pitted dates to the mixture after you've rubbed in the butter. Mix well to distribute the fruit, then proceed with the recipe.

CHEESE SCONES

MAKES 12

INGREDIENTS

250 g (9 oz/2 cups) self-raising flour
1 teaspoon baking powder
½ teaspoon dry mustard
30 g (1 oz) unsalted butter, chilled and cubed
25 g (1 oz/¼ cup) grated parmesan cheese
90 g (3¼ oz/¾ cup) finely grated cheddar cheese
250 ml (9 fl oz/1 cup) milk

METHOD

1 Preheat the oven to 220°C (425°F/Gas 7). Lightly grease a baking tray or line with baking paper. Sift the flour, baking powder, mustard and a pinch of salt into a bowl. Using your fingertips, rub in the butter until the mixture resembles fine breadcrumbs. Stir in the parmesan and 60 g (2¼ oz/½ cup) of the cheddar cheese, making sure they don't clump together. Make a well in the centre.

2 Add almost all the milk and mix with a flat-bladed knife, using a cutting action, until the dough comes together in clumps. Use the remaining milk if necessary. With floured hands, gently gather the dough together, lift out onto a lightly floured surface and pat into a smooth ball. Do not knead or the scones will be tough.

3 Pat the dough out to a 2 cm (¾ inch) thickness. Using a floured 5 cm (2 inch) cutter, cut the dough into rounds. Gather the trimmings and, without over-handling, press out as before and cut more rounds. Place the rounds close together on the tray and sprinkle with the remaining cheese. Bake for 12–15 minutes, or until risen and golden brown. Serve the scones warm or at room temperature.

PUMPKIN SCONES

MAKES 12

INGREDIENTS

250 g (9 oz) butternut pumpkin (squash), cubed
250 g (9 oz/2 cups) self-raising flour
1 teaspoon baking powder
pinch freshly grated nutmeg
30 g (1 oz) unsalted butter, chilled and cubed
2 tablespoons soft brown sugar
125 ml (4 fl oz/½ cup) milk
milk, extra, to glaze

METHOD

1 Steam the pumpkin for 12 minutes, or until soft, then drain well and mash until smooth. Cool to room temperature. Preheat the oven to 220°C (425°F/Gas 7). Lightly grease a baking tray or line with baking paper.

2 Sift the flour, baking powder and a pinch of salt into a bowl and add the nutmeg. Using your fingertips, rub the butter into the flour, then stir in the sugar and make a well in the centre. Mix the milk into the pumpkin, then add the mixture to the well in the flour. Mix with a flat-bladed knife, using a cutting action, until the dough comes together in clumps. With floured hands, gather the dough together (it will be very soft) and lift out onto a lightly floured surface. Do not knead or the scones will be tough.

3 Pat the dough out a 2 cm (¾ inch) thickness. Using a floured 5 cm (2 inch) cutter, cut the dough into rounds. Gather the trimmings and, without over-handling, press out as before and cut out more rounds. Place the rounds close together on the tray and brush with extra milk. Bake for 12–15 minutes, or until risen and golden brown. Serve warm or at room temperature.

BASIC MUFFINS

Wonderfully simple, muffins can be plain, sweet or savoury. Master the basic muffin, then experiment with different flavour combinations and enjoy them for breakfast, snacks, lunch or dinner.

MAKES 12

INGREDIENTS

- 310 g (11 oz/2½ cups) self-raising flour
- 115 g (4 oz/½ cup) caster (superfine) sugar
- 375 ml (13 fl oz/1½ cups) milk
- 2 eggs, lightly beaten
- 1 teaspoon vanilla extract
- 150 g (5½ oz) unsalted butter, melted and cooled

METHOD

1. Preheat the oven to 200°C (400°F/Gas 6). Lightly grease a 12-hole standard muffin tin, or line the muffin holes with paper cases.
2. Sift the flour into a bowl to aerate the flour and ensure a light muffin. Add the sugar to the bowl and stir through the flour. Make a well in the centre. Combine the milk, eggs and vanilla. Pour the liquid into the well in the flour and add the cooled butter. Melted butter doesn't always combine well with other liquids so it is often added separately. Fold the mixture gently with a metal spoon until just combined. Be careful not to overbeat or the muffins will become tough and rubbery. The mixture should still be lumpy at this stage.
3. Divide the mixture among the holes using two metal spoons — fill each muffin hole to three-quarters full.
4. Bake the muffins for 15–20 minutes, or until they are risen, golden and come away slightly from the sides of the holes. Test them by pressing lightly with your fingertips — they are cooked when they feel firm, and spring back. Another test is to insert a skewer into the centre — if it comes out clean they are ready. Most muffins should be left in the tin for a couple of minutes once out of the oven, but don't leave them too long or trapped steam will make the bases soggy. Using a flat-bladed knife, loosen the muffins and transfer to a wire rack. Serve the muffins warm or cool. Decorate with icing if desired.

VARIATIONS

The basic muffin recipe can be adapted to add many flavours. You can use the same tin but the muffin holes will be quite full.

CHOC CHIP MUFFINS: Add 260 g (9¼ oz/1½ cups) choc chips to the flour and replace the caster sugar with 95 g (3¼ oz/½ cup) soft brown sugar.

BLUEBERRY MUFFINS: Add 300 g (10½ oz/2 cups) blueberries to the flour. If fresh blueberries are not in season, frozen ones can be used. Add them while still frozen to avoid streaking the batter.

BANANA MUFFINS: Add an extra 55 g (2 oz/¼ cup) caster (superfine) sugar and ½ teaspoon mixed spice to the flour and 240 g (8½ oz/1 cup) mashed ripe banana to the batter. Use only 250 ml (9 fl oz/1 cup) milk. Proceed with the recipe.

PECAN MUFFINS: Replace the caster sugar with 140 g (5 oz/¾ cup) soft brown sugar. Add 90 g (3¼ oz/¾ cup) chopped pecans with the flour. Mix to distribute, then proceed with the recipe.

APPLE CINNAMON MUFFINS

MAKES 12

INGREDIENTS

- 400 g (14 oz) tin pie apple
- 310 g (11 oz/2½ cups) self-raising flour
- 2 teaspoons ground cinnamon
- 125 g (4½ oz/⅔ cup) soft brown sugar
- 350 ml (12 fl oz) milk
- 2 eggs
- 1 teaspoon vanilla extract
- 150 g (5½ oz) unsalted butter, melted and cooled
- 60 g (2¼ oz/½ cup) walnuts, finely chopped

METHOD

1. Preheat the oven to 200°C (400°F/Gas 6). Lightly grease a 12-hole standard muffin tin or line the muffin holes with paper cases. Place the pie apple in a bowl and break it up with a knife.
2. Sift the flour and cinnamon into another bowl and add the sugar. Make a well in the centre. Whisk together the milk, eggs and vanilla and pour into the well. Add the cooled melted butter.
3. Fold the mixture gently with a metal spoon until just combined. Add the apple and stir it through the mixture. Do not overmix — the mixture will still be slightly lumpy.
4. Fill each muffin hole with the mixture (the holes will be quite full, but don't worry because these muffins don't rise as much as some) and sprinkle with the walnuts. Bake for 20–25 minutes, or until golden. Leave in the tin for 5 minutes, then turn out onto a wire rack to cool.

STRAWBERRY AND PASSIONFRUIT MUFFINS

MAKES 12

INGREDIENTS

- 215 g (7¾ oz/1¾ cups) self-raising flour
- 1 teaspoon baking powder
- ½ teaspoon bicarbonate of soda (baking soda)
- 55 g (2 oz/¼ cup) caster (superfine) sugar
- 175 g (6 oz/1 cup) chopped strawberries
- 125 g (4½ oz) tin (or fresh) passionfruit pulp
- 1 egg
- 185 ml (6 fl oz/¾ cup) milk
- 60 g (2¼ oz) unsalted butter, melted and cooled
- icing (confectioners') sugar, to dust

METHOD

1. Preheat the oven to 210°C (415°F/Gas 6–7). Lightly grease a 12-hole standard muffin tin or line the muffin holes with paper cases.
2. Sift the flour, baking powder, bicarbonate of soda, sugar and a pinch of salt into a bowl. Mix in the strawberries. Make a well in the centre.
3. Add the passionfruit pulp and the combined egg and milk. Pour the cooled melted butter into the flour mixture all at once and lightly stir with a fork until just combined. Do not overmix — the mixture will still be slightly lumpy.
4. Divide the mixture evenly among the holes, filling each hole to about three-quarters full. Bake for 15 minutes, or until golden. Leave in the tin for 5 minutes, then turn out onto a wire rack to cool. Dust with icing sugar.

BUTTERMILK

Originally, buttermilk was the by-product of the butter-making process — the liquid left after cream is churned into butter. Today it is made from pasteurised skim milk to which an acid-producing bacteria is added, thickening it and giving it its characteristic tanginess. Using buttermilk instead of milk in baked goods such as muffins or scones results in a softer texture and a good crust, and also adds to the flavour.

FRIANDS

Friands (pronounced free-onds) are small oval-shaped cakes, traditionally made with ground almonds, and baked in special-purpose oval tins called friand tins or barquette moulds. Sometimes the same mixture is baked in a rectangular tin and is then named Financier, meaning 'gold ingot', which the shape resembles. Both are very popular in cafés and come in a variety of flavours. The tins can be purchased from kitchenware shops. Friands will keep, stored in an airtight container, for up to 4 days, or frozen for up to 3 months.

‹ ALMOND FRIANDS

MAKES 10

INGREDIENTS

150 g (5½ oz) unsalted butter
90 g (3¼ oz/1 cup) flaked almonds
4 tablespoons plain (all-purpose) flour
165 g (5¾ oz/1⅓ cups) icing (confectioners') sugar, plus extra for dusting
5 egg whites

METHOD

1 Preheat the oven to 210°C (415°F/Gas 6–7). Lightly grease ten 125 ml (4 fl oz/½ cup) friand tins. Melt the butter in a small saucepan over medium heat, then cook until the butter turns a deep golden colour — this should take only a few minutes. Remove the pan from the heat and strain to remove any residue (the colour will deepen on standing). Set aside to cool.
2 Process the almonds in a food processor until finely ground. Put into a bowl and sift the flour and icing sugar into the same bowl.
3 Put the egg whites in a separate bowl and whisk with a fork until just combined and bubbles start to form. Add to the flour mixture, along with the butter. Mix together with a metal spoon until.
4 Sit the friand tins on a baking tray, then pour the mixture into each tin until it is three-quarters full. Bake in the centre of the oven for 10 minutes, then reduce the heat to 180°C (350°F/Gas 4) and bake for 5 minutes, or until a skewer inserted into the centre comes out clean. (They should split across the top slightly when cooked.)
5 Remove from the oven and leave in the tins for 5 minutes, then turn out onto a wire rack to cool. Dust with icing sugar before serving.

NOTE: It is important that your oven has reached its correct temperature before cooking the friands. Cooking them in an oven that isn't hot enough will result in friands with a pale colour, and a wet, buttery and dense texture.

PISTACHIO FRIANDS

MAKES 10

INGREDIENTS

165 g (5¾ oz/1⅓ cups) icing (confectioners') sugar, plus extra for dusting
40 g (1½ oz/⅓ cup) plain (all-purpose) flour
125 g (4½ oz/1 cup) ground pistachio nuts (see Note)
160 g (5¾ oz) unsalted butter, melted
5 egg whites, lightly beaten
½ teaspoon vanilla extract
55 g (2 oz/¼ cup) caster (superfine) sugar
35 g (1¼ oz/¼ cup) chopped pistachio nuts

METHOD

1 Preheat the oven to 190°C (375°F/Gas 5). Lightly grease ten 125 ml (4 fl oz/½ cup) friand tins.
2 Sift the icing sugar and flour into a bowl. Add the ground pistachios, butter, egg whites and vanilla and stir with a metal spoon until just combined.
3 Spoon the mixture into the prepared tins, place on a baking tray and bake for 15–20 minutes, or until a skewer inserted into the centre of a friand comes out clean. Leave in the tins for 5 minutes, then turn out onto a wire rack to cool.
4 Put the caster sugar and 60 ml (2 fl oz/¼ cup) water in a small saucepan and stir over low heat until the sugar has dissolved. Increase the heat, then boil for 4 minutes, or until thick and syrupy. Remove from the heat and stir in the chopped pistachios, then, working quickly, spoon the mixture over the tops of the friands. Dust with icing sugar before serving.

NOTE: Nuts can be ground in a clean coffee grinder or using a food processor. Using the pulse button, process in short bursts until the nuts resemble breadcrumbs; do not overprocess or the nuts will become oily. If the recipe uses sugar, it helps to add a little to the nuts when processing.

MADELEINES

These petite, sponge-like cakes are baked in ribbed, scallop-shaped cake moulds. They vary in size and are usually flavoured with lemon, orange or vanilla. It is thought they may have been named after Madeleine Palmier, a nineteenth century French pastry cook.

MAKES 12

INGREDIENTS

- 125 g (4½ oz/1 cup) plain (all-purpose) flour
- 2 eggs
- 170 g (6 oz/¾ cup) caster (superfine) sugar
- 185 g (6½ oz) unsalted butter, melted and cooled
- 1 teaspoon finely grated orange zest
- icing (confectioners') sugar, to dust

METHOD

1. Preheat the oven to 180°C (350°F/Gas 4). Lightly grease a 12-hole madeleine tin or shallow patty pan. Lightly dust the tin with flour and shake off any excess.
2. Sift the flour three times onto baking paper. Combine the eggs and sugar in a heatproof bowl. Place the bowl over a pan of simmering water, making sure the bowl does not touch the water, and beat the mixture using a whisk or electric beaters until thick and pale yellow. Remove the bowl from the heat and continue to beat the mixture until cooled slightly and increased in volume. Add the flour, butter and orange zest to the bowl and gently fold in with a metal spoon until just combined.
3. Spoon the mixture carefully into the madeleine holes. Bake for 10–12 minutes, or until lightly golden. Carefully remove from the tin and transfer to a wire rack to cool. Dust with icing sugar and eat on the day of baking.

FINGER BUNS

MAKES 12

INGREDIENTS

- 500 g (1 lb 2 oz/4 cups) plain (all-purpose) flour
- 35 g (1¼ oz/⅓ cup) milk powder
- 1 tablespoon dried yeast
- 115 g (4 oz/½ cup) caster (superfine) sugar
- 60 g (2¼ oz/½ cup) sultanas
- 60 g (2¼ oz) unsalted butter, melted
- 1 egg, lightly beaten
- 1 egg yolk, extra, to glaze
- 1 quantity glacé icing (page 531)

METHOD

1. Mix 375 g (13 oz/3 cups) of the flour with the milk powder, yeast, ½ teaspoon salt, sugar and sultanas in a large bowl. Make a well in the centre. Combine the butter, egg and 250 ml (9 fl oz/1 cup) warm water and add all at once to the flour. Stir for 2 minutes, or until well combined. Add enough of the remaining flour to make a soft dough.
2. Turn out onto a lightly floured surface. Knead for 10 minutes, or until the dough is smooth and elastic, adding more flour if necessary. Place in a large, lightly oiled bowl and brush the surface with oil. Cover with plastic wrap and leave in a draught-free place for 1 hour, or until well risen.
3. Lightly grease two large baking trays. Preheat the oven to 180°C (350°F/Gas 4). Punch down the dough and knead for 1 minute. Divide into 12 pieces. Shape each into a 15 cm (6 inch) long oval. Put the dough on the trays 5 cm (2 inches) apart. Cover and set aside in a draught-free place for 20–25 minutes, or until well risen.
4. Mix the extra egg yolk with 1½ teaspoons water and brush over the dough. Transfer to the oven and bake for 12–15 minutes, or until firm and golden. Transfer to a wire rack to cool, then spread pink glacé icing over the tops of the buns. Serve buttered.

ECCLES CAKES

MAKES ABOUT 25

INGREDIENTS

- 150 g (5½ oz/1 cup) currants
- 95 g (3¼ oz/½ cup) mixed peel
- 1 tablespoon brandy
- 1 tablespoon sugar
- ½ teaspoon ground cinnamon
- 500 g (1 lb 2 oz) block ready-made puff pastry, thawed
- 1 egg white, lightly beaten
- 2 teaspoons sugar, extra, to sprinkle

METHOD

1. Preheat the oven to 210°C (415°F/Gas 6–7). Lightly grease two baking trays.
2. To make the filling, combine the currants, mixed peel, brandy, sugar and cinnamon in a bowl. Divide the pastry into three and roll each piece out to a 3 mm (⅛ inch) thickness. Using an 8 cm (3¼ inch) cutter, cut nine circles from each sheet of pastry.
3. Place 2 level teaspoons of the filling on each circle. Bring the edges of the rounds up together and pinch to seal. Turn, seam side down, and roll out to 1 cm (½ inch) thick ovals. Place on the trays, brush the tops with egg white and sprinkle with extra sugar. Make three slashes across the top of each cake, then bake for 15–20 minutes, or until golden. Serve warm.

CHELSEA BUN

MAKES 8

INGREDIENTS

- 2 teaspoons dried yeast
- 1 teaspoon sugar
- 310 g (11 oz/2½ cups) plain (all-purpose) flour, sifted
- 125 ml (4 fl oz/½ cup) milk, warmed
- 185 g (6½ oz) unsalted butter, cubed
- 1 tablespoon sugar, extra
- 2 teaspoons finely grated lemon zest
- 1 teaspoon mixed spice
- 1 egg, lightly beaten
- 45 g (1½ oz/¼ cup) soft brown sugar
- 185 g (6½ oz/1 cup) mixed dried fruit
- 1 tablespoon milk, extra to glaze
- 2 tablespoons sugar, extra to glaze

ICING

- 60 g (2¼ oz/½ cup) icing (confectioners') sugar
- 1–2 tablespoons milk

METHOD

1. Combine the yeast, sugar and 1 tablespoon of the flour in a small bowl. Add the milk and mix until smooth. Leave in a warm, draught-free place for 10 minutes, or until bubbles appear on the surface. The mixture should be frothy and slightly increased in volume. If your yeast doesn't foam, it is dead, so you will have to discard it and start again. Place the remaining flour in a large bowl and rub in 125 g (4½ oz) of the butter with your fingertips. Stir in the extra sugar, lemon zest and half the mixed spice. Make a well in the centre, add the yeast mixture and egg and mix. Gather together and turn out onto a lightly floured surface.
2. Knead for 2 minutes, or until smooth, then shape into a ball. Place in a lightly oiled bowl. Cover with plastic wrap or a damp tea towel and leave in a draught-free place for 1 hour, or until well risen. Punch down and knead for 2 minutes, or until smooth.
3. Preheat the oven to 210°C (415°F/Gas 6–7). Lightly grease a baking tray. Beat the remaining butter with the brown sugar in a small bowl using electric beaters until light and creamy. Roll the dough out to a 25 x 40 cm (10 x 16 inch) rectangle. Spread the butter mixture all over the dough to within 2 cm (¾ inch) of the edge of one of the longer sides. Spread with the combined fruit and remaining spice. Roll the dough from the long side, firmly and evenly, to enclose the fruit. Use a sharp knife to cut the roll into eight slices about 5 cm (2 inch) wide. Arrange the slices, close together and with the seams inwards, on the tray. Flatten slightly.
4. Cover and set aside in a draught-free place for 30 minutes, or until well risen. Transfer to the oven and bake for 20 minutes, or until brown and cooked. When almost ready, stir the extra milk and sugar for glazing in a small saucepan over low heat until the sugar dissolves and the mixture is almost boiling. Brush over the hot buns. Cool.
5. To make the icing, mix the icing sugar and milk, stir until smooth, then drizzle over the buns.

LAMINGTONS

MAKES 16

INGREDIENTS

185 g (6½ oz/1½ cups) self-raising flour
40 g (1½ oz/⅓ cup) cornflour (cornstarch)
185 g (6½ oz) unsalted butter, softened
230 g (8½ oz/1 cup) caster (superfine) sugar
2 teaspoons vanilla extract
3 eggs, lightly beaten
125 ml (4 fl oz/½ cup) milk
185 ml (6 fl oz/¾ cup) whipping cream

ICING

500 g (1 lb 2 oz/4 cups) icing (confectioners') sugar
40 g (1½ oz/⅓ cup) unsweetened cocoa powder
30 g (1 oz) unsalted butter, melted
170 ml (5½ fl oz/⅔ cup) milk
270 g (9½ oz/3 cups) desiccated coconut

METHOD

1 Preheat the oven to 180°C (350°F/Gas 4). Lightly grease a shallow 23 cm (9 inch) square cake tin and line the base and sides with baking paper.
2 To make the cake, sift the flour and cornflour into a large bowl. Add the butter, sugar, vanilla, egg and milk. Using electric beaters, beat on low speed for 1 minute, or until the ingredients are just moistened. Increase the speed to high and beat for 3 minutes, or until free of lumps and increased in volume. Pour into the tin and smooth the surface. Bake for 50–55 minutes, or until a skewer inserted into the centre of the cake comes out clean. Leave the cake in the tin for 3 minutes before turning out onto a wire rack to cool.
3 Using a serrated knife, trim the top of the cake until flat. Trim the crusts from the sides, then cut the cake in half horizontally. Using electric beaters, beat the cream in a small bowl until stiff peaks form. Place the first layer of cake on a board and spread it evenly with cream. Place the remaining cake layer on top. Cut the cake into 16 squares.
4 To make the icing, sift the icing sugar and cocoa into a heatproof bowl and add the butter and milk. Sit the bowl over a saucepan of simmering water, making sure the base of the bowl does not touch the water, and stir until the icing is smooth and glossy, then remove from the heat.
5 Place 90 g (3¼ oz/1 cup) of the coconut on a sheet of baking paper. Using two spoons, dip a piece of cake in chocolate icing, then hold the cake over a bowl and allow the excess to drain. (Add 1 tablespoon boiling water to the icing if it seems too thick.) Roll the cake in the coconut, then place on a wire rack. Repeat with the remaining cake, adding extra coconut for rolling as needed.

NOTE: If you cook the cake a day ahead, it will be easier to cut and won't crumble as much.

ROCK CAKES

MAKES ABOUT 20

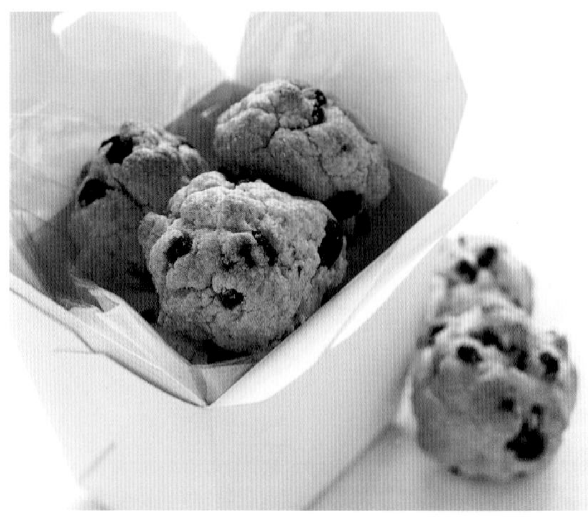

INGREDIENTS

250 g (9 oz/2 cups) self-raising flour
90 g ($3\frac{1}{4}$ oz) unsalted butter, chilled and cubed
115 g (4 oz/$\frac{1}{2}$ cup) caster (superfine) sugar
95 g ($3\frac{1}{4}$ oz/$\frac{1}{2}$ cup) mixed dried fruit
$\frac{1}{2}$ teaspoon ground ginger
1 egg
60 ml (2 fl oz/$\frac{1}{4}$ cup) milk

METHOD

1. Preheat the oven to 200°C (400°F/Gas 6). Grease two baking trays.
2. Sift the flour into a large bowl and rub in the butter with your fingertips until the mixture resembles fine breadcrumbs. Stir in the sugar, fruit and ginger.
3. Whisk the egg into the milk in a bowl, add to the dry ingredients and mix to a stiff dough. Drop rough heaps of the mixture, about 3 tablespoons at a time, onto the prepared trays. Transfer to the oven and bake for 10–15 minutes, or until golden. Remove from the tray and cool on a wire rack.

BUTTERFLY CUPCAKES

MAKES 12

INGREDIENTS

120 g ($4\frac{1}{4}$ oz) unsalted butter, softened
145 g ($5\frac{1}{2}$ oz/$\frac{2}{3}$ cup) caster (superfine) sugar
185 g ($6\frac{1}{2}$ oz/$1\frac{1}{2}$ cups) self-raising flour
125 ml (4 fl oz/$\frac{1}{2}$ cup) milk
2 teaspoons vanilla extract
2 eggs
125 ml (4 fl oz/$\frac{1}{2}$ cup) whipping cream
105 g ($3\frac{3}{4}$ oz/$\frac{1}{3}$ cup) strawberry jam
icing (confectioners') sugar, to dust

METHOD

1. Preheat the oven to 180°C (350°F/Gas 4). Line a 12-hole shallow patty pan or mini muffin tin with paper cases.
2. Put the butter, sugar, flour, milk, vanilla and eggs in a bowl. Using electric beaters, beat on low speed for 2 minutes, or until well mixed. Increase the speed and beat for 2 minutes, or until pale and smooth.
3. Divide the mixture evenly among the cases and bake for 20 minutes, or until cooked and golden. Transfer to a wire rack to cool completely.
4. Whip the cream to soft peaks. Using a small sharp knife, cut shallow rounds from the top of each cake, then cut these in half. Spoon $\frac{1}{2}$ tablespoon of the cream into the cavity in each cake, then top with 1 teaspoon of jam. Position two halves of the cake tops in the jam in each cake to resemble butterfly wings. Dust the cakes with icing sugar before serving.

CHOCOLATE BROWNIES

MAKES 24

INGREDIENTS

- 40 g (1½ oz/⅓ cup) plain (all-purpose) flour
- 60 g (2¼ oz/½ cup) unsweetened cocoa powder
- 440 g (15½ oz/2 cups) sugar
- 120 g (4¼ oz/1 cup) chopped pecans or walnuts
- 250 g (9 oz) dark chocolate, chopped into small pieces
- 250 g (9 oz) unsalted butter, melted
- 2 teaspoons vanilla extract
- 4 eggs, lightly beaten

METHOD

1. Preheat the oven to 180°C (350°F/Gas 4). Lightly grease a 20 x 30 cm (8 x 12 inch) cake tin and line with baking paper, leaving the paper hanging over on the two long sides.
2. Sift the flour and cocoa powder into a bowl and add the sugar, nuts and chocolate. Mix together and make a well in the centre.
3. Pour the butter into the dry ingredients with the vanilla and eggs and mix well. Pour into the tin, smooth the surface and bake for 50 minutes (the mixture will still be a bit soft on the inside). Chill for at least 2 hours before lifting out, using the paper as handles, and cutting into pieces.

RHUBARB SLICE

MAKES ABOUT 25 PIECES

INGREDIENTS

- 300 g (10½ oz) rhubarb, trimmed and cut into 5 mm (¼ inch) slices
- 115 g (4 oz/½ cup) caster (superfine) sugar
- 185 g (6½ oz) unsalted butter, chopped
- 230 g (8½ oz/1 cup) caster (superfine) sugar, extra
- ½ teaspoon vanilla extract
- 3 eggs
- 90 g (3¼ oz/¾ cup) plain (all-purpose) flour
- ¾ teaspoon baking powder
- 1 tablespoon sugar
- icing (confectioners') sugar, to dust

METHOD

1 Combine the rhubarb and sugar in a bowl and set aside, stirring occasionally, for 1 hour, or until the rhubarb has released its juices and the sugar has dissolved. Strain, discarding the liquid.

2 Preheat the oven to 180°C (350°F/Gas 4). Grease a 20 x 30 cm (8 x 12 inch) shallow cake tin with butter. Line the base with baking paper, leaving the paper hanging over on the two long sides.

3 Cream the butter, extra sugar and vanilla in a bowl using electric beaters until pale and fluffy. Add the eggs one at a time, beating well after each addition. Sift the flour and baking powder over the mixture, then stir to combine. Spread the mixture evenly over the base of the prepared tin, then put the rhubarb over the top in a single layer. Sprinkle with the sugar.

4 Bake for 40–45 minutes, or until golden. Leave to cool slightly in the tin, then carefully lift out and cut into squares. Dust with icing sugar and serve with cream. The rhubarb slice is best eaten on the day it is made.

RHUBARB

Although botanically classified as a vegetable, rhubarb is used in cooking as fruit. Rhubarb is usually sold with its leaves on, and although this helps prevent the stalks from wilting, the leaves should be removed before cooking as they contain poisonous oxalic acid. The edible part of rhubarb is the crisp, pink or red stalks. These can be cut into pieces and stewed or used in pies, crumbles, ice creams and jams. Any tough stalks should be peeled first to remove the tough fibres.

CARAMEL SLICE

MAKES 20 PIECES

INGREDIENTS

125 g (4½ oz/1 cup) self-raising flour
90 g (3¼ oz/1 cup) desiccated coconut
115 g (4 oz/½ cup) caster (superfine) sugar
125 g (4½ oz) unsalted butter, melted

CARAMEL FILLING

400 g (14 oz) tin sweetened condensed milk
20 g (¾ oz) unsalted butter
2 tablespoons golden syrup

CHOCOLATE TOPPING

150 g (5½ oz) dark chocolate, chopped
20 g (¾ oz) Copha (white vegetable shortening)

METHOD

1 Preheat the oven to 180°C (350°F/Gas 4). Lightly grease an 18 x 28 cm (7 x 11¼ inch) shallow cake tin and line with baking paper, leaving the paper hanging over on the two long sides.
2 Sift the flour into a bowl, then mix in the coconut and sugar. Add the melted butter and stir thoroughly. Press the mixture firmly into the tin and bake for 12–15 minutes, or until lightly golden. Allow to cool.
3 To make the caramel filling, place all the ingredients in a small saucepan over low heat. Slowly bring to the boil, stirring constantly, then boil gently, stirring, for 4–5 minutes, or until lightly caramelised. Quickly pour over the cooled base, spreading evenly. Bake for 10 minutes, then set aside to cool.
4 To make the chocolate topping, place the dark chocolate and Copha in a heatproof bowl. Half-fill a saucepan with water and bring to the boil. Remove the pan from the heat. Sit the bowl over the saucepan of water, making sure the base of the bowl does not touch the water. Stir occasionally until the chocolate and Copha have melted. Spread the chocolate topping over the cooled caramel, then refrigerate for 20 minutes, or until set. Lift the slice from the tin, using the paper as handles. To serve, cut into pieces with a hot, dry knife.

PLUM AND ALMOND SLICE

MAKES 9

INGREDIENTS

165 g (5¾ oz) unsalted butter, cubed and softened
145 g (5½ oz/⅔ cup) caster (superfine) sugar
2 eggs
60 g (2¼ oz/½ cup) plain (all-purpose) flour
40 g (1½ oz/⅓ cup) cornflour (cornstarch)
2 tablespoons rice flour
1½ tablespoons thinly sliced glacé ginger
820 g (1 lb 13 oz) tin plums in syrup, drained, seeded and halved
90 g (3¼ oz/1 cup) flaked almonds
1 tablespoon honey, warmed

METHOD

1 Preheat the oven to 180°C (350°F/Gas 4). Lightly grease a 20 cm (8 inch) square cake tin and line with baking paper, leaving the paper hanging over the edge of the tin on all sides.
2 Cream the butter and sugar in a small bowl using electric beaters until light and fluffy. Add the eggs one at a time, beating well after each addition. Sift the flours over the mixture and fold into the mixture with the ginger. Spread into the tin. Arrange the plum halves on top, pressing them in. Scatter with the flaked almonds, pressing in gently, then drizzle with the honey.
3 Bake for 1 hour 10 minutes, or until firm and golden. Cover the top with foil if the slice starts to brown too much. Cool in the tin, then lift out, using the paper as handles. Cut into pieces. Store the slice for 4–5 days in an airtight container in the refrigerator.

••BISCUITS••

The word 'biscuit' originally referred to a tough, dry rusk. French for 'twice cooked', biscuits were baked in long rolls, sliced and baked again so they would last a long time. Today, biscuits come in all forms — sweet or savoury, chewy, soft or crisp, plain or flavoured. In America, biscuits are called cookies, a word derived from the Dutch *koekge*, meaning 'little cake'. In England, they're called biscuits, and in Australia it can be either.

HOW TO... MAKE PERFECT BISCUITS

* Some recipes can be made using a food processor, however biscuit dough should not be overworked or an excess of gluten will develop, resulting in a tough biscuit. Only use a processor to rub the fat into the flour. When the liquid is added, pulse briefly until the mixture just adheres, then turn out onto a work surface to bring together into a smooth, soft ball, without kneading.
* Make sure the oven shelves are set at an equal distance apart if cooking more than one tray at a time. Often the tray underneath will require a longer cooking time. If you have time, cook the biscuits in batches. Alternatively, switch the trays halfway through cooking time.
* Biscuits spread during baking, some more than others. Most average-sized baking trays fit three rows of five biscuits, with the biscuit mixture spaced about 5 cm (2 inches) apart.
* When dropping the dough onto the tray using tablespoons, it is easier and less messy to use two tablespoons, one to measure accurately and the other to push the dough off the spoon onto the tray.
* Always place biscuit dough onto a cold baking tray. If baking in batches, allow the tray to cool before adding the next batch.
* Always bake for the minimum time given. If more cooking is needed, cook for only 2 minutes more and then retest (biscuits can be underdone one minute and then burnt the next).

ALMOND MACAROONS

MAKES 40 SMALL OR 20 LARGE

INGREDIENTS

- 115 g (4 oz) ground almonds
- 230 g (8½ oz/1 cup) caster (superfine) sugar
- 2 egg whites
- 1 tablespoon plain (all-purpose) flour
- 1 teaspoon vanilla extract
- 1 teaspoon finely grated orange or lemon zest (optional)

METHOD

1. Preheat the oven to 160°C (315°F/Gas 2–3). Grease two baking trays and line them with baking paper.
2. Using electric beaters, beat the almonds, sugar and egg whites for 5 minutes. Add the flour and vanilla and beat until smooth. Add the zest if using. Drop 1 or 2 level teaspoons of the mixture onto the trays, 3 cm (1¼ inches) apart, and bake for 10–12 minutes for the small macaroons or 15–18 minutes for the large ones, until firm. Cool on the trays, then transfer to a wire rack to cool.

(pictured page 5)

LANGUES DE CHAT

French for 'cat's tongues', these delicate biscuits may be served with ice cream, sorbet or as a light biscuit with tea or coffee. The biscuits are piped into finger-like shapes onto baking trays or cooked in special trays with shallow indentations in it. Langues de chat are sometimes called 'lady fingers', but these are usually fatter and more spongy.

MAKES 24

INGREDIENTS

- 75 g (2½ oz) unsalted butter, softened
- 80 g (2¾ oz/⅓ cup) caster (superfine) sugar
- 2 egg whites
- 75 g (2½ oz) plain (all-purpose) flour, sifted

METHOD

1. Preheat the oven to 220°C (425°F/Gas 7). Line two baking trays with baking paper.
2. Cream the butter and sugar in a small bowl with electric beaters until light and fluffy. Whisk the egg whites in another small bowl with a fork until frothy, then gradually add to the butter mixture, beating well after each addition. Lightly fold in the sifted flour and a pinch of salt until well combined.
3. To make even-sized langues de chat, draw with a pencil 8 cm (3 inch) lines at intervals on the baking paper. Turn the paper over. Use the lines as a guide to pipe the mixture, leaving a space for expansion. You will be able to fit about 12 biscuits per tray. If your trays are small, cook them in batches. Spoon the mixture into a piping (icing) bag fitted with a 1 cm (½ inch) plain tube, and pipe 8 cm (3 inch) lengths onto the trays. Transfer to the oven and bake for 6–7 minutes, or until cooked through and lightly brown around the edges. Cool on the trays for 2 minutes, then transfer to a wire rack to cool completely.

‹ FLORENTINES

MAKES 12

INGREDIENTS

- 55 g (2 oz) unsalted butter
- 45 g (1½ oz/¼ cup) soft brown sugar
- 2 teaspoons honey
- 25 g (1 oz/¼ cup) flaked almonds, roughly chopped
- 2 tablespoons chopped dried apricots
- 2 tablespoons chopped glacé cherries
- 2 tablespoons mixed peel
- 40 g (1½ oz/⅓ cup) plain (all-purpose) flour, sifted
- 120 g (4¼ oz) dark chocolate, broken into small pieces

METHOD

1 Preheat the oven to 180°C (350°F/Gas 4). Line two large baking trays with baking paper. Place the butter, sugar and honey in a saucepan and stir over low heat until the butter is melted and all the ingredients have combined. Remove from the heat and add the almonds, apricots, glacé cherries, mixed peel and flour. Mix well.

2 Place level tablespoons of the mixture well apart on the trays. Flatten the biscuits into 5 cm (2 inch) rounds, then gently reshape before cooking. Bake for 10 minutes, or until lightly browned. Cool slightly on the tray before transferring to a wire rack to cool completely.

3 Put the dark chocolate in a heatproof bowl. Bring a small saucepan of water to the boil, remove from the heat and place the bowl over the pan, making sure the base of the bowl does not touch the water. Stir until melted. Spread on the base of each florentine and, using a fork, make a wavy pattern on the chocolate before it sets. Let the chocolate set before serving.

JAM DROP BISCUITS

MAKES ABOUT 45

INGREDIENTS

- 250 g (9 oz) unsalted butter, softened
- 140 g (5 oz) icing (confectioners') sugar
- 1 egg yolk, lightly beaten
- 90 g (3¼ oz/⅓ cup) cream cheese, softened and cut into chunks
- 1½ teaspoons vanilla extract
- 1 teaspoon finely grated lemon zest
- 350 g (12 oz/2¾ cups) plain (all-purpose) flour, sifted
- ¼ teaspoon baking powder
- ½ teaspoon bicarbonate of soda (baking soda)
- 2 tablespoons each apricot, blueberry and raspberry jam

METHOD

1 Preheat the oven to 180°C (350°F/Gas 4) and grease three baking trays.

2 Cream the butter, icing sugar and egg yolk in a bowl using electric beaters until pale and fluffy, then beat in the cream cheese, vanilla and lemon zest until smooth. Combine the flour, baking powder, bicarbonate of soda and ¼ teaspoon salt in a large bowl and, using a wooden spoon, gradually stir into the creamed mixture until a soft dough forms. Set aside for 5–10 minutes, or until the dough firms up.

3 Break off small (15 g/½ oz) pieces of dough, shape into balls and flatten slightly to make 4 cm (1½ inch) rounds. Transfer to the prepared trays and make a small indent in the centre of each with your thumb. Spoon ¼ teaspoon of apricot jam into one-third of the biscuits, ¼ teaspoon blueberry jam into one-third, and ¼ teaspoon of raspberry jam into the remaining biscuits.

4 Bake for 10–12 minutes, or until light golden. Cool on the trays for 2 minutes, then transfer to a wire rack to cool completely. These biscuits are best eaten the same day but will keep, stored in an airtight container, for up to 2 days.

CHOCOLATE CHIP COOKIES

MAKES 40

INGREDIENTS

185 g (6½ oz/1½ cups) plain (all-purpose) flour
90 g (3¼ oz/¾ cup) unsweetened cocoa powder
280 g (10 oz/1½ cups) soft brown sugar
180 g (6½ oz) unsalted butter, cubed
150 g (5½ oz) dark chocolate, chopped
3 eggs, lightly beaten
265 g (9½ oz/1⅔ cups) chocolate chips

METHOD

1 Preheat the oven to 180°C (350°F/Gas 4). Line two baking trays with baking paper.
2 Sift the flour and cocoa powder into a large bowl, add the brown sugar and make a well in the centre.
3 Combine the butter and dark chocolate in a small heatproof bowl. Half-fill a saucepan with water and bring to the boil. Remove the pan from the heat. Sit the bowl over the saucepan of water, making sure the base of the bowl does not touch the water. Stir occasionally until the chocolate and butter have melted and are smooth. Mix well.
4 Add the butter and chocolate mixture and the egg to the dry ingredients. Stir with a wooden spoon until well combined, but do not overmix. Stir in the chocolate chips.
5 Drop tablespoons of the mixture onto the prepared trays, allowing room for spreading. Bake for 7–10 minutes, or until firm to the touch. Cool on the trays for 5 minutes, then transfer to a wire rack to cool completely. Store in an airtight container.

MACADAMIA BISCUITS

MAKES ABOUT 60

INGREDIENTS

180 g (6½ oz) unsalted butter, softened
185 g (6½ oz/1 cup) soft brown sugar
1 teaspoon vanilla extract
1 egg
280 g (10 oz/2¼ cups) plain (all-purpose) flour
1 teaspoon baking powder
45 g (1½ oz/½ cup) desiccated coconut
70 g (2½ oz/½ cup) macadamia nuts, roasted and chopped

METHOD

1 Cream the butter and sugar in a small bowl using electric beaters until light and fluffy. Add the vanilla and egg and beat until well combined. Transfer to a large bowl and add the sifted flour and baking powder, the coconut and macadamia nuts. Using a flat-bladed knife, mix to a soft dough. Gather together, then divide the mixture into two portions.
2 Place one portion of the dough on a sheet of baking paper and press lightly until the dough is 30 cm (12 inches) long and 4 cm (1½ inches) thick. Fold the paper around the dough and roll neatly into a log shape. Twist the edges of the paper to seal. If you like you can shape the log into a triangular shape, to give triangle-shaped biscuits when sliced. Repeat the process with the other portion of dough. Refrigerate the dough for 30 minutes, or until firm.
3 Preheat the oven to 180°C (350°F/Gas 4). Line two baking trays with baking paper. Cut the logs into slices about 1 cm (½ inch) thick. Place the slices on the prepared trays, leaving 3 cm (1¼ inches) between each. Bake for 10–15 minutes, or until golden. Cool on the trays for 5 minutes, then transfer to a wire rack to cool completely. Store in an airtight container.

ANZAC BISCUITS

These biscuits were developed at the time of the First World War and sent in food parcels to the ANZACS (Australian and New Zealand Army Corps). They are a crisp, long-lasting biscuit made without eggs, which were in short supply at that time.

MAKES 25

INGREDIENTS

- 125 g (4½ oz/1 cup) plain (all-purpose) flour
- 140 g (5 oz/⅔ cup) sugar
- 100 g (3½ oz/1 cup) rolled (porridge) oats
- 90 g (3¼ oz/1 cup) desiccated coconut
- 125 g (4½ oz) unsalted butter, cubed
- 90 g (3¼ oz/¼ cup) golden syrup or dark corn syrup
- ½ teaspoon bicarbonate of soda (baking soda)
- 1 tablespoon boiling water

METHOD

1 Preheat the oven to 180°C (350°F/Gas 4). Line two baking trays with baking paper.

2 Sift the flour into a large bowl. Add the sugar, oats and coconut and make a well in the centre. Put the butter and golden syrup in a small saucepan and stir over low heat until the butter has melted and the mixture is smooth. Remove from the heat.

3 Dissolve the bicarbonate of soda in the boiling water and add immediately to the butter mixture. It will foam up instantly. Pour into the well in the dry ingredients and stir with a wooden spoon until well combined.

4 Drop level tablespoons of mixture onto the trays, allowing room for spreading. Gently flatten each biscuit with your fingertips. Bake for 20 minutes, or until just browned. Cool on the trays for a few minutes, then transfer to a wire rack to cool completely. Store in an airtight container.

OATCAKES

MAKES 14

INGREDIENTS

- 250 g (9 oz/2 cups) medium oatmeal
- ½ teaspoon baking powder
- 2 teaspoons soft brown sugar
- 60 g (2¼ oz) butter, melted
- oatmeal, extra for sprinkling

METHOD

1 Preheat the oven to 180°C (350°F/Gas 4). Line two baking trays with baking paper.

2 Combine the oatmeal, baking powder, sugar and a pinch of salt in a large bowl. Make a well in the centre and add the melted butter and 125 ml (4 fl oz/½ cup) hot water.

3 Using a flat-bladed knife, mix to form a dough. Gather the dough together and turn onto a surface lightly sprinkled with extra oatmeal, then press into a flattish round.

4 Roll the dough out to a thickness of 5 mm (¼ inch), sprinkling with extra oatmeal. Cut the dough into 6 cm (2½ inch) rounds with a biscuit cutter. Place on the baking trays, leaving room for spreading. Bake for 25 minutes, or until golden. Cool on the trays for 5 minutes, then transfer to a wire rack to cool completely. Store in an airtight container.

BISCOTTI

MAKES 20

INGREDIENTS

375 g (13 oz/3 cups) plain (all-purpose) flour
170 g (6 oz/¾ cup) caster (superfine) sugar
3 eggs
½ teaspoon baking powder
½ teaspoon vanilla extract
150 g (5½ oz/1 cup) blanched almonds

METHOD

1 Preheat the oven to 180°C (350°F/Gas 4) and line two baking trays with baking paper.
2 Sift the flour into a large bowl or food processor, add the sugar, eggs, baking powder, vanilla and a pinch of salt and mix or process until you have a smooth dough. Transfer to a floured work surface and knead in the almonds.
3 Divide the dough into two pieces and roll each one into a log about 20 cm (8 inches) long. Put on the prepared baking trays and press down gently along the top to flatten the logs slightly. Bake for 25 minutes, or until the dough is lightly golden. Take the logs out of the oven and leave to cool slightly. Reduce the oven to 170°C (325°F/Gas 3).
4 Cut each log into 1 cm (½ inch) thick slices on the diagonal, then lay the slices back on the baking tray and return to the oven. Cook for another 15 minutes, or until they start to brown and are dry to the touch. Transfer to a wire rack to cool completely. Store in an airtight container.

MELTING MOMENTS

These small, crisp, round biscuits are made from butter, sugar, egg, vanilla and flour. Fresh from the oven, they are soft and pliable, but become brittle after a few minutes. As their name suggests they melt in your mouth when eaten. The version, given here, is more like a very crumbly shortbread, often sandwiched together with a cream filling such as passionfruit.

MAKES 14

INGREDIENTS

250 g (9 oz) unsalted butter, softened
40 g (1½ oz/⅓ cup) icing (confectioners') sugar
1 teaspoon vanilla extract
185 g (6½ oz/1½ cups) self-raising flour
60 g (2¼ oz/½ cup) custard powder

PASSIONFRUIT FILLING

60 g (2¼ oz) unsalted butter
60 g (2¼ oz/½ cup) icing (confectioners') sugar
1½ tablespoons passionfruit pulp

METHOD

1 Preheat the oven to 180°C (350°F/Gas 4). Line two baking trays with baking paper.
2 Cream the butter and icing sugar in a bowl using electric beaters until light and fluffy, then beat in the vanilla. Sift in the flour and custard powder and mix with a flat-bladed knife, using a cutting motion, to form a soft dough.
3 Roll level tablespoons of dough into balls (you should have 28) and place on the trays, leaving room for spreading. Flatten slightly with a floured fork. Bake for 20 minutes, or until lightly golden. Cool on the trays for a few minutes, then transfer to a wire rack to cool completely.
4 To make the passionfruit filling, beat the butter and icing sugar in a bowl using electric beaters until light and creamy, then beat in the passionfruit pulp. Use to sandwich the biscuits together. Leave to firm up a little before serving.

CLASSIC SHORTBREAD

MAKES 16 WEDGES

INGREDIENTS

225 g (8 oz) unsalted butter
115 g (4 oz/½ cup) caster (superfine) sugar, plus extra for dusting
225 g (8 oz/1¾ cups) plain (all-purpose) flour
115 g (4 oz/⅔ cup) rice flour

METHOD

1 Preheat the oven to 190°C (375°F/Gas 5). Lightly grease two baking trays.
2 Cream the butter and sugar in a bowl using electric beaters until pale and fluffy. Sift in the flour, rice flour and a pinch of salt and, using a wooden spoon, stir into the creamed mixture until it resembles fine breadcrumbs. Transfer to a lightly floured work surface and knead gently to form a soft dough. Cover with plastic wrap and refrigerate for 30 minutes.
3 Divide the dough in half and roll out one half on a lightly floured work surface to form a 20 cm (8 inch) round. Carefully transfer to a prepared tray. Using a sharp knife, score the surface of the dough into eight equal wedges, prick the surface lightly with a fork and, using your fingers, press the edges to form a fluted effect. Repeat this process using the remaining dough to make a second round. Lightly dust the shortbreads with the extra sugar.
4 Bake for 18–20 minutes, or until the shortbreads are light golden. Remove from the oven and while still hot, follow the score marks and cut into wedges. Cool on the trays for 5 minutes, then transfer to a wire rack to cool completely. The shortbread will keep, stored in an airtight container, for up to 1 week.

GINGERBREAD PEOPLE

MAKES 16

INGREDIENTS

125 g (4½ oz) unsalted butter, softened
60 g (2¼ oz/⅓ cup) soft brown sugar
90 g (3¼ oz/¼ cup) golden syrup
1 egg, lightly beaten
250 g (9 oz/2 cups) plain (all-purpose) flour
30 g (1 oz/¼ cup) self-raising flour
1 tablespoon ground ginger
1 teaspoon bicarbonate of soda (baking soda)
1 tablespoon currants

ICING

1 egg white
½ teaspoon lemon juice
155 g (5½ oz/1¼ cups) icing (confectioners') sugar, sifted
assorted food colourings

METHOD

1 Preheat the oven to 180°C (350°F/Gas 4). Line two baking trays with baking paper.
2 Cream the butter, sugar and golden syrup in a small bowl with electric beaters until light and fluffy. Add the egg gradually, beating well after each addition. Transfer to a large bowl. Sift the dry ingredients onto the butter mixture and mix with a knife until just combined. Combine the dough with well-floured hands. Turn onto a floured surface and knead for 1–2 minutes, until smooth. Roll out the dough on a board, between two sheets of baking paper, to 5 mm (¼ inch) thick. Refrigerate on the board for 15 minutes to firm.
3 Cut the dough into shapes with a 13 cm (5 inch) gingerbread person cutter. Press the remaining dough together and re-roll. Cut out shapes and place the biscuits on the trays. Place currants as eyes. Bake for 10 minutes, or until lightly browned. Cool completely on the trays.
4 To make the icing, beat the egg white with electric beaters in a small, clean, dry bowl until foamy. Gradually add the lemon juice and icing sugar and beat until thick and creamy. Divide the icing among several bowls. Tint the mixture with food colourings and spoon into small paper piping (icing) bags. Seal the open ends, snip the tips off the bags and pipe on faces, bows and buttons.

GINGER

The knobbly, beige-coloured rhizome of a tropical plant, ginger is indigenous to Southeast Asia but now grows all over the world in tropical climates. Unless very fresh, ginger needs to be first peeled, then grated or sliced. If it is fibrous, it may be easier to grate it, preferably with a ginger grater. Store fresh ginger in the fridge tightly wrapped in plastic wrap. Dried ginger is mainly used in baked goods such as gingerbread, ginger cake and biscuits.

GINGERNUTS

MAKES 50

INGREDIENTS

- 250 g (9 oz/2 cups) plain (all-purpose) flour
- ½ teaspoon bicarbonate of soda (baking soda)
- 1 tablespoon ground ginger
- ½ teaspoon mixed spice
- 125 g (4½ oz) unsalted butter, chopped
- 185 g (6½ oz/1 cup) soft brown sugar
- 60 ml (2 fl oz/¼ cup) boiling water
- 1 tablespoon golden syrup or dark corn syrup

METHOD

1. Preheat the oven to 180°C (350°F/Gas 4). Line two baking trays with baking paper.
2. Sift the flour, bicarbonate of soda, ginger and mixed spice into a large bowl. Add the butter and sugar and rub into the flour with your fingertips until the mixture resembles fine breadcrumbs. Pour the boiling water into a small heatproof bowl, add the golden syrup and stir until dissolved. Add to the flour and mix to a soft dough with a flat-bladed knife.
3. Roll into balls using 2 heaped teaspoons of mixture at a time. Place on the trays, allowing room for spreading, and flatten out slightly with your fingertips. Bake for 15 minutes, or until the biscuits are well coloured and firm. Repeat with the remaining mixture. Cool on the trays for 10 minutes, then transfer to a wire rack to cool completely. Store in an airtight container.

NOTE: Make icing by combining 2–3 teaspoons lemon juice, 60 g (2¼ oz/½ cup) sifted icing (confectioners') sugar and 10 g (¼ oz) melted unsalted butter in a bowl. Mix until smooth, then spread over the biscuits and allow to set.

BRANDY SNAPS

MAKES 15

INGREDIENTS

- 60 g (2¼ oz) unsalted butter
- 2 tablespoons golden syrup or dark corn syrup
- 60 g (2¼ oz/⅓ cup) soft brown sugar
- 30 g (1 oz/¼ cup) plain (all-purpose) flour
- 1½ teaspoons ground ginger

METHOD

1. Preheat the oven to 180°C (350°F/Gas 4). Line two baking trays with baking paper.
2. Put the butter, golden syrup and sugar in a small saucepan and stir over low heat until the butter has melted and the sugar has dissolved. Remove from the heat and add the sifted flour and ginger. Stir with a wooden spoon to combine the ingredients, taking care not to overmix.
3. For each brandy snap, drop 3 level teaspoons of the mixture onto each tray 12 cm (4½ inches) apart. Bake for 5–6 minutes, or until lightly browned. Leave the biscuits on the trays for 30 seconds then, while still hot, lift one biscuit off the tray, using a large flat knife or spatula, and wrap it around the handle of a wooden spoon. (If they cool too much, return them to the oven for a few minutes to warm, then try again.) Slide the biscuit off the spoon and set aside to cool while you curl the remaining brandy snaps. If desired fill with cream or ice cream.

••CAKES••

Cake-making is a symbol of celebration: we bake them for parties, weddings, birthdays, christenings and religious festivals, and yet cakes are also a symbol of an everyday celebration, as we take time out to enjoy them with a morning coffee or when friends drop by. Cakes come in myriad shapes, sizes, textures and flavours and we love them all for their sweet indulgence.

ANGEL FOOD CAKE

Angel food cake is a light sponge cake made with egg whites but no yolks or fats. The cake relies on air beaten into the egg whites (usually 10 to 12) to make it rise. Traditionally, it is baked in an angel cake tin or ring mould as this allows the cake to cook evenly. In contrast to the delicate colour and texture of angel food cake is devil's food cake — a dense, rich chocolate cake.

SERVES 10–12

INGREDIENTS

- 125 g (4½ oz/1 cup) self-raising flour
- 345 g (12 oz/1½ cups) caster (superfine) sugar
- 12 egg whites
- 1½ teaspoons cream of tartar
- ½ teaspoon vanilla extract
- ¼ teaspoon almond extract
- sliced strawberries, to serve
- icing (confectioners') sugar, to dust

METHOD

1. Preheat the oven to 180°C (350°F/Gas 4). Have an ungreased angel cake tin ready.
2. Sift the flour and 170 g (6 oz/¾ cup) of the sugar together four times. Using electric beaters, beat the egg whites with the cream of tartar and ¼ teaspoon salt until stiff peaks form. Beat in the remaining sugar, 1 tablespoon at a time. Fold in the vanilla and almond extracts. Sift one-quarter of the flour and sugar mixture onto the egg white and, using a spatula, gradually fold in. Repeat with the remaining flour and sugar.
3. Spoon the mixture into the tin and bake for 35–40 minutes, or until puffed and golden and a skewer inserted into the centre of the cake comes out clean. Turn upside down on a wire rack and leave in the tin until cool. Gently shake to remove the cake. Arrange the strawberries around the top of the cake and dust with icing sugar before serving.

CREAM OF TARTAR

Cream of tartar is a fine white powder made from the crystals that are deposited in wine barrels. The crystals are purified and ground to form cream of tartar, which is used to stabilise the egg whites beaten into cakes such as sponge and angel food cakes, and to stop the sugar in candy from crystallising. Cream of tartar is the acidic ingredient in baking powder, which activates the bicarbonate of soda.

CAKE MIXING METHODS

There are three major methods for mixing a cake and each one produces a cake with a slightly different texture.

* Creamed cakes, with their high percentage of fat, have a short, soft crumb.
* Whisked cakes are made with lots of eggs, which aerate the batter. They tend to rise dramatically in the oven and although they fall back a little once cooked their texture remains light and fluffy.
* Cakes made using the melt-and-mix method, where the butter and sugar are melted together, produces a particularly moist, dense crumb. Often highly spiced, these wonderfully moist cakes keep well and the flavour improves with time.

GENOISE SPONGE

Genoise is a light, airy sponge-like cake that relies on air beaten into the eggs to make it rise. A genoise is not a true sponge cake, as it is made with butter. Genoise is traditionally made in a moule-à-manqué mould, a French cake tin with slightly sloping sides. The cake can be flavoured with chocolate, almonds or liqueurs. Make genoise on the day you want to eat it, or freeze it straight away as it doesn't have enough fat to make it last for more than 2 to 3 days.

SERVES 10–12

INGREDIENTS

290 g (10¼ oz/2⅓ cups) plain (all-purpose) flour
8 eggs
220 g (7¾ oz) caster (superfine) sugar
100 g (3½ oz) unsalted butter, melted and cooled
icing (confectioners') sugar, to dust

METHOD

1 Preheat the oven to 180°C (350°F/Gas 4). Lightly grease one 25 cm (10 inch) Genoise tin or two shallow 22 cm (8½ inch) round cake tins with melted butter. Line the base with baking paper, then grease the paper. Dust the tin with a little flour, shaking off any excess.
2 Sift the flour three times onto a piece of baking paper. Combine the eggs and sugar in a large heatproof bowl. Place the bowl over a saucepan of simmering water, making sure the base of the bowl does not touch the water, and beat using electric beaters for 8 minutes, or until the mixture is thick and fluffy. Remove from the heat and beat for a further 3 minutes.
3 Add the butter and flour. Using a large metal spoon, fold in quickly and lightly until the mixture is just combined. Spread the mixture evenly into the tin. Bake for 25 minutes, or until the sponge is lightly golden and has shrunk slightly from the side of the tin. Leave the cake in the tin for 5 minutes, then turn out onto a wire rack to cool. Dust with icing sugar just before serving.

CLASSIC SPONGE

SERVES 8

INGREDIENTS

75 g (2½ oz) plain (all-purpose) flour
150 g (5½ oz) self-raising flour
6 eggs
220 g (7¾ oz) caster (superfine) sugar
2 tablespoons boiling water
160 g (5¾ oz/½ cup) strawberry jam
250 ml (9 fl oz/1 cup) whipping cream
icing (confectioners') sugar, to dust

METHOD

1 Preheat the oven to 180°C (350°F/Gas 4). Lightly grease two 22 cm (8½ inch) sandwich tins or round cake tins and line the bases with baking paper. Dust the tins with a little flour, shaking off any excess.
2 Sift the flours together three times onto a piece of baking paper. Beat the eggs in a large bowl using electric beaters for 7 minutes, or until thick and pale. Gradually add the sugar to the egg, beating thoroughly after each addition. Using a large metal spoon, quickly and gently fold in the sifted flour and boiling water.
3 Spread the mixture evenly into the tins and bake for 25 minutes, or until the sponges are lightly golden and shrink slightly from the sides of the tins. Leave the sponges in their tins for 5 minutes, then turn out onto a wire rack to cool.
4 Spread jam over one of the sponges. Whip the cream in a small bowl until stiff peaks form, then spoon into a piping (icing) bag and pipe rosettes over the jam. Place the other sponge on top. Dust with icing sugar before serving.

STRAWBERRY SWISS ROLL

SERVES 6–8

INGREDIENTS

caster (superfine) sugar, to sprinkle
3 eggs, separated
115 g (4 oz/½ cup) caster (superfine) sugar, extra
90 g (3¼ oz/¾ cup) self-raising flour, sifted
185 ml (6 fl oz/¾ cup) whipping cream
1 tablespoon caster (superfine) sugar, extra
160 g (5¾ oz/½ cup) strawberry jam
250 g (9 oz/1⅔ cups) strawberries, quartered

METHOD

1 Preheat the oven to 200°C (400°F/Gas 6). Sprinkle a tablespoon of sugar over a piece of baking paper 30 x 35 cm (12 x 14 inches), resting on a tea towel.
2 Brush a 25 x 30 cm (10 x 12 inch) Swiss roll tin (jelly roll tin) with oil or melted butter and line with baking paper.
3 Beat the egg whites in a clean, dry bowl until soft peaks form. Gradually add the extra ½ cup sugar and beat until dissolved. Beat in the lightly beaten egg yolks until thick.
4 Fold in the flour and 2 tablespoons hot water. Spread into the tin and bake for 8–10 minutes, or until firm and golden. Turn out onto the sugared paper and peel the paper from the base. Using the tea towel as a guide, roll up loosely from the narrow end. Leave for 20 minutes, or until cooled, then unroll. (This prevents the sponge cracking when rolled with filling.)
5 Whip the cream and extra tablespoon of sugar until soft peaks form. Spread the roll with jam and top with the cream and strawberries. Re-roll and chill before serving.

APPLE AND SPICE TEACAKE

SERVES 8

INGREDIENTS

180 g (6½ oz) unsalted butter, softened
95 g (3¼ oz/½ cup) soft brown sugar
2 teaspoons finely grated lemon zest
3 eggs, lightly beaten
125 g (4½ oz/1 cup) self-raising flour
75 g (2½ oz/½ cup) wholemeal flour
½ teaspoon ground cinnamon
125 ml (4 fl oz/½ cup) milk
400 g (14 oz) tin pie apple
¼ teaspoon mixed spice
1 tablespoon soft brown sugar, extra
25 g (1 oz/¼ cup) flaked almonds

METHOD

1 Preheat the oven to 180°C (350°F/Gas 4). Grease the base and side of a 20 cm (8 inch) spring-form cake tin, and line the base with baking paper.
2 Cream the butter and sugar in a small bowl using electric beaters until light and fluffy. Beat in the lemon zest. Add the eggs gradually, beating thoroughly after each addition. Transfer the mixture to a large bowl. Using a metal spoon, fold in the sifted flours and cinnamon alternately with the milk. Stir until the mixture is just combined and almost smooth.
3 Spoon half the mixture into the tin, top with three-quarters of the apple, then the remaining cake mixture. Press the remaining apple around the edge of the top. Combine the mixed spice, extra sugar and flaked almonds and sprinkle over the top of the cake.
4 Bake for 1 hour, or until a skewer inserted into the centre of the cake comes out clean. Leave in the tin for 15 minutes, then turn out onto a wire rack to cool.

RICOTTA, ORANGE AND WALNUT CAKE

SERVES 6–8

INGREDIENTS

150 g (5½ oz/1½ cups) walnut halves
150 g (5½ oz) unsalted butter, softened
150 g (5½ oz/⅔ cup) caster (superfine) sugar
5 eggs, at room temperature, separated
finely grated zest of 1 large orange
1 teaspoon lemon juice
200 g (7 oz) ricotta cheese
60 g (2¼ oz/½ cup) plain (all-purpose) flour
dark unsweetened cocoa powder, for dusting

CANDIED ORANGE ZEST

1 large orange
250 ml (9 fl oz/1 cup) orange juice
115 g (4 oz/½ cup) caster (superfine) sugar

METHOD

1 Preheat the oven to 200°C (400°F/Gas 6). Grease a 22 cm (8½ inch) spring-form cake tin.
2 Spread the walnuts on a baking tray and toast for 5 minutes. Use a sharp knife to roughly chop two-thirds of the walnuts. Set aside. Finely chop the remaining walnuts in a food processor and use to coat the inside of the cake tin in a thick layer. Reduce the oven to 190°C (375°F/Gas 5).
3 Cream the butter and 90 g (3¼ oz/heaped ⅓ cup) of the sugar in a large bowl with electric beaters until pale and fluffy. Add the egg yolks, orange zest, lemon juice, ricotta, flour and reserved walnuts. Gently mix until well combined.
4 Whisk the egg whites in a large bowl until soft peaks form. Gradually add the remaining sugar and whisk until stiff. Using a metal spoon, fold a large scoop of egg white into the ricotta mixture. Carefully fold in the remaining egg white. Spoon into the cake tin and level the surface. Bake for 35–40 minutes, or until the cake is set and the surface is golden. Cool in the tin for 15 minutes before turning out.
5 To make the candied zest, peel the orange, discarding the pith. Cut the zest into long, very thin strips. Put in a bowl, cover with boiling water and soak for 3–4 minutes, then drain and dry on paper towels. Combine the orange juice and sugar in a small saucepan, stirring to dissolve the sugar, then bring to the boil, add the zest and simmer for 5 minutes. Remove the zest with tongs and spread on a plate to cool.
6 To serve, dust the centre of the cake with the cocoa, leaving 5 cm (2 inches) around the rim uncovered. Arrange the zest around the rim.

TYPES OF MADEIRAS

When cooking with Madeira, it is important to use the type specified in the recipe or to choose one that is similar in flavour.

Sercial is the driest of the Madeiras and is often drunk as an apéritif. In cooking, it is used as a flavouring, particularly for savoury dishes. Verdelho is medium-sweet and sometimes served as a wine to go with the soup course or as an after-dinner drink, usually with Madeira cake. Bual is a medium-sweet blend, used to flavour desserts and cakes and as an after-dinner drink. The richest and darkest variety is Malmsey. It has fruity, liqueur-like qualities and is used to flavour desserts and as an after-dinner drink with fruit, nuts and cakes.

MADEIRA CAKE

This rich butter cake was popular in Victorian England. Madeira cake does not contain Madeira, but is so named because it is often served with a glass of Madeira.

SERVES 8

INGREDIENTS

- 185 g (6½ oz) unsalted butter, softened
- 170 g (6 oz/¾ cup) caster (superfine) sugar
- 3 eggs, lightly beaten
- 2 teaspoons finely grated orange or lemon zest
- 155 g (5½ oz/1¼ cups) self-raising flour, sifted
- 125 g (4½ oz/1 cup) plain (all-purpose) flour, sifted
- 2 tablespoons milk

METHOD

1. Preheat the oven to 160°C (315°F/Gas 2–3). Grease a 20 x 10 x 7 cm (8 x 4 x 2¾ inch) loaf (bar) tin and line the base and sides with baking paper.
2. Cream the butter and sugar in a small bowl using electric beaters until light and fluffy. Add the eggs gradually, beating thoroughly after each addition. Add the orange zest and beat until combined. Transfer to a large bowl. Using a metal spoon, fold in the flours and milk. Stir until smooth. Spoon into the prepared tin and smooth the surface.
3. Bake for 50 minutes, or until a skewer inserted into the centre of the cake comes out clean. Leave in the tin for 10 minutes, then turn out onto a wire rack to cool.

ORANGE POPPY SEED CAKE

SERVES 8–10

INGREDIENTS

- 185 g (6½ oz/1½ cups) self-raising flour
- 35 g (1¼ oz/⅓ cup) ground almonds
- 40 g (1½ oz/¼ cup) poppy seeds
- 185 g (6½ oz) unsalted butter
- 145 g (5½ oz/⅔ cup) caster (superfine) sugar
- 80 g (2¾ oz/¼ cup) apricot jam or marmalade
- 2–3 teaspoons finely grated orange zest
- 80 ml (2½ fl oz/⅓ cup) orange juice
- 3 eggs, lightly beaten
- 1 quantity cream cheese icing (page 531)
- orange zest, to decorate (optional)

METHOD

1. Preheat the oven to 180°C (350°F/Gas 4). Grease a deep 20 cm (8 inch) round cake tin and line with baking paper.
2. Sift the flour into a bowl and add the almonds and poppy seeds. Make a well in the centre.
3. Place the butter, sugar, jam, orange zest and juice in a saucepan. Stir over low heat until the butter has melted and the mixture is smooth. Gradually add the butter mixture to the dry ingredients, whisking until smooth. Add the egg and whisk until combined. Pour into the tin and bake for 50–60 minutes, or until a skewer inserted into the centre of the cake comes out clean. Leave in the tin for 10 minutes, then turn out onto a wire rack to cool.
4. Spread the icing over the cooled cake. Decorate with strips of orange zest, if desired.

POUND CAKE

Originating in the eighteenth century, a pound cake is made with equal weights of flour, butter, eggs and sugar. Traditionally it was a pound of each, so made a very big cake. Today the pound cake has many variations, some adding lemon, brandy or spices, some separating the eggs and whisking the whites to add air to the cake, others contain no fat at all. Pound cakes are usually baked in a loaf tin.

‹ POUND CAKE

MAKES 2 LOAVES OR 1 ROUND CAKE

INGREDIENTS

- 375 g (13 oz) unsalted butter, softened
- 345 g (12 oz/1½ cups) caster (superfine) sugar
- 1 teaspoon vanilla extract
- 6 eggs, lightly beaten
- 375 g (13 oz/3 cups) plain (all-purpose) flour, sifted
- 1 teaspoon baking powder
- 60 ml (2 fl oz/¼ cup) milk
- icing (confectioners') sugar, to dust

METHOD

1 Preheat the oven to 180°C (350°F/Gas 4). Grease the base and sides of two 21 x 10 x 7 cm deep (8¼ x 4 x 2¾ inch) loaf (bar) tins or a 24 cm (9½ inch) round cake tin. Line the base of the tins with baking paper.

2 Cream the butter and sugar in a small bowl using electric beaters until the mixture is light and fluffy. Beat in the vanilla, then add the eggs gradually, beating thoroughly after each addition. Transfer to a large bowl. Using a metal spoon, fold in the sifted flour and baking powder alternately with the milk. Stir until the mixture is just combined and almost smooth.

3 Spoon the mixture into the prepared tins and smooth the surface. Bake for 45–50 minutes for the loaves or 55 minutes for the round cake, or until a skewer inserted into the centre of the cake comes out clean. Leave in the tins for 10 minutes, then turn out onto a wire rack to cool. Lightly dust the top with icing sugar just before serving.

CINNAMON TEACAKE

SERVES 8

INGREDIENTS

- 60 g (2¼ oz) unsalted butter, softened
- 125 g (4½ oz) caster (superfine) sugar
- 1 egg, lightly beaten
- 1 teaspoon vanilla extract
- 90 g (3¼ oz/¾ cup) self-raising flour
- 30 g (1 oz/¼ cup) plain (all-purpose) flour
- 125 ml (4 fl oz/½ cup) milk

TOPPING

- 20 g (¾ oz) unsalted butter, melted
- 1 tablespoon caster (superfine) sugar
- 1 teaspoon ground cinnamon

METHOD

1 Preheat the oven to 180°C (350°F/Gas 4). Grease a 20 cm (8 inch) round shallow cake tin and line the base with baking paper.

2 Cream the butter and sugar in a small bowl using electric beaters until light and fluffy. Add the egg gradually, beating thoroughly after each addition. Beat in the vanilla, then transfer to a large bowl. Using a metal spoon, fold in the sifted flours alternately with the milk. Stir until the mixture is smooth.

3 Spoon into the prepared cake tin and bake for 30 minutes, or until a skewer inserted into the centre of the cake comes out clean. Leave in the tin for 5 minutes, then turn out onto a wire rack.

4 To make the topping, brush the warm cake with the butter and sprinkle with the combined sugar and cinnamon.

‹ BANANA CAKE

SERVES 8

INGREDIENTS

125 g (4½ oz) unsalted butter, softened
115 g (4 oz/½ cup) caster (superfine) sugar
2 eggs, lightly beaten
1 teaspoon vanilla extract
4 very ripe bananas, mashed
1 teaspoon bicarbonate of soda (baking soda)
125 ml (4 fl oz/½ cup) milk
250 g (9 oz/2 cups) self-raising flour, sifted
½ teaspoon mixed spice
1 quantity butter frosting (page 531)
15 g (½ oz/¼ cup) flaked coconut, toasted

METHOD

1 Preheat the oven to 180°C (350°F/Gas 4). Grease a 20 cm (8 inch) round cake tin and line the base with baking paper.
2 Cream the butter and sugar in a small bowl using electric beaters until light and creamy. Add the egg gradually, beating thoroughly after each addition. Add the vanilla and banana and beat until combined. Transfer to a large bowl.
3 Dissolve the bicarbonate of soda in the milk. Using a metal spoon, gently fold the sifted flour and mixed spice alternately with the milk into the banana mixture. Stir until all the ingredients are just combined and the mixture is smooth. Spoon into the prepared tin and smooth the surface. Bake for 1 hour, or until a skewer inserted into the centre of the cake comes out clean. Leave in the tin for 10 minutes, then turn out onto a wire rack to cool completely.
4 Spread the frosting over the cooled cake using a flat-bladed knife and sprinkle with the toasted coconut flakes.

CARROT CAKE

SERVES 8–10

INGREDIENTS

125 g (4½ oz/1 cup) self-raising flour
125 g (4½ oz/1 cup) plain (all-purpose) flour
2 teaspoons ground cinnamon
1 teaspoon ground ginger
½ teaspoon ground nutmeg
1 teaspoon bicarbonate of soda (baking soda)
250 ml (9 fl oz/1 cup) oil
185 g (6½ oz/1 cup) soft brown sugar
4 eggs
175 g (6 oz/½ cup) golden syrup or dark corn syrup
390 g (13¾ oz/2½ cups) grated carrot
60 g (2¼ oz/½ cup) chopped pecans
1 quantity cream cheese icing (page 531)
ground nutmeg, extra to sprinkle

METHOD

1 Preheat the oven to 160°C (315°F/Gas 2–3). Grease a 23 cm (9 inch) round cake tin and line the base and side with baking paper.
2 Sift the flours, cinnamon, ginger, nutmeg and bicarbonate of soda into a large bowl and make a well in the centre.
3 Whisk together the oil, sugar, eggs and golden syrup until combined. Add this mixture to the well in the flour and gradually stir with a metal spoon until smooth. Stir in the carrot and nuts, then spoon into the tin and smooth the surface. Bake for 1½ hours, or until a skewer inserted into the centre of the cake comes out clean. Leave in the tin for 15–20 minutes, then turn out onto a wire rack to cool completely.
4 Spread the icing over the cake using a flat-bladed knife and sprinkle with nutmeg.

PINEAPPLE UPSIDE-DOWN CAKE

SERVES 8

INGREDIENTS

- 90 g (3¼ oz) unsalted butter, melted
- 95 g (3¼ oz/½ cup) soft brown sugar
- 440 g (15½ oz) tin pineapple rings in juice
- 6 red glacé cherries
- 125 g (4½ oz) unsalted butter, extra, softened
- 170 g (6 oz/¾ cup) caster (superfine) sugar
- 2 eggs, lightly beaten
- 1 teaspoon vanilla extract
- 185 g (6½ oz/1½ cups) self-raising flour
- 60 g (2¼ oz/½ cup) plain (all-purpose) flour
- 30 g (1 oz/⅓ cup) desiccated coconut

METHOD

1. Preheat the oven to 180°C (350°F/Gas 4). Pour the butter into a 20 cm (8 inch) round cake tin, brushing some of it up the side, but leaving most on the base. Sprinkle the brown sugar over the base.
2. Drain the pineapple, reserving 125 ml (4 fl oz/½ cup) of the juice. Arrange the pineapple rings over the base of the tin (five on the outside and one in the centre) and put a cherry in the centre of each ring.
3. Cream the extra butter and sugar in a small bowl until light and creamy. Add the egg gradually, beating well after each addition. Add the vanilla and beat until combined. Transfer the butter mixture to a large bowl. Using a metal spoon, fold in the sifted flours, then add the coconut and reserved pineapple juice. Stir until the mixture is just combined and almost smooth. Spoon into the tin over the pineapple rings. Indent the centre slightly with the back of a spoon so the cake has a reasonably flat base. Bake for 50–60 minutes, or until a skewer inserted into the centre of the cake comes out clean. Leave in the tin for 10 minutes, then turn out onto a wire rack.

HUMMINGBIRD CAKE

SERVES 8

INGREDIENTS

- 2 ripe bananas, mashed
- 130 g ($4\frac{3}{4}$ oz/$\frac{1}{2}$ cup) drained and crushed tinned pineapple (see Note)
- 285 g ($10\frac{1}{4}$ oz/$1\frac{1}{4}$ cups) caster (superfine) sugar
- 210 g ($7\frac{1}{2}$ oz/$1\frac{2}{3}$ cups) self-raising flour
- 2 teaspoons ground cinnamon or mixed spice
- 170 ml ($5\frac{1}{2}$ fl oz/$\frac{2}{3}$ cup) oil
- 60 ml (2 fl oz/$\frac{1}{4}$ cup) pineapple juice
- 2 eggs

ICING

- 60 g ($2\frac{1}{4}$ oz) unsalted butter, softened
- 125 g ($4\frac{1}{2}$ oz/$\frac{1}{2}$ cup) cream cheese, softened
- 185 g ($6\frac{1}{2}$ oz/$1\frac{1}{2}$ cups) icing (confectioners') sugar
- 1–2 teaspoons lemon juice

METHOD

1 Preheat the oven to 180°C (350°F/Gas 4). Lightly grease a 20 cm (8 inch) square cake tin and line with baking paper.

2 Put the banana, pineapple and sugar in a large bowl. Add the sifted flour and cinnamon or mixed spice. Stir together with a wooden spoon until well combined.

3 Whisk together the oil, pineapple juice and eggs. Pour onto the banana mixture and stir until combined and the mixture is smooth.

4 Spoon into the tin and smooth the surface. Bake for 1 hour, or until a skewer inserted into the centre of the cake comes out clean. Leave in the tin for 15 minutes, then turn out onto a wire rack to cool.

5 To make the icing, beat the butter and cream cheese using electric beaters until smooth. Gradually add the icing sugar alternately with the lemon juice. Beat until thick and creamy.

6 Spread the icing thickly over the top of the cooled cake, or thinly over the top and side.

NOTE: If you are unable to buy crushed pineapple, use pineapple rings chopped very finely. Buy the fruit in natural juice rather than syrup and reserve the juice when draining to use in the recipe.

GLACE CHERRIES

These are cherries that have been candied to produce a glossy appearance, and are often dyed red, green or yellow. Undyed, they are a more natural dark-red colour. The cherries are picked just before they are ripe and stored in brine until needed. They are then pitted and candied by boiling them in sugar syrup. Use glacé cherries for baking, in biscuits or Christmas cake, in desserts, or as a decoration on small cakes.

BLUEBERRY CRUMBLE CAKE

SERVES 8–10

INGREDIENTS

125 g (4½ oz/1 cup) plain (all-purpose) flour
110 g (3¾ oz/¾ cup) wholemeal flour
230 g (8½ oz/1 cup) caster (superfine) sugar
2½ teaspoons baking powder
½ teaspoon ground cinnamon
150 g (5½ oz/1 cup) blueberries
1 egg, at room temperature
185 ml (6 fl oz/¾ cup) milk
80 ml (2½ fl oz/⅓ cup) oil
1 teaspoon vanilla extract
finely grated zest of 1 lemon
thick (double) cream, to serve

TOPPING

60 g (2¼ oz/½ cup) chopped pecans
60 g (2¼ oz/⅓ cup) soft brown sugar
30 g (1 oz/¼ cup) plain (all-purpose) flour
150 g (5½ oz/1 cup) blueberries
2 tablespoons oil

METHOD

1 Preheat the oven to 190°C (375°F/Gas 5). Grease a 20 cm (8 inch) spring-form cake tin.
2 Sift the flours, sugar, baking powder and cinnamon into a large bowl. Return the husks to the bowl. Toss the blueberries through the flour mixture. Whisk together the egg, milk, oil, vanilla and lemon zest. Pour into the dry ingredients and stir to combine. Pour the mixture into the prepared tin.
3 To make the topping, combine the pecans, brown sugar, flour and blueberries in a bowl and sprinkle evenly over the cake. Drizzle the oil over the topping. Bake the cake for 50–55 minutes, or until a skewer inserted into the centre of the cake comes out clean. Serve the cake warm with a dollop of cream.

WHOLE ORANGE AND ALMOND CAKE

SERVES 8–10

INGREDIENTS

2 large oranges
5 eggs
250 g (9 oz/2½ cups) ground almonds
220 g (7¾ oz/1 cup) sugar
1 teaspoon baking powder
icing (confectioners') sugar, to dust
thick (double) cream, to serve

METHOD

1 Grease a 22 cm (8½ inch) spring-form cake tin and line the base with baking paper.
2 Scrub the orange skins under warm running water with a soft bristle brush to remove the wax coating. Put the whole oranges in a saucepan, cover with water and boil for 1 hour. Remove from the water and set aside to cool.
3 Preheat the oven to 180°C (350°F/Gas 4). Using a plate to catch any juice, cut the cooked oranges into quarters and remove any seeds. Put the orange quarters, including the skin, into a food processor or blender and process until the oranges turn to a pulp.
4 Beat the eggs in a large bowl with electric beaters until light and creamy. Add the orange pulp and any reserved juice, the ground almonds, sugar and baking powder to the bowl. Mix thoroughly, then pour into the prepared tin.
5 Bake for 1 hour, or until the cake is firm to touch and lightly golden. Cook the cake a little longer if it is still wet. Leave in the tin for 10 minutes, then remove from the tin and leave to cool completely. Dust with sifted icing sugar and serve with cream.

PANFORTE

Panforte is a medieval recipe from the twelfth or thirteenth century, a speciality of Siena in Italy, where nearly every shop seems to feature it. This rich cake is sold in huge wheels of both blonde and dark panforte (the latter made by adding cocoa) and will keep for about 2 weeks.

MAKES 1 CAKE

INGREDIENTS

- 4 small sheets rice paper (see Note)
- 100 g (3½ oz/¾ cup) skinned hazelnuts
- 100 g (3½ oz/⅔ cup) blanched almonds
- 1 teaspoon each whole coriander seeds, cloves, and black peppercorns
- ¼ teaspoon grated nutmeg
- 1 teaspoon ground cinnamon
- 50 g (1¾ oz/¼ cup) chopped dried figs
- 1 tablespoon unsweetened cocoa powder
- 200 g (7 oz) roughly chopped mixed peel
- finely grated zest of 1 lemon
- 50 g (1¾ oz) plain (all-purpose) flour
- 150 g (5½ oz) sugar
- 4 tablespoons clear honey
- 40 g (1½ oz) unsalted butter
- icing (confectioners') sugar, to dust

METHOD

1. Butter and line the base of a 20 cm (8 inch) spring-form cake tin with rice paper. Cut a few thin strips to line the side as well. Preheat the oven to 150°C (300°F/Gas 2) and lightly brown the hazelnuts and almonds on a baking tray for 6–8 minutes. Check often, as the nuts can burn very quickly. Allow to cool.
2. Grind the whole spices together in a spice grinder or using a mortar and pestle. Put the nuts in a metal or china bowl with the spices, figs, cocoa, mixed peel, lemon zest and flour and mix together.
3. Put the sugar, honey and butter in a heavy-based saucepan over low heat to melt, briefly stirring the butter into the sugar as it just starts to melt. Do not stir again or the sugar will crystallise. Bring to the boil and cook until the syrup reaches 113°C (235°F) on a sugar thermometer, or a little of the syrup dropped into cold water forms a soft ball when moulded between your finger and thumb.
4. Immediately pour the syrup into the nut mixture and mix well, working quickly as it will soon cool and stiffen. Pour into the prepared tin and smooth the top with a spatula.
5. Bake for about 15 minutes. Unlike other cakes, this will not colour or seem very firm, even when cooked, but will begin to harden as it cools. Allow to cool a little in the tin until it is firm enough to enable the side of the tin to be removed. If the mixture is still quite soft when cooled, place in the fridge to set. To serve, dust the top heavily with icing sugar.

NOTE: Rice paper is not actually made from rice but from the pith of a small tree. The thin edible paper is essential here, as the cake is so sticky that it is almost impossible to remove the paper once it is cooked. Rice paper is available from cake decorating stores and delicatessens.

CHOCOLATE

The process needed to transform the cacao bean (cocoa in English) into that smooth, delicious end result known as chocolate is long and complicated, and the block of chocolate, so ubiquitous now, was not perfected until the 1840s. The beans are fermented, dried and roasted, and the exposed nibs ground with water to make chocolate liquor. From this comes cocoa butter, as well as a paste that can be dried to make cocoa powder. It is cocoa butter, combined with ground beans and other ingredients such as sugar, that produces chocolate.

TYPES OF CHOCOLATE

COUVERTURE (COATING OR DIPPING) CHOCOLATE

This has a higher percentage of cocoa butter and is not as stable as dark chocolate, so it needs to be tempered before use. (Tempering is a process whereby chocolate is stabilised by melting it, then cooling it before use.) Couverture chocolate is used mainly by the catering industry as it melts and coats easily, and has a glossy finish and an intense chocolate flavour.

MILK CHOCOLATE

Has milk solids added to it. It is sweet and creamy and not as intensely chocolate flavoured as dark chocolate.

DARK (PLAIN), SEMI-SWEET AND BITTER-SWEET CHOCOLATE

These have vanilla, sugar and cocoa butter added to them. Their sugar content varies slightly, but they are interchangeable in recipes. Good-quality chocolate is glossy, smooth and slightly red in colour. It snaps cleanly, melts easily, has a sweet, fruity smell, and real flavours (vanilla, nutmeg) are used to make it.

COMPOUND (BAKING) CHOCOLATE

This type of chocolate usually contains vegetable fat instead of cocoa butter and doesn't have the same depth of flavour or body as dark chocolate. Because it doesn't need to be tempered to make it stable, it is often used for chocolate decorations.

WHITE CHOCOLATE

Made from cocoa butter and milk solids, it is not strictly chocolate as it doesn't contain cocoa liquor. It needs to be treated with more care, as it will seize more easily than dark chocolate.

HOW TO... MELT CHOCOLATE

When melting chocolate, always use a clean dry bowl. Water or moisture will make chocolate seize (turn into a thick mass that won't melt) and overheating will make it scorch and taste bitter. If the chocolate does seize, add a few drops of vegetable oil and stir until smooth.

METHOD

1 Chop the chocolate finely and put it in a heatproof bowl. Sit the bowl over a saucepan of barely simmering water. Alternatively, take the pan of boiled water off the heat.
2 Leave the chocolate to soften, then stir until smooth. Don't let water or steam get in the bowl or the chocolate will seize.
3 Remove the chocolate from the saucepan to cool, or leave in place if you want to keep the chocolate liquid.

MUD CAKE

SERVES 8–10

INGREDIENTS

- 250 g (9 oz) unsalted butter
- 250 g (9 oz) dark chocolate, broken
- 2 tablespoons instant coffee powder
- 155 g (5½ oz/1¼ cups) self-raising flour
- 155 g (5½ oz/1¼ cups) plain (all-purpose) flour
- 60 g (2¼ oz/½ cup) unsweetened cocoa powder
- ½ teaspoon bicarbonate of soda (baking soda)
- 550 g (1 lb 4 oz/2½ cups) sugar
- 4 eggs
- 2 tablespoons oil
- 125 ml (4 fl oz/½ cup) buttermilk
- 1 quantity chocolate glaze (page 531)
- chocolate shards, to decorate

METHOD

1. Preheat the oven to 160°C (315°F/Gas 2–3). Grease a deep 22 cm (8½ inch) round cake tin. Line the base and side with baking paper, extending at least 2 cm (¾ inch) above the rim.
2. Put the butter, chocolate, coffee and 185 ml (6 fl oz/¾ cup) hot water in a saucepan over low heat, and stir until melted and smooth. Remove from the heat.
3. Sift the flours, cocoa and bicarbonate of soda into a large bowl. Stir in the sugar and make a well in the centre. Add the combined eggs, oil and buttermilk and, using a large metal spoon, slowly stir in the dry ingredients, then the melted chocolate mixture until combined. Spoon the mixture into the prepared tin and bake for 1 hour 40 minutes, or until a skewer inserted into the centre of the cake comes out clean. Leave in the tin to cool completely, then turn out onto a wire rack.
4. Sit the wire rack over a baking tray. Pour the chocolate glaze over the cake, making sure the side is evenly covered, then decorate with chocolate shards.

FLOURLESS CHOCOLATE CAKE

SERVES 10

INGREDIENTS

- 250 g (9 oz) dark chocolate, chopped
- 100 g (3½ oz) caster (superfine) sugar
- 100 g (3½ oz) unsalted butter, cubed
- 1 tablespoon coffee-flavoured liqueur
- 125 g (4½ oz) ground hazelnuts
- 5 eggs, separated
- icing (confectioners') sugar, to dust

METHOD

1. Preheat the oven to 180°C (350°F/Gas 4). Grease a 23 cm (9 inch) spring-form cake tin and line the base with baking paper.
2. Place the chocolate, sugar, butter and liqueur in a heatproof bowl. Bring a small saucepan of water to the boil, then reduce the heat to a gentle simmer. Sit the bowl over the saucepan, making sure the base of the bowl does not touch the water. Stir occasionally to ensure even melting. When fully melted, remove from the heat and mix thoroughly.
3. Transfer the chocolate mixture to a large bowl. Stir in the ground hazelnuts, then beat in the egg yolks, one at a time, mixing well after each addition. In a clean, dry bowl, whisk the egg whites until they form stiff peaks. Stir a tablespoonful of the whisked egg whites into the chocolate, then gently fold in the rest using a large metal spoon or rubber spatula.
4. Pour the mixture into the prepared tin and bake for 50–60 minutes, or until a skewer inserted into the centre of the cake comes out clean. Leave in the tin for 10 minutes, then remove from the tin and leave to cool completely. Dust with icing sugar before serving.

SACHER TORTE

This Viennese cake, created by chef Franz Sacher in the nineteenth century, is a rich chocolate cake covered with a chocolate glaze. The cake may be sliced into three layers, with each layer spread with jam, and traditionally the word 'Sacher' is piped in chocolate across the top of the cake. It is still served in Vienna's Hotel Sacher.

SERVES 10

INGREDIENTS

125 g (4½ oz/1 cup) plain (all-purpose) flour
30 g (1 oz/¼ cup) unsweetened cocoa powder
230 g (8½ oz/1 cup) caster (superfine) sugar
100 g (3½ oz) unsalted butter
80 g (2¾ oz/¼ cup) strawberry jam
4 eggs, separated

GANACHE TOPPING

170 ml (5½ fl oz/⅔ cup) cream
80 g (2¾ oz/⅓ cup) caster (superfine) sugar
200 g (7 oz) dark chocolate, chopped

METHOD

1 Preheat the oven to 180°C (350°F/Gas 4). Lightly grease a 20 cm (8 inch) round cake tin and line with baking paper.
2 Sift the flour and cocoa into a large bowl and make a well in the centre. Combine the sugar, butter and half the jam in a small saucepan. Stir over low heat until the butter has melted and the sugar has dissolved, then add to the flour with the lightly beaten egg yolks and stir until just combined.
3 Beat the egg whites in a small, dry, clean bowl using electric beaters until soft peaks form. Stir one-third of the egg white into the cake mixture, then fold in the rest in two batches. Pour into the prepared tin and smooth the surface. Bake for 40–45 minutes, or until a skewer inserted into the centre of the cake comes out clean. Leave in the tin for 15 minutes, then turn out onto a wire rack to cool completely.
4 To make the ganache topping, put the cream, sugar and chocolate in a small saucepan over low heat, and stir until melted and smooth. Trim the top of the cake so that it is flat, then turn it upside down on a wire rack over a tray. Melt the remaining jam and brush it over the cake. Pour most of the topping over the cake and tap the tray to flatten the surface. Place the remaining mixture in a piping (icing) bag and pipe 'Sacher' on the top of the cake.

COCOA POWDER

Cocoa powder is a by-product of the manufacture of chocolate, and is made by pressing chocolate liquor, the first stage in turning cocoa beans into chocolate, until it gives up cocoa butter and a paste, which, when dried and powdered, becomes cocoa. Cocoa is used to flavour biscuits, puddings and sauces or mixed with hot milk and sugar to make hot cocoa. In the 1800s, a Dutch chemist perfected a screw press that enabled the cocoa to be extracted more efficiently, and a process of further treating it to produce a darker, milder cocoa known as 'Dutched' cocoa, which dissolves more easily and is used for drinking or baking.

BLACK FOREST CAKE

Black Forest cake (sometimes called gâteau) is probably one of the most famous cakes in the world. It originated in Swabia, Germany, in the Black Forest region. In Germany, it is known as 'Black Forest Torte'.

SERVES 8–10

INGREDIENTS

- 125 g (4½ oz) unsalted butter, softened
- 230 g (8½ oz/1 cup) caster (superfine) sugar
- 2 eggs, lightly beaten
- 1 teaspoon vanilla extract
- 40 g (1½ oz/⅓ cup) self-raising flour
- 125 g (4½ oz/1 cup) plain (all-purpose) flour
- 1 teaspoon bicarbonate of soda (baking soda)
- 60 g (2¼ oz/½ cup) unsweetened cocoa powder
- 185 ml (6 fl oz/¾ cup) buttermilk

TOPPING

- 100 g (3½ oz) dark chocolate
- 100 g (3½ oz) milk chocolate
- cherries with stalks, to decorate

FILLING

- 60 ml (2 fl oz/¼ cup) Kirsch
- 750 ml (26 fl oz/3 cups) cream, whipped
- 425 g (15 oz) tin pitted morello or black cherries, drained

METHOD

1. Preheat the oven to 180°C (350°F/Gas 4). Lightly grease a deep, 20 cm (8 inch) round cake tin. Line the base and side with baking paper.
2. Using electric beaters, beat the butter and sugar until light and creamy. Add the egg gradually, beating thoroughly after each addition. Add the vanilla and beat until well combined. Transfer to a large bowl. Using a metal spoon, fold in the sifted flours, bicarbonate of soda and cocoa alternately with the buttermilk. Mix until combined and the mixture is smooth.
3. Pour the mixture into the prepared tin and smooth the surface. Bake for 50–60 minutes, or until a skewer inserted into the centre of the cake comes out clean. Leave in the tin for 30 minutes, then turn out onto a wire rack to cool completely.
4. When cold, cut horizontally into three layers, using a long serrated knife. The easiest way to do this is to rest the palm of one hand lightly on top of the cake while cutting into it. Turn the cake every few strokes so the knife cuts in evenly all the way around the edge. When you have gone the whole way round, cut through the middle. Remove the first layer so it will be easier to see what you are doing while cutting the next one.
5. To make the topping, leave the chocolate in a warm place for 10 minutes, or until soft but still firm. With a vegetable peeler, and using long strokes, shave curls of chocolate from the block. If the block is too soft, chill it to firm it up.
6. To assemble, place one cake layer on a serving plate and brush liberally with Kirsch. Spread evenly with one-fifth of the whipped cream. Top with half the cherries. Continue layering with the remaining cake, liqueur, cream and cherries, finishing with the cream on top. Spread the remaining cream evenly on the outside of the cake. Coat the side with chocolate shavings by laying the shavings on a small piece of baking paper and then gently pressing them into the cream. If you use your hands, the chocolate will melt. Decorate the top of the cake with more chocolate shavings and cherries on stalks.

INDIVIDUAL CHRISTMAS CAKES

MAKES 12

INGREDIENTS

60 g (2¼ oz/¼ cup) chopped glacé apricots
110 g (3¾ oz/½ cup) chopped glacé pineapple
100 g (3½ oz/½ cup) chopped glacé figs
320 g (11¼ oz/2 cups) chopped raisins
250 g (9 oz/1⅔ cups) currants
185 ml (6 fl oz/¾ cup) bourbon
250 g (9 oz) unsalted butter, chopped
230 g (8½ oz/1 cup) dark brown sugar
180 g (6½ oz/½ cup) treacle or molasses
4 eggs
310 g (11 oz/2½ cups) chopped pecans
185 g (6½ oz/1½ cups) plain (all-purpose) flour
60 g (2¼ oz/½ cup) self-raising flour
2 teaspoons ground nutmeg
2 teaspoons ground ginger
2 teaspoons ground cinnamon
125 ml (4 fl oz/½ cup) bourbon, extra

HOLLY LEAVES AND BERRIES (OPTIONAL)
60 g (2¼ oz) ready-made almond icing
icing (confectioners') sugar
green and red food colouring

SOFT ICING-COVERED CAKES
100 g (3½ oz/⅓ cup) apricot jam
1.2 kg (2 lb 10 oz) soft icing
thin ribbon, to decorate

ROYAL ICING-COVERED CAKES
1 egg white
250 g (9 oz/2 cups) icing (confectioners') sugar, sifted
2–3 teaspoons lemon juice

METHOD

1 Cut the glacé fruits into small pieces. Place in a bowl with the raisins, currants and bourbon and mix. Cover and leave to soak overnight.

2 Preheat the oven to 150°C (300°F/Gas 2). Lightly grease twelve 250 ml (9 fl oz/1 cup) muffin holes and line the bases with a circle of baking paper. Beat the butter, sugar and treacle in a bowl. Add the eggs, one at a time, beating well after each addition. Transfer to a bowl, stir in the soaked fruit mixture, pecans and the sifted dry ingredients and mix. Spoon the mixture evenly into the muffin holes, and smooth the surface. Bake for 1–1¼ hours, or until a skewer inserted into the centre comes out clean. Cover the top of the cakes with foil if over-browning. Brush the tops of the cakes with half the extra bourbon while hot, cover with baking paper, then seal with foil and cool in the tins before turning out. Brush with the remaining bourbon, wrap firmly in plastic and leave for two weeks before decorating. When decorating, the base will become the top.

3 If you like, make leaves and berries to decorate. To make the leaves, knead 50 g (1¾ oz) of the almond icing until soft. Roll out on a surface dusted with icing sugar until very thin. Cut out the leaves using a cutter or template. Dry on baking paper. Brush the edges with green food colouring. Knead a little red colouring into the remaining icing and roll into balls to make berries.

4 To make the soft icing-covered cakes, melt the jam until runny, strain and brush some all over each cake. Roll out 100 g (3½ oz) of the soft icing on a surface dusted with icing sugar until large enough to cover one cake. Place the icing over the cake and ease over the side, pressing lightly, then trim from around the base. If desired, wrap a ribbon around the cake and secure with a paste of water and icing sugar. Use the paste to secure two holly leaves and berries to the top. Repeat with the remaining cakes and icing.

5 To make the royal icing-covered cakes, lightly beat the egg white. Gradually add the icing sugar, beating to a smooth paste. Add the lemon juice until slightly runny. Spread a tablespoon of icing over each cake, letting some drizzle down the sides. Secure holly leaves and berries on the top just before the icing sets.

DUNDEE CAKE

This fruit cake, named after the town of Dundee in Scotland, is lighter than the traditional Christmas cake and is made as a general eating cake rather than for special occasions.

MAKES 1

INGREDIENTS

250 g (9 oz) unsalted butter
230 g (8½ oz/1 cup) soft brown sugar
4 eggs, lightly beaten
125 g (4½ oz/1 cup) raisins
125 g (4½ oz/1 cup) sultanas
185 g (6½ oz/1¼ cups) currants
60 g (2¼ oz/⅓ cup) mixed peel
60 g (2¼ oz/¼ cup) chopped glacé cherries
100 g (3½ oz/1 cup) ground almonds
90 g (3¼ oz/¾ cup) slivered almonds
185 g (6½ oz/1½ cups) plain (all-purpose) flour
60 g (2¼ oz/½ cup) self-raising flour
2 tablespoons rum
100 g (3½ oz/⅔ cup) blanched whole almonds

METHOD

1 Preheat the oven to 150°C (300°F/Gas 2). Grease and line a 20 cm (8 inch) round tin (see below).
2 Cream the butter and sugar in a small bowl with electric beaters until light and creamy. Gradually add the eggs, beating well after each addition. Transfer to a large bowl and add the fruits, mixed peel and nuts. Using a metal spoon, fold in the sifted flours alternately with the rum. Stir to just combine. Do not overmix.
3 Spoon into the tin and smooth the surface. Arrange the whole almonds in a pattern over the top of the cake. Wrap the outside of the tin (see Note) and sit the cake tin on several layers of newspaper in the oven. Bake for 2–2½ hours, or until a skewer comes out clean when inserted into the centre of the cake. Leave the cake in the tin for at least 4 hours before turning out.

NOTE: Because of the long cooking time, fruit cakes require extra protection, both around the side and under the base. Wrap a few layers of newspaper around the outside of the tin, secure with kitchen string, and sit the tin on layers of newspaper in the oven. The oven temperature is low, so this is quite safe.

HOW TO... LINE A CAKE TIN

Before you mix your cake, line the tin and make sure the oven rack is positioned so the cake will sit in the centre of the oven. Fruit cakes need a double layer of baking paper for the collar and base. The collar gives extra protection during baking.

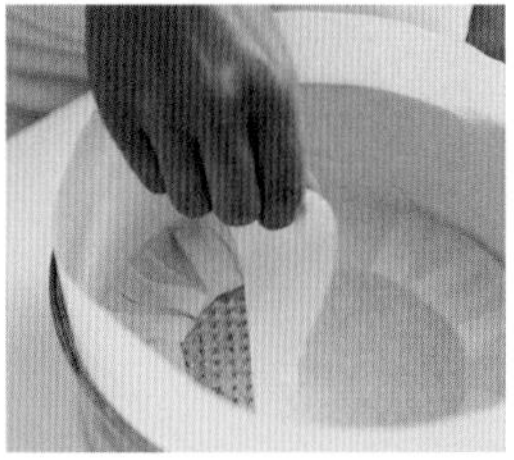

METHOD

1 Lightly grease the cake tin. Cut a double layer of baking paper into a strip long enough to fit around the outside of the tin and tall enough to come 5 cm (2 inches) above the edge of the tin. Fold down a cuff about 2 cm (¾ inch) deep along the length of the strip, along the folded edge. Make cuts along the cuff, cutting up to the fold line, about 1 cm (½ inch) apart. Fit the strip around the inside of the tin, with the cuts on the base, pressing the cuts out at right angles so they sit flat around the base.
2 Place the cake tin on a doubled piece of baking paper and draw around the edge. Cut out and sit the paper circles in the base of the tin.

ICING

Icing, sometimes called frosting, is a sweet, decorative covering for cakes, biscuits and buns. There are many types of icings, cooked and uncooked. Below are some basic icings and frostings that will suit most plain cakes or biscuits.

GLACE ICING

MAKES 1 QUANTITY

INGREDIENTS

155 g (5½ oz/1¼ cups) icing (confectioners') sugar
20 g (¾ oz) unsalted butter, melted
pink food colouring, or colour as desired

METHOD

1 Stir the icing sugar, butter and 2–3 teaspoons water together in a bowl until sooth. Mix in the food colouring, a few drops at a time, to achieve the desired shade of pink. Spread over finger buns or cakes.

CHOCOLATE GLAZE

MAKES 1 QUANTITY

INGREDIENTS

250 g (9 oz) dark chocolate, chopped
125 ml (4 fl oz/½ cup) cream
145 g (5½ oz/⅔ cup) caster (superfine) sugar

METHOD

1 Stir all the ingredients in a saucepan over low heat until melted. Bring to the boil, reduce the heat and simmer for 4–5 minutes. Remove from the heat and cool slightly before decorating the cake.

BUTTER FROSTING

MAKES 1 QUANTITY

INGREDIENTS

125 g (4½ oz) unsalted butter, softened
90 g (3¼ oz/¾ cup) icing (confectioners') sugar
1 tablespoon lemon juice

METHOD

1 Beat the butter, icing sugar and lemon juice using electric beaters until smooth and creamy.

CREAM CHEESE ICING

MAKES 1 QUANTITY

INGREDIENTS

175 g (6 oz) cream cheese, softened
60 g (2¼ oz) unsalted butter, softened
185 g (6½ oz/1½ cups) icing (confectioners') sugar
1 teaspoon vanilla extract
1–2 teaspoons lemon juice

METHOD

1 Beat the cream cheese and butter using electric beaters until smooth. Gradually add the icing sugar alternately with the vanilla and lemon juice, beating until light and creamy.

••SWEET PIES AND PASTRIES••

Pastries may come in many guises but they all share the same wonderful characteristics — they are at once tender and flaky, light and creamy, mouthwatering and delicate. The success to good pastry lies in the perfect combination of a meltingly crisp crust and the sublime filling it encases. We use pastry for tarts, pies, with their golden domed lids, hiding a mass of delicious soft fruits, and for little feathery light pastries, rolled or layered with nuts or fragrant spices, providing the perfect snack or appetiser.

TYPES OF PASTRY

Making pastry at home can appear daunting to a beginner, but it really is simple providing you follow a few rules and get to know your ingredients. Recipes in this book use five different types of pastry.

SHORTCRUST

The simplest and most versatile dough. It is made with flour and butter and just enough water to bind. The texture, once cooked, is light and crisp and it can be used for both sweet and savoury recipes.

SWEET SHORTCRUST

This is shortcrust pastry enriched with eggs and sugar, and used only in sweet dishes. Eggs help bind as well as add richness, and sugar sweetens the dough and provides extra crispness. Sweet shortcrust has a crumbly, biscuit-like texture.

CHOUX PASTRY

Made in a pan over heat and beaten firmly to incorporate air. Because it is a soft batter it is never rolled out, but is piped or spooned onto a baking tray. During cooking the mixture rises and the crust sets, leaving a hollow centre. This is then filled with a sweet or savoury filling.

PUFF PASTRY

Puff pastry consists of hundreds of layers of dough interlaced with butter. It is sold frozen in block form, or in ready-rolled sheets, or there is a recipe to make your own puff pastry on page 476. If using ready-made puff pastry, thaw the block pastry and roll out according to the recipe. The pastry sheets can usually be separated while still frozen, so you can thaw just the quantity required for a particular recipe. Always choose butter puff pastry, as the flavour and texture are superior to those made with commercial margarines.

FILO PASTRY

Making filo pastry can be quite challenging for the home cook, so we have given quantities for ready-made filo pastry in our recipes. Filo pastry is available fresh or frozen and is sold in packets of rolled sheets. If using frozen filo, you will need to thaw the whole packet to remove the required amount of sheets. Because filo pastry is exceptionally delicate, the sheets will crack and tear if allowed to dry out. Take one sheet at a time and keep the remainder covered with a clean, damp tea towel until required.

SHORTCRUST PASTRY

MAKES 400 G (14 OZ)

INGREDIENTS

220 g (7¾ oz/1¾ cups) plain (all-purpose) flour, sifted

150 g (5½ oz) unsalted butter, chilled and diced

¼ teaspoon salt

60 ml (2 fl oz/¼ cup) chilled water

METHOD

1 If making pastry using a food processor, put the flour, butter and salt in the food processor. Using the pulse button, process until the mixture resembles coarse breadcrumbs.

2 Add the chilled water gradually, and pulse just until a dough forms. If the mixture feels sticky, add a little more flour, 1 teaspoon at a time. If the dough is dry and not adhering, add a little more water, 1 teaspoon at a time. As soon as the mixture comes together, gently gather the dough together and lift it out onto a lightly floured surface. Press the dough into a flat, round disc. Cover with plastic wrap and refrigerate for 30 minutes.

3 If making the pastry by hand, sift the flour and salt into a large bowl and add the butter. Using your fingertips, rub the butter into the flour until the mixture resembles coarse breadcrumbs. Make a well in the centre.

4 Pour the chilled water into the well, then stir with a flat-bladed knife to incorporate the water. When the mixture starts to come together in small beads of dough, gently gather the dough together and lift it out onto a lightly floured surface. Gently press the dough together into a ball, kneading it lightly if necessary until the dough comes together. Press into a flat, round disc, cover with plastic wrap and refrigerate for 30 minutes. The dough is now ready to use. Roll out the dough and proceed as directed in the recipe.

SWEET SHORTCRUST PASTRY

MAKES 400 G (14 OZ)

INGREDIENTS

200 g (7 oz/1⅔ cups) plain (all-purpose) flour, sifted

85 g (2¾ oz/⅔ cup) icing (confectioners') sugar, sifted

100 g (3½ oz) chilled unsalted butter, chopped

1 egg yolk

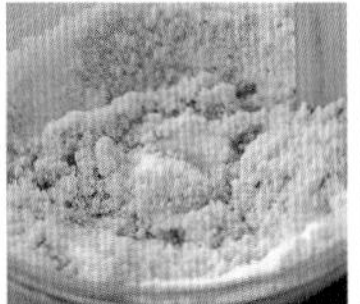

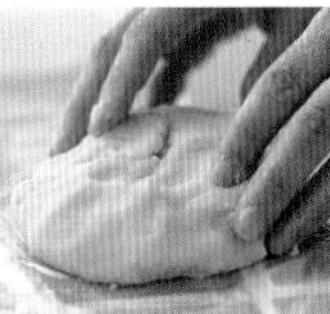

METHOD

1 If making pastry using a food processor, put the flour, icing sugar, butter and a pinch of salt in the food processor. Using the pulse button, process until the mixture resembles coarse breadcrumbs.

2 Combine the egg yolk with 3 tablespoons water in a small bowl. Add to the flour mixture and process using the pulse button, adding a little more water if necessary, until the dough just comes together. Turn out onto a lightly floured work surface and press the dough into a flat, round disc. Cover with plastic wrap and refrigerate for 30 minutes.

3 If making the pastry by hand, sift the flour, icing sugar and a pinch of salt into a large bowl, then add the butter. Using your fingertips, rub the butter into the flour until the mixture resembles coarse breadcrumbs. Make a well in the centre.

4 Combine the egg yolk with 3 tablespoons water in a small bowl. Pour it into the well, then stir with a flat-bladed knife, adding a little more water if necessary. When the mixture starts to come together in small beads of dough, gently gather the dough together and lift it out onto a lightly floured surface. Proceed as per step 2, above. The dough is now ready to use.

HOW TO... LINE A TART TIN

Metal loose-based tart tins are best to use for making tarts and pies. The metal conducts the heat well and the removable bottom makes it easy to remove the filled cooked tart without breaking it.

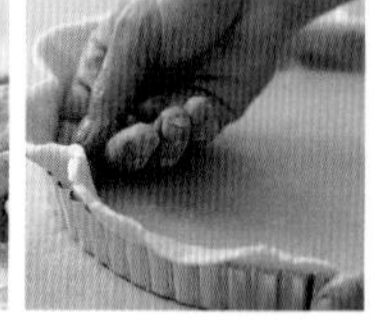

METHOD

1 Grease a metal loose-based tart tin. Lightly dust the work surface with flour and roll out the pastry until large enough to fit the tin.
2 Carefully fold the pastry back over and around the rolling pin and lift it gently from the surface. Unroll the pastry over the tin and ease it into the tin, pressing to fit the fluted side.
3 Trim the edge with a sharp knife or roll the pin across the top to cut off the excess dough. Gently push the pastry a little way above the edge of the tin.

HOW TO... BLIND BAKE

Blind baking starts cooking the pastry before the filling is put in. This stops the side collapsing as it cooks and also prevents the base becoming soggy.

METHOD

1 Line the pastry shell with a circle of baking paper and baking beads. (If you don't have baking beads, use uncooked dried beans or rice instead.)
2 Blind bake the pastry at 200°C (400°F/Gas 6) for 10–15 minutes, or until lightly cooked. Remove the paper and beads.
3 Return the pastry to the oven for 5 minutes — it should look completely dry. If you are using a very liquid filling, brush the pastry with a beaten egg while it is still hot, as this will close up any tiny holes.

TIPS FOR PERFECT PASTRY

* The kitchen needs to be as cool as possible when making pastry.
* The butter for pastry should be cold, straight from the refrigerator. Cut the butter into even-sized pieces, about 5 mm (¼ inch) thick.
* Flour should be sifted before use. This will remove any lumps and incorporate air into the flour, helping to make the dough light. For sweet shortcrust pastry, always sift icing sugar and flour to remove any lumps and help aerate them.
* If the dough is too cold to roll out it will crack easily, so leave at room temperature, still covered in plastic wrap, for 15 minutes to soften.
* Roll pastry out on a lightly floured work surface to prevent it sticking. Always roll from the middle outwards (not using a back-and-forth motion) and rotate the pastry frequently as you go to keep to the required shape. Occasionally use both hands to push the edges of the dough back inwards to help keep the shape.
* If possible, use a marble slab or a cold work surface to roll dough. This helps to keep the butter from warming up as it is rolled.
* If the dough feels really soft and starts to stick to the work surface, roll it out between two sheets of baking paper.
* Never pull or stretch pastry as you roll it or the pastry will shrink during cooking.

CHOUX PASTRY

This pastry is unlike other pastry in that the dough is cooked twice. Making choux is an exact process — weigh all the ingredients and follow the instructions to the letter.

MAKES ABOUT 50 CHOUX PUFFS OR 20 ECLAIRS

INGREDIENTS

- 100 g (3½ oz) unsalted butter
- 1 teaspoon caster (superfine) sugar
- 140 g (5 oz) plain (all-purpose) flour
- 3 eggs, lightly beaten

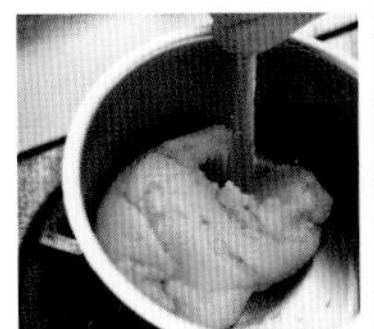

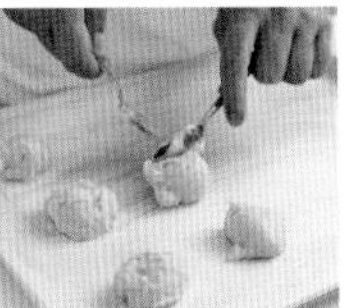

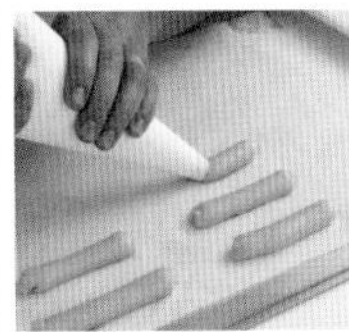

METHOD

1. Preheat the oven to 200°C (400°F/Gas 6). Lightly grease or line a baking tray with baking paper.
2. Put 250 ml (9 fl oz/1 cup) water, the butter and sugar in a small saucepan and heat until the butter has melted and the mixture has just come to the boil. Add the flour and, using a wooden spoon, stir over medium heat until the mixture comes away from the side of the saucepan, forming a ball.
3. Place the mixture into the bowl of an electric mixer fitted with a whisk attachment and allow to cool slightly. Add the eggs gradually, beating well after each addition and waiting until the egg is incorporated before adding the next. (Alternatively, you can use a hand mixer or wooden spoon to mix the ingredients.) The mixture should be thick and glossy. The pastry is now ready to use and may be piped, spooned or shaped according to the recipe you are using.
4. To make choux puffs, using 2 teaspoons, place heaped and rounded teaspoonfuls of the mixture on baking trays, spacing them 4 cm (1½ inches) apart. If desired, neaten off the tops of the mixture using a damp finger. Sprinkle the baking trays with water — this creates steam in the oven, which will help the puffs to rise. Bake for 20 minutes, then reduce the heat to 160°C (315°F/Gas 2–3) and bake for a further 20 minutes, or until puffed, golden and dry (pull one puff apart to see if it is dry inside). Turn off the oven, open the door slightly, and leave the pastries in the oven until cool.
5. To make éclairs, put the choux pastry into a piping (icing) bag fitted with a 2 cm (¾ inch) plain nozzle. Pipe 10 cm (4 inch) lengths of choux onto the baking tray, spacing them 4 cm (1½ inches) apart. Bake as for choux puffs.

TIPS FOR PERFECT CHOUX PASTRY

* Always preheat the oven before beginning to make the choux pastry, as it needs to be cooked as soon as it is shaped or piped. Likewise, prepare your equipment before you start. Line the baking tray with baking paper. If piping the dough, fit a large plain nozzle to the piping (icing) bag.
* Add the flour to the boiling mixture in one go, then immediately beat the mixture with a wooden spoon to prevent lumps forming. Stop beating as soon as the soft dough comes away from the sides of the pan and remove from the heat.
* Always allow the hot mixture to cool for 2–3 minutes before adding eggs or they can start to cook.
* The dough is ready when it is smooth and glossy. It should be piped or shaped while it is still warm.

APPLE PIE

SERVES 6

INGREDIENTS

FILLING

6 large granny smith apples, peeled, cored and cut into wedges
2 tablespoons caster (superfine) sugar
1 teaspoon finely grated lemon zest
pinch of ground cloves

PASTRY

250 g (9 oz/2 cups) plain (all-purpose) flour
30 g (1 oz/¼ cup) self-raising flour
150 g (5½ oz) chilled unsalted butter, cubed
2 tablespoons caster (superfine) sugar
80–100 ml (2½–3½ fl oz) chilled water

2 tablespoons marmalade
1 egg, lightly beaten
1 tablespoon sugar

METHOD

1 Lightly grease a 23 cm (9 inch) pie dish.

2 To make the filling, put all the ingredients in a saucepan with 2 tablespoons water. Cover and cook over low heat for 8 minutes, or until the apples are just tender, shaking the pan occasionally. Drain and cool completely.

3 To make the pastry, sift the flours into a bowl. Using your fingertips, rub in the butter until the mixture resembles fine breadcrumbs. Stir in the sugar, then make a well in the centre. Add almost all the chilled water and mix with a flat-bladed knife, using a cutting action, until the mixture comes together in beads. Add more water if the dough is too dry. Gather together and lift out onto a lightly floured work surface. Press into a ball and divide into two, making one portion a little bigger. Cover with plastic wrap and refrigerate for 20 minutes.

4 Preheat the oven to 200°C (400°F/Gas 6). Roll out the larger piece of pastry between two sheets of baking paper to line the base and side of the pie dish. Line the pie dish with the pastry. Use a small sharp knife to trim away any excess pastry. Brush the marmalade over the base and spoon the apple mixture into the shell. Roll out the other pastry portion between the baking paper until large enough to cover the pie. Brush water around the rim, then lay the pastry top over the pie. Trim off any excess pastry, pinch the edges and cut a few slits in the top to allow the steam to escape.

5 Re-roll the pastry scraps and cut into leaves for decoration. Lightly brush the top with egg, then sprinkle with sugar. Bake for 20 minutes, then reduce the oven to 180°C (350°F/Gas 4) and bake for another 15–20 minutes, or until golden.

LEMON MERINGUE PIE

SERVES 6

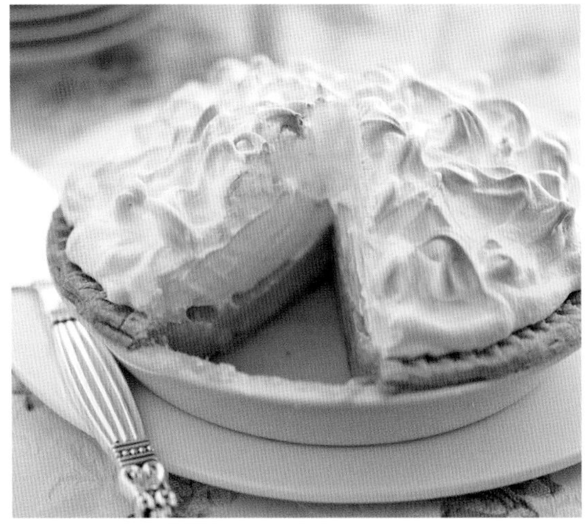

INGREDIENTS

185 g (6½ oz/1½ cups) plain (all-purpose) flour
2 tablespoons icing (confectioners') sugar
125 g (4½ oz) unsalted butter, chilled and cubed
60 ml (2 fl oz/¼ cup) chilled water

FILLING AND MERINGUE

30 g (1 oz/¼ cup) cornflour (cornstarch)
30 g (1 oz/¼ cup) plain (all-purpose) flour
230 g (8½ oz/1 cup) caster (superfine) sugar
185 ml (6 fl oz/¾ cup) lemon juice
3 teaspoons finely grated lemon zest
40 g (1½ oz) unsalted butter, chopped
6 eggs, separated
345 g (12 oz/1½ cups) caster (superfine) sugar, extra
½ teaspoon cornflour (cornstarch), extra

METHOD

1. Sift the flour and icing sugar into a large bowl. Using your fingertips, rub in the butter until the mixture resembles fine breadcrumbs. Add almost all the water and mix with a flat-bladed knife, using a cutting action, until the mixture forms a firm dough. Add more liquid if the dough is too dry. Turn onto a lightly floured surface and gather together into a ball. Roll between two sheets of baking paper until large enough to fit a 23 cm (9 inch) pie dish. Line the dish with the pastry, trim and refrigerate for 20 minutes. Preheat the oven to 180°C (350°F/Gas 4).
2. Line the pastry with a sheet of baking paper and spread a layer of baking beads or uncooked rice evenly over the paper. Bake for 10 minutes, then remove the paper and beads. Bake for a further 5–10 minutes, or until the pastry is lightly golden. Leave to cool.
3. To make the filling, put the flours and sugar in a saucepan. Whisk in the lemon juice, zest and 375 ml (13 fl oz/1½ cups) water. Whisk continually over medium heat until the mixture boils and thickens. Reduce the heat and cook for another minute, then whisk in the butter and egg yolks, one yolk at a time. Transfer to a bowl, cover the surface with plastic wrap and set aside to cool completely.
4. To make the meringue topping, increase the oven temperature to 220°C (425°F/Gas 7). Beat the egg whites in a small dry bowl using electric beaters, until soft peaks form. Add the extra sugar gradually, beating constantly until the meringue is thick and glossy. Beat in the extra cornflour. Pour the cold filling into the cold pastry shell. Spread with meringue to cover, forming peaks. Bake for 5–10 minutes, or until lightly browned. Serve hot or cold.

LEMON TART

SERVES 6–8

INGREDIENTS

PASTRY

185 g (6½ oz/1½ cups) plain (all-purpose) flour
60 g (2¼ oz/½ cup) icing (confectioners') sugar
35 g (1¼ oz/⅓ cup) ground almonds
125 g (4½ oz) unsalted butter, chilled and cubed
1 egg yolk, at room temperature

FILLING

1½ tablespoons finely grated lemon zest
80 ml (2½ fl oz/⅓ cup) lemon juice, strained
5 eggs, at room temperature
170 g (6 oz/¾ cup) caster (superfine) sugar
300 ml (10½ fl oz) cream

icing (confectioners') sugar, to dust
cream, to serve

METHOD

1 To make the pastry, sift the flour, icing sugar and ground almonds into a large bowl. Using your fingertips, rub in the butter until the mixture resembles fine breadcrumbs. Make a well in the centre, add the egg yolk and mix with a flat-bladed knife, using a cutting action, until the mixture forms a dough. Knead gently and briefly on a floured surface until the dough is smooth. Form into a ball, flatten into a disc, cover with plastic wrap and refrigerate for 30 minutes.

2 Preheat the oven to 180°C (350°F/Gas 4). Grease a 22 cm (8½ inch) loose-based tart tin. Roll out the pastry between two sheets of baking paper to a thickness of 3 mm (⅛ inch) to cover the base and side of the tin. Peel off the top sheet of baking paper, carefully invert the pastry into the tin and peel off the second sheet of paper. Press the pastry gently into the base and side, ensuring the pastry is level with the top of the tin. Trim off any excess pastry. Refrigerate for 10 minutes.

3 Line the pastry with a sheet of baking paper and spread a layer of baking beads or uncooked rice evenly over the paper. Place the tin on a baking tray and bake for 10 minutes, then remove the paper and beads. Bake for a further 10–15 minutes, or until light golden. Set aside to cool. Reduce the oven to 140°C (275°F/Gas 1).

4 To make the filling, put the lemon zest, lemon juice, eggs, sugar and cream in a bowl and whisk until combined. Set aside for 10 minutes to allow the lemon zest to infuse the mixture, then strain the mixture. Carefully pour the filling into the pastry shell and bake for 45–50 minutes, or until just set. Set aside to cool for 10 minutes, then refrigerate until cold. Dust the tart with icing sugar and serve with cream.

COOKING WITH LEMONS

* For zesting, buy unwaxed lemons or scrub the skins with warm water before you use them.
* To save cleaning fiddly citrus zest out of your grater, stick a piece of baking paper against the grater before you use it. When you pull off the paper, all the zest will come with it.
* When juicing lemons, warm them for a couple of seconds in the microwave, as this helps the juice run.

LIME CHIFFON PIE

SERVES 12

INGREDIENTS

ALMOND PASTRY

150 g (5½ oz/1¼ cups) plain (all-purpose) flour
90 g (3¼ oz) ground almonds
90 g (3¼ oz) chilled unsalted butter, chopped
1–2 tablespoons chilled water

FILLING

6 egg yolks
115 g (4 oz/½ cup) caster (superfine) sugar
100 g (3½ oz) unsalted butter, melted
80 ml (2½ fl oz/⅓ cup) lime juice
2 teaspoons finely grated lime zest
2 teaspoons powdered gelatine
125 ml (4 fl oz/½ cup) cream, whipped

METHOD

1 Sift the flour into a large bowl and add the ground almonds. Using your fingertips, rub in the butter until the mixture resembles fine breadcrumbs. Add almost all the chilled water and mix with a flat-bladed knife, using a cutting action, until the mixture forms a firm dough. Add more water if necessary. Turn onto a lightly floured surface and gather together into a ball. Roll the pastry out to fit a 23 cm (9 inch) fluted tart tin. Line the tin, trim the edges and refrigerate for 20 minutes.

2 Preheat the oven to 180°C (350°F/Gas 4). Line the pastry with a sheet of baking paper and spread a layer of baking beads or uncooked rice evenly over the paper. Bake for 20 minutes, then remove the paper and beads. Bake for a further 10–15 minutes, or until the pastry is lightly golden. Allow to cool completely.

3 To make the filling, put the egg yolks, sugar, butter, lime juice and zest in a heatproof bowl. Whisk to combine and dissolve the sugar. Sit the bowl over a saucepan of simmering water, making sure the base of the bowl does not touch the water, and stir for 15 minutes, or until the mixture thickens. Remove from the heat and cool slightly.

4 Put 1 tablespoon water in a small heatproof bowl, sprinkle the gelatine in an even layer over the surface and leave to go spongy. Do not stir. Bring a small saucepan filled with about 4 cm (1½ inches) water to the boil, remove from the heat and place the bowl into the pan. The water should come halfway up the side of the bowl. Stir the gelatine until clear and dissolved. Cool slightly, add to the lime curd and stir to combine. Cool to room temperature, stirring occasionally.

5 Fold the whipped cream through the lime curd and pour into the pastry case. Refrigerate for 2–3 hours, until set. Leave the pie for 15 minutes at room temperature before serving. Serve with extra whipped cream.

LIMES

Limes are a small green-skinned citrus fruit native to the tropics. Limes are related to the lemon, and can be used like lemons but as the juice is more acidic, usually less is needed. Both lime juice and the zest add a piquant flavour to sweet dishes such as ice cream and sorbets, as well as curries, stews and fish dishes. Like lemons, warm limes in a microwave for 2–3 seconds before squeezing them to help the juice flow.

PUMPKIN PIE

SERVES 8

INGREDIENTS

FILLING

500 g (1 lb 2 oz) pumpkin (winter squash), cubed
2 eggs, lightly beaten
140 g (5 oz/¾ cup) soft brown sugar
80 ml (2½ fl oz/⅓ cup) cream
1 tablespoon sweet sherry
1 teaspoon ground cinnamon
½ teaspoon ground nutmeg
½ teaspoon ground ginger

PASTRY

150 g (5½ oz/1¼ cups) plain (all-purpose) flour
100 g (3½ oz) unsalted butter, chilled and cubed
2 teaspoons caster (superfine) sugar
80 ml (2½ fl oz/⅓ cup) chilled water
1 egg yolk, lightly beaten, to glaze
1 tablespoon milk, to glaze

METHOD

1 Lightly grease a 23 cm (9 inch) round pie dish. Steam or boil the pumpkin for 10 minutes, or until just tender. Drain the pumpkin thoroughly, then mash and set aside to cool.

2 To make the pastry, sift the flour into a large bowl. Using your fingertips, rub in the butter until the mixture resembles fine breadcrumbs. Stir in the caster sugar. Make a well in the centre, add almost all the water and mix with a flat-bladed knife, using a cutting action, until the mixture comes together in beads. Add the remaining water if the dough is too dry.

3 Gather the dough together and roll out between two sheets of baking paper until large enough to cover the base and side of the dish. Line the dish with pastry, trim away the excess pastry and crimp the edges. If you like, make pastry decorations for the pie. Roll out the pastry trimmings to 2 mm (1⁄16 inch) thick. Using a sharp knife, cut out leaf shapes of different sizes and score vein markings onto the leaves. Refrigerate the pastry-lined dish and the leaf shapes for about 20 minutes.

4 Preheat the oven to 180°C (350°F/Gas 4). Line the pastry with a sheet of baking paper and spread a layer of baking beads or uncooked rice evenly over the paper. Bake for 10 minutes, then remove the paper and beads. Bake for a further 10 minutes, or until the pastry is lightly golden. Leave to cool. Meanwhile, place the leaves on a baking tray lined with baking paper, brush with the combined egg yolk and milk and bake for 10–15 minutes, or until lightly golden. Set aside to cool.

5 To make the filling, whisk the eggs and brown sugar in a large bowl. Add the cooled mashed pumpkin, cream, sherry, cinnamon, nutmeg and ginger and stir to combine thoroughly. Pour the filling into the pastry shell, smooth the surface with the back of a spoon and bake for 40 minutes, or until set. If the pastry edges begin to brown too much during cooking, cover the edges with foil. Allow the pie to cool to room temperature. If using leaf decorations, arrange them over the pie. Serve with ice cream or whipped cream.

TARTE TATIN

A French upside-down apple tart named after the two French sisters who first served it in their restaurant. The French give it the name of *la tarte des demoiselles Tatin*, meaning 'the tart of the two unmarried women named Tatin'. Tarte Tatin is now also made with pears, pineapple, mango or even vegetables such as shallots.

SERVES 6

INGREDIENTS

- 210 g (7½ oz/1⅔ cups) plain (all-purpose) flour
- 125 g (4½ oz) unsalted butter, chilled and cubed
- 2 tablespoons caster (superfine) sugar
- 1 egg, lightly beaten
- 2 drops vanilla extract
- 8 granny smith apples
- 110 g (3¾ oz/½ cup) sugar
- 40 g (1½ oz) unsalted butter, extra, chopped

METHOD

1. Sift the flour into a bowl. Using your fingertips, rub in the butter until the mixture resembles fine breadcrumbs. Stir in the sugar, then make a well in the centre. Add the egg and vanilla and mix with a flat-bladed knife, using a cutting action, until the mixture comes together in beads. Gather the dough together, then turn out onto a lightly floured work surface and shape into a disc. Cover with plastic wrap and refrigerate for at least 30 minutes, to firm.
2. Peel and core the apples and cut each into eight slices. Put the sugar and 1 tablespoon water in a heavy-based 25 cm (10 inch) frying pan that has a metal or removable handle, so that it can safely be placed in the oven. Stir over low heat for 1 minute, or until the sugar has dissolved. Increase the heat to medium and cook for 4–5 minutes, or until the caramel turns golden. Add the extra butter and stir to incorporate. Remove from the heat.
3. Place the apple slices in neat circles to cover the base of the frying pan. Return the pan to low heat and cook for 10–12 minutes, or until the apples are tender and caramelised. Remove the pan from the heat and leave to cool for 10 minutes.
4. Preheat the oven to 220°C (425°F/Gas 7). Roll the pastry out on a lightly floured surface to a circle 1 cm (½ inch) larger than the frying pan. Place the pastry over the apples to cover them completely, tucking it down firmly at the edges. Bake for 30–35 minutes, or until the pastry is cooked. Leave for 15 minutes before turning out onto a plate. Serve warm or cold with cream or ice cream.

NOTE: Tarte Tatin can be made in any metal pan, but there are special tins for it, similar to a frying pan but without a handle. If you don't have one, any frying pan or crepe pan with a heatproof handle will do. Ceramic dishes do not make good tarte Tatin, as the heat conduction is often not high enough to make the caramel darken.

FRUIT MINCE PIES

MAKES 24

INGREDIENTS

FRUIT MINCE

- 40 g (1½ oz/⅓ cup) raisins, chopped
- 60 g (2¼ oz/⅓ cup) soft brown sugar
- 30 g (1 oz/¼ cup) sultanas
- 50 g (1¾ oz/¼ cup) mixed peel
- 1 tablespoon currants
- 1 tablespoon chopped almonds
- 1 small apple, grated
- 1 teaspoon lemon juice
- ½ teaspoon finely grated orange zest
- ½ teaspoon finely grated lemon zest
- ½ teaspoon mixed spice
- pinch of ground nutmeg
- 25 g (1 oz) unsalted butter, melted
- 1 tablespoon brandy

PASTRY

- 250 g (9 oz/2 cups) plain (all-purpose) flour
- 150 g (5½ oz) unsalted butter, chilled and cubed
- 85 g (3 oz/⅔ cup) icing (confectioners') sugar
- 2–3 tablespoons chilled water

METHOD

1 To make the fruit mince, combine all the ingredients in a bowl, spoon into a sterilised jar and seal. You can use the fruit mince straightaway but the flavours develop if kept for a while. Keep it in a cool dark place for up to 3 months. (Use ready-made fruit mince if you are short of time.)

2 Preheat the oven to 180°C (350°F/Gas 4). Lightly grease two 12-hole shallow patty pans or mini muffin tins.

3 To make the pastry, sift the flour into a bowl. Using your fingertips, rub in the butter until the mixture resembles fine breadcrumbs. Stir in the icing sugar and make a well in the centre. Add almost all the water and mix with a flat-bladed knife, using a cutting action, until the mixture comes together in beads. Add the remaining water if the dough is too dry. Turn out onto a lightly floured work surface and gather into a ball. Roll out two-thirds of the pastry and cut out 24 rounds, slightly larger than the holes in the patty pans, with a round fluted cutter. Fit the rounds into the tins.

4 Divide the fruit mince evenly among the pastry cases. Roll out the remaining pastry, a little thinner than before, and cut 12 rounds with the same cutter. Using a smaller fluted cutter, cut 12 more rounds. Place the large circles on top of half the pies and press the edges to seal. Place the smaller circles on the remainder. Bake for 25 minutes, or until golden. Leave in the tins for 5 minutes, then lift out with a knife and cool on wire racks. Dust lightly with icing sugar.

FREEFORM BLUEBERRY PIE

SERVES 4

INGREDIENTS

185 g (6½ oz/1½ cups) plain (all-purpose) flour
60 g (2¼ oz/½ cup) icing (confectioners') sugar
125 g (4½ oz) unsalted butter, chilled and cubed
60 ml (2 fl oz/¼ cup) lemon juice
500 g (1 lb 2 oz) blueberries
30 g (1 oz/¼ cup) icing (confectioners') sugar, extra
1 teaspoon finely grated lemon zest
½ teaspoon ground cinnamon
1 egg white, lightly beaten

METHOD

1 Preheat the oven to 180°C (350°F/Gas 4). Sift the flour and icing sugar into a bowl. Using your fingertips, rub in the butter until the mixture resembles fine breadcrumbs. Make a well in the centre and add almost all the juice. Mix together with a flat-bladed knife, using a cutting action, until the mixture comes together in beads. Add the remaining juice if the dough is too dry.
2 Gently gather the dough together and lift onto a sheet of baking paper. Roll out to a circle about 30 cm (12 inches) in diameter. Cover with plastic wrap and refrigerate for 10 minutes. Put the blueberries in a bowl and sprinkle them with the icing sugar, lemon zest and cinnamon.
3 Place the pastry (still on the baking paper) on a baking tray. Brush the centre of the pastry lightly with egg white. Pile the blueberry mixture onto the pastry in a 20 cm (8 inch) diameter circle, then fold the edges of the pastry over the filling, leaving the centre uncovered. Transfer the tray to the oven and bake for 30–35 minutes, or until the pastry is golden and cooked. Dust with icing sugar and serve warm with whipped cream or ice cream.

CRANBERRY TARTLETS

MAKES 12

INGREDIENTS

½ quantity sweet shortcrust pastry (page 533)
120 g (4¼ oz) frozen cranberries, defrosted
1 tablespoon sugar
2 tablespoons seedless berry jam
100 g (3½ oz) mascarpone cheese

METHOD

1 Preheat the oven to 180°C (350°F/Gas 4). Lightly grease 12 tartlet tins.
2 Roll out the pastry and cut out 12 circles using a 7 cm (2¾ inch) fluted cutter and line the tins, Prick the pastries all over with a fork and bake for 12–15 minutes, or until cooked and golden.
3 Put the cranberries in a saucepan with the sugar and jam. Stir over low heat, taking care not to break up the cranberries. Cool.
4 To fill the tartlets, spread a teaspoon of the mascarpone into the base of the pastries. Arrange the cranberries and syrup over the top.

NOTE: Alternatively, use halved strawberries. Melt the jam and brush it over the fruit.

PORTUGUESE CUSTARD TARTS

MAKES 12

INGREDIENTS

- 150 g (5½ oz/1¼ cups) plain (all-purpose) flour
- 25 g (1 oz) Copha (white vegetable shortening), chopped and softened
- 30 g (1 oz) unsalted butter, chopped and softened
- 220 g (7¾ oz/1 cup) sugar
- 500 ml (17 fl oz/2 cups) milk
- 30 g (1 oz/¼ cup) cornflour (cornstarch)
- 1 tablespoon custard powder
- 4 egg yolks
- 1 teaspoon vanilla extract

METHOD

1 Sift the flour into a large bowl and add about 185 ml (6 fl oz/¾ cup) water, or enough to form a soft dough. Gather the dough into a ball, then roll out on baking paper to form a 24 x 30 cm (9½ x 12 inch) rectangle.

2 Spread the Copha over the surface. Roll up from the short edge to form a log. Roll the dough out into a rectangle again and spread with the butter. Roll up again into a roll and slice into 12 even pieces. Working from the centre outwards, use your fingertips to press each round out to a circle large enough to cover the base and side of twelve 80 ml (2½ fl oz/⅓ cup) muffin holes. Press into the holes and refrigerate while preparing the filling.

3 Put the sugar and 80 ml (2½ fl oz/⅓ cup) water in a saucepan and stir over low heat until the sugar dissolves. Stir a little of the milk with the cornflour and custard powder in a small bowl to form a smooth paste. Add to the pan with the remaining milk, egg yolks and vanilla. Stir over low heat until the mixture thickens. Transfer to a bowl, cover and cool.

4 Preheat the oven to 220°C (425°F/Gas 7). Divide the filling among the pastry bases and bake for 25–30 minutes, or until the custard has set and the tops have browned. Cool in the tins, then transfer to a wire rack.

CORNFLOUR

Cornflour (cornstarch) is a fine, white powder milled from corn and used to thicken custards and in desserts such as blancmange. Cornflour must be slaked into a liquid (first mixed with a small amount of cold water) before it is heated. Pure cornflour contains no protein (gluten) and, unlike flour, when it is cooked it will turn clear. Sauces made with cornflour will begin to thin again if cooked for too long. Some types of cornflour are milled from wheat and are labelled as 'wheaten cornflour' to prevent confusion. Pure cornflour has a stronger thickening power and produces a smoother liquid than wheaten cornflour.

WALNUT TART

SERVES 8

INGREDIENTS

- 1 quantity sweet shortcrust pastry (page 533)
- 4 eggs
- 185 g (6½ oz/1 cup) soft brown sugar
- 170 g (6 oz/½ cup) golden syrup
- 55 g (2 oz) unsalted butter, melted
- 1 teaspoon vanilla extract
- 2 tablespoons plain (all-purpose) flour
- 300 g (10½ oz) walnut halves

METHOD

1. Preheat the oven to 200°C (400°F/Gas 6). Line a 25 cm (10 inch) tart tin with the pastry and blind bake the shell (page 534). Reduce the oven to 180°C (350°F/Gas 4).
2. Whisk together the eggs, sugar, golden syrup, butter, vanilla and flour.
3. Roughly chop the walnuts, scatter over the base, then pour the filling over the top. Bake for 35–40 minutes, or until set and golden brown. Cover with foil if browning too much. Serve with cream or ice cream.

PECAN PIE

SERVES 6

INGREDIENTS

SHORTCRUST PASTRY

185 g (6½ oz/1½ cups) plain (all-purpose) flour
125 g (4½ oz) unsalted butter, chilled and chopped
2–3 tablespoons chilled water

FILLING

200 g (7 oz/2 cups) pecans
3 eggs, lightly beaten
50 g (1¾ oz) unsalted butter, melted and cooled
140 g (5 oz/¾ cup) soft brown sugar
170 ml (5½ fl oz/⅔ cup) light corn syrup
1 teaspoon vanilla extract

METHOD

1 Preheat the oven to 180°C (350°F/Gas 4). Sift the flour into a large bowl. Using your fingertips, rub in the butter until the mixture resembles fine breadcrumbs. Add almost all the water and mix with a flat-bladed knife, using a cutting action, until the mixture comes together in beads. Turn out onto a floured surface and gather into a ball.
2 Roll out the pastry to a 35 cm (14 inch) round. Line a 23 cm (9 inch) tart tin with pastry, trim the edges and refrigerate for 20 minutes. Pile the pastry trimmings together and roll out to a rectangle 2 mm (1⁄16 inch) thick, then refrigerate.
3 Blind bake the pastry for 15 minutes, then remove the paper and beads and bake for another 15 minutes (see Blind baking, page 534).
4 Spread the pecans over the cooled pastry base. Whisk together the eggs, butter, sugar, corn syrup, vanilla and a pinch of salt until well combined, then pour over the pecans.
5 Using a fluted pastry wheel, cut narrow strips from half the pastry trimmings. Cut out small stars with a cutter from the remaining trimmings. Arrange over the filling. Bake for 45 minutes, or until firm. Serve at room temperature.

BAKEWELL TART

SERVES 6

INGREDIENTS

125 g (4½ oz/1 cup) plain (all-purpose) flour
90 g (3¼ oz) unsalted butter, chilled and cubed
2 teaspoons caster (superfine) sugar
2 tablespoons chilled water

FILLING

90 g (3¼ oz) unsalted butter
80 g (2¾ oz/⅓ cup) caster (superfine) sugar
2 eggs, lightly beaten
3 drops almond extract
70 g (2½ oz/⅔ cup) ground almonds
40 g (1½ oz/⅓ cup) self-raising flour, sifted
160 g (5¾ oz/½ cup) raspberry jam
25 g (1 oz/¼ cup) flaked almonds

METHOD

1 Preheat the oven to 180°C (350°F/Gas 4). Grease a 20 cm (8 inch) round, loose-based, fluted tart tin.
2 Sift the flour into a large bowl and rub in the butter until the mixture resembles fine crumbs. Stir in the sugar. Add almost all the water and mix with a flat-bladed knife until the mixture comes together in beads, adding more water if needed. Gather the dough together and roll out between two sheets of baking paper to cover the base and side of the tin. Line the tin with the pastry, trim the edges and refrigerate for 20 minutes.
3 Blind bake the pastry for 10 minutes, then remove the paper and beads and bake for another 7 minutes (see Blind baking, page 534).
4 To make the filling, beat the butter and sugar in a small bowl until light and creamy. Add the egg gradually, beating after each addition. Beat in the almond extract. Transfer to a large bowl and fold in the almonds and flour. Spread the jam over the pastry, then spoon the almond mixture on top. Bake for 35 minutes, or until golden. Sprinkle with the flaked almonds.

BAKLAVA

MAKES 18 PIECES

INGREDIENTS

- 520 g (1 lb 2 oz/ 2¼ cups) caster (superfine) sugar
- 1½ teaspoons finely grated lemon zest
- 90 g (3¼ oz/¼ cup) honey
- 60 ml (2 fl oz/¼ cup) lemon juice
- 2 tablespoons orange flower water
- 200 g (7 oz) walnuts, finely chopped
- 200 g (7 oz) shelled pistachios, finely chopped
- 200 g (7 oz) almonds, finely chopped
- 2 tablespoons caster (superfine) sugar, extra
- 2 teaspoons ground cinnamon
- 200 g (7 oz) unsalted butter, melted
- 375 g (13 oz) filo pastry

METHOD

1 Put the sugar, lemon zest and 375 ml (13 fl oz/ 1½ cups) water in a saucepan and stir over high heat until the sugar has dissolved, then boil for 5 minutes. Reduce the heat to low and simmer for 5 minutes, or until the syrup has thickened slightly and just coats the back of a spoon. Add the honey, lemon juice and orange flower water and cook for 2 minutes. Remove from the heat and leave to cool completely.

2 Preheat the oven to 170°C (325°F/Gas 3). Combine the nuts, extra sugar and cinnamon in a bowl. Using melted butter, brush the base and sides of a 30 x 27 cm (12 x 11 inch) baking dish or tin. Cover the base with a single layer of filo pastry, brush lightly with the butter, folding in any overhanging edges. Continue layering the filo, brushing each new layer with butter and folding in the edges until 10 sheets have been used. Keep the unused filo under a damp tea towel.

3 Sprinkle half the nut mixture over the pastry and pat down evenly. Repeat the layering and buttering of 5 more filo sheets, sprinkle with the remaining nuts, then continue to layer and butter the remaining sheets, including the top layer. Press down with your hands so the pastry and nuts adhere to each other. Using a large sharp knife, cut into diamond shapes, ensuring you cut through to the bottom layer. Pour any remaining butter evenly over the top and smooth with your hands. Bake for 30 minutes, then lower the temperature to 150°C (300°F/Gas 2) and cook for another 30 minutes.

4 Immediately cut through the original diamond markings, then strain the syrup evenly over the top. Cool completely before lifting the diamonds out onto a serving platter.

NOTE: To achieve the right texture, it is important for the baklava to be piping hot and the syrup cold when pouring the syrup.

CHERRY CHEESE STRUDEL

SERVES 8–10

INGREDIENTS

500 g (1 lb 2 oz/2 cups) ricotta cheese
2 teaspoons finely grated lemon or orange zest
60 g (2¼ oz/¼ cup) sugar
40 g (1½ oz/½ cup) fresh breadcrumbs
2 tablespoons ground almonds
2 eggs
425 g (15 oz) tin pitted black cherries
2 teaspoons cornflour (cornstarch)
8 sheets filo pastry
60 g (2¼ oz) unsalted butter, melted
2 tablespoons dry breadcrumbs
icing (confectioners') sugar, to dust

METHOD

1 Preheat the oven to 180°C (350°F/Gas 4). Lightly grease a baking tray with melted butter. Combine the ricotta, zest, sugar, breadcrumbs and almonds in a bowl. Add the eggs and mix well. Drain the cherries, reserving half the juice. Blend the cornflour with the reserved cherry juice in a small saucepan. Stir over heat until the mixture boils and thickens, then cool slightly.

2 Layer the pastry sheets, brushing between each sheet with melted butter and sprinkling with a few breadcrumbs. Form a large square by placing the second sheet halfway down the first sheet. Alternate layers, brushing with melted butter and sprinkling with breadcrumbs.

3 Place the ricotta mixture along one edge of the pastry. Shape into a log and top with the cherries and syrup. Roll the pastry around the ricotta filling, folding in the edges as you roll. Finish with a pastry edge underneath. Place on the tray and bake for 35–40 minutes, or until the pastry is golden. Serve, heavily dusted with icing sugar.

NOTE: To make an apple strudel, fill the strudel with a mixture of cooked apples with some sultanas or raisins, roll and bake.

SUGAR SPICE PALMIERS

MAKES 32

INGREDIENTS

500 g (1 lb 2 oz) block puff pastry, thawed
2 tablespoons sugar
1 teaspoon mixed spice
1 teaspoon ground cinnamon
40 g (1½ oz) unsalted butter, melted
icing (confectioners') sugar, to dust

METHOD

1 Preheat the oven to 210°C (415°F/Gas 6–7). Grease two baking trays and line with baking paper. Roll out the pastry between two sheets of baking paper to make a 30 cm (12 inch) square, 3 mm (⅛ inch) thick. Combine the sugar and spices in a small bowl. Cut the sheet of pastry in half, then brush each with melted butter. Sprinkle with the sugar mixture, reserving 2 teaspoons.

2 Take one half of pastry, fold the short edges of the pastry inwards to almost meet in the centre. Fold the same way again, then fold over and place on baking paper. Repeat with the other half. Refrigerate both portions for 15 minutes. Using a small knife, cut each half into 16 slices.

3 Arrange the palmiers, cut side up, on the trays, brush with a little butter and sprinkle with the reserved sugar mixture. Bake for 20 minutes, or until golden. When cool, dust with icing sugar.

FRANGIPANE TART

Frangipane is a rich, almond-flavoured paste used in patisserie making and as a filling for croissants, Danish pastries and pithiviers. Frangipane is also the name of an almond-based crème pâtissière. The name is thought to have been derived from a sixteenth-century nobleman, Marquis Frangipani, who invented a perfume made from bitter almonds, which he used for scenting ladies' gloves.

SERVES 8

INGREDIENTS

- 65 g (2¼ oz) unsalted butter
- 65 g (2¼ oz) caster (superfine) sugar
- 1 egg
- 65 g (2¼ oz) ground almonds
- 3 drops almond extract
- 10 g (¼ oz) plain (all-purpose) flour
- 2 x 375 g (13 oz) blocks puff pastry, thawed
- 1 egg, extra, lightly beaten

METHOD

1. Preheat the oven to 220°C (425°F/Gas 7). Lightly grease a baking tray.
2. To make the frangipane, cream the butter and sugar until light and creamy. Beat in the egg, ground almonds, almond extract and flour.
3. Roll out each block of puff pastry into two 16 x 30 cm (6¼ x 12 inch) rectangles. Put one on the baking tray, spread the frangipane down the centre and brush the rim with beaten egg. Lie the other piece of pastry on top, pressing the edges to seal. Cut slits in the top and brush with a little more egg. Bake for 30 minutes, or until the pastry is crisp and golden.

MILLE FEUILLE

SERVES 6–8

INGREDIENTS

- 600 g (1 lb 5 oz) block puff pastry or 3 sheets ready-rolled, thawed
- 625 ml (21½ fl oz/2½ cups) whipping cream
- 500 g (1 lb 2 oz) small strawberries, halved
- icing (confectioners') sugar, to dust

METHOD

1. Preheat the oven to 220°C (425°F/Gas 7). Line a baking tray with baking paper. If using a block of puff pastry, cut the pastry into three and roll out to 25 cm (10 inch) squares.
2. Place one sheet of pastry on the tray, prick all over and top with another piece of baking paper and another tray and bake for 15 minutes. Turn the trays over and bake on the other side for 10–15 minutes, or until golden brown. Allow to cool and repeat with the remaining pastry.
3. Trim the edges of each pastry sheet and cut each one in half. Pour the cream into a large bowl and whisk to firm peaks. Place two of the pastry pieces on a serving dish and spoon some of the cream on top. Carefully arrange some of the strawberries over the cream, pressing them well down. Top each one with another pastry sheet and repeat with the cream and strawberries. Top with a final layer of pastry and dust with icing sugar.

PROFITEROLES

MAKES 50

INGREDIENTS

50 choux puffs (page 535)

FILLING AND TOPPING

375 ml (13 fl oz/1½ cups) milk
4 egg yolks
80 g (2¾ oz/⅓ cup) caster (superfine) sugar
30 g (1 oz/¼ cup) plain (all-purpose) flour
1 teaspoon vanilla extract
110 g (3¾ oz) dark chocolate, chopped
2 teaspoons oil

METHOD

1 To make the filling, put the milk in a small saucepan and bring to the boil. Set aside while quickly whisking the egg yolks and sugar in a bowl until combined. Whisk the flour into the egg mixture. Pour the hot milk slowly onto the egg and flour mixture, whisking constantly. Wash out the saucepan, return the milk mixture to the pan and bring to the boil, stirring with a wooden spoon until the mixture comes to the boil and thickens. Transfer to a bowl and stir in the vanilla. Lay plastic wrap directly over the surface to prevent a skin forming, then refrigerate until cold.

2 Pipe the filling into the choux puffs through a small hole in the base, using a piping (icing) bag fitted with a small nozzle.

3 Put the chocolate in a heatproof bowl with the oil. Bring a saucepan of water to the boil and remove the pan from the heat. Sit the bowl over the saucepan, making sure the base of the bowl does not touch the water. Stir occasionally until the chocolate has melted. Stir until smooth and dip the profiterole tops in the chocolate. Allow to set completely before serving.

CHOCOLATE ECLAIRS

MAKES 20

INGREDIENTS

20 choux éclairs (page 535)

FILLING AND TOPPING

300 ml (10½ fl oz) cream, whipped
150 g (5½ oz) dark or milk chocolate, chopped

METHOD

1 Split each éclair, removing any uncooked dough, and fill with whipped cream.

2 Put the chocolate in a heatproof bowl. Bring a saucepan of water to the boil and remove the pan from the heat. Sit the bowl over the saucepan, making sure the base of the bowl doesn't touch the water. When the chocolate has softened, stir occasionally until the chocolate has melted. Spread the melted chocolate over the tops of the éclairs.

CHAPTER ELEVEN

DESSERTS

••CUSTARDS AND CREAMS••

Eggs, sugar and milk: the foundation for sublime silky-smooth custards, as well as the basis for so many other favourite desserts, such as ice creams or soufflés. Whip in a little cream or add a fragrant vanilla bean and transform custards into velvety-smooth desserts such as bavarois and blancmange.

CUSTARD

A custard is a sweetened, milk-based dessert made with eggs and often flavoured with vanilla. Thin, or pouring, custards such as crème anglaise are cooked on the stovetop over low heat, and stirred continuously to prevent lumps from forming. They must be cooked with vigilance or they will curdle. Other custards are made with a wine base, such as zabaglione or sabayon, while others are thickened with flour, usually cornflour. Baked custards are cooked in a bain-marie or water bath so the mixture cooks gently and doesn't bubble.

If you aren't going to use the custard immediately, cover the surface with either a dusting of sugar, a disc of baking paper, or lay a piece of plastic wrap flat on the surface to prevent a skin forming. If it does form a skin, put the custard in the blender and blend until smooth.

HOW TO... MAKE PERFECT CUSTARD

* To make a smooth velvety custard, of whichever type, the golden rule is to keep the heat low. Never let custard overcook or you will end up with a pan full of scrambled eggs.
* When stirring custard, make sure the wooden spoon passes through the middle of the pan and around the edge, where the custard is hottest and so will thicken quickest. Keep stirring to ensure the custard thickens evenly.
* If there is any milk protein on the base of the saucepan, rinse it out before returning the custard to the pan, as this may cause the custard to catch on the bottom.
* If the custard curdles a little, try removing it from the heat, adding a teaspoon of iced water and beating well. This will prevent further curdling but will not make a smooth custard.
* Alternatively, make custard using a double boiler or use a metal bowl set over a saucepan of simmering water (don't let the bowl touch the water) for a more gentle heat.

POURING CUSTARD

MAKES 400 ML (14 FL OZ)

INGREDIENTS

3 egg yolks
2 tablespoons caster (superfine) sugar
375 ml (13 fl oz/1½ cups) milk

METHOD

1 Put the egg yolks in a bowl with the sugar and beat with a balloon whisk until light and fluffy. When properly beaten, the mixture will fall in a ribbon that will hold its shape for a few seconds.
2 Pour the milk into a saucepan and bring to scalding point — small bubbles will appear around the edge. Stir if a skin appears to be forming. Pour into the egg mixture, whisking until well combined.
3 Return the custard to the cleaned saucepan and stir over low heat. Keep the custard below simmering point, as the egg yolks will thicken evenly if heated slowly. To prevent lumps forming, stir continuously. The custard is ready when it forms a coating on the back of a spoon. Run your finger through the custard on the back of the spoon — it should leave a clear line.
4 When the custard is ready, either pour it quickly through a sieve into a bowl or plunge the base of the saucepan into iced water to stop the cooking process. If chilling the custard, lay a piece of baking paper or plastic wrap directly over the surface to prevent a skin forming. If keeping the custard warm, put it in a bowl over a pan of hot water.

NOTE: For vanilla custard, add a split vanilla bean to the milk when you scald it and leave to infuse for 15–30 minutes. Remove the bean before adding the milk to the eggs. Alternatively, add 1 teaspoon vanilla extract to the finished custard. If you add it earlier, it will evaporate.

BAKED CUSTARD

SERVES 4

INGREDIENTS

melted butter, for brushing
3 eggs
80 g (2¾ oz/⅓ cup) caster (superfine) sugar
500 ml (17 fl oz/2 cups) milk
125 ml (4 fl oz/½ cup) cream
1½ teaspoons vanilla extract
ground nutmeg

METHOD

1 Preheat the oven to 160°C (315°F/Gas 2–3). Brush four 250 ml (9 fl oz/1 cup) ramekins or a 1.5 litre (6 cup) ovenproof dish with a little melted butter.
2 Whisk together the eggs and sugar in a large bowl until combined. Put the milk and cream in a small saucepan and stir over medium heat for 3–4 minutes, or until the mixture is warmed through, then stir into the egg mixture with the vanilla. Strain into the prepared ramekins or dish and sprinkle with the nutmeg.
3 Put the ramekins in a deep roasting tin and add enough hot water to come halfway up the sides of the ramekins. Bake for 25 minutes for the individual custards, 30 minutes for the large custard, or until it is set and a knife inserted into the centre comes out clean. Remove the custards from the roasting tin and leave for 10 minutes before serving.

NOTE: The custard is cooked when the centre is set but still wobbles when the mould is shaken. The custard will stiffen as it cools.

ZABAGLIONE

This classic Italian dessert is made of warmed and whisked Marsala or wine, egg yolks and sugar beaten over hot water until it forms a light, foamy custard. Some versions fold in whipped cream. Zabaglione is served as a dessert with biscuits or as a sauce over fruit, cake, ice cream or pastries.

SERVES 4

INGREDIENTS

- 6 egg yolks
- 3 tablespoons caster (superfine) sugar
- 125 ml (4 fl oz/½ cup) sweet Marsala
- 250 ml (9 fl oz/1 cup) whipping cream

METHOD

1. Combine the egg yolks and sugar in a large heatproof bowl set over a saucepan of barely simmering water, making sure the base of the bowl does not touch the water. Using a balloon whisk or electric beaters, whisk the egg yolk and sugar mixture. When the mixture is tepid, add the Marsala and whisk for another 5 minutes, or until it has thickened. Don't stop whisking and don't allow the bowl to become too hot or the eggs will scramble. The final result will be creamy, pale and mousse-like.
2. Whip the cream until soft peaks form. Gently fold in the egg yolk mixture. Pour the zabaglione into four glasses and serve.
3. For chilled zabaglione, place the glasses, covered with plastic wrap, in the refrigerator and chill for at least 1 hour.

› BLANCMANGE

SERVES 6

INGREDIENTS

- 100 g (3½ oz/⅔ cup) blanched almonds
- 250 ml (9 fl oz/1 cup) milk
- 115 g (4 oz/½ cup) caster (superfine) sugar
- 3 teaspoons powdered gelatine
- 310 ml (10¾ fl oz/1¼ cups) whipping cream
- crystallised violets, to decorate (optional)

METHOD

1. Grease six 125 ml (4 fl oz/½ cup) fluted moulds or ramekins. Process the almonds and 60 ml (2 fl oz/¼ cup) water in a small food processor until finely chopped and paste-like. With the motor running, gradually add the milk.
2. Pour into a small saucepan, add the sugar and stir over low heat until the sugar has completely dissolved. Allow to cool.
3. Strain the milk through a sieve lined with muslin. Twist the muslin tightly to extract as much milk as possible — you should have about 125 ml (4 fl oz/½ cup) of almond milk.
4. Put 60 ml (2 fl oz/¼ cup) cold water in a small heatproof bowl, sprinkle the gelatine in an even layer over the surface and leave to sponge. Do not stir.
5. Bring a small saucepan filled with about 4 cm (1½ inches) water to the boil, remove from the heat and place the bowl into the pan. The water should come halfway up the side of the bowl. Stir the gelatine until clear and dissolved, then stir the gelatine mixture through the almond milk. Allow to cool completely.
6. Whip the cream until firm peaks form, then fold in the almond mixture. Pour into the moulds and refrigerate for 6–8 hours, or until set.
7. To unmould, loosen the edge with your fingertip and turn out onto a plate. If the blancmange do not unmould easily, wipe the outside of the moulds with a cloth dipped in hot water. Decorate with the crystallised violets if using.

BLANCMANGE

A semi-solid dessert, blancmange is similar to custard but thickened with cornflour or gelatine and set in moulds. In medieval England, blancmange was a savoury dish, a thick gruel made with almonds, milk, rice and chicken or fish — all white or pale ingredients — and hence its French name, blancmange, meaning 'eat white'. Blancmange is often served with a tart sauce or fruit to counterbalance its richness.

TYPES OF CREAMS

pouring cream

POURING
This cream has a higher butterfat content than English single cream and American light cream (both of which cannot be whipped). The butterfat content varies from 35–48 per cent. Reduced fat cream has a minimum of 25 per cent fat. Light cream has about 18 per cent fat.

whipping cream

WHIPPING
Whipping cream must have at least 35 per cent butterfat to trap air and hold it in place. It whips more slowly than double cream and so incorporates more air. Whipping cream in America may have only 30 per cent butterfat with added vegetable fat to make it whip.

thick cream

THICK (DOUBLE)
This cream has a minimum butterfat content of 48 per cent. Known as heavy cream in America, double cream in the United Kingdom and thick cream in Australia, some have gelatine added to them to give them more body.

EXTRA THICK
This is double cream that has been homogenised and is a spooning consistency. It doesn't need to be whipped.

extra thick cream

CLOTTED OR SCALDED
This is the thickest, yellowest cream of all with the highest butterfat content of about 55 per cent.

SOUR CREAM
Originally made by leaving cream at room temperature to sour, today it is made by adding a culture to cream. It is thickened and slightly acidic because the milk sugar (lactose) converts to lactic acid. Low-fat varieties are now available.

clotted cream

CREME FRAICHE
French for 'fresh cream', this is actually a type of cultured cream. It has a slightly nutty, sharp flavour without being too sour. Unlike sour cream, it is ideal in sauces because it can boil without curdling. Use it as you would fresh cream over stewed fruits or serve with desserts such as crumbles or rich chocolate cakes.

HOW TO... WHIP CREAM
For best results, first chill the mixing bowl in the fridge and make sure the cream is chilled as well. For maximum volume, use a balloon whisk and beat well. You can use an electric whisk, but be careful you don't overbeat the cream and end up with butter. Cream for whipping must have at least 35 per cent butterfat for it to whip.

STRAWBERRIES ROMANOFF

SERVES 4

INGREDIENTS

375 g (13 oz) strawberries
55 g (2 oz/¼ cup) caster (superfine) sugar
60 ml (2 fl oz/¼ cup) Cointreau or kirsch
300 ml (10½ fl oz) whipping cream

METHOD

1 Hull and roughly chop the strawberries, leaving 2 whole strawberries for garnishing. Put the chopped strawberries in a bowl with the sugar and liqueur and stir to combine. Cover and refrigerate overnight.
2 Whip the cream until stiff peaks form and stir in half the strawberries. Place the remaining strawberries in the base of four glasses and divide the strawberry and cream mixture over the top. Halve the remaining strawberries and use to garnish.

VANILLA PANNA COTTA

SERVES 4

INGREDIENTS

450 ml (16 fl oz) thick (double) cream
4 tablespoons caster (superfine) sugar
vanilla extract, to taste
1¼ teaspoons powdered gelatine
raspberries, to serve

METHOD

1 Put the cream and sugar in a saucepan and stir over low heat until the sugar has dissolved. Bring to a boil, then reduce the heat and simmer for 3 minutes, adding a few drops of vanilla.
2 Sprinkle the gelatine in an even layer over the hot cream and leave it to sponge for a minute, then stir it into the cream until dissolved.
3 Pour the cream mixture into four 125 ml (4 fl oz/½ cup) metal dariole moulds, cover each with plastic wrap, and refrigerate until set.
4 Unmould the panna cotta by wrapping the moulds in a cloth dipped in hot water and then tipping them gently onto individual plates. Serve garnished with raspberries.

NOTE: Don't be tempted to use more gelatine than specified or your panna cotta may become rubbery.

RHUBARB FOOL

A classic British dessert, fools are made with puréed fruit folded into whipped cream or custard. Fool is traditionally made with gooseberry, but any fruit such as rhubarb, lime or raspberries can be used. Like other desserts such as flummery, trifle and nonsense, fool may have got its name for being a light, frivolous dessert.

SERVES 6

INGREDIENTS

- 1 kg (2 lb 4 oz) rhubarb, trimmed and chopped
- 2 tablespoons orange juice
- 55 g (2 oz/¼ cup) caster (superfine) sugar
- 100 ml (3½ fl oz) whipping cream
- 200 ml (7 fl oz) custard

METHOD

1. Put the rhubarb in a saucepan with the orange juice and sugar. Cover and cook over low heat for 20 minutes, or until the rhubarb is tender. Leave to cool a little.
2. Transfer the rhubarb to a food processor and process to form a purée. Transfer to a bowl.
3. Whip the cream until soft peaks form, then fold the cream into the rhubarb purée along with the custard. Serve chilled in dessert glasses.

CHILLED ORANGE CREAMS

SERVES 6

- 125 ml (4 fl oz/½ cup) blood orange juice
- 3 teaspoons powdered gelatine
- 4 egg yolks
- 115 g (4 oz/½ cup) caster (superfine) sugar
- 310 ml (10¾ fl oz/1¼ cups) milk
- 1 teaspoon finely grated blood orange zest
- 250 ml (9 fl oz/1 cup) whipping cream

METHOD

1. Chill a large bowl in the freezer. Lightly grease six 125 ml (4 fl oz/½ cup) ramekins or dariole moulds with flavourless oil.
2. Pour the orange juice into a small heatproof bowl, sprinkle the gelatine in an even layer over the surface and leave to sponge. Do not stir.
3. Bring a large saucepan filled with about 4 cm (1½ inches) water to the boil, remove from the heat and carefully lower the gelatine bowl into the water. The water should come halfway up the side of the bowl. Stir the gelatine until dissolved, then cool slightly.
4. Whisk the egg yolks and sugar in a small bowl until thick. Heat the milk and orange zest in a saucepan and gradually pour onto the egg mixture while whisking. Return the mixture to the pan and stir until the custard coats the back of the spoon. Do not allow it to boil. Add the gelatine mixture and stir.
5. Pour the mixture immediately through a strainer into the chilled bowl. Cool, stirring occasionally, until beginning to thicken.
6. Whip the cream until soft peaks form and fold gently into the custard. Spoon into the greased ramekins and chill to set. Serve with wedges of blood orange or thin strips of zest.

YOGHURT

Yoghurt is fermented and coagulated milk, which results when milk sugar (lactose) is converted to a lactic acid, producing a bacterial change. Yoghurt can occur naturally or be made commercially by adding active bacteria such as *Lactobacillus bulgaricus* and *Streptococcus thermophilus* to milk.

In the Western world, yoghurt is usually eaten as a dessert or for breakfast but in the Middle East, Central Asia and India it is a much more important food and is eaten as an accompaniment to meals, or used for marinating and cooking meat, or as a sauce.

HOME-MADE NATURAL YOGHURT

MAKES 1.25 LITRES (5 CUPS)

INGREDIENTS

- 1 litre (35 fl oz/4 cups) full-cream milk
- 2 tablespoons non-heat-treated fresh plain yoghurt or dried culture
- 5 tablespoons skim milk powder (optional)

METHOD

1. Put the milk in a saucepan and slowly bring to the boil. Cool to 45°C (113°F). Stir in the yoghurt or dried culture. Add the skim milk powder, if desired, to make a thicker, creamier yoghurt.
2. Cover, then wrap in a thick cloth and set aside in a warm place at a constant temperature, between 40°C and 46°C (104°F and 115°F), for 5–6 hours, or until set. Refrigerate.
3. To make fruit yoghurt, stir in lightly crushed raspberries or strawberries, or stir through fruit poached in syrup.

LASSI

A refreshing yoghurt drink popular in India and the Middle East, lassi is often flavoured with mango or rosewater, or with herbs and spices such as cumin or mint. Lassi is the ideal drink to have with curries as the fat in the yoghurt helps dissolve the fiery hot capsaicin found in chillies. When making lassi, use creamy, full-fat yoghurt because the ice will dilute its flavour.

To make a rosewater lassi, blend 350 g (12 oz) yoghurt, 1 tablespoon rosewater, 3 tablespoons thick (double) cream and 4 tablespoons sugar. Add 8 ice cubes and blend until frothy — the ice won't all break up. Serves 2

To make a mango lassi, blend 350 g (12 oz) yoghurt, the flesh of 1 mango and 3 tablespoons thick (double) cream. Add 8 ice cubes and blend until frothy. Serves 2

BAVAROIS

Also known as Bavarian cream, this classic creamy dessert is made from rich vanilla-flavoured custard, which is lightened with whipped cream to produce a creamy and velvety-smooth dessert. Vanilla, chocolate, orange, coffee and fruit purées are popular flavours and these are added to the egg-custard base before it is poured into a decorative mould to set.

‹ VANILLA BAVAROIS

SERVES 4

INGREDIENTS

- 685 ml (23 fl oz/2¾ cups) milk
- 1 vanilla bean
- 1 cinnamon stick
- 6 egg yolks
- 145 g (5 oz/⅔ cup) caster (superfine) sugar
- 3 teaspoons powdered gelatine
- 185 ml (6 fl oz/¾ cup) whipping cream
- raspberry coulis (page 649), to serve

METHOD

1. Gently heat the milk, vanilla bean and cinnamon stick in a saucepan until almost boiling. Remove from the heat and set aside for 5 minutes. Remove the cinnamon stick and vanilla bean.
2. Whisk the egg yolks and sugar until thick and pale. Gradually whisk in the milk. Pour into a large clean saucepan and stir continuously over low heat until the mixture thickens. Do not boil. Remove from the heat. Cover the surface with plastic wrap to prevent a skin forming.
3. Put 2 tablespoons water in a small heatproof bowl, sprinkle the gelatine in an even layer over the surface and leave to sponge. Bring a saucepan filled with 4 cm (1½ inches) water to the boil, remove from the heat and carefully lower the gelatine bowl into the water. The water should come halfway up the side of the bowl. Stir the gelatine until dissolved. Whisk the gelatine into the custard. Cover as before and leave to cool.
4. Beat the cream until soft peaks form and then fold the cream into the custard. Spoon into four 250 ml (9 fl oz/1 cup) dariole moulds or ramekins, then refrigerate overnight. Unmould the bavarois (see right) and serve with the coulis.

CHOCOLATE BAVAROIS

SERVES 6

INGREDIENTS

- 200 g (7 oz) dark chocolate, chopped
- 375 ml (13 fl oz/1½ cups) milk
- 4 egg yolks
- 80 g (2¾ oz/⅓ cup) caster (superfine) sugar
- 1 tablespoon powdered gelatine
- 310 ml (10¾ fl oz/1¼ cups) whipping cream

METHOD

1. Combine the chocolate and milk in a small saucepan. Stir over low heat until the chocolate has melted and the milk just comes to the boil. Remove from the heat.
2. Beat the egg yolks and sugar until combined. Gradually add the hot chocolate milk, whisking until combined. Return to a clean saucepan and cook, stirring, over low heat until the mixture thickens enough to coat the back of the spoon. Do not allow to boil. Remove from the heat.
3. Put 2 tablespoons water in a small heatproof bowl, sprinkle the gelatine in an even layer over the surface and leave to sponge. Stir into the hot chocolate mixture until dissolved.
4. Refrigerate until the mixture is cold but not set, stirring occasionally. Beat the cream until soft peaks form, then fold into the chocolate mixture in two batches. Pour into six 250 ml (9 fl oz/1 cup) dariole moulds and refrigerate overnight, until set.

HOW TO... REMOVE THE MOULD

To remove desserts such as bavarois from their moulds onto a serving plate, first tilt the mould or ramekin slightly on its side. Use your finger to gently pull the bavarois away from the edge, allowing air to enter and break the suction. Turn the bavarois out onto a plate. If it does not come out straight away, wipe a cloth dipped in hot water around the outside of the mould.

CREME BRULEE

Crème brûlée has been known in England since the seventeenth century. The dish is thought to have been invented at Trinity College, Cambridge, where it was named 'burnt cream'. Before serving, the top is sprinkled with granulated sugar or brown sugar and heated, often with a blowtorch or under a grill, to form a crisp caramel topping. The French translation, crème brûlée, is now generally used.

SERVES 6

INGREDIENTS

- 750 ml (26 fl oz/3 cups) cream
- 2 vanilla beans
- 8 egg yolks
- 115 g (4 oz/½ cup) sugar
- 3 teaspoons sugar, extra

METHOD

1. Gently heat the cream and vanilla beans in a large heavy-based saucepan until almost boiling. Remove from the heat and set aside to infuse for 30 minutes. Remove the vanilla beans.
2. Beat or whisk the egg yolks and sugar in a large bowl until thick and pale. Add the cream, then pour into a clean saucepan over low heat and stir until the mixture thickens slightly and coats the back of a wooden spoon. Do not boil or you will curdle the mixture. Remove from the heat and divide among six 170 ml (5½ fl oz/⅔ cup) ramekins. Cover with plastic wrap and refrigerate for at least 3 hours, or overnight.
3. Just before serving, preheat the grill (broiler) to very hot. Sprinkle a layer of sugar about 3 mm (⅛ inch) thick over the surface of the brûlées. To do this, put the ramekins on a sheet of baking paper and sift the sugar over — you can pour the unused dry sugar off the baking paper back into your container.
4. Place the ramekins in a large baking dish and pack ice around the sides to prevent the custards being heated. Place under the grill until the sugar caramelises into an even sheet. Keep watching or you may burn the caramel. The sugar needs to caramelise quickly so that the custard doesn't have time to melt. If your grill does not get particularly hot (restaurants use special hot grills called salamanders) you might want to invest in a mini blowtorch which also does the job well. Play the flame evenly over the surface. Do not put too much sugar on or the crust will be too thick to break with a spoon.
5. Chill the crème brûlées until you serve them but not for longer than an hour or the crust will soften. Serve with biscotti or fresh fruit if desired.

CREME CARAMEL

SERVES 6

INGREDIENTS

250 ml (9 fl oz/1 cup) milk
250 ml (9 fl oz/1 cup) cream
350 g (12 oz/1½ cups) caster (superfine) sugar
1 teaspoon vanilla extract
4 eggs, lightly beaten
80 g (2¾ oz/⅓ cup) caster (superfine) sugar, extra

METHOD

1. Preheat the oven to 200°C (400°F/Gas 6). Put the milk and cream in a saucepan and gradually bring to the boil.
2. Put the sugar in a frying pan and cook over medium heat for 8–10 minutes. Stir occasionally as the sugar melts to form a golden caramel. The sugar may become lumpy — break up any lumps with a wooden spoon. Remove from the heat and pour the caramel into six 125 ml (4 fl oz/½ cup) ramekins or moulds.
3. Combine the vanilla, eggs and extra sugar in a bowl. Remove the milk and cream from the heat and gradually add to the egg mixture, whisking well. Pour the custard mixture evenly over the caramel.
4. Place the ramekins in a baking dish and pour in boiling water until it comes halfway up the sides of the ramekins. Bake for 20 minutes, or until set.
5. To serve, use a flat-bladed knife to run around the edges of the ramekin and carefully turn the crème caramel out onto a serving plate.

NOTE: When making caramel, watch it carefully. The sugar will take a while to start melting, but once it starts, it will happen quickly. Stir occasionally to ensure the sugar melts evenly.

❮ RASPBERRY FLUMMERY

In medieval England, flummery was made by boiling oatmeal, which was then strained to give a thickened jelly-like substance. Later, flummery became a richer dish of cream flavoured with spices and almonds or wine. Today, flummery is usually based on milk or berry fruits and thickened with gelatine or cornflour.

SERVES 4

INGREDIENTS

- 600 g (1 lb 5 oz) raspberries
- 230 g (8 oz/1 cup) caster (superfine) sugar
- 2½ teaspoons powdered gelatine
- whipped cream, to serve

METHOD

1. Put the raspberries and sugar in a saucepan and crush the raspberries. Bring to the boil and simmer for 2 minutes.
2. Put 80 ml (2½ fl oz/⅓ cup) water in a bowl, sprinkle the gelatine in an even layer over the surface and leave to sponge. Stir the sponged gelatine into the hot raspberries, stirring to melt the gelatine.
3. Strain the mixture through a fine sieve into a bowl. Pour into four glasses and refrigerate overnight to set. Serve with whipped cream.

LEMON PASSIONFRUIT SYLLABUB

SERVES 8–10

INGREDIENTS

- 2 teaspoons finely grated lemon zest
- 80 ml (2½ fl oz/⅓ cup) lemon juice
- 115 g (4 oz/½ cup) caster (superfine) sugar
- 125 ml (4 fl oz/½ cup) dry white wine
- 8 passionfruit
- 500 ml (17 fl oz/2 cups) thick (double) cream
- julienned lemon zest, to garnish

METHOD

1. Combine the lemon zest, juice, sugar and wine in a bowl and set aside for 10 minutes.
2. Cut the passionfruit in half and push the pulp through a sieve to remove the seeds. Add half the pulp to the lemon and wine mixture.
3. Beat the cream until soft peaks form. Gradually beat in the lemon and passionfruit syrup until all the syrup is added (the mixture will have the consistency of softly whipped cream). Stir in the remaining passionfruit, cover and refrigerate for 1 hour.
4. Spoon the mixture into chilled wine or dessert glasses and decorate with the julienned lemon zest. Serve with a sweet biscuit.

JUNKET

This sweet, silky milk dessert is made by curdling milk with rennet and allowing the curds and whey to set. Sometimes the curds may be broken up and drained before serving. The milk is often sweetened and flavoured and, when set, is served cold. Today, junket is usually made using a commercially produced packet mix or junket tablets.

To make junket, warm 550 ml (19 fl oz) full-cream milk to hand hot, then add 2 junket tablets and 2 teaspoons caster (superfine) sugar. Pour the mixture into a dish and refrigerate until set. Top with whipped cream and sprinkle with ground cinnamon or nutmeg. Serves 4

••MOUSSES AND SOUFFLES••

There is sometimes confusion about the difference between a soufflé and a mousse. Basically, a soufflé is hot and a mousse is cold. From the French meaning froth or foam, a mousse is a light, soft and airy dish, held up by gelatine and egg white and won't collapse like a hot soufflé, which is held up by hot air.

MASCARPONE AND STRAWBERRY MOUSSE

SERVES 6

INGREDIENTS

80 g (2¾ oz/⅓ cup) caster (superfine) sugar
1 tablespoon powdered gelatine
500 g (1 lb 2 oz) strawberries, hulled
250 g (9 oz) mascarpone cheese
halved strawberries, to garnish

METHOD

1 Combine the sugar and 125 ml (4 fl oz/½ cup) water in a small saucepan. Stir over low heat for 3 minutes, or until the sugar has dissolved. Sprinkle the gelatine in an even layer over the sugar mixture, leave to sponge, then stir for 2 minutes, or until the gelatine has dissolved. Set aside to cool.
2 Put the strawberries in a food processor and process until smooth. Add the mascarpone and process until well combined. With the motor running, add the gelatine mixture in a slow stream. Pour the mixture into a 1 litre (35 fl oz/4 cup) mould. Refrigerate overnight, or until set.
3 To serve, dip the base of the mould in hot water for 10 seconds, then invert the mousse onto a plate. Garnish with the halved strawberries.

› MIXED BERRY MOUSSE

SERVES 6

INGREDIENTS

300 g (10½ oz) fresh or thawed frozen mixed berries, such as raspberries, blackberries and blueberries
140 g (5 oz/⅔ cup) sugar
3 teaspoons powdered gelatine
150 ml (5 fl oz) whipping cream
4 egg whites

METHOD

1 Put the berries and sugar in a saucepan. Stir over low heat for 5 minutes, or until the sugar has dissolved. Push the berries through a sieve into a bowl and allow to cool. Discard the seeds and pulp.
2 Put 80 ml (2½ fl oz/⅓ cup) hot water in a small heatproof bowl, sprinkle the gelatine in an even layer over the surface and leave to sponge. Pour it into the berry liquid, stirring well to combine.
3 Whip the cream until soft peaks form. In a separate clean dry bowl, beat the egg whites until soft peaks form. Gently fold the cream and egg whites through the berry mixture.
4 Spoon into six 185 ml (6 fl oz/¾ cup) ramekins, cover and refrigerate overnight, or until set.

WHITE CHOCOLATE AND RASPBERRY MOUSSE

SERVES 4

INGREDIENTS

- 150 g (5½ oz) white chocolate, chopped
- 150 ml (5 fl oz) cream, at room temperature
- 4 eggs, separated
- 250 g (9 oz) raspberries, crushed
- raspberries, to garnish

METHOD

1. Put the chocolate in a heatproof bowl over a saucepan of simmering water, making sure the base of the bowl doesn't touch the water. Leave the chocolate until it has softened, then stir occasionally until melted.
2. Allow the chocolate to cool slightly, then stir in the cream. Stir the egg yolks into the chocolate.
3. Beat the egg whites in a clean dry bowl just until soft peaks form, then fold into the chocolate mixture. Fold in the crushed raspberries.
4. Spoon into four ramekins or serving dishes, cover and refrigerate for 4 hours, or until set. Garnish with extra raspberries before serving.

PASSIONFRUIT MOUSSE

SERVES 10

INGREDIENTS

- 4 eggs, at room temperature, separated
- 170 g (6 oz/¾ cup) caster (superfine) sugar
- 185 ml (6 fl oz/¾ cup) passionfruit juice, strained (see Note)
- 2 tablespoons powdered gelatine
- 300 ml (10½ fl oz) whipping cream

METHOD

1. Put the egg yolks and sugar in a heatproof bowl and whisk with electric beaters until thick and pale. Stir in the passionfruit juice. Place the bowl over a saucepan of simmering water, making sure the base of the bowl doesn't touch the water. Stir with a wooden spoon for 6–8 minutes, or until the mixture is thick enough to coat the back of the spoon.
2. Sprinkle the gelatine over 60 ml (2 fl oz/¼ cup) hot water and stir to dissolve. Add the gelatine to the passionfruit mixture, stirring to combine. Set aside to cool.
3. Whip the cream until soft peaks form. In a separate clean dry bowl, beat the egg whites until soft peaks form. Gently fold the cream and egg whites through the passionfruit mixture. Pour into ten 125 ml (4 fl oz/½ cup) dariole moulds and refrigerate for 4 hours, or until set.
4. To serve, dip the base of each mould in hot water for 5 seconds and then invert the mousse onto a plate. Serve drizzled with extra passionfruit if desired.

NOTE: You will need about 20 fresh passionfruit or 2 x 170 g (6 oz) tins of passionfruit pulp.

CHOCOLATE MOUSSE

SERVES 8

INGREDIENTS

- 300 g (10½ oz) dark chocolate, chopped
- 30 g (1 oz) unsalted butter
- 2 eggs, lightly beaten
- 60 ml (2 fl oz/¼ cup) cognac
- 4 egg whites
- 100 g (3½ oz) caster (superfine) sugar
- 500 ml (17 fl oz/2 cups) whipping cream

METHOD

1. Put the chocolate in a heatproof bowl over a saucepan of simmering water, making sure the base of the bowl doesn't touch the water. Leave the chocolate until it has softened, then stir occasionally until melted. Add the butter and stir until melted. Remove the bowl from the saucepan and cool for a few minutes. Add the eggs and cognac and stir to combine.
2. Beat the egg whites in a clean dry bowl until soft peaks form, adding the sugar gradually. Whisk one-third of the egg white into the chocolate mixture to loosen it and then fold in the remainder with a large metal spoon or spatula.
3. Whip the cream and fold into the mousse. Pour into glasses or a large bowl, cover and refrigerate for at least 4 hours, or until set.

SOUFFLES

Fluffy and light as air, a soufflé makes a spectacular showpiece on the dinner table. Soufflés are made with either a sweet or savoury base into which beaten egg whites are gently folded. A soufflé is held up by the beaten egg whites and hot air. As it cooks, the air within it expands and pushes the mixture outwards, sometimes as much as doubling its height.

HOW TO MAKE... A PERFECT SOUFFLE

* To get the best rise out of a soufflé, you'll need a straight-sided ceramic soufflé dish. If the mixture comes more than two-thirds the way up the dish, you will need to make a collar (page 68).
* It is important that the egg whites are not too soft or the soufflé will not rise; and not too stiff or they will not mix into the base well and the cooked soufflé will contain blobs of white egg.
* When beating egg whites, make sure your bowl is stainless steel or glass, and that it is very clean and dry — any hint of grease will prevent the egg white from foaming.
* The egg white must be at room temperature before beating, then beat with a balloon whisk or electric beaters. Beat slowly until the whites start to become a frothy foam, then increase the speed a little. When the foam forms soft peaks, add the sugar gradually. Continue beating until the mixture is glossy — don't overbeat or it will become grainy and not rise well.
* Some fruit may have a higher sugar content and cause the top of the soufflé to brown too quickly. If so, rest a piece of foil on top of the soufflé.
* When the soufflé is ready, it should have a pale gold crust and not wobble too much. It should be served immediately, as soufflés wait for no one.

HOT CHOCOLATE SOUFFLE

SERVES 6

INGREDIENTS

175 g (6 oz) dark chocolate, chopped
5 egg yolks, lightly beaten
55 g (2 oz/¼ cup) caster (superfine) sugar
7 egg whites
icing (confectioners') sugar, to dust

METHOD

1 To prepare the soufflé dish, brush the inside of six 250 ml (9 fl oz/1 cup) soufflé dishes with softened butter, then pour in a little caster sugar. Shake the dishes to coat them in the sugar. Tip out any excess. Prepare a paper collar to come 3 cm (1¼ inches) above the rim (page 68). Preheat the oven to 190°C (375°F/Gas 5) and put a baking tray in the oven to heat up.

2 Put the chocolate in a heatproof bowl over a pan of simmering water, making sure the base of the bowl isn't touching the water. Stir occasionally until the chocolate has melted. Stir in the egg yolks and sugar. Transfer to a large bowl.

3 Beat the egg whites in a large bowl until firm peaks form. Fold a third of the beaten egg white through the chocolate mixture to loosen it. Using a metal spoon, fold through the remaining egg white until just combined. Spoon the mixture into the dishes, place on the tray and bake for 12–15 minutes, or until well risen and just set.

4 Cut the string and remove the collars. Serve immediately, dusted with sifted icing sugar.

BERRY SOUFFLE

SERVES 6

INGREDIENTS

- 55 g (2 oz) unsalted butter
- 3 tablespoons plain (all-purpose) flour
- 250 ml (9 fl oz/1 cup) milk
- 115 g (4 oz/½ cup) caster (superfine) sugar
- 250 g (9 oz) berries, such as blackberries, raspberries or blueberries, or a mixture
- 1 tablespoon berry-flavoured liqueur or brandy such as framboise eau de vie (optional)
- 4 egg yolks
- 6 egg whites
- icing (confectioners') sugar, to dust

WARM BERRY SAUCE

- 80 g (2¾ oz/⅓ cup) caster (superfine) sugar
- 300 g (10½ oz) frozen mixed berries, such as blackberries, raspberries or blueberries (thawed, juice retained)
- 1 tablespoon berry-flavoured liqueur or brandy

METHOD

1 Preheat the oven to 190°C (375°F/Gas 5). Melt the butter in a saucepan over low heat. Use a little of it to brush the insides of six 250 ml (9 fl oz/1 cup) soufflé dishes, then sprinkle them with a little caster sugar. Shake the dishes to coat them evenly in the sugar. Tip out any excess sugar.

2 Return the remaining butter to the heat. Add the flour to the pan and cook for 1 minute, stirring until it begins to change colour and thickens a little. Remove from the heat and gradually add the milk, stirring constantly. Stir in the sugar and ½ teaspoon salt. Return to low heat and whisk until the mixture is smooth and has come to the boil.

3 Remove from the heat and cool for 5 minutes. Meanwhile, purée the mixed berries until smooth, then pour the purée through a sieve to remove any seeds. Add to the milk mixture, along with the liqueur, if using. Mix well.

4 Lightly beat the egg yolks, then beat into the berry mixture until smooth. Whisk the egg whites in a clean dry bowl until stiff peaks form. With a metal spoon, fold one-quarter of the egg white through the base mixture to loosen it slightly. Gently fold in the remaining egg white. Spoon the soufflé mixture into the prepared dishes. Smooth the top and run a finger around the edge of each dish to help the soufflés rise evenly. Bake for 13–15 minutes, or until the soufflés are well risen and firm to touch.

5 Meanwhile, make the berry sauce. Put the sugar and 100 ml (3½ fl oz) water in a saucepan and bring to the boil, stirring to dissolve the sugar. Boil for 2 minutes. Add the berries and liqueur. Reduce the heat and simmer for 10 minutes. Cool slightly. Dust the berry soufflés with icing sugar and serve immediately, with the sauce poured over the top.

••TRIFLES••

A family favourite, trifles are seen in many forms, usually made with a sponge soaked with sherry, liqueur or fruit juice, and layered with various combinations of fruit, custard and cream. Though jelly is often added, it is not an original ingredient. The word comes from *trufle*, an old French word meaning something of little importance.

SHERRY TRIFLE

SERVES 6

INGREDIENTS

4 slices Madeira cake, pound cake or trifle sponges
60 ml (2 fl oz/¼ cup) sweet sherry or Madeira
250 g (9 oz) raspberries
125 ml (4 fl oz/½ cup) whipping cream
25 g (1 oz/¼ cup) flaked almonds, to decorate
strawberries or raspberries, to decorate

CUSTARD

4 eggs
2 tablespoons caster (superfine) sugar
2 tablespoons plain (all-purpose) flour
500 ml (17 fl oz/2 cups) milk
¼ teaspoon vanilla extract

METHOD

1. Put the cake slices in a glass serving bowl and sprinkle with the sherry. Scatter the raspberries over the top and crush them gently into the sponge with the back of a spoon, leaving some of them whole.
2. To make the custard, combine the eggs, sugar and flour together in a bowl. Heat the milk in a saucepan, pour it over the egg mixture, stir well and pour the mixture back into a clean pan. Cook over medium heat until the custard boils and thickens and coats the back of a spoon. Stir in the vanilla, cover the surface with plastic wrap and leave to cool.
3. Pour the cooled custard over the raspberries and leave to set in the fridge. The custard will firm up but not become solid.
4. Before serving, whip the cream and spoon it over the custard. Decorate the trifle with almonds and strawberries.

NOTE: You can use 500 ml (17 fl oz/2 cups) prepared custard instead of making your own.

ZUPPA INGLESE

Translated as 'English soup', zuppa inglese is the Italian version of a trifle — so heavily covered in custard that it looks like a soup. Some versions are made with macaroons instead of sponge cake.

SERVES 6

INGREDIENTS

CUSTARD
6 large egg yolks
115 g (4 oz/½ cup) caster (superfine) sugar
2 tablespoons cornflour (cornstarch)
1 tablespoon plain (all-purpose) flour
625 ml (21 fl oz/2½ cups) milk
½ vanilla bean or 1 teaspoon vanilla extract

1 sponge cake, thickly sliced
170 ml (5½ fl oz/⅔ cup) rum, Marsala or grappa
200 g (7 oz) raspberries
400 g (14 oz) blackberries
2 teaspoons caster (superfine) sugar
250 ml (9 fl oz/1 cup) cream, whipped

METHOD

1 To make the custard, whisk the egg yolks with the sugar until pale and fluffy. Add the cornflour and flour and mix well. Put the milk in a saucepan with the vanilla bean and bring just to the boil. Pour into the egg mixture, whisking as you do so. Pour the custard back into the cleaned saucepan and gently bring to the boil, stirring. Once the mixture is just boiling, take it off the heat and stir for a few minutes. Pour the custard into a bowl and cover with plastic wrap.
2 Place a few pieces of sponge cake on each serving plate (use deep plates) and brush with two-thirds of the alcohol. Soak for 10 minutes.
3 Put the berries in a saucepan with the remaining alcohol and the sugar. Gently warm through so that the sugar just melts, then set aside to cool. Spoon over the cake, then pour the custard over the top. Serve the whipped cream on the side.

QUICK RATAFIA TRIFLES

SERVES 4

INGREDIENTS

20 ratafia biscuits
1 tablespoon ratafia liqueur or sherry
125 g (4½ oz) strawberries, chopped
125 g (4½ oz) raspberries, chopped
500 ml (17 fl oz/2 cups) custard
raspberries, to garnish

METHOD

1 Put five ratafia biscuits in the base of each of four dessert glasses. Drizzle a little of the liqueur into each glass.
2 Combine the chopped berries and divide among the glasses. Pour over the custard and leave to set in the fridge. Serve the trifles garnished with the raspberries.

NOTES: Ratafia is a sweet, brandy-based liqueur flavoured with fruit or almonds.
Ratafia biscuits are small biscuits flavoured with bitter almond and similar to a macaroon. They are eaten with liqueurs, as well as used as the basis for trifles. If unavailable, use macaroons or Italian amaretti biscuits.

TIRAMISU

Tira mi su means 'pick me up' in Italian and this is how the dessert started life — as a nourishing dish to be eaten when feeling low. It originated in Venice, but now is popular worldwide. Tiramisu is made from sponge fingers soaked in coffee and an alcohol such as Marsala, and layered with a mascarpone cheese mixture. You can also make a fruit version, using framboise and puréed raspberries instead of Marsala or brandy and coffee.

SERVES 4

INGREDIENTS

- 5 eggs, separated
- 170 g (6 oz/¾ cup) caster (superfine) sugar
- 300 g (10½ oz) mascarpone cheese
- 250 ml (9 fl oz/1 cup) cold strong coffee
- 3 tablespoons sweet Marsala or brandy
- 36 small sponge fingers (lady fingers)
- 80 g (2¾ oz) dark chocolate, finely grated

METHOD

1. Beat the egg yolks with the sugar until the sugar has dissolved and the mixture is light and fluffy and leaves a ribbon trail when dropped from the whisk. Add the mascarpone and beat until the mixture is smooth.
2. Whisk the egg whites in a clean dry glass bowl until soft peaks form. Fold the egg whites into the mascarpone mixture.
3. Pour the coffee into a shallow dish and add the brandy. Dip enough biscuits to cover the base of a 25 cm (10 inch) square dish into the coffee. The biscuits should be fairly well soaked but not so much so that they break up. Arrange the biscuits in one tightly packed layer in the base of the dish.
4. Spread half the mascarpone mixture over the layer of biscuits. Add another layer of soaked biscuits and then another layer of mascarpone, smoothing the top layer neatly. Dust with the grated chocolate before serving.

NOTE: The flavours will be better developed if you can make the tiramisu a few hours in advance or even the night before. If you have time to do this, don't dust with the chocolate, but cover with plastic wrap and chill. Dust with the grated chocolate just before serving.

SPONGE FINGERS

Also called lady fingers, savoiardi or savoy biscuits, these are finger-like strips of sponge cake made by piping the mixture into thin lines about 10 cm (4 inches) long, then sprinkling them with sugar. The cooked biscuits are light and crisp and used to accompany desserts such as mousses, fruit desserts and ice creams, as a border for cold charlottes or as a base for trifles and tiramisu. They can also be bought ready-made from supermarkets.

••MERINGUE••

Meringue is a miraculous mixture of egg whites and sugar whipped together until soft or firm, depending on the recipe, and used both cooked and uncooked in many desserts such as pavlova, meringues and baked Alaska.

MERINGUE NESTS

Meringue nests, once cooled, can be filled with thick custard or whipped cream, and topped with sliced fresh fruit or stewed rhubarb or apple. Alternatively, pipe the meringue into small mounds using a star nozzle (pictured opposite), and serve plain or sandwiched together with whipped cream.

MAKES 4 NESTS OR 30 SMALL MERINGUES

INGREDIENTS

2 egg whites, at room temperature
115 g (4 oz/½ cup) caster (superfine) sugar

METHOD

1 Preheat the oven to 150°C (300°F/Gas 2). Line a baking tray with baking paper. If making nests, mark out four 9 cm (3½ inch) circles on the back of the paper.
2 Put the egg whites in a large clean dry bowl. Using electric beaters, whisk the egg whites until soft peaks form. Gradually add the sugar, beating well after each addition, until the mixture is thick and glossy. Do not overbeat.
3 For the nests, spread 1 tablespoon of the meringue evenly over each of the circles to a thickness of 5 mm (¼ inch). Put the remaining meringue in a piping (icing) bag fitted with a 1 cm (½ inch) star nozzle. Pipe the mixture around the edge of the meringue circles to make a nest 1–2 cm (½–¾ inch) high. For the small meringues, pipe small rosettes onto the baking paper. Bake for 30–35 minutes for the nests, or 10–15 minutes for the small meringues, or until lightly golden. Leave the meringues to cool completely in the oven. Once cooled, transfer to an airtight container until required.

COOKING TIPS

* It's important to cook meringue or pavlova for the right amount of time — if syrupy droplets appear on the outside of the meringue, it is overcooked; if liquid oozes out, it is undercooked.
* For ordinary meringue, the sugar is added in at least two batches and beaten until the sugar dissolves and stabilises the whites.
* Meringue should be thick and shiny and hold its shape when piped. It might not work as well on a humid day, as it may break down.

HAZELNUT MERINGUE STACK

SERVES 8

INGREDIENTS

- 300 g (10½ oz) hazelnuts
- 8 egg whites, at room temperature
- 350 g (12 oz/1½ cups) caster (superfine) sugar
- 2 teaspoons vanilla extract
- 2 teaspoons white vinegar
- 600 g (1 lb 5 oz) sour cream
- 200 ml (7 fl oz) cream, whipped
- 230 g (8 oz/1¼ cups) soft brown sugar
- whipped cream, extra
- chopped hazelnuts, to garnish

METHOD

1. Preheat the oven to 180°C (350°F/Gas 4). Roast the hazelnuts on a baking tray for 5–10 minutes, or until golden. Tip the nuts onto a tea towel and rub vigorously to remove the skins. Transfer to a food processor and chop until finely ground.
2. Reduce the oven to 150°C (300°F/Gas 2). Line four baking trays with baking paper and draw a 21 cm (8¼ inch) diameter circle on the back of each piece of paper.
3. Beat the egg whites in a large, clean dry bowl until soft peaks form. Gradually add the caster sugar, beating well after each addition, until the meringue is stiff and glossy. Fold in the ground hazelnuts, vanilla and vinegar.
4. Divide the meringue evenly among the four circles on the baking paper and carefully spread it to the edge of each. Bake for 45 minutes, or until crisp. Turn off the oven and leave the meringues to cool in the oven, with the door ajar.
5. To make the filling, put the sour cream, whipped cream and brown sugar in a bowl and stir until combined. Sandwich together the meringue circles with the filling. Decorate with the extra whipped cream and chopped hazelnuts.

› GRANDMOTHER'S PAVLOVA

SERVES 6–8

INGREDIENTS

- 4 egg whites, at room temperature
- 230 g (8 oz/1 cup) caster (superfine) sugar
- 2 teaspoons cornflour (cornstarch)
- 1 teaspoon white vinegar
- 250 ml (9 fl oz/1 cup) whipping cream
- fruit such as strawberries, kiwi fruit and banana, to decorate
- pulp from 3 passionfruit, to decorate

METHOD

1. Preheat the oven to 160°C (315°F/Gas 2–3). Line a 33 x 28 cm (13 x 11¼ inch) baking tray with baking paper.
2. Put the egg whites and a pinch of salt in a large, clean stainless steel or glass bowl. Using electric beaters, slowly beat the egg white until the whites start to become a frothy foam, then increase the speed until the bubbles in the foam have become small and even-sized. When soft peaks have just formed, add the sugar gradually, beating constantly after each addition, until the mixture is thick and glossy and all the sugar has dissolved. Don't overbeat or the mixture will become grainy.
3. Using a metal spoon, fold in the sifted cornflour and the vinegar. Spoon the mixture into a mound on the prepared tray. Lightly flatten the top of the pavlova and smooth the sides, making upward strokes around the edge. (The pavlova should be about 2.5 cm/1 inch high.) Bake for 1 hour, or until pale cream and crisp on the outside. Remove from the oven while warm and carefully turn upside down onto a plate.
4. Lightly whip the cream until soft peaks form and spread over the soft centre of the pavlova. Decorate with halved strawberries, sliced bananas and kiwi fruit. Drizzle over the passionfruit pulp. Cut into wedges to serve.

PAVLOVA

Named for the Russian ballerina Anna Pavlova, pavlova is made from a meringue base, slightly indented in the middle and filled with whipped cream and fruit such as strawberries, passionfruit and kiwi fruit. Meringue connoisseurs will debate over the merits of the crunchy brittle variety over the 'grandmother's pavlova', with its crisp outer shell and gooey chewy centre. The addition of cornflour and vinegar gives the meringue a soft, marshmallow centre.

BAKED ALASKA

SERVES 6–8

INGREDIENTS

- 2 litres (8 cups) vanilla ice cream
- 250 g (9 oz) mixed glacé fruit, finely chopped
- 125 ml (4 fl oz/½ cup) Grand Marnier or Cointreau
- 2 teaspoons finely grated orange zest
- 60 g (2¼ oz) almonds, toasted and finely chopped
- 60 g (2¼ oz) dark chocolate, finely chopped
- 1 sponge or butter cake, about 350 g (12 oz), cut into 3 cm (1¼ inch) slices
- 3 egg whites
- 170 g (6 oz/¾ cup) caster (superfine) sugar

METHOD

1. Line a 2 litre (8 cup) pudding basin with damp muslin. Allow half of the ice cream to soften just enough that you can fold in the glacé fruit along with 2 tablespoons of the liqueur and 1 teaspoon of the orange zest. Spoon the ice cream over the base and up the sides of the basin, then freeze until hard.
2. Soften the remaining ice cream and fold in the almonds, chocolate, remaining liqueur and orange zest. Add to the frozen shell, filling it and smoothing the surface. Working quickly, evenly cover the ice cream with a layer of cake. Cover with foil and freeze for 2 hours.
3. Preheat the oven to 220°C (425°F/Gas 7). Beat the egg whites in a clean dry bowl until soft peaks form. Gradually add the sugar, beating well after each addition. Beat for 4–5 minutes, or until the meringue is thick and glossy.
4. Carefully unmould the ice cream onto a flat ovenproof dish and gently remove the muslin. Quickly spread the meringue over the top, completely covering the ice cream. Bake for 5–8 minutes, or until the meringue is lightly browned. Serve immediately.

OEUFS A LA NEIGE

SERVES 4–6

INGREDIENTS

- 4 eggs, at room temperature, separated
- 230 g (8 oz/1 cup) caster (superfine) sugar
- 750 ml (26 fl oz/3 cups) milk
- 1 vanilla bean, split lengthways
- 115 g (4 oz/½ cup) caster (superfine) sugar, extra

METHOD

1. Beat the egg whites in a clean dry bowl until soft peaks form. Gradually add 80 g (2¾ oz/⅓ cup) of the sugar, beating well after each addition, until the meringue is stiff and glossy.
2. Combine the milk, another 80 g (2¾ oz/⅓ cup) of the sugar and the vanilla bean in a large frying pan and bring to a simmer. Using two dessertspoons, mould the meringue into 16 egg shapes and lower in batches into the simmering milk. Poach for 5 minutes, or until firm to touch, turning once during cooking (be careful as the meringues are delicate and crumble easily). Remove with a slotted spoon and set aside. Strain the milk into a bowl.
3. Whisk the egg yolks with the remaining sugar until thick and pale. Gradually pour the milk into the egg yolk mixture, whisking to combine. Pour the mixture into a saucepan and stir over low heat until the custard thickens and coats the back of a wooden spoon. Do not boil the custard. Pour the custard into shallow serving dishes and cool. When the custard is completely cold, arrange the poached meringues on top.
4. Stir the extra caster sugar with 2 tablespoons water in a small pan over low heat until the sugar has dissolved, then bring to the boil and simmer until the syrup turns golden brown. Working quickly and carefully, drizzle the toffee over the meringues and custard.

NOTE: Oeufs à la neige means 'snow eggs' and is sometimes known as floating islands.

MARBLED MERINGUES WITH RASPBERRY CREAM

MAKES 20

INGREDIENTS

4 egg whites
230 g (8 oz/1 cup) caster (superfine) sugar
2 teaspoons cornflour (cornstarch)
1 teaspoon white vinegar
pink food colouring
300 ml (10½ fl oz) whipping cream
2 tablespoons icing (confectioners') sugar, sifted
1 teaspoon vanilla extract
150 g (5½ oz) fresh raspberries

METHOD

1. Preheat the oven to 150°C (300°F/Gas 2). Cut out two pieces of baking paper large enough to line 2 baking trays. Draw ten 5 cm (2 inch) circles on the back of each piece of paper.
2. Put the egg whites in a clean dry bowl. Using an electric beater beat the whites until soft peaks form. Gradually add the sugar, 1 tablespoon at a time, whisking well after each addition until the mixture is smooth and glossy. Sift in the cornflour, then fold in the vinegar. Sprinkle over a few drops of food colouring and fold through, marbling the mixture.
3. Pipe small mounds onto the baking paper, filling in the circle outlines. Put some food colouring into a bowl and dip a blunt knife into the colouring, then into the meringues, drawing swirls of colour through them.
4. Reduce the oven to 140°C (275°F/Gas 1) and bake for 1 hour. Turn off the oven and leave the meringues to cool.
5. Whisk together the cream, icing sugar and vanilla until soft peaks form. Put the raspberries in a bowl and gently crush with the end of a rolling pin. Fold into the cream. Sandwich the cooled meringues together with the raspberry cream. Serve within 2 hours of making.

••JELLY••

Sparkling, translucent, wobbly jellies aren't just for the children — jellies made from champagne or clear fruit juices and set with berries or other fruit in a mould or wine glasses can make a showy centrepiece, and a refreshing and light finish to a meal.

JELLY

Jellies are made with a setting agent such as gelatine, agar-agar or pectin. Some are made by boiling fruit juice and allowing it to set using its natural pectin, others are made with fruit juice and using a setting agent such as gelatine, or they may be made with commercially prepared cubes or crystals that are stirred into boiling water and then set in the fridge. Fruit jellies can be made with a variety of fruit, but fruit such as pineapple, papaya, kiwi fruit and figs won't work in jellies as these fruit all contain enzymes that will eat the protein in gelatine, preventing it from setting.

HAS YOUR JELLY LOST ITS WOBBLE?

Jellies should be firm enough to hold their shape so they can be turned out of their mould without collapsing but, of course, the whole point of a jelly is that it should wobble! If your jelly is too firm to wobble, it may simply be too cold. Jellies become very firm on chilling and may need to be brought back to room temperature to regain their wobble.

GELATINE

Gelatine is a colourless, almost flavourless protein best known as a setting agent for jellies, but also used in desserts such as creamy bavarois or cheesecakes. Gelatine is available as powder or granules and in clear sheets or leaves. As a rule, 6 sheets of gelatine is equal to 3 teaspoons of powdered gelatine or a 10 g (¼ oz) sachet. This is enough to soft-set 500 ml (17 fl oz/2 cups) of liquid.

HOW TO... USE SHEET GELATINE

METHOD

1. Put the gelatine sheets in cold water and soak for 1 minute, or until they are floppy.
2. Squeeze out any excess water and then stir the sheets straight into a hot liquid to dissolve them.

HOW TO... USE POWDERED GELATINE

METHOD

1. Put 60 ml (2 fl oz/¼ cup) water into a glass bowl and sprinkle on the gelatine evenly. Leave the gelatine to sponge, without stirring — it will swell.
2. Add the sponged gelatine to a hot liquid and stir well to dissolve it (or place the bowl over hot water and stir until the gelatine has dissolved).

BERRIES IN CHAMPAGNE JELLY

SERVES 8

INGREDIENTS

- 1 litre (35 fl oz/4 cups) champagne or sparkling white wine
- 1½ tablespoons powdered gelatine
- 220 g (7¾ oz/1 cup) sugar
- 4 strips lemon zest
- 4 strips orange zest
- 250 g (9 oz) small strawberries, hulled and halved
- 250 g (9 oz) blueberries

METHOD

1. Pour 500 ml (17 fl oz/2 cups) champagne into a bowl and let the bubbles subside. Sprinkle the gelatine in an even layer over the surface and leave to sponge — do not stir.
2. Put the remaining champagne in a large saucepan with the sugar, lemon and orange zests, and heat gently, stirring constantly for 3–4 minutes, until the sugar has dissolved.
3. Remove the saucepan from the heat, add the gelatine mixture and stir until thoroughly dissolved. Allow the jelly to cool completely, then remove the lemon and orange zests.
4. Divide the berries among eight 125 ml (4 fl oz/½ cup) stemmed wine glasses and gently pour the jelly over the top. Refrigerate for 6 hours, or overnight, until the jelly has fully set. Remove from the refrigerator 15 minutes before serving.

FRUIT JUICE JELLY

MAKES 6

INGREDIENTS

- 750 ml (26 fl oz/3 cups) sweetened fruit juice (except pineapple)
- 1–2 tablespoons liqueur (optional)
- 4½ teaspoons powdered gelatine

METHOD

1. Pour 250 ml (9 fl oz/1 cup) of the fruit juice into a saucepan (and add the liqueur if you like). Sprinkle the gelatine in an even layer over the surface and leave to sponge — do not stir.
2. Heat the juice over low heat, then stir in the gelatine until completely dissolved. Stir in the remaining juice, then pour into jelly moulds. Refrigerate for 6 hours, or overnight, until the jelly has fully set. Turn the jellies out onto a plate.

NOTE: Some fruit juices take longer to set than others and jellies that have alcohol in them take longer to set than those that don't.

HOW TO... TURN JELLY OUT OF THE MOULD

To turn out the jelly, use a wet finger to pull it away from the mould all the way around. Invert onto a plate and give the whole thing a firm shake to break the airlock — you should hear a squelching noise. If this fails, wrap a warm cloth around the mould for a few seconds and try again. If the jelly seems to have melted too much, refrigerate it again until it sets. If you are turning the jelly out onto a plate, remember that unless you wet the plate first, the jelly will stick and you won't be able to move it. You can, of course, eat jelly out of the dish it is made in.

••PANCAKES AND BATTERS••

Crepes are made using a sweetened batter of flour, milk, melted butter and eggs. At their simplest, they are eaten with a dusting of sugar and a squeeze of lemon, or they can be wrapped around a filling or soaked in a sauce. Thicker batters are used to make pancakes, pikelets and waffles.

BASIC CREPES

MAKES 18

INGREDIENTS

- 300 g (10½ oz/2½ cups) plain (all-purpose) flour
- 3 eggs, lightly beaten
- 200 ml (7 fl oz) milk combined with 250 ml (9 fl oz/1 cup) water
- 50 g (1¾ oz) unsalted butter, melted
- caster (superfine) sugar, to serve
- lemon juice, to serve

METHOD

1 Sift the flour into a large bowl with a pinch of salt and make a well in the centre.

2 Gradually whisk in the beaten egg, drawing the flour in from the edges. As the batter becomes thicker, gradually add the combined milk and water, and whisk until the batter is smooth and free of lumps.

3 Pour in the melted butter and stir to combine. The batter should be the consistency of pouring cream. Transfer to a jug for easy pouring, cover and set aside for 30 minutes.

4 Heat a 20 cm (8 inch) crepe pan or non-stick frying pan and brush lightly with melted butter.

5 Pour in a little batter, swirling to thinly cover the base, and pour any excess batter back into the jug. Thin the batter with 1–2 tablespoons water if it is too thick.

6 Cook until the edges just begin to curl and lift off the pan, then turn and brown the other side. Transfer to a plate and cover with a tea towel while cooking the remaining batter, greasing the pan when necessary. Stack the crepes between baking paper to prevent them sticking together. To serve, roll up or fold into quarters and sprinkle with caster sugar and lemon juice. Serve with whipped cream if desired.

HOW TO... MAKE PERFECT CREPES

* Most recipes will ask you to set the batter aside to rest for 30 minutes or so. Why? This gives the starch in the flour time to expand and allows the gluten to relax, making for a much lighter batter.
* Your batter should be of a creamy pouring consistency; if not, add a little water until it's right. Be careful, as it is much easier to thin batter than it is to thicken it.
* When cooking crepes, the classic crepe pan is the best pan for the job. Non-stick pans also work well, but they tend not to brown the crepes as well. You may find that the first crepe is a disaster — don't despair, just throw it away and try again.
* Leftover crepes can be stacked with baking paper between them, wrapped in foil and frozen in an airtight bag.

CHOCOLATE CREPES

MAKES 8–10

INGREDIENTS

60 g (2¼ oz/½ cup) plain (all-purpose) flour
1 tablespoon unsweetened cocoa powder
2 eggs
250 ml (9 fl oz/1 cup) milk
2 tablespoons caster (superfine) sugar
3 oranges
160 g (5½ oz) dark chocolate, chopped
185 ml (6 fl oz/¾ cup) cream
125 g (4½ oz/½ cup) crème fraîche

METHOD

1 Sift the flour and cocoa into a large bowl with a pinch of salt and make a well in the centre.
2 Gradually whisk in the combined eggs, milk and sugar, drawing the flour in from the edges, and whisking until the batter is smooth and free of lumps. Transfer to a jug, cover and set aside for 30 minutes.
3 Meanwhile, cut a 1 cm (½ inch) slice from the ends of each orange. Cut the skin away in a circular motion, cutting only deep enough to remove all the white membrane and skin. Cut the flesh into segments between each membrane. (Do this over a bowl to catch any juice.) Place the segments in a bowl with the juice. Cover with plastic wrap and refrigerate.
4 Heat a 20 cm (8 inch) crepe pan or non-stick frying pan over medium heat and brush lightly with melted butter.
5 Pour 2–3 tablespoons of batter into the pan, swirling to thinly cover the base, and pour any excess batter back into the jug. Cook for 1 minute, or until the edges just begin to curl and lift off the pan, then turn and cook the other side. Transfer to a plate and cover while cooking the remaining batter, greasing the pan when necessary. Stack the crepes between baking paper to prevent them sticking together.
6 To make the sauce, drain the oranges and reserve the juice. Combine the juice in a saucepan with the chocolate and cream. Stir over low heat until the chocolate has melted and the mixture is smooth.
7 To assemble the crepes, place a heaped teaspoon of crème fraîche on a quarter of each crepe. Fold the crepe in half, and then in half again. Place two crepes on each serving plate. Spoon the warm chocolate sauce over the crepes and serve with the orange segments.

CREPES SUZETTE

SERVES 4–6

INGREDIENTS

1 quantity basic crepes (page 586)

SAUCE
125 g (4½ oz) unsalted butter
115 g (4 oz/½ cup) caster (superfine) sugar
finely grated zest of 1 orange
185 ml (6 fl oz/¾ cup) orange juice
60 ml (2 fl oz/¼ cup) Cointreau
2 tablespoons brandy

METHOD

1 Have the crepes cooked and ready beside you.
2 To make the sauce, put the butter, sugar, orange zest, juice and Cointreau in a large frying pan and simmer for 2 minutes. Add the crepes one at a time to the pan, placing each one flat, then folding it into quarters and pushing to one side.
3 Pour the brandy over the crepes and, with care, ignite the crepes, either with a gas flame or a match. (Keep a lid large enough to cover the pan beside you in case you need to smother the flame.) Repeat with the remaining crepes. Serve the crepes and sauce on warmed plates, with ice cream if desired.

BLINTZES

These are thin pancakes, similar to a crepe, filled with either a sweet or savoury filling. The pancake is folded into a rectangular packet and baked or fried until golden brown. Blintzes are of Eastern European origin and are traditionally eaten at Shavuot, the Jewish celebration held after Passover, when it is customary to eat dairy products. Typically, they are filled with fresh cheese, sprinkled with cinnamon and served with sour cream.

RICOTTA BLINTZES

MAKES ABOUT 14

INGREDIENTS

125 g (4½ oz/1 cup) plain (all-purpose) flour
2 eggs
310 ml (10¾ fl oz/1¼ cups) milk
30 g (1 oz) unsalted butter, melted
melted butter, extra, for brushing
icing (confectioners') sugar, to dust

RICOTTA FILLING

60 g (2¼ oz) raisins
1 tablespoon orange liqueur, such as Grand Marnier or Cointreau (optional)
375 g (13 oz/1½ cups) ricotta cheese
80 g (2¾ oz/⅓ cup) caster (superfine) sugar
1 tablespoon finely grated lemon zest
2 tablespoons lemon juice

METHOD

1 Sift the flour into a large bowl and make a well in the centre. Gradually whisk in the combined eggs and milk until the batter is smooth and free of lumps. Stir in the melted butter, transfer to a jug, cover and set aside for 30 minutes.
2 Heat a crepe pan or non-stick frying pan and brush lightly with melted butter. Pour enough batter into the pan, swirling to thinly cover the base, and pour any excess batter back into the jug. Cook for 30 seconds, or until golden brown and completely set on the upper part. Transfer to a plate and cover while cooking the remaining batter, greasing the pan when necessary. Stack the crepes between baking paper to prevent them sticking together.
3 To make the ricotta filling, put the raisins in a bowl with the liqueur, if using, and stir to combine. Set aside for 30 minutes. Using electric beaters, beat the ricotta, sugar, lemon zest and juice for 1–2 minutes, or until smooth. Stir in the raisins and liqueur.
4 Preheat the oven to 160°C (315°F/Gas 2–3). Place a heaped tablespoon of filling on the centre of each crepe, then fold into a flat parcel. Place the filled crepes, folded side down, in a greased ovenproof dish in a single layer. Brush each crepe lightly with the melted butter. Cover with foil and bake for 10–15 minutes, or until hot. Serve with a light dusting of sifted icing sugar.

NOTE: Ricotta blintzes can be assembled several hours in advance and heated just before serving.

PANCAKE STACK

Pancakes are traditionally served on Shrove Tuesday to celebrate renewal, family life and hopes for future good fortune and happiness.

MAKES 9 PANCAKES

INGREDIENTS

- 185 g (6½ oz/1½ cups) self-raising flour
- 1 teaspoon baking powder
- 2 tablespoons caster (superfine) sugar
- 2 eggs, lightly beaten
- 250 ml (9 fl oz/1 cup) milk
- 60 g (2¼ oz) unsalted butter, melted
- 100 g (3⅓ oz) unsalted butter, whipped, to serve
- maple syrup, to serve

METHOD

1. Sift the flour, baking powder, sugar and a pinch of salt into a bowl. Make a well in the centre.
2. Mix together the eggs, milk and melted butter in a jug and pour into the well all at once, whisking to form a smooth batter. Cover the bowl with plastic wrap and set the batter aside for 20 minutes.
3. Heat a frying pan over low heat and brush lightly with melted butter or oil. Pour 60 ml (2 fl oz/¼ cup) of the batter into the pan and swirl gently to create a pancake about 10 cm (4 inches) in diameter. Cook for 1 minute, or until the underside is golden. Turn the pancake over and cook the other side very quickly — about 10 seconds. Transfer to a plate and keep warm while cooking the remaining batter.
4. Serve the pancakes stacked, topped with whipped butter and drizzled with maple syrup.

WAFFLES

Waffles are a crisp cake made by cooking batter on a special purpose waffle iron, which gives the waffle a honeycombed pattern. Waffles are traditionally served with a sweet sauce such as maple syrup, and cream or ice cream, or you can drizzle them with a warm chocolate sauce and top with vanilla ice cream.

MAKES 8

INGREDIENTS

- 250 g (9 oz/2 cups) self-raising flour
- 1 teaspoon bicarbonate of soda (baking soda)
- 2 teaspoons sugar
- 2 eggs
- 90 g (3¼ oz) unsalted butter, melted
- 440 ml (15½ fl oz/1¾ cups) buttermilk
- maple syrup or warm chocolate fudge sauce (page 647), to serve

METHOD

1. Sift the flour, bicarbonate of soda, sugar and a pinch of salt into a large bowl and make a well in the centre.
2. Whisk the eggs, melted butter and buttermilk in a jug and gradually pour into the well, whisking until the batter is just smooth. Set aside for 10 minutes. Preheat the waffle iron.
3. Brush the waffle iron with melted butter. Pour about 125 ml (4 fl oz/½ cup) batter (the amount will vary according to your waffle iron) into the centre and spread the batter almost to the corners of the grid.
4. Cook the waffle for about 2 minutes, or until golden and crisp. Keep the cooked waffles warm while cooking the remaining mixture. Serve with maple syrup or chocolate sauce, and vanilla ice cream if desired.

MAPLE SYRUP

Maple syrup and maple sugar are made from the sap of certain species of maple trees found only in Canada and parts of North America. A hole is cut into the trunk of the tree, the sap runs down a metal spigot, and is caught in buckets or collection tubes below. Maple sap is watery, almost flavourless, and needs to be reduced to roughly a quarter of its volume to produce maple syrup, and further reduced to produce maple sugar. Large quantities of sap are needed to produce only a small amount of maple syrup, one of the main reasons that the syrup is so expensive.

Maple syrup can be used as a sweetener like honey as well as a pouring syrup. It goes well with waffles and pancakes, can be used as a glaze for ham, or in desserts and baking. Pure maple syrup is expensive and its price tag is a good indication that what you are buying is 100 per cent pure. Less expensive versions may be synthetically reproduced or the syrup may be mixed with corn syrup.

PIKELETS WITH JAM

MAKES 18

INGREDIENTS

125 g (4½ oz/1 cup) self-raising flour
1 tablespoon caster (superfine) sugar
185 ml (6 fl oz/¾ cup) milk
1 egg
jam, to serve

METHOD

1. Sift the flour, sugar and a pinch of salt into a large bowl and make a well in the centre. Whisk the milk and egg in a jug and slowly pour into the well, whisking to form a smooth batter.
2. Heat a non-stick frying pan over medium heat and brush lightly with melted butter or oil.
3. Drop level tablespoons of the batter into the frying pan, allowing room for spreading (you will probably fit about four pikelets in the pan at a time). Cook the pikelets for about 30 seconds, or until small bubbles begin to appear on the surface and the underneath has turned golden brown. Turn the pikelets over and cook the other side.
4. Transfer to a plate or wire rack to cool, and repeat with the remaining batter. Serve the pikelets topped with jam, and with whipped cream if desired.

BLINIS

Blinis are small yeast savoury pancakes originally from Russia and make from buckwheat flour. Traditionally they are topped with sour cream and strips of smoked salmon or caviar, or for sweet toppings try homemade fruit jams with crème fraîche, or mascarpone cheese and thinly sliced pear.

MAKES ABOUT 40

INGREDIENTS

200 g (7 oz/1½ cups) buckwheat flour
125 g (4½ oz/1 cup) plain (all-purpose) flour
2 teaspoons dried yeast
625 ml (21 fl oz/2½ cups) warm milk
2 tablespoons unsalted melted butter
3 eggs, separated

METHOD

1. Sift the buckwheat and plain flours into a large non-metallic bowl. Add the yeast and a pinch of salt and mix well. Make a well in the centre and pour in the warm milk. Mix to a batter and beat for a couple of minutes to get rid of any lumps. Cover the bowl with plastic wrap and leave to rise for 1–2 hours, by which stage it should have formed a bubbly batter.
2. Using a fork, beat the bubbles out of the batter. Add the melted butter and 3 egg yolks and beat them in. In a separate bowl, whisk the 3 egg whites until stiff peaks form, then gently fold into the batter. Set aside for 10 minutes.
3. Grease a heavy-based frying pan (or, even better, a blini pan), add spoonfuls of the batter and fry until bubbles rise to the surface and the underside is brown.
4. Flip the blini over and cook the other side for about 1 minute until brown. Repeat with the rest of the batter. (If you don't need to use the full amount, any leftover blinis can be frozen.) Serve with a sweet or savoury topping.

CHURROS

Churros is a popular breakfast snack in Spain and is usually eaten with a rich, thick hot chocolate. The batter is piped through a star-shaped nozzle, cut into lengths, and deep-fried until golden and crisp. The churros is then sprinkled with icing sugar, or a mixture of sugar and ground cinnamon or nutmeg.

SERVES 4

INGREDIENTS

- 30 g (1 oz) unsalted butter
- 150 g (5½ oz) plain (all-purpose) flour
- ½ teaspoon finely grated orange zest
- ¼ teaspoon caster (superfine) sugar
- 2 eggs
- 1 litre (35 fl oz/4 cups) vegetable oil, for deep-frying
- icing (confectioners') sugar, to dust or 115 g (4 oz/½ cup) caster (superfine) sugar mixed with 1 teaspoon ground cinnamon

METHOD

1. Put the butter, flour, orange zest, caster sugar and a pinch of salt in a heavy-based saucepan with 170 ml (5½ fl oz/⅔ cup) water. Stir over low heat until the butter softens and forms a dough with the other ingredients. Keep cooking for 2–3 minutes, stirring constantly, until the dough forms a ball around the spoon and leaves a coating on the base of the pan.
2. Transfer the dough to a food processor and, with the motor running, add the eggs. Do not overprocess. If the dough is too soft to snip with scissors, return it to the pan and cook, stirring, over low heat until it is firmer. Spoon the dough into a piping (icing) bag fitted with a 5 mm (¼ inch) star nozzle.
3. Put the oil in a deep heavy-based saucepan and heat to 180°C (350°F), or until a cube of bread dropped into the oil turns golden brown in 15 seconds. Pipe lengths of batter 6–8 cm (2½–3 inches) long into the oil, a few at a time — pipe with one hand and cut the batter off using scissors in the other hand. Fry for about 3 minutes, or until the churros are puffed and golden, turning once or twice. Transfer to paper towels to drain.
4. While still hot, toss the churros in either icing sugar or the sugar and cinnamon mixture and serve at once.

BANANA FRITTERS

SERVES 4

INGREDIENTS

- 125 g (4½ oz/1 cup) self-raising flour
- 1 egg, beaten
- 185 ml (6 fl oz/¾ cup) soda water
- 20 g (¾ oz) unsalted butter, melted
- oil, for deep-frying
- 4 firm bananas
- butterscotch sauce (page 646), to serve
- ice cream, to serve

METHOD

1. To make the batter, sift the flour into a bowl and make a well in the centre. Add the egg and soda water and whisk until smooth. Whisk in the melted butter.
2. Fill a deep heavy-based saucepan one-third full of oil and heat to 200°C (400°F), or until a cube of bread dropped into the oil turns golden brown in 5 seconds.
3. Cut each banana into thirds and add to the batter in batches. Use a spoon to coat the banana in the batter, then, using a slotted spoon, carefully lower the banana into the hot oil in batches. Cook each batch for 2–3 minutes, turning them carefully, until the fritters are puffed and golden brown. Drain on paper towels.
4. Serve the fritters hot, drizzled with butterscotch sauce, and with ice cream.

••FRUIT DESSERTS••

Fresh fruit — from a crisp, sweet apple, to a bowl of fresh berries or the rich extravagance of a perfectly ripe fig — is the simplest dessert we have, and it can be one of the most stunning. From here it is but a tiny step to baking, grilling, poaching in a boozy syrup, or combining fruit in a salad or compote, served with a dollop of thick cream.

NECTARINES AND PEACHES

Nectarines are smooth-skinned stone fruit similar to, but distinctly different in flavour to, peaches, to which they are related. Their colour ranges from silvery white or yellowy orange to pinkish red. The white-fleshed varieties are considered the best and are usually the most expensive. Press gently along the seam to see that they are ripe. While they will soften at room temperature, they won't ripen further after picking.

Peaches can be either slipstone (flesh separating easily from the stone) or clingstone (flesh clinging to the stone). Among the many varieties, white-fleshed peaches are considered to be the best eating. Peaches spoil quickly so only buy as needed. They should last 3–4 days at room temperature, unless already very ripe. If stored in the fridge, remove before eating as they are less flavoursome when chilled. The flesh can turn brown on contact with air, so prepare as needed or sprinkle the flesh with a little lemon juice.

AMARETTI-STUFFED NECTARINES

SERVES 4

INGREDIENTS

- 100 g (3½ oz) amaretti biscuits
- 4 tablespoons mascarpone cheese
- 4 firm slipstone nectarines
- 1 tablespoon soft brown sugar
- extra mascarpone, to serve

METHOD

1. Preheat the oven to 180°C (350°F/Gas 4).
2. Put the amaretti biscuits in a plastic bag and crush with a rolling pin. Transfer to a bowl with the mascarpone and stir to combine.
3. Cut the nectarines in half, remove the stones and put them in an ovenproof dish. Pile the mascarpone and amaretti mixture into the nectarine cavities. Sprinkle with the sugar and bake for 8–10 minutes. Serve with a dollop of extra mascarpone.

PEACH MELBA

SERVES 4

INGREDIENTS

- 300 g (10½ oz) fresh raspberries, or thawed frozen raspberries
- 2 tablespoons icing (confectioners') sugar
- 330 g (11½ oz/1½ cups) sugar
- 1 vanilla bean, split lengthways
- 4 firm peaches
- vanilla ice cream, to serve

METHOD

1. Put the raspberries and icing sugar in a food processor and purée. Pass the raspberry through a sieve and discard the seeds.
2. Put the sugar, vanilla bean and 625 ml (21 fl oz/ 2½ cups) water in a saucepan over low heat and stir until the sugar has completely dissolved.
3. Bring the sugar syrup to the boil and add the peaches, ensuring they are covered with the syrup. Simmer for 5 minutes, or until tender, then remove the peaches with a slotted spoon and carefully remove the skin.
4. Put a scoop of ice cream on a plate, add a peach then spoon the raspberry purée over the top.

PEACHES POACHED IN WINE

SERVES 4

INGREDIENTS

- 4 firm slipstone peaches
- 500 ml (17 fl oz/2 cups) dessert wine, such as Sauternes
- 60 ml (2 fl oz/¼ cup) orange liqueur, such as Cointreau
- 220 g (7¾ oz/1 cup) sugar
- 1 cinnamon stick
- 1 vanilla bean, split lengthways
- 8 small mint leaves
- mascarpone cheese or crème fraîche, to serve

METHOD

1. Peel the skin off the peaches (see below). Cut in half and carefully remove the stones.
2. Put the wine, liqueur, sugar, cinnamon stick and vanilla bean in a deep frying pan, large enough to hold the peach halves in a single layer. Heat the mixture, stirring until the sugar dissolves. Bring to the boil, then reduce the heat and simmer for 5 minutes. Add the peaches and simmer for 4 minutes, turning them over halfway through. Remove and leave to cool. Simmer the syrup for 6–8 minutes to thicken. Strain and set aside.
3. Arrange the peaches on a plate, cut side up. Spoon the syrup over the top and garnish each half with a mint leaf. Serve the peaches warm or chilled with mascarpone or crème fraîche.

HOW TO... PEEL STONE FRUIT

The skin of stone fruit can be difficult to remove. One of the easiest ways to remove it is to first blanch the fruit in boiling water, but take care not to leave the fruit in the water for too long or it will start to cook. First score a tiny cross at the base of the fruit and put into boiling water for 10 seconds for ripe fruit and up to 20 seconds for less ripe fruit. Using a slotted spoon, transfer each one carefully to a bowl of iced water to cool. Carefully loosen the skin at the cross using a small knife, then peel away the skin.

FRESH FRUIT COMPOTE

SERVES 6

INGREDIENTS

- 6 apricots
- 6 peaches
- 170 g (6 oz/¾ cup) sugar
- 24 pitted cherries
- zest of 1 orange, cut into very thin strips
- 80 ml (2½ fl oz/⅓ cup) dessert wine (optional)

METHOD

1. Peel the apricots and peaches (page 595) and cut into thick slices.
2. Put the sugar and 500 ml (17 fl oz/2 cups) water in a saucepan, bring to the boil and cook for 1 minute. Add the apricots, peaches, cherries and orange zest. Simmer for 2–3 minutes, or until the fruit is tender. Remove the fruit from the pan and simmer the syrup until it thickens. Add the dessert wine if you like.
3. Return the fruit to the syrup in the pan to warm. Serve either chilled or warm for breakfast or dessert, with cream, or sprinkled with cinnamon and sugar.

NOTE: You can use any fresh fruit in season, such as apples, pears or plums.

QUINCE

The quince is a fragrant relative of the apple, held sacred by the ancient Greeks as the fruit of Aphrodite, goddess of love. Golden when ripe, and often coated in a soft grey down, their flesh is firm, dryish and rarely softens sufficiently to eat raw. Quinces can be baked, stewed or poached, all of which make the flesh meltingly soft. When buying quinces choose the smoother, larger varieties, as these are easier to prepare and less wasteful. They go brown instantly when cut, so rub the cut surfaces with lemon juice.

QUINCE PASTE

SERVES 8–10

INGREDIENTS

3 large quinces
about 660 g (1 lb 7 oz/3 cups) sugar (see Notes)

METHOD

1 Wash the quinces, put them in a large pan and cover with water. Simmer for 30 minutes, until tender, then drain. Peel and core the quinces then push them through a sieve or potato ricer.
2 Weigh the fruit pulp, then put the pulp in a heavy-based saucepan and add the same weight of sugar. Cook over low heat, stirring occasionally with a wooden spoon, for 3½–4½ hours, or until very thick. Pour into a shallow 28 x 18 cm (11¼ x 7 inch) rectangular tin lined with plastic wrap. Allow to cool.

NOTES: The amount of sugar given above is a guide only and will vary depending on the size of the quinces. The amount of sugar you use should equal the weight of quince pulp. You can measure this once strained.
Quince paste, known as membrillo in Spain, can be kept for several months in a tightly sealed container. Serve with cheese and crackers, game or pâté.

POACHED QUINCE ON BRIOCHE

SERVES 8

INGREDIENTS

2 large quinces
lemon juice, for brushing
350 g (12 oz/1½ cups) caster (superfine) sugar
1 vanilla bean
1 cinnamon stick
1 cardamom pod
8 slices brioche
ground cinnamon, to sprinkle
caster (superfine) sugar, to sprinkle

METHOD

1 Peel and core the quinces, then cut them into quarters. Brush the flesh with a little lemon juice to prevent them turning brown.
2 Put 350 ml (12 fl oz) water, the sugar, vanilla bean, cinnamon stick and cardamom pod in a saucepan. Bring to the boil, stirring until the sugar has dissolved. Add the quinces, cover and simmer for 2–3 hours, or until very tender. Drain and simmer the cooking liquid until reduced to a syrup, then strain.
3 Toast the brioche slices and butter lightly. Sprinkle with a little cinnamon and caster sugar and top with the poached quince. Drizzle some syrup over the top and serve hot or cold.

PEARS

The pear is one of the most widely eaten fruits, after apples. Most varieties eaten today are the results of crosses developed in the seventeenth and eighteenth centuries in Europe and America as growers tried to develop a variety that was free of the tiny, hard grains within its cells that made pears gritty. Choose smooth, firm but not hard pears. Cut just before eating, or sprinkle with lemon juice to stop the flesh oxidising.

TYPES OF PEARS

WINTER NELIS
Small pear with a rough skin and spicy, juicy flesh.

PACKHAM'S
Large pear with green-yellow skin. Slow to ripen but has very soft, smooth flesh. A good dessert pear.

WILLIAM (BARTLETT)
Golden yellow skin, smooth white flesh, although some varieties are red (pictured below). Highly aromatic, slightly musky pear. Good dessert and cooking pear.

CONFERENCE
Easily recognised by its long thin shape and russet skin. It is sweet, juicy and refreshing. A good all-purpose pear.

COMICE
Large round pear with a short neck. Considered to be one of the finest pears in the world, it is exceptionally juicy. Often the variety served for dessert with cheese.

BEURRE
A juicy pear. Includes beurre bosc and beurre d'Anjou.

CORELLA
Small with a pretty green skin and pink blush; very white juicy flesh.

POACHED PEARS

SERVES 4

INGREDIENTS

- 300 g (10½ oz/1⅓ cups) sugar
- 2½ tablespoons lemon juice
- ½ cinnamon stick
- 4 cloves
- 1 vanilla bean
- 4 pears

METHOD

1. Use a saucepan large enough to hold 4 upright pears, plus their stalks. Put the sugar and 750 ml (26 fl oz/3 cups) water in the pan over low heat, stirring until the sugar has dissolved. Bring to the boil, add the lemon juice, cinnamon stick, cloves and vanilla bean.
2. Peel the pears, keeping their stalks attached. Place them upright in the saucepan, cover and poach very gently for 30–45 minutes, or until tender. Remove the pears to serving bowls and simmer the syrup until it is slightly thickened.
3. Spoon a little syrup over the pears. Serve warm or chilled with whipped cream or mascarpone.

winter nelis

packham's triumph

red william

conference

beurre bosc

corella

PEARS BELLE-HELENE

SERVES 6

INGREDIENTS

- 6 pears
- 360 g (12¾ oz/1⅔ cups) sugar
- 2 cinnamon sticks
- 2 cloves
- 6 scoops vanilla ice cream
- 250 ml (9 fl oz/1 cup) dark chocolate sauce (page 647)

METHOD

1. Peel the pears, leaving the stalks attached. Slice a small piece off the base of each pear so it sits flat, then remove the core, using a small knife.
2. Use a saucepan large enough to hold all the pears or cook them in two batches. Put the sugar, cinnamon sticks and cloves in the pan along with 750 ml (26 fl oz/3 cups) water. Stir over low heat until the sugar dissolves, then bring the syrup to the boil. Add the pears and simmer for 10 minutes, or until tender. Remove the pears with a slotted spoon and leave to cool.
3. Put a scoop of ice cream on each plate and make a hollow in each scoop with the back of a spoon. Stand the pears in the hollow and coat with the chocolate sauce.

GRILLED ORANGES WITH CARAMEL MINT BUTTER

SERVES 4

INGREDIENTS

- 80 g (2¾ oz/⅓ cup) caster (superfine) sugar
- 60 ml (2 fl oz/¼ cup) cream
- 45 g (1½ oz) unsalted butter, chopped
- 2 teaspoons finely grated orange zest
- 2 tablespoons finely chopped mint
- 6 oranges, peeled and segmented (see opposite)
- cream or mascarpone cheese, to serve

METHOD

1. Put the sugar and 60 ml (2 fl oz/¼ cup) water in a small saucepan over very low heat. Heat, shaking the pan occasionally, until the sugar dissolves (do not stir). Increase the heat, bring to the boil and cook until the sauce is deep golden.
2. Remove from the heat and gradually add the cream (the mixture will become lumpy and may spit, so be careful). Return to the heat and stir until the caramel dissolves. Add the butter, orange zest and mint and whisk until blended. Transfer to a bowl and refrigerate.
3. Preheat the grill (broiler) to hot. Arrange the orange segments slightly overlapping in a gratin or pie dish. Dot the top of the oranges with the caramel butter, then grill (broil) until the butter has melted. Serve with cream or mascarpone.

CLEMENTINES IN BRANDY

A clementine is a cross between a mandarin and a bitter Seville orange. To bottle clementines in brandy, wash enough small clementines to fill a 2 litre (8 cup) sterilised jar. Dissolve 1 kg (2 lb 4 oz) sugar in 1 litre (35 fl oz/4 cups) water, bring to the boil and simmer for 5 minutes. Prick the fruit all over with a needle, then put them in the syrup. Simmer for 1 hour, remove the fruit from the syrup and place in the jar. Simmer the syrup until thick, then add 500 ml (17 fl oz/2 cups) brandy. Cool, then pour over the fruit. Leave the fruit to infuse for 1 week.

ORANGES

Sweet oranges are eaten fresh and used in sorbets and granitas, and their aromatic zest can be used in sweet and savoury dishes. To use the zest in cooking, scrub, wash and dry the orange first. Grate the zest, but make sure you don't remove the bitter white pith, or use a zester to scrape down the side of the orange. Use a pastry brush to brush all the loose bits off the grater. If using the zest in a sweet dish, rub a sugar cube over the orange before grating it to extract the oils. Use a sharp knife or vegetable peeler to slice off pieces of orange zest, then cut it into fine strips and use these as decoration. Blanch the strips to make them more tender, if you prefer.

TYPES OF ORANGES

BLOOD

These have lots of red pigment in the flesh and skin, which gives the appearance of blood. They are rich, sweet and aromatic, but their season is short.

blood orange

SWEET

Including Valencia, these have smoother, firmer skin than the navel and more seeds. They are eaten fresh, used in sorbets and granitas, squeezed for their juice, or their aromatic zest can be used in baking or added to meat and fish stews and soups.

sweet orange

NAVEL

This orange is characterised by a navel-like depression at its base. It has a slightly pebbly skin and bright-orange colour and is nearly always seedless. It is ideal for desserts or eating fresh.

navel orange

BITTER

Bitter oranges are usually cooked and used in marmalades or dishes such as duck à l'orange. They have a thick zest, tough membrane and lots of seeds. The aromatic oils extracted from the skin are used to make Grand Marnier, Cointreau and Curaçao.

HOW TO... SEGMENT ORANGES

This simple technique cuts the orange into neat segments, and removes the tough membrane. Work over a bowl to collect the juice.

METHOD

1. Cut a thin slice from each end of the orange. Stand the fruit upright and slice off the skin and pith following the curve of the fruit.
2. Holding the orange in one hand, slice down the side of each segment to the core to free it from its membrane. Continue to work around the fruit, folding the membranes back as you release each segment. Once you have removed the orange segments, squeeze the core and membranes over the bowl to collect any remaining juice.

DATES

Date palms have been cultivated for their fruit for more than 5000 years. Although now grown commercially in many countries, the date palm is native to the Middle East where its fruit is held in high esteem and the tree honoured with the title of 'tree of life'. The Greek word *daktulos*, meaning 'finger', is thought to be the origin of its name, referring to the shape of the fruit. Green when unripe, dates turn pale honey to brown when ripened, though colour, texture and flavour can vary. Common date varieties include medjool, halawy and the highly prized degletnoor.

Store fresh dates at room temperature, or in an airtight container in the fridge. Store dried dates in an airtight container in a cool, dark place. Choose fresh dates with skin that is translucent when held to the light.

POACHED DATES

SERVES 4

INGREDIENTS

- 220 g (7¾ oz/1 cup) sugar
- 2 Earl Grey tea bags
- 2 cardamom pods
- 1 vanilla bean, split lengthways
- 16 fresh or dried dates, stoned

METHOD

1. Put the sugar and 500 ml (17 fl oz/2 cups) water in a saucepan with the tea bags, cardamom pods and vanilla bean. Boil for 5 minutes, then remove the tea bags.
2. Add the dates and poach for 2–3 minutes. Serve hot or cold with cream or mascarpone if desired.

FIGS

There are over a hundred varieties of figs, and these vary in colour from pale green and golden yellow to brown, red or purple. Some of the varieties of fig include the caprifig, smyrna, san pedro and common fig. When buying fresh figs, select firm, unblemished fruit that yield to gentle pressure. Peel the fruit (some thin-skinned varieties may be eaten with their skins on), cut off the stems and eat raw; slice and add to a cheeseboard or fruit salad; or lightly poach them. Because they are highly perishable, they are often dried or candied.

STUFFED FIGS

SERVES 6

INGREDIENTS

- 175 g (6 oz/½ cup) honey
- 125 ml (4 fl oz/½ cup) sweet dark sherry
- ¼ teaspoon ground cinnamon
- 18 large dried figs
- 18 whole blanched almonds
- 100 g (3½ oz) dark chocolate, cut into shards
- thick (double) cream, to serve (optional)

METHOD

1. Combine the honey, sherry, cinnamon and figs with 375 ml (13 fl oz/1½ cups) water in a large saucepan. Bring to the boil over high heat, then reduce the heat and simmer for 10 minutes. Remove the pan from the heat and set aside for 3 hours. Remove the figs with a slotted spoon, reserving the liquid.
2. Preheat the oven to 180°C (350°F/Gas 4). Return the pan of liquid to the stovetop and boil over high heat for 5 minutes, or until the liquid has reduced and is syrupy, then set aside. Snip the stems from the figs with scissors, then cut a slit in the top of each fig with a small sharp knife. Push an almond and a few shards of chocolate into each slit. Place the figs in a lightly buttered dish and bake for 15 minutes, or until the chocolate has melted.
3. Serve three figs per person with a little of the syrup drizzled over, and a dollop of cream.

FIGS IN HONEY SYRUP

SERVES 4

INGREDIENTS

- 12 fresh whole figs
- 100 g (3½ oz/⅔ cup) blanched whole almonds, toasted
- 110 g (3¾ oz/½ cup) sugar
- 115 g (4 oz/⅓ cup) honey
- 2 tablespoons lemon juice
- 6 cm (2½ inch) strip lemon zest
- 1 cinnamon stick
- 250 g (9 oz/1 cup) Greek-style yoghurt

METHOD

1. Cut the stems off the figs and make a small crossways incision 5 mm (¼ inch) deep on top of each. Push an almond into each fig. Roughly chop the remaining almonds.
2. Put 750 ml (26 fl oz/3 cups) water in a large saucepan, add the sugar and stir over medium heat until the sugar dissolves. Increase the heat and bring to the boil. Stir in the honey, lemon juice, strip of lemon zest and cinnamon stick. Reduce the heat to medium, place the figs in the saucepan and simmer gently for 30 minutes. Remove the figs with a slotted spoon and place in a large serving dish.
3. Boil the liquid in the pan over high heat for 15–20 minutes, or until thick and syrupy. Remove the cinnamon and lemon zest. Cool the syrup slightly and pour over the figs. Sprinkle with the chopped almonds and serve with the yoghurt.

SUMMER PUDDING

SERVES 4–6

INGREDIENTS

- 150 g (5½ oz) blackcurrants
- 150 g (5½ oz) redcurrants
- 150 g (5½ oz) raspberries
- 150 g (5½ oz) blackberries
- 200 g (7 oz) strawberries, hulled and quartered or halved
- caster (superfine) sugar, to taste
- 6–8 slices good-quality white bread, crusts removed

METHOD

1 Put all the berries, except the strawberries, in a large saucepan with 125 ml (4 fl oz/½ cup) water and heat gently until the berries begin to collapse. Add the strawberries and turn off the heat. Add the sugar, to taste (how much you need will depend on how ripe the fruit is). Set aside to cool.

2 Line six 150 ml (5 fl oz) moulds or a 1 litre (35 fl oz/4 cup) pudding basin with the bread. For the small moulds, use 1 slice of bread for each, cutting a circle to fit the bottom and strips to fit the sides. For the large pudding basin, cut a large circle out of 1 slice for the bottom and cut the rest of the bread into fingers. Drain a little juice off the fruit mixture. Dip one side of each piece of bread in the juice before fitting it, juice side down, into the moulds, leaving no gaps. Do not squeeze it or flatten it or the bread will not absorb the juices as well.

3 Fill the centre of the bread-lined moulds with the fruit and add a little juice. Cover the top with a layer of dipped bread, juice side up, and cover with plastic wrap. Put a plate, which fits inside the large pudding basin, onto the plastic wrap, then weigh it down. If using small moulds, stack them on top of each other to weigh them down. Refrigerate overnight. Carefully turn out the pudding and serve with any leftover fruit mixture. Serve with whipped cream if desired.

HOW TO... STEM CURRANTS

Currants are often sold still attached to the stalk, and the easiest way to remove them is to slide the tines of a fork down either side of the stalk, popping off the berries on either side. This is called 'strigging' or stemming (the word 'strig' was the sixteenth century name for a stalk).

LOGANBERRIES

A berry first raised in the garden of Judge Logan in California, these berries are thought to be a hybrid of the raspberry and blackberry. Resembling both in flavour, loganberries can be used as you would raspberries, and are delicious both raw and cooked. Like most berries, loganberries are available in summer. Store in the vegetable crisper and wash just before use.

STRAWBERRIES WITH BALSAMIC VINEGAR

This might seem an odd combination, but this dish has been served in Italy since Renaissance times. The balsamic vinegar adds an acidic piquancy to the berries. Serve with mascarpone cheese, ice cream or whipped cream to counterbalance the flavours.

SERVES 6

INGREDIENTS

- 500 g (1 lb 2 oz) strawberries, hulled and halved
- 60 ml (2 fl oz/¼ cup) good-quality balsamic vinegar
- 2 tablespoons caster (superfine) sugar
- 2 teaspoons lemon juice
- 1 small handful small mint leaves

METHOD

1. Put the strawberries in a glass bowl. Heat the balsamic vinegar, sugar and lemon juice in a small saucepan, stirring until combined. Remove from the heat and leave to cool.
2. Pour the balsamic vinegar mixture over the strawberries, add the mint and toss. Cover with plastic wrap and marinate in the fridge for at least 1 hour.

RED FRUIT SALAD

SERVES 6

INGREDIENTS

- 55 g (2 oz/¼ cup) caster (superfine) sugar
- 125 ml (4 fl oz/½ cup) dry red wine
- 1 star anise
- 1 teaspoon finely grated lemon zest
- 250 g (9 oz) strawberries, hulled and halved
- 150 g (5½ oz) blueberries
- 150 g (5½ oz) raspberries or mulberries
- 250 g (9 oz) cherries
- 5 small red plums (about 250 g/9 oz), stones removed, quartered

METHOD

1. To make the syrup, put the sugar, wine, star anise, lemon zest and 125 ml (4 fl oz/½ cup) water in a small saucepan. Bring to the boil over medium heat, stirring to dissolve the sugar. Boil the syrup for 3 minutes, then set aside to cool for 30 minutes. When cool, strain the syrup.
2. Mix the fruit together in a large bowl and pour on the red wine syrup. Mix well to coat the fruit in the syrup and refrigerate for 1½ hours. Serve the fruit dressed with a little syrup and with plain yoghurt or ice cream if desired.

FRUIT IN EAU DE VIE

FILLS A 1 LITRE (35 FL OZ/4 CUP) JAR

INGREDIENTS

250 g (9 oz) strawberries, hulled and halved
150 g (5½ oz) raspberries
150 g (5½ oz) blackberries
2 tablespoons caster (superfine) sugar
eau de vie (see Note)

METHOD

1 Layer the berries with the sugar in a 1 litre (35 fl oz/4 cup) glass jar until two-thirds full.
2 Pour in enough eau de vie to cover the berries. Put a lid on and store in a cool, dark place for at least 4 weeks. Serve with some of the syrup and whipped cream.

NOTE: Literally meaning 'water of life', eau de vie is the French term given to any strong, colourless brandy distilled from the fermented juice of fruit. Common examples include kirsch made from cherries, and framboise made from raspberries. Eau de vie is used to flavour desserts, pastries, sorbets or compotes, or can be drunk as an apéritif.

LEMONGRASS AND GINGER FRUIT SALAD

SERVES 4

INGREDIENTS

55 g (2 oz/¼ cup) caster (superfine) sugar
2 cm (¾ inch) piece ginger, thinly sliced
1 lemongrass stem, bruised and halved
1 large passionfruit
½ honeydew melon
1 large mango
1 small fresh pineapple
12 fresh lychees
1 small handful mint, shredded

METHOD

1 Put the sugar, ginger and lemongrass in a small saucepan, add 125 ml (4 fl oz/½ cup) water and stir over low heat to dissolve the sugar. Bring to the boil and cook for 5 minutes, or until the liquid has reduced to about 80 ml (2½ fl oz/⅓ cup). Cool, then strain the syrup and add the passionfruit pulp.
2 Peel and seed the melon and cut the flesh into large cubes. Peel the mango and cut the flesh into cubes (see below). Peel, halve and core the pineapple and cut into cubes. Peel the lychees, make a slit in the flesh and remove the seeds.
3 Put the fruit in a large serving bowl. Pour the syrup over the fruit. Garnish with the mint.

HOW TO... PEEL A MANGO

The best way to eat a mango or to cut the flesh into cubes is to cut it into a 'hedgehog'. First slice off the two cheeks of the unpeeled mango, close to the stone and, without cutting the skin, score the flesh in a crosshatched pattern. Push the skin inside out so the cubes of mango flesh pop out. It is then very easy to scoop the cubes of mango off the skin with a spoon or eat the fruit, as it is, straight off the skin.

MELON

Like other members of the melon family — cucumber, squash and zucchini — melons grow along the ground. Varieties abound, so there's nearly always one in season. Watermelons, however, are not true melons, they just share the same name.

If storing cut melon in the fridge, wrap it well or its strong smell may flavour other foods that are stored there. Melons are best served at room temperature, so remove them from the fridge about 30 minutes before you are ready to serve.

Pictured clockwise from bottom left: netted (musk) melon; seedless watermelon; white honeydew; watermelon; yellow honeydew, whole and cut.

TYPES OF MELONS

WINTER MELON

This variety of sweet melon has smooth yellow or yellow and green skin. Honeydew is a type of winter melon. It is a smooth yellow- or white-skinned melon with pale yellow-green flesh. Honeydew melon is best eaten when really ripe.

MUSK MELON

This variety of melon has a lovely musky smell when ripe. The skin has an irregular netted pattern, with either bright orange or pale green flesh. Galia, a variety of musk melon, is a spherical melon with a netted pattern on its skin. As it ripens, its skin turns from dark green to golden. These melons are also known as rockmelons, netted melons or commercially as canteloupe in America.

CANTELOUPE MELON

These small, round melons have grey-green skin with segmented grooves along the skin. The fragrant flesh is orange-yellow and very sweet. This group of melons includes chanterais and ogen, a melon first cultivated in Israel, with green skin and pale green, sweet flesh.

WATERMELON

Watermelon is so named because of its high water content of 92 to 95 per cent. They have sweet dark pink to red flesh, which contains seeds, although seedless varieties have been cultivated. Watermelon is best served lightly chilled and cut into wedges. Not just the sweet flesh, but all parts are edible: the seeds may be dried, roasted and salted or the rind may be pickled.

HOW TO... BUY A RIPE MELON

A ripe melon should give slightly at the base (opposite to the stalk). When buying a melon, hold it to your nose and smell it — a ripe melon will have a lovely musky 'melony' smell.

It is difficult to tell if a watermelon is ripe but if buying it whole, tap the fruit — it should sound hollow like a drum. The area where the melon rested on the ground should be pale yellow, not white or green.

APPLES

Apples were one of the earliest cultivated fruits, and today there are around 8000 varieties to choose from. High in vitamin C and fibre, apples are a healthy snack, and are a useful ingredient in both sweet and savoury dishes. To stop apple slices turning brown, brush them with lemon juice or use them as soon as you slice them.

TYPES OF APPLES

EATING

Good eating (dessert) apples are sweet and often slightly acidic. They can be sliced and tossed in salads, or served with a cheese platter. As these apples have a high sugar content, they hold their shape well and are perfect for use in baked pies and tarts, or if fried and caramelised, are excellent with pork or chicken. Good eating apples include: braeburn, fuji, discovery, empire, red delicious, royal gala, russet and lady william.

COOKING AND EATING

Apples suitable for cooking, such as those used to make purées or crumbles, are more acidic and become soft and break up when stewed or baked. Some apples are good for both cooking and eating: spartan, golden delicious (hold their shape well), cox's orange pippin, rome, granny smith (good for purée), pink lady, jonagold and jonathan.

COOKING

Apples such as bramley, grenadier and newton wonder are usually very sour and are best used as cooking apples. These apples make excellent purées because their flesh breaks down easily.

HOW TO... STORE APPLES

Don't store apples next to ethylene-sensitive fruit and vegetables, such as beans, broccoli and zucchini, because the ethylene gas given off by apples causes these fruit and vegetables to deteriorate faster. Similarly, one bad apple in a bag will give off lots of ethylene, causing the other apples to go bad. Apples store well at room temperature, but will maintain their crisp texture for longer if kept in the vegetable crisper of the fridge.

red delicious

fuji

jonathan

golden delicious

granny smith

pink lady

bramley

royal gala

lady william

BAKED APPLES

Remove the cores from 4 eating apples. Mix 4 tablespoons sultanas with 1 tablespoon softened butter and a large pinch of mixed spice. Stuff the cores and bake at 180°C (350°F/Gas 4) for 30 minutes, or until tender. Serves 4

••BAKED DESSERTS••

Baked desserts are the stuff of childhood dreams — comfort food to warm and nurture; often an irresistible combination of autumn fruits and buttery doughs. But that's not to say this is strictly a cold-weather chapter — the truly dedicated can enjoy their crumbles, cobblers, betties and other baked puddings all year round.

CHERRY CLAFOUTIS

A clafoutis (pronounced 'clafootee') is a classic French batter pudding. Traditionally, but unwisely, the cherry stones are left in but you can use pitted cherries if you prefer. Other berries such as blueberries, blackberries or raspberries may be used. Use a shallow pie plate or the top will not turn golden brown.

SERVES 6–8

INGREDIENTS

- 500 g (1 lb 2 oz) fresh cherries, or 800 g (1 lb 12 oz) tin pitted cherries
- 60 g (2¼ oz/½ cup) plain (all-purpose) flour
- 75 g (2½ oz/⅓ cup) sugar
- 4 eggs, lightly beaten
- 250 ml (9 fl oz/1 cup) milk
- 25 g (1 oz) unsalted butter, melted
- icing (confectioners') sugar, to dust

METHOD

1. Preheat the oven to 180°C (350°F/Gas 4). Brush a 23 cm (9 inch) glass or ceramic shallow pie plate with melted butter.
2. Pit the cherries and spread them onto the pie plate in a single layer. If using tinned cherries, drain them thoroughly in a sieve before spreading in the plate. If they are still wet, the juices will leak into the batter.
3. Sift the flour into a bowl, add the sugar and make a well in the centre. Gradually add the combined egg, milk and butter, whisking until smooth and free of lumps.
4. Pour the batter over the cherries and bake for 30–35 minutes, or until the batter has risen and is golden. Remove from the oven and dust generously with icing sugar. Serve immediately with cream or ice cream.

CHERRIES

Cherries are a glossy deep-red stone fruit, related to the plum, peach and apricot. There are more than 1000 varieties, which can be broadly grouped into three types: sweet, sour and hybrids. Sweet cherries can be eaten raw or cooked, and include napoleon, bing and rainier. Sour cherries are usually cooked in pies, added to jams or used as an accompaniment to savoury dishes, and include the morello and montmorency. Hybrids, such as duke cherries can be used for both eating and cooking.

Buy cherries with their stems on and use any without their stems first as they don't last as long. The stems should be pliable: brown, brittle stems indicate the cherries are old. Store sweet cherries in the fridge for up to 1 week; sour cherries will keep for several weeks.

APPLE COBBLER

SERVES 6

INGREDIENTS

1 kg (2 lb 4 oz) cooking apples, peeled and cored
55 g (2 oz/¼ cup) caster (superfine) sugar
25 g (1 oz) unsalted butter, melted
1 teaspoon finely grated orange zest
2 tablespoons orange juice

TOPPING

85 g (3 oz/⅔ cup) self-raising flour
40 g (1½ oz/⅓ cup) plain (all-purpose) flour
50 g (1¾ oz) unsalted butter, chopped
2 tablespoons caster (superfine) sugar
1 egg, lightly beaten
2–3 tablespoons milk
1 teaspoon raw (demerara) sugar

METHOD

1 Preheat the oven to 180°C (350°F/Gas 4). Cut the apples into 8–12 wedges and combine them with the sugar, butter, orange zest and juice in a large bowl. Mix well until all the apple pieces are thoroughly coated. Transfer to a 1.5 litre (6 cup) ovenproof dish about 5 cm (2 inches) deep, cover with foil and bake for 40 minutes, or until the apples are tender, stirring once halfway through cooking.

2 When the apples have been cooking for about 30 minutes, start to prepare the topping. Sift the flours into a bowl and rub the butter into the mixture until it resembles fine breadcrumbs. Stir in the sugar and make a well in the centre of the mixture. Using a flat-bladed knife, stir in the egg and enough milk to make a mixture of thick dropping consistency.

3 Take the apples out of the oven, remove the foil and drop spoonfuls of the mixture onto the cooked apples, covering the surface. Sprinkle with the raw sugar and return to the oven. Bake for 35 minutes, or until the top is golden and cooked. Serve hot with cream or custard.

RHUBARB CRUMBLE

SERVES 4–6

INGREDIENTS

1 kg (2 lb 4 oz) rhubarb, trimmed, cut into pieces
140 g (5 oz/⅔ cup) sugar
100 g (3½ oz) unsalted butter, chopped
90 g (3¼ oz/¾ cup) plain (all-purpose) flour
75 g (2½ oz/⅓ cup) raw (demerara) sugar
10 amaretti biscuits, crushed
2 tablespoons golden syrup or pure maple syrup
3 amaretti biscuits, extra, crushed
200 ml (7 fl oz) thick (double) cream

METHOD

1 Preheat the oven to 200°C (400°F/Gas 6). Put the rhubarb in a saucepan with the sugar. Stir over low heat until the sugar has dissolved, then cover and simmer for 8–10 minutes, or until the rhubarb is soft. Taste the rhubarb — you may need to add a little more sugar. Spoon the rhubarb into a deep 1.5 litre (6 cup) ovenproof dish.

2 Rub the butter into the flour until the mixture resembles fine breadcrumbs, then stir in the raw sugar and biscuits. Sprinkle over the rhubarb and bake for 15 minutes, or until golden brown.

3 Swirl the golden syrup and extra biscuits through the cream, and serve with the rhubarb crumble.

APPLE AND PASSIONFRUIT CRUMBLE

SERVES 4–6

INGREDIENTS

- 4 passionfruit
- 4 green apples, such as granny smiths
- 55 g (2 oz/¼ cup) caster (superfine) sugar, plus 80 g (2¾ oz/⅓ cup)
- 60 g (2¼ oz/1 cup) shredded coconut
- 90 g (3¼ oz/¾ cup) plain (all-purpose) flour
- 80 g (2¾ oz) unsalted butter, chopped

METHOD

1. Preheat the oven to 180°C (350°F/Gas 4). Grease a 1 litre (35 fl oz/4 cup) ovenproof dish.
2. Sieve the passionfruit, discarding the pulp, and place the juice in a bowl. Peel, core and thinly slice the apples and add to the passionfruit juice, along with the 55 g (2 oz/¼ cup) of sugar. Mix well, then transfer the mixture to the prepared dish.
3. Combine the shredded coconut, flour, extra sugar and butter in a bowl and rub together until the mixture resembles breadcrumbs. Pile on top of the apple mixture.
4. Bake the crumble for 25–30 minutes, or until the topping is crisp and golden. Serve with thick cream or ice cream.

CHERRY SLUMP

SERVES 6

INGREDIENTS

- 500 g (1 lb 2 oz) fresh or tinned cherries, pitted
- caster (superfine) sugar, to taste
- 185 g (6½ oz/1½ cups) self-raising flour
- 1 teaspoon baking powder
- 50 g (1¾ oz) unsalted butter, chopped
- 55 g (2 oz/¼ cup) raw (demerara) sugar
- 150 ml (5 fl oz) cream

METHOD

1. Put the cherries and 60 ml (2 fl oz/¼ cup) water in a large saucepan. Cook for 5 minutes over medium heat, until the cherries have begun to soften. Add the caster sugar, to taste, and transfer to a 1 litre (35 fl oz/4 cup) ovenproof dish. Preheat the oven to 200°C (400°F/Gas 6).
2. Sift the flour, baking powder and a little salt into a large bowl. Add the butter and raw sugar and rub in the butter using your fingertips until the mixture resembles fine breadcrumbs. Pour in the cream and stir well to mix everything together — you should have a spreadable mixture.
3. Cover the cooled cherries with blobs of the topping mixture, leaving small gaps between each. Bake for 25 minutes, or until the topping is puffed and golden. Serve with whipped cream.

COBBLERS, SLUMPS, GRUNTS AND CRUMBLES

These are simple fruit desserts, with a topping, served straight from the oven. Cobblers are made in a deep dish filled with fruit and topped with dough. The dough is shaped into overlapping circles or squares and, when baked and brown, the topping looks similar to cobblestones. Fruit such as plums, apples and mixed berries are typically used. Slumps and grunts are similar to cobblers, but some versions are cooked on the stovetop. The fruit supposedly 'grunts' as it cooks. A crumble, or crisp, is a dessert of cooked fruit topped with a crumbly mixture of butter, flour and sugar. The crumble is baked in the oven until the topping is crisp and golden. Sometimes nuts and oats are added to the crumble mixture, or the crumble may be made using biscuit crumbs, muesli or breadcrumbs. Apples, rhubarb and blueberries are popular fruit used in crumbles.

APPLE BETTY

This classic North American dessert, in its many guises, usually consists of sliced or puréed fruit mixed with spices and sugar and layered with breadcrumbs. The main characteristic of this pudding is that the breadcrumbs are layered with the fruit, not just sprinkled over the top.

SERVES 4–6

INGREDIENTS

- 5 cooking apples, peeled, cored and chopped
- 100 g (3½ oz) unsalted butter
- 95 g (3¼ oz/½ cup) soft brown sugar, plus 1 tablespoon
- finely grated zest of 1 lemon
- ¼ teaspoon ground cinnamon
- pinch of ground nutmeg
- 240 g (8½ oz/3 cups) fresh breadcrumbs

METHOD

1. Put the apples in a saucepan with 1 tablespoon of the butter, 1 tablespoon of the brown sugar and the lemon zest, cinnamon and nutmeg. Cook over medium heat for 10–15 minutes, or until the apples are very soft.
2. Preheat the oven to 180°C (350°F/Gas 4). Melt the remaining butter in a frying pan over low heat and add the breadcrumbs and the remaining brown sugar. Toss everything together until all the crumbs are coated, and continue tossing while you fry the crumbs until golden brown.
3. Spread a third of the buttered breadcrumbs in a 1 litre (35 fl oz/4 cup) ovenproof dish and add half the apples. Repeat with another third of the crumbs and the remaining apples, then finish with a layer of crumbs. Bake for 20 minutes, or until the top is crisp and golden brown. Serve with cream or ice cream.

LEMON DELICIOUS

SERVES 4

INGREDIENTS

60 g (2¼ oz) unsalted butter, at room temperature
170 g (6 oz/¾ cup) caster (superfine) sugar
3 eggs, separated
1 teaspoon finely grated lemon zest
40 g (1½ oz/⅓ cup) self-raising flour, sifted
60 ml (2 fl oz/¼ cup) lemon juice
185 ml (6 fl oz/¾ cup) milk
icing (confectioners') sugar, to dust

METHOD

1 Preheat the oven to 180°C (350°F/Gas 4). Grease a 1 litre (35 fl oz/4 cup) ovenproof dish.
2 Using electric beaters, beat the butter, sugar, egg yolks and lemon zest in a small bowl until the mixture is light and creamy. Transfer to a bowl. Add the flour and stir with a wooden spoon until just combined. Add the lemon juice and milk and stir to combine.
3 Put the egg whites in a small, dry bowl. Using electric beaters, beat the egg whites until firm peaks form. Using a large metal spoon, fold a third of the egg white into the butter and flour mixture. Gently fold in the remaining egg white, being careful not to overmix.
4 Spoon the mixture into the dish and place the dish in a deep baking tin. Pour boiling water into the tin to come one-third of the way up the side of the dish. Bake for 40 minutes, or until the top of the pudding is golden, risen and is firm to the touch. Divide among bowls, and spoon some sauce on each. Dust with icing sugar and serve with whipped cream or ice cream.

EVE'S PUDDING

SERVES 4–6

INGREDIENTS

500 g (1 lb 2 oz) cooking apples, peeled, cored and thickly sliced
2 tablespoons sugar
125 g (4½ oz) unsalted butter, softened
115 g (4 oz/½ cup) caster (superfine) sugar
2 eggs
1 teaspoon vanilla extract
125 ml (4 fl oz/½ cup) milk
185 g (6½ oz/1½ cups) self-raising flour, sifted

METHOD

1 Preheat the oven to 180°C (350°F/Gas 4). Grease a 1.5 litre (6 cup) ovenproof dish and line the base with baking paper.
2 Put the apple, sugar and 1 tablespoon water into a saucepan. Cover and cook over medium heat for 12 minutes, or until the apples are soft. Spoon the apples into the prepared dish.
3 Beat the butter and sugar until light and creamy. Add the eggs, one at a time, beating well after each addition. Using a large metal spoon, fold in the combined vanilla and milk alternately with the flour. Spoon the mixture over the apples and smooth the top. Bake for 40–45 minutes, or until the pudding is cooked when tested with a skewer.

QUEEN OF PUDDINGS

SERVES 6

INGREDIENTS

80 g (2¾ oz/1 cup) fresh breadcrumbs
500 ml (17 fl oz/2 cups) milk, scalded
2 eggs, separated
75 g (2½ oz/⅓ cup) sugar
3 tablespoons strawberry jam
150 g (5½ oz) strawberries, sliced

METHOD

1. Preheat the oven to 180°C (350°F/Gas 4). Grease a ceramic pie dish or ovenproof dish.
2. Put the breadcrumbs in a bowl with the hot milk and leave for 10 minutes. Beat the egg yolks with half the sugar and stir into the breadcrumb mixture. Spoon the custard mixture into the prepared dish and bake for 45 minutes, or until firm. Reduce the oven to 160°C (315°F/Gas 2–3).
3. Combine the jam and strawberries and spread over the custard mixture.
4. Using an electric mixer, beat the egg whites in a clean dry bowl until stiff peaks form, then beat in the remaining sugar to form a meringue. Spread the meringue over the jam and strawberries. Bake for 8–10 minutes, or until the meringue is set and lightly browned. Serve hot or warm.

APPLE CUSTARD PUDDING

SERVES 6

INGREDIENTS

180 g (6½ oz) unsalted butter, softened
115 g (4 oz/½ cup) caster (superfine) sugar
2 eggs
155 g (5½ oz/1¼ cups) self-raising flour, sifted
30 g (1 oz/¼ cup) custard powder
30 g (1 oz/¼ cup) ground almonds
250 ml (9 fl oz/1 cup) cream
4 cooking apples
2 tablespoons sugar

CUSTARD

1½ tablespoons custard powder
125 ml (4 fl oz/½ cup) milk
1 tablespoon sugar
90 g (3¼ oz/⅓ cup) sour cream

METHOD

1. To make the custard, combine the custard powder and a little of the milk and mix until smooth. Stir in the remaining milk. Pour into a saucepan, add the sugar and sour cream and stir over medium heat until the custard thickens and boils. Remove from the heat and cover the surface with plastic wrap.
2. Preheat the oven to 180°C (350°F/Gas 4). Beat the butter and sugar together until light and creamy. Add the eggs one at a time, beating well after each addition. Fold in the flour, custard powder and almonds alternately with the cream.
3. Place half the pudding mixture in a 2 litre (8 cup) ovenproof dish and spoon the custard over it. Top with the remaining mixture — smooth it with the back of a spoon. Bake for 45–50 minutes, or until the pudding is firm to the touch.
4. Peel, core and thinly slice the apples and put them in a pan with the sugar and 2 tablespoons water. Bring to the boil, then cover, reduce the heat and simmer for 10 minutes, until tender. Serve the pudding with the warm stewed apples.

APPLE CHARLOTTE

SERVES 8

INGREDIENTS

- 1.25 kg (2 lb 12 oz) cooking apples, peeled, cored and sliced
- 115 g (4 oz/½ cup) caster (superfine) sugar
- 1 tablespoon finely grated lemon zest
- 1 cinnamon stick
- 30 g (1 oz) unsalted butter
- 1 loaf sliced white bread, crusts removed
- softened butter

METHOD

1. Put the sliced apples in a large saucepan with the sugar, lemon zest, cinnamon stick and butter. Cook over low heat for about 10 minutes, stirring occasionally, until the apples are tender and the mixture is thick.
2. Preheat the oven to 200°C (400°F/Gas 6). Brush eight 125 ml (4 fl oz/½ cup) fluted moulds or ramekins with melted butter, or use a 1.25 litre (5 cup) charlotte tin or pudding basin.
3. To make the mini charlottes, cut out 16 rounds of bread, spread with the butter and put a round in each mould, buttered side down. Cut the remaining bread into wide strips, butter and use to line the sides of the moulds, either cutting to fit, or overlapping a little, with the buttered side against the mould. Spoon the apple into the bread-lined moulds, pressing down firmly. Put the remaining buttered rounds of bread on top, buttered side up. Press down firmly and bake for 15 minutes, or until golden.
4. For the large charlotte, cut a round of bread to fit the base, and wide strips to line the side. Leave enough bread to cover the top. Butter the bread and line the mould, overlapping the strips a little. Fill with the apple, put the remaining buttered rounds of bread on top, buttered side up, and bake for 30–40 minutes. Cover if it starts to overbrown. Cool a little before turning out. Serve with cream or ice cream.

❮ BREAD AND BUTTER PUDDING

SERVES 4

INGREDIENTS

- 60 g (2¼ oz) mixed raisins and sultanas
- 2 tablespoons brandy or rum
- 30 g (1 oz) unsalted butter
- 4 slices good-quality white bread or brioche loaf (see Note)
- 3 eggs
- 3 tablespoons caster (superfine) sugar
- 750 ml (26 fl oz/3 cups) milk
- 60 ml (2 fl oz/¼ cup) cream
- ¼ teaspoon vanilla extract
- ¼ teaspoon ground cinnamon
- 1 tablespoon raw (demerara) sugar

METHOD

1. Soak the raisins and sultanas in the brandy for about 30 minutes. Butter the slices of bread and cut each piece into eight triangles. Arrange the bread in a 1 litre (35 fl oz/4 cup) ovenproof dish.
2. Mix the eggs with the sugar, then add the milk, cream, vanilla and cinnamon and mix well. Drain the raisins and sultanas and add any soaking liquid to the custard.
3. Scatter the soaked raisins and sultanas over the bread and pour the custard over the top. Cover with plastic wrap and refrigerate for 1 hour.
4. Preheat the oven to 180°C (350°F/Gas 4). Remove the pudding from the refrigerator and sprinkle with the raw sugar. Transfer to the oven and bake for 35–40 minutes, or until the custard is set and the top is crunchy and golden.

NOTE: Instead of using sultanas and bread separately, you can use a good-quality raisin bread or brioche, as pictured. Use good-quality bread for this recipe. Ordinary sliced white bread will tend to go a bit gluggy when it soaks up the milk.

SELF-SAUCING CHOCOLATE PUDDING

SERVES 4–6

INGREDIENTS

- 125 g (4½ oz/1 cup) self-raising flour
- 40 g (1½ oz/⅓ cup) unsweetened cocoa powder
- 290 g (10¼ oz/1¼ cups) caster (superfine) sugar
- 1 egg
- 125 ml (4 fl oz/½ cup) milk
- 60 g (2¼ oz) unsalted butter, melted
- 1 teaspoon vanilla extract
- icing (confectioners') sugar, to dust

ORANGE CREAM

- 310 ml (10¾ fl oz/1¼ cups) whipping cream
- 1 teaspoon finely grated orange zest
- 1 tablespoon icing (confectioners') sugar
- 1 tablespoon orange liqueur, such as Grand Marnier

METHOD

1. Preheat the oven to 180°C (350°F/Gas 4). Grease a 2 litre (8 cup) ovenproof dish.
2. Sift the flour and 2 tablespoons of the cocoa into a large bowl. Stir in 115 g (4 oz/½ cup) of the sugar and make a well in the centre.
3. Put the egg in a bowl and lightly beat in the milk, butter and vanilla. Pour the egg and milk mixture into the well in the flour and stir until smooth, but do not overmix. Pour into the prepared dish.
4. Dissolve the remaining cocoa and sugar in 625 ml (21 fl oz/2½ cups) boiling water. Pour this gently over the back of a spoon over the pudding mixture. Transfer to the oven and bake for 40 minutes, or until a skewer comes out clean when inserted into the pudding.
5. To make the orange cream, beat the cream, orange zest, icing sugar and liqueur with electric beaters until soft peaks form.
6. Dust the pudding with sifted icing sugar and serve immediately with the orange cream.

••CHEESECAKES••

Cheesecakes are one of the earliest baked desserts — it is thought that the ancient Romans were the first to bake cheese into small cakes. It was the Americans who developed one of the versions popular today — a pastry or biscuit crumb base filled with a creamy cheese (usually cream, cottage or ricotta cheese) and egg mixture. The New York cheesecake, one of the most famous versions, is made with cream cheese and cream or sour cream. Usually cheesecakes are baked, but sometimes gelatine is added to the mixture and the cheesecake is left to set in the fridge. Before the cheesecake is set, it may be flavoured with cocoa, fruit purée or caramel, or fruit such as pears, apples or berries may be added.

BAKED CHEESECAKE WITH SOUR CREAM

SERVES 8–10

INGREDIENTS

250 g (9 oz) plain sweet biscuits
1 teaspoon mixed spice
100 g (3½ oz) unsalted butter, melted

FILLING

500 g (1 lb 2 oz) cream cheese, softened
145 g (5 oz/⅔ cup) caster (superfine) sugar
1 teaspoon vanilla extract
1 tablespoon lemon juice
4 eggs

TOPPING

250 g (9 oz/1 cup) sour cream
½ teaspoon vanilla extract
3 teaspoons lemon juice
1 tablespoon caster (superfine) sugar
ground nutmeg, to sprinkle

METHOD

1 Lightly grease a 20 cm (8 inch) spring-form cake tin and line the base with baking paper. Finely crush the biscuits in a food processor or place them in a sealed plastic bag and crush them with a rolling pin. Transfer to a bowl, add the mixed spice and butter and stir until the crumbs are all moistened. Spoon the mixture into the tin and press firmly onto the base and up the side to create an even shell. Refrigerate for 20 minutes, or until firm. Preheat the oven to 180°C (350°F/Gas 4).

2 To make the filling, beat the cream cheese with electric beaters until smooth. Add the sugar, vanilla and lemon juice, then beat until smooth. Add the eggs, one at a time, beating well after each addition. Pour the filling carefully over the crumbs and smooth the surface. Transfer to the oven and bake for 45 minutes, or until just firm to touch.

3 To make the topping, combine the sour cream, vanilla, lemon juice and sugar in a bowl. Spread the topping over the hot cheesecake. Sprinkle with nutmeg and return to the oven for another 7 minutes. Turn off the oven and leave to cool with the door ajar. When cool, refrigerate until firm. Decorate with strawberries if desired.

COOKING TIPS

* The different cheeses used in cheesecake recipes have varying moisture and fat contents and are not interchangeable. Using the wrong kind of cheese may result in a cheesecake that separates or sinks.
* Cool the cheesecake in the oven with the door slightly ajar. If the cheesecake is cooled too quickly, the top may crack.
* When cutting cheesecake, dip the knife into hot water, then dry it: the cheesecake will then be easier to cut without the cheese sticking to the knife.

NEW YORK CHEESECAKE

SERVES 10–12

INGREDIENTS

BASE

60 g (2¼ oz/½ cup) self-raising flour
125 g (4½ oz/1 cup) plain (all-purpose) flour
55 g (2 oz/¼ cup) caster (superfine) sugar
1 teaspoon finely grated lemon zest
80 g (2¾ oz) unsalted butter, chopped
1 egg

FILLING

750 g (1 lb 10 oz) cream cheese, softened
230 g (8 oz/1 cup) caster (superfine) sugar
30 g (1 oz/¼ cup) plain (all-purpose) flour
2 teaspoons finely grated orange zest
2 teaspoons finely grated lemon zest
4 eggs
170 ml (5½ fl oz/⅔ cup) whipping cream

375 ml (13 fl oz/1½ cups) whipping cream
candied citrus zest, to serve (optional) (see below)

METHOD

1 To make the base, combine the flours, sugar, lemon zest and butter in a food processor and process for about 30 seconds, until crumbly. Add the egg and process briefly until the mixture just comes together. Turn out onto a lightly floured surface and gather together into a ball. Cover with plastic wrap and refrigerate for about 20 minutes, or until the mixture is firm.

2 Preheat the oven to 210°C (415°F/Gas 6–7). Lightly grease a 23 cm (9 inch) spring-form cake tin. Roll the pastry between two sheets of baking paper until large enough to fit the base and side of the tin. Ease into the tin and trim the edges. Line the pastry with baking paper and fill with baking beads or rice. Blind bake for 10 minutes, then remove the paper and beads. Flatten the pastry lightly with the back of a spoon and bake for another 5 minutes. Set aside to cool.

3 Reduce the oven to 150°C (300°F/Gas 2). To make the filling, beat the cream cheese, sugar, flour and orange and lemon zest until smooth. Add the eggs, one at a time, beating well after each addition. Beat in the cream, then pour the cheese filling over the pastry and bake for about 1½ hours, or until almost set. Turn off the oven and leave to cool with the door ajar. When cool, refrigerate until firm.

4 Whip the cream and spoon it in small mounds around the outside of the cheesecake. Top the cream with candied zest if using.

CANDIED CITRUS ZEST

Remove the zest from 3 oranges, 3 lemons or 3 limes (or a mixture of each) and cut into julienne strips (or use a zester). Put the zest in a saucepan with a little water and bring to the boil. Simmer for 1 minute, then drain the water and repeat the boiling process. This will get rid of any bitterness in the zest and syrup. Drain, then put 220 g (7¾ oz/1 cup) sugar and 60 ml (2 fl oz/¼ cup) water in the pan and stir until the sugar has dissolved. Add the zest and bring to the boil, then reduce the heat and simmer for 5–6 minutes, or until it looks translucent — don't overcook or it will caramelise. Drain the zest and dry on baking paper (you can use the syrup to drizzle over the cheesecake if you like).

FROZEN HONEY PRALINE CHEESECAKE

SERVES 8–10

INGREDIENTS

100 g (3½ oz) flaked almonds
165 g (5¾ oz/¾ cup) sugar
225 g (8 oz) plain sweet biscuits
100 g (3½ oz) unsalted butter, melted

FILLING

250 g (9 oz) mascarpone cheese
250 g (9 oz) cream cheese, softened
400 ml (14 fl oz) tin sweetened condensed milk
90 g (3¼ oz/¼ cup) honey
310 ml (10¾ fl oz/1¼ cups) whipping cream
2 teaspoons ground cinnamon

METHOD

1 Preheat the oven to 150°C (300°F/Gas 2). To make the praline, spread the almonds on a foil-lined, greased baking tray. Put the sugar in a pan with 125 ml (4 fl oz/½ cup) water and stir over low heat until the sugar has dissolved. Bring to the boil, then simmer without stirring until the toffee is golden brown. Pour over the almonds, then set aside to cool and harden before breaking into pieces.
2 Lightly grease a 23 cm (9 inch) spring-form cake tin and line the base with baking paper. Reserve about half the praline and finely chop the rest with the biscuits in a food processor. Stir in the butter. Spoon the mixture into the tin and press firmly onto the base and up the side. Bake for 15 minutes, then leave to cool.
3 To make the filling, process the mascarpone and cream cheese in a food processor until soft and creamy. Add the condensed milk and honey. Whip the cream until soft peaks form and then fold into the cream cheese. Pour into the tin, sprinkle with cinnamon and swirl gently with a skewer. Freeze for several hours, or until firm. Decorate with the remaining praline.

PEAR AND GINGER CHEESECAKE

SERVES 10

INGREDIENTS

250 g (9 oz) plain sweet biscuits
2 tablespoons ground ginger
100 g (3½ oz) unsalted butter, melted

FILLING

3–4 firm ripe pears
230 g (8 oz/1 cup) caster (superfine) sugar
2 tablespoons lemon juice
500 g (1 lb 2 oz) cream cheese, softened
2 eggs
2 tablespoons ground ginger
300 g (10½ oz) sour cream

METHOD

1 Lightly grease a 23 cm (9 inch) spring-form cake tin and line the base with baking paper.
2 Finely crush the biscuits with the ginger in a food processor. Add the butter and mix well. Spoon into the tin and press firmly onto the base and up the side. Refrigerate for 10 minutes. Preheat the oven to 150°C (300°F/Gas 2).
3 To make the filling, peel, core and thinly slice the pears and put them with half the sugar, the lemon juice and 375 ml (13 fl oz/1½ cups) water in a saucepan. Bring to the boil, then reduce the heat and simmer until the pears are tender but not breaking up. Strain and set aside to cool.
4 Process the cream cheese and remaining sugar in a food processor until light and smooth. Mix in the eggs and ginger. Add the sour cream and process to combine. Arrange the pears over the base, pour the filling over the top and bake for 1 hour, or until set. Turn off the oven and leave to cool with the door ajar. When cool, refrigerate until firm. Serve with whipped cream.

NOTE: For a stronger ginger flavour, use gingernuts instead of plain biscuits for the base.

••STICKY AND STEAMED PUDDINGS••

Whether dense and rich or light and cakey, steamed or sticky puddings are one of the oldest, most traditional desserts. Eat just one sticky mouthful — perhaps with butterscotch, dark chocolate or a rich brandy sauce to soak into the sponge — and it's not too difficult to understand why these puddings are so irresistible.

HOW TO... STEAM A PUDDING

Originally, pudding mixture was tied in a cloth and suspended from a wooden spoon in a pan of boiling water to cook. Now, we use pudding basins, available in ceramic, glass, steel and aluminium. Ceramic ones don't have a lid but are the best insulators and let the pudding cook through without overcooking the edges.

PREPARING THE BASIN

First you will need a pudding basin with the right capacity. Measure this by filling it with water from a measuring cup. If your basin is too small, your pudding will expand right out of it.

Next, you need a large saucepan with a tight-fitting lid. The pan should comfortably hold a trivet or upturned saucer with the basin on top, with space for the lid to fit properly. You can use a steamer to cook puddings, and collapsible metal vegetable steamers can have their handles unscrewed so that you can stand a basin on them. Mini puddings can be cooked in a bamboo steamer or bain-marie in the oven.

Prepare the pudding basin by greasing it and placing a circle of baking paper in the bottom. Next, place a sheet of foil on the work surface, then a sheet of baking paper on top of it (a few dabs of oil on the foil will hold the paper in place). Grease the paper. Make a large pleat across the width of the foil and paper to allow for expansion as the pudding rises and pushes against it. Place the empty basin in the pan on top of its trivet and pour in cold water to come halfway up the side of the basin. Remove the empty pudding basin from the pan and put the water on to boil.

COVERING THE BASIN

Prepare the pudding mixture and spoon it into the basin, smoothing the top. Put the foil and paper across the top of the basin, foil side up, and smooth it down the side — don't press it onto the pudding. If you are using a metal basin, just clip on the lid. If not, tie a double piece of string around the rim of the basin. Tie the string in a knot, then, using another double piece of string, tie a handle onto the string around the basin — this will enable you to lift the pudding in and out of the water. The covering should be fairly watertight to keep the mixture dry.

STEAMING THE PUDDING

Lower the pudding carefully into the boiling water and reduce the heat to a fast simmer. Cover with the lid and cook as directed. Keep an eye on the water level and top it up with boiling water (to keep the cooking temperature constant) when necessary. When the cooking time is up, remove the basin from the pan and take off the foil and paper cover. If the pudding is a solid one, test it with a skewer (a fruit pudding, however, may leave the skewer sticky if you hit a piece of fruit) or press the top gently — it should be firm in the centre and well risen. If the pudding is not cooked, re-cover it and continue cooking. Leave for 5 minutes, then invert onto a plate. If the pudding is reluctant to come out of the basin, run a flat-bladed knife around the edge.

JAM PUDDING

SERVES 6

INGREDIENTS

- 160 g (5½ oz/½ cup) berry jam
- 185 g (6½ oz) unsalted butter, softened
- 170 g (6 oz/¾ cup) caster (superfine) sugar
- 1 teaspoon vanilla extract
- 3 eggs
- 60 g (2¼ oz/½ cup) plain (all-purpose) flour
- 125 g (4½ oz/1 cup) self-raising flour

METHOD

1. Preheat the oven to 180°C (350°F/Gas 4). Lightly grease a 1.75 litre (7 cup) pudding basin or six 250 ml (9 fl oz/1 cup) dariole or fluted moulds.
2. Spoon the jam evenly into the base of the pudding basin or moulds.
3. Beat the butter, sugar and vanilla with electric beaters for 1–2 minutes, or until light and creamy. Add the eggs one at a time, beating well after each addition. Using a metal spoon, gently fold in the combined sifted flour, a quarter at a time.
4. Spoon the mixture into the basin or moulds and smooth the surface. Cover with a piece of greased foil and baking paper, pleated in the middle. Secure with string (see opposite).
5. Put the pudding basin or moulds in a large deep baking tin. Pour in enough boiling water to come halfway up the side of the basin. Bake for 45 minutes (or 35 minutes for the smaller moulds), or until a skewer inserted into the pudding comes out clean.
6. Leave the pudding in the basin for 5 minutes before loosening the side with a knife and turning out onto a serving plate. Serve with custard, cream or ice cream.

SUSSEX POND PUDDING

SERVES 4–6

INGREDIENTS

- 340 g (12 oz/2¾ cups) self-raising flour
- 170 g (6 oz) suet or unsalted butter, frozen
- 150 ml (5 fl oz) milk
- 250 g (9 oz) unsalted butter, cubed
- 250 g (9 oz) raw (demerara) sugar
- 1 thin-skinned lemon

METHOD

1. Grease a 1.5 litre (6 cup) pudding basin and place in a saucepan on a trivet. Pour in enough water to come halfway up the side of the basin. Remove the basin and put the water on to boil. Place a sheet of foil on a work surface and put a sheet of baking paper on top. Grease the paper. Make a large pleat in the centre of the foil and paper (page 624).
2. Sift the flour into a large bowl, wrap one end of the frozen suet or butter in foil and grate into the flour. Mix into the flour, then mix in the milk and 150 ml (5 fl oz) water, using a flat-bladed knife. Bring together with your hands.
3. Keep one-quarter of the pastry aside for the lid and roll the rest into a 25 cm (10 inch) circle, leaving the middle thicker than the edges. Lift this into the basin and press upwards against the side until it fits, leaving a little bit above the rim.
4. Put half the butter and sugar in the basin, prick the lemon all over with a skewer and add to the basin with the rest of the butter and sugar. Fold the edge of the pastry into the basin and brush with water. Roll out the remaining pastry to form a lid and press firmly onto the rim of the pastry. Place the foil and paper over the basin, foil side up. Tie a double piece of string around the rim, knot tightly and, using another double piece of string, tie a handle onto the string to make it easier to remove when the pudding is ready. Lower the basin into the water. Cover the pan with a lid and steam for 3–4 hours, topping up the water as necessary.
5. Invert the pudding onto a plate with a rim. When cut, the juices will flow out to form the 'pond'.

WHAT IS SUET?

Suet is the firm white fat that surrounds the kidneys of beef and mutton. It has excellent cooking properties: it is stiff and melts slowly, and is used in many traditional British dishes to make pastry, suet puddings and mincemeat. It is the preferred fat for pastries as it gives them a good 'short' texture. Suet can be bought commercially in packages, usually granulated and coated with flour. Most butchers will supply fresh suet, which can be grated either by hand or in a food processor. You may need to order suet from your butcher ahead of time. Store it in the freezer to make it easier to grate.

SPOTTED DICK

Spotted Dick is a traditional British pudding made with a sweet suet pastry crust, which is rolled out and filled (spotted) with raisins or sultanas, currants and sugar, then rolled into a log. A similar pudding, spotted dog, has raisins mixed into the pudding. Because the differences between the two are so minimal, the names are often used interchangeably.

SERVES 4

INGREDIENTS

185 g (6½ oz/1½ cups) plain (all-purpose) flour
1½ teaspoons baking powder
110 g (3¾ oz/½ cup) sugar
1½ teaspoons ground ginger
160 g (5½ oz/2 cups) fresh breadcrumbs
60 g (2¼ oz/½ cup) sultanas
110 g (3¾ oz/¾ cup) currants
125 g (4½ oz) suet (see box, opposite), grated
2 teaspoons finely grated lemon zest
2 eggs, lightly beaten
170 ml (5½ fl oz/⅔ cup) milk

METHOD

1 Sift the flour, baking powder, sugar and ginger into a large bowl. Add the breadcrumbs, sultanas, currants, suet and lemon zest. Mix thoroughly with a wooden spoon.
2 Combine the egg and milk, add to the dry ingredients and mix well. Add a little more milk if necessary, then set aside for 5 minutes.
3 Lay a sheet of baking paper on the work surface and form the mixture into a roll shape about 20 cm (8 inches) long. Roll the pudding in the paper and fold up the ends — do not wrap it too tight as the pudding will expand as it cooks. Wrap in a tea towel, put it in the top of a bamboo or metal steamer, cover and steam over boiling water for 1½ hours. Do not let the water boil dry — replenish with boiling water as the pudding cooks. Unmould the pudding onto a plate and slice. Serve with custard or cream.

PECAN AND MAPLE SYRUP PUDDING

SERVES 8–10

INGREDIENTS

200 g (7 oz) unsalted butter, softened
230 g (8 oz/1 cup) caster (superfine) sugar
4 eggs, lightly beaten
1 teaspoon vanilla extract
375 g (13 oz/3 cups) self-raising flour, sifted
200 g (7 oz) pecans, chopped
½ teaspoon ground cinnamon
finely grated zest of 1 lemon
185 ml (6 fl oz/¾ cup) milk
250 ml (9 fl oz/1 cup) maple syrup

METHOD

1 Preheat the oven to 180°C (350°F/Gas 4). Beat the butter and sugar until creamy. Gradually beat in the eggs, then the vanilla. Combine the flour, three-quarters of the pecans, cinnamon and lemon zest and fold in, alternating with spoonfuls of milk, until smooth.
2 Grease a 2.25 litre (9 cup) pudding basin and line the base with a circle of baking paper. Pour three-quarters of the maple syrup into the basin and add the remaining pecans. Fill with the pudding mixture and pour the rest of the syrup over the top.
3 Cover with foil and put in a large baking tin. Pour enough water into the tin to come halfway up the side of the basin, then bake for 2 hours, or until a skewer inserted into the pudding comes out clean. Turn out onto a large serving plate. Serve with ice cream or cream.

SAGO PLUM PUDDING

SERVES 6–8

INGREDIENTS

65 g (2¼ oz/⅓ cup) sago
250 ml (9 fl oz/1 cup) milk
1 teaspoon bicarbonate of soda (baking soda)
140 g (5 oz/¾ cup) dark brown sugar
160 g (5¾ oz/2 cups) fresh breadcrumbs
60 g (2¼ oz/½ cup) sultanas
75 g (2½ oz/½ cup) currants
80 g (2¾ oz/½ cup) chopped dried dates
2 eggs, lightly beaten
60 g (2¼ oz) unsalted butter, melted and cooled
raspberries, to garnish
blueberries, to garnish
icing (confectioners') sugar, to dust
brandy cream sauce (page 649), to serve

METHOD

1 Combine the sago and milk in a bowl, cover and refrigerate overnight.
2 Lightly grease a 1.5 litre (6 cup) pudding basin with butter and line the base with baking paper. Place the empty basin in a large saucepan on a trivet and pour in enough cold water to come halfway up the side of the basin. Remove the basin and put the water on to boil.
3 Transfer the soaked sago and milk to a large bowl and stir in the bicarbonate of soda until dissolved. Stir in the sugar, breadcrumbs, dried fruit, eggs and butter and mix well. Spoon into the prepared basin and smooth the surface with wet hands.
4 Cover the basin (page 624) and make a string handle. Lower the basin into the boiling water, reduce to a fast simmer and cover the saucepan with a tight-fitting lid. Cook for 3½–4 hours, or until a skewer inserted into the pudding comes out clean. Check the water level hourly and top up with boiling water as necessary. Carefully remove the pudding basin from the saucepan, remove the coverings and leave for 5 minutes before turning out the pudding onto a large serving plate. Loosen the edges with a knife, if necessary.
5 Serve the pudding garnished with raspberries and blueberries and lightly dusted with icing sugar. Serve hot with the brandy cream sauce if desired.

CHOC FUDGE PUDDINGS

SERVES 8

INGREDIENTS

150 g (5½ oz) unsalted butter, softened
170 g (6 oz/¾ cup) caster (superfine) sugar
100 g (3½ oz) dark chocolate, melted and cooled (page 524)
2 eggs
60 g (2¼ oz/½ cup) plain (all-purpose) flour
90 g (3¼ oz/¾ cup) self-raising flour
30 g (1 oz/¼ cup) unsweetened cocoa powder
1 teaspoon bicarbonate of soda (baking soda)
125 ml (4 fl oz/½ cup) milk
chocolate fudge sauce (page 647), to serve

METHOD

1 Preheat the oven to 180°C (350°F/Gas 4). Grease eight 250 ml (9 fl oz/1 cup) dariole moulds.
2 Using electric beaters, beat the butter and sugar until light and creamy. Add the melted chocolate, beating well. Add the eggs one at a time, beating well after each addition.
3 Sift together the flours, cocoa and bicarbonate of soda, then gently fold into the chocolate mixture. Add the milk and fold through. Half-fill the moulds, then cover with pieces of greased foil and place in a deep roasting tin. Pour in enough hot water to come halfway up the sides of the moulds. Bake for 35–40 minutes, or until a skewer inserted into the centre comes out clean. Turn out onto serving plates and drizzle with the chocolate sauce. Serve with whipped cream.

TREACLE AND GOLDEN SYRUP

Treacle is the liquid collected at the end of the sugarcane refining process. Black treacle is the darkest and has a burnt, almost bitter taste. Light treacle, known as golden syrup, is the lightest and is sweet. In America, treacle is known as molasses, the darkest being blackstrap molasses. Treacle is used in baking: dark treacle adds flavour and colour; golden syrup is milder. Treacle puddings and tarts use golden syrup and a little dark treacle to get a balance of sweetness and flavour.

GOLDEN SYRUP DUMPLINGS

SERVES 4

INGREDIENTS

- 125 g (4½ oz/1 cup) self-raising flour
- 40 g (1½ oz) unsalted butter, chopped
- 1 egg
- 1 tablespoon milk

SYRUP

- 220 g (7¾ oz/1 cup) sugar
- 40 g (1½ oz) unsalted butter
- 2 tablespoons golden syrup
- 60 ml (2 fl oz/¼ cup) lemon juice

METHOD

1. Sift the flour and a pinch of salt into a bowl. Rub in the butter until fine and crumbly, and make a well. Using a flat-bladed knife, stir in the combined egg and milk to form a soft dough.
2. Put the syrup ingredients in a pan with 500 ml (17 fl oz/2 cups) water and stir over medium heat until the sugar has dissolved. Bring to the boil, then gently drop dessertspoons of the dough into the syrup. Cover and reduce the heat to simmer for 20 minutes, or until a knife inserted into a dumpling comes out clean. Spoon the dumplings into bowls and drizzle with the syrup. Serve with cream or ice cream if desired.

STICKY DATE PUDDING

SERVES 6–8

INGREDIENTS

- 375 g (13 oz) pitted dates, chopped
- 1½ teaspoons bicarbonate of soda (baking soda)
- 1 teaspoon grated ginger
- 90 g (3¼ oz) unsalted butter
- 230 g (8 oz/1 cup) caster (superfine) sugar
- 3 eggs
- 185 g (6½ oz/1½ cups) self-raising flour
- ½ teaspoon mixed spice
- caramel sauce (page 646), to serve

METHOD

1. Preheat the oven to 180°C (350°/Gas 4). Grease and line a deep 23 cm (9 inch) cake tin.
2. Put the dates in a pan with 435 ml (15 fl oz/ 1¾ cups) water. Bring to the boil, then remove from the heat, add the bicarbonate of soda and ginger and leave to stand for 5 minutes.
3. Cream together the butter, sugar and 1 egg. Beat in the remaining eggs, one at a time. Fold in the sifted flour and mixed spice, add the date mixture and stir until well combined. Pour into the tin and bake for 55–60 minutes, or until cooked through. Leave to stand for 5 minutes, then turn out onto a serving plate. Serve immediately with the caramel sauce and ice cream or cream.

••RICE PUDDINGS••

Wherever there is rice, there is rice pudding: from the schoolrooms of England to the breakfast tables of Asia. Rice puddings can be baked on the stovetop or in the oven, with flavourings often suited to the particular country or region. In countries with a strong Spanish influence, rice pudding is flavoured with cinnamon and citrus zest. In Thailand there is a sweet, sticky version using black or jasmine rice and coconut milk. And India has its own rice pudding, kheer, spiced with cardamom, topped with almonds and sultanas, and decorated with gold or silver leaf for special occasions.

HOW TO... COOK RICE PUDDING

Rice pudding should be creamy and tender, but not mushy. The texture is affected by several variables: the cooking method, the type of rice and the amount of eggs used — though extra eggs add richness to the custard, they also make the pudding firmer.

Cooking rice pudding on the stovetop results in a softer and creamier pudding than those baked in the oven. The constant stirring involved with the stovetop method releases a lot of starch into the pudding, providing extra creaminess. For this reason it is sometimes referred to as creamed rice. The baked version, however, develops a lovely golden crust on top and is generally firm enough to be able to cut through with a spoon.

WHICH RICE?

The texture and creaminess will also depend on the type of rice used — generally the rounder and fatter the grain the higher the starch content and the more liquid the grain will absorb. Most rice puddings use short- or medium-grain rice, though some use arborio rice because it releases more starch than other varieties.

THE RIGHT TOOLS

For a stovetop pudding, use a large heavy-based saucepan to promote even heat distribution and prevent the rice from sticking to the bottom of the pan, and use a wooden spoon for stirring. A baked version requires a ceramic or glass baking dish which also doubles as a serving dish.

BAKED RICE PUDDING

SERVES 4

INGREDIENTS

- 55 g (2 oz/¼ cup) short- or medium-grain rice
- 420 ml (14½ fl oz/1⅔ cups) milk
- 1½ tablespoons caster (superfine) sugar
- 60 ml (2 fl oz/¼ cup) cream
- ¼ teaspoon vanilla extract
- ¼ teaspoon ground nutmeg
- 1 bay leaf

METHOD

1. Preheat the oven to 150°C (300°F/Gas 2). Grease a 1 litre (35 fl oz/4 cup) ovenproof dish.
2. Put the rice, milk, sugar, cream and vanilla in a bowl and stir to combine. Pour into the prepared dish. Dust the surface with the nutmeg and float the bay leaf on top.
3. Put the dish into a larger baking tin and pour in enough hot water to come halfway up the side of the ovenproof dish. Bake for about 2 hours, or until the top is a deep golden colour and a knife inserted comes out clean. Serve hot.

ITALIAN RICE PUDDING

SERVES 4

INGREDIENTS

625 ml (21 fl oz/2½ cups) milk
250 ml (9 fl oz/1 cup) cream
1 vanilla bean, split lengthways
50 g (1¾ oz) caster (superfine) sugar
¼ teaspoon ground cinnamon
pinch of ground nutmeg
1 tablespoon finely grated orange zest
60 g (2¼ oz/½ cup) sultanas
2 tablespoons brandy or sweet Marsala
110 g (3½ oz/½ cup) risotto rice

METHOD

1 Put the milk, cream and vanilla bean in a heavy-based saucepan over medium heat. Bring just to the boil, then remove from the heat. Stir in the sugar, cinnamon, nutmeg and orange zest and set aside.
2 Soak the sultanas in the brandy. Meanwhile, add the rice to the infused milk and return to the heat. Bring to a simmer and stir slowly for about 35 minutes, or until the rice is creamy. Stir in the sultanas and remove the vanilla bean at the end. Serve warm or cold.

SPANISH RICE PUDDING

SERVES 6

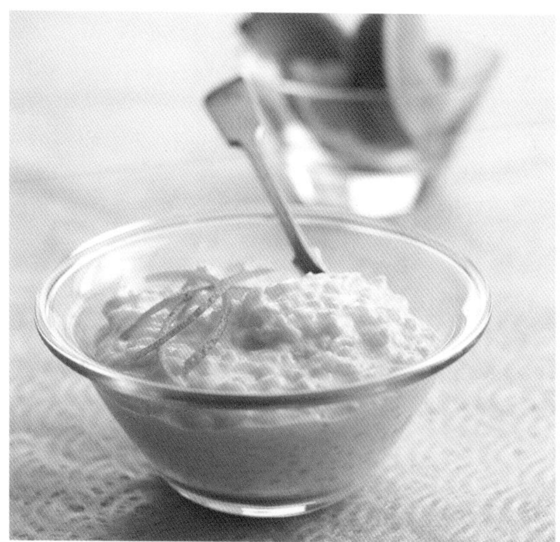

INGREDIENTS

1.25 litres (5 cups) milk
220 g (7¾ oz/1 cup) arborio rice
1 large strip orange zest, pith removed
1 cinnamon stick
1 teaspoon vanilla extract
145 g (5 oz/⅔ cup) caster (superfine) sugar
julienned strips of orange zest, to garnish

METHOD

1 Put the milk, rice, strip of orange zest, cinnamon stick, vanilla, sugar and a pinch of salt in a large heavy-based saucepan. Stir over high heat until the sugar has dissolved, then bring just to the boil. Reduce the heat and simmer, stirring regularly, for 50 minutes, or until the rice is tender but not mushy. Stirring not only helps stop the rice from sticking to the pan, but also helps produce a very creamy texture.
2 Remove the strip of orange zest and the cinnamon stick using tongs. Serve the rice pudding warm or cold, garnished with the julienned orange zest.

COCONUT SAGO PUDDINGS WITH GUAVA

SERVES 8

INGREDIENTS

250 ml (9 fl oz/1 cup) coconut milk
60 g (2¼ oz/¼ cup) grated palm sugar (jaggery) or soft brown sugar
1 lemongrass stem, bruised and halved
250 g (9 oz/1¼ cups) sago
1 teaspoon finely grated lime zest
1 egg white
4 guavas, thinly sliced

LIME SYRUP

450 g (1 lb/2 cups) caster (superfine) sugar
1 tablespoon finely shredded ginger
finely grated zest of 2 limes

METHOD

1 Lightly grease eight 125 ml (4 fl oz/½ cup) dariole moulds. Put the coconut milk, palm sugar and lemongrass in a saucepan with 750 ml (26 fl oz/3 cups) water. Bring just to the boil. Add the sago and lime zest and cook over low heat, stirring, for 35–40 minutes, or until the sago is thick and clear.

2 Remove from the heat and cool slightly. Remove the lemongrass. Using an electric mixer, beat the egg white in a clean dry bowl until stiff peaks form, then gently fold into the sago. Spoon the mixture into the prepared moulds, cover with plastic wrap and chill for 3 hours, or until firm.

3 Meanwhile, to make the lime syrup, put the sugar and 250 ml (9 fl oz/1 cup) water in a saucepan and stir over low heat until the sugar has dissolved. Bring to the boil and cook for 10 minutes, without stirring, until the syrup thickens. Add the ginger and lime zest and cook for another 5 minutes.

4 Stand the moulds in hot water for 20 seconds before turning out onto serving plates. Arrange the sliced guava on the plate and pour the lime syrup over the puddings.

GUAVA

There are many varieties of these tropical fruit, and these vary in size and shape, but generally the fruit is round or oval and has a thin skin and fragrant, slightly acid flesh, which can vary in colour from red to pinkish yellow or cream. The flavour is slightly different with each variety and may taste of either lemon, strawberry or pineapple. Peel the fruit first, then eat raw or cooked, add to fruit salads or platters or use in fools, juices, jellies and ice creams. The flavour can be quite strong and may overpower more subtle fruit. Make sure the fruit is ripe or it will be very astringent. Ripen at room temperature until soft, then store in the fridge.

SAGO AND TAPIOCA

Sago is a starch extracted from various Southeast Asian palms. It is dried and formed into small balls, called pearl sago, by pushing through a sieve. Pearl sago is commonly made into milky baked or steamed puddings in the West. In Southeast Asia, sago is used both as a flour and in pearl form for desserts. Sago is sold in supermarkets and health food stores. It is white when uncooked but goes transparent when cooked.

Tapioca is a starch extracted from the cassava plant. The tubers are pulped and dehydrated and the dried starch, the tapioca, is formed into whitish beads of various sizes called 'pearl tapioca'. It is also made into flour or flakes, or granulated to make 'instant tapioca'. Tapioca can be used as a thickener in desserts and pearl tapioca is used in puddings or baked egg custard puddings.

SAGO PUDDING

SERVES 6

INGREDIENTS

- 125 ml (4 fl oz/½ cup) golden syrup
- 75 g (2½ oz) sago
- 420 ml (14½ fl oz/1⅔ cups) milk
- 330 ml (11¼ fl oz/1⅓ cups) cream
- 2 eggs, lightly beaten
- 1 teaspoon vanilla extract
- 1 teaspoon finely grated lemon zest
- 2 teaspoons lemon juice

METHOD

1. Preheat the oven to 170°C (325°F/Gas 3).
2. Put the golden syrup, sago, milk and cream in a saucepan and bring to the boil, stirring. Reduce the heat and simmer for 10 minutes, then remove the pan from the heat and leave to cool.
3. Stir in the egg, vanilla, lemon zest and juice. Transfer the mixture to a 1 litre (35 fl oz/4 cup) ovenproof dish and bake for 1 hour, or until the sago is soft and the top is golden.

LIME AND COCONUT RICE PUDDINGS

SERVES 4

INGREDIENTS

- 200 ml (7 fl oz) milk
- 2 x 400 ml (14 fl oz) tins coconut cream
- finely grated zest of 1 lime
- 60 ml (2 fl oz/¼ cup) lime juice
- 3 kaffir lime leaves, halved
- 140 g (5 oz/⅔ cup) medium-grain rice
- 100 g (3½ oz/¾ cup) grated palm sugar (jaggery) or soft brown sugar
- toasted shredded coconut, to garnish

METHOD

1. Put the milk, coconut cream, lime zest, lime juice and lime leaves in a large saucepan and bring to the boil. Add the rice and stir to combine. Reduce the heat to low and simmer, stirring occasionally, for 25–30 minutes, or until the rice is tender.
2. Remove the saucepan from the heat and add the sugar, stirring until the sugar has dissolved and the mixture is creamy.
3. Remove the lime leaves and divide the rice pudding among four 250 ml (9 fl oz/1 cup) heatproof glasses or ramekins. Serve warm or cold, garnished with shredded coconut.

THAI STICKY RICE WITH MANGO

SERVES 4

INGREDIENTS

- 200 g (7 oz/1 cup) glutinous (sticky) rice
- 170 ml (5½ fl oz/⅔ cup) coconut milk
- 1 tablespoon grated palm sugar (jaggery) or soft brown sugar
- 2 large ripe mangoes
- 170 ml (5½ fl oz/⅔ cup) coconut cream mixed with ¼ teaspoon salt, to garnish

METHOD

1. Put the rice in a bowl and pour in cold water to come 5 cm (2 inches) above the rice. Soak for at least 3 hours, or overnight.
2. Drain and transfer to a steamer lined with a double thickness of muslin. Spread the rice in the steamer. Bring the water in the bottom of the steamer to a rolling boil. Taking care, set the rice over the water. Lower the heat, cover and steam for 20–25 minutes, or until the rice swells and is glistening and tender. The cooking time will vary depending on the soaking time. Check and replenish the water every 10 minutes or so. When the rice is cooked, tip it onto a large tray and spread it out to help it cool quickly.
3. While the rice is cooking, stir the coconut milk, sugar and ½ teaspoon salt in a small saucepan over low heat until the sugar has dissolved. As soon as the rice is cooked, use a wooden spoon to gently mix it in with the coconut milk. Set aside for 15 minutes.
4. Peel the mangoes and slice off the two cheeks from each, removing as much flesh as you can in large pieces. Avoid cutting close to the stone where the flesh is fibrous. Slice each cheek lengthways and crossways into cubes.
5. Arrange the mango on a serving plate. Spoon a portion of the sticky rice near the mango and spoon the coconut cream garnish over the rice.

PALM SUGAR

Palm sugar, or jaggery, is a dark, unrefined sugar obtained from the sap of sugar palm trees. The sap is collected from the trees and boiled until it turns into a thick, dark syrup. It is then poured into moulds, where it dries to form dense, heavy cakes. Palm sugar is widely used in Southeast Asian dishes, not only in sweet dishes but to balance the flavours in savoury dishes. The easiest way to use it is to shave the sugar off the cake with a sharp knife or grate it. Buy palm sugar in blocks or jars from Asian grocery stores and some supermarkets. If unavailable, any full-flavoured brown sugar can be used as a substitute.

STICKY BLACK RICE

SERVES 6–8

INGREDIENTS

- 400 g (14 oz/2 cups) black rice
- 3 fresh pandanus leaves (see Notes)
- 500 ml (17 fl oz/2 cups) coconut milk
- 80 g (2¾ oz/⅔ cup) grated palm sugar (jaggery)
- 55 g (2 oz/¼ cup) caster (superfine) sugar
- coconut cream, to serve
- tropical fruit, to serve

METHOD

1. Put the rice in a large glass or ceramic bowl and cover with water. Leave to soak for 8 hours, or preferably overnight. Drain, then put in a saucepan with 1 litre (35 fl oz/4 cups) water and slowly bring to the boil. Cook at a low boil, stirring frequently, for 20 minutes, or until tender, then drain.
2. Pull your fingers through the pandanus leaves to shred them and then tie them in a knot. Pour the coconut milk into a large saucepan and heat until almost boiling. Add the palm sugar, caster sugar and pandanus leaves and stir until the sugars have dissolved.
3. Add the cooked rice to the pan of coconut milk and cook, stirring, for 8 minutes without boiling. Turn off the heat, cover and leave for 15 minutes for the rice to absorb the flavours. Remove the pandanus leaves.
4. Spoon into bowls and serve warm with coconut cream. Serve with fresh tropical fruit such as mango, papaya, banana, pineapple or lychees.

NOTES: The long flat leaves of the pandanus are crushed and used as a flavouring in many Thai sweets. They are sold fresh, frozen, dried or as a flavouring essence or paste. If unavailable, substitute 1 teaspoon vanilla extract.
Don't refrigerate the sticky rice or it will dry out.

KHEER

This is the Indian version of rice pudding. It is exotically delicious, rich and creamy, with the cardamom and almonds giving it a distinctive flavour and texture.

SERVES 6

INGREDIENTS

- 150 g (5½ oz/¾ cup) basmati rice
- 20 cardamom pods
- 2.5 litres (10 cups) milk
- 30 g (1 oz/⅓ cup) flaked almonds
- 165 g (5¾ oz/¾ cup) sugar
- 30 g (1 oz/¼ cup) sultanas

METHOD

1. Wash the rice, then put it in a large bowl and cover with water. Leave to soak for 30 minutes, then drain well. Remove the seeds from the cardamom pods and lightly crush them in a spice grinder or using a mortar and pestle.
2. Put the milk in a large heavy-based saucepan and bring to the boil. Add the rice and cardamom, then reduce the heat and simmer for 1½–2 hours, or until the rice has a creamy consistency. Stir occasionally to stop the rice sticking to the pan.
3. Dry-fry the almonds in a frying pan for a few minutes over medium heat.
4. Add the sugar, almonds and sultanas to the rice, reserving some almonds and sultanas for garnish. Stir into the rice, then divide among bowls. Serve warm, garnished with the almonds and sultanas.

··ICE CREAM··

Ice cream, gelato and sorbet are elegant, simple desserts that can easily be made at home by hand or with an ice-cream maker. Ice cream gets its smooth, creamy texture by churning or whisking the mixture as it freezes to break up the ice crystals. Ice-cream machines do the churning for you, but the hand-made method gives equally good results.

TYPES OF ICE CREAMS

Ice cream in its original form is a frozen dessert based on milk or cream, sometimes thickened with eggs. Other types of ice cream include semifreddo, parfait, Indian kulfi and Italian gelato, as well as ice creams made with yoghurt or tofu (bean curd). Sorbets and granitas are actually based on water ices and generally do not contain dairy products. These are usually made from fruit pulp or juice.

ICE CREAM SAFETY

Ice creams, if handled incorrectly, can be a perfect breeding ground for bacteria. Bacteria are normally killed when heated to a high enough temperature, and made inactive when cooled down enough or frozen. It is the temperatures between these points that are a problem, especially blood temperature. Custards should be cooled as quickly as possible and dairy products kept well chilled until used. Ice cream that has been thawed slightly and then refrozen should be eaten quickly and not thawed again. If thawed completely, the ice cream should be thrown away. All equipment should be thoroughly washed after use and the machine may benefit from being sterilised.

HOW TO... STORE ICE CREAM

Store homemade ice cream in plastic or metal freezerproof containers filled almost to the lid, allowing a little room for expansion when the ice cream freezes. Cover the surface of the ice cream with baking paper to stop crystals forming, then a lid.

Homemade ice creams made with raw eggs should be eaten in 2–3 days. Those without eggs will keep longer but their flavour may change as they age.

VANILLA BEANS

True vanilla comes from the pod of a climbing orchid vine. The beans are picked when green, then left to sweat and dry in the sun, causing them to shrivel, turn deep brown and acquire a light coating of white vanillin crystals. True vanilla is expensive, partly because of the labour-intensive methods of obtaining it and partly because the flowers are hand-pollinated on the one day of the year that they open. Good-quality vanilla beans have a warm, caramel vanilla aroma and flavour, and should be soft, not hard and dry. Bury a bean in a jar of sugar and let the flavours infuse the sugar, or infuse the whole bean in hot milk and use for custards and ice cream. For extra flavour, use the tip of a knife to slice down the bean to allow some of the tiny, potently flavoured seeds to escape. Vanilla is also distilled into pure vanilla extract (or essence). Synthetic or imitation vanilla flavouring is also available and this must be labelled as such. It is cheaper than pure vanilla extract and the flavour is inferior.

VANILLA ICE CREAM

SERVES 4

INGREDIENTS

250 ml (9 fl oz/1 cup) milk
250 ml (9 fl oz/1 cup) cream
1 vanilla bean, split lengthways
6 egg yolks
115 g (4 oz/½ cup) caster (superfine) sugar

METHOD

1 Combine the milk and cream in a saucepan and add the vanilla bean. Bring to the boil, then remove from the heat and set aside for 10 minutes.
2 Using a wire whisk, beat the egg yolks and sugar together in a bowl for 2–3 minutes, until thick and pale, then whisk in the warm milk mixture. Scrape the seeds from the vanilla bean into the mixture. Discard the bean.
3 Wash the pan, and pour the mixture into it. Stir over very low heat for 5–10 minutes until thickened. To test, run a finger through the mixture across the back of the wooden spoon — if it leaves a clear line, the custard is ready.
4 Pour the custard into a shallow metal container, cover the surface of the custard with plastic wrap or baking paper and freeze for about 2 hours, until almost frozen. Scoop into a chilled bowl and beat with electric beaters until smooth, then return to the tray and freeze again. Repeat this step twice more before transferring to a storage container. Cover the surface with baking paper or plastic wrap to stop ice crystals forming on the surface, then a lid. Alternatively, pour the mixture into an ice-cream machine and churn following the manufacturer's instructions.
5 Ice cream is best served slightly softened for the full flavour to be appreciated. Transfer the ice cream to the refrigerator for about 15 minutes before serving.

CHOCOLATE ICE CREAM

SERVES 4

INGREDIENTS

8 egg yolks
115 g (4 oz/½ cup) caster (superfine) sugar
2 tablespoons unsweetened cocoa powder
500 ml (17 fl oz/2 cups) milk
250 ml (9 fl oz/1 cup) cream
1 vanilla bean, split lengthways
250 g (9 oz) good-quality dark chocolate, chopped

METHOD

1 Put the egg yolks in a large heatproof bowl and gradually whisk in the sugar. Continue to whisk until the sugar has dissolved and the mixture is thick and pale. (Do not use an electric mixer as this will incorporate too much air into the mixture.) Stir in the sifted cocoa.
2 Combine the milk, cream and vanilla bean in a saucepan. Bring to the boil, scrape the seeds out of the vanilla bean into the milk, and discard the empty bean.
3 Gently whisk the hot milk into the egg yolk mixture. Place the bowl over a saucepan of simmering water, and stir constantly over low heat for about 20 minutes, or until the custard coats the back of a wooden spoon. Do not allow the mixture to boil or the eggs will curdle. Remove from the heat, strain and pour into a clean bowl. Chill a deep 20 cm (8 inch) square cake tin in the freezer.
4 Put the chocolate in a heatproof bowl. Bring a small saucepan of water to the boil, remove from the heat and place the bowl over the pan, making sure the base of the bowl does not touch the water. Stir until melted. Add the warm chocolate to the warm custard and stir constantly until the chocolate has mixed through. Allow to cool.
5 Pour the cooled mixture into the chilled container, cover and freeze until the ice cream has just set. Remove from the freezer and spoon into a large bowl. Beat with a wooden spoon or electric beaters until smooth and thick, then return to the container. Repeat the freezing and beating twice more, then cover with a layer of baking paper and freeze overnight, or until completely set. Alternatively, pour the mixture into an ice-cream machine and churn following the manufacturer's instructions.
6 Remove from the freezer and place in the refrigerator for about 20 minutes before serving, to allow the ice cream to soften slightly.

BANANA SPLIT

SERVES 4

INGREDIENTS

200 g (7 oz) dark chocolate, chopped
185 ml (6 fl oz/¾ cup) cream
30 g (1 oz) butter
4 ripe bananas, halved lengthways
12 scoops vanilla ice cream
chopped peanuts, to serve

METHOD

1 Put the chocolate, cream and butter in a saucepan and stir over low heat until the chocolate has melted and is smooth. Remove from the heat and cool slightly.
2 Place one split banana on each side of a flat glass dish. Place three scoops of ice cream between the banana pieces and pour the chocolate sauce over the top. Sprinkle with the chopped nuts.

LYCHEE AND STRAWBERRY ICE CREAM

SERVES 6–8

INGREDIENTS

250 g (9 oz/1⅔ cups) strawberries
170 g (6 oz/¾ cup) caster (superfine) sugar
565 g (1 lb 4 oz) tin lychees in syrup
375 ml (13 fl oz/1½ cups) milk
500 ml (17 fl oz/2 cups) whipping cream
6 egg yolks, at room temperature

METHOD

1 Reserve 50 g (1¾ oz/⅓ cup) of the strawberries for decoration. Hull and roughly chop the remaining strawberries and put in a bowl, along with any juices. Sprinkle with 1 tablespoon of the sugar and set aside for 30 minutes. Drain and finely chop the lychees, reserving 125 ml (4 fl oz/ ½ cup) of the syrup.

2 Put the milk, cream and remaining sugar in a saucepan over medium heat. Cook, stirring constantly, for a few minutes, or until the sugar has dissolved and the milk is just about to boil. Remove from the heat.

3 Whisk the egg yolks in a bowl for 1 minute, or until combined, then add 60 ml (2 fl oz/¼ cup) of the hot milk mixture. Stir to combine, then pour into the remaining milk mixture. Return the saucepan to low–medium heat and cook, stirring constantly with a wooden spoon, until the mixture thickens and coats the back of the spoon. Do not allow the mixture to boil. Strain through a fine sieve and set aside to cool.

4 Gently stir the strawberries and any juice, lychees and lychee syrup into the custard to combine. Transfer the mixture to a shallow metal container, cover and freeze until the ice cream begins to set around the edges. Remove from the freezer and spoon into a large bowl. Beat with a wooden spoon or electric beaters until smooth and thick, then return to the container. Whisk every couple of hours until the ice cream is frozen and creamy in texture. Alternatively, pour the mixture into an ice-cream machine and churn following the manufacturer's instructions.

5 Remove from the freezer and place in the refrigerator for about 20 minutes before serving, to allow the ice cream to soften slightly. Serve garnished with the reserved strawberries.

LYCHEES

About the size of a small plum, the lychee has a knobbly, red or rust-coloured leathery skin, which encases a sweet and fragrant creamy flesh around a hard stone. Lychees are important in Chinese cuisine as they are said to promote fertility and good luck. Eat them fresh or add to fruit salads and ice creams, purée or poach in a light syrup. Because fruit with green skins won't ripen once picked, buy lychees at their peak — when their skin is red. As the fruit ages, its skin becomes more brittle and brown. Lychees are also available tinned and dried.

CHOCOLATE SEMIFREDDO

SERVES 10

INGREDIENTS

- 500 ml (17 fl oz/2 cups) thick (double) cream
- 145 g (5 oz/⅔ cup) caster (superfine) sugar
- 50 g (1¾ oz) unsweetened cocoa powder
- 4 eggs, separated
- 60 ml (2 fl oz/¼ cup) brandy
- 3 tablespoons icing (confectioners') sugar
- 150 g (5½ oz) hazelnuts

METHOD

1. Line a 1.5 litre (6 cup) loaf (bar) tin with two long strips of foil.
2. Heat 200 ml (7 fl oz) of the cream in a small saucepan. Combine the sugar, cocoa and egg yolks in a bowl. Pour the hot cream on top and mix well. Pour back into the pan and cook over low heat, stirring, until the mixture is thick enough to coat the back of a wooden spoon. Stir in the brandy and remove from the heat. Cover with plastic wrap and cool for 30 minutes.
3. Whisk the egg whites in a clean dry bowl until stiff peaks form. Whip the remaining cream in a large bowl until soft peaks form. Add the icing sugar and continue whipping until stiff and glossy.
4. To skin the hazelnuts, toast them under a hot grill (broiler) for 2 minutes (turn after 1 minute). Tip into a cloth and rub the husks off. Roughly chop.
5. Lightly fold the chocolate custard into the cream, then fold in the egg whites. Gently fold in the hazelnuts. Spoon into the tin and cover with foil. Freeze for 24 hours. Serve in slices.

› PRALINE ICE CREAM

SERVES 4

INGREDIENTS

- 200 g (7 oz) blanched almonds
- 200 g (7 oz) sugar
- 4 eggs, separated
- 2 tablespoons caster (superfine) sugar
- 300 ml (10½ fl oz) thick (double) cream, lightly whipped

METHOD

1. To make the praline, put the almonds in a hot frying pan over medium heat and dry-fry until well browned. Remove the almonds from the pan and set aside. Melt the sugar in a saucepan over medium heat until golden, without stirring. Take the pan off the heat and immediately stir in the almonds.
2. Spoon the nut mixture onto a greased baking tray and leave to harden. When the praline is hard, break into pieces and crush in a food processor or place in a bag and crush with a rolling pin.
3. To make the ice cream, whisk the egg yolks with the sugar until pale. Fold in the cream and crushed praline.
4. In a clean dry bowl, whisk the egg whites until stiff peaks form, then gently fold into the praline mixture. Transfer to a shallow metal tray and freeze, whisking hourly for 6–8 hours, or until the ice cream is frozen and creamy. Alternatively, pour the mixture into an ice-cream machine and churn following the manufacturer's instructions.

PRALINE

Traditionally made with almonds, a praline can be any nut coated in caramelised sugar and left to harden. Once hardened, the mixture can be eaten as is, or crushed and added to other dishes such as ice cream, cakes and patisserie, or used as a filling or coating for chocolates. Praline is also the name of a type of chocolate.

KULFI

This simple, elegant ice cream from India is made by boiling milk until it reduces and condenses, then flavouring it with ingredients such as cardamom and pistachio nuts or almonds. Kulfi is traditionally set in cone-shaped moulds.

SERVES 8

INGREDIENTS

- 40 g (1½ oz/¼ cup) pistachio nuts
- 1.5 litres (6 cups) milk
- 8 cardamom pods
- 115 g (4 oz/½ cup) caster (superfine) sugar
- ½ teaspoon finely grated lime zest

METHOD

1. Preheat the grill (broiler) to medium. Spread the pistachios on a baking tray and place under the grill for about 3 minutes, or until aromatic and lightly toasted. Set aside to cool slightly, then roughly chop the nuts.
2. Put the milk and cardamom pods in a large heavy-based saucepan. Bring to the boil, making sure that the milk doesn't boil over. Reduce the heat and simmer for 15–20 minutes, or until the liquid has reduced by one-third. Strain the mixture into a container suitable for freezing. Add the sugar and stir until it has dissolved. Stir in half the chopped pistachios and the lime zest. Set aside to cool for 30 minutes. Store the remaining pistachios in an airtight container.
3. Freeze the kulfi until almost firm, stirring every 30 minutes. (This can take 3–6 hours, depending on the freezer.) Rinse eight 170 ml (5½ fl oz/⅔ cup) dariole moulds with cold water and shake out the excess. Pack the kulfi into the moulds and freeze until completely firm.
4. Remove the moulds from the freezer 5 minutes before serving. To turn out the kulfi, briefly dip the moulds in very hot water, then invert them onto serving plates. Sprinkle the reserved pistachios over the top before serving.

PARFAIT

The base of a parfait is an egg custard to which cream and flavourings such as coffee (its traditional flavour), alcohol, fruit or chocolate are added. The mixture is poured into a loaf tin or the traditional parfait tin. An American parfait is similar to an ice-cream sundae.

SERVES 4

INGREDIENTS

- 1 tablespoon instant espresso coffee
- 150 g (5½ oz) sugar
- 4 egg yolks
- 250 ml (9 fl oz/1 cup) whipping cream

METHOD

1. Combine the coffee and sugar in a pan with 200 ml (7 fl oz) water and dissolve over low heat.
2. Put the egg yolks in a heatproof bowl and whisk until pale and light. Whisk in the coffee syrup a little at a time. Place the bowl over a saucepan of simmering water and cook, stirring, until the mixture coats the back of a wooden spoon. Remove from the heat and beat with electric beaters until doubled in volume. Chill until cold.
3. Whip the cream to soft peaks, then fold into the egg mixture. Pour into a loaf (bar) tin lined with plastic wrap and freeze for at least 2 hours. Transfer to the fridge for 10 minutes before turning out and cutting into slices.

GELATO, SORBET AND GRANITA

* Gelato is the Italian name for an ice cream based on an egg custard mixture. Italians are discerning about ice cream and flavours tend to be fresh and aromatic, often based on fruit.
* Sorbets are water-based ices made without dairy products or egg yolks, but may contain egg whites. Sorbet has a fine, grainy texture and is eaten both as a dessert and as a palate cleanser between meals.
* Granitas are an Italian ice confection with a coarse texture. The mixture is still-frozen, not churned like other ice creams, and the ice crystals are broken up by beating them with a fork. Granitas are traditionally flavoured with lemon or coffee.

COFFEE GELATO

SERVES 6

INGREDIENTS

- 5 egg yolks
- 125 g (4½ oz) sugar
- 500 ml (17 fl oz/2 cups) milk
- 125 ml (4 fl oz/½ cup) espresso coffee
- 1 tablespoon coffee-flavoured liqueur, such as Tia Maria

METHOD

1 Whisk the egg yolks and half the sugar together until pale and creamy. Put the milk, coffee and remaining sugar in a saucepan and bring to the boil. Pour the milk mixture over the egg mixture and whisk to combine. Pour back into the cleaned saucepan and cook over low heat, stirring continuously with a wooden spoon until the mixture is thick enough to coat the back of the spoon — do not allow the custard to boil.

2 Strain the custard into a bowl and cool over ice. Stir in the liqueur.

3 Pour the mixture into a metal tray, cover with plastic wrap and freeze. Stir every 30 minutes with a whisk during freezing to break up the ice crystals and give a better texture. Keep in the freezer until ready to serve. Alternatively, pour the mixture into an ice-cream machine and churn following the manufacturer's instructions.

LEMON GELATO

SERVES 6

INGREDIENTS

- 5 egg yolks
- 125 g (4½ oz) sugar
- 500 ml (17 fl oz/2 cups) milk
- 2 tablespoons finely grated lemon zest
- 185 ml (6 fl oz/¾ cup) lemon juice
- 60 ml (2 fl oz/¼ cup) thick (double) cream

METHOD

1 Whisk the egg yolks and half the sugar together until pale and creamy. Put the milk, lemon zest and remaining sugar in a saucepan and bring to the boil. Pour the milk mixture over the egg mixture and whisk to combine. Pour back into the cleaned saucepan and cook over low heat, stirring continuously with a wooden spoon until the mixture is thick enough to coat the back of the spoon — do not allow the custard to boil.

2 Strain the custard into a bowl, mix in the lemon juice and cream and then cool over ice.

3 Pour the mixture into a metal tray, cover with plastic wrap and freeze. Stir every 30 minutes with a whisk during freezing to break up the ice crystals and give a better texture. Keep in the freezer until ready to serve. Alternatively, pour the mixture into an ice-cream machine and churn following the manufacturer's instructions.

BLACKCURRANT SORBET

SERVES 4

INGREDIENTS

- 230 g (8 oz/1 cup) caster (superfine) sugar
- 30 g (1 oz) liquid glucose (see Note)
- 350 g (12 oz) blackcurrants, stalks removed
- 1 tablespoon lemon juice
- 2 tablespoons crème de cassis

METHOD

1. Put the sugar and glucose in a saucepan with 225 ml (8 fl oz) water. Heat gently to dissolve the sugar, then increase the heat and boil for 2–3 minutes. Cool completely.
2. Put the blackcurrants and lemon juice in a blender with half of the cooled syrup and mix to a thick purée. (Alternatively, push the fruit through a sieve to purée and then mix with the lemon juice and syrup.) Add the remaining syrup and the crème de cassis and mix well.
3. Pour the mixture into a metal tray, cover and freeze. Stir every 30 minutes with a whisk during freezing to break up the ice crystals and give a better texture. Freeze overnight with a layer of plastic wrap over the surface and the lid on the container. Alternatively, pour the mixture into an ice-cream machine and churn following the manufacturer's instructions. Keep in the freezer until ready to serve.

NOTE: We've used glucose for this sorbet because it stops the sugar crystallising and gives a good texture. To weigh glucose without it running everywhere, measure the sugar into the pan of the scales, then make a hollow in the middle and pour in the glucose.

MANGO SORBET

SERVES 4

INGREDIENTS

- 350 g (12 oz/1½ cups) caster (superfine) sugar
- 125 ml (4 fl oz/½ cup) lime juice
- 5 mangoes, about 1.5 kg (3 lb 5 oz) (see Note)

METHOD

1. Put the sugar and 625 ml (21 fl oz/2½ cups) water in a saucepan. Stir over low heat until the sugar dissolves, then bring to the boil. Reduce to a simmer for 15 minutes, then stir in the lime juice.
2. Peel the mangoes and remove the flesh from the stones. Chop the flesh and place in a heatproof bowl. Add the syrup and leave to cool.
3. Put the mango mixture in a blender, blend until smooth, then pour into a metal tray and freeze for 1 hour. Return to the blender and blend until smooth. Pour back into the tray and return to the freezer. Repeat this twice more. For the final freezing, place in an airtight container and cover the sorbet with baking paper and lid. Allow the sorbet to soften slightly before serving.

NOTE: Use frozen mango if fresh is not available. Use 1 kg (2 lb 4 oz) frozen mango cheeks, softened, 170 g (6 oz/¾ cup) caster sugar and 60 ml (2 fl oz/¼ cup) lime juice.

COFFEE GRANITA

SERVES 6

INGREDIENTS

170 g (6 oz/¾ cup) caster (superfine) sugar
1½ tablespoons unsweetened cocoa powder
1.25 litres (5 cups) strong espresso coffee, chilled

METHOD

1 Put the sugar and cocoa in a large saucepan, gradually add 125 ml (4 fl oz/½ cup) water and stir over low heat until the sugar has dissolved. Bring to the boil, then reduce the heat and simmer for 3 minutes.
2 Remove from the heat and add the coffee. Pour into a shallow metal tray. Freeze for 1 hour, or until just frozen around the edges. Scrape the ice crystals back into the mixture with a fork. Repeat this process every hour, scraping the frozen edges, at least twice more, or until the mixture has even-sized ice crystals.
3 Using a fork, work the granita into fine crystals and return to the freezer for 1 hour before serving. Spoon into glasses to serve.

NOTE: This is extremely hard when frozen, so should be put into a shallow tray and broken up when partially frozen. It is difficult to break up if frozen in a deep container.

WATERMELON GRANITA

SERVES 4

INGREDIENTS

450 g (1 lb) watermelon (rind and seeds removed)
1 tablespoon liquid glucose or caster (superfine) sugar
½ teaspoon lemon juice

METHOD

1 Purée the watermelon flesh in a blender or food processor, or chop it finely and push it through a metal sieve to remove the seeds and fibre. Transfer to a bowl.
2 Put the glucose, lemon juice and 80 ml (2½ fl oz/⅓ cup) water in a small saucepan and heat for 4 minutes. Pour the liquid over the watermelon and stir well.
3 Pour into a shallow metal tray. Freeze for 1 hour, or until just frozen around the edges. Scrape the ice crystals back into the mixture with a fork. Repeat this process every hour, scraping the frozen edges, at least twice more, or until the mixture has even-sized ice crystals. Serve immediately or beat well with a fork and refreeze until you are ready to serve.
4 To serve, scrape the granita into serving dishes with a fork, or serve in scoops in a tall glass.

NOTE: For a refreshing flavour, add 2 tablespoons chopped mint when freezing the last time.

••SWEET SAUCES••

Sinfully rich creamy sauces flavoured with caramel or chocolate, perhaps a dash of your favourite liqueur stirred in, are perfect poured over ice cream, pancakes or baked fruit. For something light, try fresh, fruity sauces, which can be made with just about any fruit in season. Drizzle them over ice cream or yoghurt, or serve with chocolate or sponge cakes.

BUTTERSCOTCH SAUCE

MAKES ABOUT 400 ML (14 FL OZ)

INGREDIENTS

- 60 g (2¼ oz) unsalted butter
- 115 g (4 oz/⅓ cup) golden syrup
- 60 g (2¼ oz/⅓ cup) soft brown sugar
- 55 g (2 oz/¼ cup) caster (superfine) sugar
- 170 ml (5½ fl oz/⅔ cup) cream
- ½ teaspoon vanilla extract

METHOD

1 Put the butter, golden syrup and sugars in a small pan. Stir over low heat for 2–3 minutes, or until the sugar has dissolved. Increase the heat a little and simmer for 3–5 minutes. Remove from the heat and stir in the cream and vanilla.

CARAMEL SAUCE

MAKES ABOUT 300 ML (10½ FL OZ)

INGREDIENTS

- 125 ml (4 fl oz/½ cup) cream
- 100 g (3½ oz) unsalted butter
- 95 g (3¼ oz/½ cup) soft brown sugar

METHOD

1 Combine the cream, butter and sugar in a saucepan and stir over medium heat, without boiling, until the sugar has dissolved. Reduce the heat and simmer gently for 3–4 minutes. Serve over waffles, pancakes or ice cream.

DULCE DE LECHE

Dulce de leche is an Argentinian speciality originally made by caramelising sugar in milk for many hours. Today, it is often made by boiling a tin of sweetened condensed milk to thicken and reduce the milk. When cooled, it can be eaten from the tin, used as a dip for fruit or spooned over ice cream.

To make dulce de leche, pierce the top of a tin of condensed milk a few times (so the tin won't explode when it is heated). Put the tin in a saucepan of boiling water: the water should reach halfway up the side of the tin. Simmer for about 2½ hours, keeping an eye on the water so it doesn't boil dry. For a more solid dulce de leche, simmer for up to 4 hours. Stir well before serving.

CHOCOLATE FUDGE SAUCE

MAKES ABOUT 300 ML (10½ FL OZ)

INGREDIENTS

150 g (5½ oz/1 cup) chopped dark chocolate
30 g (1 oz) unsalted butter
2 tablespoons golden syrup
150 ml (5 fl oz) cream

METHOD

1 Combine all the ingredients in a saucepan and heat gently until the chocolate has melted and the sauce is smooth. Continue to heat, stirring, until the sauce almost reaches boiling point. Remove from the heat. Serve warm.

MILK CHOCOLATE AND FRANGELICO SAUCE

MAKES 185 ML (6 FL OZ/¾ CUP)

INGREDIENTS

100 g (3½ oz/¾ cup) chopped milk chocolate
60 ml (2 fl oz/¼ cup) thick (double) cream
2 tablespoons Frangelico (see Note)

METHOD

1 Put the chocolate in a heatproof bowl. Put the cream in a small saucepan and bring just to the boil. Reduce the heat, then pour the hot cream over the chocolate, leave for 2 minutes, then stir until smooth.
2 Remove from the heat, stir in the Frangelico, then continue to stir occasionally until the sauce has cooled a little. Serve warm.

NOTE: Frangelico is a hazelnut flavoured liqueur; you can substitute Amaretto (bitter almond liqueur), if preferred.

DARK CHOCOLATE SAUCE

MAKES ABOUT 400 ML (14 FL OZ)

INGREDIENTS

150 g (5½ oz/1 cup) chopped dark chocolate
300 ml (10½ fl oz) cream
2 tablespoons caster (superfine) sugar

METHOD

1 Put the chocolate in a heatproof bowl. Put the cream in a small saucepan and bring to the boil. Reduce the heat, then add the sugar and stir until dissolved. Pour the hot cream over the chocolate, leave for 2 minutes, then stir until smooth. Serve warm.

NOTE: You can stir in a spoonful of any liqueur you like. Try Baileys Irish Cream or Tia Maria.

VANILLA CHOCOLATE HAZELNUT SAUCE

MAKES 500 ML (17 FL OZ/2 CUPS)

INGREDIENTS

300 ml (10½ fl oz) cream
1 vanilla bean
200 g (7 oz/1⅓ cups) chopped white chocolate
30 g (1 oz) toasted hazelnuts, chopped

METHOD

1 Put the cream into a small saucepan. Split the vanilla bean and scrape the seeds into the cream. Add the bean and bring to the boil. Remove the pan from the heat, cover and leave for 10 minutes, then strain.
2 Put the chocolate in a heatproof bowl, reheat the cream, then pour the cream over the chocolate. Leave for 2 minutes, then stir until the chocolate has melted. Stir in the hazelnuts.

MANGO CITRUS SAUCE

MAKES 325 ML (11 FL OZ)

INGREDIENTS

300 g (10½ oz) chopped mango flesh (1 mango)
80 ml (2½ fl oz/⅓ cup) orange juice
juice of 1 lime
1–2 tablespoons icing (confectioners') sugar (optional)

METHOD

1 Combine the chopped mango, orange juice and lime juice in a food processor. Process until the mixture is smooth. Sweeten to taste with the icing sugar, if needed.

PASSIONFRUIT AND PALM SUGAR SAUCE

MAKES 125 ML (4 FL OZ/½ CUP)

INGREDIENTS

50 g (1¾ oz/⅓ cup) grated palm sugar (jaggery) or soft brown sugar
170 ml (5½ fl oz/⅔ cup) passionfruit pulp (about 8 large passionfruit)

METHOD

1 Combine the sugar and 150 ml (5 fl oz) water in a saucepan. Cook over low heat for 5 minutes, or until the sugar has dissolved. Add the passionfruit pulp, bring to a simmer and cook for 10–15 minutes, or until the sauce has reduced and thickened slightly.
2 Strain the sauce, pressing firmly on the pulp to extract all the juice. Return 1 tablespoon of the seeds back to the sauce, stir to combine well, then cool. Serve over ice cream or waffles or with baked cheesecake.

SPICED BLUEBERRY SAUCE

MAKES 250 ML (9 FL OZ/1 CUP)

INGREDIENTS

300 g (10½ oz/2 cups) fresh or frozen blueberries
55 g (2 oz/¼ cup) caster (superfine) sugar
1 cinnamon stick
2 strips orange zest
1 strip lemon zest
1 teaspoon lemon juice

METHOD

1 Combine the blueberries, sugar, cinnamon stick, strips of orange and lemon zests, lemon juice and 2 tablespoons water in a saucepan over low heat. Cover and cook, stirring occasionally, for 2–3 minutes, or until the sugar has dissolved.
2 Bring to a simmer and cook for 5 minutes, or until the blueberries are soft and the sauce has thickened slightly. Remove the cinnamon stick and zest. Cool a little before serving.

CINNAMON PEAR SAUCE

MAKES 750 ML (26 FL OZ/3 CUPS)

INGREDIENTS

3 just under-ripe pears
230 g (8 oz/1 cup) caster (superfine) sugar
juice of ½ lemon
2 cinnamon sticks

METHOD

1 Peel, core and chop the pears and put them in a saucepan with 350 ml (12 fl oz) water. Add the sugar, lemon juice and cinnamon sticks. Bring to the boil, then reduce the heat and simmer for 10 minutes, or until the pears are soft. Remove the cinnamon sticks.
2 Purée the sauce in a blender until smooth. Serve warm over ice cream, fruit or puddings.

STRAWBERRY COULIS

MAKES 250 ML (9 FL OZ/1 CUP)

INGREDIENTS

250 g (9 oz) strawberries, hulled
2 tablespoons icing (confectioners') sugar
2 teaspoons lemon juice
1–2 teaspoons Grand Marnier (optional)

METHOD

1 Put the strawberries in a food processor with the icing sugar, lemon juice and liqueur, if using. Process until smooth. Strain through a fine sieve if desired.

NOTE: Use raspberries to make a raspberry coulis. Adjust the quantity of icing sugar depending on the sweetness of the raspberries.

BRANDY CREAM SAUCE

MAKES ABOUT 400 ML (14 FL OZ)

INGREDIENTS

2 eggs, separated
80 g (2¾ oz/⅓ cup) caster (superfine) sugar
80 ml (2½ fl oz/⅓ cup) brandy (see Note)
250 ml (9 fl oz/1 cup) cream, lightly whipped

METHOD

1 Beat the egg yolks and sugar until the mixture is thick and creamy and the sugar has dissolved. Stir in the brandy and fold in the cream.
2 Beat the egg whites in a clean dry bowl until soft peaks form. Gently fold the egg whites into the sauce and serve immediately. Serve with plum pudding or with chocolate pudding, fresh or poached fruit, or fruit pies.

NOTE: Whisky or Calvados can be used instead of brandy.

SPICY PEACH SAUCE

MAKES 420 ML (14½ FL OZ/1⅔ CUPS)

INGREDIENTS

500 g (1 lb 2 oz) peaches
½ vanilla bean
2 cloves
1 cinnamon stick
3 tablespoons sugar

METHOD

1 Put the peaches in a bowl, cover with boiling water and leave for 20 seconds. Drain, then peel and chop them (page 595). Put the peaches in a saucepan with 250 ml (9 fl oz/1 cup) water, the vanilla bean, cloves and cinnamon stick. Bring to the boil, then reduce the heat and simmer for 15–20 minutes, or until tender.
2 Add the sugar and stir over low heat until the sugar has dissolved. Increase the heat and simmer for 5 minutes. Remove the vanilla bean, cloves and cinnamon stick and cool slightly. Blend in a food processor or blender. Strain through a fine sieve before serving.

RHUBARB SAUCE

MAKES 375 ML (13 FL OZ/1½ CUPS)

INGREDIENTS

350 g (12 oz) rhubarb, chopped
95 g (3¼ oz/½ cup) soft brown sugar
¼ teaspoon mixed spice

METHOD

1 Put the chopped rhubarb in a saucepan with the sugar, 250 ml (9 fl oz/1 cup) water and the mixed spice. Slowly bring to the boil, stirring to dissolve the sugar. Simmer for 10 minutes, stirring often, until the rhubarb is tender. Push through a sieve and serve hot or cold.

••SWEET TREATS••

Soft ball and hard ball — these sound more like sports games than cooking terms, but these are the descriptions for the various stages of cooking with sugar. Once armed with the basics, you'll be able to make all manner of delicious treats — fudge, marshmallows, caramels and toffees. Wrap your sweets in cellophane or stack them in a decorative box to give to friends or family for special occasions.

SUGAR

Sugar cane was first cultivated in India more than 2000 years ago. In the seventh century, the Persians set up sugar refineries, and it is from their word for it, 'sakar', that we get the English name. Sugar, like spices, reached the Western world via the Arab trade routes, and when it first appeared, was considered an exotic and prohibitively expensive commodity, often called 'white gold'. Until the eighteenth century when sugar cane from the West Indies became more plentiful and less expensive, food was sweetened with honey, fruit syrups and maple syrup.

Sugar is made by extracting crystals from sugar cane juice. The crystals obtained after the first extraction are golden brown and contain some molasses. Refined white sugar is often made from sugar crystals that have been chemically treated and bleached

HOW TO... MAKE SUGAR SYRUP

Sugar syrups are solutions of sugar dissolved in water, which vary in their concentration of sugar to water. Lighter syrups are used for poaching fruits while heavy sugar syrups, made with more sugar, are used to make confectionery and caramels.

For the home cook, a sugar thermometer is helpful in determining the exact temperature and stages of the boiled syrup. To make a sugar syrup, put the sugar and water into a saucepan and dissolve the sugar over low heat. Wash down the side of the pan with a wet brush to dissolve any crystals. To make the syrup stronger, bring the mixture to the boil and keep boiling until you reach the following stages (the recipe will specify which stage you need to reach):

THREAD
(106–113°C/223–235°F) At this point, the syrup will form threads when dropped from a spoon into water. Use as a poaching syrup.

SOFT BALL
(112–116°C/234–240°F) A blob of syrup dropped in water will form a very soft ball. Use for Italian meringue, fondant and fudge.

HARD BALL
(121–130°C/250–266°F) A hard blob will form. Use for toffee, hard caramels and marshmallow.

SOFT CRACK
(132–143°C/270–289°F) The ball of sugar will stretch to form threads. Use for butterscotch and nougat.

HARD CRACK (BRITTLE)
(149–157°C/300–315°F) The ball can be stretched and snapped. Use for barley sugar and glazed fruits.

CARAMEL
(160–177°C/320–350°F) The sugar syrup starts to change colour, getting darker as it cooks. Stop it cooking by putting the base of the saucepan into cold water. Re-melt as necessary. Use for praline, spun sugar and caramel sauces.

NOUGAT

MAKES 1 KG (2 LB 4 OZ)

INGREDIENTS

- 450 g (1 lb/2 cups) sugar
- 250 ml (9 fl oz/1 cup) liquid glucose
- 175 g (6 oz/½ cup) honey (preferably blossom honey)
- 2 egg whites
- 1 teaspoon vanilla extract
- 125 g (4½ oz) unsalted butter, softened
- 60 g (2¼ oz) almonds, unblanched, toasted
- 100 g (3½ oz) glacé cherries

METHOD

1. Grease a 28 x 18 cm (11¼ x 7 inch) baking dish or tin and line with baking paper.
2. Place the sugar, glucose, honey, 60 ml (2 fl oz/¼ cup) water and ¼ teaspoon salt in a heavy-based saucepan and stir over low heat until dissolved. Bring to the boil and cook at a rolling boil for 8 minutes, or until the mixture forms a hard ball when tested in a small amount of water, or reaches 122°C (252°F) on a sugar thermometer. The correct temperature is very important, otherwise the mixture will not set properly.
3. Beat the egg whites in a clean dry bowl until stiff peaks form. Slowly pour a quarter of the syrup onto the egg whites in a thin stream and beat for up to 5 minutes, or until the mixture holds its shape. Place the remaining syrup over the heat and cook for 2 minutes (watch that it doesn't burn), or until a small amount forms brittle threads when dropped in cold water, or reaches 157°C (315°F) on a sugar thermometer. Pour slowly onto the meringue mixture with the beaters running and beat until the mixture is very thick.
4. Add the vanilla and butter and beat for another 5 minutes. Stir in the almonds and cherries using a metal spoon. Turn the mixture into the dish and smooth the top. Refrigerate for 4 hours, or until firm. Turn out onto a large chopping board and with a sharp knife cut into 4 x 2 cm (1½ x ¾ inch) pieces. Wrap each piece in cellophane and store in the fridge.

CREAMY COCONUT ICE

MAKES 30 PIECES

INGREDIENTS

250 g (9 oz/2 cups) icing (confectioners') sugar
¼ teaspoon cream of tartar
400 g (14 oz) tin sweetened condensed milk
315 g (11 oz/3½ cups) desiccated coconut
2–3 drops pink food colouring

METHOD

1 Grease a 20 cm (8 inch) square cake tin and line the base with baking paper.
2 Sift the icing sugar and cream of tartar into a bowl. Make a well and add the condensed milk. Using a wooden spoon, stir in half the coconut, then the remaining coconut. Mix well with your hands. Divide in half and tint one half pink. Using your hands, knead the colour through evenly.
3 Press the pink mixture over the base of the tin, cover with the white mixture and press down firmly. Refrigerate for 1–2 hours, or until firm. Remove from the tin, remove the paper and cut into pieces. Store in an airtight container in a cool place for up to 3 weeks.

VANILLA FUDGE

MAKES 12 PIECES

INGREDIENTS

460 g (1 lb/2 cups) caster (superfine) sugar
250 ml (9 fl oz/1 cup) cream
1 teaspoon vanilla extract

METHOD

1 Grease a 21 x 11 cm (8¼ x 4¼ inch) loaf (bar) tin. Line the base with baking paper, extending over two sides.
2 Place the sugar, cream and a pinch of salt in a heavy-based saucepan. Stir over low heat, without boiling, until the sugar has dissolved. Increase the heat slightly, until the mixture is just simmering. Cover and cook for 3 minutes.
3 Remove the lid and clean the sugar from the side of the pan with a wet pastry brush. Do not stir the mixture. Continue to boil the mixture for 10 minutes, or until it reaches 115°C (239°F) on a sugar thermometer. If you don't have a thermometer, drop a little mixture into a glass of cold water. It should form a soft ball when squeezed between your thumb and forefinger.
4 Remove from the heat, cool slightly and stir in the vanilla. Beat with electric beaters for 1–2 minutes, or until the mixture loses its gloss and begins to thicken. Quickly pour into the tin and smooth the top. Cover and leave to set. Cut into small squares. Refrigerate for up to 1 week.

PEANUT BUTTER FUDGE

Melt 90 g (3¼ oz) sugar and 500 ml (17 fl oz/2 cups) milk in a saucepan and boil for 4 minutes. Add 110 g (3¾ oz) unsalted butter, ¼ teaspoon vanilla extract and 4 tablespoons peanut butter. Beat the mixture with a wooden spoon over medium heat until it thickens and darkens — this will take about 35–40 minutes. Pour the mixture into a lightly greased 17 cm (6½ inch) square tin. Cut into slices when set.

HARD CARAMELS

MAKES 49

INGREDIENTS

- 220 g (7¾ oz/1 cup) sugar
- 90 g (3¼ oz) unsalted butter
- 2 tablespoons golden syrup or dark corn syrup
- 80 ml (2½ fl oz/⅓ cup) liquid glucose
- 90 ml (3 fl oz) sweetened condensed milk
- 250 g (9 oz) dark chocolate, chopped

METHOD

1. Grease the base and sides of a 20 cm (8 inch) square cake tin, then line with baking paper and grease the paper.
2. Combine the sugar, butter, golden syrup, glucose and condensed milk in a heavy-based saucepan. Stir over medium heat without boiling until the butter has melted and the sugar has dissolved completely. Clean the sugar crystals from the side of the pan with a wet pastry brush. Bring to the boil, reduce the heat slightly and boil, stirring, for 10–15 minutes, or until it reaches 122°C (252°F) on a sugar thermometer. If you don't have a thermometer, drop a little mixture into a glass of cold water. It should form a hard ball when squeezed between your thumb and forefinger. Remove from the heat immediately.
3. Pour into the tin and leave to cool. While the caramel is still warm, score into 49 squares with an oiled knife. When cold, cut through completely into squares.
4. Line two baking trays with foil. Place the chocolate in a small heatproof bowl. Bring a saucepan of water to the boil, then remove the pan from the heat. Sit the bowl over the pan, making sure the base of the bowl does not touch the water. Stir until the chocolate has melted. Remove from the heat and cool slightly. Using two forks, dip the caramels one at a time into the chocolate to coat. Lift out, drain the excess chocolate, then place on the trays and leave to set.

PEANUT BRITTLE

MAKES ABOUT 500 G (1 LB 2 OZ)

INGREDIENTS

- 450 g (1 lb/2 cups) sugar
- 185 g (6½ oz/1 cup) soft brown sugar
- 175 g (6 oz/½ cup) golden syrup
- 60 g (2¼ oz) unsalted butter
- 400 g (14 oz/2½ cups) roasted, unsalted peanuts

METHOD

1. Line the base and sides of a shallow 30 x 25 cm (12 x 10 inch) cake tin with foil or baking paper. Grease the foil with melted butter or oil.
2. Combine the sugars, golden syrup and 125 ml (4 fl oz/½ cup) water in a large heavy-based pan. Stir over medium heat without boiling until the sugar has completely dissolved. Clean the sugar from the side of the pan with a wet pastry brush. Add the butter and stir until melted. Bring to the boil, reduce the heat slightly and boil without stirring for 15–20 minutes. The mixture must reach 150°C (302°F) on a sugar thermometer, or a little dropped into cold water will be brittle and not sticky. Remove from the heat.
3. Add the nuts and fold in, tilting the pan to help mix — don't overmix or it will crystallise. Pour into the tin and smooth the surface with a buttered spatula. Leave the tin on a wire rack for the brittle to cool. Break into pieces when almost set. Store in an airtight container for up to 3 weeks.

RICH CHOCOLATE TRUFFLES

MAKES ABOUT 30

INGREDIENTS

185 ml (6 fl oz/¾ cup) thick (double) cream
400 g (14 oz) dark chocolate, grated
70 g (2½ oz) unsalted butter, chopped
2 tablespoons Cointreau
dark unsweetened cocoa powder, for rolling

METHOD

1. Put the cream in a small saucepan and bring to the boil. Remove from the heat and stir in the chocolate until it is completely melted. Add the butter and stir until melted. Stir in the Cointreau. Transfer to a large bowl, cover and refrigerate for several hours or overnight, or until the mixture is firm enough to roll.
2. Quickly roll tablespoons of the mixture into balls, and refrigerate until firm. Roll the balls in the cocoa, shake off any excess and return to the refrigerator. Serve at room temperature.

NOTE: The truffle mixture can be made and rolled up to 2 weeks ahead. You will need to roll the balls in cocoa again close to serving time.

CHOCOLATE CARAMEL CUPS

MAKES 24

INGREDIENTS

150 g (5½ oz/1 cup) dark chocolate melts (buttons)
80 g (2¾ oz) Mars® bar, chopped
60 ml (2 fl oz/¼ cup) cream
50 g (1¾ oz/⅓ cup) white chocolate melts (buttons)

METHOD

1. Put the dark chocolate in a small heatproof bowl. Bring a small saucepan of water to the boil and remove from the heat. Sit the bowl over the pan, making sure the base of the bowl does not touch the water. Stir occasionally until the chocolate has melted and the mixture is smooth.
2. Brush a thin layer of chocolate inside 24 small foil confectionery cases. Stand the cases upside down on a wire rack to set. (Return the bowl of remaining chocolate to the pan of steaming water for later use.)
3. Combine the Mars bar and cream in a small saucepan and stir over low heat until the Mars bar has melted and the mixture is smooth. Transfer to a bowl and leave until just starting to set, then spoon into each foil case, leaving about 3 mm (⅛ inch) of space at the top.
4. Spoon the reserved melted chocolate into the caramel cases and allow the chocolate to set. Melt the white chocolate in the same way as the dark chocolate. Place in a small paper piping (icing) bag and drizzle patterns over the cups. Carefully peel away the foil when the chocolate has set.

NOTE: Caramel cups can be made up to 3 days ahead. Ensure the chocolate is set before piping the white chocolate on the top.

RUM BALLS

MAKES ABOUT 25

INGREDIENTS

- 200 g (7 oz) dark chocolate, finely chopped
- 60 ml (2 fl oz/¼ cup) cream
- 30 g (1 oz) unsalted butter
- 50 g (1¾ oz) chocolate cake crumbs
- 2 teaspoons dark rum
- 90 g (3¼ oz/½ cup) chocolate sprinkles

METHOD

1. Line a baking tray with foil. Place the chocolate in a heatproof bowl. Combine the cream and butter in a small saucepan and stir over low heat until the butter melts and the mixture is just boiling. Pour the hot cream mixture over the chocolate, and stir until the chocolate melts and the mixture is smooth.
2. Stir in the cake crumbs and rum. Refrigerate for 20 minutes, stirring occasionally, or until just firm enough to handle.
3. Roll heaped teaspoons of the mixture into balls. Spread the chocolate sprinkles on a sheet of baking paper. Carefully roll each rum ball in the sprinkles, then place on the tray. Refrigerate for 30 minutes, or until firm. Serve in paper confectionery cases.

ROCKY ROAD

MAKES ABOUT 30 PIECES

INGREDIENTS

- 250 g (9 oz) pink and white marshmallows, halved
- 160 g (5½ oz/1 cup) unsalted peanuts, roughly chopped
- 105 g (3½ oz/½ cup) glacé cherries, halved
- 60 g (2¼ oz/1 cup) shredded coconut
- 350 g (12 oz) dark chocolate, chopped

METHOD

1. Line the base and two opposite sides of a shallow 20 cm (8 inch) square cake tin with foil.
2. Put the marshmallows, peanuts, cherries and coconut into a large bowl and mix well.
3. Put the dark chocolate in a small heatproof bowl. Bring a small saucepan of water to the boil and remove from the heat. Sit the bowl over the pan, making sure the base of the bowl does not touch the water. Stir occasionally until the chocolate has melted. Pour the chocolate over the marshmallow mixture and mix.
4. Spoon into the prepared tin and press evenly over the base. Refrigerate for several hours, or until set. Lift out of the tin, then peel away the foil and cut the rocky road into small pieces. Store in an airtight container in the refrigerator.

MARZIPAN

A paste of ground almonds and sugar, marzipan is sold in block form or made into varying miniature shapes of fruit, vegetables or animals. It is used in baking, as a tart filling, to stuff dates and sweetmeats, or can be rolled out into thin sheets to decorate and cover fruit cakes and cassata. Though marzipan is often said to have been named after the Latin *marci panis* (Mark's bread), it is more likely to have come from the Middle East, where it was originally made from sugar, ground almonds and rosewater. It was regarded as a delicacy and sometimes covered with gold leaf.

WHITE CHRISTMAS

MAKES 24 PIECES

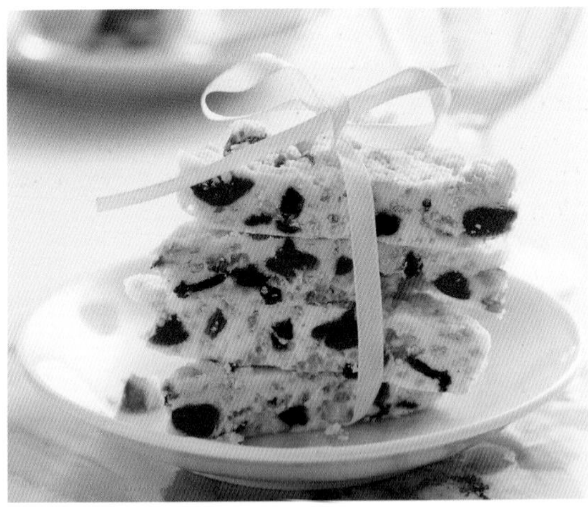

INGREDIENTS

- 45 g (1½ oz/1½ cups) puffed rice cereal
- 100 g (3½ oz/1 cup) milk powder
- 125 g (4½ oz/1 cup) icing (confectioners') sugar
- 90 g (3¼ oz/1 cup) desiccated coconut
- 80 g (2¾ oz/⅓ cup) chopped red glacé cherries
- 80 g (2¾ oz/⅓ cup) chopped green glacé cherries
- 55 g (2 oz/½ cup) sultanas
- 250 g (9 oz) Copha (white vegetable shortening)

METHOD

1. Line a shallow 28 x 18 cm (11¼ x 7 inch) cake tin with foil. Put the puffed rice, milk powder, icing sugar, coconut, glacé cherries and sultanas in a large bowl and stir. Make a well in the centre.
2. Melt the Copha over low heat, cool slightly, then add to the well in the puffed rice mixture. Stir with a wooden spoon until all the ingredients are moistened.
3. Spoon the mixture into the prepared tin and smooth the surface. Refrigerate for 30 minutes, or until completely set. Remove from the tin, and peel away and discard the foil. Cut into 24 small triangles to serve.

MINI CHRISTMAS TRUFFLE PUDDINGS

MAKES ABOUT 44

INGREDIENTS

- 500 g (1 lb 2 oz) fruit cake
- 2 tablespoons desiccated coconut
- 80 ml (2½ fl oz/⅓ cup) dark rum
- 30 g (1 oz/⅓ cup) flaked almonds, toasted and crushed
- 400 g (14 oz/2⅔ cups) dark chocolate melts (buttons), melted
- 2 teaspoons oil
- 150 g (5½ oz) white chocolate, melted
- 1 stick of angelica (see Note), chopped
- 8 red glacé cherries, chopped

METHOD

1. Finely chop the fruit cake in a food processor. Combine in a bowl with the coconut, rum, almonds and 150 g (5½ oz) of the melted dark chocolate, and mix thoroughly. Roll 2 teaspoons of the mixture at a time into balls. Place on a baking tray covered with baking paper.
2. Place the remaining melted dark chocolate and oil in a small bowl and stir well. Sit each truffle on a fork and dip in the chocolate to coat. Carefully remove, allowing any excess to drain away. Place back on the paper and leave to set. Do not refrigerate.
3. When the chocolate is set, spoon the white chocolate into a small piping (icing) bag or a small plastic bag, snip off the end of the bag and drizzle chocolate on top of each 'pudding' and down the sides (to look like custard). Before the chocolate sets, decorate with small pieces of angelica and cherry.

NOTE: Angelica is a herb that resembles a parsley plant. Its most popular use is in cake decoration, where its green stalks are blanched, then candied in sugar to produce a vivid green colour. Angelica is sold in health food or cake decorating stores.

TOFFEE APPLES

MAKES 12

INGREDIENTS

12 small red or green apples, very crisp
900 g (2 lb/4 cups) sugar
2 tablespoons white vinegar
red or green food colouring

METHOD

1 Line two 33 x 28 cm (13 x 11¼ inch) baking trays with foil. Grease the foil lightly with oil.
2 Wipe the apples well with a clean dry towel. Push a wooden lolly stick or thick skewer into the stem end of each apple.
3 Put the sugar, vinegar and 500 ml (17 fl oz/2 cups) water in a large, heavy-based saucepan. Stir over medium heat, without boiling, until the sugar has completely dissolved. Clean the sugar crystals from the side of the pan with a wet pastry brush. Add the food colouring.
4 Bring to the boil, then boil without stirring for 15–20 minutes, or until the mixture reaches 150°C (302°F) on a sugar thermometer. If you don't have a sugar thermometer, drop a little mixture into a glass of cold water. The toffee will be brittle and have reached hard crack stage. Remove from the heat immediately.
5 Dip the apples, one at a time, into the toffee to coat. (The apples need to be at room temperature when they are dipped into the hot toffee. If they are too cold, the toffee will form bubbles on the surface.) Lift out and twist quickly to coat evenly. Drain, then place on the trays. Leave to set at room temperature. When set, wrap each toffee apple in cellophane and tie with ribbon. Toffee apples can be made up to 3 days ahead.

TURKISH DELIGHT

Turkish delight is the Western name for *rahat lokum,* meaning 'rest for the throat'. The sweet is made by slowly boiling a mixture of syrup and cornflour, sometimes with honey, fruit juice or mastic until gummy and gel-like. The mixture is often flavoured with orange or rosewater or mint, or may include nuts such as pistachios or almonds. The set mixture is cut into squares and rolled in icing sugar.

MAKES 25 PIECES

INGREDIENTS

900 g (2 lb/4 cups) sugar
125 g (4½ oz/1 cup) cornflour (cornstarch)
1 teaspoon cream of tartar
2 tablespoons rosewater
red food colouring
40 g (1½ oz/⅓ cup) icing (confectioners') sugar
2 tablespoons cornflour (cornstarch), extra

METHOD

1 Pour 625 ml (21 fl oz/2½ cups) water into a large, heavy-based saucepan and bring to the boil. Add the sugar and stir until thoroughly dissolved. Remove from the heat.
2 In a large bowl, blend the cornflour and cream of tartar with 250 ml (9 fl oz/1 cup) cold water. Gradually add the blended cornflour to the sugar syrup, then return the saucepan to medium heat and stir until the mixture boils. Reduce the heat and cook very slowly for 45 minutes, stirring often. During this time, the colour will change from cloudy to clear and golden and the mixture will thicken.
3 Add the rosewater and a few drops of food colouring, then pour onto a lightly oiled 30 x 20 cm (12 x 8 inch) tray and leave to set. When firm and cool, cut into 2.5 cm (1 inch) squares and toss in the combined icing sugar and extra cornflour.

CHAPTER TWELVE

JAMS AND PRESERVES

••JAMS••

Jam is made by boiling fruit with sugar, and is set by pectin, which will either be present in the fruit or added. Jams are used as spreads, as an ingredient in tarts and steamed puddings or as filling in cakes.

WHICH FRUIT TO CHOOSE

Choose firm just-ripe fruit for making jam, as overripe fruit lack the pectin needed for setting. Some fruit are quite low in pectin, such as blackberries, cherries, figs and nectarines, or have none at all and need the addition of pectin-containing fruit (such as apples or citrus fruit) or juice or commercial setting agents to help them set.

The acidity of the fruit acts as both a preservative and a setting agent. Fruit that have low acid levels, such as apricots, figs, kiwi fruit, strawberries and pears, can be supplemented with lemon juice or by adding fruit that are high in acid, such as cherries, blackberries, blackcurrants, citrus or green apples.

SUGAR AND PECTIN

Sugar not only sweetens jam but it also works with pectin as a setting agent, and inhibits the growth of microorganisms. Jams must contain over 55 per cent sugar to inhibit the growth of microorganisms, so the amount of sugar needed to preserve the fruit will depend on its natural sweetness. Follow the recipe carefully as using too much sugar will cause the jam to crystallise; too little sugar and the jam won't set.

Pectin is found in the skin, flesh and seeds of most fruits in varying degrees. It is particularly high in citrus pith and apple skin.

HOW TO... TEST FOR SETTING POINT

To test if your jam is cooked, lift up the wooden spoon and see if the jam falls off it in drips or sheets. When it falls in sheets, drip a little onto a chilled plate. Return the plate to the freezer to cool for 30 seconds, then push your finger through the jam: if it wrinkles up as you push, it's ready.

HOW TO... STERILISE JARS

Jars must always be sterilised before jams are put in them for storage, or bacteria will multiply. Always use sterilised containers with the correct lid or seal. The jars can be sterilised in an oven or in boiling water.

To sterilise jars in the oven, preheat the oven to 160°C (315°F/Gas 2–3). Place clean, dry jars and lids on a tray and heat in the oven for 10 minutes. Cool slightly, then fill with the warm jam or preserve and put the lid on. As the fruit cools, it will form a vacuum, which will help preserve them.

To sterilise in boiling water, put a wire rack in the bottom of a saucepan. Put washed jars on the rack and cover with water. Bring to the boil and boil rapidly for 10 minutes. Lids and rubber seals should be added for a few seconds. Lift the jars out and drain upside down. Place on a tray and dry in a cool oven.

RASPBERRY JAM

FILLS SEVEN 250 ML (9 FL OZ/1 CUP) JARS

INGREDIENTS

1.5 kg (3 lb 5 oz) raspberries
80 ml (2½ fl oz/⅓ cup) lemon juice
1.5 kg (3 lb 5 oz) sugar

METHOD

1. Put the raspberries and lemon juice in a large heavy-based saucepan. Gently stir over low heat for 10 minutes, or until the raspberries have softened. Warm the sugar by spreading it in a large baking dish and heating in a 120°C (235°F/Gas ½) oven for 10 minutes, stirring occasionally.
2. Add the sugar to the saucepan and stir, without boiling, for 5 minutes, or until the sugar has completely dissolved.
3. Put two small plates in the freezer. Bring the jam to the boil and boil for 20 minutes, then start testing the jam for setting point. Place a little jam on a cold plate and place in the freezer for 30 seconds. When setting point is reached, a skin will form on the surface and the jam will wrinkle when pushed with your finger. Remove any scum from the surface.
4. Pour into hot, sterilised jars. Turn the jars upside down for 2 minutes, then invert and leave to cool. Label and date. Store in a cool, dark place for 6–12 months.

(pictured above left)

PEAR AND GINGER CONSERVE

FILLS SIX 250 ML (9 FL OZ/1 CUP) JARS

INGREDIENTS

- 1.5 kg (3 lb 5 oz) beurre bosc pears
- 60 ml (2 fl oz/¼ cup) lemon juice
- 1 teaspoon finely grated lemon zest
- 1.5 kg (3 lb 5 oz) sugar
- 150 g (5½ oz) glacé ginger, finely chopped

METHOD

1. Put two small plates in the freezer. Peel, halve and core the pears. Cut the flesh into 1.5 cm (⅝ inch) pieces. Place the cores and seeds on a piece of muslin, gather up and tie securely with string. Add to a large heavy-based saucepan with the fruit, lemon juice and zest, and 250 ml (9 fl oz/1 cup) water.
2. Bring to the boil, then reduce the heat and simmer for 20–25 minutes, or until the pear is soft. Warm the sugar by spreading it in a large baking dish and heating in a 120°C (235°F/Gas ½) oven for 10 minutes, stirring occasionally.
3. Add the sugar and glacé ginger and stir over low heat, without boiling, for 5–10 minutes, or until the sugar has dissolved. Return to the boil and boil for 20–25 minutes, stirring often. Remove any scum during cooking. When the conserve falls from a tilted wooden spoon in thick sheets without dripping, start testing for setting point.
4. Remove from the heat, place a little conserve onto one of the cold plates and place in the freezer for 30 seconds. A skin will form on the surface and the conserve will wrinkle when pushed with your finger when setting point is reached. Discard the muslin bag. Remove any scum from the surface.
5. Spoon immediately into hot, sterilised jars. Turn the jars upside down for 2 minutes, then invert and leave to cool. Label and date. Store in a cool, dark place for 6–12 months. Refrigerate after opening and keep for up to 6 weeks.

APRICOT AND ALMOND JAM

FILLS EIGHT 250 ML (9 FL OZ/1 CUP) JARS

INGREDIENTS

- 500 g (1 lb 2 oz) dried apricots
- 1.5 kg (3 lb 5 oz) sugar
- 45 g (1½ oz/½ cup) flaked almonds

METHOD

1. Put the dried apricots in a large non-metallic bowl. Add 2 litres (8 cups) water and leave to soak overnight.
2. Put two small plates in the freezer. Pour the apricots and water into a large heavy-based saucepan. Bring slowly to the boil, then reduce the heat and simmer, covered, for 45 minutes, or until the fruit is soft. Warm the sugar by spreading it in a large baking dish and heating in a 120°C (235°F/Gas ½) oven for 10 minutes, stirring occasionally.
3. Add the sugar to the fruit. Stir over low heat, without boiling, for 5 minutes, or until all the sugar has dissolved. Return to the boil and boil, uncovered, for 20 minutes, stirring occasionally. When the jam falls from a tilted wooden spoon in thick sheets without dripping, start testing for setting point.
4. Remove from the heat, place a little jam onto one of the cold plates and place in the freezer for 30 seconds. A skin will form on the surface and the jam will wrinkle when pushed with your finger when setting point is reached. Cool for 5 minutes, then remove any scum from the surface of the jam.
5. Spoon into hot, sterilised jars and seal. Turn the jars upside down for 2 minutes, then invert and leave to cool. Label and date. Store in a cool, dark place for 6–12 months. Refrigerate after opening and keep for up to 6 weeks.

STRAWBERRY JAM

FILLS SIX 250 ML (9 FL OZ/1 CUP) JARS

INGREDIENTS

1.25 kg (2 lb 12 oz) sugar
1.5 kg (3 lb 5 oz) strawberries
125 ml (4 fl oz/½ cup) lemon juice

METHOD

1 Warm the sugar by spreading it in a large baking dish and heating in a 120°C (235°F/Gas ½) oven for 10 minutes, stirring occasionally. Put two small plates in the freezer.
2 Hull the strawberries and put in a large heavy-based saucepan with the lemon juice, sugar and 125 ml (4 fl oz/½ cup) water. Warm gently, without boiling, stirring carefully with a wooden spoon. Try not to break up the fruit too much.
3 Increase the heat and, without boiling, continue stirring for 10 minutes, until the sugar has thoroughly dissolved. Increase the heat and boil, without stirring, for 20 minutes. Start testing for setting point (page 660) — it could take up to 40 minutes to reach setting point. Remove from the heat and leave for 5 minutes before removing any scum that forms on the surface. Pour into hot, sterilised jars, seal and label.

BLOOD PLUM JAM

FILLS EIGHT 250 ML (9 FL OZ/1 CUP) JARS

INGREDIENTS

2 kg (4 lb 8 oz) blood plums
125 ml (4 fl oz/½ cup) lemon juice
1.5 kg (3 lb 5 oz) sugar

METHOD

1 Put two small plates in the freezer. Cut the plums in half and remove the stones. Place the plums in a large heavy-based saucepan and add 1 litre (35 fl oz/4 cups) water.
2 Bring slowly to the boil, then reduce the heat and simmer, covered, for 50 minutes, or until the fruit is soft. Meanwhile, warm the sugar by spreading it in a large baking dish and heating in a 120°C (235°F/Gas ½) oven for 10 minutes, stirring occasionally.
3 Add the lemon juice and sugar and stir over low heat, without boiling, for 5 minutes, or until all the sugar has dissolved. Bring to the boil and boil for 20 minutes, stirring often. Remove any scum from the surface during cooking with a skimmer or slotted spoon. When the jam falls from a tilted wooden spoon in thick sheets without dripping, start testing for setting point.
4 Remove from the heat, place a little jam onto one of the cold plates and place in the freezer for 30 seconds. When setting point is reached, a skin will form on the surface and the jam will wrinkle when pushed with your finger. Remove any scum from the surface.
5 Spoon immediately into hot, sterilised jars and seal. Turn the jars upside down for 2 minutes, then invert and leave to cool. Label and date. Store in a cool, dark place for 6–12 months. Refrigerate after opening and keep for up to 6 weeks.

THREE FRUIT MARMALADE

FILLS TWELVE 250 ML (9 FL OZ/1 CUP) JARS

INGREDIENTS

1 grapefruit
2 oranges
2 lemons
3 kg (6 lb 12 oz) sugar

METHOD

1 Scrub the grapefruit, oranges and lemons under warm running water with a soft-bristle brush to remove any wax coating. Slice the quartered grapefruit and halved oranges and lemons very thinly and place in a large non-metallic bowl. Put the pips on a square of muslin and tie with string. Add to the bowl with 2.5 litres (10 cups) water, cover and leave overnight.
2 Transfer the fruit and water and muslin bag to a large heavy-based saucepan. Bring slowly to the boil, then reduce the heat and simmer, covered, for 1 hour, or until the fruit is tender. Meanwhile, warm the sugar by spreading it in a large baking dish and heating in a 120°C (235°F/Gas ½) oven for 10 minutes, stirring occasionally. Put two small plates in the freezer.
3 Add the warmed sugar to the fruit all at once. Stir over low heat, without boiling, for 5 minutes, or until all the sugar has dissolved. Return to the boil and boil rapidly for 50–60 minutes. When the marmalade falls from a tilted wooden spoon in thick sheets without dripping, start testing for setting point. Remove from the heat and place a little marmalade on one of the plates and place in the freezer for 30 seconds. A skin will form on the surface and the marmalade will wrinkle when pushed with your finger when setting point is reached. Cool for 10 minutes, then remove any scum from the surface. Discard the muslin bag.
4 Spoon into hot, sterilised jars and seal. Turn the jars upside down for 2 minutes, then invert and leave to cool. Label and date for storage.

SEVILLE ORANGE MARMALADE

FILLS TEN 250 ML (9 FL OZ/1 CUP) JARS

INGREDIENTS

4 seville oranges (about 1.25 kg/2 lb 12 oz)
2–2.25 kg (4 lb 8 oz–5 lb) sugar

METHOD

1 Scrub the oranges under warm, running water with a soft-bristle brush to remove any wax coating. Cut the oranges in half, and then in half again. Slice the oranges thinly, removing and retaining the pips. Put the pips on a square of muslin and tie with string. Place the orange and muslin bag in a large non-metallic bowl. Add 2 litres (8 cups) water and leave overnight.
2 Transfer the fruit and water and muslin bag to a large heavy-based saucepan. Bring to the boil, then reduce the heat and simmer, covered, for 45 minutes, or until the fruit is tender. Meanwhile, warm the sugar by spreading it in a large baking dish and heating in a 120°C (235°F/Gas ½) oven for 10 minutes, stirring occasionally. Put two small plates in the freezer.
3 Measure the fruit and for every 250 ml (9 fl oz/1 cup) of fruit mixture add 250 g (9 oz/1 cup) of the warmed sugar. Stir over low heat, without boiling, for 5 minutes, until the sugar has dissolved. Return to the boil and boil rapidly for 30–40 minutes, stirring often. Remove any scum during cooking. When the marmalade falls from a tilted wooden spoon in thick sheets, start testing for setting point. Remove from the heat, place a little marmalade onto one of the cold plates and place in the freezer for 30 seconds. When setting point is reached, a skin will form on the surface and the marmalade will wrinkle when pushed with your finger. Discard the muslin bag. Remove any scum from the surface.
4 Spoon into hot, sterilised jars and seal. Turn the jars upside down for 2 minutes, then invert and leave to cool. Label and date for storage.

(pictured page 658)

CURD

Made from a mixture of fruit juice (usually citrus), sugar, butter and egg yolks, curds are cooked until thick and used as a spread on bread or as a filling in sweet tarts.

PASSIONFRUIT CURD

FILLS THREE 250 ML (9 FL OZ/1 CUP) JARS

INGREDIENTS

- 4 eggs
- 170 g (6 oz/¾ cup) caster (superfine) sugar
- 80 ml (2½ fl oz/⅓ cup) lemon juice
- 3 teaspoons finely grated lemon zest
- 125 g (4½ oz/½ cup) passionfruit pulp
- 200 g (7 oz) unsalted butter, chopped

METHOD

1. Beat the eggs well, then strain into a heatproof bowl, and stir in the sugar, lemon juice, lemon zest, passionfruit pulp and butter. Place the bowl over a saucepan of simmering water and stir constantly with a wooden spoon over low heat for about 15–20 minutes, or until the butter has melted and the mixture thickly coats the back of the wooden spoon.
2. Transfer the curd to a clean heatproof jug and pour into sterilised jars. Seal while hot. Turn the jars upside down for 2 minutes, invert and cool, then refrigerate. Refrigerate for up to 1 month.

LEMON CURD

FILLS TWO 250 ML (9 FL OZ/1 CUP) JARS

INGREDIENTS

- 1½ tablespoons finely grated lemon zest
- 185 ml (6 fl oz/¾ cup) lemon juice
- 185 g (6½ oz) unsalted butter, softened, chopped
- 230 g (8 oz/1 cup) caster (superfine) sugar
- 12 egg yolks, beaten

METHOD

1. Combine the lemon zest, juice, butter and sugar in a heatproof bowl. Place the bowl over a saucepan of simmering water and stir until the butter has melted and the sugar has dissolved.
2. Add the egg yolks to the bowl and stir until the mixture thickens to coat the back of the spoon. This will take about 15 minutes and the heat must be low or the mixture will curdle.
3. Strain the curd into a jug, then pour into cooled sterilised jars. Seal immediately. Store in the fridge for up to 3 weeks, unopened. Use within a week of opening.

PASSIONFRUIT

The most common variety of these tropical fruit are purple-skinned but some are yellow or orange. The pulp is sweet but tart, juicy, very fragrant and refreshing. The seeds are edible and crunchy, but if only the pulp is wanted, push the flesh through a sieve. It is hard to tell if a passionfruit is ripe — purple varieties may be ripe either when the skin is still smooth or when it starts to wrinkle (not withered). The lighter yellow varieties are ripe when smooth and have a little 'give'. Unripe passionfruit are very tart. Passionfruit pulp is available tinned or frozen.

••PRESERVES AND PICKLES••

Preserves and pickles are vegetables or fruit preserved in a bottle or container. Pickles are often simmered in brine or vinegar or a mixture of both, which prevents the growth of microorganisms. Preserves and pickles are often made when there is a glut of fruit or vegetables, to ensure supply through unseasonal months.

CURING AND PRESERVING OLIVES

Olives differ in colour at various stages of ripeness. All are inedible straight from the tree and need to be cured, then preserved in oil or brine. Green olives, the youngest, are hard and very bitter, whereas black olives are fully mature and plump. Each requires a different curing process and the resulting textures and flavours vary. Curing olives is simple but takes time and patience.

The first step in curing green olives is to leach out the bitter juices. Crack or split the olives to the stone either with a paring knife or by tapping with a wooden mallet. Put them in a bowl, then cover with cold water. Drain and cover with fresh water every day. Taste after 2 weeks and if still bitter continue soaking and changing the water. It may take up to 4 weeks. The olives can now be preserved in olive oil or in a brine solution and different herbs and aromatics can be added to infuse the olives with flavour.

A traditional method of curing black olives is simple but may take longer than the green olives to leach out the bitter juices. Completely cover black olives in cold water, cover and soak for 6 weeks. Replace the water every second day. Drain the olives, then cover with rock salt and set aside for 2 days. Rinse off all the salt and leave to dry thoroughly. As with the green olives, preserve in either olive oil or a brine solution.

HOW TO... PRESERVE OLIVES IN OIL

Spread the olives out on paper towels and leave overnight in a warm place to dry. Steep the olives in 2 parts olive oil to 1 part vinegar, seasoning with garlic, mint, peppercorns and salt, to taste. Cover, stirring occasionally, for 3 days. Transfer to sterilised glass jars and cover with olive oil. Refrigerate for up to 6 weeks. Serve the olives at room temperature.

HOW TO... PRESERVE OLIVES IN BRINE

Drain and dry the soaked olives. Make a brine solution with 10 parts water to 1 part rock salt. Bring to the boil and simmer for 5 minutes with bay leaves, citrus zest, peppercorns and herbs. Pack the olives into sterilised glass jars, cover with the brine, seal and cool completely. Store for a week before eating. Use within 1 month and refrigerate after opening.

HOW TO... MAKE HERBED OLIVES

Put 250 g (9 oz) each of cracked green and cracked kalamata olives (cracking the olives with a mallet or cutting to the stone with a small knife, allows the marinade to penetrate into the olives), 3 thyme sprigs, 1 tablespoon oregano leaves, 2 bay leaves, 2 teaspoons finely grated lemon zest and 1 teaspoon paprika in a bowl and toss to combine. Spoon into a 1 litre (35 fl oz/ 4 cup) sterilised jar and pour in 500 ml (17 fl oz/2 cups) olive oil. Marinate for 1–2 weeks in the fridge. Use the olives within 1 month and refrigerate after opening.

PICCALILLI

FILLS EIGHT 250 ML (9 FL OZ/1 CUP) JARS

INGREDIENTS

- 400 g (14 oz) cauliflower, cut into florets
- 1 Lebanese (short) cucumber, chopped
- 200 g (7 oz) green beans, cut into 2 cm (¾ inch) lengths
- 1 onion, chopped
- 2 carrots, chopped
- 2 celery stalks, chopped
- 4 tablespoons salt
- 220 g (7¾ oz/1 cup) sugar
- 1 tablespoon mustard powder
- 2 teaspoons ground turmeric
- 1 teaspoon ground ginger
- 1 red chilli, seeded and finely chopped
- 1 litre (35 fl oz/4 cups) white vinegar
- 200 g (7 oz) frozen broad (fava) beans, thawed, peeled
- 60 g (2¼ oz/½ cup) plain (all-purpose) flour

METHOD

1. Combine the cauliflower, cucumber, beans, onion, carrot, celery and salt in a large bowl. Add enough water to cover the vegetables, and top with a small upturned plate to keep the vegetables submerged. Leave to soak overnight.
2. Drain the vegetables and rinse under running water. Drain again. Combine the vegetables with the sugar, mustard, turmeric, ginger, chilli and all but 185 ml (6 fl oz/¾ cup) of the vinegar in a large pan. Bring to the boil, then reduce the heat and simmer for 3 minutes. Stir in the broad beans. Remove any scum from the surface.
3. Blend the flour with the remaining vinegar and stir it into the vegetable mixture. Stir until the mixture boils and thickens.
4. Spoon immediately into hot, sterilised jars and seal. Turn the jars upside down for 2 minutes, then invert. Label and date. Leave for 1 month to allow the flavours to develop. Refrigerate after opening and keep for up to 6 weeks.

SPICY FRUIT CHUTNEY

FILLS TEN 250 ML (9 FL OZ/1 CUP) JARS

INGREDIENTS

- 400 g (13 oz) dried apricots
- 200 g (7 oz) dried peaches
- 200 g (7 oz) dried pears
- 250 g (9 oz) raisins
- 200 g (7 oz) pitted dates
- 250 g (9 oz) onions
- 250 g (9 oz) green apples, peeled and cored
- 4 garlic cloves, finely chopped
- 1 teaspoon ground cumin
- 1 teaspoon ground coriander
- 1 teaspoon ground cloves
- 1 teaspoon ground cayenne pepper
- 600 g (1 lb 5 oz/3¼ cups) soft brown sugar
- 625 ml (21 fl oz/2½ cups) malt vinegar

METHOD

1. Finely chop the apricots, peaches, pears, raisins, dates, onions and apples. Place in a large heavy-based saucepan. Add the garlic, cumin, coriander, cloves, cayenne pepper, sugar, vinegar, 2 teaspoons salt and 750 ml (26 fl oz/ 3 cups) water to the saucepan.
2. Stir over low heat until the sugar has dissolved. Increase the heat and bring to the boil, then reduce the heat and simmer, stirring often, over medium heat for 1½ hours, or until the mixture has thickened and the fruit is soft and pulpy. Do not cook over high heat because the liquid will evaporate too quickly and the flavours will not have time to fully develop.
3. Spoon immediately into hot, sterilised jars and seal. Turn the jars upside down for 2 minutes, then invert and leave to cool. Label and date. Leave for 1 month before opening to allow the flavours to develop. Store in a cool, dark place for up to 12 months. Refrigerate after opening.

HOW TO... USE PRESERVED LEMONS

Preserved lemons are a speciality of Morocco, made by tightly packing lemon quarters in jars with salt and lemon juice. They are traditionally served with dishes such as grilled (broiled) meats or used to flavour couscous, tagines, stuffings and casseroles. They can lend an intense citrus tang to a surprising variety of savoury dishes, such as risotto, pasta and vinaigrettes. Only the zest is used in cooking. Discard the flesh and bitter pith, rinse and finely slice or chop the zest before adding it to the dish. Preserved lemons can be stored for up to 6 months in a cool, dark place.

PRESERVED LEMONS

FILLS A 2 LITRE (8 CUP) JAR

INGREDIENTS

- 10 lemons
- 300 g (10½ oz/1 cup) rock salt
- 1 teaspoon black peppercorns
- 1 bay leaf
- 250 ml (9 fl oz/1 cup) lemon juice
- olive oil

METHOD

1. Scrub the lemons under warm running water with a soft-bristle brush to remove the wax coating. Cut into quarters, leaving the base attached at the stem end. Open each lemon, remove any visible pips and pack 1 tablespoon rock salt against the cut edges of each lemon. Push the lemons back into shape and pack into a 2 litre (8 cup) sterilised jar with a clip or screw-top lid. (Depending on the size of the lemons, you may not need them all — they should be firmly packed and fill the jar.)
2. Add the black peppercorns, bay leaf and remaining salt to the jar. Fill the jar to the top with lemon juice. Seal and shake to combine all the ingredients. Leave in a cool, dark place for 6 weeks, inverting each week. (In warm weather, store in the refrigerator.) The liquid will be cloudy initially, but will clear by the fourth week.
3. To test if the lemons are preserved, cut through the centre of one of the lemon quarters. If the pith is still white, the lemons are not ready. Re-seal and leave for a week before testing again. The lemons should be soft-skinned and the pith should be the same colour as the skin.
4. Once the lemons are preserved, cover the brine with a layer of olive oil. Replace the oil each time you remove some of the lemon pieces.

ROASTED TOMATO RELISH

FILLS FOUR 250 ML (9 FL OZ/1 CUP) JARS

INGREDIENTS

- 2 kg (4 lb 8 oz) tomatoes, halved
- 2 onions, chopped
- 2 small red chillies, seeded and chopped
- 1 teaspoon paprika or Hungarian smoked paprika (see Note)
- 330 ml (11¼ fl oz/1⅓ cups) white wine vinegar
- 300 g (10½ oz/1⅓ cups) sugar
- 60 ml (2 fl oz/¼ cup) lemon juice
- 1 teaspoon finely grated lemon zest

METHOD

1. Preheat the oven to 150°C (300°F/Gas 2). Line a baking tray with foil and then baking paper. Place the tomato halves, cut side up, on the baking tray and cook for 1 hour. Scatter the onion over the top and cook for another hour.
2. Cool slightly, then remove the tomato skins and roughly chop the flesh. Place the tomato, onion, chilli, paprika, vinegar, sugar, lemon juice, lemon zest and 2 teaspoons salt into a large pan and stir until the sugar has dissolved.
3. Bring to the boil, then reduce the heat and simmer for 45 minutes, or until the relish is thick and pulpy. Stir often to prevent the relish from burning or sticking.
4. Spoon into hot, sterilised jars and seal. Turn the jars upside down for 2 minutes, then invert and leave to cool. Label and date. Leave for 1 month before opening to allow the flavours to develop. Store in a cool, dark place for up to 12 months. Refrigerate after opening for up to 6 weeks.

NOTE: If available, Hungarian smoked paprika gives this relish a lovely smoky flavour. It is available at speciality spice shops and delicatessens.

GARDEN PICKLES

FILLS A 1.25 LITRE (5 CUP) JAR

INGREDIENTS

- 280 g (10 oz) carrots, cut into short lengths
- 280 g (10 oz) pearl onions
- 225 g (8 oz) small gherkins
- 875 ml (30 fl oz/3½ cups) white wine vinegar
- 1 tablespoon sea salt
- 2 tablespoons honey
- 225 g (8 oz) stringless green beans, cut into short lengths
- 10 black peppercorns
- 6 whole cloves
- 5 juniper berries
- 2 bay leaves

METHOD

1. Preheat the oven to 120°C (250°F/Gas ½). Put the carrots, onions, gherkins, vinegar, salt and honey in a large saucepan with 600 ml (21 fl oz) water and bring to the boil. Reduce the heat and simmer for 20 minutes. Add the beans and simmer for 5 minutes, or until the vegetables are tender but still slightly crisp.
2. Drain the vegetables, reserving the liquid. Arrange the vegetables in a sterilised 1.25 litre (44 fl oz/5 cup) jar and add the peppercorns, cloves, juniper berries and bay leaves. Pour in the liquid to cover the vegetables. Seal and refrigerate for 24 hours before use.

INDEX

INDEX

Published in 2009 by Murdoch Books Pty Limited.

Murdoch Books Australia
Pier 8/9, 23 Hickson Road
Millers Point NSW 2000
Phone: + 61 (0) 2 8220 2000
Fax: + 61 (0) 2 8220 2558
www.murdochbooks.com.au

Murdoch Books UK Limited
Erico House, 6th Floor
93–99 Upper Richmond Road
Putney, London SW15 2TG
Phone: + 44 (0) 20 8785 5995
Fax: + 44 (0) 20 8785 5985
www.murdochbooks.co.uk

Chief Executive: Juliet Rogers
Publishing Director: Kay Scarlett

Editor: Kim Rowney
Design: Heather Menzies
Photographers: Alan Benson, Ben Dearnley, Jared Fowler,
Ian Hofstetter, Chris L. Jones
Stylists: Jane Collins, Michaela Le Compte, Mary Harris, Katy Holder,
Cherise Koch, Sarah de Nardi, Justine Poole
Additional writing: Jane Price
Recipes: Sophie Braimbridge, Michelle Earl, Jo Glynn, Katy Holder
and members of the Murdoch Books Test Kitchen
Production: Kita George

National Library of Australia Cataloguing-in-Publication Data

Author: Grimes, Lulu.
Title: The cook's book of everything / Lulu Grimes, edited by Kim Rowney.
ISBN: 9781741960334 (hbk.)
Notes: Includes index.
Subjects: Cookery. Cookery--Miscellanea
Other Authors/Contributors: Rowney, Kim.
Dewey Number: 641.5

A catalogue record for this book is available from the British Library.

Colour separation by Colour Chiefs.
Printed by 1010 Printing International Limited in 2009. PRINTED IN CHINA.

IMPORTANT: Those who might be at risk from the effects of salmonella poisoning
(the elderly, pregnant women, young children and those suffering from immune deficiency diseases)
should consult their doctor with any concerns about eating raw eggs.

CONVERSION GUIDE: You may find cooking times vary depending on the oven you are using.
For fan-forced ovens, as a general rule, set the oven temperature to 20°C (35°F) lower than indicated in the recipe.